ridge Imperial and Post-Colonial Studies series is a well-collection of over 100 volumes focussing on empires in world on the societies and cultures that emerged from, and chal-onial rule. The collection includes transnational, comparative tive studies, as well as works addressing the ways in which egions or nations interact with global forces. In its forma-he series focused on the British Empire and Commonwealth, now no imperial system, period of human history or part of hat lies outside of its compass. While we particularly welcome nographs of young researchers, we also seek major studies ior scholars, and welcome collections of essays with a strong cus that help to set new research agendas. As well as history, cludes work on politics, economics, culture, archaeology, liter-ce, art, medicine, and war. Our aim is to collect the most v scholarship on world history and to make this available to larly readership in a timely manner.

nation about this series at
v.palgrave.com/gp/series/13937

Cambridge Imperial and I

Series Ed

Richard Drayton, Department of Hi
London,
Saul Dubow, Magdalene Colleg
Cambridg

The Camb
established
history an
lenged, co
and conne
particular
tive years,
but there i
the world
the first m
by more se
thematic fo
the series in
ature, scien
exciting ne
a broad sch

More inforı
http://ww

Bert Becker

France and Germany in the South China Sea, c. 1840–1930

Maritime competition and Imperial Power

palgrave
macmillan

Bert Becker
Department of History
School of Humanities
University of Hong Kong
Hong Kong, Hong Kong

ISSN 2635-1633 ISSN 2635-1641 (electronic)
Cambridge Imperial and Post-Colonial Studies
ISBN 978-3-030-52603-0 ISBN 978-3-030-52604-7 (eBook)
https://doi.org/10.1007/978-3-030-52604-7

Cover image: The cargo-steamer *Amiral Latouche-Tréville* of the French shipping company Chargeurs Réunis, in service from 1904 to 1929, in the port of Haiphong, c. 1910 (Private collection Bert Becker)

This Palgrave Macmillan imprint is published by the registered company Springer Nature Switzerland AG
The registered company address is: Gewerbestrasse 11, 6330 Cham, Switzerland

Acknowledgements

When I came to Hong Kong in 2002 and took up a DAAD-funded lectureship in History and European Studies at the Department of History of The University of Hong Kong, I became interested in researching the history of European expatriate communities in the former British colony. The first opportunity arose with the 90-year anniversary of the university and the invitation from a colleague in the History Department, Peter Cunich, to contribute to the Festschrift of which he and Chan Lau Kit-ching, then head of department, were the editors. Then came the invitation from Hans Michael Jebsen, chairman of the Jebsen Group in Hong Kong (or Jebsen & Company Limited), to visit the company archives in Aabenraa, Denmark. Afterwards, he invited me to write a comprehensive academic biography about his great-grandfather, Michael Jebsen (1835–1899). The research project gave me access to extensive correspondence from the founder and first owner of the Reederei M. Jebsen (M. Jebsen Shipping Company), which is kept in the company's own archives in Denmark.

Research visits to the French National Archives in Aix-en-Provence, which hold the records of the former French colonial ministry and a large collection of newspapers published in Hanoi and Haiphong, gave access to a considerable amount of correspondence from one of the most important pioneering firms in French Indochina (and one of the main competitors of the M. Jebsen Shipping Company), the shipping company Marty et d'Abbadie, with its affiliates, the Subsidised River Shipping Service of

Tonkin and the Tonkin Shipping Company. Combined with the business correspondence of Michael Jebsen, the French records promised to provide a comprehensive and often fascinating picture of dynamic transnational interactions between European shipping and trading companies and their Chinese customers. It was also exciting to delve deeper into the biographies of their owners, especially those of the almost forgotten French shipowners, Auguste Raphael Marty (who was in his time quite a well-known figure in colonial Hong Kong) and his partner Édouard Jules d'Abbadie. The Indochina files of the German Foreign Ministry Archives in Berlin offered insights into Speidel & Company, one of the earliest and most important trading houses in French Indochina, which employed Jebsen vessels to ship rice from Saigon or Haiphong to Hong Kong. The existence and operations of this company are nowadays almost unknown even to experts of French colonial history or Vietnamese modern history. All this together finally gave me sufficient inspiration and motivation to write this book.

The research for the book took me to many different places. The most fascinating was Hanoi where I was allowed to access numerous volumes of former French colonial newspapers preserved in the National Library of Vietnam, and, years later, also to look at various records of the former French colonial government of Indochina that are in the National Archives No. 1 of Vietnam. The respective archives of the foreign ministries in Paris, Nantes and Berlin provided valuable insights into various political-diplomatic matters and the sometimes colourful reports of French and German consuls from several port cities in the South China Sea. The Main Library of The University of Hong Kong, the State Library in Berlin and the French National Library in Paris were the most important places to find an array of secondary literature that was relevant to almost all areas of the book. I am grateful for the support of staff working in the aforementioned archives and libraries.

The Faculty of Arts and the School of Humanities of The University of Hong Kong have been extremely generous in allowing study leave and providing financial assistance in support of research. The Jebsen Group provided extra funds and access to their archives. I do owe much gratitude to both.

I am especially indebted to the following colleagues in France for help with this project: Hubert Bonin, François Dremeaux and Antoine Vannière. These colleagues sent books and other publications, commented on various chapters and helped with tricky translations. I am also grateful for support of various kinds provided by my colleagues at The University of Hong Kong: John M. Carroll, Peter Cunich, James R. Fichter, Ghassan Moazzin, Robert Peckham, David Pomfret, Stefan Purwins, Maureen Sabine, Charles Schencking, Elizabeth Sinn, Paul Urbanski and Roland Vogt. My further thanks go to a number of individuals who were part of this research throughout: Mette Haugaard Bach, Ruth Clausen, Frank-Ulrich Gast, Manfred Lutz, Lena Mengelkamp, Joel Montague, Sonja Or, Quang Minh Pham, Fion So, Christy Takeuchi, Pamela Tsui, Ekin Ulas, Bowman Wu and Bamboo Yeung. I am especially grateful to Ekin Ulas who considerably contributed to improving my French language skills. I owe much gratitude to Paul Wenham who was willing to copy edit the manuscript proofs at very short notice. I am also profoundly indebted to Christiane Millenet and her father, Eduard Leopold, who provided private images for this book. Finally, I thank the series editors, the anonymous reviewer and the staff of Palgrave Macmillan for their support and patience during the time I spent working on the manuscript in Hong Kong, Berlin and Seebad Ahlbeck in 2019–2021.

Bert Becker
Hong Kong, Special Administrative Region
People's Republic of China

Contents

Abbreviations

ACM	Archives départementales de la Charente-Maritime
ADPO	Archives départementales des Pyrénées-Orientales, Perpignan
ANOM	Archives Nationales d'Outre-Mer, Aix-en-Provence
AP	Archives de Paris
BAB	Bundesarchiv, Berlin
BASF	Badische Anilin- & Soda-Fabrik
CADN	Centre des Archives Diplomatiques, Nantes
CCC	Correspondance consulaire et commerciale, 1793–1901
CGT	Compagnie Général Transatlantique
CNEP	Comptoir national d'escompte de Paris
CPC	Correspondance politique et commerciale, 1896–1918. Nouvelle Série: Chine
CSI	Carl Smith Index
DAAD	Deutscher Akademischer Austauschdienst (German Academic Exchange Service)
DDG Hansa	Deutsche Dampfschiffahrts-Gesellschaft Hansa (German Steamship Company Hansa)
EAC	East Asiatic Company
EIC	[English] East India Company
FO	Foreign Office
GGI	Gouvernement-Général de l'Indochine
GSTA	Geheimes Staatsarchiv Preußischer Kulturbesitz, Berlin
HKGG	Hong Kong Government Gazette
HKPRO	Hong Kong Public Records Office
HSBC	Hong Kong and Shanghai Banking Corporation
IG Farben	Interessengemeinschaft Farbenindustrie Aktiengesellschaft

INDO-GGI	Gouvernement-Général de l'Indochine
JJHA	Jebsen and Jessen Historical Archives, Aabenraa
LAA	Landsarkivet for Sønderjylland, Aabenraa
MAE	Centre des Archives Diplomatiques du Ministère des Affaires Étrangères, Paris
N.Y.K.	Nippon Yusen Kaisha
NAN	Nationaal Archief, Den Haag
Ø.K.	Det Østasiatiske Kompagni
PAAA	Politisches Archiv des Auswärtigen Amts, Berlin
PS	Miscellaneous files
R	Deutsches Reich
RH	Résidence de Hadong
RST	Résidence Supérieur au Tonkin
SEDT	Service de l'Enregistrement, des Douanes et du Timbre de l'Indochine
TNA	British National Archives, Kew/Surrey
VNA1	Vietnamese National Archives No. 1, Hanoi
VOC	Verenigde Oostindische Compagnie

List of Illustrations

CHAPTER 1

Introduction

Since the earliest times, the South China Sea, sometimes regarded as a "Chinese lake",[1] was a closely interconnected maritime region. It was for some two thousand years China's main gateway to the world and the main corridor for the China trade. The waterway from the Indian Ocean through the Southern Sea or South Sea (in Chinese: Nánhǎi or Nanyang; in Vietnamese: Biển Đông, the East Sea) was the essential bulk commodity carrier and the run mostly preferred by Persian, Arab, Jewish, Indian, Malay and other merchants engaged in the traditional intra-Asian trading system. The oldest shipping route, the Western one, connected several trading regions near the Straits of Malacca with the major Chinese port city of Guangzhou (Canton). It passed along the coast of present central Vietnam controlled by several Cham principalities competing against each other and struggling against expansionist moves by the rulers of northern Vietnam. Around their base in Tonkin,[2]

[1] Samuels (1982, 9–30) proposed the term "Chinese lake" for the South China Sea, being from the late tenth to the mid-fifteenth centuries "a zone of preeminent Chinese influence and power" increasingly dominated by Chinese economic interests and Chinese navies. According to the author, this period ended with the beginning of "European domination of the China coast" and China being reduced to semi-colonial status.

[2] The choice of "Tonkin" in this book derives from the French usage. Li (2011, ix–x: on the term "Tongking" meaning "Eastern Capital" in Vietnamese and its Portuguese transliteration "Tonkin").

B. Becker, *France and Germany in the South China Sea, c. 1840–1930*, Cambridge Imperial and Post-Colonial Studies,
https://doi.org/10.1007/978-3-030-52604-7_1

on the Red River Delta, traces of a very cosmopolitan society from the third century were found. An alternative route probably went in a north-easterly direction to Guangzhou, passing Hainan Island where a small Islamised Cham community was established. In the following centuries, Arabs and Persians founded large foreign communities in the main ports of Fujian (Fukien) and Chinese merchants settled in Guangdong (Kwang-tung), Hainan and further south in Java, the Philippines and other parts of Southeast Asia.

This cosmopolitan character turned the South China Sea into an "Asian Mediterranean", as Denys Lombard pointed out in his ground-breaking article of 1998. Referring to the concept of the eminent French historian Fernand Braudel, who approached the Mediterranean as a coherent geographical space, Lombard suggested also integrating southern China into the understanding of Southeast Asia: otherwise, he argued, it would be "like wanting to give an account of the Mediterranean world after removing Turkey, the Levant, Palestine and Egypt".[3] Other scholars pursued this revisionist path, demonstrating that the South China Sea remained an economically closely interconnected region, even during the following centuries.[4] The Age of Commerce of Southeast Asia (1450–1680), as Anthony Reid put it, "was one in which these maritime links were particularly active", with "interconnected maritime cities of the region" being "more dominant in this period than either before or since". This trend continued during the Chinese Century of Southeast Asia (1740–1840) which was characterised by considerable commercial expansion in the South China Sea. The vibrant economic dynamism of these periods mostly originated in the coastal regions of southern China where Chinese junk traders were the driving force in the move southwards

[3] Lombard (2007, 3–9, the quote: 4) refers to the highly influential history of the Mediterranean world by the French historian Fernand Braudel which was first published in France in 1949 and reprinted several times since; the first English edition, *The Mediterranean and the Mediterranean World in the Age of Philip II* was published by Collins in 1972–1973 and by Harper Torchboook in c. 1972. Lombard's article was first published in the French geographical journal *Hérodote* in 1998 and translated by Nola Cooke for the publication in English.

[4] In his study "The Asian Mediterranean", François Gipouloux pursued and enhanced Braudel's and Lombard's perspectives, including the "maritime corridor" which connects the basins of the Sea of Japan, the Yellow Sea, the South China Sea, the Sulu Sea and the Celebes Sea. Focusing on overlapping and cosmopolitan trading networks in history, and even today, he stressed the important role of port cities such as Hong Kong, Shanghai and Singapore (Gipouloux 2011/2009).

to purchase consumer goods for China's developing population. Consequently, these wider trading networks spanned from southern China to the mainland and insular Southeast Asia.[5]

Following this geographical understanding, Li Tana proposed comprehending the entire coastal region from the Mekong Delta in southern Vietnam to the sultanates and later British colonies of the Malay Peninsula as a single economic region, as extended "Water Frontier", an area comprising a sparsely settled coastal and riverine frontier region inhabited by people of mixed ethnicities engaged in waterborne trade in a long chain of small ports. As it was frequently accessed by Chinese junk traders, and increasingly inhabited by Chinese people, this "Water Frontier" developed into "a fluid transnational and multi-ethnic economic zone" which grew even more rapidly in the early nineteenth century when urban centres such as Saigon, Singapore and Bangkok started dominating the regions around them. Closely knitted together by the commercial activities of the Chinese and other smaller and larger merchants, the Water Frontier region became in the later eighteenth century the true foundation of the kingdoms of Nguyen Vietnam and Chakkri Siam, with their economic capitals, Saigon and Bangkok.[6] Challenging nationalist historiographies, a number of scholars developed a systematic revisionist review of Vietnam's position in the early trade networks of the South China Sea, stressing the importance of the sea in understanding Vietnamese history. The traditional national model of early Vietnamese political economy and ethnicity as basically agrarian was questioned and regional dynamics inside Southeast Asia and southern China put forward. The importance of the sea was underlined by Charles Wheeler who proposed regarding the geography of water as "an important arena for social interaction among those who would influence Vietnamese history". He stressed that in the seventeenth and eighteenth centuries the sea was of major importance for Vietnamese societies, with watercraft being the principal technology of travel and transport contributing to the intensification of intra-Asian trading networks.[7]

[5] Reid (1988, the quote: 7) and Reid (2004, 22–24, 2015, 74–76).

[6] As Li pointed out, this fact was later frequently ignored by nationalistic interpretations of this era in Vietnamese or Thai historiographies. Li (2004, 1–3). See also, Li (1998, 14–17).

[7] Wheeler (2001, chapter 2) and Wheeler (2006, 123–153, the quote: 124).

As a result of this revisionist model, it was possible to regard the southern "Water Frontier" not only as a multiethnic and open frontier society, but also the north-western part of the South China Sea, namely, the Gulf of Tonkin region, an active trading zone located in the centre of the old Western sea route which up to the fifteenth century was frequently visited by Muslim traders from South, West and Southeast Asia.[8] This zone encompassed the maritime region between the shores of Guangxi (Kwangsi), Guangdong (Kwangtung) and Hainan Island in southern China and the neighbouring coasts of northern and central Vietnam. Whether this region should be treated as a "mini-Mediterranean" remained a somewhat open question until in 2008 scholars uncovered "an overlapping historical and economic ensemble with its own long-standing integrity" making it possible to analyse "the importance of regions and regionalism in the long-term history of modern Asian states".[9] Since the history of the Gulf region was largely ignored by nation-centred studies of Chinese and Vietnamese histories, the approach of studying interregional economic interactions in the Tonkin Gulf as "a centuries-old phenomenon" resulting in "innumerable transactions between local peoples" enriched the knowledge of maritime regions around the Gulf, which had for centuries been closely interconnected beyond modern national borders.[10]

This book is based on the same notion of employing a maritime perspective when treating the South China Sea as a closely interconnected maritime region in which European shipping and trading companies acted as drivers of economic development between the mid-nineteenth and the early twentieth centuries. As for the role of port cities, it seems obvious that Hong Kong should be considered a global city or "global metropolis"[11] (and the other British colonial port city, Singapore, which

[8] Momoki (1998, 1–34), Goscha (2000, 987–1018) and Li (2006, 83–102).

[9] Li (2011, vii–viii). The first international conference to discuss whether this concept could be applied to a Southeast Asia maritime space was held in Paris in March 1997. Some discussants also highlighted the important role of single port cities, and China was regarded as a decisive long-term factor in shaping Southeast Asian societies (Ptak 1997, 45–46). The latest major contribution to the field is Wade and Chin (2019) highlighting historical interactions between China and Southeast Asia.

[10] Ptak (2008, 53–69) and Luan and Cooke (2011, 143).

[11] One of the major studies of Hong Kong's history employing an historical geography approach is expressively titled "Hong Kong as Global Metropolis" (Meyer 2000).

is not the focus of this research, undoubtedly ranks in the same category). Less globally oriented, but certainly multinational in character, the Vietnamese port cities of Saigon and Haiphong developed into meeting places of Chinese and foreign social networks of capital during the imperialist period in East Asia, resulting in a new wave of commercial expansion during the European Century of East and Southeast Asia (c. 1860–1910s).[12] As European imperial powers approached the shores of the South China Sea in the mid-nineteenth century, the capitalist modernisation of port cities and their hinterlands, and of economic structures and business networks, brought profound change to traditional societies. The South China Sea was at times home to seafarers, traders, administrators, military forces and missionaries from European countries such as Britain, France, Germany and many others. This maritime region, which brought together different groups of people in considerable numbers, also provided them with familiar European administrative and economic infrastructures. British and French colonial entities such as Hong Kong and Indochina, became little "Britains" or "Frances" where European foreigners lived and worked together in constant daily interaction with each other and Chinese and Vietnamese locals.

Without ignoring the important role of Christian missionaries in cultural transfer and intercultural exchanges of many kinds, it seems evident that the main area of such transnational interactions was economic. This took place predominantly in the areas of shipping and trade in port cities of the South China Sea. Chinese and European companies co-operated and also engaged in rivalry with each other to maximise their profits. Such interactions in the economic field happened in temporarily unstable geopolitical conditions created by European imperialism and strongly impacted economies and societies in East and Southeast Asia. Both macroeconomic changes in the global economy and major political shifts of sometimes dramatic proportions constantly outweighed and affected the highly complex microeconomic transactions in shipping and trade during the European Century, and even beyond.

This book can be regarded as a contribution to maritime history in the broadest sense. Generally, maritime history is comprehended as a field of research which covers all the dynamics arising from, and which are required by, the ways humans use the sea. In the broader sense, maritime

[12] Tønnesson (2006, 1–2).

history is a heterogeneous field including a wide range of subjects. The main topics are shipping, naval organisation and warfare at sea, empire building, overseas trade, navigation and exploration, communication and transport systems, including the study of merchant fleets and shipping companies or trading houses which served as agents for shipping lines or were themselves shipping operators. The central role of human agents in maritime dynamics is an important issue of maritime history, with the traditional focus being on shipowners, shipmasters, merchants and other leaders, but also on common and anonymous agents such as seafarers or seamen's professional organisations and even architecture, urbanisation and the representation of maritime space.[13]

With a central focus on French and German companies operating within the confines of the South China Sea, this book attempts to cover a range of topics in maritime history. As a basic methodological approach, it combines both transnational business history and imperial history. This combination allows us to escape the structures of national narratives and think more flexibly and reflexively about private business and imperial power and about various cross-connections between shipowners and traders on the one hand, who were actively involved in the operation of merchant ships and various commercial transactions, and colonial administrators and foreign consuls on the other, who represented "empire" and national interests. These cross-links looked very different in the fourport cities studied, which were characterised by the almost completely different economic policies of the British and French empires.

Transnational business history offers the chance to go beyond narrow company histories or national histories and to look into human interaction across national or imperial borders. Such cross-border flows of people, of knowledge or of specific goods, of "transnational actors or trans-boundary formations", are often difficult to grasp and to pursue, because they do not fit into national narratives and therefore often escape documentation. This requires new reading of national sources and the identification of sources from previously neglected transnational actors or "trans-boundary formations". Pierre-Yves Saunier suggested five main types of "units of understanding": individuals, organisations, topics, events and territorial regions. According to this model, transboundary formations are constructs which attempt to overcome the limitations

[13] For definitions of maritime history, see Broeze (1995), Harlaftis and Vassallo (2004) and Polónia (2010, 1–3).

of state borders and to focus instead on trans-boundary phenomena.[14] This approach requires selecting and interpreting sources with a different perspective when writing business history. It concerns stories of companies and their owners, maritime networks of exchange and established patterns of co-operation, competition and conflict as they become evident in the French and German sources used for this book. In this respect, the South China Sea can be seen as a transnational region (situated between the Chinese, British, French and Dutch empires in South East Asia) where transnational actors (private shipping and trading companies) collaborated and engaged in rivalry with or without the support of colonial powers, creating and shaping transnational connections or trans-boundary phenomena.

Transnational business history requires, to a certain extent, studying the micro-perspective of individual business actors and private companies and linking this research to interpreting their role in creating and shaping different connections together with other actors and institutions. In order to emphasise transnational constellations both within and outside the company, intensive research into the primary sources is necessary.[15] In this book, four companies and their owners and employees form the backbone of studying business networks and exchanges in the South China Sea, namely the trading company Speidel & Company in Saigon with its branches in Haiphong, Phnom Penh and Paris (whose owners came from Württemberg in south-western Germany); the trading company A. R. Marty in Hong Kong (owned by the Marty brothers from the French Pyrenees); the shipping company Marty et d'Abbadie in Haiphong with the Subsidised River Shipping Service of Tonkin and the Tonkin Shipping Company as its main affiliates (whose owners came from south-west France); and the M. Jebsen Shipping Company in Apenrade (whose owners were from Schleswig-Holstein in northern Germany and who used Hong Kong as a permanent position for their tramp steamers). Studying the histories of these companies proved to be one of the major challenges in writing this book. Speidel & Co., A. R. Marty and Marty et d'Abbadie vanished into thin air after the First World War, with all primary documentation being lost, while the M. Jebsen Shipping Company exists

[14] Saunier (2013, 99–116).

[15] Boon (2017, 515–516, 533–535).

today in name only, having sold its last ships in the late 1970s. Their physical disappearance left the companies almost completely forgotten, despite the considerable roles they had played in shipping and trade in the South China Sea. The same can be said about their owners, who have almost disappeared from the collective memory. While Michael Jebsen (1835–1899) is still well remembered by the Jebsen Group (or Jebsen & Co. Ltd.) in Hong Kong (founded in 1895 as a shipping agency and trading company by Michael Jebsen's eldest son Jacob Jebsen, and his associate, Johann Heinrich Jessen), the Speidels, Auguste Raphael Marty and Pierre Augustin Marty, and Édouard Jules d'Abbadie are known only to a few historians of French and Hong Kong colonial history or Vietnamese economic and business history. Therefore, their biographies, discovered in a variety of primary and secondary source materials, are presented in some detail in this book. Since business operations of French companies played an important role in fostering French national interests in southern China (which was considered by France as an exclusive sphere of influence), shipping and trade in the South China Sea were carefully monitored by both French and German consuls posted in the port cities of the region and by colonial administrators of French Indochina. Their reports and correspondence went regularly to their respective governments in Paris and Berlin and have therefore been preserved in French and German government archives. Furthermore, the business records of the M. Jebsen Shipping Company (of which Jebsen & Company in Hong Kong was the principal agent) have been carefully preserved both in the company's own archives and in the regional state archives of Southern Jutland, both located in Aabenraa, Denmark. To a certain extent, the French and German government and private files even enable an investigation into the backgrounds and motives of Chinese merchants in their charters and operation of steam coasters owned by European shipping companies. This fact makes them relevant when researching Chinese rice companies and other businesses. As it emerges from the sources, economic exchange between the Chinese and European companies resulted in a variety of transnational interactions that were mostly cooperative, but sometimes obstructive, as in the case of price wars, boycotts or illicit trades.

Imperial history relates to "empire" which is regarded as "one of the most powerful transnational political formations". From a transnational perspective, empire means "a wide variety of hegemonic territorial conquests that produce flows of people, goods, and ideas across frontiers".[16] In the region around the South China Sea, the largest European empire was France's colonial state in East Asia, successively extended from the 1850s to the 1890s. The territorial consolidation process of "L'Indochine Française" (French Indochina) began with the occupation of southern Vietnam, or Cochinchina, in 1858 and was finalised with the Sino-French Convention over Guangzhouwan, the French leased territory in China's Guangdong Province, in 1898. France's imperialist expansion on the Indochinese Peninsula from the 1850s forms the main context of this book in combination with the history of Franco-German political–diplomatic relations from the 1870s to the 1920s. The strained relationship between the two major European nations following the Franco-German War of 1870–1871 was the main impetus for German politicians, first and foremost Imperial Chancellor Otto von Bismarck, to have German consuls carefully monitor French policy in Indochina and throughout the South China Sea. However, Bismarck, who was mainly interested in European affairs, adhered strictly to his policy of non-intervention towards Indochina, and even supported France's imperialist ventures in the region. With the development of Speidel & Company in one of the most important trading companies operating in the French colony, and of the M. Jebsen Shipping Company, which almost dominated the tramp shipping markets of Indochina and the north-western South China Sea, German officials became increasingly interested in French activities in the region. This resulted in a fairly rich collection of documents kept in the archives of the German foreign ministry in Berlin that were used for this book. This material allows us to examine various aspects of "great politics" by the governments in Paris and Berlin and their impact on private companies operating in French Indochina and Hong Kong.

As the title of this book suggests, maritime competition and imperial power implies a certain interdependent relationship between shipping companies and colonial empires. In the nineteenth century, steamships became the symbol of modernity in transport, but also "tools or engines of empires" and even "spearheads of penetration" to open up the Chinese

[16] Iriye and Saunier (2009, 319, 325).

and other East Asian markets.[17] These political, economic and even military functions of steamships for imperialist and colonialist endeavours by European powers in East Asia form an important part of this book. The relationship between Indochina's colonial government and Marty et d'Abbadie in Haiphong serves as an example of a shipping company that, as a "state monopolist", was almost entirely reliant on financial subsidies from the colonial state. That made the firm dependent on the ups and downs of government policy and therefore very vulnerable to the point that it had to cease operations.

This book is divided into five main chapters. An introductory chapter provides a brief overview of Chinese, Vietnamese and European shipping and trade in the South China Sea before the establishment of French colonial rule in southern Vietnam. The remaining four chapters correspond to four colonial port cities in the central parts of the South China Sea, namely Hong Kong, Saigon, Haiphong and Guangzhouwan. The chapter on Hong Kong looks at the local German and French business communities and examines tramp shipping markets in East Asia and the general decline of the French mercantile marine in the late nineteenth century. France's imperialist policies in East and Southeast Asia from the 1850s to the 1890s are covered in the chapters on Saigon, Haiphong and Guangzhouwan. The first two also explore the development of Franco-German political-diplomatic relations from 1870 to 1914 and their impact on the microcosm of Cochinchina and Tonkin, the southern and northern parts of the French colonial state. In addition, both chapters address various transnational interactions between European shipping companies and Chinese merchants in the South China Sea, including boycotts and the trafficking of Vietnamese women and children. The interdependent relationship between Indochina's colonial government and Marty et d'Abbadie is evaluated in the chapters on Haiphong and Guangzhouwan. The history of the four individual companies and of their owners and employees is examined to some detail in the chapters on Hong Kong (which deals with A. R. Marty and the M. Jebsen Shipping Company), on Saigon (which is about Speidel & Company), on Haiphong (which focuses on Marty et d'Abbadie and Speidel & Company), and on Guangzhouwan (which deals with the subsidised postal steamer service of the Tonkin Shipping Company).

[17] Liu (1959), Headrick (1981), Jackson and Williams (1996), Campo (2002), Eberspächer (2004), Berneron (2007), Burgess Jr. (2016) and Reinhardt (2018).

All in all, this book attempts to contribute to maritime history with a special focus on transnational business history and imperial history. By shedding some light on almost forgotten companies that once operated in Hong Kong and French Indochina around 1900, the book hopes to draw attention to the crucial significance of private initiative and efficient co-operation between European shipowners and traders on the one hand, and Chinese merchants, ship charterers and loaders on the other. It also seeks to highlight the benefits and results of freemarket competition as has been and still is practised in Hong Kong, in contrast to economic interventions and regulations imposed by national and colonial governments, as in the case of French Indochina. With regard to Franco-German relations, the book takes up a topic that has become almost irrelevant to people in France and Germany these days. However, it is all the more part of the history of the South China Sea and its port cities. This history would be quite incomplete without knowing about the lively competition between French and German companies and their important contributions to the progress of this maritime region — despite all the pitfalls of imperialism.

References

Berneron-Couvenhes, Marie-Françoise. 2007. *Les Messageries Maritimes: L'essor d'une grande compagnie de navigation française, 1851–1894*. Paris: PUBS.

Boon, Marten. 2017. Business Enterprise and Globalization: Towards a Transnational Business History. *Business History Review* 91 (autumn): 511–535.

Brocheux, Pierre, and Daniel Hèmery. 2009. *Indochina: An Ambiguous Colonization, 1858–1954*. Berkeley: University of California Press.

Broeze, Frank (ed.). 1995. *Maritime History as the Crossroads: A Critical Review of Recent Historiography*. St. John's, Newfoundland: International Maritime Economic History Association.

Burgess Jr., Douglas R. 2016. *Engines of Empire: Steamships and the Victorian Imagination*. Stanford, CA: Stanford University Press.

Campo, Josef N.F.M. à. 2002. *Engines of Empire: Steamshipping and State Formation in Colonial Indonesia*. Hilversum: Verloren.

Eberspächer, Cord. 2004. *Die deutsche Yangtse-Patrouille: Deutsche Kanonenbootpolitik in China im Zeitalter des Imperialismus 1900–1914*. Bochum: Winkler.

Gipouloux, François. 2011. *The Asian Mediterranean: Port Cities and Trading Networks in China, Japan and Southeast Asia, 13th–21st Century*. Cheltenham, UK and Northampton, MA, USA: Edward Elgar. First published in 2009. *La Méditerranée asiatique: Villes portuaires et réseaux marchands en Chine, au Japon et en Asie du Sud-Est, XVIe-XXI siècle*. Paris: CNRS Éditions.

Goscha, Christopher. 2000. The Borders of Vietnam's Early Wartime Trade with Southern China: A Contemporary Perspective. *Asian Survey* 40 (6): 987–1018.

Harlaftis, Gelina, and Carmel Vassallo (eds.). 2004. *New Directions in Mediterranean Maritime History*. St. John's, Newfoundland: International Maritime Economic History Association.

Headrick, Daniel R. 1981. *The Tools of Empire: Technology and European Imperialism in the Nineteenth Century*. Oxford: Oxford University Press.

Iriye, Akira, and Pierre-Yves Saunier (eds.). 2009. *The Palgrave Dictionary of Transnational History*. Houndsmill: Palgrave Macmillan.

Jackson, Gordon, and David M. Williams (eds.). 1996. *Shipping, Technology and Imperialism*. Hants, UK: Scolar Press.

Li, Tana. 1998. *Nguyễn Cochinchina: Southern Vietnam in the Seventeenth and Eighteenth Centuries*. Ithaca: Cornell University Southeast Asia Program.

Li, Tana. 2004. The Water Frontier: An Introduction. In *Water Frontier: Commerce and the Chinese in the Lower Mekong Region, 1750–1880*, ed. Nola Cooke and Li Tana, 1–17. Singapore: Singapore University Press.

Li, Tana. 2006. A View from the Sea: Perspectives on the Northern and Central Vietnamese Coast. *Journal of Southeast Asian Studies* 37 (1): 83–102.

Li, Tana. 2011. Preface. In *The Tongking Gulf through History*, ed. Nola Cooke, Li Tana, and James A. Anderson, vii–x. Philadelphia: University of Pennsylvania Press.

Liu, Kwang-ching. 1959. Steamship Enterprise in Nineteenth-Century China. *The Journal of Asian Studies* 18 (4): 435–455.

Lombard, Denys. 2007. Another "Mediterranean" in Southeast Asia. *Chinese Southern Diaspora Studies* (1): 3–9. First published in *Hérodote* (88) 1998: 184–193: Une autre "Méditerranée" dans le Sud-Est asiatique.

Luan, Vu Duong, and Nola Cooke. 2011. Chinese Merchants and Mariners in Nineteenth-Century Tongking. In *The Tongking Gulf Through History*, ed. Nola Cooke, Li Tana, and James A. Anderson, 143–159. Philadelphia: University of Pennsylvania Press.

Meyer, David R. 2000. *Hong Kong as a Global Metropolis*. Cambridge: Cambridge University Press.

Momoki, Shirō. 1998. Đại Việt and the South China Sea Trade from the 10th to the 15th Century. *Crossroads* 12 (1): 1–34.

Polónia, Amélia. 2010. Maritime History: A Gateway to Global History? In *Maritime History as Global History*, ed. Maria Fusaro and Amélia Polónia, 1–20. St. John's, Newfoundland: International Maritime Economic History Association.

Ptak, Roderich. 1997. The Southeast Asian Mediterranean. *SPAFA Journal* 7 (1): 45–46.

Ptak, Roderich. 2008. The Gulf of Tongking: A Mini-Mediterranean? In *The East Asian 'Mediterranean': Maritime Crossroads of Culture, Commerce and Human Migration*, ed. Angela Schottenhammer, 53–72. Wiesbaden: Harrassowitz.

Reid, Anthony. 1988. *Southeast Asia in the Age of Commerce 1450–1680, vol. 1: The Lands Below the Winds*. New Haven and London: Yale University Press.

Reid, Anthony. 2015. *A History of Southeast Asia: Critical Crossroads*. Chichester, West Sussex: Wiley Blackwell.

Reinhardt, Anne. 2018. *Navigating Semi-Colonialism: Shipping, Sovereignty, and Nation-Building in China, 1860–1937*. Cambridge, MA and London: Harvard University Press.

Samuels, Marwyn S. 1982. *Contest for the South China Sea*. New York and London: Methuen.

Saunier, Pierre-Yves. 2013. *Transnational History*. Houndsmill: Palgrave Macmillan.

Tønnesson, Stein. 2006. The South China Sea in the Age of European Decline. *Modern Asian Studies* 40 (1): 1–57.

Wade, Geoff and James K. Chin. 2019. *China and Southeast Asia: Historical Interactions*. London and New York: Routledge.

Wheeler, Charles. 2001. *Cross-Cultural Trade and Trans-Regional Networks in the Port of Hội An: Maritime Vietnam in the Early Modern Era*. Unpublished PhD Thesis, Yale University.

Wheeler, Charles. 2006. Re-thinking the Sea in Vietnamese History: Littoral Society in the Integration of Thuận-Quảng, Seventeenth-Eighteenth Centuries. *Journal of Southeast Asian Studies* 37 (1): 123–153.

CHAPTER 2

The South China Sea in History

The Age of Commerce (1450–1680)

For centuries, the Southern Sea or South Sea (in Chinese: Nánhǎi or Nanyang; in Vietnamese: Biển Đông, the East Sea) had been a centre of vibrant commercial exchange before European ships and traders arrived on its shores. Persian merchants seemed to have initiated maritime trade on the route between the western Indian Ocean, the Bay of Bengal and the South China Sea. From the ninth century, a rather wide-ranging and sophisticated maritime trading network emerged in Asia linking ports in the Middle East, East Africa, India, Southeast Asia, China and Japan. The South China Sea was an integral part of this major trading zone and China's major access to the world. On its western shores, Dai Viet, the forerunner of modern Vietnam, became a hub for both tributary and non-tributary trade with China from the tenth century. Economic rivalry between the ports of Tonkin, on the Red River Delta, and those of South China affected commercial relations in the northern part of the South China Sea. From the tenth and eleventh centuries, Guangdong (Canton) and Xiamen (Amoy) developed into bustling economic hubs in southern China, with large foreign communities including Arabs and Persians. From the thirteenth century, Chinese migrants moved in a southern direction, settling in neighbouring regions situated in today's Cambodia, Thailand and Indonesia. Places such as Guangdong and Xiamen, Hainan Island, Java and the Philippines grew into bases for powerful Chinese

B. Becker, *France and Germany in the South China Sea, c. 1840–1930*, Cambridge Imperial and Post-Colonial Studies,
https://doi.org/10.1007/978-3-030-52604-7_2

merchants who dominated commerce between ports in China and Japan (where they met severe competition from Japanese merchants) and Southeast Asia. From the thirteenth to the sixteenth centuries, the South China Sea turned cosmopolitan and developed into a kind of "Asian Mediterranean". This process was further stimulated by a major trade boom marking the Age of Commerce of Southeast Asia (1450–1680), which provided considerable material gains to port cities in the South China Sea and urban centres in neighbouring regions (Fig. 2.1).[1]

At some time during the twelfth century, Chinese junks began operating on the route between the South China Sea and the Indian Ocean, and by the early fifteenth century Chinese maritime trade in the region had an important share. From the fourteenth century, the term "junk" appears in foreign accounts, evidence of the deep impression these ships left on Europeans when they first arrived in the region. At the time, the variety of ships visiting Southeast Asian ports was more diverse than in the Mediterranean or Atlantic. Asian shipping was dominated by large junks of 300–500 tonnes, mostly built in Malacca, Java and Siam, due to the long tradition of Chinese migrants settling in Southeast Asian port cities and creating a hybrid Sino-Southeast Asian style in shipbuilding. In 1433, for unknown reasons, Chinese shippers and traders suddenly withdrew from the long-distance trade to India, leaving the maritime region west of Malacca to Indian merchants, many of whom settled in this port city on the Straits of Malacca. While in earlier periods Arab or Southeast Asian ships were mainly operating China's maritime trade, between 1567 and 1840 this commerce was principally in the hands of Chinese shippers, mostly based in Fujian (Fukien) in Southeast China. This probably stimulated the common usage of the epithet "Chinese lake" for the South China Sea.[2]

The Age of Commerce of Southeast Asia (1450–1680) attracted traders from Portugal, who initiated the first European commercial relations with China after Portuguese forces had conquered Malacca in 1511. With their commercial bases in India, the Portuguese soon occupied an important middleman role in trading to and from China and India, in which Chinese merchants had played an important role in

[1] Lombard (2007, 6–9), Momoki (1998, 6–18), Reid (1988, 7–10) and Wade (2019, 103-113).

[2] Reid (2015, 80–81, 121, 148), Chang (2019, 221–225), Prakash (1999, 175–176) and Samuels (1982, 9).

Fig. 2.1 Map of the South China Sea, 1920s. (*Eduard Gaebler's Hand-Atlas über alle Teile der Erde*, ed. Eduard Gaebler, Leipzig: Georg Dollheimer, 1930)

the fifteenth century. When Ming China (1368–1644) permitted the Portuguese to set up a trading post at Macao, a small peninsula on the western side of the Pearl River estuary in southern China, Portuguese Macao developed into a major entrepôt from 1557 and became a base for introducing Christianity and Western knowledge into China. With its mostly floating population, the port city emerged as "a place of transience" and "an early modern cosmopolis".[3] From Macao, Chinese products such as tea, porcelain and silk were sent to Europe on behalf of the Portuguese Crown, while China received silver shipped from Japan or the Americas in Portuguese galleons. Except for this long-distance trading, private Portuguese merchants also got involved in trade within Asia in the sixteenth century and considerably enhanced the traditional intra-Asian trading system. This stimulated economic growth during the late Ming Dynasty, especially the rise of Guangzhou as a trading centre in southern China and Southeast Asia. Cantonese merchants employed Portuguese vessels to ship cargoes to the Philippines, and Chinese money-lenders helped finance Portuguese trade with Japan. In the 1620s, the trade boom in Southeast Asia reached a peak when international demand for its products increased, with pepper and spices accounting for more than half of the value of European homeward cargoes from Asia. Euro-Asian commerce operated by the Portuguese Crown was even surpassed by Portuguese intra-Asian trade, reaching very respectable proportions in terms of value, which provided huge profits for private Portuguese merchants.[4]

In the seventeenth century, European merchants' share in the intra-Asian trading system was considerably enhanced by the Dutch United East India Company (Verenigde Oostindische Compagnie, VOC). Founded in Amsterdam in 1602, the company's main goal was to break into the Portuguese monopoly in Euro-Asian commerce and to extensively participate in trade within Asia by rivalling Portuguese, British and Asian merchants. This strategic focus on intra-Asian trade made the Dutch company different from its Portuguese, British and later, French and Prussian rivals. Chinese silk, silk textiles and other Chinese goods were purchased at ports in the South China Sea and the Malay Peninsula, where

[3] Man-Cheong (2014, 143–145) and Chang (2019, 226–229).

[4] Fieldhouse (1966, 138–143), Souza (1986, 228–229), Souza (1997, 121–122), Porter (1996, 3), Wills (1998, 342–344), Coates (1999, 26–30), Prakash (1999, 178–181) and Reid (2015, 74–76).

Chinese junks traded in large numbers. In 1609, a Dutch warehouse or "factory" was founded at Hirado in south-western Japan and, in 1624, the Company established another agency in Formosa (Taiwan) in return for an informal agreement that Chinese merchants would be permitted to trade with their Dutch counterparts. Major resources for developing this trade were precious metals in Asia, namely in China, Formosa, Sumatra, Japan and Arabia. The Company's intra-Asian trading network stretching from Persia to Japan, with its centre in the East Indies (now Indonesia), and created new connections among various Asian markets and between markets in Asia and Europe. In 1637, the Company sent its first ship from Japan to the Trinh lords, a noble feudal clan and the de facto rulers of Tonkin, who were seeking military support against their rivals in the south, the Nguyen lords. In the following sixty-four years, the Company exported silver, copper coins and military goods to Tonkin in exchange for Vietnamese silk and silk goods. With their permanent residence in the capital Thang Long (later Hanoi) and large-scale commerce, the Dutch were the most influential traders in northern Vietnam. In intra-Asian trade, around 1700, Dutch Company ships were ahead of their European counterparts (the British and French Trading Companies) and all other European private traders put together when moving goods in terms of both bulk and value on voyages between Asian ports. Although this position declined to some extent in the eighteenth century due to certain developments in Asia, the Dutch United East India Company remained the only major European trading company to participate in intra-Asian trade during this period.[5]

The Dutch Company's main rival, the English East India Company (EIC), founded in London in 1600, had initially focused its attention on India to avoid conflicts of interests with the Portuguese in Macao and the Dutch in the East Indies. After the fall of the Ming Dynasty (1644), and the subsequent struggle for control of China's seaboard, Britain began to challenge Portugal and the Netherlands as the major European trading power in Asia. In 1654, the EIC was allowed to land in Macao after British ships had made their way to Chinese waters. The Portuguese territory became the headquarter of British traders when the Qing government lifted the ban on overseas commerce in 1684, opening up trade in Guangzhou to all nations (except Russia and Japan), governed

[5] Fieldhouse (1966, 144–148), Furber (1976, 272–273), Gaastra (1997, 152–156), Prakash (1999, 181–188), Hoang (2007, 127–185) and Chang (2019, 229–234).

by regulations set by the Chinese authorities. An English "factory" was established at Guangzhou in 1699, a year after France had opened a warehouse in this major port city in southern China.[6]

French policymakers acquired an active interest in East Asia after the Thirty Years' War (1618–1648) in Europe, during the reign of King Louis XIV. In contrast to British traders, who were searching for new markets, French missionaries became emissaries, representing French culture as well as Catholicism. In 1663, the Société des missions étrangères (Society of Foreign Missions) was founded in Paris and was soon, actively supported by the king, planning to make Siam a Christian stronghold and a centre of French influence in East Asia. Yet, Louis XIV's political and economic policies, which initiated several major administrative and fiscal reforms in France, also enabled him to sponsor the creation of the first Compagnie des Indes orientales (French East India Company) in 1664, the sixth such company in a series dating back to 1600. The Company's trade monopoly extended to almost the whole world, except the Atlantic, with the China Seas becoming part of its privileged area of operation, although the main bases were in India. In 1680, the first Company ship sailed from India to Siam, with the goal of setting up a trading centre, something that came to fruition five years later when the Siamese court signed a treaty granting commercial and religious concessions to France. However, in 1688, a revolution against the Siamese king, followed by the cession of almost all European contacts, led to the collapse of the French position in the country. On Siamese ships, the entire French military force was shipped to Pondicherry, a south-eastern Indian port city, which became the headquarters of the Company in 1674 and the chief French settlement in India, to where the Company's vessels mostly transported flat iron, lead and some copper, as well as foodstuffs and alcohol for French residents. Exporting French fabrics to India turned out to be very difficult because of British and Dutch competition which offered better quality and lower prices.[7]

[6] Fieldhouse (1966, 149–152), Keay (1991, 206–210); Bassett (1997, 234–236), Hsü (2000, 96–97) and Van Dyke (2005, 5–18).

[7] Furber (1976, 201–211), Manning (1997, 282–287), Haudrère (1999, 206–207), Eberstein (2007, 109) and Schopp (2018, 44–45).

When the French East India Company sent the *Amphitrite* to Guangzhou in 1698, French trade with China began.[8] The 500-tonne sailing vessel was operated by private French traders who had signed a limited agreement with the Company, leasing them the trading monopoly. Relying on private traders remained the Company's practice for voyages to China until the final ship returned from Guangzhou in 1718. In the following year, a major restructuring brought about the next Compagnie des Indes, which retained its trading monopoly for half a century and encountered various political, commercial and financial difficulties during this period. Naval conflicts with other European powers (especially with Britain and her powerful navy), the temporary low demand for French luxury goods and rising shipping costs, which accounted for two-thirds of the Company's expenses, were major factors in its relatively weak performance. After the Company proved unable to support itself financially, it gave up its trade monopoly in 1769 and opened all its East India and China trade to French citizens. In October 1776, Pierre-Charles-François Vauquelin, a long-serving employee of the Company, was appointed as the first French consul in Guangzhou. However, the consulate was abolished when the third and final Compagnie des Indes was established in 1785 as part of France's programme of fiscal reform. After the French Revolution (1789), the Company was dissolved for alleged accusations of mismanagement and speculation.[9]

[8] The best study on the French frigate *l'Amphitrite* and its voyages to Canton, including Guangzhou Bay (the later French leased territory Guangzhouwan), is Montague (2019, 144–183). In the missionary field, the Paris Foreign Mission Society had proven to be mostly unsuccessful in its efforts to bring French vicars apostolic into China. Due to Portuguese opposition in defending their right of ecclesiastical right of patronage in the Far East dating back to the late fifteenth century, the first French missionaries entered China only in 1695. French Jesuits followed soon after, and even achieved the building of the first Christian church in Beijing. The backlash against these efforts came as result of a long-fought controversy over ritualistic practices which, since 1724, had led to the virtual elimination of all overt missionary activity in China. Most of the expelled missionaries moved southward, the members of the Paris Society to Annam proper and to Cochinchina, and the Jesuits and the Portuguese clergy to Tonkin. In 1749–1750, French missionaries in Hue, the capital of Annam, played an important role in providing information to the French East India Company about trading opportunities in Annam, and also in Tonkin. At the time, the Company's expedition was negotiating a formal trade treaty with the King of Annam, but was eventually unsuccessful in achieving any agreement with the country. Cady (1954, 1–6, 10–11).

[9] Cady (1954, 11–12), Fieldhouse (1966, 155–156), Furber (1976, 119–121), Haudrère (1999, 207–211) and Schopp (2018, 51–63).

In the late seventeenth and early eighteen centuries, European trade in the South China Sea faced severe difficulties. For political reasons, the ruling Qing dynasty in China (1644–1912) wished to abandon trade in southern Chinese ports, and even forced the coastal population of Fukien to move inland. This triggered a period of decline in trade in Southeast Asia after 1650.[10] In Vietnam, the two rival states, Tonkin in the north and Cochinchina in the south (as they were labelled by Westerners), accepted European traders only because of their interest in purchasing Western guns to fight each other, but imposed crippling controls on such trade after the war had ended in 1679. This left Portuguese ships plying between Macao and the central Vietnamese port of Hoi An (near Tourane or modern Da Nang) as the only regular non-Chinese contact with Vietnam. Another token of decline was the deteriorating trade monopolies of the Dutch and English East India Companies which left room for private merchants. "Country traders" such as Asian merchants (primarily of Chinese origin) or Asian-based British or French shipowners with Asian crews or home ports, played a major role in this phase, but the Chinese profited mostly from the new developing trend in East Asian commerce. In a revisionist approach to Eurocentric histories, the period from 1740 to 1840 has been described as the "Chinese century" of Southeast Asia, stressing the dynamic role of southern Chinese merchants, miners, craftsmen, shipbuilders and agriculturalists in opening up economic frontiers in Southeast Asia.[11]

The Chinese Century (1740–1840)

The initial phase of the Chinese century partly coincided with the long reign of Emperor Qianlong (Ch'ienlung, 1736–1795) during which China enjoyed peace and prosperity before its modern decline. With a rapidly growing population, from about 150 million in 1700 to 400 million in 1850, the country experienced great migration waves moving from northern to southern China. By land, the Chinese migrated even further south, into Burma, Laos and northern Vietnam, and by sea into the remainder of Southeast Asia. The Nguyen dynasty of southern Vietnam and the Chakkri dynasty of Siam especially welcomed Chinese

[10] Reid (1997, 58–59).

[11] Reid (2015, 188–191).

migrants to expand their lands and their revenue base. By the middle of the eighteenth century, the Chinese population of Cochinchina was estimated to exceed thirty thousand. The Chinese factor, as Anthony Reid (1997) put it, was crucial to most of the increases in shipping, trading, mining and other economic activities in the regions around the South China Sea.[12]

The Chinese century was decisively influenced by the Canton Trade era, which lasted from the late seventeenth century to 1842. Guangzhou, the port city in southern China, developed into the centre of direct commerce with foreigners, which brought about the increasing arrival of foreign merchant ships and a growing expansion of the Chinese junk trade with Southeast Asia. British and other Western merchants were confined to factories, or manufactories, rented from Chinese merchant houses, specially authorised and licensed by the Qing government. For mainly geographical and political reasons, Macao was gradually replaced by Guangzhou as the sole centre of China's foreign trade. However, since Chinese authorities compelled foreigners to leave Guangzhou in the off-season to minimise conflict, the Portuguese territory remained an important place of residence for Western merchants. In the early eighteenth century, each the French and English East India Companies sent one or two ships a year to the Chinese city. "Country traders", private British merchants in India licensed by the EIC, sent ships every year to Guangzhou, where the Chinese authorities were patronising and promoting trade by different means. Other European merchants also made their way to East Asia. In 1732, the first Swedish East India Company ship arrived in Guangzhou, followed two years later by the Danish Asiatic Company. At the time, the overall volume of Guangzhou's trade had enormously expanded, with private English, French, Indian, Armenian, Muslim and other traders, who regularly visited the port city.[13]

Germans were latecomers in establishing commercial links with East Asia. In 1751, King Frederick II of Prussia (later called "the Great"), established the Königlich Preußisch-Asiatische Handlungs-Compagnie von Emden auf China (Royal Prussian-Asiatic Trading Company of

[12] Hsü (2000, 38–42), Reid (1997, 70–71), Reid (2004, 22–27) and Li (2004, 262).

[13] Hsü (2000, 142–147) and Van Dyke (2005, 5–18). On Chinese junk trading with Saigon, see Chin (2004, 61–62).

Emden for China). Based on capital from German and Dutch shareholders, the company was friendly received in the Netherlands, and even in France, where the government promised support for Prussia. The central European kingdom was regarded by France as an important political counterweight to keep in check her major European rivals, Britain and Austria. King Frederick II provided the Company, which was highly independent in its administrative and business dealings, with comprehensive trading and customs privileges. Emden, the North Sea port city, was deliberately selected as its headquarters since other Prussian seaports were located in the Baltic and restricted to the Sound as only exit passage into the Atlantic, with Denmark controlling both shores and exacting tolls from foreign shipping passing through. In 1752, the *König von Preussen*, the Company's first ship, with a freight of fine cloth, lead and cash, called at Guangzhou, marking the beginning of German commerce with East Asia. On her return voyage to Emden, the vessel carried tea, porcelain, silk and other Chinese produce. In the following years, four other Company ships made the same voyage, gaining good profits. However, Prussia's trade with China came to an abrupt end with the outbreak of the Seven Years' War (1756–1763), the first global war in history. Although French troops had occupied Emden in 1757 only temporarily, the ongoing war, for which Prussia needed all her economic resources, required King Frederick II to liquidate the Company and sell its entire fleet. Prussia emerged from the war as a major European power, but with her lands and population severely devastated, meagre domestic resources and most of her international connections severed.[14]

In the meantime, in 1757, Guangzhou had been officially designated by the Qing dynasty as China's centre of foreign trade. In 1772, King Frederick II launched the Königlich Preußische Seehandlungs-Gesellschaft (Royal Prussian Maritime Trading Company) in which he was the major shareholder. The company, with its headquarters in Prussia's capital Berlin, started operations on 1 January 1773, but was restricted to Europe given Prussia's limited economic resources, and was unable to obtain any share of the Canton trade. Nevertheless, in 1787, the Prussian government appointed the English merchant Daniel Beale to be its honorary consul in Guangzhou. He was also the first-ever consul of a German state in China, without being ever officially recognised by

[14] Eberstein (1988, 26–28), Clark (2006, 213–215) and Eberstein (2007, 42–67).

the Chinese government. Beale's main reason for seeking such a commission was to circumvent the monopoly of the English East India Company (which granted private traders operating under its licence a monopoly of all trade east of the Cape of Good Hope). A number of unlicensed British private merchants secured the consulships of other European countries in order to be permitted to stay in Guangzhou and expand their business, often serving as agency houses for companies in London and India, and engaging in lucrative trades such as opium smuggling.[15] Thanks to his commission, Beale and his partner James Cox were permitted to establish the firm Cox & Beale, which, after numerous intermediate changes in partners, became the progenitor of Jardine, Matheson & Co. (founded by William Jardine and James Matheson), the major British trading house in southern China, which was trafficking opium in China but usually traded in cotton, tea, silk and a variety of other goods. In 1799, Thomas Beale, the younger brother of Daniel, took over the Prussian consulate, with Charles Magniac as vice-consul, a principal figure in Guangzhou, who became a partner in the firm in 1804. The company, which was consequently renamed Beale, Magniac and Company, was a typical "agency house", as Michael Greenberg put it, not only trading but also performing important commercial functions, as did agents and correspondents of private firms in London and India, acting all at once "as banker, bill broker, ship owner, freighter, insurance agent [and] purveyor".[16]

The aim of private British merchants trading in Guangzhou to circumvent the monopoly of the English East India Company by taking over foreign consulates coincided with the Prussian government's interest in receiving regular news on China's political and economic affairs, and possibly opening new markets for Prussia's industries in the future. In 1792, the independent North German port city of Hamburg recorded the first arrival of a ship from Guangzhou, and of four more vessels in

[15] According to Jessica Hanser, over twenty unlicensed private traders were doing business in Guangzhou between 1761 and 1780, mostly English East India Company servants, Company ship captains and free merchants acting as brokers and bankers for wealthy clients in India. Hanser (2018, 9), Eberstein (2007, 89–90, 108–118), Hsü (2000, 166), Keay (1991, 433), Van Dyke (2005, 16) and Becker (2010, 330–332).

[16] Charles Magniac originated from the old French Huguenot family of de Magnac or Magniac, the members of which appear to have been Hugenots who escaped from Catholic France to England in the late seventeenth century. He was the eldest son of Francis Magniac who carried on a business in clocks and automata. (Steuart 1934, 5, 43), Greenberg (1951, the quote: 144) and Becker (2010, 332–333).

the following years, but which flag the ships were sailing under remains unknown. The first vessel flying the Hamburg flag left the port city for China in 1797. At the time, shipping and commerce in China and Southeast Asia was experiencing a strong and mutually influential economic upturn. The main stimulus was the increased demand for rice in southern China where population pressure and the easing of trade restrictions opened up a large market. In southern Vietnam, the number of Chinese junks increased fourfold between 1750 and 1820, and subsequently, the state revenues of the Nguyen ruler from overseas commerce in Saigon rose considerably; the same happened with the Siamese Crown's income from maritime trade, which increased from a fourth or a third to well over half. The final phase of the Chinese century was marked by constant economic growth and increasing prosperity in Southeast Asia.[17]

Meanwhile, in Europe, the French Revolution and its aftermath severely constrained shipping and commerce. Successive French governments refrained from any initiatives in East Asia, and instead focused on European affairs. The Continental System designed in 1806/07 by French Emperor Napoleon Bonaparte brought the overseas trade of continental Europe to an almost total standstill. The French policy aimed at excluding British trade from the Continent and hitting Britain's economy decisively was also imposed on Prussia, France's ally since 1806. When Britain took revenge, the last Prussian ship still operating in East Asia fell victim to a British naval attack on Batavia, the capital of the Dutch East Indies, in 1811. Under these circumstances, Beale, Magniac & Co. in Guangzhou seemed to have relinquished any visible consular activities for Prussia. Therefore, the Prussian consulate faded almost into oblivion, even after Napoleon's fall and the liberation of Europe (1814/1815). In 1822, the Royal Prussian Maritime Trading Company dispatched its first ship to Guangzhou after numerous other vessels had called at Hamburg since 1816; around three ships annually were constantly on the run between Hamburg and Guangzhou from the 1820s. It came as a great surprise to Berlin when Daniel Beale, in 1825, applied to the government to appoint his eldest son as Prussian consul in Guangzhou. The company's president, Christian Rother, was charged with approaching William Oswald, supercargo on the Company's ships sailing to China, about the matter. In 1829, when Oswald had returned from a voyage to

[17] Eberstein (1988, 28), Reid (2004, 28–32), Lieberman (1997, 35) and Li (2004, 3).

Guangzhou to report that none of the foreign consulates there had any influence on the Chinese authorities, consideration in Berlin of appointing another honorary consul came to an abrupt end. Consequently, in 1840, the proposal by Hollingworth Magniac (the younger brother of Charles Magniac) to appoint Alexander Matheson, nephew of James Matheson, and partner in Jardine, Matheson & Co., to be the consul of Prussia in Guangzhou, also met with disapproval. The Prussian government made it clear that appointing another British merchant in Guangzhou to be consul at the beginning of the "entanglement between England and China", was undesirable. This was a clear hint about the imminent outbreak of the First Opium War (1839–1842), which brought an end to the Chinese century in Southeast Asia.[18]

The Early Imperialist Age (1839–61)

Anglo-French Imperialism and German Commerce (1839–60)

The British military campaign aimed at pressuring the Qing government into compensation negotiations after the anti-opium crusade launched by the Chinese Special Imperial Commissioner, Lin Zexu, started with the public burning of the entire opium stocks at Guangzhou in March 1839. Almost one hundred foreign commercial enterprises trading on the southern China coast were directly or indirectly affected by the resulting war. The forceful British intervention in China opened up the period of European imperialism in East Asia. France turned her attention to the region soon after the outbreak of the conflict. The French foreign ministry despatched Alexandre de Challaye (the 24-year-old élève consul or student-consul), to the Philippines and from there to China. He arrived in Guangzhou in September 1840 with instructions to establish France's first professional consulate in China. One month later, French policy took a new course when François Guizot, formerly ambassador in London, began his tenure as the new French foreign minister. On Guizot's agenda was the renewal of French naval power, which required the creation of a global network that provided coal, wood and provisions. Consequently, the Division navale des mers de Chine (Naval Division of the Chinese Seas), was established. As Guizot said in the French parliament on 31 March 1842, the project to expand the navy went hand in hand with

[18] Eberstein (2007, 116–118) and Becker (2010, 331–335).

France's global expansion in terms of shipping and trade. According to the foreign minister, it was necessary "to have around the globe, at those points destined to become great centres of trade and shipping, strong and secure maritime stations capable of serving as support of our trade".[19]

On 29 August 1842, the First Opium War was settled with the signing of the Treaty of Nanjing (Nanking) between China and Britain, the first in a series of so-called "unequal treaties" imposed on China. It opened five seaports, including Guangzhou (the so-called "treaty ports"), to foreign trade, with British trade and consular representation officially sanctioned, and ceded Hong Kong Island to Britain. The general settlement was joined by the supplementary Treaty of the Bogue (signed on 18 October 1843), that laid down a set of detailed regulations about the conduct of the new order, including granting Britain the most-favoured nation treatment, through which China would confer on her any rights which might be conceded to other powers later. Such events were carefully reported by British and continental European newspapers and caused politicians and businessmen to watch developments in China with great expectations.[20] French Foreign Minister Guizot quickly reached an agreement with the British government that London would not oppose the sending of an official delegation to negotiate a commercial treaty with Beijing that gave France the same privileges as Britain. In December 1843, Guizot charged Théodore de Lagrené (the former French ambassador to Spain) with leading an official trade mission to China. The impressive delegation, which consisted of a number of officials from the French ministries of commerce and finance, representatives of several textile and other industries and of delegates from chambers of commerce of five major French cities, left France on board six naval vessels. On 24 October 1844, Lagrené managed to sign the Treaty of Whampoa, in which China granted France the same privileges as Britain. The agreement included the opening of five treaty ports to French merchants, extraterritorial privileges for French citizens, the right of France to appoint consuls and the free propagation of Catholicism in China. However, hopes of acquiring a territory like Hong Kong were dashed after Britain and Spain strongly

[19] Bensacq-Tixier (2003, 106–107) and Brocheux and Hémery (2009, 21–22, the quote: 22).

[20] Fairbank (1978, 213–223) and Hsü (2000, 184–193).

opposed such French intentions. Moreover, initial expectations of developing substantial trade with China were frustrated after delegates found the trade opportunities in the newly opened treaty ports unpromising.[21]

Within the Deutscher Bund (German Confederation, an association of thirty-nine independent German-speaking states in Central Europe formed in 1815 to replace the former Holy Roman Empire of German nation which had been dissolved in 1806), events in China had been carefully observed by manufactures and traders based in major industrial regions. A few weeks after the Treaty of Nanjing was signed, the Cologne Chamber of Commerce (Cologne had been part of the Kingdom of Prussia since 1815) submitted a memorandum to the Prussian government requesting that the Royal Prussian Maritime Trading Company send a trade mission to China to promote German exports with delegates consisting of experts from the member states of the Deutscher Zollverein (German Customs Union), the coalition of German states formed in 1833 to manage tariffs and economic policies within their territories. Around Cologne, the commercial hub of the Rhineland manufacturing district (since 1815, the Rhineland had been the most western province of Prussia), industrial development was accelerating and contributing to economic cooperation among the twenty-eight Customs Union members. The Cologne initiative was firmly supported by Saxony, another Customs Union member state, which even proposed to Prussia the establishment of common Customs Union consulates in the treaty ports of China. It was obvious that the Saxon government was keenly interested in fostering the country's important textile industry and opening up fresh business opportunities in China for its manufacturers and merchants. However, the proposals from Dresden met with great caution in Berlin, where the company's president, Christian Rother, warned strongly against excessive expectations and was only willing to send the expert Friedrich Wilhelm Grube to explore trade opportunities by boarding a Company ship carrying crude woollen goods to northern China. Grube, a medium-ranking official in the Rhineland administration, was made Prussian commercial council to provide him with a higher status for his negotiations in Beijing and sent to China in September 1843. However, his subsequent report to the Prussian government was not very encouraging when it came to the question of appointing a Customs Union consul

[21] Cady (1954, 44–69).

for China. Grube was supported in his opinion by Theodor Johns, a German merchant residing in Macao, who was charged by the Hamburg government with assessing the need for a trade agreement with China. Johns came to the conclusion that German trade at Guangzhou had no importance and that most foreign merchants knew nothing about it.[22]

Despite such gloomy perspectives, it was private initiative which brought about the first business contacts with East Asia. The first of the German merchants in China was Carl Wilhelm Engelbrecht von Pustau who began trading in Guangzhou on 1 January 1843. The establishment was supported by the Hamburg banker Salomon Heine, the uncle of the poet Heinrich Heine. In 1846, the firm Wm. Pustau & Company was registered in Hong Kong. After Pustau had returned to Europe in the 1850s, the company expanded considerably, until by 1861 it had four principal partners and a staff of twelve distributed among Guangzhou, Shanghai and Hong Kong (in 1876, the firm went bankrupt).[23] Other German pioneers in the China business were the Leipzig trading houses Carl & Gustav Harkort and C. Hirzel & Company which dispatched a private trade mission from Saxony to East Asia to explore the potential for Saxon exports. When Richard von Carlowitz, Max Harkort and Bernhard Harkort discovered promising markets in China, they decided to establish two trading companies, with Carlowitz being in charge in Guangzhou (the firm Carlowitz, Harkort & Co. was established in Guangzhou on 1 January 1846), and with the Harkorts in Shanghai. In both cities there was no German consul at all, and bearing in mind that such an honorary appointment could be advantageous, especially for a newly established business, the Leipzig merchants requested the Saxon government to charge their partners with such posts. Although Saxony preferred a joint Customs Union consulate, and filed a corresponding motion before the general meeting in Berlin in May 1846, the Hanse cities Hamburg, Bremen and Lübeck were unwilling to relinquish any of their sovereign rights for such an enterprise which would probably enhance the dominance of the stronger German states over them. Facing such opposition from small states, which nevertheless had important trading and shipping interests in East Asia, eighteen Germans residing in Guangzhou and Hong Kong, led by Carlowitz, set up a joint petition to support the

[22] Stoecker (1958, 43) and Becker (2010, 337–339).

[23] Eberstein (1988, 37).

idea which was published by two major German newspapers in October 1846. However, the Prussian government found trading opportunities in China too insignificant to justify the establishment of a salaried professional consul, and instead proposed making Carlowitz joint consul of Prussia and Saxony. When the Saxon government agreed to the idea, in May 1847 Carlowitz was appointed to the post of consul in Guangzhou, being the first German-born merchant commissioned to be a consul in China.[24]

In the 1840s and 1850s, German shipping companies and trading firms operating in the treaty ports of China clearly profited from the concessions granted by Beijing to Britain and France in the treaties of 1842/1844. The firm of Siemssen & Company was established in Guangzhou in 1846 by the Hamburg trader Georg Theodor Siemssen; F. Schwarzkopf & Company began operating in the Chinese port city in the 1850s, dealing mainly in ship stores. Although facts and figures are only sporadically available, most trading seemed to have been done through Britain, with exports of tea and spices to Hamburg and imports of German cloth into China via London. This was the result of the long series of English Navigation Acts, which required all trade between England and her colonies to be carried in English or colonial vessels. Therefore, in many cases, the Chinese purchaser thought the imported German cloth had been produced in Britain, while the German textile manufacturer was not aware of the Chinese consumers of his goods. After the British Navigation Acts were revoked in 1849, under the impact of free trade principles, direct shipping between Hamburg, the major German port city, and China became more frequent, with around twelve vessels annually on the run. The rising numbers were also due to increasing demand for coasters in East Asia, which made German sailing vessels shipping English coal to the region, and after discharging freights, engaging in tramp shipping along Chinese and other East Asian shores before returning to Europe. Tramp ships were cargo-carrying merchant vessels which did not work a regular route but could be diverted to any port to pick up available cargo. Cabotage by tramp vessels along East Asian coasts provided crucial connections between port cities around the region, linking the trade of Asian and foreign merchants with each

[24] *Börsen-Halle* (Hamburg), 31 October 1846. Beutler (1946, 1–23) and Eberstein (1988, 53–54). Smaller German states usually commissioned foreign merchants to be their consuls in China. See Becker (2010, 335–336).

other. Tramp ships went on to transport large quantities of low-value but high-bulk materials, something that became a typical pattern of the nineteenth-century global transport revolution.[25]

Usually, independent states setting up national laws or bilateral treaties to regulate foreign shipping on their shores denied foreigners the right of tramp shipping in their coastal and inland waters. However, in China, the right to engage in cabotage was tacitly granted to British and other flags in the treaties of 1842/1844. It was seemingly because of the absence of appropriate Chinese transport by water, and also the ignorance of Chinese officials, that they raised no objection to British and other vessels freely navigating in Chinese waters. Only in the treaties of 1858 did China explicitly grant navigation rights for British and French vessels, even for inland waterways. Since all treaty powers had a most-favoured-nation arrangement with China in their commercial conventions concluded after 1858, the right of cabotage was applied accordingly. Prussia and the German Customs Union states were granted this right in the Treaty of Tianjin signed with China on 2 September 1861. This enabled German vessels to gain a strong position in the cabotage of China, as shipping statistics of the Chinese Imperial Maritime Customs reveal: In 1864 and 1866, German ships, in both number and tonnage, came third to British and American flags, and even before Chinese vessels including junks, in the treaty ports of China.[26]

According to the consular report of Richard von Carlowitz submitted in early 1849, there were at the time merely thirty-three Germans, mostly from the Hanse cities, residing in China and only four German companies. However, in the 1850s, an increasing number of German merchants established themselves in Chinese treaty ports and in the British colonies of Hong Kong and Singapore, with some of them acquiring considerable capital.[27] A report from Lieutenant Reinhold von Werner (who took part in the Prussian expedition to East Asia in 1860/1861), said the following about Germans trading in East Asia:

[25] Stoecker (1958, 44–45), Stoecker (1977, 27–28), Eberstein (1988, 32–36), Bard (1993, 96–105), Armstrong (2004, 115) and Dear and Kemp (2006, 591).

[26] Otte (1930, 128), F. F. A. (1931, 251), Otte (1931, 352–353), Sze (1925, 131–136) and Hsü (2000, 189–190).

[27] Bard (1993, 103) and Stoecker (1958, 45–46).

> For fifteen to twenty years, young and enterprising merchants, on average without any capital than intellectual one, went to East India and China. At first, they were mainly attracted by the high salary, which amounts to three thousand to four thousand thalers for a useful clerk in major English houses. They are remaining in those positions for some years, acquiring some wealth with smaller businesses on the side that are permitted by their principals, learned to know local conditions and used them to establish themselves later. In this way, almost all German firms in China developed. Their founders started from nowhere, gradually worked their way up and acquired through hard diligence and business ability the honourable position and the recognition they generally enjoy now.[28]

At the time, French shipping and trade were almost non-existent in China, although the Treaty of Whampoa (1844) had set favourable conditions for French merchants in China. All the same, French politicians pursued imperialist goals in East Asia. In 1847, Foreign Minister Guizot appointed Baron Alexandre de Forth-Rouen (the former French attaché in London and then legation secretary in Lisbon) to become French minister and chargé d'affaires for China in Guangzhou. Like the British and other foreign legations, the French legation remained based in Macao. Yet, Forth-Rouen showed little interest in promoting France's interests in China. In 1851, he was replaced by Alphonse de Bourboulon (the son of a French emigrant to Hamburg in the Napoleonic era who had been French chargé d'affaires in Argentina and the United States). Appointed to Minister of the Republic in China, Bourbolon continued to reside in Macao and watched from the Portuguese territory the British bombardment of Guangzhou that followed the so-called *Arrow* incident of 1856. That event opened the Second Opium War or Arrow War (1856–1860). Taking advantage of the assassination of a French missionary in Kwangsi Province, the French government decided to join in a joint naval action with Britain and sent a task force under the command of Baron Jean-Baptiste-Louis Gros, a veteran diplomat, who was appointed to become special ambassador in April 1857. Gros co-operated closely with James Bruce, 8th Earl of Elgin, the British plenipotentiary and leader of the expedition to China, when Anglo-French forces stormed and occupied Guangzhou in December 1857. The French navy proved to be a lever to push for trading concessions from China and to support French

[28] Werner (1863, 215–216).

troops commanded by Admiral Charles Rigault de Genouilly in the invasion of central and southern Vietnam and the seizure of Saigon.[29] As a result of major military actions in northern China, Britain and France managed to secure the Treaties of Tianjin, signed on 26 and 27 June 1858 respectively. The agreements that contained the most-favoured-nation clause stipulated the opening of ten new treaty ports, the reduction of Chinese inland transit dues (likin) for foreign imports, permission for foreigners, including Catholic and Protestant missionaries, to travel in all parts of China under passports and the promise of high indemnities for Britain and France.[30]

In early 1859, the British and French governments transferred their ministers and legations from Macao to Shanghai. Soon later, Frederick Bruce (the brother of Lord Elgin, appointed British minister to China and instructed to exchange the ratifications at Beijing) and his French counterpart, Bourboulon, were confronted with the Chinese demand to let the event take place in Shanghai, which they refused. The subsequent military actions at the Taku forts resulted in heavy casualties for the British naval forces and only nominal losses for the Chinese side, which was a severe blow to British prestige in China and forced Bruce and Bourboulon to retreat to Shanghai. Lord Elgin was once again dispatched to China with an impressive naval force where he co-operated closely with French troops as they finally burned down the Summer Palace near Beijing in retaliation for continuing Chinese resistance. On 24 October 1860, he dictated to Prince Kungthe Convention of Beijing, which established the British right to diplomatic representation in the Chinese capital. Consequently, Bruce and Bourboulon established their respective legations in Beijing in March 1861. For both Britain and France, indemnity was increased. Tianjin was declared a treaty port and Britain acquired the Kowloon Peninsula opposite Hong Kong, while France secured the right of Catholic missionaries to own properties in China. The second set of "unequal" treaties obtained from China by Britain and France during the Second Opium War (1856–1860) considerably reinforced the first ones signed after the First Opium War (1839–1842).[31]

[29] Jenkins (1973, 298–299), Walser (1992, 1) and Halpern (2001, 36–37).

[30] Cady (1954, 70–80), Bensacq-Tixier (2003, 78–80, 221–222) and Hsü (2000, 205–211).

[31] Bensacq-Tixier (2003, 81) and Hsü (2000, 212–219).

The Prussian Expedition to East Asia (1860/61)

The British and French Tianjin treaties of 1858 stimulated interest in East Asia among German politicians and businesspeople, especially in the big Hanse cities. In September 1858, the Hamburg government proposed to Bremen and Lübeck the joint securing of a similar treaty with China. August von der Heydt, Prussian trade minister and an influential Rhineland economist, urged action as soon as possible and not waiting "until the commerce of other countries had taken possession of the markets". Prussia should try to secure a similar treaty by dispatching men-of-war and a negotiator to East Asia who could make shipping and trading agreements with Japan, Siam and Hawaii. His firm call convinced the Prussian government to take up the idea, which even found strong backing from Prince William (who was to become King in 1861 and German Emperor in 1871) deputising for his older brother, King Frederick William IV, who had been incapacitated by a sequence of strokes. During his posting to the Rhineland as military governor in 1849, William had developed contacts with liberal supporters of the idea that Prussia should lead the path to the unification of the German states. In November 1858, he initiated a cabinet reshuffle which brought liberal-minded personalities into major government positions. The so-called Neue Ära (New Era) proved to be crucial in launching the official Prussian expedition to East Asia.[32]

For the new Prussian government, the traditional rivalry with Austria was a powerful factor. Since 1815, when the German Confederation was formed, the two major German states had vied for leadership and dominance of the other members. This rivalry was also expressed in foreign politics after discussion of German unification began to dominate the agendas of national and liberal movements across the member states of the German Confederation. On a global level, the Austrian Habsburg Empire had taken the lead in 1857, sending a man-of-war on a voyage of exploration around the world which was enthusiastically received by the German community of Shanghai. Acquiring new shipping and trading markets in East Asia through joint German efforts seemed a possible option to move closer towards German unification. However, when Austrian armies suffered a crushing military defeat in June 1859

[32] Stoecker (1958, 50–51, the quote: 51), Stoecker (1977, 28), Martin (1990, 35) and Clark (2006, 514).

during the Second Italian War of Independence (which threatened to dismember the Habsburg Empire), the government in Vienna decided to relinquish any plans for global endeavours. This opened the door for Prussia to strengthening her position in striving for the leadership of Germany. Presenting herself as the protagonist of overseas trading expansion, Prussia took the lead by dispatching a trading mission to East Asia. On 18 August 1859, the Prussian government decided to launch such an expedition on behalf of the German Customs Union (of which Prussia, but not Austria, was a member), with the goal of coming to shipping and trading agreements with China, Japan and Siam (Thailand). The Prussian navy agreed to provide four men-of-war for the voyage. Berlin's step was widely appreciated by the member states of the Customs Union governments, with the Hanse cities Hamburg, Bremen and Lübeck signalling strong support and promising to dispatch special delegates to join the mission, carrying with them samples of products from their industries.[33]

Count Friedrich Albrecht zu Eulenburg (the former Prussian consul-general in Antwerp and Warsaw and a commercial expert) was chosen to lead the expedition, which demonstrated the Custom Union's prime interest in promoting trading interests and not foreign political goals. Immediately after his appointment, Eulenburg, who was inexperienced in high diplomacy and unacquainted with the countries he was to visit, rushed to Paris in March 1860 to personally consult the French and British chief negotiators of the Treaties of Tianjin about the matter. On the British side, Lord Elgin promised full support for Prussia in securing from China a similar agreement to Britain. On the French side, Baron Gros went even further and proposed to Eulenburg using the opportunity to seize Formosa (Taiwan) and make the island a Prussian colony. The French diplomat pointed to the fact that treaties with East Asian governments, without establishing a German colony, would be "entirely unsuccessful for Germany's commercial relations with these countries". Gros even hinted at the possibility that French troops could occupy Cambodia when Prussia seized Formosa. It seemed that the French government was hoping of to have Prussia as an ally in realising France's

[33] Stoecker (1958, 52–54), Stoecker (1977, 28) and Martin (1990, 35–36).

imperialist projects in Southeast Asia, which were constrained by her rivalries with Britain and China.[34]

The French diplomat's ideas met with some interest in Berlin. After consulting Prince William the Prussian government, on 8 May 1860, instructed Eulenburg to search for a suitable location in East Asia for a colony and, if necessary, to leave behind a ship with a crew. Any political or military conflict with other powers was to be avoided. The expeditionary force only disposed of a tiny fleet consisting of two men-of-war (with the wooden corvette *Arcona* launched in 1858 as the largest vessel), a supply ship and a merchant vessel, carrying altogether seven hundred forty men (not all of them trained soldiers). On the other hand, the expedition leader was authorised to eventually provide military support to British and French forces for their campaign in China. Calling at Singapore, Eulenburg learned about the ongoing war in China and decided to sail to Japan first. In September 1860, his fleet entered the bay of Edo (today's Tokyo), with only three ships left after the supply vessel had sunk in a typhoon. With the strong backing of the American and French envoys, Eulenburg finally succeeded in securing a trading and friendship treaty with Japan which was signed on 24 January 1861. However, the Japanese negotiators were only prepared to sign the agreement with Prussia, arguing that they were not acquainted with the complicated conditions of other German states or the German Customs Union.[35]

In March 1861, the Prussian ships landed on the coast near Shanghai. Eulenburg and his attaches (among them Max von Brandt the later Prussian minister-resident in Tokyo and German minister in Beijing), were taken to the major Chinese port city on board a small steamer of the French navy. Therefore, he paid the first courtesy visit to Vice Admiral Auguste Léopold Protet, the commander of the French naval forces during the Second Opium War, to express his thanks. In the following month, the Prussian expedition proceeded to Tianjin where Eulenburg was received by two commissioners of Prince Kung, the reform-oriented official representative of the Chinese emperor. According to French Minister de Bourboulon, the Chinese government initially refused to accept to grant any rights to Prussia, which it had been forced

[34] Letter from Count Friedrich von Eulenburg to Foreign Minister Alexander von Schleinitz, 20 March 1860, as quoted in Stoecker (1958, 55).

[35] Stoecker (1958, 55, 269) and Martin (1990, 36).

to concede to other European powers only after heavy military defeats.[36] Therefore, the commissioners insisted on granting merely a commercial treaty, without the right to establish a Prussian legation in the Chinese capital or to provide protection to Chinese Christians. Although the British and French ministers were initially reluctant to strongly support Eulenburg's demands, fearing that Prince Kung could be overthrown by traditionalist court circles, it seems that the French government explicitly pushed Bourboulon to back the Prussian case. This finally forced his British counterpart, Frederick Bruce, to join him. Although the Chinese government tried to delay the negotiations, Eulenburg used all kinds of diplomatic pressure to achieve an agreement with Beijing. He finally succeeded in securing a convention which was in many ways identical to the second set of "unequal" treaties Britain and France had secured from China during the Second Opium War. After four months of rather unpleasant negotiations with three powers, the most important concession from Prussia the Chinese negotiators could achieve was Eulenburg's promise that a permanent Prussian legation would be established in the Chinese capital five years at the earliest after the treaty was ratified. The Tianjin Treaty signed on 2 September 1861 granted not only member states of the German Customs Union but also the Grand Duchies of Mecklenburg-Schwerin and Mecklenburg-Strelitz and the Hanse cities of Hamburg, Lübeck and Bremen most-favoured-nation treatment and Prussia the sole right to represent them at Beijing. This gave the government in Berlin a kind of supervisory function over every German residing in China. The convention, which permitted Prussia and the German Customs Union to fully profit from the British and French achievements in China during the Second Opium War, was a splendid diplomatic success for the Germans.[37]

The Sino-German treaty of 1861 (which was revised in 1880) was the basic treaty concerning trade between the two countries until 1928 when a new commercial agreement was signed between them. However, even after the military occupation of Jiaozhou (Kiaochow) Bay in Shandong (Shantung) Province (1898) and the territory's subsequent development

[36] Alphonse de Bourboulon (Beijing) to Foreign Ministry (Paris), 22 June 1861, as quoted in Cordier (1901, 139).

[37] Hsü (2000, 215), Eulenburg-Hertefeld 1900, 184, 220–286), Stoecker (1958, 57–60, 269–272), Stoecker (1977, 28–29) and Martin (1990, 37–38).

into a kind of model colony of Imperial Germany's industrial achievements,[38] the German share of China's foreign trade (4.6 per cent in 1913) remained at rather modest levels, compared to Britain (19 per cent, including dominions and without Hong Kong) or Japan (18.7 per cent). During the First World War, German trade was almost suspended but later resumed and, with 6.5 per cent in 1932, achieving a respectable share of China's external trade.[39]

At the time the Prussian expedition sailed from Japan to China to start negotiations with the Chinese government, French forces under the command of Admiral Léonard Charner launched a military offensive in Cochinchina, seizing Vietnamese defence lines at Chi Hoa in February 1861 and moving further towards My Tho, a strategic key position to the Mekong Delta, and to Cambodia. France's imperial war in East Asia attracted the attention of King William I (who had ascended the throne of Prussia in January 1861) and who instructed the admiralty to give advice about the idea of acquiring a colony for Prussia. On 17 April 1861, a memorandum was submitted to the king in which three places were highly recommended for establishing a Prussian naval base and for settling Prussian emigrants and convicts: the island of Formosa, the Salomon Islands (a small atoll in the Indian Ocean) and Patagonia (a region at the southern end of South America). Therefore, Eulenburg was advised to keep an eye on the matter but not to take any action which could possibly cause political complications or threaten his negotiations for a treaty with China. The diplomat did as instructed and only came back to the issue almost two months after the Treaty of Tianjin with China (2 September 1861) was signed. Having paid a visit to Formosa, Eulenburg found the Chinese island's ports unsuitable for a Prussian naval station and its hot and humid climate not appropriate for permanently settling Europeans. Furthermore, he even warned the Prussian government about becoming estranged from Britain and France and endangering the treaties achieved with Japan and China. Although Prince Adalbert (a cousin of King William I), the commander-in-chief of the Prussian navy, protested against abandoning the project and again floated the idea of occupying Formosa, the case was closed. On 6 January 1862, King William I decided to bury such ideas

[38] Mühlhahn (2000, 11–13) and So (2019, 1–12).

[39] Ho (1933, 112–114), Feng (1936, 4–64, 171–261), Eberstein (2007, 171–200) and Ratenhof (1987, 564–565: table 3).

and instructed the expedition to depart from the China Seas. Yet, the project of a Prussian naval station in East Asia was realised in 1869, with the arrival in Singapore of two Prussian steam corvettes flying the flag of the North German Confederation and the opening of the naval station with a depot and hospital on a small plot of land in Yokohama leased from the Japanese government in 1867.[40]

On 15 December 1861, on their return voyage to Europe, the Prussian expedition called at Bangkok, the capital of Siam, for talks about a treaty. Two weeks earlier, French consul Count Francis de Castelnau had submitted to the Siamese government an official note enquiring about the legal status of Cambodia, over which Siam and Vietnam had jointly exercised suzerainty since the early nineteenth century. The enquiry was the result of France's military advances in Cochinchina after the fall of My Tho. French gunboats had begun penetrating the interior of southern Vietnam, resulting in April 1861 in the seizure of the provincial capitals of Ba Ria, Bien Hoa and Vinh Long. According to Max von Brandt, the excessive demands of the French consul caused "concerns and indignation" in Bangkok. The situation became even more tense when in December 1861 French naval forces occupied the archipelago of Poulo Condore (Con Dao), off the coast of southern Cochinchina, which was owned by the Siamese king. "To complete the mess", as Brandt put it, on 10 December 1861 a French steamer arrived in Bangkok, bringing a Siamese diplomatic delegation back from a courtesy visit to France, with a personal letter from the French Emperor, Napoleon III. Although King Mongkut (also known as King Rama IV), received the accompanying French envoys in a private audience, he immediately thereafter left Bangkok "to escape further demands and annoyances", as Brandt noted. Therefore, the welcome for the Prussian expedition in Bangkok was very friendly, compared to the earlier responses in Japan and China. Nine days later, the king, who had returned to the capital, received Eulenburg and other official members of the Prussian expedition in a private audience. King Mongkut, who embraced Western innovations and had initiated the modernisation of his country, welcomed the coming of the Germans,

[40] Brocheux and Hémery (2009, 25), Stoecker (1958, 60–61) and Martin (1990, 38). For the Prussian naval station in Yokohama, see in this book the chapter Saigon—The Franco-German War of 1870–1871—The Navies in East Asia.

obviously hoping to win the support of Prussia and a kind of mediatory influence on France.[41]

On 24 December 1861, in the private audience with Eulenberg, King Mongkut was very pleased to learn that Prussia would "never consider establishing colonies in these regions". During the official welcome ceremony three days later, he enquired about the relationship between Britain and Prussia and was curious to learn whether the two governments would support him should other countries create difficulties with Siam. Understanding that the king had hinted at the French threat, Eulenburg replied that he could only offer the friendly services of his sovereign, if such a situation arose. This statement was welcomed by King Mongkut who, in his formal response, announced he would "nominate qualified persons to deliberate upon and finally conclude a treaty similar to those signed with the monarchs of other European countries". On 9 January 1862, when the negotiations began, some important legal issues were at first addressed (such as certain property rights of German merchants residing in Siam who demanded to acquire land wherever they wished to do), but were quickly resolved after the king had intervened to support the German claims. The Treaty between Siam and Prussia signed on 7 February 1862 came "to everyone's satisfaction", as Prussian Lieutenant Reinhold von Werner noted in his report. German residents in Siam received the same legal rights as their British and French counterparts. Due to the fact that such clauses were also part of the other treaties signed in the wake of the Second Opium War, British, French and German traders were put on an equal legal footing in Japan, China and Siam.[42]

In January 1862, at the opening session of the Prussian diet, King William I described the series of treaties with East Asian countries as major achievements of his government. The left-liberal parliamentarian Rudolf Virchow (a renowned physician and co-founder of the German Progressive Party) hailed the success of the expedition to East Asia, calling it "a German national issue". Due to such widespread agreement, the diet unanimously ratified the treaties. Rudolf von Delbrück (a strong promoter of free trade and the first president of Bismarck's chancery later), judged

[41] Werner (1863, 282), Brandt (1901–1, 247–249, the quotes: 248–249), Martin (1990, 39) and Eberstein (2007, 200–202).

[42] Eulenburg-Hertefeld (1900, the citation: 352), Brandt (1901–1, 257–259, 265–266, 290–291), Martin (1990, 39–40, the quote: 40) and Werner (1863, 513, the quote: 528).

in his memoirs published in 1905 that funds for the expedition had been "very well employed", adding that "the advantage immediately catching one's eye was the position which we, as a great power, gained regarding the East Asian empires, next to Great Britain, France, Russia and America, in the political representation of all parts of Germany which did not include Austria, something that Austria was not able to prevent". He added that Prussia had been "the carrier of the real interests of Germany in the Far East".[43] His remark clearly showed the political dimension of the expedition for the global power position of Prussia, and for the unification of Germany under Prussian leadership which was to begin soon after the expedition returned home. Eulenburg was appointed Prussian interior minister on 8 December 1862, serving under Bismarck for almost sixteen years. Other members of the expedition including Max von Brandt also made it into high political, administrative or military positions. The treaties of 1861–1862 with Japan, China and Siam remained up until the 1920s the legal basis of Germany's relations with the three East Asian countries.

References

Armstrong, John. 2004. The Role of Short-Sea, Coastal, and Riverine Traffic in Economic Development since 1750. In *Maritime History as World History*, ed. Daniel Finamore, 115–129. Salem: Peabody Essex Museum & University Press of Florida.

Bard, Solomon. 1993. *Traders of Hong Kong: Some Foreign Merchant Houses, 1841–1899*. Hong Kong: Urban Council.

Bassett, D.K. 1997. The Trade of the English East India Company in the Far East, 1623–84. In *European Commercial Expansion in Early Modern Asia*, ed. Om Prakash, 208–236. Aldershot, Hampshire: Variorum.

Becker, Bert. 2010. The Merchant-Consuls of German States in China, Hong Kong and Macao (1787–1872). In *Consuls et services consulaires aux XIXe siècle/Consulship in the 19th Century/Die Welt der Konsulate im 19. Jahrhundert*, ed. Jörg Ulbert and Lukian Prijac, 329–351. Hamburg: DOBU.

Bensacq-Tixier, Nicole. 2003. *Dictionnaire du corps diplomatique et consulaire français en Chine (1840–1911)*. Paris: Les Indes Savantes.

[43] Stoecker (1958, the quote of Virchow: 61), Delbrück (1905–2, the quote: 184) and Martin (1990, 41).

Beutler, Heinz. 1946. *Hundert Jahre Carlowitz & Co., Hamburg und China: Ein Beitrag zur wirtschaftsgeschichtlichen Entwicklung des deutschen Chinahandels*. PhD Thesis, University of Hamburg.

Brandt, Max von. 1901. *Dreiunddreissig Jahre in Ost-Asien: Erinnerungen eines deutschen Diplomaten*, vol. 1. Leipzig: Georg Wigand.

Brocheux, Pierre, and Daniel Hèmery. 2009. *Indochina: An Ambiguous Colonization, 1858–1954*. Berkeley: University of California Press.

Cady, John Frank. 1954. *The Roots of French Imperialism in Eastern Asia*. Ithaca, NY: Cornell University Press.

Chang, Pin-tsun. 2019. The Rise of Chinese Mercantile Power in Maritime Southeast Asia c.1400–1700. In *China and Southeast Asia: Historical Interactions*, ed. Geoff Wade and James K. Chin, 221–240. London and New York: Routledge.

Chin, James Kong. 2004. The Junk Trade between South China and Nguyen Vietnam in the Late Eighteenth and Early Nineteenth Centuries. In *Water Frontier: Commerce and the Chinese in the Lower Mekong Region, 1750–1880*, ed. Nola Cooke and Li Tana, 53–66. Singapore: Rowman & Littlefield.

Clark, Christopher. 2006. *Iron Kingdom: The Rise and Downfall of Prussia, 1600–1947*. Cambridge, MA: Harvard University Press.

Coates, Austin. 1999. *A Macao Narrative*. Hong Kong: Oxford University Press.

Cordier, Henri. 1901. *Histoire des Relations de la Chine avec les Puissances Occidentales 1860–1900: L'Empereur T'oung Tché (1861–1875)*. Paris: Félix Alcan.

Dear, I.C.B., and Peter Kemp, eds. 2006. *The Oxford Companion to Ships and the Sea*. Oxford: Oxford University Press.

Delbrück, Rudolf von. 1905. *Lebenserinnerungen, 1817–1867*. 2 vols. Leipzig: Duncker & Humblot.

Eberstein, Bernd. 1988. *Hamburg-China: Geschichte einer Partnerschaft*. Hamburg: Christians.

Eberstein, Bernd. 2007. *Preußen und China: Eine Geschichte schwieriger Beziehungen*. Berlin: Duncker & Humblot.

Eulenburg-Hertefeld, Graf Philipp zu, ed. 1900. *Ost-Asien 1860–1862 in Briefen des Grafen Fritz zu Eulenburg*. Berlin: Mittler und Sohn.

Fairbank, John K. 1978. The creation of the treaty system. In: *The Cambridge History of China*, vol. 10, 1, ed. Denis Twitchett and John Fairbank, 213–263. Cambridge: Cambridge University Press.

Feng, Djen. 1936. *The Diplomatic Relations between China and Germany since 1898*. Shanghai: The Commercial Press.

F. F. A. 1931. Foreign Shipping in Chinese Waters. *Chinese Economic Journal* 9 (3): 249–258.

Fieldhouse, D.K. 1966. *The Colonial Empires: A Comparative Survey from the Eighteenth Century*. New York: Delacorte Press.

Furber, Holden. 1976. *Rival Empires of Trade in the Orient, 1600–1800.* Minneapolis: University of Minnesota Press.

Gaastra, Femme S. 1997. The Dutch East India Company and its Intra-Asiatic Trade in Precious Metals. In *European Commercial Expansion in Early Modern Asia*, ed. Om Prakash, 151–166. Aldershot, Hampshire: Variorum.

Greenberg, Michael. 1951. *British Trade and the Opening of China, 1800–42.* Cambridge: Cambridge University Press.

Halpern, Paul. 2001. The French Navy, 1880–1914. In *Technology and Naval Combat in the Twentieth Century and Beyond*, ed. Philipps Payson O'Brien, 36–52. Abingdon and New York: Routledge.

Hanser, Jessica. 2018. British Private Traders between India and China. In *The Private Side of the Canton Trade, 1700–1840: Beyond the Companies*, ed. Paul Arthur Van Dyke and Susan E. Schopp, 7–20. Hong Kong: Hong Kong University Press.

Haudrère, Philippe. 1999. The French India Company and Its Trade in the Eighteenth Century. In *Merchants, Companies and Trade: Europe and Asia in the Early Modern Era*, ed. Sushil Chaudhury and Michel Morineau, 202–211. Cambridge: Cambridge University Press.

Hoang, Anh Tuan, *Silk for Silver: Dutch-Vietnamese Relations, 1637–1700.* Leiden and Boston: Brill.

Hsü, Immanuel C. Y. 2000. *The Rise of Modern China*, 6th ed. New York and Oxford: Oxford University Press.

Jenkins, Ernest H. 1973. *A History of the French Navy: From its Beginnings to the Present Day.* London: Macdonald and Jane's.

Keay, John. 1991. *The Honourable Company: A History of the English East India Company.* New York: Macmillan.

Lieberman, Victor. 1997. Mainland-Archipelagic Parallels and Contrasts, c.1750–1850. In: *The Last Stand of Asian Autonomies: Responses to Modernity in the Diverse States of Southeast Asia and Korea, 1750–1900,* ed. Anthony Reid, 27–53. Houndsmill: Macmillan Press.

Li, Tana. 2004. Rice from Saigon: The Singapore Chinese and the Saigon Trade of the Nineteenth Century. In *Maritime China in Transition 1750–1850*, ed. Wang Gungwu and Ng Chin-keong, 261–270. Wiesbaden: Harrassowitz.

Lombard, Denys. 2007. Another "Mediterranean" in Southeast Asia. *Chinese Southern Diaspora Studies* (1): 3–9. First published in *Hérodote* (88) 1998: 184–193: Une autre "Méditerranée" dans le Sud-Est asiatique.

Man-Cheong, Iona. 2014. Macao: an early modern cosmopolis. In *Macao – The Formation of a Global City,* ed. C.X. George Wei, 143–155. London and New York: Routledge.

Manning, Catherine. 1997. French Country Trade on Coromandel (1720–50). In *European Commercial Expansion in Early Modern Asia*, ed. Om Prakash, 282–292. Aldershot, Hampshire: Variorum.

Martin, Bernd. 1990. The Prussian Expedition to the Far East (1860–1862). *The Journal of the Siam Society* 78 (1): 35–42.

Montague, Joel. 2019. The Glorious Beginning and Dismal End of the French Frigate "l'Amphitrite". In *Études Historiques et Culturelles de Kouang-Tchéou-Wan: Actes de la Première Conférence Académique Internationale sur l'Histoire et la Culture de Kouang-Tchéou-Wan*, vol. 1, ed. Wang Qin Feng, 144–183 (English version), 184–222 (Chinese version by Angel Xiao). Zhanjiang: Lingnan Normal University.

Mühlhahn, Klaus. 2000. *Herrschaft und Widerstand in der „Musterkolonie" Kiautschou: Interaktionen zwischen China und Deutschland, 1897–1914.* Munich: R. Oldenbourg.

Otte, Friedrich. 1930. Shipping in China and Chinese Shipping Abroad. *Chinese Economic Journal* 6 (2): 123–152.

Otte, Friedrich. 1931. Shipping Policy in China. *Chinese Economic Journal* 8 (4): 346–358.

Ping-Yin, Ho. 1933. A Survey of Sino-German Trade. *Chinese Economic Journal* 13 (2): 111–140.

Porter, Jonathan. 1996. *Macau: The Imaginary City*. Boulder: Westview.

Prakash, Om. 1999. The Portuguese and the Dutch in Asian Maritime Trade: A Comparative Analysis. In *Merchants, Companies and Trade: Europe and Asia in the Early Modern Era*, ed. Sushil Chaudhury and Michel Morineau, 175–188. Cambridge: Cambridge University Press.

Ratenhof, Udo. 1987. *Die Chinapolitik des Deutschen Reiches 1871 bis 1945: Wirtschaft-Rüstung-Militär.* Boppard am Rhein: Harald Boldt.

Reid, Anthony. 1988. *Southeast Asia in the Age of Commerce 1450–1680, vol. 1: The Lands below the Winds.* New Haven/London: Yale University Press.

Reid, Anthony. 1997. A New Phase of Commercial Expansion in Southeast Asia, 1760–1850. In *The Last Stand of Asian Autonomies: Responses to Modernity in the Diverse States of Southeast Asia and Korea, 1750–1900*, ed. Anthony Reid, 57–81. Houndsmill/London: MacMillan.

Reid, Anthony. 2004. Chinese Trade and Southeast Asian Economic Expansion in the Later Eighteenth and Early Nineteenth Centuries: An Overview. In *Water Frontier: Commerce and the Chinese in the Lower Mekong Region, 1750–1880*, ed. Nola Cooke and Li Tana, 21–34. Singapore: Rowman & Littlefield.

Reid, Anthony. 2015. *A History of Southeast Asia: Critical Crossroads*. Chichester, West Sussex: Wiley Blackwell.

Samuels, Marwyn. 1982. *Contest for the South China Sea*. New York and London: Methuen.

Schopp, Susan E. 2018. French Private Trade at Canton, 1698–1833. In *The Private Side of the Canton Trade, 1700–1840: Beyond the Companies*, ed. Paul Arthur van Dyke and Susan E. Schopp, 43–63. Hong Kong: Hong Kong University Press.

Momoki, Shiro. 1998. Dai Viet and the South China Sea Trade. *Crossroads* 12 (1): 1–34.
So, Fion Wai Ling. 2019. *Germany's Colony in China: Colonialism, Protection and Economic Development in Qingdao and Shandong, 1898–1914*. Abingdon and New York: Routledge.
Souza, George Bryan. 1986. *The Survival of Empire: Portuguese Trade and Society in China and the South China Sea, 1630–1754*. London: Cambridge University Press.
Souza, George Bryan. 1997. Portuguese Country Traders in the Indian Ocean and the South China Sea, c. 1600. In *European Commercial Expansion in Early Modern Asia*, ed. Om Prakash, 69–80. Aldershot, Hampshire: Variorum.
Steuart, James, ed. 1934. *Jardine, Matheson & Co., Afterwards Jardine, Matheson & Co., Limited: An Outline of the History of a China House for Hundred Years, 1832–1932*. Hong Kong: Self-Published.
Stoecker, Helmuth. 1958. *Deutschland und China im 19. Jahrhundert: Das Eindringen des deutschen Kapitalismus*. Berlin: Rütten & Loening.
Stoecker, Helmuth. 1977. Germany and China, 1861–94. In *Germany in the Pacific and Far East, 1870–1914*, ed. John A. Moses and Paul M. Kennedy, 26–39. St. Lucia, Queensland: University of Queensland Press.
Sze, Tsung-yu. 1925. *China and the Most-favored-nation Clause*. New York: Fleming H. Revell (reprint Taipei: Ch'eng Wen Publishing, 1971).
Van Dyke, Paul A. 2005. *The Canton Trade: Life and Enterprise on the China Coast, 1700–1845*. Hong Kong: Hong Kong University Press.
Wade, Geoff. 2019. Ming China and Southeast Asia in the Fifteenth Century. In *China and Southeast Asia: Historical Interactions*, ed. Geoff Wade and James K. Chin, 87–129. London and New York: Routledge.
Walser, Ray. 1992. *France's Search for a Battle Fleet: Naval Policy and Naval Power, 1898–1914*. New York: Garland.
Werner, Reinhold. 1863. *Die preussische Expedition nach China, Japan und Siam in den Jahren 1860, 1861 und 1862, Reisebriefe*, 2. Leipzig: Brockhaus.
Wills, John E. 1998. Relations with Maritime Europeans, 1514–1662. In *The Cambridge History of China*, vol. 8, 2, ed. Denis Twitchett and John Fairbank, 333–375. Cambridge: Cambridge University Press.

CHAPTER 3

Hong Kong

The German Business Community

In 1842, Britain formally acquired sovereignty over Hong Kong after taking it from China under the terms of the Treaty of Nanjing that settled the First Opium War (1839–1842). From the beginning, the British regarded Hong Kong, which was declared a crown colony, as their emporium of trade in East Asia. Starting in the 1840s, Chinese traders from Guangzhou and other ports in China also came to the colony or dispatched family members to operate as merchants; the number of Chinese trading firms including compradors (middlemen) and brokers reached had 128 by 1861. Most of Hong Kong residents were Chinese, whose share of the total population of Hong Kong remained around 95 per cent from the 1860s until the 1920s. During this period, the number of non-Chinese residents increased almost sevenfold from about 3,000 to 20,000, with a slump during the First World War, when many of them left the colony. A small part of this group of foreigners consisted of German and French nationals. There is generally little information available on the whereabouts of the expatriate communities in Hong Kong, which until the present day formed only a tiny, but often financially potent group of businesspeople in the former British colony. Their reasons for coming to Hong Kong were manifold, but certainly based on a number of economic and political considerations. Hong Kong enjoyed a status backed by the full legal and military authority of the sovereign

B. Becker, *France and Germany in the South China Sea, c. 1840–1930*, Cambridge Imperial and Post-Colonial Studies,
https://doi.org/10.1007/978-3-030-52604-7_3

nation. This made it attractive for British and foreign companies alike and paved the way for the formation of Hong Kong as the hub of East Asian shipping, trade and finance. Free-market economy or laissez-faire policy and social non-interventionism had been the guidelines of the economic policies of Hong Kong's colonial governments since the founding of the colony. As a free port, with tariffs imposed on only certain imported goods such as petroleum and liquor, Hong Kong's governments encouraged free-trade contact between an isolated city with few domestic resources and the rest of the globe. Combined with the practice of social non-interventionism, the role of government was primarily to maintain, through the enactment and enforcement of laws, an orderly environment in which a free market could operate smoothly.[1]

Such advantages drew various merchants from around the globe to Hong Kong. Among the traditional British firms in China, namely Jardine, Matheson & Company, and Dent & Company (the major opium traders in the Far East), established themselves in Hong Kong immediately after the founding of the crown colony, turning the port city, as David R. Meyer puts it, into "a pivot of the information network in Asia". Market information concerning opium crop reports, auctions, market trends and government reports was included in instructions to commanders of its vessels plying the China coast, in formal business circulars for distribution in Asia, Europe and North America and in confidential letters to customers. Political and commercial news from Hong Kong also circulated in newspapers such as the *China Mail*, which began publication in 1845. With the opening of the Hong Kong Club (1846), the local branch of the Royal Asiatic Society (1847) and the Hong Kong Chamber of Commerce (1861), all sorts of information on economic, political, and social exchanges among traders and government officials was generated and soon made known in ports in the South China Sea and beyond its shores.[2] From the beginning, British firms dominated in Hong Kong, but were soon joined by an international group that included representatives from India, Europe and the United States. Hong Kong developed into the first meeting place between foreign and Chinese social networks of capital in Asia, providing crucial information to companies

[1] Boxer (1961, 2–4), Sayer (1975, 138–139), Cheng (1980, 33–37), Lau and Kuan (1988, 18–33), Meyer (2000, 114–115) and Carroll (2005, 16–18).

[2] Meyer (2000, 1–4, the quote: 58).

inside and beyond Asia for access to the most sophisticated global information. This strategic advantage enabled Hong Kong firms to dominate decision-making about the control of the exchange of commodity and financial capital.[3]

German trading firms established in Guangzhou since the 1840s successively opened branches in Hong Kong or moved their headquarters to the port city, thereby developing into "an integral part of the multifaceted and multicultural nature of the British Empire".[4] In this respect, the German firms were transnational actors engaging in multiple interactions with other businesspeople from Europe, Asia and the Americas. The first ones to establish branches in Hong Kong were Wm. Pustau & Company, registered in Hong Kong in 1846 (three years after being founded in Guangzhou). This firm was followed by Siemssen & Company in 1848, Schwarzkopf & Company (or anglicised: Blackhead & Company) in 1854, Carl Boediker & Company in 1860 and Arnhold, Karberg & Company in 1865. Other German merchants came directly to the British colony, such as Eduard Schellhass from Hamburg, who established Schellhass & Company in 1861, or Hermann Melchers from Bremen, who founded Melchers & Company in 1866. Up until the early 1880s, around twenty German companies established their headquarters or set up branch offices in the British colony, a number which remained fairly stable until the First World War.[5] In 1897, there were twenty-one German wholesale trade companies, five agents for money exchange, shipping and securities and eight shops employing 180, mainly German staff. According to Hermann Schumacher, a professor of law and national economics at Kiel University who paid a study visit to Hong Kong in 1897, "German merchants in Hong Kong were on an almost equal footing with the English, and leaving Parsees [or Parsis, members of an Indian ethnic minority] and Indian Jews aside, they are far beyond all other nations together".[6] Britain's own loss of industrial leadership,

[3] Meyer (2000, 52–61), Gipouloux (2011, 13, 22–23) and Carroll (2005, 16–32).

[4] Tsang (2004, 56–62), Carroll (2007, 66–69), Meyer (2000, 57–61) and Davis et al. (2012, the quote: 1).

[5] Bard (1993, 96–105), Smith, Carl T. (1994, 1–55), Mak (2005, 61–83), Becker (2004, 91–113) and Manz (2014, 39). See also, Jarvis and Lee (2008, 1–2) and Davis et al. (2012, 1–17).

[6] Henderson (1975, 239–240) and Schumacher (1900, 23–25). This account is based on a survey conducted by Consul Loeper on behalf of the German foreign ministry. BAB,

and Germany's rise as an industrial power, were reflected in the relatively large number of German firms in Hong Kong, which almost equalled the number of British companies in the colony.

Most of the German firms were engaged in the import and export trade, many being agents for German and other foreign manufacturers, whose products were imported through the British colony into China. These firms also exported considerable quantities of Chinese produce through Hong Kong to European and other countries. Among the German firms were several trading houses acting as brokers for shipping companies, such as Wieler & Co.; Melchers & Co.; Siemssen & Co.; Eduard Schellhass & Co.; Carlowitz & Co.; Lauts, Wegener & Co. and Jebsen & Co. German influence was present even outside its own companies. After the establishment of the Hong Kong Chamber of Commerce (1861), a German national became an elected member of the board, and almost forty years later, two Germans were among the nine members. Four Germans served as board members of the Hong Kong and Shanghai Banking Corporation (HSBC), the most important bank in the colony, and three sat on the seven-person board of the Hong Kong & Whampoa Dock Company, the largest dockyard in East Asia for the maintenance of British warships. There were several German directors in other British firms making considerable investments in them. In 1900, the German presence in Hong Kong increased with the opening of a branch of the Deutsch-Asiatische Bank (German Asiatic Bank, founded in 1889 in Shanghai with the participation of Deutsche Bank, one of the largest banks in Imperial Germany).[7] The important role such capital played for Hong Kong's economic position should be labelled as "participatory colonialism", as this author puts it. This variant of colonialism was a specific form of German economic participation in Britain's formal empire in Hong Kong. It meant collaborating with institutions such as the chamber of commerce, investing capital in major British firms, and last but not least, being actively present in the competitive markets of Hong Kong, China and Southeast Asia. In this way, German (and

R 901-8598: Attachment to report of Consul Loeper (Hong Kong) to Chancellor von Hohenlohe-Schillingsfürst (Berlin), 19 December 1897.

[7] Müller-Jabusch (1940, 141–142), Roll (1957, 293) and Plumpe (30–31, 44–45).

other) merchants were transnational actors who contributed considerably to British imperialism.[8]

On the other hand, this "German penetration of British and empire markets", as Cain and Hopkins put it, seemed to have contributed to rising Anglo-German political-diplomatic conflict before the outbreak of the First World War. It was certainly triggered by Germany's decision to build a large navy, which was regarded by Britain as a challenge to her own sea power and as "a threat greater than anything Britain had faced in over a century".[9] However, economic rivalry between Britain and Germany, which was global in scope, was the major reason for the growing dispute, which was only softened by the generally rapid growth of international trade in the final years before the war. From 1860 to 1913, Germany's foreign trade quadrupled, with an annual increase of 4 per cent; since the 1880s, Germany had been the third-largest exporter worldwide (only surpassed by Britain and the United States). Compared to France, whose share of global trades decreased from 12.7 per cent (1875) to 7.6 per cent (1913), Germany's share grew from 11.8 to 12.5 per cent in this period. From 1880 to 1913, German exports rose by 245 per cent, American ones by 195 per cent and British ones by 122 per cent, with France's increasing by 98 per cent.[10]

In Hong Kong and other port cities in East Asia, Chinese compradors employed by German and other foreign firms served as important "intermediaries" for business relations with Chinese merchants. As John Carroll stresses, "the comprador system was crucial to the rise of Sino-foreign commerce in modern China". According to a French observer who visited China in the mid-1890s, the comprador was "the interested agent, person in charge, del credere agent, between the Asian and the European; it is the necessary instrument of the obligatory intermediary of all transactions".[11] Named after the Portuguese word for "buyer" or "purchaser", Chinese compradors became business assistants or business managers in Western companies, where they usually handled the firms' import-export transactions. Since Westerners were not acquainted with local languages, customs or business conditions in China, the comprador system became

[8] Becker (2004, 100–101) and Davis et al. (2012, 17).

[9] Cain and Hopkins (2016, 421–427, the quotes: 423 and 424).

[10] Henderson (1975, 111–242), Bonin (1988, 17, 42) and Nipperdey (1998, 276).

[11] Carroll (2005, 33–35, the quote: 33) and Dujardin-Beaumetz (1897–1898, 496).

especially important in Hong Kong, where most of the foreign firms that did business in China were located. With the increasing diversification of foreign companies after the 1860s, many compradors became multifunctional managers who handled the transaction business and all matters concerning shipping and insurance. Among the German firms in Hong Kong, Jebsen & Company (founded in 1895), hired its first comprador after the firm had become principal agent of Badische Anilin- & Soda-Fabrik (BASF), the chemical producer located in Ludwigshafen, Germany, for Hong Kong and China. However, when this Chinese merchant proved to be a private gambler who encountered huge financial losses, Jebsen & Co. discharged him from his duties and instead hired the eldest son of a Chinese businessman whom the firm's partners had known for many years. Chau Yue Teng soon gave evidence of his high reliability and trustworthiness and remained in the firm's service until 1914. After the First World War, Chau provided Jacob Jebsen with considerable working capital to help him restart his business in Guangzhou. He established his own shipping agency and trading house, operating in the South China Sea, and became an important member and social leader of Hong Kong society.[12]

In sharp contrast to their enormous economic potential inside the colony, Germans in Hong Kong were a very small group. According to the Hong Kong government census of 20 January 1897, the colony's total population of 241,762 people overwhelmingly consisted of Chinese (96.49 per cent), of which Germans, with 208 residents, represented a tiny minority (0.08 per cent). Inside the group of Europeans and Americans (1.49 per cent of Hong Kong's total population), Germans had a 5.73 per cent share. According to a list by local historian Carl T. Smith, there were 170 Germans in Hong Kong in 1871, 188 in 1881, and 292 in 1896, of which most were males (69.5 per cent). In the following fifteen years, these numbers remained relatively stable, with a total of 342 Germans (62.5 per cent males) in 1911. With the expulsion of almost the entire German community at the outbreak of the First World War, the total number decreased to only three in 1921. After German companies were permitted to return to Hong Kong in late 1922, the number of Germans increased to 156 in 1931, most of whom were

[12] Becker (2017, 118–125).

males.[13] In view of the lack of further statistical evidence, the evaluation of different sources permits the conclusion that three distinct groups of Germans resided in Hong Kong in the late nineteenth and early twentieth century, namely merchants (including medical doctors), seafarers and missionaries.[14] German merchants were divided into an upper class of owners and/or managers of wholesale businesses residing permanently or only temporarily in the colony. Another group comprised middle-class merchants, mostly clerks hired by German and other firms, or storekeepers and landlords and doctors. Although there are a few accounts on German companies and detailed facts and figures about the German business community, the daily life of German merchants is often neglected in consular correspondence or travel reports. The following excerpts are from an unpublished manuscript of 1910 written by Walther Dübgen, a German clerk in Hong Kong:

> Generally, office hours are from 9 to 1, and after the tiffin [light midday meal] from 2 or 2.30 until 5. On Saturday afternoon, only German companies are working; for the Englishman, Saturdays are reserved for sports. The aforementioned office hours should not be taken as on the dot, often we arrive earlier than at 9, shorten our tiffin break and stay until 7 or 7.30 in the evening, according to the requirements of work. On the other hand, if there is little to do, we do not strictly keep to office hours and sit out our time, as it is often common in Europe, but leave once finished. Actually, working is freer. Bosses do not try to act as being unapproachable and give staff a free hand, as long as they do their job. It is not unusual to occasionally leave the office for a short time to visit a next-door friend or to get shaved.[15]

The few married Germans residing in Hong Kong lived rather remote family lives, having single houses in quarters of the city of varying respect ability, according to their financial means. German bachelors usually resided in boarding houses operated by British property owners. According to Dübgen, such accommodation offered the chance to learn or to improve their English and to make contacts. On the other hand,

[13] *Hong Kong Blue Book for the Year 1897* (1897, M1) and Smith, Carl T. (1994, 3: Number of German residents in Hong Kong 1871–1931).

[14] For overviews of the German community in Hong Kong, see Roll (1957, 293), Smith, Carl T. (1994), Mak (2000, 2005) and Speitkamp (2000).

[15] Dübgen (1910, 59–60).

bachelors who got along well with each other or who hoped to do so, often jointly leased private residences. In the 1890s, the owners of Jebsen & Co., Jacob Jebsen and Johann Heinrich Jessen, rented a house called Sans Souci in Robinson Road and established a mess hall, frequently inviting guests to opulent dinners with drinks for which they charged very little. Drinks were more expensive than locally purchased food. Larger messes had honorary mess wards (in German: Messwarte) chosen from its own members on a rotating basis and responsible for bookkeeping and supervising Chinese staff (called "boys") who purchased food and other items. Messes had Chinese cooks and were usually less costly than feeding in boarding houses, as long as they worked economically. Two or three Chinese "coolies" in each residence were charged with cleaning matters, and each European had a "boy" for personal services. This provided more freedom for bachelors, as Dübgen noted: "They are able to do what they want, yet later when returning to civilised Europe from the half-civilised Far East, they get used to life in the country of their childhood only with difficulty".[16]

The earliest German institution in Hong Kong was the Medical Hall, founded in 1853, in which several physicians from Germany and Austria practiced until the outbreak of the First World War. The social epicentre of the German business community in Hong Kong was Club Germania, located in Wanchai district and founded in November 1859. Some years later (in 1865), the rather unpretentious building was relinquished for a new one, situated at the top of Wyndham Street just south of D'Aguilar Street. Its construction was commissioned by the German merchant Gustav Overbeck, partner in the British firm Dent & Co., the Prussian honorary vice-consul and honorary consul for Austria in Hong Kong.[17] With the increasing German expatriate community, the club decided to erect a new building on the east side of Wyndham Street off Queens Road. This brick building in Gothic style, designed by British architects, was opened on 2 February 1872 in the presence of Governor Sir Richard Graves Macdonnell and a large number of local residents. It had a main hall with a billiard room and a reading room on each side, a library and a concert hall which could accommodate 275 persons, a drawing room and a dining room for sixty persons on either side. In

[16] Hänisch (1970, 42) and Dübgen (1910, 65–66).

[17] Becker (2010b, 342).

Fig. 3.1 Club Germania in Hong Kong, c. 1910 (Private collection Bert Becker)

the rear of the building were four bowling alleys. After thirty years, the premise had become too small, and a new and more impressive club building was erected at Kennedy Road. On 31 December 1902, in his inaugural speech, club President Georg Harling emphasised its character as "the centre of Germanness, as centre of unity and harmony". In 1908, the club had 139 present, 101 absent, and nine associate members, almost exclusively businesspeople.[18] When comparing these numbers with the total number of Germans in Hong Kong at the time, it is evident that around two-thirds of Germans residing in Hong Kong counted among the upper and middle class (Fig. 3.1).

Another group of German residents was connected in some way or other with merchant shipping: shipmasters and ship officers, navigators and machinists of steamships operating under the German and other flags, or technicians employed by dockyards and other workshops in Hong Kong. It was not unusual for masters to be accompanied by their families

[18] Smith, Carl T. (1994, 9–13), *Der Ostasiatische Lloyd*, 23 January 1901, Wright, Arnold and Cartwright, H. A. (1908, 171) and Mak (2005, 74).

to avoid longstanding separation; yet, in these cases, wives and children had principally to remain ashore. In October 1897, Michael Jebsen told one of his captains that he was powerless to act when "the masters of my shipping company take their respective wives to China and reside ashore, be it in Hong Kong or elsewhere". He would even allow that "wives occasionally join the ship for a short voyage, something that would be dealt with in more detail by Jebsen & Co. in Hong Kong". On the other hand, the shipowner made it clear that he was not prepared to allow wives "to go as permanent passengers".[19]

German shipmasters had their captain's club in Hong Kong, about which little is known. Furthermore, there existed Club Eintracht (in English: Club Unity), established in 1892 by German navigators and machinists, which had 250 members in 1898, of which 150 resided permanently in Hong Kong, many with their families.[20] Machinists were also employed in businesses other than aboard steamers, such as ship chandleries, factories, mechanical workshops or steam-powered mills. Members of the Jebsen family illustrate this: The second son of the shipowner Michael Jebsen, Heinrich Jebsen, a mechanical technician, was co-owner of the ship chandler Chr. Witzke and Company in Kowloon. The firm, established by Christian Witzke from Flensburg, existed up until the First World War, specialising in repairing ships, boilers, engines and similar items.[21]

The smallest group of Germans in Hong Kong consisted of missionaries of both sexes in the service of German and Swiss missionary societies. Their base was the Foundling Home Bethesda (established in 1861), where Chinese female orphans received care and education. Pastor Ernst Klitzke, house father of Bethesda, started public church services soon after his arrival in Hong Kong in 1867. Regular Sunday services were attended by both Germans residents and German sailors temporarily staying in the colony. In 1873, Klitzke was the initiator of an informal church community of which he was made pastor. This congregation faded almost into oblivion after Klitzke passed away in 1881. The situation of German families residing in Hong Kong was highlighted by Pastor Theodor Kriele

[19] JJHA, A01-01-310: Michael Jebsen (Apenrade) to Captain C. Möller (Hong Kong), 20 October 1897.

[20] *South China Morning Post*, 12 June 1913 and *Hansa. Deutsche Nautische Zeitschrift*, 14 May 1898.

[21] Becker (2012, 590–593).

in his report of 1899, in which he dealt specifically with the colony's education system and the lack of a German school in Hong Kong. While wealthy parents usually hired private German teachers, less affluent families sent their children to missionary schools, private boarding schools or even Chinese schools. This situation, regarded as unsatisfactory, resulted in local Germans founding, on 30 October 1899, the Deutsche Kirchen- und Schulgemeinde (German Church and School Congregation), for which Kriele was hired as both pastor and teacher. He was also charged with missionary work for German seafarers temporarily staying in Hong Kong. For helping the school to start operating, several German company owners and Consul Dr. Friedrich Rieloff searched for the necessary financial means. In June 1899, the consul, in his letter to the foreign ministry in Berlin, pointed to the fact that many German families were required to leave Hong Kong because of the lack of a German school. Stating that such a school would not only be in the interests of individual families "but also in the interest of sustaining and strengthening Germanness here at this most important point of East Asia", the consul requested a government subsidy for the school project. Soon after, Emperor William II authorised the sum of 1,500 marks for the year 1899.[22]

In February 1901, the German Church and School Congregation had around three hundred members, but only a few contributed financially to the operation of the school which depended on membership fees, school fees and government grants. Other than the lack of sufficient funding, the number of children attending school remained very small (14 in 1901, 22 in 1903). This resulted from the fact that only European children (but no Chinese or other nationalities) between six and fourteen years of age were permitted to enrol in the congregation's school. Another negative factor was the frequent fluctuation in pupils due to the high living costs in Hong Kong which severely constrained the stays of German middle-class families. This made it almost impossible for teachers, basically only Pastor Kriele and his wife, to offer stringent teaching. When the Krieles returned to Germany in 1905, the school in effect closed down, despite some basic teaching offered by missionaries continuing for another two years. Other activities such as regular Sunday church services or christenings and marriages were more popular among German residents of Hong Kong. Entire crews of the men-of-war of the German East Asian naval squadron

[22] Plag (1969, 149–150), Stone (2013, 1–33) and Becker (2015, 59–64).

regularly attended church services or other cultural activities. The congregation served as a kind of social epicentre outside Club Germania which remained exclusively reserved for the business community.[23]

On 4 August 1914, the outbreak of war between Britain and Germany resulted in widespread uncertainty among Germans and German companies in Hong Kong. Several male members of the German expatriate community were called up for military service in Kiaochow, the German leasehold in Shandong Province. Others left Hong Kong and made their way back to Europe to join the war. Yet, Governor Sir Francis Henry May pledged his word to Consul Arthur von Voretzsch that Germans were permitted to remain in the colony under parole. Only four German residents were arrested in the following days, but thirty German passengers on board an American liner sailing from San Francisco and calling Hong Kong on its way to Manila were detained in barracks. Before the consul departed from Hong Kong on 11 August, he named the American Consul-General, Geo E. Anderson, as being in charge of German interests. During a courtesy visit to the governor, Anderson learned that May had received instructions from London to grant the German merchants very extensive relief for trading in view of their important business position in Hong Kong. As the consul-general reported, the governor said: "We do not wish to lose you". He even asked to be informed when Germans felt improperly treated by Englishmen. In Anderson's opinion, May had expressed his personal disposition towards the Germans which appeared to be meant honestly.[24]

In the first weeks of August 1914, rumours spread among the Chinese in Hong Kong that the German East Asian naval squadron was going to bombard the colony as a result of an alleged defeat of the British navy in the North Sea. Another rumour was that an attempt had been made to assassinate the governor, who was alleged since then to be in hospital. This prompted many to leave for the Chinese mainland. Whether Germans were behind the false rumours, or Chinese robber gangs keen on plundering the valuables of fleeing Chinese, could not be verified.[25] The Hong Kong government continued to treat the remaining German and Austrian

[23] Becker (2015, 64–66, 72–79, 83–84).

[24] *Hong Kong Daily Press*, 11 August 1914. Selby (1988). PAAA, R 86155: Otto Struckmeyer (Shanghai), February 1915: Report on Hong Kong from the outbreak of the war to the expulsion of the Germans, in *Protest der deutschen Firmen Hongkongs gegen die Maßnahmen der englischen Regierung nebst Bericht und Anlagen* (5–11).

[25] *Hong Kong Daily Press*, 13 August 1914.

citizens in the colony rather leniently, informing German firms which had branches or partners in Germany that any transactions with them required permission since this would be regarded as trading with the enemy of the British Empire. However, since very large British interests were involved in their trading, which could cause disturbance in Hong Kong's trade and global British trade, certain limited permission was granted to the affected German firms. Those purely local German firms with no partners in Germany or Austria were allowed to carry on trading, like any friendly alien, but were required to pay all money received by them into certain approved banks so that none of it would be able to reach Germany. This policy, under which Britain still adhered to free and fair trading, was reiterated in the Legislative Council session on 6 October 1914 which discussed the bill "concerning trading with the enemy" introduced by Governor May. Despite critics in the British and Chinese merchant community pointing to the expulsion of British businessmen from Germany and Austria, and therefore demanding similar measures be taken in the British Empire, the governor refused to make any changes to his firm instructions from London. Against three dissenting votes, the bill was passed.[26]

In October 1914, with British citizens being increasingly interned in Germany and British warships and merchant vessels attacked by German men-of-war (the cruiser *Emden* sank fifteen British merchant ships in the Indian Ocean), the attitude in London towards German and Austrian subjects residing in Hong Kong changed. On 24 October 1914, Governor May told members of the German community that he had received orders from London to intern Germans up to the age of forty-five, expel the others and charge British firms in Hong Kong with liquidating German businesses. According to a German report, the governor said the following: "I have received these instructions from my government and, being the officer of the government, I have to carry them out. I know it won't be for the benefit of the colony".[27] On 27 October 1914, the governor informed the Legislative Council of the new policy announcing the forced departure or internment of the remaining

[26] *Hong Kong Daily Press*, 7 October 1914.

[27] PAAA, R 86155: Otto Struckmeyer (Shanghai), February 1915: Report on Hong Kong from the outbreak of the war to the expulsion of the Germans, in *Protest der deutschen Firmen Hongkongs gegen die Maßnahmen der englischen Regierung nebst Bericht und Anlagen* (5–11).

German residents of the colony. Consequently, their trading should cease and their various firms had to be wound up. For this purpose, May introduced the "Alien Enemies (Winding up) Ordinance", giving the government the necessary power to start appointing liquidators which would act on behalf of the "alien enemies" when liquidating their property or business in Hong Kong. The bill, which was passed by the council, concerned "such alien enemies as may be ordered to quit the Colony or may be detained or may be absent from the Colony".[28]

The remaining members of the German community regularly met in Club Germania to discuss the matter, with American Consul-General Anderson joining the meetings. On 30 October 1914, twenty-three German companies, including The Medical Hall, submitted a formal protest letter to the consul-general. The signatories voiced their "very keen disappointment at the sudden and most unexpected change", pointing to the fact that they had been established in the colony for over thirty years, and some of them up to fifty, and even close on seventy years. Their important participation in the progress of Hong Kong and the expansion of British interests was expressed as follows:

> Whilst naturally trading for their own benefit, they think that they may justly claim to have contributed in no small way to the development, growth and prosperity of the Colony, and in their capacity as peaceful traders they consider themselves and their businesses a valuable asset to the Colony. It has taken decades of hard and strenuous work to create such an asset, which they consider particularly valuable to the Colony since they have as impartial traders been instrumental to a great extent in attracting to this port business from and with all quarters of the globe, thereby promoting British trade more than that of any other nation.[29]

However, the protest remained unsuccessful. Between 26 October and 1 November 1914, eighty-one German and Austrian residents of Hong Kong were interned in a camp in Hung Hom Bay, Kowloon, together

[28] *Hong Kong Daily Press*, 28 and 29 October 1914.

[29] PAAA, R 86155: Protest resolution of German firms in Hong Kong, 30 October 1914, in *Protest der deutschen Firmen Hongkongs gegen die Maßnahmen der englischen Regierung nebst Bericht und Anlagen* (attachment 35, 57–58). This resolution was signed by partners of some of the longest-established German firms such as Siemssen & Co. (1848), F. Blackhead & Co. (1854), Carl Boediker & Co. (1860), Arnhold, Karberg & Co. (1865) and Melchers & Co. (1866).

with crews of captured German merchant ships and a number of German travellers, around three hundred prisoners-of-war in total.[30] When the Legislative Council debated the Alien Enemies (Winding up) Amendment Ordinance on 4 December 1914, further details of the liquidation of German property in Hong Kong were settled, with the bill passing unanimously. According to a German assessment issued in 1915, the bill was intended to capture German trade since it enabled the liquidators, British companies in Hong Kong, to take over agencies or business connections of German firms. "Since in the course of decades, many German firms had built up an important business especially with England, they are worst affected and specifically in fields for which they cannot find any substitute in Germany", the evaluation claimed. For the author, a former member of the German business community in Hong Kong, it was obvious that since the outbreak of the war British competitors had been successful in getting "foreign agencies and connections off German firms, with the Hong Kong government strongly supporting these actions by making it impossible to Germans to transfer their agencies to neutrals, and even British staff of their firms".[31]

In the aftermath of the First World War, in late 1922, the Hong Kong government permitted German companies to re-establish themselves in the colony. Several trading firms returned, but there were also new ones such as IG Farben, the chemical and pharmaceutical conglomerate (formed in 1925), making Jebsen & Co. (the owners of which had become Danish citizens after the cession of North Schleswig to Denmark in 1920 as consequence of a plebiscite stipulated by the Treaty of Versailles), their sub-agents for southern China. Other German manufacturers also had local firms as agents, while Siemens & Halske, the leading German electro-technical producer, reopened its own sales office.[32] There were probably about 120 German residents in 1928, mostly businessmen with their families; their number increased to about 200 in 1933, which signalled that the German community had reached half the number

[30] In February 1916, most of the Germans and Austrians were transferred to another camp in Australia. For details of the Hung Hom Bay Camp, see Hänisch (1970, 136–145), Selby (1988) and Smith, Carl T. (1994, 54–55).

[31] *Hong Kong Daily Press*, 4 December 1914. PAAA, R 86155: Otto Struckmeyer (Shanghai), February 1915: Report on Hong Kong from the outbreak of the war to the expulsion of the Germans.

[32] Roll (1957, 293–294) and Miller and Wasmuth (2008, 49).

of the pre-war population. The tennis club in Kowloon, founded in 1927, became the centre of the German expatriate community before the Deutscher Klub (German Club) was established in the town centre in 1931. After Adolf Hitler took power in Germany, the Club, in late 1933, had 142 members and took care of "Germanness, sports and sociability".[33] According to the Bremen merchant Walter Sporleder, who resided in Hong Kong at the time, "the national celebrations, the special winter parties and diligent sport activities witnessed the will and courage to live, the again increasing ability, and also a certain prosperity of the Hong Kong Germans".[34] An overview of Germans firms operating in South China and Hong Kong, published in 1934, listed twenty-six firms, most of which had already been established in Hong Kong before the First World War.[35]

Tramp Shipping Markets in East Asia

From the 1840s until the Second World War, tramp shipping was the most common form of operation in intra-Asian shipping markets. According to statistics, the largest share of ocean-going (including coastal shipping or cabotage) and river shipping activities was held by foreign companies. Foreigners were usually unilaterally denied shipping rights in countries' coastal and inland waters, but China was forced to grant them due to the series of unequal treaties signed with Western powers following the Sino-British Treaty of Tianjin (26 June 1858). Since all treaty powers had a most-favoured nation agreement with China in their commercial conventions concluded after 1858, the right of cabotage was applied accordingly. Yet, the strong position of Western shipping in Chinese and other Asian waters was due not only to political reasons but mainly to the technological superiority of foreign sailing vessels, and later, foreign steamships. In contrast to traditional Chinese junks dominating shipments of inexpensive, bulk commodities, steamships offered competitive transport for both low- and high-value commodities, sufficient insurance and reliable timetables almost independent of weather conditions, sea currents

[33] PAAA, Peking II-1604: Attachment to the Report of the German Consulate in Hong Kong, 12 December 1933.

[34] Hänisch (1970, 185) and Sporleder (1976, 266–283, the quote: 271).

[35] *The Germans and Their Activities in South China & Hong Kong* (1934, 1: Index).

or other unpredictable natural events. Therefore, the expansion of steam navigation into Chinese waters was both a political and a commercial process. Steam tramps or steam coasters carrying Chinese-owned goods met the existing transport requirements of Chinese merchants, mainly low-cost Chinese merchant firms with limited capital, which were part of well-functioning domestic and international social networks of capital in Asia. They competed well in the unspecialised, small-scale commodity intra-Asian trades for which regular and irregular transport such as small- and medium-sized steam coasters were chartered. In this area, Chinese and foreigners worked in close co-operation, resulting in the greater part of the cargoes of foreign vessels engaged in China's domestic trade being carried on behalf of Chinese merchants.[36]

According to statistics from the Chinese Imperial Maritime Customs, foreign merchant ships flying flags of the different German littoral states, in both number and tonnage, came third to British and American flags in the open ports of China in 1864 and 1866, even before Chinese vessels, including junks. In 1868, Britain had a share of 52.2 per cent of foreign shipping in China, the United States 35 per cent, Germany 73 per cent and Japan 0.1 per cent. The relatively strong position of American and German sailing vessels in intra-Asian coastal shipping decreased until the mid-1870s, when British steamships became dominant in the market. The crucial turning point was the opening of the Suez Canal (1869), an all-steamer route, which contributed to the sudden decline in the importance of the sailing ship as a major world carrier. A further factor was the invention of the compound engine and its mass introduction, reducing the fuel consumption of steamers by nearly half and making it possible for steamships to challenge sailing vessels as cargo carriers on almost all of the world's major shipping routes. Steamship building increased enormously, especially in Britain, and many new steamer lines were formed in the years following the opening of the canal. The China Navigation Company, launched in 1872 by the British entrepreneur John Swire, soon became the major shipping line in East Asia, forming the core business of the future multinational trading house of Butterfield & Swire. In 1873, the China Merchants Steam Navigation Company appeared as

[36] Sze (1925, 131–136), Boxer (1961, 35–36), and Hsiao (1974, 239–261: Number and Tonnage of Vessels, 2). Interport Trade [1872–1948]. Allen and Donnithorne (1954, 127–128, 131–132), Meyer (2000, 100–103), Gipouloux (2011, 187–198) and Reinhardt (8–9).

a Chinese rival, initiated by the influential politician Li Hongzhang (Li Hung-chang; sometimes called the "Bismarck of China"), and financed by Chinese merchants in the treaty ports.[37] In 1881, Jardine, Matheson & Company, famous for its opium trading and smuggling, set up the Indo-China Steam Navigation Company, which developed into one of the major shipping lines in the region.[38] Britain's share of China's foreign shipping rose to 85.7 per cent in 1882, while Germany had a share of only 7 per cent in that year. The "Big Three" operated intra-Asian regular lines running to a fixed schedule in particular trades and dominating the coastal and riverine traffic until the early twentieth century. To regulate competition between them and intercontinental lines (such as the Messageries Maritimes, the Hamburg-Amerika Linie (Hamburg-America Line) and the Norddeutscher Lloyd (North German Lloyd) operating a number of important feeder lines in East Asia closely linked with their intercontinental services), conference agreements introduced steamship pools, joint-purse agreements and cargo pools from the 1870s. The agreements reflected the impact of growing pressure on intra-Asian freight markets, something that was further propelled by the continuing intrusion of European tramp steamers into the region.[39]

The earlier strong position of German merchant ships declined between 1868 (7.3 per cent) and 1892 (6.4 per cent), especially in direct and return voyages between Europe and China. This was mainly due to the retarded switch from sail to steam among German shipping companies and the opening of the Suez Canal. British, French and American intercontinental steamers pushed aside German flags, which even affected tramp shipping markets. German consuls posted to Chinese ports told the government that more steamships instead of sailing ships needed to be employed in the trade if they were to compete successfully with other lines. Finally, Hamburg pioneered the dispatching of steamships to East Asia, followed in 1877 by Flensburg, the major port of Schleswig-Holstein.[40] With the worsening freight rates in Europe at the time, a reflex of the protectionist policies of major European

[37] Liu (1959, 439–452), Lai (2004, 301–303) and Reinhardt (2018, 77–85).

[38] Fletcher (1958, 556–573), Marriner and Hyde (1967), Harlaftis and Theotokas (2002, 18–22), Liu (1964, 49–77), Keswick (1982, 36) and Blake (1999, 230–231).

[39] Hyde (1973, 32–37), Henderson (1975, 201–203), Scholl (1984, 30–54) and Armstrong (2009b, 77).

[40] Spethmann (2002, 50–51).

countries, including Germany, and the consequent overproduction of steamers, a number of shipping companies were prompted to dispatch their vessels to East Asia. From the mid-1880s, German steam tramps specially fitted for intra-Asian coastal shipping subsequently increased in numbers in Asian waters. In 1881, the Reederei M. Jebsen (M. Jebsen Steam Shipping Company), established in Apenrade, Schleswig-Holstein, sent the first steam coaster to Hong Kong. The Chinesische Küstenfahrt-Gesellschaft (Chinese Coastal Shipping Company), headquartered in Hamburg, started operating four steam tramps in Chinese waters in 1887; after the firm merged with the Hamburg-based Dampfschiffs-Gesellschaft Swatow (Swatow Steam Shipping Company) in 1895, it took over from it six steamers, bringing its fleet to ten ships in 1898. At the time, the Dampfschiffahrts-Gesellschaft von 1869 (Steam Shipping Company of 1869), headquartered in Flensburg, operated five steamers in East Asia; the Asiatische Küstenfahrt-Gesellschaft (Asiatic Coastal Shipping Company), in Hamburg, had four ships in Chinese waters; the M. Struve Shipping Company in Blankenese (a port close to Hamburg), owned three vessels; and three smaller firms (two of which were based in Schleswig-Holstein), the J. P. Massmann Shipping Company in Heiligenhafen, the company of J. D. Bischoff in Bremen and the firm of Heinrich Schuldt in Flensburg had one steamer each, and even sailing ships operating in East Asia. In 1899, the Rickmers Shipping Company in Bremerhaven began to dispatch its first two small steam tramps to Chinese waters and, until 1903, sent seven more of this type specially equipped for coastal shipping. Until the First World War, German shipping companies frequently sent steam coasters to the Far East, where they were chartered by Chinese merchants in time charter and serviced routes between Hong Kong and ports in southern and northern China and other parts of East Asia.[41] In intra-Asian markets, German tramps were usually employed in time charters, shipping mainly bulk goods such as rice, bamboo, jute, copra and mixed cargoes, but occasionally also passengers, presumably Chinese emigrants ("coolies").[42] In 1902, Germany's

[41] *Hansa. Deutsche Nautische Zeitschrift*, 8 July 1899, Becker (2012, 249–251, 255–256, 363–364) and Leonhard (2009, 146–147). BAB, R 901-76697: German Consulate-General for China (Shanghai) to Foreign Ministry (Berlin), 27 March 1923: Report on shipping in China.

[42] On the distinction between Chinese emigration movements and "coolie trade", see Sinn (2013, 50–53).

share of foreign shipping in China had considerably increased (16.2 per cent), almost equalling Japan's (16.5 per cent). However, with Japan's massive expansion into intra-Asian shipping and trading after the Russo-Japanese War (1904–1905), the German share fell to 8.6 per cent (1913), while Japan's grew strongly to 31.9 per cent. After the First World War, which brought German merchant shipping in East Asia to a complete standstill, pre-war numbers could not be attained, even with a remarkable increase in the 1920s. With 1.9 per cent (1924) and 3.2 per cent (1928), Germany's share of shipping in China lagged far behind the respective totals of Britain (51.5 and 48.3) and Japan (32.1 and 33.6) in those years, but came close to that of the United States (5.9 and 5.5).[43]

Steam tramps or steam coasters (besides the traditional Chinese junks and European sailing ships), capable of picking up freight and passengers at widely scattered ports and transporting them all around the region, played a crucial and increasing role in East Asia's shipping and economic development from the 1870s, after the Suez Canal opened. Tramping was, as Michael M. Miller states, "a constant struggle to position ships where freight was abundant and competitors' ships were not, where rates therefore were high not low, where voyages contracted would not undercut arrival in time for seasonal trade, where going for a 'spot loading' was better than fixing a cargo in advance".[44] Since tramps were generally not plying any regular route but rather worked whatever cargo and route were available, mutual pricing was "a nightmare" and tramp conferences "were unlikely to succeed", explains John Armstrong.[45] However, when regular lines were operated in coastal shipping, a shipping conference, a combination of tramp shipping companies, sometimes prevented ruinous competition against each other. Such an arrangement was somewhat similar to the agreements — so-called conferences — among liner companies in overseas shipping running to a fixed schedule in a particular trade on a given route. A shipping conference usually had two main goals. The first was to regulate rivalry between the regular companies themselves so as to obtain and maintain reasonable rates of freight. Consequently, unified rates were charged and the trade was divided either by fixing the number of sailings for each line

[43] Ratenhof (1987, 567: table 5).

[44] Miller (2012, 95).

[45] Armstrong (2009a, 77).

during a specific period, allocating certain ports to each company, or by pooling an agreed proportion of freight receipts. The second goal was to limit the entry of outside shipping interests, and this was usually achieved by the use of a deferred rebate system.[46] In the South China Sea, this was practised at certain times on the run between Haiphong and Hong Kong when the M. Jebsen Shipping Company and the Tonkin Shipping Company agreed on more or less equal freight and passage prices for their steam tramps, to avoid relentless competition as in other shipping markets of East Asia.

Highly competitive tramp shipping markets were normally divided into two different types of charter markets, the trip (or voyage) charter market and the time charter market. Under the first type of contract, which was typical of tramp shipping, the charterer hired the ship for only one voyage to carry his cargo at an agreed rate per tonne. Under the second, the shipowner provided the crew and all other requirements for operating the ship. The charterer became the disponent owner and was allowed to send the vessel anywhere and load it with all kinds of merchandise. Under this type of contract, the charterer commonly hired the ship at an agreed monthly rate over a period of three, six, or twelve months, though shorter or longer periods were also possible. The time charter option permitted the operation of regular lines in coastal shipping, something that was highly profitable when agricultural bulk cargoes were frequently transported from agriculturally producing regions to consuming and distributing markets (e.g. from Burma, Siam, French Indochina, the Dutch East Indies and southern China to Hong Kong and other major ports. In bulk trades such as rice, tea, sugar, beans, grain, raw cotton, coal, wood, iron and kerosene, tramps were particularly important.[47]

After the Sino-Japanese War (1894–1895), which opened up the Chinese market to foreign industry and commerce, the "Big Three" and other foreign shipping companies (mainly from Japan,[48] Norway,[49] and Germany) had more and even larger steamers constructed to satisfy the

[46] Fairbank (1973, 24–26), Miller (2012, 180–181) and Reinhardt (94–124).

[47] Armstrong (2009b, 91–102) and Becker (2010a, 274–275).

[48] Wray (1984, 388–394).

[49] Norway, an independent European state after the dissolution of the Swedish-Norwegian union in 1905, possessed by 1880 a merchant marine with the third greatest tonnage in the world. By 1902, most Norwegian ships calling at Asian ports were steamers

growing needs of Chinese merchants in intra-Asian shipping markets. With the global economic boom from 1895 to 1913, the overall competition in shipping markets strongly increased. Although German flags in Chinese ports rose in number and tonnage, Japanese steamships pushed them into fourth place in 1900. In the port's statistics of Hong Kong, the German flag ranked better, which reflected the growing importance of the colony as a port-of-call of intercontinental shipping lines and as intra-Asian shipping hub. In 1909, 735 German vessels, with a tonnage of 1,176,322 tonnes, called at the port of Hong Kong, numerically only surpassed by 4.931 British ships, of 5.722.084 tonnes, and 493 Japanese vessels, of 1,283.330 tonnes (France had fifth place on this list just behind the Chinese flag). The higher tonnage of the Japanese mercantile marine signalled the increasingly stronger performance of Japan in East Asian shipping markets since the Russo-Japanese War (1904–1905). Germany's position changed drastically with the outbreak of the First World War and the disappearance of her merchant navy from the oceans. In 1921, the first German ships turned up in Chinese waters, and four years later, seventy-eight German vessels, of 332.495 tonnes, entered the port of Hong Kong (which gave the German flag numerically eighth place behind Britain, Japan, China, United States, the Netherlands, France and Norway). This ranking remained the same in 1930 when 170 German vessels, of 631.474 tonnes, called at Hong Kong. Compared to 1909, the number of German vessels had drastically decreased and their tonnage fell to slightly more than half of what it had been in 1909. These numbers reflected the very slow recovery of the German mercantile marine after the First World War and the impact of the Global Great Depression (1929) on shipping markets worldwide.[50]

The M. Jebsen Shipping Company

Coastal shipping was a century-old and traditional occupation of people living in the coastal regions of the Baltic Sea. However, some port cities such as Flensburg and Apenrade also employed sailing ships for overseas trade. In the 1850s, Apenrade, a small Baltic port town in the duchy of

in intra-Asian trades, the most visited ports were Hong Kong, Bangkok, Shanghai, Singapore and Saigon. Brautaset and Tenold (2010, 207, 217–221).

[50] Otte (1930, 128–134); *Hong Kong Blue Books for the Years 1909, 1925 and 1930.* Scholl (1984, 55–59), Scholl (1990, 91–100) and Rübner and Scholl (2009).

Schleswig, at the time a part of the Kingdom of Denmark, became the leading shipping centre in the duchy, offering shipping services carrying a variety of cargoes from Europe to East Asia and engaging in the coastal trade, with Hong Kong as a major hub; between 1850 and 1880, there were sometimes half a dozen Apenrade vessels anchored in Hong Kong harbour at any one time. One of the German merchant vessels calling at Hong Kong in the 1860s was under the command of Michael Jebsen, born in Apenrade on 27 September 1835. Following the traditions of his hometown, Jebsen became a sailor and shipmaster. However, due to the fact that he was from a German-minded family and personally suffered under Danish rule in Schleswig, Jebsen swore never to command a ship flying the Danish flag. Therefore, he acquired Hamburg citizenship and was sailing a ship under the Hamburg flag when calling at the port of Hong Kong on 5 September 1864. On board *Notos* was a cargo of rice from Bangkok, the last port of call, which Jebsen had purchased on his own account, hoping to find purchasers in Hong Kong. Ten months earlier, in November 1863, *Notos*, owned by the Hamburg-based shipping company Hastedt & Company, had been dispatched with different piece goods destined for Australia. After discharging the freight in Adelaide, Jebsen sailed to Singapore to engage in the highly profitable coastal shipping in East Asia. In the British colony, he was able to get a contract for a full rice shipment from Bangkok to Hong Kong. It was Jebsen's first experience with freight markets in the China seas.[51]

At the time, the switch from sail to steam as a technology for ships was looming. In Apenrade, the local shipbuilding industry specialising in building fast, high-quality sailing ships, was the town's core employment sector. Active or retired masters were owners of the largest local shipping companies, and a good many Apenrade citizens were co-owners (in German: Partenreeder) of vessels, receiving a share of the profits. For many, shipping was not merely a business but the major source of their income and, furthermore, an important factor in their identity. The local economy's strong focus on shipbuilding and shipping using sailing ships, plus a certain degree of emotional affiliation with such traditions, made it very difficult for Apenrade to switch to the new steam technology when it became more common in the shipping industry in the 1870s. The complex network of investors hampered the switch to steamers because it

[51] Becker (2012, 89–97).

required investment in ships that were direct competitors of sailing ships. However, in Britain, but also in Germany's major North Sea ports and some larger Baltic Sea ports such as Flensburg, larger investor groups, mainly from the commerce and finance sectors, put money into shipyards to build iron steamships, and into steam shipping companies. When establishing the Partenreederei M. Jebsen (also called Reederei M. Jebsen: M. Jebsen Shipping Company), in the traditional form of a partnership on 23 November 1878, Michael Jebsen was following the practices of his hometown.[52]

Due to the negative attitude of local investors towards steam, Jebsen was not able to secure sufficient capital in Apenrade and had to find it elsewhere. Of the fifty shares of the steamer, called *Signal*, which Jebsen bought at a Flensburg shipyard, he and his brother-in-law, Jes Nicolai Jessen, took twelve; the rest were sold to business friends in London, Hamburg, Kiel, Rotterdam and Flushing. Due to the general oversupply of new steamships, the global recession and decreasing freight rates, it was difficult for Jebsen to find investors at all. He became managing shipowner (Korrespondentreeder), of the ship employing the *Signal* in coastal shipping in the Baltic and other European seas. For the next steamers, the *Vorwärts* and the *Triumph*, built by the Howaldt Shipyard at Kiel in 1879 and 1881, Jebsen found investors again exclusively among his network of business friends. In this group, a core of substantial shareholders, tied to him by family bonds, continued to invest in new vessels in his growing fleet for more than a quarter of a century. Until Michael Jebsen died in 1899, the brothers, Carl and Gustav Diederichsen, coffee merchants in Hamburg, remained the chief investors. Their relatives, the shipbuilders Georg, Bernhard, and Hermann Howaldt, were the main suppliers of new steamers for the M. Jebsen Shipping Company. This well-functioning triangular network of Apenrade, Hamburg and Kiel was the basic factor in frequently supplying the firm with the most advanced steam technology and gaining high profits in competitive shipping markets.[53]

The beginning of Michael Jebsen's involvement with tramp shipping in East Asia was marked by the *Vorwärts* calling at Hong Kong in June 1881. The steam tramps of the M. Jebsen Shipping Company were

[52] The early history of the M. Jebsen Shipping Company is dealt with in Hieke (1953), Hänisch (1970, 25–32), Schmelzkopf (1994, 27–50), Miller and Wasmuth (2008, 8–21), Becker (2010a, 245–302; 2012, 165–370) and So (2019, 29–54).

[53] Hieke (1953, 37–38), Becker (2012, 191–231) and So (2019, 33–43).

specially equipped for shipping bulk goods (rice, coal, wood, vegetables and cattle), with a low draught capable of entering the typically very shallow Chinese and Indochinese ports. Jebsen's modern fleet mainly consisted of medium-sized steam coasters which were chartered by Chinese and European merchants to transport all sorts of cargo and passengers between coastal ports in East Asia. Starting in March 1895, the principal agent of the M. Jebsen Shipping Company was Jebsen & Company in Hong Kong, owned by his eldest son Jacob (1870–1941) and his son's business associate Johann Heinrich Jessen (1865–1931). During his term as member of the German national parliament,[54] Michael Jebsen profited from the close interplay with his son to gain a degree of influence on the German government, both in the interests of shipping companies operating in East Asian and of his own company. He used his professional expertise as a shipowner and his influence as a politician to demand from Berlin a more efficient consular service for German merchant vessels in East Asia, considerable government subsidies for the postal steamer lines of the North German Lloyd to East Asia and Australia and for the postal steamer service at the northern Chinese coast, mainly between Shanghai and Jiaozhou (Kiaochow), which was operated by his company from 1898 to 1901.[55] Furthermore, Jebsen's political connections, and the close interplay with his son in Hong Kong, explain to some extent the influence Jebsen & Co. had on German consuls in the South China Sea being charged with promoting German shipping and trading interests in the region. After his death on 30 September 1899 in Berlin, Jebsen & Co. was no longer able to profit from Michael Jebsen's lobbying in the German capital.

During Michael Jebsen's lifetime, the traditional form of a partnership, in which each ship was owned by a group of different investors, remained unchanged, making joint decisions on larger repairs or sales of vessels often cumbersome, or sometimes even impossible. Furthermore, operating fixed liner routes in East Asia, such as between Hong Kong and Haiphong, Shanghai and Jiaozhou (Kiaochow), and between Shantou (Swatow) and Deli, the port city on Sumatra, in the Dutch East Indies,

[54] Active in local politics from the early 1880s, Michael Jebsen became a member of the National Liberal Reichstag Party in 1890, was re-elected in 1893 but lost his seat in 1898; until his death on 30 September 1899 he held a seat for his party in the Prussian Diet. Becker (2012, 371–555).

[55] Becker (2009, 205–229) and So (2019, 43–47).

it became increasingly difficult to distribute sufficient dividends for each single vessel servicing a line; sometimes, ships did not make profits at all. This was aggravated by difficulties in crediting to the account of single ships the purchase of lighters or storage places to transport and store cargoes. In these circumstances, the M. Jebsen Shipping Company was transformed into a joint-stock company in 1911. In 1885, after all ships had been transferred to Hong Kong, its steamer fleet numbered eight; in 1903–1904, the company reached its peak with 17 ships, and by 1913, it had 11 ships.[56]

Jacob Friedrich Christian Jebsen (the eldest son of Michael Jebsen), born on 27 December 1870 in Apenrade, studied chemistry at universities in Karlsruhe and Berlin in 1889–1890, hoping for good career prospects. The chemical industry was one of Germany's key businesses, globally renowned for its fast progress, quality and versatility. An eye injury during a chemical experiment forced him to drop out of university, however. At his father's shipping company in Apenrade, and at the firm of Adolf Deppe, shipping agent and shipbroker in Antwerp, Belgium, Jacob pursued a commercial apprenticeship before leaving for Hong Kong in 1894 to look for a position in a German shipbroker's business closely connected with the M. Jebsen Shipping Company. However, he was not successful and therefore joined forces with a distant relative, Johann Heinrich Jessen (nephew of his uncle Jes Nicolai Jessen), who was working for a German company in Shanghai at the time. On 1 March 1895, they set up Jebsen & Co. in Hong Kong as principal agent of the M. Jebsen Shipping Company in Apenrade. This establishment was certainly impacted by the outcome of the Sino-Japanese War (1894–1895), which had put the Chinese empire on the brink of extinction, and peace negotiations started almost three weeks later. In the peace treaty of Shimonoseki signed on 17 April 1895, China agreed to permit Japan to establish industries on its territory, something that was also applied to other treaty powers, with the most-favoured nation clause as stipulated in the unequal treaties of Western powers with China. This concession opened up major Chinese markets, thus offering entirely new fields of business for foreign companies which until then had been restricted to the treaty ports. Such favourable prospects doubtless motivated the founders of Jebsen & Co. to take the decision to establish their own company in Hong Kong which

[56] Becker (2012, 173–191) and So (2019, 53–58).

initially depended entirely on profits of commissions secured from the M. Jebsen Shipping Company. "There was rarely a war that had as many winners as the one of 1894-95", states Jürgen Osterhammel.[57] The main winners were European nations such as France and Germany and, to a lesser extent, the Jebsen and Jessen families which profited from new markets in East Asia.

The healthy profits of the shipping business provided the basis for Jebsen & Co. to become active in trading. The company started to import textiles from Manchester, selling them to Chinese merchants operating in Hong Kong, China and French Indochina. In 1897, Jebsen & Co. were made agents of Badische Anilin- & Soda-Fabrik (BASF), the major chemical producer in Ludwigshafen, Germany. After Jiaozhou Bay became a German leasehold colony in 1898, Jacob Jebsen and Johann Heinrich Jessen joined with Heinrich Diederichsen, the brother of Carl and Gustav Diederichsen, a coal trader and shipowner in Kiel, to establish the partnership firm Diederichsen, Jebsen & Company in Jiaozhou. When the successful association ended after ten years, mainly due to friction over strategic decisions taken by Heinrich Diederichsen, the two partners founded Jebsen & Jessen in Hamburg as import agents of Asian products for European markets.[58] Jebsen & Co. headquartered in Hong Kong established branches in Shanghai (1903), Guangzhou and Tianjin (1907) focusing on importing German industrial products to China and exporting Chinese products to Germany. With the outbreak of the First World War, Jacob Jebsen (who was staying in Hong Kong at the time) was interned in October 1914, as were many other German businessmen treated as enemies by the British authorities. Jebsen & Co. was forcefully, but legally, liquidated in Hong Kong and Jacob Jebsen was transferred to an Australian prisoner-of-war camp in February 1916. He returned to Apenrade in the summer of 1919, shortly before his hometown became a part of Denmark as a consequence of the plebiscite of February 1920 in North Schleswig. Their new status as Danish citizens (which was not much liked by the two partners), favoured the reopening of Jebsen & Co. in Guangzhou (1922) and in Hong Kong (1923) where the firm was the agent of major German and Danish industries such as IG Farben, the electrical company of Robert Bosch, the automobile producer Daimler-Benz,

[57] Osterhammel (1989, 203).

[58] Hänisch (1970, 52–62, 104–110) and So (2019, 58–75).

the Rickmers Shipping Company from Bremerhaven and the Maersk Line from Copenhagen. The Jebsen steamers were mostly destroyed in war-related incidents or were confiscated during the conflict, and the company did not recover from these losses: in East Asia in the 1920s, the M. Jebsen Shipping Company operated only five vessels under the Danish and German flags, less than half the size of its pre-war fleet.[59]

Asian Crews and European Shipmasters

In the late nineteenth century and early twentieth centuries, it was customary for European shipping companies operating steam coasters in intra-Asian trading to have Chinese, Indian or Malayan crews. When the ships arrived in Asia the entire European crews — seamen, stokers, trimmers and others — were usually discharged and replaced by "native" crewmen. Reports from German consuls in China and Japan suggest that around 80 per cent of all German coasters sailed with Asian seafarers employed as stokers and trimmers, but also as ordinary seamen, stewards and carpenters. In Hong Kong, Chinese crewmen especially were accepted as "excellent labourers, as for diligence, willingness and bodily care", the Rickmers Shipping Company reported from Bremerhaven. In 1919, about 115,000 young men, mainly originating from Guangzhou and small villages in the Pearl River Delta, made up a reserve of maritime workers who were employed as seamen on European vessels in Hong Kong.[60] Through the intervention of so-called "boarding masters", recruiting agents and owners of houses in Hong Kong who offered accommodation and provisions, shipmasters hired uniform groups of Chinese as deck and engine room crews. Since family members or inhabitants of the same villages were grouped together, crew members were rather homogenous, a factor which obviously contributed to discipline on board. This was further enhanced by the fact that Asian crews did not consume large quantities of alcohol, as European crews commonly did. Hiring Chinese crews was a common practice in most of the ports of

[59] Schmelzkopf (1994, 46–47) and Becker (2012, 578–580).

[60] BAB, R 901-75936: Rickmers Shipping Company (Bremerhaven) to Foreign Ministry (Berlin), 15 February 1897. Chan (1991, 145–181), Chesneaux (1968, 40) and Amenda (2011, 46–48).

China around 1900, establishing an international labour market for ship crews.[61]

The main reason for shipowners hiring local crews was the cost factor. This was especially so in times such as the 1890s, when the Mexican silver dollar, the commonly used currency for paying ship crews in most parts of East Asia, declined in value. Chinese crews seem to have received only 50 to 60 per cent of the pay earned by their German and other European counterparts.[62] Michael Jebsen was well aware of the advantages Chinese crews offered. Before the departure of his first steamer to China, he instructed one of his masters to get rid of his Dutch crew and replace them with Malayans or Chinese "because you would come off cheaper that way".[63] A Chinese stoker aboard a German coaster between 1880 and 1906 earned an average of 18 to 20 dollars per month. In 1880, when the dollar was equivalent to 4 marks, the savings for shipowners were relatively small. The pay for a Chinese stoker was between 72 and 80 marks, while his German counterpart earned 83 marks on average. With the sharp devaluation of the Mexican silver dollar in the 1890s, the employment of Chinese crews became more profitable for shipowners.[64] Compared to a German crew, a Chinese crew earned more or less the same as long as the exchange rate of the dollar remained stable, namely equivalent to 4 marks. However, with the decline of the dollar after 1893, Jebsen was able to save costs when hiring Chinese. Pointing to the unaffected purchasing power of the dollar, he put forward the argument that, on the China coast "for the Chinese, the equivalent remains almost the same because the dollar keeps its dollar value there".[65]

An additional important factor which helped to limit expenses was the fact that the monthly board for Chinese crews was included in their wages,

[61] Rübner (1997, 16–17).

[62] Conrad (2006, 248–250).

[63] JJHA, A01-01-313: Michael Jebsen (Apenrade) to Captain Heinrich Evers (Hong Kong), 4 August 1881.

[64] Küttner (2000, 9, 98). The monthly wages in 1897 for Chinese crew members aboard Jebsen's ships were: stokers 18 dollars, trimmers 16 dollars, seamen 20 dollars, cook 20 dollars, crew's cook 2 dollars and steward 9 dollars. JJHA, A01-01-237: Franz Engelbrecht (on behalf of Michael Jebsen) to the Hamburg Chamber of Commerce, 12 February 1897.

[65] JJHA, A01-01-237: Franz Engelbrecht (on behalf of Michael Jebsen) to the Apenrade Magistrate, 6 March 1897.

and this meant that the Chinese purchased their own food which was prepared by the crew's Chinese cook. The result was that the costs for the board of Chinese crews were 75 per cent lower than for European crews. However, in the early 1880s Jebsen still paid board for his Chinese crews which was almost equivalent to that paid for Europeans, but this generous spending seems to have been reduced, and later completely abolished when economic circumstances were difficult.[66] When Jebsen discovered in 1893 that the ship's carpenter on one of his steamers was a European whose board cost 30 dollars per month on the ship's account, he wrote to the captain that "a Chinese might have filled equally well this vacancy", and informed him that 800 marks annually could have been saved had he instead hired a Chinese carpenter.[67] The cost factor was so important in keeping the ship profitable that earlier payments for the board of Chinese crew members were subject to rigorous saving measures. In 1897, Jebsen reported that the Chinese in his ships "cater for themselves in the way that is customary in their country".[68]

However, the commonest and most influential argument for employing Chinese stokers and trimmers was the claim that they were more resistant to heat than Europeans.[69] Temperatures in the engine rooms of steamships were very high, usually between 40 and 50 degrees, and could rise up to 70 degrees in tropical climates. Medical research confirmed the allegedly physical superiority of non-Europeans for this work, but a more likely explanation was that the lighter clothing and better nutrition of Asian workers helped them to withstand the risk of heat-stroke. When the German Social Democratic Party began to protest against the employment of Asian crews by German shipping companies, arguing that this practice would reduce work opportunities and result in the lowering of pay for German seamen, shipowners referred to "the dictates of humanity" when making use of Asian stokers on account of their much

[66] Küttner (2000, 101). JJHA, A01-01-307: Michael Jebsen (Apenrade) to Captain Friedrich Boysen (Hong Kong), 18 June 1883.

[67] JJHA, A01-01-228: Michael Jebsen (Apenrade) to Captain Jürgen Bruhn (Hong Kong), 19 July 1893.

[68] JJHA, A01-01-237: Franz Engelbrecht (on behalf of Michael Jebsen) to the Apenrade Magistrate, 6 March 1897.

[69] Amenda (2011, 47–48).

greater resistance to heat.[70] Jebsen supported this notion, which was widespread among shipowners. In the Reichstag debate of 15 January 1892, he referred to his personal experiences reporting that European stokers in East African waters, in the Red Sea, and elsewhere would not stand the climate nor work. His accountant followed this argument, pointing in 1897 to "the greater insensitiveness" of Chinese stokers against high temperatures in the engine and boiler rooms.[71] This was obviously disguising the real facts. In the business correspondence of the M. Jebsen Shipping Company, such humanitarian arguments did not matter at all and only the financial advantages of Chinese crews played a role. When one of his captains reported that he had discharged the European crew in Hong Kong and hired a Chinese crew, Jebsen praised "the very considerable savings, apart from the advantage to have tranquillity and peace on board".[72]

One of the main challenges for managing owners of a fleet of steam tramps fleet operating thousands of miles from the companies' headquarters was to instruct and control the shipmasters. The intermittent character of this relationship meant that immense trust had to be placed in a single individual who was primarily an employee. Confidence in a shipmaster was so important because in all the longer-distance trades he had to be a person who could be relied upon to handle both navigational and commercial functions. Once the ship had passed beyond the confines of the port he was "master next god", a term describing his omnipotence aboard, and it was difficult for anyone to control his actions.[73] This reality made trust an absolute necessity, especially when, as in the case of the M. Jebsen Shipping Company, the vessels did not frequently return to their home ports but remained for years at a distant station such as Hong Kong. Jebsen once made clear to a master who was on his way to China that "it is not sufficient for the master to steer his ship in an orderly manner over the seas but he must also pay proper attention and make arrangements at port", something that he found was "unfortunately

[70] *Hansa. Deutsche Nautische Zeitschrift*, 15 September 1900. Küttner (2000, 82–87) and Conrad (2006, 251–252).

[71] Becker (2012, 293). JJHA, A01-01-237: Franz Engelbrecht (on behalf of Michael Jebsen) to the Apenrade Magistrate, 6 March 1897.

[72] JJHA, A01-01-225: Michael Jebsen (Apenrade) to Captain Jürgen Bruhn (Hong Kong), 18 May 1892.

[73] Davis (1972, 159–168).

(…) not always done". He further explained to him that, on the coast of China "you are mainly left to yourself".[74]

Since confidence in a person was usually enhanced through personal acquaintance, it is not surprising that most of the masters on Jebsen's ships came from his hometown of Apenrade or the neighbouring regions. Many began service as helmsmen on board Jebsen steamers and were promoted to master if a vacancy occurred.[75] The long-term relationships with his masters did not prevent Jebsen from being highly critical of them when he thought that they had neglected their duties. Many of his letters contain strong complaints about the behaviour of his masters, sometimes in an abusive tone. This was regarded as necessary by Jebsen because when a ship was chartered the master was the principal representative of the shipping company in his relations with the charterer, and he therefore carried a dual responsibility. Ralph Davis summed up these tasks as follows: "On the one hand, he had to comply in all respects with the charter-party, going to the places specified in it, accepting instructions from the charterers' agents, providing services for unloading and loading if agreed. On the other, he had to watch his owners' interests to see that charter-party conditions were not broken. For practical purposes, it may be said that usually the charterers' instructions replaced those of his owners for the conduct of the affairs of the voyage". In East Asia, however, when the Chinese charterer or his shipping comprador (middleman) was aboard, as sometimes happened, it lifted from the master a certain degree of responsibility.[76]

The most repetitive topic in Jebsen's letters to his masters was economy on board. "Order and thriftiness are qualities that can never be exercised too much", he once stated.[77] He regarded it as his duty constantly to make his masters aware of these necessities. Especially during economic downturns in the shipping market, his appeals for thriftiness were a constant refrain in his correspondence. If an accident occurred, the master was the first person to be questioned and made responsible for any loss or damage to the vessel and its cargo, or for other financial consequences.

[74] JJHA, A01-01-214: Michael Jebsen (Apenrade) to Captain W. Zerrahn, 29 May, 2 June and 16 June 1884.

[75] Hieke (1953, 99).

[76] Davis (1972, 167–168).

[77] JJHA, A01-01-214: Michael Jebsen (Apenrade) to Captain Friedrich Boysen (Hong Kong), 20 July 1884.

When the *Triumph,* under the command of Captain Jürgen Bruhn, ran aground in the Hainan Strait in early 1891, causing extensive damage to the ship with repair costs of around 33,000 dollars, it was the worst accident suffered by the Jebsen fleet up till that time. The annoyed shipowner sent a strong letter to Bruhn stating that "for years the steamers of my company have been employed on this route, but soon after you joined this misfortune happened". He assumed that Bruhn's carelessness was to blame for the accident because the extent of the damage suggested that the ship was running at full speed when the accident occurred. Although his co-owners had suggested giving Bruhn the sack, Jebsen settled it with a reproach, but warned the master that any further problem of this sort would lead to his dismissal.[78]

In the 1890s, during the depression, Jebsen was even more mistrustful of his masters. A whole series of letters calling for more economy on board and appealing to the duties of masters was dispatched. After his son Jacob became the principal shipping agent for the Jebsen fleet based in Hong Kong, he frequently wrote to him warning of the misbehaviour of masters and giving him advice on how to deal with them. Jebsen's negative stance towards his masters was obviously influenced by his own experiences as a shipmaster, but also by the information and impressions he received through the masters' letters. It is difficult to come to a final judgement, but there was certainly some truth in his criticism of the masters' practices and behaviour. He felt increasingly helpless, however, about making any fundamental changes regarding their malpractices. After Jebsen & Co. was founded in Hong Kong in 1895, taking over the supervision of the steamers operating in East Asia, the situation considerably improved, resulting in fewer complaints from the shipowner about the masters.[79]

The French Business Community

In December 1845, Auguste Haussmann arrived in Hong Kong. The Alsatian textile manufacturer, an influential member of the Mulhouse Chamber of Commerce, was part of the official French mission of Théodore Lagrené charged with concluding a commercial treaty with

[78] JJHA, A01-01-316, Michael Jebsen (Apenrade) to Captain Jürgen Bruhn (Hong Kong), 11 March 1891.

[79] Becker (2012, 272–273).

China securing for France the same privileges as Britain had obtained in the Treaty of Nanjing (1842) after the First Opium War. On 24 October 1844, the French diplomat, accompanied by several industrialists and merchants, succeeded in signing the Treaty of Whampoa in which China granted, among other things, the opening of five treaty ports for French merchants, extraterritorial privileges for her citizens and the right of France to appoint consuls in these ports. To learn more about shipping and trade, the delegates visited treaty ports in China, Macao and Hong Kong. At the time, the British colony had a total population of almost 24,000, mainly Chinese and some Indians, and 1,800 garrisoned troops; the 595 European residents comprised 455 men, 90 women and 50 children. In his travel report, Haussmann noted that the twenty-five trading firms established in Hong Kong, and a large number of other companies, had their headquarters in Guangzhou and branches in Shanghai. "Hong Kong is the political rather than the commercial abode of the English merchants in China", he added. The French merchant was convinced that Hong Kong was "too close to the huge market of Guangzhou to be ever able to acquire a great importance, if not for opium sales". Generally, he found that China treaty ports trade held limited promise for France, with little business available for her merchants and seafarers.[80]

In 1846, France exported mainly manufactured products such as silk, foil, cotton and woollen fabrics (394 million francs), followed by wines, knick-knacks, haberdashery, furniture (28 million francs), decorated skins (27 million francs), linen and hemp materials (26 million), paper and its applications (21 million francs), pottery, glass and crystal (55 million francs). Imports into France consisted mainly of raw materials needed for her industries, namely cotton (114 million francs), cereals (100 million francs), silks (77 million francs), ordinary woods (52 million francs), sugar from the French colonies (49 million francs), wool (37 million francs), coal (29 million francs), oleaginous grain (27 million francs), olive oil (26 million francs), tobacco and raw skins (both 25 million francs) and indigo (12 million francs). China, the main exporter of tea and silks and a major importer of opium, seemed not to offer much opportunity for commercial exchange with France. In his other book on China, published in 1864, Haussmann admitted that "our country consumes little tea; our colonies do not export any opium, not any cotton wool; in contrast, we

[80] Cady (1954, 44–69), Endacott (1995, 65), Drémeaux (2012, 30–31) and Haussmann (1848, 303–304).

ourselves, like China, produce silk, and our cotton and woollen fabrics are more expensive than those of the English and the Americans. We see that nature and circumstance created obstacles to the development of our trade with the Far East". However, the textile manufacturer added that in previous years, imports of Chinese raw silks into France had sizeably increased.[81]

Such cautious comments on France's commercial relations with China were indicative of the future size and composition of the French business community in Hong Kong. It was rather a small group in the nineteenth and early twentieth centuries, mainly consisting of French Catholic clergy, the agents of Messageries Maritimes and the Banque de l'Indochine (Bank of Indochina), and a handful of retailers, often commission agents for French and other companies exporting a range of products to the British colony which were often re-exported to China and other destinations in East Asia. However, information on French merchants in the available primary and secondary sources is very scanty, and there is frequent confusion over their nationality because Swiss and Belgian businessmen often had French-sounding names.[82]

To begin with banking, the Comptoir d'escompte de Paris (since 1889: Comptoir national d'escompte de Paris or CNEP), the major French credit bank in East Asia, which established its Hong Kong branch in 1862, remained for many years the only French financial institution in the British colony. After the establishment of the Saigon branch of the Banque de l'Indochine (Bank of Indochina) in 1875, both banks closely co-operated in promoting French interests in East Asia, especially in Cochinchina and during the Sino-French War over Tonkin (1884–1885). In 1894, the Bank of Indochina took over the CNEP agency and

[81] Haussmann (1864, 105). France's main trading partners were the United States, Britain, the Kingdom of Sardinia and other parts of Italy, Belgium, the German Customs Union, the Kingdom of Hanover and the Hanseatic cities, Spain, Algeria, Switzerland, Russia, Turkey, French possessions in the Indian Ocean, British India, Brazil and the Spanish colonies in America, and the Netherlands. Levasseur (1912, 236–241).

[82] For the history of the French community in Hong Kong, see Castel (1957); Dremeaux (2012) providing a comprehensive overview and many details. On the French clergy, see Dremeaux (2012), Chu (2005, 89) and Le Pichon (2006). For France's consulate in Hong Kong until the early 1920s, see the master thesis of Mouries (1991), which is exclusively based on the Hong Kong files of the government-general of Indochina kept at ANOM; these files contain little information on the French business community in Hong Kong. For the history of Banque de l'Indochine in Hong Kong, see the comprehensive and detailed study of Bonin (2020, 85–176) based on the bank's records.

established itself in Hong Kong. The impetus behind this step was French Foreign Minister Gabriel Hanotaux and his imperial ambitions regarding China in the wake of the Sino-Japanese War (1894–1895). The Hong Kong branch, initially "a mere tool" of the bank's main branches in French Indochina, China and Singapore, developed, as Hubert Bonin explains, into an access road to the foreign exchange market, thanks to the colony's eminent role as a major trading hub in the region. This gave the branch an important position vis-a-vis its counterparts in Saigon and Guangzhou and satisfied "French economic patriotism" (Bonin). With Hong Kong being the major export destination for rice from Saigon and Haiphong (416,843 tonnes in 1902) - China and Japan were much less important for Indochina's rice exports (51,383 tonnes in 1902) - the branch joined the lucrative business (which was mainly in the hands of British and Chinese banks) to provide loans to Chinese rice merchants in Saigon and Haiphong.[83]

Without its main customer base of Chinese traders in Indochina, Guangzhou and Hong Kong, the Bank of Indochina would have suffered a cruel fate. French shipping and commerce in the British colony remained at a very modest level up to the 1930s, with imports from Indochina being the only sizeable trade. The earliest French traders recorded in Hong Kong by name in the files of France's consulate in Hong Kong were J. Ullmann and Auguste Raphael Marty, with their warehouses in Queen's Road, which were almost destroyed by the great fire of Christmas Day 1879. The Marty brothers, Auguste Raphael and Pierre Augustin, with their firm A. R. Marty, continued to be mentioned occasionally in consular correspondence from the late 1880s, often in conjunction with their shipping business. With French consuls' growing concern about their country's weak performance in the Hong Kong and China markets, reports about French businesses became more frequent. In April 1884, Consul Dejardin sent a list of Frenchmen representing certain branches of French trade to the foreign minister, adding

[83]Meuleau (1990, 153–155), Bonin (2020, 89–99, the quotes: 92 and 99) and Diplomatic and Consular Reports (1906, 10).

that the "small French community of Hong Kong is industrious and prosperous; its commercial value is relatively important, and the professional education of each of its members is above average".[84]

Although the aforementioned list of French firms is not preserved in the records of the foreign ministry in Paris, another register is found there. In December 1886, Consul J. Rigoreau provided extra information about an unnamed French firm in Hong Kong dealing in "jewellery, watchmaking, toys, spectacle trade, fantasy articles, etc. – retail selling" and was "furthermore, selling liquids". However, he added that this company's business operations of this company "were not very extended and their credit was limited". The brief list includes three French firms — H. Fournier & Company, Guieu Frères, and A. R. Marty — and the British firm Lane, Crawford & Company, the oldest department store in Hong Kong, founded by T. A. Lane and Ninian Crawford in 1850, which was selling French products. About three years later, Acting Consul Vinarona believed it "very necessary to have a company in Hong Kong specialised in selling French goods: our country sells very little directly to Hong Kong; with the exception of wines, cans and some foods, French articles reaching this place are usually sent from England". He reported that French manufacturers were prepared only to pay commission to an agent established in France, while British and German producers found this extra intermediary costly and unnecessary, and therefore had lower costs. Vinarona considered that an "error", deriving from "a lacking spirit of initiative" and suggesting instead another way of doing business: "Commission paid to agents from both sellers and purchasers in different forms, would be sufficient to assure the foreign purchaser of a normal profit on imported French goods". For such transactions, he proposed the same four firms as Consul Rigoreau had done in 1886, recommending that French producers establish direct business transactions with them and praising their "good reputation for honourability and solvency".[85]

[84]Bonin (2020, 107–108). MAE, CCC, 137-3 Hong Kong: Consul Joseph Plichon (Hong Kong) to Foreign Minister Waddington (Paris), 4 January 1879; Consul Dejardin (Hong Kong) to Foreign Minister Ferry (Paris), 23 April 1884.

[85]MAE, CCC, 137-3 Hong Kong: Consulate chancellor J. Rigoreau (Hong Kong) to Foreign Minister Flourens (Paris), 30 December 1886. MAE, CCC, 137-4 Hong Kong: Acting Consul Vinarona (Hong Kong) to Foreign Minister Spuller (Paris), 1 February 1890. On Lane, Crawford & Co., see Wright and Cartwright (1908, 214).

In August 1890, referring to the register of French firms in Hong Kong, published on 3 April by the *Moniteur Officiel du Commerce*, Acting Consul Georges Gueyraud announced major changes in "our small French community". The firm of H. Fournier, which sold mainly French wines, liqueurs and different cans and foods, and which was enjoying prosperity, had been liquidated after its sole owner passed away. Guieu Frères (Guieu Brothers) had relinquished their stocks of wines, cans, cheeses and delicatessens to G. Gérault, an employee of their Shanghai branch. A new French-Swiss firm, named Rosselet & Company, had recently been created with the intention of combining its watchmaking trade, established by Rosselet some years earlier, with selling good brands of wine, liqueur and canned foods, in the same way Fournier had specialised in French brands. The consul also pointed to the French company Ullmann which dealt in clocks, toys, perfumeries and Paris articles [fashion and jewellery] "which would be induced to represent other branches of our industry". Finally, he praised A. R. Marty and Lane Crawford & Co. as "always justifying their excellent reputation".[86]

In the following years, several French industrialists approached the consulate in the British colony, seeking commercial information. Whether this resulted in any business transactions was not recorded in consular correspondence from Hong Kong kept in France's foreign ministry archival files preserved up to 1901. An important incentive to enhance trade with China was the trading mission of twelve delegates from six major French cities (Bordeaux, Lille, Lyon, Marseille, Roubaix and Roanne) initiated by the Lyon Chamber of Commerce and supported by the governor-general of Indochina. Since May 1896, the delegates A. Vial from Lille and Louis-M. Rabaud from Bordeaux had inspected several port cities along the Chinese coast. Rabaud, an expert in colonial trade, was assigned to to draft a detailed report on Hong Kong which was later included in the mission's comprehensive documentation. He devoted around ten pages to shipping and twenty to trade but remained largely silent about French commerce, except for mentioning French woollen fabrics imported to Hong Kong and exports of Chinese human hair to France. He concluded as follows: "Except silks, not many goods are sent

[86]MAE, CCC, 137-4 Hong Kong: Acting Consul Gueyraud (Hong Kong) to Foreign Minister Ribot (Paris), 5 and 13 August 1890.

to France; they are rather sent to England where the markets for the products of the Far East are located. Our industry is forced to go there to get their supplies".[87]

This observation was confirmed by the French consulate's commercial report for 1895, which pointed to the fact that "a large proportion of French products destined for the Far East pass through London" because this voyage was "more economical than that from Marseille". The weak presence of French industrial products in Hong Kong's large trading market place was attributed to the poor performance of France's mercantile marine. The report hinted at "the scant importance of our flag vis-à-vis those of other nations" and "our marked inferiority as transporters" to explain the low volume of French trade with China.[88] "Currently, no effort is made in Hong Kong to start selling our national products, given that no one has a direct interest occupying himself with that", Léon Leroux stated bluntly in the summer of 1897. Hinting at the commercial agent of the British consulate in Shanghai who was successful in having sample collections from Britain sent to compare them with similar Chinese products, the consul suggested doing likewise with French goods. He was convinced that an "active Frenchman, with a good mind and acquainted with business in the Far East" would have "a serious chance of success, and certainly be of great service to our national production". However, Leroux had little optimism about such possibilities when considering the highly valuable financial transactions in Hong Kong of major British, German and other enterprises. He wrote: "Under these conditions, it is only the companies with large capital that are able to work safely. The Germans well understood this situation and they organised themselves to deal with it. Helped considerably by the low freight rates of their shipping companies, they rapidly increase the openings to all forms of German manufacturing goods."[89]

[87] MAE, CCC, 137-4 Hong Kong: Acting Consul Gueyraud (Hong Kong) to Foreign Minister Ribot (Paris), 20 February, 6 and 18 March, 28 April 1891. Martonne (1897, 273-276) and Rabaud (1898, 177, the quote: 182, 184). In the whole of China, the Lyon delegation counted 363 British firms, 99 German and 29 French ones. Poidevin (1998, 157).

[88] MAE, CCC, 137-5 Hong Kong: Report on Commercial Situation of Hong Kong, 31 December 1895.

[89] MAE, CCC, 137-6 Hong Kong: Consul Leroux (Hong Kong) to Foreign Minister Hanotaux (Paris) [undated: late July 1897], with Report on Commercial and Shipping Movements in Hong Kong in 1896.

An active French businessman of the kind the consul hoped for was Louis Sculfort, a banker and general trader from Lyon, France's second-largest city. Sculfort was one of the delegates of the trading mission from the Lyon Chamber of Commerce visiting various parts of China and Hong Kong in 1895-1896. In the mission's very detailed report, Sculfort contributed the section dealing with monetary circulation in China and the consequences for China of the decreasing silver standard. Furthermore, he provided extra notes on the operations of Chinese banks in Chóngqìng (Chungking), a municipality at the confluence of the Yangzi (Yangtze) and Jialing rivers in the south-western province of Sichuan (or Szechwan). His good knowledge of China's economy may have prompted Sculfort's decision to establish, in September 1898, an import and export firm in Hong Kong under the name of L. Sculfort & Company. This was obviously a bold attempt to rectify the lack of a French business presence in East Asia, which had been identified in the report as one of the major reasons for France's commercial shortcomings in the region.[90]

In 1898–1899, France's seizure of Guangzhouwan, located in China's Guangdong Province, captured Sculfort's attention. Approaching Chinese merchants in and around the leased French territory, he succeeded in getting twelve of them to invest in the French-Chinese Syndicate, a joint-stock company registered in Hong Kong, which primarily aimed to develop French shipping and trade in southern China. This company, established by Sculfort and two other French traders in Hong Kong, Paul Lemaire and M. Leborgne, assigned one quarter of its shares to Chinese merchants. After founding his own trading firm under the name of P. Lemaire & Co. in Paris, Lemaire took over the Syndicate in July 1900, as well as the shipping service between Hong Kong and Guangzhouwan. When Louis Sculfort left Hong Kong permanently in April 1904 for unknown reasons, Paul Lemaire also became the owner of L. Sculfort & Co.[91]

In 1899, Sculfort and the French engineer Francis Laur founded the journal *La Chine Nouvelle: Revue Illustrée d'Extrême Orient*, with monthly or bimonthly editions published in Hong Kong. Sculfort was

[90] Sculfort (1898, 399–423) and Raquez (1900, 66).

[91] ANOM, INDO-GGI-5087: Note of Louis Sculfort (Naozhou, Guangzhouwan), 19 February 1900, Louis Sculfort (Hong Kong) to Governor-General Doumer, 25 February 1900. *La Chine Nouvelle: Revue Illustrée d'Extrême Orient* (1900, no. 9: August–September).

made director in the British colony and Laur served as editor based in Paris, writing articles about French politics in China and related issues while Sculfort contributed information on China's politics, economy and society, as well as reports about Chinese regions and cities, and on trade between Indochina and China. The special issue of 15 April 1900, to which Sculfort contributed two essays, paid significant attention to the economic development of Guangzhouwan, the French leased territory in Guangdong Province. About China's future, Sculfort optimistically predicted in June 1900 that through the Chinese merchant class "China will be transformed and experience real and definitive contact with the civilised world".[92]

In 1902, when Japan achieved a share of 16.5 per cent, and Germany of 16.2 per cent in China's foreign shipping, and with these flags also strongly present in the port of Hong Kong, French consuls became more and more alarmed. In October 1901, Consul Gaston-Ernest Liébert informed Paris about the results of the latest census, which included the inhabitants of Hong Kong Island and Kowloon (but not of the New Territories, acquired in 1898). Among the Europeans and Americans, consisting of a total of 5,808 residents, the French had a share of 103 persons (against 89 in 1897) and the Germans of 337 (against 208 in 1897). Even more impressive was the sharply increasing number of Japanese residents, counting 218 persons (against 63 in 1897). For the consul, the growing presence of Germans and Japanese was clear proof of "the vivid development of commercial transactions of Germany and Japan in the China Seas during the last years for which Hong Kong became the great entrepot". Similar concerns were common among French consuls worldwide, affecting the French press and public opinion. Several reports blamed Germany's strong commercial competition in global markets for France's declining trade. Initiatives taken by French ministries and chambers of commerce to improve the situation often failed to produce results. As Hubert Bonin explains, except for cars and weapons, French industry maintained its tradition of producing luxury goods, resulting in the country falling behind its global competitors. With an insufficient mercantile marine and an incomplete maritime network,

[92] *La Chine Nouvelle: Revue Illustrée d'Extrême Orient* (1900), no. 5 (special issue); (1900, no. 7, the quote: 83). This journal seems to have ceased publication after about one year, with the final number 9 published in August–September 1900.

France "seemed to lack dynamism, trying to take refuge behind hard protectionism".[93]

Except for occasional advertisements for shops run by French owners published in the English-language press in Hong Kong, little additional information can be found about the French business community in any official documents or other publications. Consular files from Hong Kong, limited to the period from 1858 to 1901 and kept in the archives of the French foreign ministry, contain only one item of correspondence about social activities, namely celebrations on the occasion of the French National Holiday on 14 July 1892. The smallness of the French community (89 members in 1897 and 103 in 1901, about one-third of the size of the German community) gave the celebration the character of "a real family party" which was the case "this year as in the preceding ones", Consul Gueyraud reported. However, by publicly inviting all local French residents, and also French travellers, to the reception in the consulate the day before, Gueyraud was certainly well aware of the consequences. Not only French residents but most of his colleagues from the consular corps and a number of British civil servants and foreign residents turned up at his house to convey their wishes for the prosperity of France. In the port of Hong Kong, the French mail steamers *Salazie* and *Haiphong* dressed ship in honour of the occasion, *The Hong Kong Daily Press* reported. The first one was "gay with bunting as she steamed out of the harbour for Shanghai in the morning". Gueyraud enclosed the article in his report for Foreign Minister Alexandre Ribot and did not forget to ask to have sent on the good wishes of his guests "to the President of the Republic with the expression of our profound respect". Since the one-hundred-and-third anniversary of the destruction of the Bastille, as the unrounded number suggests, hardly justified such public celebrations that year, the reason for initiating the event was to be found elsewhere. It probably had to do with Gueyraud's request to the foreign ministry concerning his rather modest earnings as a second-class consul which were in stark contrast to the high living expenses and additional costs for official representations he had to meet in the British colony. On 26 June 1891, Gueyraud had alerted the ministry that the city was "the most expensive one in the Far East", pointing to his obligation "to continuously

[93] Ratenhof (1987, 567, table 5). MAE, CCC, 137-6 Hong Kong: Consul Liébert (Hong Kong) to Foreign Minister Delcassé (Paris), 5 October 1901. Bonin (1988, 42–43, the quote: 42).

receive French officers and travellers of distinction, not to speak of foreign consuls and all the important personalities of the British colony". To publicly celebrate the French National Day in the following year, and to keep Paris informed of the well-received event, was certainly helpful to his request. Six weeks later, Gueyraud was promoted to first-class consul and received an allowance of 5,000 francs to cover his large expenses in Hong Kong.[94]

According to information provided by Consul Gueyraud in 1892, the French community in Hong Kong consisted of seafarers (in French: marins), missionaries and traders. These three very distinct groups constituted the main pillars of the French presence in Hong Kong before the First World War, and even later. The seafarers were mostly officers and crews of French merchant ships and men-of-war in France's East Asian naval squadron that frequently called at the British colony for repairs or provisions. With respect to trading, the earlier focus on importing French luxury goods had prevailed. In 1912, the company Louis Rondon, which the Bank of Indochina had earlier assisted in its exports to Hong Kong, opened a warehouse in the colony to stock foodstuffs and spirits (among them two hundred bottles of Hennessy cognac) after the firm was made the agent of Hennessy for China. The First World War severely interrupted global trade relations, affecting France. In 1919, the French community in Hong Kong had seventy members engaged in about fifteen import and export firms, as well as other organisations. This number indicated that the French community had more than doubled since 1914, with six new firms being established. In 1923, the French trading house Optorg, which had done business in Russia, established branches in Hong Kong and Shanghai to import wool cloth, spirits and champagne and pharmaceutics. The colony continued to serve as a base for French traders to serve the local needs of Hong Kong's wealthier population, provide a kind of platform to distribute French products in markets in China and other locations in East Asia, and to transfer East Asian commodities from Hong Kong to France.[95]

[94] Bensacq-Tixier (2003, 278–279, the quoted letter of 26 June 1891: 279).

[95] *Hong Kong Daily Press*, 13 and 15 July 1892. MAE, CCC, 137-4 Hong Kong: Consul Gueyraud (Hong Kong) to Foreign Minister Ribot (Paris), 16 July 1892. Castel (1957, 289), Dremeaux (2014, 12–13) and Bonin (2020, 90 and 115).

Auguste Raphael Marty (1841–1914)

On 17 August 1841, Raphael Augustin Marty (later called Auguste Raphael Marty) was born in Porta, a mountain village of 939 inhabitants located in the French eastern Pyrenees. The family name Marty, often deriving from the first name Martin, originated mainly from the southern Pyrenees and is still common nowadays in France, with over 31,000 bearers of the name. His father was a 32-year-old farmer, Joseph Marty, and his mother was a 28-year-old knitter, Marguerite Garréta. More than eleven years later, his brother, Pierre Augustin Marty, (later called A. Pierre Marty or Pierre Marty) was born in Porta on 10 November 1852.[96]

Auguste Raphael Marty had a difficult youth. From 1845 to about 1855, his home region, which was heavily agricultural, went through a series of economic and food crises caused by the potato blight spreading from Ireland. The European potato failure, and the subsequent grain crisis, harshly affected harvests in the Pyrenees, leading to a sharp decrease food supplies and rising prices, finally forced the French government to import potatoes from far-away regions such as southern Russia and the Americas. The next crisis struck when cholera spread in the Pyrenees between 1854 and 1857, causing increasing mortality among the population due to low hygiene standards and insufficient medical care.[97] The ongoing economic crises of those years undoubtedly impacted the livelihood of the Marty family. In a longer obituary of Auguste Raphael Marty published twenty-five years after his death, the anonymous author, obviously a former acquaintance in Haiphong, explained that Marty lacked "evidently a general schooling for which a probably difficult youth had not left him the time; in this way, despite an excellent memory, his knowledge was fragmentary, dispersed and not interconnected. However, he did not cease increasing it to his best. I saw him hastily taking improvised notes, with a pencil on his white cuffs; and everything interested him, he did not stop asking questions to people capable of answering him". The

[96] APO: Registre d'état civil de la commune de Porta: Raphaël Augustin Marty (9NUM2E2888), Pierre Augustin Marty (9NUM2E2889). Pelissier (1986, 260) and Mergnac (1999, 215).

[97] Soulet (2004, 328–384).

writer also noted that Marty resided in Bordeaux in 1861, doing "the most modest trades".[98]

Both the food and health crises were powerful factors in the mass emigration from the Pyrenees reaching its climax between 1846 and 1855, with 1,614 people a year on average leaving the region. Bordeaux was the place for migrants to leave for Spain and Algeria, and more distant destinations such as North and South America or East Asia. The south-western French port city on the Garonne River, close to the Atlantic coast, traditionally a major trading hub for wine exports and for sugar and slaves from the West Indies, had at an early stage established commercial connections with Portuguese and Spanish business networks operating in the Indian Ocean, in Macao and in the Philippines. In 1854, one of the major wholesale companies of Bordeaux, A. Eymond & Delphin Henry, was the first to launch a shipping line to Hong Kong and Shanghai, operating several owned or chartered vessels. The firm, which operated a branch in Bangkok, took the next step in October 1859 when announcing the new "Ligne de Chine" (China Line), with Singapore, Manila, Hong Kong, Macao and Shanghai as ports of call. The shipping line made direct migration to East Asia departing from Bordeaux much more convenient than in earlier times.[99]

Among the early French migrants to East Asia was Étienne (or Estevan) Garréta (or Garreta), uncle of Auguste Raphael Marty. From 1859 to 1864, he was listed as a resident of Macao, and thereafter he was registered in Hong Kong as a merchant residing in Hollywood Road.[100] On 19 October 1866, the retailer passed away in the British colony, leaving behind effects worth over 43,000 dollars which were put by the Probate Court under the administration of Albert Emile Vaucher, a Swiss merchant and commission agent, at the time associated with George Blakeway under the firm of Vaucher & Company. Less than a year later, on 23 September 1867, the Hong Kong Supreme Court declared the company bankrupt. This information was probably the decisive trigger

[98] *Bulletin Trimestriel de la Société Amicale des Anciens Tonkinois* (1940, 11).

[99] Denis (1965, 77). On French migration to East Asia and French Indochina, see Gantès (2002, 15–28).

[100] *The Hong Kong Directory* (1859, 17), *The China Directory for 1861* (1861, 49), *The China Directory for 1862* (1862, 65), *The Chronicle and Directory for China, Japan and the Philippines for 1864* (1864, 155) and *The Hong Kong Government Gazette* (1865, Jury list: 75).

for Garréta's nephew, Auguste Raphael Marty, residing in Bordeaux at the time, to leave for Hong Kong. In December 1867, Marty arrived in the British colony, and in the following month, Vaucher was deprived of the administration of the belongings of the late Garréta. On 11 May 1868, the 26-year-old Marty was formally granted letters of administration of his uncle's estate, and thereby inherited sufficient capital to start up his own business.[101]

In Hong Kong, Marty initially joined a partnership with the watchmaker James Henri Barrelet to establish the clothes shop Barrelet & Marty. When the company was dissolved on 1 January 1871, Marty remained responsible only for debts contracted in Hong Kong. The following month, he was listed as a commission agent in Queen's Road, Central district. When his brother, Pierre Augustin Marty, arrived in Hong Kong in August 1871, he immediately started business with him, resuming the small shop of Matilda Vise specialised in selling Japanese wares and French boots and shoes. On 7 October 1871, he advertised as follows in a local newspaper: "A. R. Marty, successor of M. Vise & Co., 92, Queen's Road, has received a large assortment of large and small Japanese Tea Sets, Toilette and Dinner SETS, Porcelain and Lacquered Vases, of every size. A very fine choice of Japanese IVORY and BRONZE inlaid. European GOODS".[102]

In the following years, Pierre Augustin Marty was frequently listed as an assistant at his brother's firm. The Marty brothers seemed to have co-operated very well in running a growing business and extending their commercial connections to China, the Philippines and northern Vietnam. The obituary of Auguste Raphael Marty says he "went to offer his merchandises to Chinese shopkeepers, took the launch to Macao, to Guangzhou, and went around – not without risk sometimes – the narrow little streets of the capital of the South [Guangzhou], with bundles of fabrics, of ribbons, of threads and of haberdashery". In 1873, Pierre Augustin Marty was registered additionally as a storekeeper in

[101] *The Hong Kong Government Gazette*, 2 February 1867 and 28 September 1867, 351. CADN, I 3 B: Consul Léon Leroux (Hong Kong) to Foreign Minister Delcassé (Paris), 3 August 1898.

[102] *Bulletin Trimestriel de la Société Amicale des Anciens Tonkinois* (1940, 8). *Hong Kong Daily Press*, 9 January 1871 and 7 October 1871. *Hong Kong Government Gazette*, 26 February 1870: Jury List, 79 and 1 March 1873: Jury List, 87. *Hong Kong Weekly Press*, 1 February 1909.

Manila associated with Auguste Raphael Marty. When the northern Vietnamese port city of Haiphong was declared a French concession (1875), the Marty brothers opened a branch in the port city, frequently shipping all kinds of industrial goods from Hong Kong to local French and Chinese merchants and transporting rice and other natural products to the British colony. The firm A. R. Marty specialised in importing Japanese and Chinese wares and curios, selling them in their shops located at 92, 24 and 44, Queen's Road.[103]

Like the warehouses of several other French merchants, Marty's stocks were under severe threat when a great fire broke out on Christmas Day 1878. Thanks to the active support of five French shipmasters and their crews, among them Captain Pasqualini, commander of the Messageries Maritimes liner *Peiho*, and forty-five men of his crew, the flames were extinguished and the warehouses saved. According to French consul Joseph Plichon who co-ordinated the rescue operation, the fire destroyed almost four hundred houses and caused immense material losses and was "the most terrible incident here since the founding of the colony".[104]

In August 1884, Auguste Raphael Marty, in his capacity as commission agent, submitted to Consul Léon Dejardin a collection of samples of principal articles imported from Europe to Hong Kong such as cotton fabrics and threads of cotton, and woollen fabrics from British and German manufacturers. He informed the French consul that most cotton fabrics came from Manchester, the threads from Manchester and Bombay, British India, and the woollen fabrics from England and Germany. Some rare pieces of French origin were imported together with the British articles for consumption by Europeans, "being both limited in number and very attentive for the collection". Furthermore, Marty made Dejardin aware of the fact that the other articles being specially prepared for the Chinese market had to conform to customs and traditions regarding the length and width of pieces and so forth. He said that both observing Chinese rituals and offering low prices were "indispensable conditions". Furthermore, he presented some Chinese

[103] *The Chronicle and Directory for China, Japan and the Philippines* (1875, 211; 1876, 212; 1877, 217; 1879, 215; 1882, 244). *Bulletin Trimestriel de la Société Amicale des Anciens Tonkinois* (1940, 8).

[104] *Hong Kong Daily Press*, 27 December 1878. MAE, CCC, 137-3 Hong Kong: Consul Plichon (Hong Kong) to Foreign Minister Duc Decazes (Paris), 4 January 1879.

industry products — opium lamps, toiletries, combs, papers and buttons — which European industry could possibly try to imitate. In his letter to the French foreign minister, Dejardin was only cautiously optimistic about the chances of French producers in competing against their British and German counterparts, pointing to the two countries' long-established business relations with China. However, he suggested making the Chinese products available to French manufacturers and merchants who should "judge whether French competition is possible, and whether French imports would have chances of success".[105]

In spring 1882, France had launched military action in Tonkin, resulting in armed conflict with Vietnamese and Chinese troops. The Marty brothers were obviously on the alert about trading opportunities which the French occupation of the region would offer their business. Consul Dejardin, who was in close contact with French naval forces operating in the South China Sea, noted several voyages of Auguste Raphael Marty to China and Tonkin. In early 1883, when the British colony was the major supply centre for the French expeditionary troops engaged in the Tonkin campaign, the consul hired Pierre Augustin Marty as substitute chancellor. He praised his "local experience and diligence" as being "of great help for me" but was concerned about the fact that his new staff was "all the time absorbed, as myself, by the expedition of urgent matters which keep coming since some months". The main supplier for the French forces was the Saigon firm Roque Frères (Roque Brothers), represented in Haiphong and in Hong Kong by the company A. R. Marty. Dejardin remained silent about his chancellor's close links with the latter firm when informing the foreign minister that "important deals for the provisions of the expeditionary corps in foods and equipment" included "a lot of purchases in Hong Kong (steam launches, supplies), and in Shanghai (horses and horse tacks)". Other French companies in Saigon were almost excluded from this business, the consul said, "because the purchaser of the transactions of the expeditionary corps operates a steamship line to Hong Kong where preferably supplies are acquired".[106]

[105] MAE, CCC, 137-3 Hong Kong: Consul Dejardin (Hong Kong) to Foreign Ministry (Paris), 16 August 1884.

[106] Brocheux and Hémery (2009, 42–44). MAE, CCC, 137-3 Hong Kong: Consul Sienkiewicz (Hong Kong) to Foreign Ministry (Paris), 22 January 1883, Consul Dejardin (Hong Kong) to Foreign Ministry (Paris), 13 June 1883 and 16 July 1883.

During the subsequent Tonkin and Keelung campaigns (1884–1885), French troops were predominantly supplied by the firm A. R. Marty in Hong Kong and Haiphong. Initial contacts between the firm and the general staff of Admiral Amédée Courbet had been established by Marty's accountant, previously a long-serving shipbroker's clerk of Nantes and well acquainted with chartering ships and supplying the French navy. Courbet made it clear that the French naval squadron, for reasons of confidentiality, wished to purchase its provisions from a Frenchman based in Hong Kong, but not from a British firm. Although Marty initially hesitated to accept such a voluminous commission, he finally agreed to supply the naval squadron with coal, food and other provisions. In March 1885, Consul Dejardin called Marty the "official supplier of the French vessels" when informing Hong Kong's Colonial Secretary Sir William Henry Marsh, about Chinese "coolies" loading a French man-of-war in the port which was supervised by Marty's clerk Heinrich Zimmermann. Marty's involvement in France's war with Vietnam and China was also well known, as the 1884 trade report prepared by German consul Karl Theodor Speidel in Saigon made evident. During the Keelung campaign in the spring of 1885, A. R. Marty chartered the German steamer *Ingraban*, of the J. P. Massmann Shipping Company from Heiligenhafen, Schleswig-Holstein, to frequently ship provisions including coal to Formosa where Pierre Augustin Marty managed a branch of the company. In June 1885, after French naval forces had captured the Pescadores Islands in the Taiwan Strait and established a small garrison, Auguste Raphael Marty dispatched his Hong Kong accountant to serve as agent for Admiral Sébastian Lespès, the successor of Courbet (who had died of cholera). Yet, with some irregularities in the accounts being detected, the squadron decided to cease collaborating with Marty. Probably a more compelling reason for terminating the connection with A. R. Marty was the actual end of the Sino-French War after the Treaty of Hue (or Patenôtre Treaty) which came into effect in June 1885, allowing the French to take over the whole of Vietnam. For the Marty brothers, the Sino-French War ended up having provided them with enormous profits for their company.[107]

[107] Brocheux and Hémery (2009, 45), Goscha (2017, 66) and *Bulletin Trimestriel de la Société Amicale des Anciens Tonkinois* (1940, 9). PAAA, R 251851: Trade Report for 1884 of Consul Karl Theodor Speidel (Saigon), undated. *Hong Weekly Press*, 1 February 1909.

The company A. R. Marty in Hong Kong became main agent of Marty et d'Abbadie when the joint firm was established in Haiphong in 1886. The first paddle steamers of the Service Subventionné des Correspondances Fluviales du Tonkin (Subsidised River Shipping Service of Tonkin), the major affiliate of Marty et d'Abbadie, were purchased at British wharfs in Hong Kong. In 1888, A. R. Marty was registered as a shipping agent of "Hong Kong and Tonkin steamers", which gave the firm's staff practical experience with the profitable chartering business.[108] His customers were mainly Chinese merchants employing foreign steam coasters to transport all kinds of cargoes around the region. Since 1884, Marty had regularly chartered small- and medium-sized steamships from German and Danish shipping companies, among them steam tramps of the M. Jebsen Shipping Company and Danish shipping companies based in Randers, Jutland. After the acquisition of two British-built merchant steamers in 1893, Marty was able to establish the Compagnie de Navigation Tonkinoise (Tonkin Shipping Company) in Haiphong, another affiliate of Marty et d'Abbadie, of which the firm A. R. Marty was the sole agent in Haiphong and Hong Kong. For more than twenty years, this shipping company operated a small fleet of steam coasters on the run between Haiphong and Hong Kong. The service, operated under the French flag, was the only one of its kind in the South China Sea at the time. From 1900, it also operated the subsidised postal steamer service linking Haiphong with Guangzhouwan, the French leased territory in China's Guangdong Province.[109]

A. R. Marty in Hong Kong had several Chinese staff supervised by the Chinese comprador[110], and also European staff.[111] Since 1914, the firm

[108] *The Chronicle and Directory for China*, etc. (1888, 316).

[109] Becker (2019, 199).

[110] The Comprador department of the company A. R. Marty consisted among others of the following Chinese staff members: Lam Chau Chuen, 1905 member of the comprador department (according to HKPRO-CSI): CS/I003/00021715.GIF); Che Mau Hing (1915 as comprador (CS/I001/00006259.GIF and CS/I001/00006253.GIF and CS/I001/00003991.GIF); Leung Kin Hau, 1915 as assistant comprador (CS/I003/00025723.GIF); Lo Kung Tao, 1915 as accountant (CS/I004/00031911.GIF); Wong Kan Yan (1915 as shroff (CS/I005/00048201.GIF); Pang Ching San (1915 as shipping shroff (CS/I004/00,037625.GIF).

[111] The following Europeans worked for A. R. Marty (according to HKPRO-CSI): Thomas Manuel, 1875 as assistant (CS/I013/00123977.GIF); Antonio Marcal Carneiro, 1882–1883 as assistant (CS/I021/00203111.GIF); Alphonse Jules Levesque,

had established branches in Haiphong,[112] Haikou (Hoihow) on Hainan Island,[113] Beihai (Pakhoi) and Guangzhouwan. In the obituary for Marty published in 1940, the anonymous writer was rather critical about Marty's personnel, stating that he "retained of his beginnings in the small businesses the habit of only wanting third-rate staff: he never knew how to surround himself with people of real value who would have had to be paid a bit more, or at least did not keep them; in this way he never had a real management, as businesses of such importance would have needed but which perpetual replacements and certain deficiencies harmed".[114]

Due to the lack of a personal archive of Marty, his private life remains somewhat obscure, with only a few facts known. Auguste Raphael Marty was unmarried and had an illegitimate child with Eugenia Felicia Portier. On 19 June 1870, their daughter was born in Hong Kong and baptised as Clotilde Emmanuelle Marty at the Roman Catholic Cathedral of the Immaculate Conception (located from 1843 to 1886 in Wellington

1883–1884 as assistant (CS/I012/00119135.GIF); Heinrich Zimmermann, 1885–1886 as assistant (CS/I016/00154625.GIF); Gumelsindo Jesus Sequeira, 1886-c. 1919 as assistant, later as manager (*Hong Kong Government Gazette (HKGG)*, Supplement, 28 February 1919: Jurors List of 1919, 92); Lara Banguin Sequeira, 1887–1890 and 1897–1899 as assistant (CS/I027/00260685.GIF); José Maria Passos, 1887 as assistant (CS/I024/00239547.GIF); Auguste Trante, 1892–1895 as assistant (CS/I015/00148049.GIF); José Gonsalves dos Remedios, 1892–1896 as assistant (*HKGG*, 27 February 1892: Jury List for 1892, 195; *HKGG*, 25 February 1893: Jury List for 1893, 132; *HKGG*, 24 February 1894: Jury List for 1894, 96; *HKGG*, 2 March 1895: Jurors List for 1895, 136; *HKGG*, 15 February 1896: Jurors List for 1896, 160); Pedro Nolasco Sequeira, 1895–1898 as assistant (CS/I027/00260777.GIF); Francisco Quintino Ronaldo Xavier, 1897–1902 as clerk (CS/I028/00273801.GIF); José Maria da Silva Rozario, 1898–1901 as clerk (CS/I026/00256237.GIF); Louis Jules Martel, 1899–1900 as clerk (CS/I013/00124467.GIF); Nicolau Gabriel Marques, 1901–1902 as clerk (CS/I024/00231574.GIF); José Daniel Pompilio de Souza, 1902 as clerk (*HKGG*, 1 March 1902: List of Jurors for 1902, 222); Henri Barbey, 1908–1913 as clerk (*Hong Kong Telegraph*, 13 September 1911).

[112] The Haiphong branch of the company A. R. Marty was managed by Etienne Rousé, the first husband of Marty's only daughter. French Vice-Consul Hauchecorne called Rousé "a good colleague" of Marty, stating that "some claimed he could become one day his successor; however, the loss of Rousé "was difficult for him [and] diminished somewhat the enthusiasm of the old shipowner." On 16 June 1907, Rousé passed away in Haiphong. *South China Morning Post*, 19 June 1907. MAE, CPC-552: Vice-Consul Hauchecorne (Hoihow) to Foreign Minister Delcassé (Paris), 31 December 1914.

[113] The Hoihow branch was managed by F. C. Binder who passed away in Hoihow on 1 November 1905. *South China Morning Post*, 4 November 1905.

[114] *Bulletin Trimestriel de la Société Amicale des Anciens Tonkinois* (1940, 11).

Street). She married twice; her first husband was Etienne Rousé (who passed away in 1907), the Haiphong manager of the company A. R. Marty. Her second husband was Raymond René Sallé, prosecutor-general of French Indochina in Saigon, who had an adopted child called Régina. On 6 February 1909, the wedding contract was registered by a notary in Paris. In 1922, the family left Indochina to reside in France. On 25 May 1930, Clotilde Emmanuelle Marty passed away in Seysses, a commune near Toulouse in the Haute-Garonne department in south-western France.[115]

After establishing his private residence at Haiphong, Auguste Raphael Marty resided most of his life in the French colonial port city, paying regular visits to Hong Kong. On 15 December 1914, Marty died in Haiphong at the age of seventy-three after catching a severe cold during a trip to Do Son, a popular resort, about twenty kilometres from Haiphong. "Bronchial trouble developed and pneumonia set in, but the symptoms were not considered serious until Sunday, when the illness became acute", reported the *South China Morning Post* in Hong Kong. On 17 December 1914, Marty was buried in Haiphong.[116] At Marty's death, the *North China Herald* called the company "one of the best-known French firms in the Far East", adding that Marty was "highly esteemed by all who knew him, and his death is regretted by a wide circle of friends".[117] The company A. R. Marty was continued by Raymond René Sallé, Marty's son-in-law.[118]

In 1940, the aforementioned obituary of Auguste Raphael Marty was published in the newsletter of the Haiphong-based association of Old Tonkinese (of which Marty had been a member). The late French merchant and shipowner was characterised as follows:

[115] HKPRO-CSI: CS/I013/00124670.GIF. MAE, CPC-552: Vice-Consul Hauchecorne (Hoihow) to Foreign Minister Delcassé (Paris), 31 December 1914 and 27 July 1915. VNA1, SEDT-2885: Succession of Clotilde Emmanuelle Marty, 24 November 1930.

[116] *South China Morning Post*, 17 December 1914. The 1914 editions of *Le Courrier d'Haiphong* and *L'Avenir du Tonkin* are neither available in ANOM (Aix-en-Provence) nor in the National Library of Vietnam (Hanoi); the only useable obituary on Marty was published in 1940. The European cemetery of Haiphong does not exist any longer.

[117] *North China Herald and Supreme Court & Consular Service*, 26 December 1914.

[118] *South China Morning Post*, *Hong Kong Daily Press*, *China Mail*, all dated 17 December 1914.

> He was a great worker, of fair spirit, clear-sighted, energetic, [and] bold. He was also of a remarkable composure and personal courage. (…) He had also a good heart. Not that he was tritely kind and lenient for small services, because alone for carrying out many things he was passably bad-tempered; but he knew how to discern the efforts to make, the people who deserved it, and the real misfortunes to relieve, and did often more than one expected of him from his abrupt appearances. In short, he was made for a new world, a country in creation, rather than for an already organised and ranked society; also, he succeeded even better in Tonkin than in Hong Kong where he had issue to comply himself to the quasi obligatory ways of English businesspeople, to their prejudices and to their sort of life. He was a great independent as well as a bold one and a relentless one. Without having perhaps, the sympathies of everyone, he had at least their esteem, and after a long life of constant work, his death seemed, 25 years ago, like a loss for a country to which he had provided enormous services by bringing to it all his work and all his resources.[119] (Fig. 3.2)

Marty's younger brother, Pierre Augustin Marty, had stayed in Hong Kong after the end of the Sino-French War (1885), working in his brother's company. He was married to Maria Martha Joanne Yvonne Marty, born Barbier; the couple had four daughters.[120] Michelle Marty, the first daughter, was thirty-three when she began teaching at Belilios School, a governmental school for girls in Hong Kong opened in 1890, with English as the medium of instruction. She later taught French at St. Stephen's College for Girls, where she became residential warden. In 1939, she was appointed to teach in the Faculty of Arts of the University of Hong Kong (as a part-time lecturer in French) and took over the role of "Advisor to Women Students", expected to advise students who required her assistance, to help in the organisation of social activities,

[119] *Bulletin Trimestriel de la Société Amicale des Anciens Tonkinois* (1940, 11–12). Another, although very brief description of Auguste Raphael Marty was provided by the Frenchman J. Brien visiting Hong Kong in 1901 on his way to Indochina. He called Marty an "honourable French merchant" describing him as follows: "Mr Marty was very clever, very perspicacious, I would gladly say, very wily (…)". Brien (1916, 18–19).

[120] The children of Pierre and Martha Marty were Michaela Petronilla Catharine Marty (called Michelle, born on 23 May 1896 and baptised on 22 October 1896), Margarita Luisa Rosalina Marty (born and baptised on 7 February 1897), Carmen Yvonne Raphaella Marty (born on 4 (?) July 1901), and Farinella Alex Martha Marty (born on 29 July 1903). HKPRO-CSI: CS/1013/00124671.GIF.

Fig. 3.2 Auguste Raphael Marty (1841–1914), c. 1910 (*Bulletin Trimestriel de la Société Amicale des Anciens Tonkinois* 9, 1940)

and to be an intermediary between women students and the University authorities. Staci Ford described Michelle Marty as a person who "understood the importance of creating an intellectual space for women because much of the physical space of the University was still dominated by men". According to Hong Kong historian Peter Cunich, after the seizure of Hong Kong by Japanese forces (December 1941), Michelle Marty "used her French nationality to secure her freedom, although not without a 'tremendous row' with the Japanese official in charge of registering third nationals".[121]

Pierre Augustin Marty was a well-known figure in Hong Kong's European society. One of his oldest friends, whom he came to know in 1885 was Eugenio Zanoni Volpicelli, from 1899 to 1919 the Italian consul, and for some time, Marty served as vice-consul of Italy. From 1901 to 1907, he was also vice-consul of Spain in Hong Kong and Guangzhou. He was friendly with L. Berindoague, from 1896 to 1919 director of the Banque de l'Indochine (Bank of Indochina) in Hong Kong.[122] On 22 January 1909, after a short illness, Marty passed away in Hong Kong at the age of fifty-six. The *Hong Kong Daily Press* called him "one of the best known and esteemed members of the community". The next day, the funeral service in the Roman Catholic Cathedral was well-attended by consuls, French and Spanish residents, Catholic clergy and numerous other residents of Hong Kong. His coffin was wrapped in the Spanish flag. "Beautiful wreaths and floral anchors and crosses" were sent by many others, with Governor Sir Frederick Lugard at the top of the list, as well as British and German firms such as Jebsen & Co. and Wendt & Co., the staff of the Banque de l'Indochine, and also the Chinese staff of the company A. R. Marty. Consul Liébert called Marty a "brave Français" (good Frenchman), expressing his sympathy with the family. On 30 January 1909, the parochial church of Haiphong held a service for his soul's rest.[123] Pierre Augustin Marty was buried in St. Michael's Catholic Cemetery in Happy Valley on Hong Kong Island; his grave was later removed.

The Decline of the French Flag

Since the 1840s, Hong Kong had emerged as the most important port of call for intercontinental and intra-Asian shipping lines, and for all sorts of

[121] Hoe (1991, 215–217, 221), Boxer (2001, 122), Cunich (2012, 351, 360, the quote: 405) and Ford (2002, 130). After 1940, Michelle Marty was the only female member of the Free French Committee in Hong Kong, taking an active part in broadcasting a radio programme to French Indochina. Thanks to François Dremeaux for this information.

[122] *Hong Kong Daily Press*, 25 January 1909. Bonin (2020, 91).

[123] *Hong Kong Daily Press*, 25 January 1909; *The Singapore Free Press and Mercantile Advertiser*, 2 February 1900. *L'Avenir du Tonkin*, 27 January 1909.

vessels employed in coastal shipping in East Asia. This fact was highlighted by Ernest Godeaux, the first French consul appointed to Hong Kong, in April 1863 when setting up a comprehensive report on the British colony for the foreign ministry in Paris. With respect to shipping, he called for an increased presence of French merchant vessels when noting the following:

> In short, these days, thanks to its geographic situation, to its harbour able to admit and to shelter an immense number of ships, to absolute security and liberty from which benefit transactions there, to communications by steamships for which it is the centre, to the healthiness of its climate, thanks to these various advantages which it gathers at the same time, the island of Hong Kong became the site of considerable traffic, the entrepot [warehouse or depot] of southern China, as much for the products from Europe, America and the Indies as for Chinese goods themselves. (…) According to lists of the colonial government that do not contain junks and native lorchas [sailing vessels with a junk rig and batten sails], which numbers, by the way, drop from day to day, it follows that the maritime movement of the port of Victoria [de-facto capital of Hong Kong, present-day Central district] in 1862, when only considering loaded vessels, constituted an amount of 2,080 voyages and 993,000 tonnes, that being 288 voyages and 91,000 tonnes more than in 1861. The links maintained with the coasts of China and Formosa represent more than half of this movement; then follows particularly England with its possessions India and Australia, the United States and Siam. (…) By these numbers we see the considerable development which exchanges with the China coast took in 1862, and perhaps, Your Excellency, you will consider that we would have reason to call the attention of our shipowners to this fact. The Chinese perfectly understand nowadays the advantage that foreign ships have over their junks, as much to security as to speediness of transports, and native shipping tends to disappear more and more before foreign shipping in ports-of-call. Therefore, European flags are destined to reap the benefits of the development of trading relations between these ports, and it would be desirable that our merchant navy has its share in that. The profits made by some ships we have in these seas which are engaged in the said operations, should encourage our shipowners.[124]

[124] MAE, CCC, 137-1, Hong Kong 1858–1869: Consul Ernest Godeaux (Hong Kong) to Foreign Minister Édouard Drouyn de Lhuys (Paris), 17 April 1863. On Godeaux, Ernest-Napoléon-Marie (1833–1906): Bensacq-Tixier (2003, 266–269).

According to the information of the Hong Kong harbour master, most ships calling at the colony in 1862 arrived with cargoes from China and Formosa, India, Singapore, Siam and Britain. The overwhelming majority of them were leaving with freights to the same destinations except for Britain. Such numbers clearly indicated Hong Kong's major position as a shipping hub, with foreign flags having an important share in this traffic. The British flag dominated in Hong Kong, with a rounded share of 46 per cent of ships entered and 45 per cent cleared at the port; other flags had the following rounded proportions: American flag (18 per cent each), various German flags, of which Hamburg had the absolute lion's share (15 per cent each), Siamese flag (6 per cent each), Danish flag (4 per cent each), French and Spanish flags (both 3 per cent each), and Portuguese flag (1 per cent each). Of the French ships (37 in total) calling at Hong Kong in 1862, thirty-two arrived with cargoes and five in ballast, certainly mainly sailing ships operating in intra-Asian trades.[125] Some of them seemed to be engaged in shipping Chinese emigrants ("coolies") to destinations in Southeast Asia such as Singapore or the Dutch East Indies.[126] The French occupation of southern Vietnam in the late 1850s and early 1860s provided France's shipping companies with a permanent base in Southeast Asia, permitting more extended coastal shipping operations. Despite such an advantage, as the statement of Consul Godeaux makes obvious, certain weaknesses in France's merchant fleet made it difficult for French shipowners to fully profit from the new geopolitical situation in the South China Sea. The major exception was the highly subsidised French shipping company Messageries Impériales (later named Messageries Maritimes), calling at Saigon and Hong Kong with passenger and cargo liners since 1862. French merchant shipping in the South China Sea remained more or less in the hands of this major French shipping company or was an ad hoc business of individual French shipowners operating from France.

In 1860, France owned the third-largest mercantile marine in the world, with a share of 7.2 per cent of global tonnage, surpassed only by Britain (35.06 per cent) and the United States (19.2 per cent). Its

[125] MAE, CCC, 137-1, Hong Kong 1858–1869: Robert McMurdo, Acting Harbour Master (Hong Kong), tables no. 1, 2, and 3: Annex to report of Consul Ernest Godeaux (Hong Kong) to Foreign Minister Édouard Drouyn de Lhuys (Paris), 17 April 1863 (the tables do not differentiate between sailing ships and steamers).

[126] *Hong Kong Daily Press*, 19 May 1865.

merchant navy consisted almost entirely of sailing ship tonnage (93.1 per cent), a proportion which decreased in the following four decennia (85.5 per cent in 1870, 43.8 per cent in 1910) but was relatively much larger than the British one (80.4 per cent in 1870, 0.9 per cent in 1910). Finally, 1890 signalled the turning point in the technological transfer from sail to steam, with steamships having a 62.9 per cent share of tonnage in the British mercantile marine; the French share of steam tonnage was 52.9 per cent at the time.[127] Furthermore, France fell to fifth place in the global statistics of shipping tonnage, surpassed by Norway and Germany, with Japan reaching in 1900 fourth place worldwide, even before the United States. In 1910, the French merchant navy still had an impressive proportion of sailing ships (43.8 per cent), compared to Japan (25 per cent), Germany (17.4 per cent) or Britain (1 per cent). Although its total steam tonnage increased 12-fold (from 68,025 tonnes to 815, 567 tonnes) in the period from 1860 to 1910, the relative position of France in global shipping fell from third place in 1860 (after Britain and the United States) to sixth place in 1910 behind Britain, the British Empire, Germany, Japan and Norway, because the mercantile marines of those countries grew faster than France's. This decline was especially striking in relation to Germany. In 1880, the French steamer fleet was almost one-third larger than the German steamer fleet, but thirty years later, it was only one-third its size.[128]

In the South China Sea, postal subsidies paid by the French government to Messageries Maritimes to run large passenger liners on intercontinental routes or by French Indochina to the Tonkin Shipping Company of Auguste Raphael Marty, and to the French East Asiatic Company to operate the Guangzhouwan postal steamer service secured the continuing presence of the French flag in ports of the region before and after the First World War. This fact was reflected in the port statistics of Hong Kong. In 1909, 446 French vessels, of 551,005 tonnes, called at the British colony, giving the French flag numerically fifth ranking in the harbour master's statistics. This remained the same in 1913, mainly due to the regular intercontinental passenger liners of Messageries Maritimes and

[127] British tonnage refers to shipping tonnage of the United Kingdom, excluding tonnages of British possessions and the British Empire. Percentages are calculated from numerical figures provided by Kirkaldy (1919, Appendix XVII: Net Tonnage of the Leading Mercantile Fleets of the World from 1850 to 1910).

[128] Aldcroft (1968, 327, Table 1) and Smith, Michael S. (1994, 11).

the cargo-steamers of Chargeurs Réunis servicing the route from France to East Asia. Compared to British and other shipping companies, with their strong positions in intercontinental services and intra-Asian shipping, the French flag performed rather modestly, something that did not considerably improve in the wake of the First World War when German shipping companies had lost their pre-war position. In the 1920s, the ships of Messageries Maritimes (which was de facto nationalised at the time), Chargeurs Réunis, the Compagnie Indochinoise de Navigation, the Société Maritime Indochinoise, and the Société Anonyme Pannier and Cie. were frequently calling at Hong Kong. With French Indochina's close proximity considerably contributing to French vessels operating in the South China Sea, the French flag maintained its sixth place in the port statistics behind Britain, Japan, China, United States and the Netherlands in 1925 and 1930, thereby almost retaining its pre-war ranking in Hong Kong.[129]

The reasons for the relative decline of the French mercantile marine had been described, with interrelated geographical, cultural, political and economic factors being included. Fernand Braudel, in his seminal study on France's identity, explained that the French coast was divided into two rather different maritime sections, on the one hand, the Atlantic, the Channel and the North Sea, and on the other hand, the Mediterranean. This required two fleets, resulting in France's maritime power being affected by "a sort of structural weakness" to which was added the lack of "a grand maritime policy". The country's achievements on the sea were "scarcely equal to those on dry land", concluded Braudel. According to the memoires of Pierre-Victor Malouet, published in 1868, who served in the French navy and later became a French parliamentarian, the basic problem was the "regime of absolute power" with "the weight of taxes provoked by demands for luxuries" and "a virtually constant state of war". He was convinced that only "an industrious freedom to speculate can create a class of wealthy capitalists without whom we shall never obtain that commercial activity which multiplies and sends abroad the products of the interior; we have not yet seen in our national councils nor in our nation's habits that spirit of enterprise and economy necessary to create and maintain a large merchant navy, the only solid foundation of maritime might". The failure of France to become the leading

[129] *Hong Kong Blue Books for the Years 1909, 1925 and 1930.* Castel (1957, 289) and Dremeaux (2012, 88; 2014, 11–13).

economic power of Europe considerably contributed to the country's inability to establish a large merchant navy, as Britain did from the eighteenth century and Germany from the mid-nineteenth century. Étienne Taillemite, a French archivist and historian, posed the provocative question whether the French were "allergic to international maritime trade". He pointed to the fact that irrespective of political systems, French policy-makers displayed an unfortunate lack of coherence and methods in their foreign politics towards the rest of the world which led to severe failures in France's maritime policies.[130]

When looking at the overall reasons for France's decline as a maritime power in the late nineteenth century, various factors played a role. Despite natural disadvantages and political failures, the major French ports in 1789 (the year of the French Revolution) were well integrated into international trading networks and actively contributed to the dynamical commercial sector of the pre-industrial world. Shipbuilding in France almost equalled Britain. However, the French Revolutionary Wars (1792–1802) and the subsequent Napoleonic Wars (1803–1815) impeded the development of France's merchant navy and caused an almost total interruption of her commercial relations with the overseas world. The French flag disappeared more or less completely from the oceans. With peace in 1814, France's mercantile marine recovered, but was never able to make up the ground lost to Britain. Although the government made some efforts to re-establish broken links, particularly with the Far East and Spanish America, reconstructing permanent naval stations created by King Louis XVI and supporting attempts by merchants from Bordeaux, it proved to be both a difficult and a long-term operation to recover lost markets. Furthermore, after 1815, French assemblies elected by property qualification were dominated by property owners little concerned with commercial questions. Therefore, maritime interests based in port cities were hardly noticeable in French politics.[131]

French port cities, where the mercantile marine was based and concentrated, were generally not well situated geographically, mainly lacking industrialised and export-driven hinterlands like those of Britain or Germany. An exception seemed to be Le Havre, near the Atlantic

[130] Braudel (1988, 325–328, the quote of Malouet [1868, 173–174]: 327-328) and Taillemite (2006, 21–25).

[131] Clapham (1968, 243).

coast which, in the early nineteenth century, was poised to become the prime port in Europe, with prosperous commercial links to the Americas (between 1820 and 1913, more than two million emigrants shipped through Le Havre), active business ties to Rouen and Paris and railroad lines in an eastward direction to industrial centres in Alsace and Germany. However, by the end of the nineteenth century, it was obvious that Le Havre, and also Dunkerque, were too far south to benefit from major transatlantic commercial flows, unlike their North Sea rivals Antwerp, Rotterdam, Bremen and Hamburg. Although Le Havre counted the enormous Paris basin as its hinterland, it shared this traffic with Rouen. Both French ports lacked efficient waterways and railways linking them to their respective hinterlands. In 1870, Le Havre was the seventh port of Europe in terms of transport volume, but had declined to ninth in 1901, despite the fact that it was the home port of two major French shipping companies, the Compagnie Général Transatlantique (CGT, established in 1855 as Compagnie Général Maritime) and the Chargeurs Réunis, founded in 1872 to provide regular steamer services between Le Havre and South America; in 1901, the company started a regular service to East Asian ports.[132] Besides difficulties arising from international conditions and geopolitical changes, the port of Le Havre owned by the French state increasingly suffered from a lack of investment in its maritime infrastructures and, even worse, from severe competition from Antwerp and Rotterdam which offered more advanced facilities and also more efficient transport links to their respective German hinterlands.[133]

Marseille, the other major French port city, always remained peripheral in relation to Europe's industrial and urban centres, sharing to some extent the same fate as the entire Mediterranean, becoming a second-tier location for the global circulation of goods and people. Except for Lyon, the second-largest urban agglomeration in France, Marseille lacked any major industrial centre in its vicinity, and the poorly navigable Rhone was not comparable to the Elbe or the Rhine in Germany. In 1870, Marseille was the third port of Europe in terms of transport volume, but fell to sixth in 1901, although it was the home port of the Compagnie Fraissinet (Fraissinet Company), the well-known trading and shipping

[132] On the history of Chargeurs Réunis, see Beaugé and Cogan (1984) and Smith, Michael S. (1994).

[133] Miller (2006, 126–128), Taillemite (2006, 27) and Marnot (2020, 60–62, table 2: 60).

company founded in 1836, and of the major French shipping company, the Messageries Maritimes (established in 1851 as Messageries Nationales, later Messageries Impériales, since 1871 called Messageries Maritimes).[134] Initial hopes in Marseille business circles that the Suez Canal (developed by the former French diplomat Ferdinand de Lesseps and opened in 1869) would lead to more profitable commercial ties with Asia remained largely unfulfilled. With French shareholders having the major stake in the enterprise, the canal was an all-steamer route contributing to the increasing decline of the sailing ship as a major world carrier, and to lower freight rates for transports between Western Europe and East Asia. This was triggering severe competition for Marseille from other Mediterranean ports such as Genoa, Venice and Trieste. With increased coal prices at Marseille, and severe British competition on the route, Fraissinet's direct steam shipping line to India, and later to China and Japan, proved to be unprofitable. It was finally the vessels of Messageries Maritimes (strongly supported by the French government, with 30 per cent of the company's annual receipts coming from postal subsidies by 1879) which turned Marseille into the most important transit hub for serving France's imperialist and colonial expansion, with thousands of administrators, colonists, troops and tourists passing through the port city on their way to and from Africa, Indochina, China and other parts of East Asia. Furthermore, the relative decline and weak economic performance of both Marseille and Le Havre were due to the fact that most headquarters of the shipping companies operating from these ports were based in Paris, which deprived the two cities of a powerful political base able to promote and defend their local maritime interests. Michael M. Miller concluded as follows: "Le Havre and Marseille were thus big international ports, but less so than their main competitors. Hinterlands, business inhibitions, colonial preferences and the preponderance of Paris kept them focused on France, curbing greater possibilities". According to Bruno Marnot, the development of Le Havre and Marseille served "as a symbol of the demotion of French ports". From the nineteenth century up to the First World War, successive French parliamentary assemblies proved to be rather uninterested in France's commercial ports, which suffered from permanent underinvestment and other financial and political obstacles. This negligence resulted in major French maritime infrastructures being undersized,

[134] On the history of Messageries Maritimes, see Bois (1992), Berneron-Couvenhes (2000), Berneron-Couvenhes (2007) and Dremeaux (2014).

and therefore disadvantaged in their competition with other ports in Europe.[135]

The decline of France's mercantile marine has consistently been attributed to ill-advised French government policies, especially the highly complex system of subsidies to shipbuilders and fleet operators first established in 1881 and afterwards renewed in 1891, 1893, 1902 and 1906. It began after the Franco-German War of 1870–1871 and the heavy financial burden of the war indemnity imposed on France. With the goal of protecting French wharfs from foreign competition, the law of 30 January 1872, prepared by a special parliamentary commission, drastically increased import duties on sailing ships and steamers built abroad. Consequently, imports of foreign vessels diminished from 35,000 tonnes (1872) to 15,000 tonnes (1876) and 19,000 tonnes (1878). French wharfs exploiting the favourable situation increased their prices for newly built ships, which made it much less attractive for French shipowners to purchase vessels constructed in France. This resulted in reduced sales of French-built tonnage, diminishing from 50,000 tonnes (1872) to 21,000 tonnes (1878). On the other hand, beginning in 1872–1873, French shipowners turned to buy used and older foreign vessels totalling 138,058 tonnes (including 51,070 steam tonnage) and operated them under French flag. They usually chose out-of-date and inexpensive ships (mostly steamers from Britain) to compensate for France's high import fees. This led to France's sailing tonnage rapidly diminishing from 917,633 tonnes (1870) to 641,539 tonnes (1880), faster than that of her neighbours. Her sailing tonnage decreased by 30 per cent, that of Britain by around 15 per cent, while that of Germany actually increased by 6.7 per cent. The only positive effect of the French law of 1872 was that a larger number of foreign steamships were imported into France, resulting in the general modernisation of the French mercantile marine. In 1879, for the first time, France's newly registered steam tonnage (22,000 tonnes) surpassed the newly registered sailing ship tonnage (20,000 tonnes). Although steam tonnage had a mere 30.2 per cent in 1880, the general tendency of French shipowners to employ the more efficient steam technology was

[135] Miller (2006, 126–128), Miller (2012, 56–59, the quote: 59) and Marnot (2020, 60–63, 80, table 2: 60, the quote: 63).

obvious. It enabled the French mercantile marine to effectively compete against rivals, not only in domestic trade but in global transport, too.[136]

The French subsidy law of 29 January 1881 was an attempt to further enhance the global competitiveness of its merchant vessels by introducing a navigation bounty exclusively for long sea voyages (navigation au long cours). The number of sea miles sailed was calculated according to the distance between the ports of departure and arrival, measured on a direct maritime line. Vessels of French construction received twice the bounty for vessels of foreign construction. Therefore, the new legislation was a stimulus for the French shipbuilding industry in two ways: First, by the direct bounty on the construction, and second, because the bounties on navigation were fixed at a higher rate for ships of French origin. This led to the excessive growth of shipbuilding on French wharfs in the early 1880s, without resulting in a strong increase in total tonnage (only 2.6 per cent in ten years). However, in 1890, French steam tonnage exceeded sailing ship tonnage, demonstrating that France's mercantile marine had been successfully renewed and modernised, possibly even at a faster pace than without the navigation bounties. On the other hand, the share of steamers built in French yards had declined considerably, to one-third of France's total steam tonnage, which showed that French shipping companies still preferred to acquire steam vessels abroad, preferably at British wharfs offering more competitive prices. Compared to Britain's merchant fleet (1890: 7.9 million tonnes, of which 5.04 million was steam tonnage), the French mercantile marine (944,000 tonnes, of which 499,921 was steam tonnage) was very small. However, in contrast to Germany's merchant navy (1.43 million tonnes, of which 723,652 was steam tonnage), the French merchant fleet looked much less inferior.[137]

Another major step to further promote global competitiveness of the merchant navy was the French subsidy law of 30 January 1893. This stipulated the slight increase in the construction bounty and fixed the navigation bounty at a much higher rate. The most important amendment was that foreign-built vessels were excluded from the navigation bounty. This gave French steamship yards a kind of monopoly in shipbuilding, resulting in cartelisation and drastically increased prices for

[136] Raffalovich (1888, 147–148), Colin (1901, 182–187), Seilhar (1903, 206), Guggenmusz (1914, 31–33) and Kirkaldy (1919, Appendix XVII).

[137] Raffalovich (1888, 149–151), Guggenmusz (1914, 78–85), Kirkaldy (1919, Appendix XVII) and Smith, Michael S. (1994, 15).

newly constructed French steamers, often 30 to 80 per cent above costs at comparable British yards. Consequently, shipowners began ordering from French yards the more inexpensive sailing vessels rather than the pricy steamships, or instead of buying new ones, they continued to purchase inexpensive older steamers abroad. With much lower construction prices and running costs of sailing ships compared to steamers, the navigation bounty of 1893 even contributed to higher profits for French sailing shipowners. Thus, at a time when most countries were discarding their sailing fleets, France continued to build sailing vessels on a considerable scale. Although the French mercantile marine slightly increased (1900: 1.02 million tonnes, of which 527,551 tonnes was steam tonnage), it fell far behind its British (9.3 million tonnes, of which 7.2 million tonnes was steam tonnage) and German (1.94 million tonne, of which 1.3 tonnes was steam tonnage) competitors, especially in the proportions of sailing ship and steamship tonnages. Furthermore, with increasing purchases of older and cheaper foreign-built steamers by French shipping companies, the overall modernisation of the French merchant navy slowed down considerably.[138]

The following amendments to the subsidy laws of 1902 and 1906, which attempted to tackle the weaknesses of the bounty system, did not help to considerably improve the global competitiveness of the French merchant navy. In 1910, France (1.4 million tonnes, of which 815,567 was steam tonnage) still lagged far behind Britain (11.5 million, of which 10.4 million was steam tonnage) and Germany (2.9 million tonnes of which 2.3 million was steam tonnage), and was surpassed by Japan (1.6 million tonnes, of which 1.2 million was steam tonnage) and even Norway (1.5 million tonnes, of which 897,440 was steam tonnage). The very modest rise of France's merchant navy, with its relatively high proportion of sailing vessels compared to other fleets, was probably the result of the bounty system imposed by politics combined with the tendencies of France's larger commercial policy, which did not favour maritime industries, including shipbuilding facilities and shipping companies. Geographical and cultural factors, as described earlier, contributed to the decline of France as a maritime power in the late nineteenth and early

[138] Kirkaldy (1919, Appendix XVII), Clapham (1968, 243–244) and Aldcroft (1968, 336).

twentieth centuries.[139] In 1905, Royal Meeker, an American economist, concluded that subsidies were turning French marine transport into a "giant infant industry whose weakness increases with its growth".[140]

References

Archival Sources

Archives départementales des Pyrénées-Orientales, Perpignan (ADPO)

Registre d'état-civil de la commune de Porta.

Archives nationales d'outre-mer, Aix-en-Provence (ANOM)

Gouvernement-Général de l'Indochine (INDO-GGI).

Bundesarchiv, Berlin (BAB)

Deutsches Reich: R.

Centre des Archives Diplomatiques, Nantes (CADN)

Consulat Hong Kong, Série I 3 B: Affaires politiques et commerciales (août-octobre 1898).

Centre des Archives Diplomatiques du Ministère des Affaires Étrangères, Paris (MAE)

Correspondance consulaire et commerciale (CCC), 1793–1901.

Hong Kong Public Records Office (HKPRO)

Carl Smith Index (CSI).

[139] Clapham (1968, 244–245, 355–358) and Aldcroft (1968, 336).

[140] Meeker (1905, 84).

Jebsen and Jessen Historical Archives, Aabenraa (JJHA)

Letter Copy Books (A01-01).

Politisches Archiv des Auswärtigen Amts, Berlin (PAAA)

Deutsches Reich: R.

Vietnamese National Archives One, Hanoi (VNAi)

Service de l'Enregistrement, des Douanes et du Timbre de l'Indochine (SEDT).

Secondary Sources

Aldcroft, Derek H. 1968. The Mercantile Marine. In *The Development of British Industry and Foreign Competition 1875–1914: Studies in Industrial Enterprise*, ed. Derek H. Aldcroft, 326–363. London: Allen & Unwin.

Alderton, Patrick, and Rowlinson, Merwyn. 2002. The Economics of Shipping Freight Markets. In *The Handbook of Maritime Economics and Business*, ed. Costas Th. Grammenos, 157–185. London: LLP.

Allen, George Cyril, and Audrey G. Donnithorne. 1954. *Western Enterprise in Far Eastern Economic Development*. London: Allen & Unwin.

Amenda, Lars. 2011. "Chinese Quarters": Maritime Labor, Chinese Migration, and Local Imagination in Rotterdam and Hamburg, 1900–1950. In *Chinatowns in a Transnational World: Myths and Realities of an Urban Phenomenon*, ed. Vanessa Künnemann and Ruth Mayer, 45–61. New York and Abingdon: Routledge.

Armstrong, John. 2009a. Conferences in British Nineteenth-Century Coastal Shipping. In *The Vital Spark: The British Coastal Trade 1700–1930*, ed. John Armstrong, 77–90. St. John's, Newfoundland: International Maritime Economic History Association.

Armstrong, John. 2009b. Coastal Shipping: The Neglected Sector of Nineteenth-Century British Transport History. In *The Vital Spark: The British Coastal Trade 1700–1930*, ed. John Armstrong, 91–102. St. John's, Newfoundland: International Maritime Economic History Association.

Bard, Salomon. 1993. *Traders of Hong Kong: Some Foreign Merchant Houses 1841–1899*. Hong Kong: Urban Council.

Beaugé, Jean, and René-Pierre Cogan. 1984. *Histoire Maritime des Chargeurs Réunie et leur Filiales Françaises*. Paris: Barré et Dayez.

Becker, Bert. 2004. German Business in Hong Kong Before 1914. *Journal of the Royal Asiatic Society Hong Kong Branch* 44: 91–113.

Becker, Bert. 2009. The German Colony of Kiaochow and Its Postal Steamer Service, 1898–1914. *International Journal of Maritime History* 21 (1): 201–238.

Becker, Bert. 2010a. Coastal Shipping in East Asia in the Late Nineteenth Century. *Journal of the Royal Asiatic Society Hong Kong Branch* 50: 245–302.

Becker, Bert. 2010b. The Merchant-Consuls of German States in China, Hong Kong and Macao (1787–1872). In *Consuls et services consulaires aux XIXe siècle/Consulship in the 19th Century/Die Welt der Konsulate im 19. Jahrhundert*, ed. Jörg Ulbert and Lukian Prijac, 329–351. Hamburg: DOBU.

Becker, Bert. 2012. *Michael Jebsen: Reeder und Politiker 1835–1899: Eine Biographie*. Kiel: Ludwig.

Becker, Bert. 2015. Die Deutsche Kirchen- und Schulgemeinde zu Hongkong 1900–1914. In *Gemeinsam Unterwegs: 50 Jahre Evangelische Gemeinde Deutscher Sprache in Hongkong 1965–2015*, ed. Hanns Hoerschelmann and Bert Becker, 54–102. Hong Kong: Evangelische Gemeinde Deutscher Sprache in Hong Kong.

Becker, Bert. 2017. Western Firms and Their Chinese Compradors: The Case of the Jebsen and Chau Families. In *Meeting Place: Encounters Across Cultures in Hong Kong, 1841–1984*, ed. Elizabeth Sinn and Christopher Munn, 106–130. Hong Kong: Hong Kong University Press.

Becker, Bert. 2019. French Kwang-chow-wan and British Hong Kong: Politics and Shipping, 1890s–1920s. In *British and French Colonialism in Africa, Asia and the Middle East: Connected Empires across the Eighteenth to the Twentieth Centuries*, ed. James R. Fichter, 181–221. Cham: Palgrave Macmillan.

Bensacq-Tixier, Nicole. 2003. *Dictionnaire du corps diplomatique et consulaire français en Chine (1840–1911)*. Paris: Les Indes Savantes.

Berneron-Couvenhes, Marie-Françoise. 2000. The Internationalisation of Messageries Maritimes Steamship Company from 1851 to 1914: The Defense of the French Flag Overseas. In *Transnational Companies (19th–20th Centuries)*, ed. Hubert Bonin, et al., 289–300. Paris: Plage.

Berneron-Couvenhes, Marie-Françoise. 2007. *Les Messageries Maritimes: L'essor d'une grande compagnie de navigation française, 1851–1894*. Paris: PUBS.

Blake, Robert. 1999. *Jardine Matheson: Traders of the Far East*. London: Weidenfeld & Nicolson.

Bois, Paul. 1992. *Le Grand Siècle des Messageries Maritimes*. Marseille: Chambre de Commerce et de l'Industrie de Marseille-Provence.

Bonin, Hubert. 1988. *Histoire économique de la France depuis 1880*. Paris: Masson.

Bonin, Hubert. 2020. *French Banking and Entrepreneurialism in China and Hong Kong from the 1850s to 1980s*. Abingdon, Oxon, and New York: Routledge.

Boxer, Baruch. 1961. *Ocean Shipping in the Evolution of Hong Kong*. Chicago: University of Chicago.

Boxer, Charles R. 2001. *An Uncommon Life: Soldier, Historian, Teacher, Collector, Traveller*. Lisbon: Fundacao Oriente.

Braudel, Fernand. 1988. *The Identity of France, vol. 1: History and Environment*. New York: Harper & Row.

Brautaset, Camilla, and Stig Tenold. 2010. Lost in Calculation? Norwegian Merchant Shipping in Asia, 1870–1914. In *Maritime History as Global History,* ed. Maria Fusaro and Amélia Polónia, 203–221. St. John's, Newfoundland: International Maritime Economic History Association.

Brien, J. 1916. *Souvenirs d'Extrême-Orient: Une Mission en Chine*, vol. 2. Paris: Les Œuvres Nouvelles.

Brocheux, Pierre, and Daniel Hèmery. 2009. *Indochina: An Ambiguous Colonization, 1858-1954*. Berkeley: University of California Press.

Bulletin Trimestriel de la Société Amicale des Anciens Tonkinois, vol. 9. 1940. Un des créateurs de Haiphong, 8–12. Hanoi: G. Taupin.

Cady, John Frank. 1954. *The Roots of French Imperialism in Eastern Asia*. Ithaca, NY: Cornell University Press.

Cain, P.J., and A.G. Hopkins. 2016. *British Imperialism 1688–2015*. London and New York: Routledge.

Carroll, John M. 2005. *Edge of Empires: Chinese Elites and British Colonials in Hong Kong*. Cambridge, MA and London: Harvard University Press.

Carroll, John M. 2007. *A Concise History of Hong Kong*. Hong Kong: Hong Kong University Press.

Castel, A. 1957. The French Community in Hong Kong. In *Hong Kong Business Symposium*, ed. J.M. Braga, 289–290. Hong Kong: South China Morning Post.

Chan, Wai Kwan. 1991. *The Making of Hong Kong Society: Three Studies of Class Formation in Early Hong Kong*. Oxford: Clarendon Press.

Cheng, Tong Yung. 1980. *The Economy of Hong Kong*. Hong Kong: Far East Publications.

Chesneaux, Jean. 1968. *The Chinese Labor Movement, 1919–1927*. Stanford: Stanford University Press.

Chu, Cindy Yik-yi. 2005. Catholic Church Between Two World Wars. In *Foreign Communities in Hong Kong, 1840s–1950s*, ed. Cindy Yik-yi Chu, 85–109. New York: Palgrave Macmillan.

Clapham, J.H. 1968. *The Economic Development of France and Germany 1815–1914*, 4th ed. Cambridge: Cambridge University Press.

Colin, Ambroise. 1901. *La Navigation Commerciale au XIXe Siècle*. Paris: Rousseau.

Conrad, Sebastian. 2006. *Globalisation and the Nation in Imperial Germany*. Cambridge: Cambridge University Press.

Cunich, Peter. 2012. *A History of The University of Hong Kong, vol. 1: 1911–1945*. Hong Kong: Hong Kong University Press.

Davis, John R., Stefan Manz, and Margrit Schulte Beerbühl, eds. 2012. *Transnational Networks: German Migrants in the British Empire, 1670–1914*. Leiden: Brill.

Davis, Ralph. 1972. *The Rise of the English Shipping Industry in the Seventeenth and Eighteenth Centuries*. Newton Abbot: David & Charles.

Denis, Étienne. 1965. *Bordeaux et la Cochinchine sous la Restauration et le Second Empire*. Bordeaux: Delmas.

Diplomatic and Consular Reports. 1906. *Trade of Indo-China for the Years 1903–04*. London: Foreign Office.

Drémeaux, François, ed. 2012. *Hong Kong: French Connections: From the 19th Century to the Present Day*. Hong Kong: Bonham Media.

Drémeaux, François. 2014. *Les Messageries Maritimes à Hong Kong 1918–1941*. Scientrier: GOPE.

Dübgen, Walther. 1910. *Hongkong-Skizzen, vol. 1*. Unpublished manuscript.

Dujardin-Beaumetz. 1897–1898. Le Commerce de la Chine avec L'Étranger. *Bulletin de la Société de Géographie Commerciale de Paris* 19: 477–511.

Endacott, G.B. 1995. *A History of Hong Kong*. Hong Kong: Hong Kong University Press.

Fairbank, Francis E. 1973. *Far Eastern Trade 1860–1914*. London: Adam & Charles Black.

Feuerwerker, Albert. 1983. The Foreign Presence in China. *The Cambridge History of China*, vol. 12 (1): 128–207. Cambridge: Cambridge University Press.

Fletcher, Max E. 1958. The Suez Canal and World Shipping, 1869–1914. *The Journal of Economic History* 18 (4): 556–573.

Ford, Staci. 2002. Women, Gender, and HKU. In *An Impossible Dream: Hong Kong University from Foundation to Re-establishment, 1910–1950*, ed. Kit-ching Chan Lau and Peter Cunich, 119–138. Hong Kong: Oxford University Press.

Gantès, Gilles de. 2002. Migration to Indochina: Proof of the Popularity of Colonial Empire? In *Promoting the Colonial Idea: Propaganda and Visions of Empire in France*, ed. Tony Chafer and Amanda Sackur, 15–28. Houndsmill: Palgrave.

Gipouloux, François. 2011. *The Asian Mediterranean: Port Cities and Trading Networks in China, Japan and Southeast Asia, 13th–21st Century*. Cheltenham, UK and Northampton, MA: Edward Elgar.

Goscha, Christopher. 2017. *The Penguin History of Modern Vietnam*. Milton Keynes: Penguin.

Gregg, E.S. 1921. Vicissitudes in the Shipping Trade, 1870–1920. *The Quarterly Journal of Economics* 35 (4): 603–617.

Guggenmusz, Franz. 1914. *Die Unterstützung der französischen Handelsmarine durch Prämien*. Hamburg: L. Friedrichsen.

Hänisch, Adolf von. 1970. *Jebsen & Co. Hongkong: China-Handel im Wechsel der Zeiten 1895–1945*. Apenrade: Self-Published.

Harlaftis, Gelina, and John Theotokas. 2002. Maritime Business During the 20th Century: Continuity and Change. In *The Handbook of Maritime Economics and Business*, ed. Costas Th. Grammenos, 9–34. London: LLP.

Haussmann, Auguste. 1848. *Voyage en Chine, Cochinchine, Inde et Malaisie*. Paris: Sagnier et Bray.

Haussmann, Auguste. 1864. *La Chine: résumé historique de l'insurrection et des évènements qui ont eu lieu dans ce pays, depuis le commencement de la guerre de l'opium jusqu'en 1857*. Paris: Gustave Barba.

Henderson, William Otto. 1975. *The Rise of German Industrial Power 1834–1914*. London: Temple Smith.

Hieke, Ernst. 1953. *Die Reederei M. Jebsen A. G., Apenrade*. Hamburg: Hamburgische Bücherei.

Hoe, Susanna. 1991. *The Private Life of Old Hong Kong: Western Women in the British Colony 1841–1941*. Hong Kong: Oxford University Press.

Hong Kong Blue Book for the Years 1897, 1909, 1913, 1925 and 1930. Hong Kong: Hong Kong Government Reports Online (1842–1941).

Hsiao, Liang-Lin. 1974. *China's Foreign Trade Statistics, 1864–1949*. Cambridge, MA: Harvard University Press.

Hyde, Francis E. 1973. *Far Eastern Trade, 1860–1914*. London: A. and C. Black.

Jarvis, Adrian, and Robert Lee, eds. 2008. *Trade, Migration and Urban Networks in Port Cities, c. 1640–1940*. St. John's, Newfoundland: International Maritime Economic History Association.

Keswick, Maggie, ed. 1982. *The Thistle and the Jade: A Celebration of 150 Years of Jardine, Matheson & Co*. London: Octopus Books.

Kirkaldy, Adam Willis. 1919. *British Shipping: Its History, Organisation and Importance*. London: Kegan Paul.

Küttner, Sibylle. 2000. *Farbige Seeleute im Kaiserreich: Asiaten und Afrikaner im Dienst der deutschen Handelsmarine*. Erfurt: Sutton.

Lai, Chi-Kong. 2004. From Seagoing Junk to Modern Enterprise: The Transition of Steamship Business, 1826–1873. In *Maritime China in Transition 1750–1850*, ed. Wang Gungwu and Ng Chin-keong, 299–316. Wiesbaden: Harrassowitz.

Lau, Siu-Kai, and Hsin-Chi Kuan. 1988. *The Ethos of the Hong Kong Chinese*. Hong Kong: The Chinese University Press.

Le Pichon, Alain. 2006. *Béthanie & Nazareth: French Secrets from a British Colony*. Hong Kong: The Hong Kong Academy for Performing Arts.

Leonhard, Melanie. 2009. *Die Unternehmerfamilie Rickmers 1834–1918: Schiffbau, Schifffahrt, Handel*. Bremen: H. M. Hauschild.

Levasseur, E. 1912. *Histoire du Commerce de la France*, vol. 2. Paris: Arthur Rousseau.

Liu, Kwang-ching. 1959. Steamship Enterprise in Nineteenth-Century China. *The Journal of Asian Studies* 18 (4): 435–455.

Liu, Kwang-ching. 1964. British-Chinese Steamship Rivalry in China, 1873–85. In *The Economic Development of China and Japan*, ed. C.D. Cowan, 49–77. New York: Allen & Unwin.

Mak, Ricardo K.S. 2005. Nineteenth-Century German Community. In *Foreign Communities in Hong Kong, 1840s–1950s*, ed. Cindy Yik-yi Chu, 61–83. New York: Palgrave Macmillan.

Mak, Ricardo K.S. 2000. Business for Business Sake: German Merchants in Nineteenth Century Hong Kong. In *Sino-German Relations Since 1800: Multidisciplinary Explorations*, ed. Ricardo K.S. Mak and Danny S.L. Paau, 31–52. Frankfurt am Main: Lang.

Malouet, Pierre-Victor. 1868. *Mémoires,* vol. 1, ed. by his grandson. Paris: Didier.

Manz, Stefan. 2014. *Constructing a German Diaspora: The "Greater German Empire", 1871–1914.* New York and Abingdon: Routledge.

Marnot, Bruno. 2020. Croissance et déclassement: le sous-investissement dans les grands ports de commerce français au XIXe siècle. In *L'Économie Maritime en France: histoire, enjeux, perspectives*, ed. Stéphane Becuwe and Bertrand Blancheton, 57–82. Paris: Ellipses.

Marriner, Sheila, and Francis E. Hyde. 1967. *The Senior: John Samuel Swire, 1825–1898: Management in Far Eastern Shipping Trades*. Liverpool: Liverpool University Press.

Martonne, Edouard-Guillaume. 1897. La mission lyonnaise d'exploration en China. *Annales de Géographie* 6 (27): 273–276.

Meeker, Royal. 1905. *History of Shipping Subsidies*. New York: The Macmillan Co.

Mergnac, Marie-Odile., ed. 1999. *Les noms de famille du Sud-Ouest*. Paris: Archives & Culture.

Meuleau, Marc. 1990. *Des Pionniers en Extrême-Orient: Histoire de la Banque de l'Indochine (1875–1975).* Paris: Fayard.

Meyer, David R. 2000. *Hong Kong as a Global Metropolis*. Cambridge: Cambridge University Press.

Miller, Laura, and Arne Cornelius Wasmuth. 2008. *Three Mackerels: The Story of the Jebsen and Jessen Family Enterprise*. Hong Kong: Hongkongnow.com.

Miller, Michael B. 2006. L'énigme de la marine marchande française au XXe siècle. *Revue d'Histoire Maritime* 5: *La Marine marchande française de 1850 à 2000*: 119–134.

Miller, Michael B. 2012. *Europe and the Maritime World: A Twentieth-Century History*. Cambridge: Cambridge University Press.

Mouries, Frederic. 1991. *Le Consulat de France à Hong-Kong et l'Indochine 1863–1921.* Master Thesis, Université de Provence, Aix-en-Provence.

Müller-Jabusch, Maximilian. 1940. *Fünfzig Jahre Deutsch-Asiatische Bank 1890–1939.* Berlin: Otto von Holten.

Nipperdey, Thomas. 1998. *Deutsche Geschichte 1866–1918, vol. 1: Arbeitswelt und Bürgergeist.* Munich: Beck.

Osterhammel, Jürgen. 1989. *China und die Weltgesellschaft: Vom 18. Jahrhundert bis in unsere Zeit.* Munich: Beck.

Otte, Friedrich. 1930. Shipping in China and Chinese Shipping Abroad. *Chinese Economic Journal* 6 (2): 123–152.

Pelissier, Jean-Pierre. 1986. *Paroisses et communes de France: Dictionnaire d'histoire administrative et démographique: Pyrénées-Orientales.* Paris: Éditions du Centre National de la Recherche Scientifique.

Plag, Albrecht. 1969. "Bethesda" and the Berliner Frauenverein für China. *Journal of the Hong Kong Branch of the Royal Asiatic Society* 9: 149–150.

Plumpe, Werner. 2004. Deutsche Bank in East Asia 1872–1988. In *Deutsche Bank in East Asia*, ed. The Historical Association of Deutsche Bank, 21–86. Munich and Zürich: Piper.

Poidevin, Raymond. 1998. *Les Relations Économiques et Financières entre la France et l'Allemagne de 1898 à 1914.* Paris: Comité pour l'Histoire économique et financière de la France.

Rabaud, Louis-M. 1898. Rapport sur Hong-Kong. In *La Mission Lyonnaise d'Exploration Commerciale en Chine 1895–1897*, ed. Chambre de Commerce de Lyon, 157–189. Lyon: A. Rey.

Raffalovich, M. Arthur. 1888. The Effects of Shipping Bounties. *Journal of the Royal Statistical Society* 51 (1): 141–154.

Raffi, Gilles. 1994. *Haiphong: origines, conditions et modalités du développement jusqu'en 1921.* PhD Thesis, Université de Provence.

Raquez, Alfred. 1900. *Au pays de pagodes: notes de voyage.* Shanghai: Presse Orientale.

Ratenhof, Udo. 1987. *Die Chinapolitik des Deutschen Reiches 1871 bis 1945: Wirtschaft - Rüstung – Militär.* Boppard am Rhein: Harald Boldt.

Reinhardt, Anne. 2018. *Navigating Semi-Colonialism: Shipping, Sovereignty, and Nation-Building in China, 1860–1937.* Cambridge, MA and London: Harvard University Press.

Roll, Christian. 1957. German Business in Hong Kong. In *Hong Kong Business Symposium*, ed. J.M. Braga, 293–294. Hong Kong: South China Morning Post.

Rübner, Hartmut, and Lars Scholl. 2009. Major German Shipping Lines During the 1920s and 1930s. *International Journal of Maritime History* 21 (1): 27–54.

Rübner, Hartmut. 1997. Lebens- und gewerkschaftliche Organisationsbedingungen chinesischer Seeleute in der deutschen Handelsflotte. Der maritime Aspekt der Ausländerbeschäftigung vom Kaiserreich bis in den NS-Staat. *Internationale wissenschaftliche Korrespondenz zur Geschichte der deutschen Arbeiterbewegung (IWK)* 1: 1–41.

Sayer, Geoffrey Robley. 1975. *Hong Kong 1862–1919: Years of Discretion*. Hong Kong: Hong Kong University Press.

Schmelzkopf, Reinhart. 1994. Reederei Michael Jebsen, Apenrade/Aabenraa. *Strandgut* 33: 27–50.

Scholl, Lars. 1984. Struktur und Wandel in der deutschen Handelsschiffahrt. 1815–1918. *Scripta Mercaturae* 18 (2): 30–60.

Scholl, Lars. 1990. Struggling Against the Odds: The German Merchant Marine in the Inter-War Period. In *Shipping and Trade (1750–1950)*, ed. Lewis R. Fischer and Helge W. Nordvik, 91–100. Leuven: Leuven University Press.

Schumacher, Hermann. 1900. Deutschlands wirtschaftliche Interessen in Hongkong. In *Beiträge zur Flottennovelle 1900*, ed. Nauticus, 23–34. Berlin: Ernst Siegfried Mittler und Sohn.

Sculfort, Louis. 1898. Rapport sur la circulation monétaire en Chine et les conséquences de la baisse de l'argent, 399-416; Note sur les opérations de banques chinoises de Tchoung-king, 417–423. In *La Mission Lyonnaise d'Exploration Commerciale en Chine 1895–1897*, ed. Chambre de Commerce de Lyon. Lyon: A. Rey.

Seilhar, Léon de. 1903. Untersuchung über die Lage der französischen Handelsflotte und der französischen Seeleute. In *Die Lage der in der Seeschiffahrt beschäftigten Arbeiter*, vol. 1, ed. Verein für Sozialpolitik, 199–217. Leipzig: Duncker & Humblot.

Selby, Anne. 1988. When Germans were unwelcome in Hong Kong. *South China Morning Post*, 25 June.

Sinn, Elizabeth. 2013. *Pacific Crossing: California Gold, Chinese Migration and the Making of Hong Kong*. Hong Kong: Hong Kong University Press.

Smith, Carl T. 1994. The German Speaking Community in Hong Kong 1846–1918. *Journal of the Royal Asiatic Society Hong Kong Branch* 34: 1–55.

Smith, Michael S. 1994. Unlikely Success: Chargeurs Réunis and the Marine Transport Business in France, 1872–1914. *Entreprises et Histoire* 6: 11–27.

So, Fion Wai Ling. 2019. *Germany's Colony in China: Colonialism, Protection and Economic Development in Qingdao and Shandong, 1898–1914*. Abingdon and New York: Routledge.

Soulet, Jean-François. 2004. *Les Pyrénées au XIXe siècle: L'éveil d'une société civile*. Bordeaux: Éditions Sud Ouest.

Speitkamp, Winfried. 2000. The Germans in Hong Kong, 1860–1914: Social Life, Political Interest and National Identity. In *Sino-German Relations Since 1800: Multidisciplinary Explorations*, ed. Ricardo K.S. Mak and Danny S.L. Paau, 53–71. Frankfurt am Main: Lang.

Spethmann, Catharina. 2002. *Schiffahrt in Schleswig-Holstein 1864–1939*. PhD Thesis, University of Kiel.

Sporleder, Walter. 1976. *Hong Kong zu meiner Zeit 1928–1939*. Bremen: Self-Published.

Stoecker, Helmuth. 1958. *Deutschland und China im 19. Jahrhundert: Das Eindringen des deutschen Kapitalismus*. Berlin: Rütten & Loening.

Stone, Julia. 2013. *Chinese Basket Babies: A German Missionary Foundling Home and the Girls It Raised (1850s–1914)*. Wiesbaden: Harrassowitz.

Sze, Tsung-Yu. 1925. *China and the Most-Favored Nation Clause*. New York: Fleming H. Revell (reprint 1971, Taipei: Ch'eng Wen Publishing).

Taillemite, Étienne. 2006. Les Français furent-ils allergiques au commerce maritime international ? *Revue d'Histoire Maritime* 5 : *La Marine marchande française de 1850 à 2000*: 21–28.

The China Directory for 1861. 1861. Hong Kong: A. Shortrede.

The China Directory for 1862. 1862. Hong Kong: A. Shortrede.

The Chronicle and Directory for China, Corea, Japan, the Philippines, Cochin-China, Annam, Tonquin, Siam, Borneo, Straits Settlements, Malay States, etc. for the year 1888. 1888. Hong Kong: Daily Press.

The Chronicle and Directory for China, Japan and the Philippines for 1864. 1864. Hong Kong: Daily Press.

The Chronicle and Directory for China, Japan and the Philippines for 1875. 1875. Hong Kong: Daily Press.

The Chronicle and Directory for China, Japan and the Philippines for 1876. 1876. Hong Kong: Daily Press.

The Chronicle and Directory for China, Japan and the Philippines for 1877. 1877. Hong Kong: Daily Press.

The Chronicle and Directory for China, Japan and the Philippines for 1882. 1882. Hong Kong: Daily Press.

The Germans and Their Activities in South China & Hong Kong. 1934. Supplement to the Guangzhou Daily Sun. Guangzhou: The National Publishers.

The Hong Kong Directory. 1859. Hong Kong: Armenian Press.

The Hong Kong Government Gazette. 1865. Hong Kong Government Reports Online (1842–1941).

Thieß, Karl. 1907. *Deutsche Schiffahrt und Schiffahrtspolitik der Gegenwart*. Leipzig: Teubner.

Tsang, Steve. 2004. *A Modern History of Hong Kong*. Hong Kong: Hong Kong University Press.

Wray, W.D. 1984. *Mitsubishi and the N.Y.K., 1870–1914: Business Strategies in the Japanese Shipping Industry*. Cambridge, MA: Harvard University Press.

Wright, Arnold, and H.A. Cartwright, eds. 1908. *Twentieth Century Impressions of Hongkong, Shanghai, and other Treaty Ports of China: Their History, People, Commerce, Industries, and Resources*. London: Lloyd's Greater Britain Publishing Company.

CHAPTER 4

Saigon

Cochinchina (1840–1870)

French Naval Expansion in Southern Vietnam

From the seventeenth century onwards, the Red River Delta ceased to be the beating heart of Vietnamese civilisation. The city of Hue emerged to supplement Hanoi (Thăng Long), and the southern or inner region (Đàng Trong) was clearly distinct from the northern or outer region (Đàng Ngoài). While the northern section was commonly called "Tonkin" by Europeans, the southern part was known as "Cochinchina"; the name "Vietnam" was generally used by the Chinese Qing court when recognising the whole country as a vassal kingdom. Southernmost Vietnam, with its principal city, Saigon, was initially called Lower Cochinchina (in French: Basse-Cochinchine) by the French; in 1862, this region was inaugurated as "French Cochinchina", and later simply called Cochinchina[1] (Fig. 4.1).

[1] The term Vietnam was changed by the Hue court to Dai Viet (Greater Viet) in 1813. However, in 1838, Emperor Minh Mang (1820–1841) altered the kingdom's name to Dai Nam (the Greater South) which was used by the Nguyen rulers until mid-1945. The word Vietnam entered popular usage in the 1910s, 1920s and 1930s and was often used by nationalists for the nation-state they proclaimed as independent in 1945. Li (1998, 12), Taylor (2013, 398) and Goscha (2017, xxiii).

B. Becker, *France and Germany in the South China Sea, c. 1840–1930*, Cambridge Imperial and Post-Colonial Studies,
https://doi.org/10.1007/978-3-030-52604-7_4

Fig. 4.1 Detail of a map of French Indochina, showing Cochinchina with Saigon, 1920s (*Newnes' Citizen's Atlas of the World*, ed. by John Bartholomew, London: The Home Library Book Co., c. 1923/24)

When Emperor Tu Duc (1847–1883), of the Nguyen dynasty, ascended to the throne, Vietnam was a military state running from the Red River basin to the Mekong Delta. The real threat to the country came from the French whose influence had frequently spread in Vietnam through missionaries and merchants since the early nineteenth century. During the First Opium War (1839–1842), French and British warships began to appear regularly in Vietnamese waters, with the French navy actively searching for a permanent base after the end of the war. In 1847, French men-of-war bombarded Da Nang (Tourane), the central

Vietnamese port city, killing hundreds of local people, in retaliation for the arrest of the French missionary Dominique Lefèbvre. Tu Duc's return to the anti-Christian policy of the 1830s resulted in an edict of 1848 prescribing the death penalty for foreign missionaries. This was extended to Vietnamese Catholic clergy three years later. In 1852, two French missionaries were executed in Tonkin, and the execution of Vietnamese priests resumed. This triggered the attention of the French navy and of President Louis-Napoléon who, in the same year, adopted the title Emperor Napoleon III and proclaimed the Second Empire.[2] Under her new ruler, France resumed not only a more active role in European politics but also an aggressive attitude in the Far East. As a logical addition to the expedition in China, Napoleon III, in mid-July 1857, decided on military intervention in Vietnam. After the Treaty of Tianjin with China was signed in June 1858, Admiral Rigault de Genouilly received orders to take some of his ships south to conquer Tourane (Da Nang), a strategically important port city located near the Vietnamese capital Hue, and to negotiate a protectorate treaty or an agreement similar to that which France had imposed on China. Spain joined the expedition, dispatching Spanish and Philippine soldiers, which increased the French naval force consisting of fourteen ships and around three thousand troops. In August 1858, Da Nang was seized, but with the Vietnamese court at Hue still refusing to give in, the French decided to strike further south, at Saigon. Unlike Hue, this Vietnamese city was accessible from the sea by the Saigon River and also had an economically important function, with its extended rice industry supplying markets in central and southern Vietnam. On 17 February 1859, Saigon was occupied and brought under French control, despite strong resistance by Vietnamese forces around the city.[3]

In November 1860, Justin Prosper Chasseloup-Laubat, later known as "the first founder of French Indochina", was appointed as the new navy and colonial minister and took immediate action.[4] Admiral Léonard

[2] Corfield (2009, 18–19), Taylor (2013, 430–441), Goscha (2017, 53–57) and Stovall (2015, 96).

[3] Brocheux and Hèmery (2009, 24–25), Hsü (2000, 212–215) and Jenkins (1973, 300–301).

[4] *Dictionnaire des Ministres de 1789 à 1989* (1990, 241–242).

Charner, commander of the Far East naval squadron and the French expeditionary corps in China, with his flag in the steam frigate *Impératrice-Eugénie*, was ordered to turn south to Vietnam where a small French-Spanish force, surrounded by Vietnamese troops, was being maintained with great difficulty. In February 1861, the strongly fortified Vietnamese lines around Saigon and its counterpart, the Chinese town of Cholon, were taken; two months later, My Tho, the strategically important province offering access to the delta and Cambodia, was seized, followed by the French occupation of three south-eastern provincial capitals. When Charner left for France, in August 1861 Admiral Louis Bonard became the first French governor of Cochinchina, facing a deeply divided Hue court which was severely hampered by serious revolts among Vietnamese Catholics in Tonkin. Forced to decide between two enemies, the Hue court finally signed a peace agreement with the French. The Treaty of Saigon (5 June 1861) formally ceded the Vietnamese south-eastern provinces of My Tho (or Dinh Thuong), Gia Dinh and Bien Hoa to France, along with the archipelago of Poulo Condor (Con Doa). Furthermore, the agreement opened Da Nang and the northern Vietnamese port cities of Ba Cat and Quang Yen to foreign trade, granted freedom of navigation for French ships on all branches of the Mekong, declared religious freedom in the Vietnamese empire and forced Vietnam to abandon its suzerainty over Cambodia. The new colony, called Cochinchina or French Cochinchina (in French: Cochinchine française), was for twenty years exclusively ruled by French admirals (1859–1879), becoming a symbol of France's "naval expansion".[5]

From 1860, Navy and Colonial Minister Chasseloup-Laubat was for almost seven years not only the spiritual driving force behind the first phase of French expansion in Vietnam but also gained a reputation as "one of the best ministers with technical expertise of the Second Empire"

[5] Goscha (2017, 57–60, the quote: 58) and Brocheux and Hèmery (2009, 21). The name "Cochinchina", when first recorded by a European in 1515, referred to Dai Viet in general. The suffix "China" was used to distinguish it from the similarly called south-western Indian town Cochin or Kochi. In 1679, when the Pope approved the founding of a separate apostolic vicariate of Cochinchina, the name was formalised in European usage. At about the same time, the Vietnamese began to call this southern region Dang Trong (meaning "inner region"), and the northern region Dang Ngoai (meaning "outer region"). After the French conquest, "Cochinchina" (in French "Cochinchine") came to refer exclusively to the southernmost part of Vietnam while the central part was called "Annam" and the northern part "Tonkin". Li (1998, 12–14).

by modernising the navy and making it one of the best in the world.[6] The French navy had a long and proud tradition which, for the first time, had been shattered during the Napoleonic wars (1803–1815) by British sea power. As a symbol of renewed French maritime power, the Divison navale des mers de Chine (Naval Division of the Chinese Seas) was established in 1840. Focusing on the construction of steamships in the extensive naval building programmes of 1846–1851 proved well-suited when the Crimean War (1853–1856) involved the French fleet. Naval warfare provided a testing ground for modern technologies such as screw-driven steamers and ships built of iron. The little ironclad, screw-driven French gunboats employed during bombardments proved highly effective. In the following years, navies worldwide underwent important technical change. Based on findings from the Crimean War, French naval builders in 1859 produced *La Gloire*, an armoured frigate, using the experience gained with these gunboats. She was armoured from stem to stern, with a speed of thirteen knots, and carried fourteen rifled and breech-loading guns firing shells instead of shot. Britain's reaction in 1860 was the *Warrior*, larger and faster but less armoured or manoeuvrable. In 1860, France was equal to Britain in older men-of-war, and even ahead of her in new ones and in her construction programme.[7]

Thanks to the ambitious programme of naval construction launched in 1862, France aimed to play a leading role in applying technology to naval warfare. By 1870, sail had given way to steam in French men-of-war, providing her with a fleet of modern armoured steam vessels that were technologically more advanced than their British counterparts. Although the French navy was much smaller in size than the British, this technical superiority caused widespread fear and envy in Britain and other naval nations worldwide. Despite the Anglo-French alliance in the Crimean War, and their joint expedition to China (1857–1858), French service and popular journals displayed lively anti-British sentiments that discussed options for meeting and beating Britain at sea. In the Second Opium War (1856–1860), the French navy was a wedge used to push for trading concessions from China and to aid French troops led by Admiral Rigault de Genouilly that were invading Vietnam and occupying

[6] *Dictionnaire des Ministres de 1789 à 1989* (1990, 241–242).

[7] Jenkins (1973, 298–299) and Walser (1992, 1–2).

Saigon.[8] However, from the outset, French warships operating in East Asian waters depended on the British network of bases able to provide wood, coal and supplies.[9]

Traders in Saigon

During the Chinese century (1740–1840), Saigon had developed into a trading centre for bulk goods (rice, sugar and salt) with other ports in Southeast Asia, especially Singapore. This trend continued in the following years: from 1841 to 1845, rice exports to the British colony rose about tenfold, combined with a strong increase in shipping. In 1860, Saigon was declared a free port by the French and opened to general trade. Rice remained the main export article in the 1860s, being sold at once for cash or transported to China in speculative ventures. The other major share was held by Britain and Singapore, from where a large share was re-exported to neighbouring countries. A small portion of direct rice exports also went to Europe (excluding Britain). In 1869, Saigon became the foremost global rice port. The import trade was almost entirely in the hands of Chinese merchants whose operating costs were so low, European merchants at Saigon could not profitably import goods directly from Europe. In the 1860s, except for the importation of French wines and a few other articles, almost all imports (especially British cotton manufactures) passed through Singapore, from where Chinese merchants shipped all kinds of goods on board vessels owned by Singaporean Chinese. On the other hand, Cochinchina was increasingly able to establish a direct export trade with Europe, leading to a decrease in Singapore's imports of about 27 per cent.[10] This trend was mainly due to growing business activities among European traders in Saigon[11] (Fig. 4.2).

Immediately after the French navy's invasion of southern Vietnam and seizure of Saigon in 1858, British trading companies based in Hong Kong became the first to establish branches in Saigon, such as

[8] Jenkins (1973, 298–299), Walser (1992, 1) and Halpern (2001, 36–37).

[9] Fichter (2012, 183–184).

[10] Saigon's main imports included textiles (cotton, calicoes and silks), flour, wheat, tobacco and opium; the port's exports were mainly rubber, maize, fish products, pepper, cane sugar, fruits and skins. Wong (1960, 157–158), Fourniau (2002, 114), Goscha (2017, 74–76) and Vo (2011, 82–84).

[11] For overviews of European trading in French Indochina in the nineteenth and early twentieth century, see Vorapheth (2004) and Morlat (2016).

Fig. 4.2 The port of Saigon on the Saigon River (Sông Sài Gòn), c. 1890 (Courtesy of Eduard Leopold, Coburg)

Wm. G. [William Garner] Hale & Company (1858), Jardine, Matheson & Company (1859), Dent & Company (1860), and Butterfield & Swire (1865). This signalled the French navy's strong dependence on British coal supplies and other provisions. Since the coal needed for fuelling steamships was of good quality and at low prices only available in Cardiff, Wales, France depended on British supplies to provide her warships operating in Asia with coal. British competition also hampered French shipowners and traders based in Bordeaux who were charged with supplying provisions to French troops and opening up new commercial opportunities in East Asia. In spring 1861, dissatisfaction with the situation prompted the Bordeaux and Marseille Chambers of Commerce to jointly submit a complaint to Minister Chasseloup-Laubat requesting equitable treatment from the French government in supplying the French navy.[12]

Since the eighteenth century, Bordeaux had developed into the most important French "colonial port", with strong commercial links to the Caribbean. After the Napoleonic Wars (1815), the local economy was based on numerous industries producing foodstuffs, much of it in cans, and on the building of sailing ships which triggered the establishment of thirteen foundries and forges. To satisfy the demand for fuel, Bordeaux became an important coal port and a major importer, which prompted the construction of railway lines connecting the somewhat remotely located riverine port city to the rest of France. During the French Second Empire and the early Third Republic, Bordeaux experienced the most dynamic foreign trade, with growth rates of 8.51 net tonnes (1850–1855), 4.84 net tonnes (1860–1865), 6.41 net tonnes (1865–1870), 4.38 net tonnes (1870–1875) and 9.37 net tonnes (1875–1880). After the seizure of Saigon, traders from Bordeaux became pioneers in establishing the first French companies in Cochinchina which were branches of shipping and/or trading companies based in Bordeaux, namely A. Eymond & Delphin Henry (1860), Chabert (1860), Édouard Renard & Company (1861), Denis Frères and Roque Frères (both founded in 1862); the only exception was the company of Émile Luro (1863) originating from Lyon, the second-largest French city.[13] A. [Alain] Eymond & Delphin Henry, since 1854 one of the major wholesale businesses of Bordeaux, came first, operating with self-owned and chartered vessels a regular shipping service from the French port city to Hong Kong and Shanghai. Thanks to its Bangkok branch, the firm was well acquainted with shipping and trading conditions in Asia and was one of the first enterprises to sail up the Saigon River. On 14 June 1861, A. Eymond & Delphin Henry announced the launch of the Ligne de Chine (China Line), a regular service every 45 days from Bordeaux to Singapore, Siam, Cochinchina and ports in China. The vessels not only carried British coal for French warships and military supplies for the French forces, but also cargoes of various goods to be delivered to

[12] Denis (1965, 74) and Morlat (2016, 412). On the dependency of the French navy on British infrastructures in Asia in the 1850–1860s, see (Fichter 2012, 183–203).

[13] Bonin and Marnot (2007, 3, 8–9), Vorapheth (2004, 43–48) and Bonin (2008, 247–252). For Denis Frères, see Bonin (1999, 109–112) and Boissarie (2010–2011, 116–126).

local Chinese shopkeepers. In Saigon, these Chinese traders operated as middlemen, reselling imported products to French soldiers and also to the local Vietnamese and Chinese. The initial expectations of A. Eymond & Delphin Henry that the ships would return to Bordeaux with Vietnamese commodities to be sold profitably on European markets proved premature when agricultural products were spoilt during long and dangerous voyages and other shipping companies appeared as strong competitors in the market. Facing the numerous difficulties hindering their businesses in Cochinchina, A. Eymond & Delphin Henry, which possessed the lion's share of French transport to East Asia, established a proper agency in Saigon in early 1862 and the year after, next to it, a shop selling Paris articles [fashion and jewellery] and provisions for ships. In 1862, the Saigon branch of A. Eymond & Delphin Henry was made agent of the French bank Comptoir d'escompte de Paris which since 1860 had expanded overseas, establishing branch offices in Shanghai and Calcutta (1860), the French colony of La Réunion (1861), Bombay and Hong Kong (1862).[14] In the same year, Messageries Impériales (later called Messageries Maritimes), the major French shipping company, established its service between Marseilles and East Asia, employing the steamer *L'Impératrice Eugénie* and other liners, and integrating Saigon into the transnational networks of Europe and East Asia.[15]

Almost simultaneously with British and French traders, German merchants established trading firms in Saigon. The first one was Gustav Behre from Altona (the major port city of the Duchy of Holstein, at the time formally a part of the Kingdom of Denmark, located next to Hamburg) and Wilhelm Kufeke from Hamburg who jointly founded Behre & Company (1860). Due to their contacts with several Hamburg shipping and trading firms or their respective branches in Singapore and Hong Kong, Behre & Co. took up wholesale trading which gave them a strong position among local exporters. On 13 March 1863, Behre passed away in Saigon, and the merchant Georg Niederberger (who was from the Grand Duchy of Baden) became a partner of Kufeke[16]; he was later joined

[14] In 1864, Eymond & Henry lost the agency when Comptoir d'escompte de Paris, focusing on financing intercontinental commercial transactions, established its own agency in Saigon. Denis (1965, 77–79, 81–91, 98, 367–368), Meuleau (1990, 29), Brötel (1996, 234), Brocheux and Hèmery (2009, 23) and Bonin (2020, 54–55).

[15] Berneron-Couvenhes (2000, 291–292).

[16] Georg Niederberger was from Freiburg (a major town in the south-western part of the Grand Duchy of Baden). In 1839, he became an apprentice in a Paris trade firm,

by Emil Saltzkorn. When Niederberger permanently left Saigon in 1873, Saltzkorn took over the sole management of the firm. In 1875, Saltzkorn made August Bauermeister his associate and remained in Saigon until 1882; the Cholon branch of the firm was managed by Bruno Röver. For unknown reasons, Bauermeister liquidated Behre & Co. in the autumn of 1884 to become associate and manager of the new Haiphong branch of Speidel & Company.[17]

The other pioneering German firm (founded in Saigon in 1861) was Kaltenbach, Engler & Company. Its owners, Gustav Kaltenbach and Friedrich Engler, were relatives and came from Laufen (a village located in the most south-western part of the Grand Duchy of Baden, near the French and Swiss borders). In 1848, Gustav Kaltenbach began an apprenticeship in Paris and in the 1850s went to Singapore to set up a shop selling bookbinding articles. When Friedrich Engler came to the British colony, he was made partner, with the shop being extended to general retail trading. With France's acquisition of Cochinchina, the partners, hoping for fresh business opportunities, opened the Saigon branch, soon expanding into wholesale trade including, from 1864, supplying provisions to the French colonial government. While Kaltenbach was managing his firm in Singapore, Engler made Johann Mettler (a Swiss national from Zug, Switzerland) his partner of the Saigon branch (which, in 1867, traded under the name of Kaltenbach, Engler & Mettler). In November 1866, the firm had won the call for tender for supplying provisions to the French naval station of Saigon for a period of two years, thanks to the discount of twenty per cent the firm had granted. In 1869, the company traded under the name Kaltenbach, Engler & Speidel, making it evident that instead of Mettler, Karl Theodor Speidel was partner. When this partnership was terminated at an unknown date, Friedrich Engler made his

acquiring professional skills and knowledge of the French language. When Kufeke retired to Hamburg in late 1865, Niederberger became sole owner and manager of Behre & Company. GSTA, III. HA, II, 729: Ambassador Count von Bernstorff (London) to the Foreign Ministry (Berlin), 6 December 1865; Minister-Resident von Redlich (Hamburg) to the Foreign Ministry (Berlin), 12 December 1865. Denis (1965, 334).

[17]BAB, R 901-12817: Consul Bauermeister (Saigon) to Foreign Ministry (Berlin), 29 February 1884. According to information of Karl Theodor Speidel, in 1887, there were two German firms in Saigon, while "the third and little important one" was "in liquidation" — a clear hint that legal issues took time before Behre & Co. was finally abolished. BAB, R 901-9501: Consul Karl Theodor Speidel (Saigon) to Chancellor von Bismarck (Berlin), 15 July 1887.

son Eduard an associate and continued to trade in Saigon, with the firm's headquarter established in Frankfurt am Main.[18]

French trading firms in Saigon also hired German merchants. When Hilaire and Octavien Lafon, the Saigon managers of A. Eymond & Delphin Henry, decided to leave the firm at the end of 1865, the French company made as new partners the Prussian nationals Hugo Räuber (from Hamburg) and Johannes Schwanbeck (from Stettin, the major Pomeranian port city at the Oder River near the Baltic Sea coast).[19] Räuber's previous experience with consular matters gained in Mexico gave him sufficient motivation to approach, in August 1865, the ministry of foreign affairs in Berlin to apply for the (not yet existing) post as honorary Prussian consul for Cochinchina.[20] This caused ministry officials to seek information from Prussian consuls posted in Hamburg, Bremen and Bordeaux about A. Eymond & Delphin Henry, and additionally on German companies trading in Cochinchina. According to Emil Baron von Richthofen, Prussian minister-resident in Hamburg, A. Eymond & Delphin Henry ran risky businesses and were therefore morally dubious. Julius Michaelsen, Prussian merchant-consul in Bordeaux, reported that local business circles were divided in their opinion about the firm's honesty and respectability, pointing to the fact that the owners, with their very important shipping business, were probably not rich enough to engage in such voluminous business affairs. Based on this information, the Prussian Trade Minister, Heinrich Count von Itzenplitz, in his November 1865 report to Bismarck, repudiated Räuber's application, pointing to the

[18] In 1863, Kaltenbach returned to Paris where the year after he married a Swiss national (born in Appenzell, Switzerland, and raised in the French capital). After another term of three years in Singapore, he returned to Paris from where he managed his companies in East Asia, until he passed away in Geneva, Switzerland, in 1913. GSTA, III. HA, II, 729: Consul-General von Redlich (Hamburg) to Minister-President von Bismarck (Berlin), 12 and 23 December 1865; PAAA, R 251848: Friedrich Engler and Gustav Kaltenbach (Freiburg) to the Baden Foreign Ministry, 10 June 1871. Denis (1965, 91–92, 335 and 342) and Vorapheth (2004, 46: Table 2).

[19] GSTA, III. HA, II, 729: Announcement of A. Eymond & Delphin Henry, Ligne de Chine (Bordeaux-Saigon), 15 June 1865.

[20] Hugo Räuber (born in 1830 in Marienwerder, Western Prussia), was an apprentice in Stettin and later joined wholesale trading companies in Hamburg, Bordeaux and in Tampico (Mexico). In the latter place, he assisted his employer who served as Prussian consul in practically managing routine consular matters. GSTA, III. HA, II, 729: Hugo Räuber (Hamburg) to Director von Philipsborn, Foreign Ministry (Berlin), 23 August 1865.

fact that there were apparently a number of German merchants in Saigon who possessed longer experience of local conditions combined with sufficient personal qualifications and a respected business position. He stressed that German business communities contacted by the consuls had "generally urgently" expressed the wish to establish a Prussian consulate in Cochinchina, and so further enquiries about German merchants in Saigon were needed.[21]

Initially, Kaltenbach, Engler & Co. attracted the attention of Prussia's ministry of trade, but finally Behre & Co. received the strongest backing from German business circles. Although Albrecht Count von Bernstorff, Prussia's ambassador in London, described commercial ties between Cochinchina and Europe as "until now, negligible", he nevertheless recommended Behre & Co. for the post, describing the firm as "the most important and most respectable" German trading house in Saigon. He was joined by Wilhelm Redlich, Prussian consul-general in Hamburg, who said the firm was considered prosperous and provided very reliable and efficient services. According to Redlich, Wilhelm Kufeke (whom he had recently met in person) enjoyed "a very respectable reputation" in Hamburg, which gave him sufficient reason to conclude that Georg Niederberger too had a respectable character. The meeting with the consul-general seemed to have provided strong motivation to Kufeke to directly approach the Prussian government, warmly recommending his business partner for the post in Saigon. This advocacy paved the way to the appointment of Niederberger. After Paris had agreed, Minister-President Otto von Bismarck proposed Niederberger to King William I. The formal letter stressed the importance of the country's trading and shipping connections which "would make desirable the establishment of a Prussian consulate in the French colony Saigon (Cochinchina)". On 1 January 1867, Niederberger assumed office as Prussian consul.[22]

[21] GSTA, III. HA, II, 729: Minister-Resident Baron von Richthofen (Hamburg), 12 September 1865, and Consul Michaelsen (Bordeaux), 23 September 1865, to Foreign Ministry (Berlin); Minister Count von Itzenplitz (Berlin) to Minister-President von Bismarck (Berlin), 20 November 1865.

[22] On 29 August 1865, King William I issued the appointment of Niederberger to Prussian consul for Cochinchina. The French foreign ministry's exequatur was sent through the Naval Ministry to Governor de La Grandière who on 28 November 1865 provided Niederberger with this French authorisation. GSTA, III. HA, II, 729: Consul Delius (Bremen) to the Foreign Ministry (Berlin), 30 November and 2 December 1865; Ambassador Count von Bernstorff (London) to the Foreign Ministry (Berlin), 6 December

Prussian Reports on Cochinchina

In June 1866, without notifying the Vietnamese government, Governor Pierre-Paul de La Grandière ordered French navy troops to annex three more provinces in southern Vietnam (Vinh Long, Chau Doc and Ha Tien) in the western part of the Mekong Delta.[23] This new phase of France's naval expansion attracted attention in Hong Kong. On 22 November 1866, *The China Mail* published a highly critical article about Saigon's economic and social conditions. The author, an anonymous "Gentleman" who seemed to have recently paid a visit to the riverine port city, described it as "an uncommonly hot and not over healthy place" in which fever, dysentery, liver complaints and sunstroke occurred on a regular basis. According to him, the Vietnamese were "lazy and indolent to excess", while the Chinese forming the largest local group were "active and intelligent" and "the go-betweens in transactions of natives [Vietnamese] and Europeans", having "by degrees monopolised as it were the entire commerce of Cochinchina". Therefore, the writer stated, the Chinese had "to a certain extent, the advantage over Europeans" who, "hampered by heavier expenses and not acquainted with the language, meet with more obstacles in their endeavours to acquire an independence". Looking to merchants and traders, he found that the different nationalities were "unfortunately a preventive to any nearer approach" so that sociability was scarcely present in Saigon. Concerning the countryside around the city, the article expressed some hope for the future when describing it as "fertile and rich in every respect" so that "with the requisite capital (…), trade would be properly developed".[24]

This highly critical article may have prompted the Prussian Consul to Japan, Max von Brandt, to pay a personal visit to Saigon only a few months later. The diplomat was commonly regarded as an expert

1865; Consul-General Redlich (Hamburg) to the Foreign Ministry (Berlin), 12 December 1865; Wilhelm Kufeke (Hamburg) to the Foreign Ministry (Berlin), 18 December 1865; Director von Philipsborn, Foreign Ministry (Berlin), to Prussian Envoy Baron von der Goltz (Paris), 12 January 1866 and 31 March 1866; Director von Philipsborn (Berlin) to Minister-President von Bismarck, 21 August 1866; Bismarck (Berlin) to King William I, 27 August 1866; Appointment Certificate for Georg Niederberger, 29 August 1866; Envoy Baron von der Goltz (Paris) to the Foreign Ministry (Berlin), 5 October 1866; Georg Niederberger (Saigon) to the Foreign Ministry (Berlin), 15 January 1867.

[23] Brocheux and Hèmery (2009, 26–27), Corfield (2009, 20–21) and Goscha (2017, 60).

[24] *The China Mail*, 22 November 1866.

for East Asia after joining the Eulenburg expedition in 1860/61, and consequently as a result of the treaty with Japan, being appointed the first Prussian consul in Tokyo. According to his memoirs published in 1901, Brandt was convinced that the further development of Prussia's trade and shipping in East Asia required a naval base. In the autumn of 1866, he met King William I and Crown Prince Frederick William (the later Emperor Frederick III) to discuss related projects such as annexing the island of Formosa for this purpose. For several reasons, Brandt firmly rejected this plan and made his viewpoint clear in January 1867 during a conversation with Prince Adalbert (a cousin of King William I), naval theorist and the supreme commander of the Prussian navy.[25] The following month, before returning to Asia, he tried in vain to meet Bismarck who was sick and not receiving visitors. Only in Marseille, before boarding the liner of Messageries Imperiales, did Brandt receive a personal letter in which Bismarck wished him the best in expanding "the field of our national interests in the Far East".[26]

After arriving in Hong Kong, Brandt used the wait for the connecting steamer to Japan to visit Saigon in March 1867. In his subsequent report, the diplomat was entirely silent about Consul Niederberger who had assumed office some weeks earlier (but was probably absent from Saigon at the time). Brandt, who was fluent in French, described the situation of Cochinchina as "far from appearing satisfactory" because most sums were spent on the 10,000 troops and the crews of 25 gunboats and six men-of-war, barely half of whom were fit for service due to fever, dysentery, liver disease and cholera. Furthermore, after visiting Saigon's main military hospital, where he observed that one hundred beds had been prepared for the wounded, he pointed to the fact that continuous skirmishing with the Vietnamese and Cambodians had cost the lives of many French soldiers. Commenting on Saigon's economic situation, Brandt stressed that import trade from Singapore was entirely in the hands of local Chinese, and export trade — rice, dried fish and silk — was "almost exclusively done by two German companies employing a larger number of German vessels". He found very few other European settlers, mostly low-class Frenchmen, as he called them, but more Chinese emigrating

[25] Brandt (1901, vol. 2, 138, 140–146).

[26] Brandt (1901, vol. 2, the quote: 138–139, in Bismarck to Brandt, 12 February 1867).

in large numbers to Vietnam each year and the only ones doing good business. According to Brandt, this fact made it impossible to settle Europeans in Cochinchina, and thereby bring considerable financial means to the colony.[27] His report submitted to Berlin was probably the earliest and most up-to-date account of Saigon and Cochinchina which Bismarck received, providing him with first-hand information on the French colony.

Meanwhile, Consul Niederberger had more positive impressions of Cochinchina. The first annual report submitted by the Saigon consulate for the years 1866–1867 was published in *Preußisches Handels-Archiv*, the official weekly of Prussia's trade ministry. After surveying the colony's acquisition by force, and its geographical features, the consul provided detailed information on shipping — German flags came third after the French and British in 1866 — trading and currency conditions, concluding that most trades were in the hands of Chinese, making it difficult for the few European companies to compete against them. Employing Chinese as middlemen (compradors), European merchants had hardly any contact with the Vietnamese, Niederberger admitted. Looking to the future, the consul was optimistic that rice from Cochinchina, which in 1867 was for the first time shipped directly to Europe, would further contribute to Saigon's economic upturn.[28] In the same year, Niederberger was appointed honorary North German Consul in Saigon after the establishment of the North German Confederation, "the extended arm of Prussia", as Christopher Clark put it.[29] Shortly after, he went on leave to Europe, charging his associate in Behre &

[27] BAB, R 901-12806: Max von Brandt (Hong Kong) to Bismarck (Berlin), 3 April 1867. In his memoirs published in 1901, Brandt wrote about French Indochina several times, without ever coming back to his extremely negative report on Saigon of March 1867.

[28] Niederberger's report, of 30 September 1867, in *Preußisches Handels-Archiv* (1868, February, no. 8, 243–245).

[29] Clark (2007, the quote: 546). In the wake of the Prussian-Austrian War of 1866, the Norddeutscher Bund (North German Confederation) was established, consisting of Prussia and smaller North German states; its constitution became effective on 1 July 1867 and Bismarck resumed office as Federal Chancellor of the Confederation. These changes required to accordingly amend Prussia's consular service. PAAA, R 251848: Appointment of Georg Niederberger to Consul of the North German Confederation in Saigon (Berlin), 15 April 1868, Oath of Office of Georg Niederberger (Saigon), 27 June 1868, Consul Niederberger (Saigon) to Bismarck (Berlin), 27 July 1868. GSTA, III. HA, II, 729: Rudolf von Delbrück (Berlin) to Bismarck (Berlin), 8 September 1868. Denis (1965, 334).

Co., Carl Wilhelm Adolf Grandhomme, with the consulate.[30] In January 1869, Grandhomme submitted the second annual report of the Saigon consulate to Prussia's trade ministry. The rather brief article pointed to the smaller rice harvest in 1868 resulting in less business, but nevertheless highlighted increasing rice exports to the French colonies of Mauritius and Bourbon. With respect to shipping, the German flag again held third place in the port of Saigon. Both exports and imports were developing satisfactorily, resulting in lower expenditure on her colony. Based on these findings, Grandhomme judged Cochinchina's situation as "generally favourable". In May 1869, the report was published in *Preußisches Handels-Archiv*.[31]

German Merchants in Local Politics

On 8 May 1867, Governor La Grandière appointed naval doctor Louis Turc, third-class inspector of Indigenous Matters in the colonial government, to the post of commissaire municipal (municipal commissioner) of Saigon. The municipal commission, the earliest political body in the town elected by universal suffrage, was formally established on 17/18 June 1867 in an extraordinary session attended by the commissioner (also called president), twelve municipal councillors and six administrative salaried staff.[32] In July 1867, following an important diplomatic success, the French protectorate over Cambodia was established, with three Khmer provinces (Battambang, Sisophon and Siem Reap) being handed over to Siam as compensation. The temporary halt to France's naval expansion in Indochina provided a breathing space to further develop urban structures in Saigon.[33] The local assembly reconvened on 19 November 1867, with nine councillors being present, mostly

[30] Carl Wilhelm Adolf Grandhomme (born in 1838 in Usingen, a small town in the Duchy of Nassau, located in today's Hesse) was an apprentice in trading houses in Rotterdam, Antwerpen, Hamburg, Paris and London before becoming partner in Behre & Co. in Saigon. PAAA, R 251848: Consul Niederberger (Saigon) to Bismarck (Berlin), 27 July 1868, Carl Wilhelm Adolf Grandhomme (Saigon) to Bismarck (Berlin), 1 March 1869.

[31] PAAA, R 251848: Annual Report of the Consulate of the North German Confederation in Saigon for 1868, January 1869. Published in *Preußisches Handels-Archiv* (1869, May, 520–521).

[32] Baudrit (1936, vol. 2, 7, 60), Fourniau (2002, 205–209) and Vo (2011, 77).

[33] For the development of Saigon as French colonial city, see Barrelon (1999, 1–29), Guillaume (1985, 181–192), Fourniau (2002, 208–209) and Vo (2011, 75–87).

French military personnel, but also including the French trader Étienne Denis, of the firm Denis Frères (Denis Brothers), and the German merchants Friedrich Engler and Georg Niederberger. The participation of the latter two signalled the important positions of Kaltenbach, Engler & Co., and of Behre & Co. in the French colony. Despite the fact that Niederberger had been Prussian honorary consul for more than ten months, Governor La Grandière obviously had no reservations at all in appointing him to Saigon's municipal commission. In this session, the reorganisation of the local police force, composed of fourteen Europeans and some Asian officers, was discussed, its numbers being regarded as insufficient for safeguarding security in a town inhabited by people of different ethnicities.[34] Discussing politically sensitive issues within the commission, which was partly composed of German members, signalled the high degree of trust the French governor had in them. It represented a certain form of "participatory colonialism" which was in some way comparable, though on a much more limited scale, to the participation of German businessmen in British businesses and economic organisations in Hong Kong.[35] In French Cochinchina, German merchants became members of the Saigon Chamber of Commerce (established in 1867) and, as mentioned earlier, were invited to join the municipal commission as councillors (since 1869 called municipal council). In 1870, at the outbreak of the Franco-German War, the manager of the bank Comptoir d'escompte de Paris was C. Fritsch, a Prussian citizen. This shows that Germans were actively involved, for about three years (until the Franco-German War), in participating in important public institutions of the French colony and operating the agency of the most important French bank, thereby contributing to the city's early economic and urban development.

Constructing Saigon's basic infrastructure was on the agenda of the local assembly in these early years. During the commission session of 17 August 1867, some councillors raised concerns about the Great Canal shortly before the start of the dry season, when the Canal would become impassable by boat. After the commission had unanimously voted to urgently transfer the question to the president, Louis Turc promised to quickly find a solution. With no obvious answer available, the councillors Friedrich Engler and Salnave (probably a French merchant) informed

[34] Baudrit (1936, vol. 2, 70–84: Session of 19 November 1867, with names of councillors and voting results: 84).

[35] About "participatory colonialism" of German merchants in Hong Kong, see Becker (2004, 100–101).

the commission on 18 February 1868 about the great inconvenience encountered by residents required to extend their journeys by several hundred meters in order to pass the Canal. Their joint proposal to ask the local administration to very quickly build a footbridge for pedestrians was unanimously supported by the commission.[36] On 13 April 1868, the commission reconvened to discuss the governor's urgent request to install a ferry connection between the town and the small island in the river on which the liners of Messageries Impériales disembarked passengers and cargoes, and floating landing stages used by other vessels to discharge carriages and animals. Present were Turc and seven councillors, among them Engler and Niederberger. Discussing the question, French and German merchants were unanimously of the opinion that a ferry would be insufficient to establish commercial flows between the two points; instead, they called for the construction of a bridge to the island. To meet the governor halfway, the commission finally decided, six votes to three, that a ferry should be operated while awaiting the construction of a bridge.[37] In the session of 10 June 1868, Major Bouvet, engineer and army officer, announced that the networks of pipes in Saigon were under construction but criticised the fact there was no levelling plan for the whole town. By seven votes to one, the commission decided to urgently request such a plan from the administration (however, it was not until 1871 that such plans were provided for further discussion).[38] The production of clean drinking water, an urgent issue for Saigon, was raised in the session of 20 November 1868. In view of the insufficient quality of the water at some times of the year, Engler demanded that the colonial administration should take care of this matter as soon as possible. The following month, the commission reserved the sum of 10,000 francs to study the question of drinking water, which was mainly responsible for the bad reputation of heath conditions in Cochinchina and Saigon.[39]

In the summer of 1869, the municipal commission of Saigon was reorganised. The president changed his title to "mayor" and the body its name to "municipal council", with one half of members appointed by the

[36] Baudrit (1936, vol. 2, 89–90: Sessions of 17 August 1867 and 18 February 1868).

[37] Baudrit (1936, vol. 2, 107–109: Session of 13 April 1868).

[38] Baudrit (1936, vol. 2, 218–219: Sessions of 10 June 1868 and 27 March 1871).

[39] Baudrit (1936, vol. 1, 79: Sessions of 20 November 1868 and 14 December 1869) and Vo (2011, 78).

governor, without the distinction of class and nationality, and the other half nominated by universal suffrage; the term of office was limited to two years. As the first Vietnamese councillor, the scholar Petrus Truong Vin Ky was directly appointed by Acting Governor Gustave Ohier. The reform also gave the governor the right to exercise his power of veto regarding the council's decisions. Further amendments restricting the council's authority were introduced by the imperial decree of 21 August 1869, providing extra powers to the governor, abolishing regular sessions of the council and forbidding it to spontaneously make resolutions.[40] These measures were aimed at transforming the council into a purely consultative body of the colonial government of Cochinchina. Therefore, a councillor (whose name was not recorded in the registers) who had recently learned of the decree, used the session of 27 November 1869 to sharply criticise the planned reforms, calling them "incompatible with a council elected by universal suffrage".[41] However, any attempts undertaken in the following weeks to reach an understanding between the council and the governor remained unsuccessful. In the meantime, Niederberger, after staying for months at the French company Buisman & Company in Paris, had returned to Saigon. In February 1870, he submitted his resignation as councillor to Governor René de Cornulier-Lucinière, who had assumed office the month before. As Niederberger explained in his letter, his "numerous occupations neither allow me to regularly attend sessions of the Municipal Council nor to deal with details which the interest of the town demands". The German merchant possibly had political motives in relinquishing his post as a Saigon councillor, but there is no evidence for his motivation in the records consulted.[42] With the outbreak of the Franco-German War a few weeks later, the short phase of participatory colonialism by Germans in French Cochinchina came to an abrupt end.

[40] Fourniau (2002, 208) and Vo (2011, 77).

[41] Baudrit (1936, vol. 2, 9: Session of 10 June and 1 October 1869, and vol. 2, 9–11: Session of 27 November 1869).

[42] Niederberger had stayed in Paris from October 1868 to August 1869. On 19 May 1870 (some weeks before the outbreak of the Franco-German War), he sent a letter to the governor informing that the North German consulate's chancellery in Saigon had been officially opened on this day. PAAA, R 251848: Georg Niederberger (Paris) to Chancellor von Bismarck (Berlin), 21 October 1868 and 12 July 1869. ANOM, INDO-GGI-11659: Consul Niederberger (Saigon) to Governor de Cornulier-Lucinière (Saigon), 22 February 1870 and 19 May 1870.

The Franco-German War of 1870–1871

Saigon in the War

On 29 July 1870, initial news about the outbreak of the Franco-German War was made known in Singapore, the first East Asian port of call of steamships from Europe. Telegrams arrived on the French merchant steamer *La Sarthe*, sailing from Toulon, which had learned the fact at Galle, the southern port of British Ceylon. Information rapidly spread that French warships were instructed to intercept German commerce on all waters and privateer merchant vessels flying the North German flag. Ferdinand von der Heyde, honorary consul of the North German Confederation in Singapore, having received official instructions from Berlin to warn North German shipmasters of the risk of being captured by French warships operating in the region, decided to act immediately. Fearing that *La Sarthe* might be carrying telegraphic orders for the French governor in Saigon to seize North German merchant ships in the port, Heyde dispatched a trustworthy messenger on a private steamer bound for China which dropped him off at the mouth of the Saigon River and proceeded on her voyage; from there, the agent continued his journey upriver by boat, arriving in Saigon on 3 August 1870. Having accomplished his secret mission, he returned to Singapore by the homeward French mail steamer.[43] Thanks to the consul's independent action (which was later made known to the governor of Cochinchina) German merchants and shipmasters in Saigon knew about the outbreak of the war two days before local French residents.[44]

On 5 August 1870, the Franco-German War became generally known in Saigon when *La Sarthe* called at the port, with telegrams from Galle, Ceylon. The same day, Governor de Cornulier-Lucinière formally notified Niederberger and instructed him to haul down the flag of the North German Confederation. However, being well aware of the importance of the German merchants, the governor made it clear that German nationals residing in Cochinchina would be allowed to peacefully continue their businesses as long as they did not commit any hostile act. He also let it be known that he would grant North German vessels currently in Saigon a certain grace period to leave port unharmed. Reacting quickly, Niederberger informed the colonial government that several North German

[43] *Straits Times Overland Journal* (Singapore), 12 August 1870.

[44] Bouault (1929, 601: Letter of Governor de Cornulier-Lucinière [Saigon] to the Colonial Minister [Paris], 30 August 1870).

ships chartered with cargoes for Saigon were expected to call at the port in the coming days, and that, after discharging and loading new freight, they were bound to return to China. Because these vessels had left ports on the China coast before being informed of the state of war, the consul asked for them to be allowed to call at Saigon for discharging and loading; he also requested passports to protect them against seizure so that they would be able to reach their final destination safely.[45] The following day, the governor issued a proclamation stating that North German vessels then in the port would be allowed fifteen days to leave, and that all vessels then on their way to the port, not being aware of the war, would be allowed the same grace. Furthermore, on leaving, they were to be provided with a letter of "safe conduct", valid for six days from Cape Saint Jacques (Vung Tau) near the mouth of the Saigon River. Therefore, French men-of-war were to be instructed not to follow any of them with a view to capturing them at the expiration of the period.[46] Because *La Sarthe,* after leaving Saigon on the evening of 6 August 1870, had called at the port of Hong Kong bringing official instructions to North German honorary consul Theodor Eimbcke to warn masters of North German ships of their risk,[47] the governor's announcement meant that North German vessels which had left Hong Kong before 6 August were considered not to have received the advice about the war, and were allowed time for departure, and on leaving received the "safe conduct" passport, available for six days.[48] In the next two days, Niederberger, now a private citizen, was busy requesting these documents for four vessels under the North German flag; for two of them, he recorded some details: *G. C. Lorenz Meyer,* owned by the Saigon merchant August Behn, and *Pyrmont*, of the Laeisz Shipping Company (Reederei F. Laeisz in Hamburg), both loaded to Hong Kong with rice.[49]

[45] ANOM, INDO-GGI-11647: Consul Niederberger (Saigon) to Director of the Interior (Saigon), 6 and 7 August 1870.

[46] *The North-China Herald and Supreme Court & Consular Gazette* (Shanghai), 25 August 1870; *Hong Kong Daily Press*, 1 September 1870 (both newspapers reprinted in French the proclamation of 6 August 1870); *The Straits Times* (Singapore), 27 August 1870;

[47] *Hong Kong Daily Press*, 6 August 1870.

[48] *Hong Kong Daily Press*, 1 September 1870.

[49] ANOM, INDO-GGI-11647: Consul Niederberger (Saigon) to Director of the Interior (Saigon), 7 and 8 August 1870.

Meanwhile, the first steps were taken to place Cochinchina in a proper state of defence against any probable assailants. "Saigon is heavily fortified because the French fear an uprising of the Annamite [Vietnamese]", reported Captain Heinrich Köhler, commander of the Prussian naval station. Besides the impressive number of both military and police forces stationed in Cochinchina, on 8 August 1870, by order of the director of Naval Construction, a volunteer company was recruited from dockyard workers and contracted for six months to provide further defence for the colony. Redoubts were thrown up on either bank of the river, and a frigate, mounting forty guns and manned by 500 men, was anchored in the stream, about midway between Cape Saint Jacques and the town.[50] With such careful preparations ongoing, on 15 August 1870, the fête of Emperor Napoleon Bonaparte (who was born on that day in 1769) was celebrated in Saigon in the usual manner: a review of the troops at half past six in the morning, followed by the celebration of a high mass in the cathedral and two salutes; in the afternoon, a regatta was held on the river and games played on shore; and in the evening, a grand ball and supper were given at Government House.[51]

In the second half of August 1870, at a distance of from 15 to 20 sea miles from Saigon, the French aviso gunboat *Ségond* captured the two North German vessels *Georg*, from Cardiff to Shanghai with coal, and *Turandot*, from Hamburg to Hong Kong and Shanghai with general cargo, expedited mainly by German firms. The masters and crews were taken on board the *Ségond*, French prize crews were put on the captured vessels and the chief officers retained on board to navigate them into Saigon. On arrival, the eighteen men were handed over free to the private charge of former North German consul Niederberger. After promising the colonial government that he would send the crews at his own expense on the first neutral steamer leaving Saigon, the sailors escaped the fate of

[50] BAB, R 901-86576: Captain Köhler (Yokohama) to the Navy Supreme Command (Berlin), 21 September 1870. In July 1870, French forces stationed in Cochinchina comprised of 30 navy infantry companies, one regular indigenous infantry company, two mounted artillery batteries, one gendarmerie squadron and one section of spahis (light cavalry regiment), one company of conductive gunners and 4,000 indigenous militiamen. The local naval station had three aviso (dispatch boats), 18 gunboats and ten steam dinghies. Bouault (1929, 601–602: *Annual Report to the Colonial Minister*). *The North-China Herald and Supreme Court & Consular Gazette*, 25 August 1870.

[51] *Hong Kong Daily Press*, 1 September 1870.

being treated as prisoners-of-war, with some even remaining on board their ships.[52]

The rather relaxed atmosphere in Saigon changed when in early September 1870 news arrived from Paris about the extreme rigour with which French citizens in Germany were being treated, while at the time Germans in France were not being molested or restricted, an irritating fact that, on 25 July, was complained about in the French council of ministers. As punitive reaction to the expulsion of French officials from Prussia, Emperor Napoleon III decided that during the war North German consuls should immediately cease their duties on French territory, and that instead US consuls should be charged with representing the interests of German citizens who were allowed to remain in French colonies. Consequently, on 28 July, Naval and Colonial minister Charles Rigault de Genouilly (the former governor of Cochinchina) notified the colonial government to execute the imperial order in the French colony accordingly.[53] When the official despatch arrived in Saigon, the governor, on 6 September 1870, decreed that in future Friedrich Wilhelm Speidel, the consular agent of the United States in Saigon, should be charged with representing the interests of Prussian residents in Cochinchina.[54]

On 17 June 1870, James Grey Jewell, the American consul in Singapore in 1870/71, had appointed Friedrich Wilhelm Speidel (a citizen of the Kingdom of Württemberg) to be a consular agent of the United States in Cochinchina. In this capacity, Speidel was, on 6 September, formally charged by the governor to represent the interests of Prussian residents. Despite the fact that Speidel was not from Prussia but from another German state, he was nevertheless a German national whose home country was at the time allied with Prussia in her war with France. When assuming his new duties, Speidel informed the governor that he would "willingly accept the position as interim consul", although he was

[52] *The Straits Times* (Singapore), 3, 10, and 24 September 1870. PAAA, R 251848: Consul Niederberger (Saigon) to Chancellor von Bismarck (Berlin), 13 September 1870.

[53] PAAA, R 251848: Minister Rigault de Genouilly (Paris) to Governor de Cornulier-Lucinière (Saigon), 28 July 1870; Consul Niederberger (Saigon) to Chancellor von Bismarck (Berlin), 13 September 1870. *Hong Kong Daily Press*, 5 September 1870.

[54] ANOM, INDO-GGI-11653: Consul Grey Jewell (Singapore) to Governor de Cornulier-Lucinière (Saigon), 17 June 1870; PAAA, R 251848: Decree of Governor de Cornulier-Lucinière (Saigon), 6 September 1870; Consul Niederberger (Saigon) to Chancellor von Bismarck (Berlin), 13 September 1870.

"by no means authorised by the American or the Prussian government". Speidel also took charge of sailors from the captured German vessels *Georg* and *Turandot*, sending them off on a French transport ship bound for Singapore. Carrying seven other Germans, as well as French invalids, *Creuse* called at the British colony on 18 September. On their arrival, the Germans were transferred to Consul von der Heyde.[55]

At the same time, breaking news about the war became known in Saigon. On 17 September 1870, the Singapore-based journal *The Straits Times* published telegrams from Paris and London, dated 4 September, reporting the capitulation of the French army in the battle of Sedan, the capture of Emperor Napoleon III by Prussian forces and the declaration of the fall of the empire by Jules Favre in France's legislative body. That these events were known in Saigon only a few days later is made evident by the fact that, on 22 September, in the town's municipal council, an unnamed councillor was pointing to "a liberal breeze shaking our homeland" and consequently suggesting a fresh approach towards the governor to safeguard the rights of the council. When this initiative also failed, on 14 October the councillors Jules Blancsubé and Émile Luro resigned from their offices, leading to the resignation of all remaining members. In the following month, a new municipal council was appointed by the governor.[56]

With the regular Messageries Impériales liner calling at Saigon on 25 September, the latest news from Europe was confirmed by telegrams, dated 5 September, reporting the announcement of the French Republic, the general refusal of any idea of the cession of French territory and Empress Eugenie's presence in Hastings in England, after fleeing from Paris.[57] Such information had hardly an effect on the Vietnamese inhabitants of Saigon, who, according to the governor, remained "calm and

[55] ANOM, INDO-GGI-11647: Consul Speidel (Saigon) to Governor de Cornulier-Lucinière (Saigon), 8 September 1870. *The Straits Times* (Singapore), 24 September 1870.

[56] *The Straits Times* (Singapore), 17 September 1870. Baudrit (1936, vol. 2, 12–14: Session of 22 September 1869, and 14: Session of 14 October 1869, and 14–15: Sessions of 14 October 1870 and of 9 November 1870); Vo (2011, 77).

[57] *Hong Kong Daily Press*, 1 October 1870. Bouault (1929, 605–606) and Meyer (1999, 78).

seemed little preoccupied with events in France, at least the ones living in the town [of Saigon] and the main centres".[58] The situation remained peaceful for several weeks, even after the governor on 20 October received official confirmation from Paris about the change of government; the next day, his immediate reaction was to remove portraits of Napoleon III and to announce the Republic before the troops and the citizens of Saigon.[59] Five days later, the governor informed the Vietnamese Emperor Tu Duc of the events, pointing to "the unfortunate results of the start of the war with Prussia" and explaining France's military defeats with the fact that "the intelligence of Emperor Napoleon had decreased before the years of age".[60] Tu Duc's reply demanding the return of the six lost provinces to Vietnam for the promise of continuing good relations with France was regarded as arrogant by Governor de Cornulier-Lucinière. It also raised concerns derived from rumours that the emperor was planning to conspire with Germans in the region to send against Cochinchina a Vietnamese army assisted by 1,200 - 1,500 German troops. As evidence, the governor, in his letter to Paris, pointed to reports that the Vietnamese government had purchased ammunition and weapons in Hong Kong, and was sending secret emissaries around Cochinchina calling for uprisings against the French. Such rumours were enhanced by the earlier arrest of the Prussian Müller, for many years an assistant in a French trading company in Saigon, who had made a recreation trip through Cochinchina. When he was seen with a map of the region, local police suspected him of being a spy. On 26 October 1870, Müller was arrested and imprisoned in the citadel of Bien Hoa; he was released only on 25 March 1871 when it officially became known in Saigon that France had agreed to peace terms at Versailles.[61]

[58] Bouault (1929, 606: Letter of Governor de Cornulier-Lucinière [Saigon] to Navy and Colonial Minister [Paris], 28 September 1870).

[59] Meyer (1996, 52–53). In the session of 9 November 1870, Saigon's municipal council also decided to change some streets' names. Baudrit (1936, vol. 2, 15: Session of 9 November 1870).

[60] Bouault (1929, 605–606: Governor de Cornulier-Lucinière [Saigon] to the Vietnamese Government [Hue], 25 October 1870). Meyer (1999, 81).

[61] Bouault (1929, 604–605: Governor de Cornulier-Lucinière [Saigon] to Navy and Colonial Minister [Paris], 9 November 1870). Meyer (1999, 82). BAB, R 901-86576: Consul von der Heyde (Singapore) to Chancellor von Bismarck (Berlin), 7 November 1870.

Actual events, as well as rumours, provided sufficient motivation for the governor to inform German merchants in early November 1870 that he was no longer able to protect them, and strongly recommending that they leave Cochinchina. Soon after, Consul von der Heyde reported from Singapore that some Germans had already arrived in the British port, with the remaining ones daily expecting they would all be expelled. On 4 November 1870, the Saigon Electors' Committee, exclusively composed of French nationals, having discussed the current situation, decided by a majority of votes (with only one dissenting vote) to request the governor to order "the immediate expulsion of all German citizens whose governments are at war with France". According to Niederberger's later report, it was the leading German merchants in Saigon who especially caused the "jealousy of French trading firms", prompting the leaders of the French pro-republican party "to suggest to the government the outrageous regulation". Consequently, on 8 November 1870, Governor de Cornulier-Lucinière gave official notice to all Germans residing in Cochinchina that they had to leave the colony within seven days. This decision triggered a protest campaign. The following day, American consular agent Friedrich Wilhelm Speidel reminded the governor of his status when he submitted a support letter issued by United States consul Jewell in Singapore in which Jewell expressed his hope that there would be no reason to apply the expulsion decree to Speidel; the support letter was obviously prepared in advance as an immediate response to such an event. The other sharp protest came from the British firm Wm. G. Hale & Company which submitted two strong pleas to allow their Saigon representative, C. Saltzkorn, from Hamburg, to remain there in the interests of the company. Protests reached their climax when, on 11 November 1870, Speidel submitted to the governor the joint protest petition of fourteen German residents who had personally appeared in his office to put down the following statement: "We protest against our expulsion from Saigon by decree of the French government dated 8 November, and we further protest each one individually, and for all therein concerned, against all losses, damages, disadvantages of whatever kind and nature which have arisen and will still arise for us by this expulsion". In his accompanying letter, Speidel made it clear that he, in his capacity as American consular agent charged with German interests, had to join, and would join, this protest "since indeed no act justifies this measure against the citizens of the belligerent states residing in Cochinchina".[62]

The protest campaign was strengthened by other individual protest notes, including the one from ex-consul Niederberger, but it was all in vain. On 15 November 1870, most of the remaining German nationals left Saigon on board vessels bound for Singapore and Hong Kong. As Niederberger reported, two or three of the German trading firms with only German staff were "especially badly affected after being forced to entirely close down their businesses, while the majority of expellees consisted of assistants able to again fill their posts once permitted to return to Saigon". While for those expellees heading to Singapore, the voyage ended safely, with Consul von der Heyde having promised support and accommodation, the others — around nine merchants and assistants— were less lucky when the British steamer *United Service* sailing to Hong Kong suddenly had to return to Saigon due to bad weather and technical damage. While the vessel was permitted to complete repairs in the port, the Germans were not allowed to land after being informed by the governor that they would be treated as spies. Therefore, they had to stay on board for eight days before the *United Service* was able to resume her voyage to Hong Kong.[63]

Before the vessel finally departed from Saigon, extra controversy was sparked by the alleged misbehaviour of C. Fritsch, the Prussian manager of the bank Comptoir d'escompte de Paris. After the expulsion decree had been issued, Fritsch, in a personal meeting with Governor de Cornulier-Lucinière, had informed him of his earlier application for French citizenship, the official confirmation of which he was still awaiting; he

[62] BAB, R 901-86576: Consul von der Heyde (Singapore) to Chancellor von Bismarck (Berlin), 7 November 1870. PAAA, Peking II-261: Niederberger (Singapore) to Captain Köhler (Yokohama), 26 December 1870. ANOM, INDO-GGI-11647: Electors' Committee of Saigon to Governor de Cornulier-Lucinière (Saigon), 4 November 1870; Friedrich Wilhelm Speidel (Saigon) to Governor de Cornulier-Lucinière (Saigon), 9 and 11 November 1870 (the last letter includes the protest petition of 9 November 1870); Wm. G. Hale & Co. (Saigon) to Governor de Cornulier-Lucinière (Saigon), 9 and 10 November 1870. Bouault (1929, 603).

[63] ANOM, INDO-GGI-11647: Protest letters (Saigon, 9 November 1870) of B. D. Mehrens, Hermann Pohl, and Georg Niederberger and Wilhelm Kufeke (signed by his attorney Carl Wilhelm Adolf Grandhomme). BAB, R 901-86576: Consul von der Heyde (Singapore) to Chancellor von Bismarck (Berlin), 7 November 1870. PAAA, Peking II-261: Niederberger (Singapore) to Captain Köhler (Yokohama), 26 December 1870. *The Straits Times* (Singapore), 26 November and 10 December 1870.

also promised to completely abandon Prussian citizenship. Consequently, the governor granted Fritsch an extra month's stay in Cochinchina. However, when official confirmation of Fritsch's naturalisation did not arrive in due course, the governor ordered the bank manager to prepare for departure. The instruction led Fritsch to warn the governor of possible negative consequences, if the bank, "the only credit institution in Cochinchina", cease operations. Then, he added, "this trouble would be even greater when rice shipments begin, shipments which generally need the intervention of capital from the Comptoir". However, Governor de Cornulier-Lucinière kept to his line which prompted Fritsch, on the morning of 29 November 1870, to enter the bridge of the *United Service* to loudly read to the Germans the governor's reply and to ask them to inform the Hong Kong manager of Comptoir d'escompte de Paris about the matter. According to a local French resident observing the incident, Fritsch, after reading the letter, made a vile gesture and said "Voila". Then, the German merchant Grandhomme went up the bridge and read the letter " constantly laughing, which caused other Germans to look like joking around". This incident was quickly reported to A. Fangellies, the commander-in-chief of the French troops. The same day, Fritsch, in his reply, rejected the accusations stating that he being "too full of respect for the government of Cochinchina" was "incapable of such a disgrace". However, the explanation did not satisfy the governor, and Fritsch had to leave Saigon with the next French mail steamer bound for Hong Kong. He was sent away without even being permitted to make arrangements for the transfer of his business before his successor arrived.[64]

When he learned about the events in Saigon, Captain Köhler, the commander of the *Hertha* anchored at Yokohama, the site of the Prussian naval station in East Asia, sent a personal letter to Governor Cornulier-Lucinière referring to the expulsion "of German residents of the colony in masses". Pointing to "this imitation of mass expulsions of peaceful [German] citizens" from France, he made clear that Germany could leave

[64] ANOM, INDO-GGI-11647: C. Fritsch (Saigon) to Governor de Cornulier-Lucinière (Saigon), 23 November 1870; A. Fangellies, Commander-in-Chief (Saigon) to Governor de Cornulier-Lucinière (Saigon), 28 and 29 November 1870; statement of C. Fritsch (Saigon), 29 November 1870. *Hong Kong Daily Press*, 13 December 1870.

the judgement on this issue "to the civilised world"[65]— a direct reference to previous French accusations against the allegedly uncivilised behaviour of German troops in France.[66] After returning to Saigon, Consul Niederberger, in his first post-war report on the years 1870–1871, explained that, following the outbreak of the Franco-German War, local Germans residents had to suffer from "unpopularity and much hostility", which was increasing following the proclamation of the French Republic. He added that French citizens of Saigon, "partly for other reasons than patriotism", had demanded the Germans' expulsion.[67] Indeed, at the time, anti-German sentiment ran high in Saigon resulting, on 28 November 1870, in the municipal council's decision to grant voting rights exclusively to the French citizens of Saigon and also to permit only them to remain members of the Saigon Chamber of Commerce. This was a clear signal that the brief phase of participatory colonialism by Germans in Saigon had ended.[68]

War Aims and Peace Terms

On 15 July 1870, the French National Assembly backed the decision by Emperor Napoleon III's government to declare war on the North German Confederation. This provoked German national sentiment into turning against France, which was regarded as an aggressive and offensive power. It also inspired the debate on war aims or peace terms among the public of several German states. Patriotic fever and national enthusiasm spread among political groups and societal classes in all German states,

[65] ANOM, INDO-GGI-11647: Captain Köhler (Yokohama) to Governor de Cornulier-Lucinière (Saigon), 24 November 1870 (this letter is in German, with an attached translation into French; a copy of the German letter is in PAAA, Peking II-261).

[66] Such a judgement was provided by the *Hong Kong Daily Press* which was rather critical over the treatment of the Saigon Germans. On 13 December 1870, a few days after the arrival of several deported Germans on board *United Service* (9 December 1870), the journal pointed to the fact that "there were about 25 to 30 Germans and 2,000 French troops, so that no disturbance could be looked for; while, it might be imagined steps could easily be taken to intercept any information which it was considered undesirable to allow to go out of the Colony". The writer concluded that "the whole affair is very much to be regretted, as it hardly seems, on calm reflection, that there was any reason for so strong a measure".

[67] *Preußisches Handels-Archiv* (January 1873, 2, 34–41).

[68] Baudrit (1936, vol. 2, 16: Session of 28 November 1870).

and also among Germans abroad. In the south-western regions bordering France, directly affected by invasion of French troops in the initial phase of the war, press articles appeared hinting about the fact that France's easternmost provinces, Alsace and Lorraine, had historically been part of the German Empire. After the victories of the German armies in early August 1870, such voices, in a considerable number of brochures and numerous press articles of various different political sympathies, and mostly published in southern Germany and the Rhineland, became increasingly popular, demanding the "reclamation" of these territories and "secure borders" for the future. On 7 August, Bismarck, chancellor of the North German Confederation, made the first recorded, and rather passing, remark about Alsace and a possible annexation to a small circle of confidants.[69] After King William I of Prussia and his closest advisors had agreed to make territorial claims on France in the interests of "better protecting southern Germany", on 25 August the Chancellor gave instructions on launching a press campaign in newspapers close to the government. An article published on 1 September justifying the annexation claim, drafted by Moritz Busch, press agent of the Confederation's foreign ministry, and sanctioned by Bismarck, was the first semi-official statement on the issue.[70] Two weeks later, on 13 and 16 September, the Prussian government sent official circulars to the country's diplomatic missions explaining its position. With respect to war aims, the letter warned of illusions about permanent peace and of a possible speedy new French attack "entirely independent from claims" Prussia would ask from France. In his clarification, sent four weeks later to the Prussian ambassador in London, the Chancellor stated that the "strategic security of Germany" was the only important factor standing "in contrast to more far-reaching demands that, from other points of view, had been many times expressed".[71]

Bismarck's remark certainly hinted at press statements making more expansive requests for French territory. The lead was taken by Bremen shipowner Peter Rickmers (the company founder's second eldest son, who was married to a French woman and who took an active interest in politics, science and literature in addition to attending to the shipping business). In late 1869, Rickmers had returned from a world trip,

[69] Kolb (1990, 147).

[70] *Norddeutsche Allgemeine Zeitung*, 1 September 1870; Busch (1899, vol. 1, 122–124).

[71] Kolb (1990, 161: Chancellor von Bismarck [Berlin] to Ambassador Count von Bernstorff [London], 15 October 1870).

having visited Japan, China, East India and Saigon. At the time, the entire fleet of the Rickmers firm was shipping tea from Shanghai or Foochow to London or New York. After the outbreak of the war, Peter Rickmers was a prominent figure in inspiring public discussion about German colonies in the press and at public meetings.[72] His first article, published in the Hamburg newspaper *Börsen-Halle* on 6 September 1870, pointed to the critical importance of Saigon, as a French naval station in East Asia, for crippling German shipping in these waters: "Even when our shipmasters accept a cargo, taking the risk of privation, the local merchants do not dare to entrust them with their goods, fearing seizure by the French". When asking the rhetorical question whether this important naval station causing "to us such enormous losses" should remain in French hands, the writer also provided the answer: "This can, this may, and this will never be accepted by Germany". Rickmers proposed to consider as possible acquisitions the entire French fleet, Alsace and parts of Lorraine and the French colonies of Cochinchina and Réunion. For several months, Rickmers' far-reaching suggestions were the focus of attention in German newspapers.[73]

When shortly after, news arrived from Singapore that the German merchant vessels *Georg* and *Turandot* had been captured near Saigon by French men-of-war and taken to the colonial port city, the *Börsen-Halle* published a reader's letter considering the captures as "spoken evidence for the importance of this port in the event of war". The anonymous reader strongly repudiated the idea of acquiring Réunion, which he regarded as unsuitable for several reasons. Instead, the French possessions of Pondicherry and Tranquebar on the eastern Indian coast were urgently proposed as extremely valuable trading stations. However, the reader was even more enthusiastic about Saigon being "for us Germans an exceptionally important place" since "the local trade is mainly done by

[72] In 1834, the Rickmers shipyard was founded in Bremerhaven, which became the nucleus of the later shipping company. In 1863, Peter Rickmers married Sophie Bourard, daughter of François Henry Bourard, mayor of Cognac and member of the department council of Charente. He met his future wife in 1862 during a commercial apprenticeship in France. Rickmers (1934, 21, 26).

[73] *Hamburgische Börsen-Halle,* 6 September 1870. The writer's name was not made known in the article. The leaflet on "the French naval station Saigon in Cochinchina", which was produced in support of the Reichstag petition of 26 November 1870, provided a slightly revised version of the article. It was signed by Peter Rickmers and directly refered to the article of 6 September and also to the following discussion in the press.

Germans, and by Germans the colony is enriched".[74] On 18 September, the newspaper *Kreuz-Zeitung* (known as the voice of the Prussian conservatives) continued the discussion, demanding "to not conclude peace with France without colonial acquisitions for Germany". Another journal, the *National-Zeitung*, followed on two days later when the travel writer Ernst von Weber took up Rickmer's ideas, suggesting that annexing Alsace and Lorraine would be insufficient as war compensation and that France should do "a larger penance". Germany was "in need of colonies", Weber stated, while also presenting the possible solution: France possessed in Cochinchina "a colony, the acquisition of which would be of incalculable importance for Germany's future". He made it clear that "everyone acquainted with the constant increase of trade in East Asia, and who also knew which enormous development was possible in the future" should urge Germany "to acquire such a favourable mercantilist, and also strategically important position" which was to become "the core of a future German-Indian colonial empire".[75] However, virulent opposition to such plans was expressed by the Hamburg Chamber of Commerce which regarded the idea as "very alarming for the interests of the whole of Germany" and pleading "to counter the project by proper and practical explanation in public journals".[76]

Empress Eugenie and the Cochinchina Offer

On 1–2 September 1870, the Battle of Sedan resulted in the capture of the French Emperor and large numbers of his troops and effectively decided the war in favour of Prussia and its allies. When Napoleon III was taken as a prisoner to Germany, Empress Eugenie took over as regent but, after hostile crowds had gathered near her palace, she fled the French capital to settle in England, where she resided at Camden Place in Chislehurst, Kent. In the meantime, on 4 September, a group of republican deputies proclaimed the return of the Republic and the creation of a Government of National Defence. The most outstanding figures of the new regime were Jules Favre who became foreign minister, and

[74] *Hamburgische Börsen-Halle,* 19 September 1870 (the sent in letter is of 7 September 1870).

[75] The statement of Ernst von Weber was published in *National-Zeitung* on 20 September 1870 and reprinted in Körner (1908, the quote: 325–326).

[76] Baasch (1915, 317), Baasch (1925, 360) and Stoecker (1958, 77).

Léon Gambetta who took over France's domestic affairs. Although the governor of Paris and commander of troops in the capital, General Louis-Jules Trochu, instituted by Napoleon III, remained in office after siding with the revolutionaries, the provisional cabinet was made up almost entirely of convinced republicans. When this news arrived at the German military headquarters in Reims, on 6 September, Bismarck took the view that instead of the new provisional regime, only Napoleon's government was legitimatelyable to enter international negotiations. His position was formally released to the French press in Reims and published on 11 September. However, when the Chancellor tried to find out Napoleon's attitude to entering into negotiations, he learned that the former emperor was unwilling to do so. Furthermore, the fact could not be ignored that the Republican government was officially recognised by the United States, Switzerland and other countries, although they refrained from such formal step in order to maintain normal relations with the new rulers. With neutral powers such as Britain, Austria-Hungary, Italy and Russia, Foreign Minister Favre immediately initiated contacts, requesting them to act as mediators in France's relations with Prussia. His main goal was to conclude peace as soon as possible and, despite disastrous military defeats, without any territorial losses for France. Not awaiting the powers' reactions, Favre, on 6 September, published a circular that committed his government to an entirely intransigent position in its peace terms. The key sentence was: "We will not cede neither an inch of our territory nor a stone of our fortresses". Almost the entire cabinet, and also General Trochu, agreed to this wording, which was greeted with enthusiastic acclamation in the French public. However, the circular brought an end to any mediation attempt by neutral powers, who regarded such efforts as hopeless from the start. For Bismarck, this was the trigger to publish the aforementioned two explanatory circulars, of 13 and 16 September, accusing the French government of inciting public sentiment, of nourishing hopes of foreign intervention and of not adequately preparing the people for serious peace negotiations with Germany.[77]

Facing the German armies approaching Paris, Favre tried to hold a direct meeting with Bismarck. On 17 September, with the siege ring almost completed, the French government and almost all foreign diplomats left the French capital for Tours. On 19 and 20 September, the

[77] Kolb (1990, 221–231), Roth (1990, 101–140) and Howard (1967).

French foreign minister met the Chancellor at the German headquarters near Paris to negotiate an armistice maintaining the military status quo, and also to find out the German peace terms. Bismarck made it clear that Germany would demand the cession of Alsace and parts of Lorraine with Strasbourg and Metz. However, it seems that the Chancellor was prepared to reduce the demands to Strasbourg and its suburbs should the French principally agree to territorial cessions. Concerning the armistice terms, Bismarck was also ready to compromise, but found Favre largely unco-operative and still insisting on the military status quo. Finally, the foreign minister returned to Paris and published his report on the meeting which brought him high popularity in the French public. The French cabinet, without discussing Bismarck's proposals, rejected his armistice terms, and, on 22 September, Favre informed the Chancellor accordingly. These steps made it clear that the French government was not prepared to make any compromises to end the war and would stick to the maximum terms for armistice and peace.[78]

In late September and in October 1870, the diplomatic struggle between France and Germany prompted different personalities to initiate exploratory talks, kicking up a lot of dust at the time and later. The most mysterious was Edouard Regnier, an amateur politician of the sort that sometimes turns up in time of crisis and at favourable moments and is able to play a certain role. Determined to restore the Second French Empire, Regnier went to Hastings, the residence of the exiled Empress Eugenie, to submit to her, on 12 September 1870, a memorandum explaining possible ways to recover her crown. Although his plea for an audience was repeatedly rejected, Regnier managed by a to have Louis-Napoleon ruse, the imperial prince, sign a postcard of Hastings. After leaving immediately for France, he made his way to the German headquarters at Versailles where Bismarck was at the time negotiating with Favre about the armistice terms. Regnier, pretending to be an envoy of Empress Eugenie, presented the postcard of Hastings signed by the Prince. Although the Chancellor knew that Regnier had no real authority and came without concrete proposals, he thought that the Frenchman might be useful to send to him (Bismarck) a person with full powers who was able to negotiate on behalf of the exiled monarchs. The Chancellor thought of Marshall François-Achille Bazaine, the commander of the French Rhine Army, who was

[78] Kolb (1990, 231, 236–245).

hardly aware of the turbulent events in Paris and therefore had avoided clear statements on whether he recognised the new revolutionary government or instead remained loyal to the regency of Empress Eugenie as the legitimate French government. The Rhine Army, with 170,000 troops in the fortress of Metz, was still intact, but the strong siege ring drawn by around 200,000 Prussian troops commanded by Prince Frederick Charles made any breakout attempt futile. Due to this siege by German troops, since the beginning of September 1870, the Rhine Army had no reliable communication with the outside world.[79]

When Regnier promised to meet either Napoleon III or Marshall Bazaine to present his plans, he was allowed to leave Versailles for Metz where he arrived on 23 September 1870. The Marshall agreed to Regnier's proposal to dispatch to Empress Eugenie a general of the Rhine Army to provide her with first-hand information on the difficult military situation at Metz and to ask for her opinion about possible political talks between Bazaine and the Germans at Versailles. The chosen but obviously unwilling envoy was General Charles Bourbaki, the commander of the Imperial Guard who immediately left for Chislehurst. His mission ended in complete failure because he did not fully inform Eugenie about the precarious situation of the Rhine Army nor about Bazaine's plans to initiate talks with the Germans. His only wish was to return to Metz as soon as possible. Meanwhile, Regnier met again with Bismarck but had neither authority nor concrete proposals from Bazaine at hand. When the Chancellor enquired by telegraph about Bazaine's attitude to the military and political situation, Prince Frederick Charles said the Marshall demanded a grant to his army of safe conduct to leave Metz, without surrendering the fortress, but did not answer the political questions. Therefore, on 30 September, Regnier was told to immediately leave the German headquarters the same day. Bismarck replied to a memorandum of Napoleon III of 25 September, in which the exiled Emperor demanded that the Rhine Army remain intact, which he deemed necessary to secure peace and order in France should Paris fall and anarchy break out. Since Napoleon III offered no adequate compensation for his obvious wish to use the army to restore his dynasty, Bismarck made it clear that only after the former emperor agree to the German peace terms could negotiations be entered into. After the failed talks with Favre, the fruitless

[79] Paz (1965, 227–240) and Kolb (1990, 257–259).

mission of Bourbaki and the unsuccessful approach to Bazaine through Regnier, Bismarck decided not to take any new action but to simply await the surrender of the Rhine Army whose provisions at Metz were running out quickly. It was obvious to the German headquarters, and even to Napoleon III and Eugenie, that the marshal was pressed for time and badly needed a political agreement with Bismarck to avoid the unconditional surrender of the last intact French army.[80]

On 10 October 1870, both Marshall Bazaine and Empress Eugenie, acting independently of each other but out of the same reason, roused themselves to try to save the Rhine Army. The adjutant general, Baron Napoleon Boyer, was despatched from Metz to Versailles, arriving at the German headquarters on 14 October. There, he learned of Bismarck's terms for a military convention which would give the Rhine Army safe conduct to leave Metz with their arms and materials. The Chancellor flatly rejected the idea, insisting on first discussing political matters such as peace terms. Since the French revolutionary government had proven to be intransigent on the issue, Bismarck tried to make the former imperial dynasty a power factor willing and also able to negotiate with him. Therefore, the main reason for possibly offering support to Napoleon III to restore his throne was to find the best available or fastest way to achieve a peace agreement with France, based on the German peace terms. The Chancellor explained to Boyer, that, first, the Rhine Army had to publicly declare allegiance to the government of Empress Eugenie; second, that the Empress had to publicly ask the French people to voice their opinion about France's future political system; and, third, that a representative of her government should sign an agreement which would generally accept the German peace terms. After Boyer had met King William I, Crown Prince Frederick William, and the Prussian commanders Helmuth Count von Moltke and Albrecht Count von Roon, he returned to Metz to discuss the proposal with the commanders of the Rhine Army. The commanding officers, facing the almost total depletion of provisions, urgently dispatched Boyer to the Empress, requesting her to mediate a military convention, without making any political concessions. However, under such conditions, the mission was unlikely to succeed. Boyer had talks with the Empress, with exiled politicians of the Second Empire and even with Count von Bernstorff, the North German ambassador in

[80] Kolb (1990, 260–265).

London. On 23 October, upon her own request, Eugenie met Bernstorff in person. It was obvious to the ambassador that Eugenie aimed to win time for the Rhine Army when requesting a fortnightly armistice and new provisions without offering any return favours such as obligating herself to the German peace terms, or to immediately and publicly addressing the French nation to regain her power. The Empress' only motive was to keep intact the Rhine Army and not to harm, for her own political interests, the ongoing efforts of the revolutionary government to defend France. On the same day, when Bismarck was telegraphically informed by the ambassador about the points to be discussed at the meeting with Eugenie, he knew already that a political solution was not achievable, informing Marshall Bazaine accordingly. On 24 October 1870, the commanders of the Rhine Army prepared for surrender.[81]

On the same day, Théophile Gautier, the son of the renowned French poet Pierre Jules Théophile Gautier (1811–1872), had a personal meeting with Bismarck at Versailles. This was another attempt by the Empress to find a solution with the German Chancellor for the catastrophic situation facing France. Gautier, the personal envoy of Empress Eugenie, had been charged with informing Bismarck about the utmost sacrifices she was thinking of being able to make in the name of France. Before leaving Chislehurst, Gautier had received concrete instructions for his mission from Eugène Rouher, the former president of the French senate who was also residing in exile. After a long and adventurous journey, Gautier arrived at Versailles on 23 October, with a personal letter from the Empress to King William I which was to inform him about the peace terms she was willing to negotiate. Three major territorial and financial concessions should be offered: First, France would agree that Strasburg was to be declared a "Free City" surrounded by territory sufficient for its material and financial needs; second, the nation would be prepared to pay reparations, and, third, she would offer to the Germans the cession of Cochinchina.[82]

On 24 October 1870, at half past-four, Gautier was received by Bismarck in the Chancellor's private residence at Versailles. The

[81] Kolb (1990, 265–270).

[82] On the question of Alsace, Gautier's list of concessions slightly differed from a letter he wrote on 25 October 1870 (which seemed to have been checked for accuracy by Bismarck) to an unknown addressee and his more detailed report published in 1903. Kolb (1990, 266).

Frenchman described him as “having a tall figure, large shoulders appearing to be even larger because of the style of his uniform, with his red and bloated face, his jaw reminding one of a bulldog which really gave him a wild expression”. He found that Bismarck’s harsh voice was well matched to his outward appearance: “He speaks without emphasis, rather slow, and a very correct French with a slight accent. His style is extremely good, sometimes even artistically, and each word describes very carefully the thought he wants to express”. The envoy passed to Bismarck the letter for King William I. The Chancellor enquired about Gautier’s journey, gladly learning that his visitor had been orderly treated by German troops when passing through the lines. Then Bismarck informed Gautier about his negotiations since 10 October (the time of Gautier’s departure from London) and the failed mission of Boyer to Chislehurst. The envoy also learned that the Chancellor was partially familiar with Eugenie’s peace terms but wished to again listen to them. Gautier presented the terms, emphasising the heavy toll the reparations would take on the French people and asking, if this “ransom” and the complete exhaustion deriving from it would not suffice for the victor as guarantee for any revenge by France.

Finally, Théophile Gautier offered France’s cession of Cochinchina. He described the colony as a very hopeful possession that, being wisely administrated by the French navy, was already covering the expenses made for it. It was even providing a surplus for France. Bismarck who uninterruptedly listened to Gautier, slightly shrugged his shoulders when hearing the word “Cochinchina”. As Gautier later reported, the Chancellor, “driven by the old instinct of Prussian frugality that had not yet been replaced by German imperial megalomania (…), with a touch of humility” remarked the following: “Oh! Oh! Cochinchina! This is a well big piece for us; we are not rich enough to afford the luxury of colonies!”[83] With these words spoken, the first meeting ended. After the Chancellor had conversed with King William I, he informed Gautier soon after in a second meeting that the offered concessions were inacceptable, especially those concerning Alsace, and they would allow France at some future time to again take up an offensive attitude to Germany. “Should the King and I return home without bringing back Alsace, stones would

[83] The French version of Bismarck’s remark reads as follows: “Oh! oh! la Cochinchine! C’est un bien gros morceau pour nous; nous ne sommes pas assez riches pour nous offrir le luxe de colonies!” Gautier (Fils) (1903, 786). The German translation: Bismarck (1924, 382).

be cast on us", Bismarck stated. Gautier found this remark "open, honest and clear in its will to insist on Alsace under all circumstances". The Chancellor stressed that this will was imposed by events, namely as an "inevitable result of fatality". Finally, Gautier noted that Bismarck, with a compassionate tone, said the following: "I respect the Empress, I deplore the misfortunes of France, but you must well understand by yourselves that it is impossible for us not to strangle you. I am really sorry about that!"[84] With this statement, the meeting ended remaining secret at the time. In 1903, Gautier published a comprehensive report on the background and course of his journey to Bismarck and about his talks and impressions at the German headquarters in Versailles.[85]

The Debate on Cochinchina

Since the meeting between Bismarck and Gautier was not made public, the debate about Cochinchina as a possible war gain to demand from France went on. The first to again propose the idea was Peter Rickmers, supported by Alexander Georg Mosle (a Bremen merchant and deputy of the Bremen diet and a member of the local Chamber of Commerce). In late November 1870, Rickmers and Mosle drew up the petition "concerning the acquisition of the naval station of Saigon" which was signed by 35 Bremen firms and three Berlin firms, and even the well-known jurist Franz Philipp von Holtzendorff (an extraordinary professor in Berlin and author of several major works on legal subjects). The petitioners declared that the establishment of a German naval station at Saigon was "the key to the Chinese-Japanese waters" and would "conform to great national interests such as the world position of the new Germany". Repudiating any colonial interests, the petition emphasised the interests of the German merchant navy: "Because Saigon is in French hands, in each only imminent war in which France participates, the great difficulty is that German shipping is entirely left fallow; the narrowly limited shipping channel to and from Chinese and Japanese ports can be

[84] The French version of Bismarck's remark reads as follows: "Je respecte l'Impératrice, je déplore les malheurs de la France, mais vous devez bien comprendre vous-mêmes qu'il est impossible de ne pas vous étrangler. J'en suis vraiment désolé!" Gautier (Fils) (1903, 788). The German translation: Bismarck (1924, 383).

[85] Gautier (Fils) (1903, 763–792); for the German translation, see Gautier (1912/13) and Bismarck (1924, 382–383).

blocked by a few war steamers operating from Saigon". However, once in German hands, Saigon would have an important role "to effectively protect, without much effort, all German interests in those regions and waters, and also against Chinese pirates". The petitioners pointed to the "very large number of German companies in Chinese ports, with scales of businesses being unsurpassed".[86]

The petition was submitted to the competent Reichstag petitions committee which unanimously voted in favour of it, being well aware that the final decision entirely rested with the Chancellor. Yet, to boost the case, the committee decided to have the petition debated and passed in the Reichstag before it was submitted to Bismarck.[87] On 30 November 1870, the petition was presented by the entrepreneur Ernst Friedrich Adickes (a local and regional politician and also national-liberal Reichstag deputy for Hanover). Adickes not only stressed the importance of Saigon for protecting Germany's merchant fleet operating in East Asia but also pointed to its strategic value for the navy that, "with a few gunboats," would be able to control the Sunda Strait between Java and Sumatra, and therefore the southern access to the South China Sea.[88] Adickes' enthusiastic plea was opposed by deputies questioning principally his arguments. The Hamburg merchant Edgar Daniel Ross (national-liberal deputy of the Hamburg diet and the Reichstag) strongly criticised colonial policies in general for their "great abuses". His viewpoint that Saigon was also an unhealthy place was taken up by the Bremen merchant Rudolf Schleiden (an international law and customs expert who served as Hanseatic consul in Washington D.C. and London before becoming a liberal-conservative Reichstag deputy in 1867). Schleiden stated that almost all German trading was done with countries for which protection by a strong fleet was unnecessary. Therefore, he made a strong plea for not being dragged into "decisively corrupting colonial policies". His warning was taken up by the merchant Hermann Henrich Meier (the founder of the Bremen bank and

[86] BAB, R 1001-7156. The petition of 26 November 1870 was also published by the Berlin Geographical Society titled *Die französische Flottenstation Saigon in Cochinchina*. This leaflet containing extra information on Saigon included a slightly revised version of Rickmer's article of 6 September 1870 published in the *Börsen-Halle*.

[87] *Stenographische Berichte Reichstag, Anlagen*, petition no. 15 (1870, 45), Stoecker (1958, 76) and Wehler (1976, 202).

[88] *Stenographische Berichte Reichstag* (1870, 40–41).

stock exchange, and the shipping company Norddeutscher Lloyd, and the national-liberal deputy for Bremen of the Reichstag). Meier made it clear that he had not signed the petition because he wished not to promote a decision which he found premature. However, the shipowner rejected Schleiden's notion that German merchant shipping was not in need of protection by the navy, pointing to the actual situation in previous weeks when French men-of-war had captured vessels flying the North German flag. He also tried to correct the negative opinions about Saigon, as expressed by the previous speakers, referring to information he had received. Meier continued his speech as follows:

> Furthermore, perhaps in the interior of the Annamite [Vietnamese] Empire, with its much-extended rice culture, it may still be that districts are not very healthy; Saigon itself, with all its large installations that the French have already created and would not require us to first build them, would certainly be very useful and suitable. So, things are at the moment, and I ask you to understand the matter from this objective, impartial position and to agree to the motion of the committee [on petitions]. Whether the Chancellor will find it suitable to make something of it in the peace treaty, or not, is well within his better discretion, and I think in this respect we can entirely be reassured. Could we get it [Saigon] without sacrifice, could we amend the Treaty [of Saigon of 5 June 1861] France concluded with the Annamite [Vietnamese] Empire so that the rural areas would be returned to it and could we merely retain Saigon, then I believe that it could be and would be rather useful in the course of time.[89]

Meier's line of argument was supported by the lawyer Johannes Miquel (the former mayor of Osnabrück, and also founder and director of a major bank in Berlin, who was both national-liberal deputy of Hanover in the Prussian diet and the Reichstag; from 1890 to 1901, he was Prussian finance minister). Miquel alluded to the acquisition of Saigon as "a hardly costly naval station in Chinese waters to protect our merchant navy", stressing the fact that German shipping during the current war was "entirely dead" in the region due to the fact that France had fortified the place with a few warships on the coast. However, he believed the final decision should be left to the Chancellor. Miquel's rather positive stance towards Saigon was strongly rejected by Leopold Baron von Hoverbeck

[89] *Stenographische Berichte Reichstag* (1870, 42).

(the left-liberal East Prussian rural estate owner). Hoverbeck was principally opposed to any discussion on such matters before the war had ended. His opinion was supported by Fritz Mende (the social-democrat deputy of Freiberg, Saxony, and co-founder and chairman of Ferdinand Lassalle's social democratic labour party). Pointing to the position of the North German government that the war with France was a purely defensive one, Mende sharply criticised any plans for territorial acquisitions. Finally, when the majority of the Reichstag voted for Hoverbeck's proposal to proceed to the order of the day, the committee's motion to pass the petition to the Chancellor was carried.[90]

Despite the parliamentary defeat, the public discussion on the possible acquisition of Saigon for Germany was far from over. On 3 December 1870, the Berlin Geographical Society decided to set up a committee with specially appointed members to further study the issue. The leading figure was the prominent ethnologist Dr. Adolf Bastian (an expert for South East Asia and East Asia, with a thorough theoretical and practical knowledge of the region acquired during extensive journeys in the 1860s). When visiting Saigon in 1863, Bastian had stayed in the mansion of Behre & Co., talking to its manager Wilhelm Kufeke and to Bishop Dominique Lefèbvre, French missionary of the Paris Foreign Missions Society. Bastian collected comprehensive information on Saigon's historical development, urban designs, trading and shipping up until 1867, which he later included in his travel report.[91] In December 1870, he and other members of the Geographical Society published, in the form of a leaflet, the memorandum *Deutschlands Interessen in Ostasien* (Germany's interests in East Asia). The declared intention was "to present a question from national-economic and geographic-historical positions that was important for the nation's interests but hardly comprehended by most people". The authors stressed that Saigon as a European possession was "one of the best located ones in the Asian seas", and since there was "little prospect of making a new acquisition there", the acquisition of a German naval station would remain "in the realm of pious hopes" should it not be realised "by coincidence or use of a favourable chance". They referred to German merchants in East Asia who unanimously had demanded the frequent presence of German warships to safeguard

[90] *Stenographische Berichte Reichstag* (1870, 43).

[91] Bastian (1868, 376, 416–418, 429–436).

merchant vessels against pirates. A naval station would have such positive effects on German shipping and trading that the navy's expenses for its installation should be compensated by Germany's increased national prosperity. The most important result would be a higher comprehension in Germany of these unknown regions, and also for German national interests in the enormous world trade. The conclusion was as follows: "Therefore, national interest in each way seems to demand a seizure in East Asian waters, not only that Germany is represented there in her position as great power but also so that industry and trade with all its inherent powers are able to develop on this fertile ground".[92]

Far-reaching colonial plans also circulated in the German headquarters at Versailles. Prince Adalbert, the commander of the Prussian navy, was the driving force behind the campaign to convince Bismarck to demand from the French revolutionary government the acquisition of Saigon. On 1 December 1870, Adalbert requested War and Navy Minister Albrecht Count von Roon to sound out Bismarck on the plan. However, he received an entirely evasive answer from the Minister arguing that colonies required a powerful fleet which Prussia or Germany neither owned nor needed.[93] On the other hand, the Admiral succeeded in winning Grand Duke Frederick I of Baden (the son-in-law of King William I) over to the idea, and he approached Crown Prince Frederick William accordingly. On 14 December, the Crown Prince noted in his war diary the following notes: "It was brought to my attention that it would be of far-reaching benefit for Germany, if we, in peace talks, would insist on the cession of a French naval station in Cochinchina which would easily provide us with an excellent harbour in those waters".[94] With the obvious goodwill of the Crown Prince, Grand Duke Frederick I, on 3 January 1871, took a fresh initiative with Rudolf von Delbrück (the influential president of the federal chancellery). The two men had recently met in person when Delbrück was on a mission to the South German states negotiating the agreements on forming the German empire. A convinced promoter of free trade, Delbrück, since 1848, had contributed

[92] Bastian (1870, 3–9, 16); *Zeitschrift der Gesellschaft für Erdkunde zu Berlin* (1871, 91, 95).

[93] Batsch (1890, 309).

[94] Meisner (1926, 275).

to extending the German Customs Union and to concluding commercial treaties with Austria-Hungary, France and other European countries. However, Delbrück bluntly told the Grand Duke "that he was a decided opponent of such stations since they would pave the way for colonies, and this he would consider to be a disaster for Germany". With his argument that colonies would require a powerful fleet, Delbrück was entirely in line with Bismarck and Roon, but he even went one step further when pointing to "excessive costs" for building a German fleet.[95]

On 27 January 1871, with an armistice agreed between Prussia and France, the future peace terms became increasingly important, and also the attention of foreign countries. The British press reported on telegrams sent from Bordeaux — since early December 1870 the seat of the French government with Léon Gambetta as minister of the interior and of war — that the German demands would not only include Alsace-Lorraine but also the French colony of Pondicherry in India, twenty warships and ten billion francs. These alleged conditions had caused the worst impression in Britain, as the German press agency Wolff reported telegraphically from London. The sensitive international situation prompted Bismarck to put an end to the discussion on far-reaching colonial plans. On 4 February, Bernstorff was instructed to put it about in the English press, "that we do not have the intention to acquire, through the peace treaty, possessions in India, East Asia and generally in overseas countries". The following day, North German Ambassador in Washington D.C., Count Friedrich von Gerolt, was briefly directed to disseminate in the American press that overseas acquisitions were not "our aim". The envoy hurried to clarify to Secretary of State Hamilton Fish, and also to the main agent of Associated Press, that the North German government was not intending to make overseas acquisitions. This news was published by New York newspapers. Bismarck's concerns about the British public mood were somewhat confirmed when Bernstorff, on 15 February 1871, gave an account of ideas seriously expressed by distinguished English personalities that, "we, with the acquisition of Pondicherry, intended to drive a wedge between the English possessions in East India, to wrest them from the English with the support of Russia, and to use the twenty warships ceded to us

[95] Oncken (1927, 287) and Lorenz (1902, 508, 516–517).

by France to prepare an invasion of Britain, perhaps even supported by America".[96]

Meanwhile, Grand Duke Frederick I of Baden had continued pressing for a colony. For this purpose, he approached Heinrich Abeken, the representative of the North German foreign ministry at the German headquarters in Versailles, who was often employed by Bismarck for setting up official despatches. On 6 February 1871, Frederick I introduced Abeken to the plans of Prince Adalbert, stressing the importance of acquiring Cochinchina: "Saigon would become the central operation point of our navy in the Far East, and even more, Cochinchina in our hands would at a stroke provide us with an important power position in East Asia that could only have beneficial effects on our already very important trade with China and Japan". He also explained that the Grand Duchy of Baden was obviously interested "since a part of our industry has active dealings with East Asia, making good businesses there". After receiving the aforementioned leaflet of the Berlin Geographical Society, Abeken promised to submit it to Bismarck and to talk to him about the issue.[97] However, the Chancellor, on 9 February, in a round with a few close friends, repudiated colonies, describing them as "care posts and nothing else", as it would be currently the case in England and Spain: "And for us in Germany, this colonial issue would be equally for us like the silky sable in Polish aristocratic families possessing no shirts".[98] On 20 February, Abeken informed Frederick I about Bismarck's position. The polite and non-committal reply was clearly aimed at satisfying the distinguished questioner when the Chancellor disclosed not to share "the slightly curt views of Delbrück" and "not to be principally opposed to acquiring overseas points, but rather to be very well-disposed towards the idea". Abeken made it clear that Bismarck was very interested in Saigon, "because German trading relations to East Asia were already were active". On the other hand, the Chancellor had stressed that any conflict with a naval power should be avoided, and therefore the question of colonies should be left to rest at the moment. According to Abeken, he remarked the following: "If such a naval station could later be gained, East Asia would certainly be

[96] Bismarck (1931, 687–688) and Stoecker (1977, 30). BAB, R 1001-7156: Baron von Gerolt (Washington, DC) to Chancellor von Bismarck (Versailles), 9 February 1871.

[97] Oncken (1927, 357–361), Stoecker (1958, 78) and Wehler (1976, 204).

[98] Busch (1899, 157).

the most suitable place". With such conciliatory statements, which were in obvious contradiction to the Chancellor's other utterances, Bismarck probably wished to put off Frederick until a distant future. The Grand Duke of Baden was well aware of this intention of the Chancellor when writing in his diary that the issue was thereby "shrugged off".[99]

In his memoirs published in 1901, Max von Brandt came back to the possible acquisition of Saigon. Pointing to the fact that higher goals had priority at the time and the German public was "not yet ripe for such questions", he regretted nevertheless that "from the point of view of colonial policy" the idea of 1871 to partly replace the French war indemnity with France's East Asian colonial empire in the making had passed by "so unheard and unconsidered". Brandt did not mention his own, very negative assessment of Saigon of March 1865 when stating that in the 1860s and 1870s, "much more would have been possible in East Asia which later proved to be impossible or only available for much higher costs or higher risks".[100] This was a clear hint about the seizure of Jiaozhou (Kiaochow) Bay in China's Shandong Province by German naval troops in 1897. By establishing a colony in this economically promising region of north-eastern China, Germany finally joined the other imperial powers in seizing a territorial foothold in East Asia, almost thirty years after Bismarck had turned down the idea of acquiring Cochinchina as the first colonial possession of Imperial Germany. Although German colonies were acquired in Africa and in the Pacific (1883–1884), Bismarck, during his term as imperial chancellor (1871–1890), predominantly remained a proponent of "free trade imperialism", mainly focusing on economic expansion overseas by employing informal means.[101]

The Navies in East Asia

In stark contrast to Britain or France, Prussia and other German littoral states lacked any noteworthy naval tradition. This created the potential danger of German coasts being blockaded by naval powers and invaded by foreign armies. However, until the early nineteenth century, Prussia

[99] Oncken (1927, 387), Lorenz (1902, 517), Stoecker (1958, 78) and Wehler (1976, 204).

[100] Brandt (1901, vol. 2, 145–146).

[101] Wehler (1976, 191–193), Baumgart (1982, 140–155), Mommsen (1993, 56–77) and Pflanze (2014, 119–142).

exclusively relied on her land troops. After France's unsuccessful continental blockade during the Napoleonic period (1799–1815), and Britain's demonstration of her naval supremacy over the French navy, Prussia revised her attitude towards naval power. In 1849, Prince Adalbert became supreme commander of the fleet, launching a naval construction programme and making Danzig (the major Baltic seaport, with a growing shipbuilding industry) the major headquarter of Prussia's new naval force. When the Crimean War (1853–1856), in which Prussia remained neutral, demonstrated the importance of steam-driven vessels, the Prussian admiralty ordered the construction of nineteen gunboats in 1859.[102] Two of these steam gunboats served to ship the Prussian expedition led by Count zu Eulenburg to East Asia in 1860–1861, which succeeded in making trading agreements with Japan, China and Siam. In January 1863, when Guido von Rehfues began his term as the first Prussian minister in Beijing, Bismarck (who had assumed office as Prussia's minister-president the year before) promised to dispatch two steam gunboats to Chinese and Japanese waters. In the following years, the *Gazelle* and the *Vineta* occasionally cruised around East Asia. For their support, a small plot of land in Yokohama, which was called Preußischer Marine Grund (Prussian Navy Ground), was, in the aftermath of the treaty with Japan (24 January 1861) leased by contract from the Japanese government to erect a naval depot and hospital. Yet, in Bismarck's opinion, this site was "neither suitable in size nor location to also satisfy the needs of a naval station on the Chinese coast".[103]

Prussia's military victory over Austria (1866) and the subsequent founding of the North German Confederation (1867) resulted in the Prussian navy becoming the core of the North German navy.[104] In 1867, the new naval law increased the tasks of the North German navy, from coastal defence and protection of the merchant marine only to offensive action, and even offensive operations against other naval powers, including attacks on coasts and ports in case of war. This inspired public calls to the government of the North German Confederation to acquire

[102] Chevalier (1873, 25) and Giersch (2009, 152–157).

[103] Stoecker (1958, 66–67, 272: Chancellor von Bismarck [Berlin] to Minister von Rehfues [Beijing], 2 April 1870). For reasons of cost, the Prussian Navy Ground was ceded in December 1867 to the Pacific Mail Steamship Company to be used as a coal depot. In return, the American company agreed to annually deliver 600 tons of best coal to Prussian or North German warships. BAB, R 901-22545.

[104] The black-white-red flag of the new North German navy combining the colours of Prussia and the Hanse cities was made the national flag of Imperial Germany in 1871.

colonial territories. The Berlin junior barrister Ernst Friedel was first to openly demand the occupation of the Chinese island of Formosa (Taiwan) to establish a "German Hong Kong" and thereby secure a fixed position for Germany in East Asia.[105] However, Bismarck regarded such colonial acquisitions as economically useless, and instead continued to support the establishment of a naval station in East Asia and in Central America to bring the North German flag to the attention of other powers and to provide support to German merchant ships in case of pirate attacks. On 23 January 1868, the North German government gave the order to permanently station in East Asia the wooden steam corvettes *Hertha* and the somewhat smaller but almost equally equipped *Medusa* (with a crew of 200–390 men and 17 cannons, reaching a maximum speed of 12 knots (22 km/h) to effectively protect North German political and trading interests. The vessels had been launched by the Royal Shipyard in Danzig in October 1864. Due to technical difficulties, the arrival of the *Medusa* in Singapore was delayed until 4 March 1869. However, this event was regarded as the launch of the Ostasiatische Schiffsstation (East Asian Naval Station) of the North German Confederation. When the *Hertha* finally called at Singapore on 12 February 1870, Captain Heinrich Köhler was made commander of the East Asian Naval Station, with Captain Marinus Struben of the *Medusa* under his command.[106]

In April 1870, Bismarck, concerned about the unfavourable location of the Prussian naval station, instructed Rehfues to approach the Chinese government to purchase or lease a territory "at a centrally located point on the Chinese coast, or on an island in its vicinity, to establish a naval depot". The Chancellor also made it clear that chiefly for political but also economic reasons, the North German Confederation would not seek sovereignty over Chinese territory and only wished to safeguard the basic requirements needed for their warships operating in East Asia. Bismarck pointed out that continuing Chinese sovereignty over this territory would be helpful should European wars have any repercussions on East Asia.[107] However, the idea met with severe concern from Minister Rehfues who warned of growing anti-foreigner sentiment in China, and

[105] Wehler (1976, 199) and Friedel (1867, 100).

[106] Fecht (1937, 349–350).

[107] Stoecker (1958, 272–274: Chancellor von Bismarck [Berlin] to Minister von Rehfues [Beijing], 2 April 1870) and Wehler (1976, 199).

therefore extended negotiations with the Chinese government, which might result in the revision of the Sino-German Treaty of Tianjin of 1861.[108] With the outbreak of the Franco-German War a few weeks later, the idea was put aside. The project of establishing a permanent German naval station in East Asia was finally realised in 1898 when, after the seizure of Jiaozhou (Kiaochow) Bay in China's north-eastern Shandong Province by German naval forces, the territory of Jiaozhou, with its port city Qingdao (Tsingtau), became the base of the German East Asia Squadron.

In 1870, the North German navy consisted of 34 warships, with *Hertha* and *Medusa* being posted to Japan. When in late July 1870, news about the Tianjin Massacre[109] arrived in Yokohama, Captain Köhler of *Hertha* set sail to Yantai (Chefoo), the port city in north-eastern Shandong Province, to join a naval demonstration by European powers demanding satisfaction from the Chinese government. In stark contrast to Prussia, the French navy had 339 men-of-war, 27 of which were part of the East Asian Squadron in 1870.[110] In Yantai, the French frigate *Venus* and the corvette *Dupleix* rode at anchor, but news of the outbreak of war in Europe had not yet arrived. On 7 August 1870, Minister von Rehfues in Beijing received the official telegram from Berlin about the outbreak of the war with France. The unusual delay of one week had been caused by broken Siberian telegraphic lines and the subsequent slow forwarding by horse. Therefore, Captain Köhler was first informed about the dramatic events by private telegrams delivered from the German consul in Tianjin. Facing French superior forces, which made it impossible to fight should the unofficial news be confirmed, Köhler, on 9 August 1870 at eleven o'clock at night, immediately set sail for Nagasaki, the nearest Japanese

[108] Stoecker (1958, 74–75).

[109] The Tianjin Massacre, the most spectacular of many Chinese attacks on Christian missionaries and converts, occurred in the summer of 1870 resulting in the death of sixty French Catholic priests and nuns. It led to intense belligerence from French diplomats and armed foreign intervention in Tianjin. Hsü (2000, 299–302).

[110] The total numbers of the French navy are from Brocheux and Hèmery (2009, 21) and Schäfer (1901, 46). See also Walser (1992, 2) and (Giersch (2009, 134) with slightly differing numbers. The total number of the North German navy is from Kriegsgeschichtliche Abteilung des Großen Generalstabes (1874, 26–27) and Giersch (2009, 152–157, with differing numbers). On the situation of the French and Prussian navies in 1870–1871, see Chevalier (1873, 22, 34) and Pohl (1918, 391).

port, to await further news, and after that joined the *Medusa* on the way to Yokohama.[111]

The *Hertha* was being chased by the *Dupleix,* commanded by Captain Sébastien Lespès. On 15 August 1870, he met Köhler in Yokohama and, surprisingly, proposed a special convention between France and the North German Confederation for China and Japan to secure the interests of the subjects of the two powers during the war. The French were obviously interested in keeping a free hand towards China to strongly pursue the Tianjin case. For the Germans, it was also desirable that similar incidents should be avoided in future to protect their own nationals. Furthermore, the plan would allow North German merchant vessels to freely operate in East Asian waters during the Franco-German War. Such an agreement seemed beneficial for both sides and would at the same time demonstrate European solidarity towards China despite the war in Europe. When Köhler reacted very positively, Lespès, on the next day, announced that he would immediately set sail for Yokohama to inform both the French minister to Japan, Maxime Outrey, and the French supreme commander in East Asia, Admiral Marie-Jules Dupré, of the plan. He said: "My particular opinion is that it would be the best thing here, but it would be necessary to settle the question as soon as possible". Köhler repeated that he "would fully agree" to such an arrangement, requesting Lespès "to make known my inclination to such a step to the French Admiral" and to take with him a letter for Captain Struben of *Medusa* repairing at Yokohama. He also dispatched a sailor of his own crew to Minister von Brandt in Tokyo to inform him about the plan. Nevertheless, Köhler took the necessary precaution by formally announcing to his crew the ship's readiness for war and reading out the war laws. When news arrived on 31 August 1870 that the *Dupleix* had been instructed to prevent under all circumstances the combining of *Hertha* and *Medusa*, Köhler, on 1 September, set sail for Yokohama to enforce such uniting "immediately and, if necessary, by force". As he reported to the navy supreme command, *Medusa* with her steam engine still under repair, was very likely to be attacked by *Dupleix* "superior in powers and speed". After a voyage of six days, during which coal was purchased at Hyogo, the port

[111] PAAA, Peking II-261: Consul Wentzel (Tianjin) to Minister von Rehfues (Beijing), 6 August 1870; Minister von Rehfues (Beijing) to Chancellor von Bismarck (Berlin), 8 August 1870; Captain Köhler (Nagasaki) to Minister von Rehfues (Beijing), 12 August 1870. Pohl (1918, 390–391).

in the Japanese Inland Sea, *Hertha* called at Yokohama where *Medusa* and *Dupleix* were anchored among other men-of-war flying the British, American, Austrian and Japanese flags. Köhler sent copies of his correspondence with the French commander to Rehfues, suggesting the taking of further steps by approaching the French minister: "The entire matter should not only be very important for the North German, but also for European commerce since the interests of various nationalities in this important point are the same. Furthermore, the *Hertha* and the *Medusa* are not able to provide sufficient protection to the large number of North German ships against the strong French squadron in East Asian waters".[112]

With respect to the sheer numbers of global naval forces, France's overwhelming superiority over Prussia was undeniable. Facing such military imbalance, and consequently the threat that German merchant ships would be captured by French men-of-war in all waters, the government in Berlin, on 18 July 1870, proclaimed, without reservation or reciprocity, the inviolability of private merchant vessels during the war. However, Paris could not be prompted to do the same, and instead stuck to the traditional right of privateering enemy vessels, crews and cargoes. Under these circumstances, merchant vessels flying the North German flag (more than four thousand ships) fled to their own or neutral ports and lay idle during the Franco-German War. With this scenario in mind, which he learned from newspapers published in China, Rehfues thought that negotiations, as proposed by Captain Köhler, would not lead to any result "after the outbreak of war and under local conditions" in East Asia.[113] His pessimism was not shared by his colleague Max von Brandt in Tokyo. After receiving Köhler's letters, Brandt, in late August 1870, had approached his French counterpart, Maxime Outrey, who took up the matter with great fervour. The diplomats invited British Minister Harry Smith Parkes to join their talks, during which they agreed

[112] PAAA, Peking II-261: Captain Lespès (Nagasaki) to Captain Köhler (Nagasaki), 16 August 1870; Captain Köhler (Nagasaki) to Captain Lespès (Nagasaki), 16 August 1870 (both letters are in English); Captain Köhler (Yokohama) to Minister von Rehfues (Beijing), 21 August 1870. BAB, R 901-86576: Captain Köhler (Yokohama) to the Navy Supreme Command (Berlin), 21 September 1870. Pohl (1918, 391–393).

[113] *Hansa* (1870, 23 October, 203–204; 6 November, 211–213; 20 November, 220–221), Brandt (1901, vol. 3, 327), Pohl (1918, 394–395), Walser (1992, 2) and Giersch (2009, 154). PAAA, Peking II-261: Minister von Rehfues (Beijing) to Captain Köhler (Nagasaki), 6 September 1870.

to await the final decisions of Admiral Dupré and both the French and German governments. For the time being, Outrey declared that the North German corvettes would have freedom of movement while Brandt promised that the German warships would not attack French merchant vessels or men-of-war "as long as they were not affronted or attacked by French vessels". This temporary Franco-German agreement gave sufficient time to most German merchant ships operating in East Asia to find protection in neutral ports. It did not prevent the French navy from capturing, in the second half of August 1870, two North German vessels in the South China Sea near Saigon and taking them as prizes to the port city. However, with the overall positive results in mind, Köhler could later state that "the main purpose of the pursued neutrality talks had been achieved". In his opinion, he was joined by Brandt who, in his report to Bismarck of 3 October 1870, pointed out that the talks allowed them "to protect our shipping companies from important losses of all our merchant vessels in these waters". However, such views were not at all shared by Rehfues who remained highly critical of the arrangement which finally failed after the French government had refused to support it. In January 1871, Rehfues let Bismarck know that "no one here in this country [China] had believed in the possibility of neutralisation and that, after the outbreak of the war, some shipmasters sentenced themselves to idleness or were forced to do so because they were unable to find any cargoes in the light of imminent danger of privation". His final verdict was even more critical when accusing Köhler of "self-delusion" arguing that "the reverse proportion of the navies and the merchant navies of the two belligerent powers excluded from the outset the possibility of neutralisation".[114]

In September 1870, after the new French government of national defence had been informed about the temporary Franco-German agreement in East Asia, Navy Minister Léon Martin Fourichon quickly disapproved of the idea and immediately informed Outrey about his decision. Accordingly, on 28 September 1870, Admiral Dupré followed, explaining

[114] BAB, R 901-86576: Captain Köhler (Yokohama) to the Navy Supreme Command (Berlin), 21 September 1870; Minister von Brandt (Tokyo) to Chancellor von Bismarck (Berlin), 3 October 1870; Minister von Rehfues (Beijing) to Chancellor von Bismarck (Berlin), 16 and 18 January 1871. PAAA, Peking II-261: Captain Köhler (Yokohama) to Minister von Rehfues (Beijing), 1 October 1870, Minister von Rehfues (Beijing) to Chancellor von Bismarck (Berlin), 3 October 1870.

that his instructions would not allow him to come to another conclusion. The French naval squadron in Japan was ordered to closely block *Hertha* and *Medusa* at Yokohama.[115] When Brandt learned about the French refusal, in a letter sent from Outrey, further talks were suspended. The last chance to strike such an agreement seemed to come when the British Foreign Minister Granville George Leveson-Gower (called Lord Granville), on 21 October 1870, was informed of the details of the Franco-German agreement by Charles-Josef Tissot, first secretary of the French embassy in London. The minister took a very positive stance, stressing "the extreme importance of showing to the Chinese, as well to the Japanese, that even when at war with each other the European powers will always be prepared to protect European interests in both countries". This was a clear hint about the much-sought European solidarity in East Asia despite the ongoing war in Europe. Consequently, Lord Granville let both Tissot and Lord Augustus Loftus, the British ambassador to the North German Confederation know that "the judicious arrangement [...] would cause great satisfaction" in Britain. He further added: "Hostile engagements near China and Japan between the naval forces of two great European powers would, without much probable advantage to either belligerent, produce effects permanently disadvantageous to European influence in those countries". With such strong British support, the North German government, on 24 October 1870, telegraphically instructed Brandt to proclaim his agreement to the neutralisation of Chinese and Japanese waters should the French minister to Japan agree to do the same.[116]

A week later, American President Ulysses S. Grant took over the role of mediator telegraphically warning, through Secretary of State Hamilton Fish, that "the hostilities between France and Germany, if conducted in Chinese waters, will operate on the minds of the Chinese to put in peril the lives of Europeans and Americans in that Empire". Grant was obviously aware of the possible dangers should solidarity between nationals

[115] Chevalier (1873, 97).

[116] PAAA, Peking II-261: Foreign Minister Favre (Paris) to Minister Washburne (Paris), 5 December 1870 (the French replies of September 1870 are mentioned in this letter; the letter is in English). BAB, R 901-86576: Minister von Brandt (Tokyo) to Chancellor von Bismarck (Berlin), 3 October 1870; Lord Granville (London) to Lord Loftus (Berlin), 21 October 1870; Federal Chancellery (Berlin) to Minister von Brandt (Yokohama), 24 October 1870. Pohl (1918, 393–394).

from Western countries in China break, but not of the existence of the temporary Franco-German neutrality agreement. George Bancroft, the US minister to Prussia, was instructed to sound out the North German government about "whether it is possible to obtain suspension of hostilities and co-operative action between the squadrons in Chinese waters, so far as the protection of the lives and property of Americans and Europeans may require". Should the reply be favourable, Bancroft was to approach Elihu B. Washburne, the US minister to France, to enable him "to ask for a like action on the part of the French government". Hermann von Thile, state secretary of the North German foreign ministry, promptly submitted confidential evidence to Bancroft on "a provisional neutrality subjected to certain conditions and particularly to ratification by the French admiral and government" and also informed Bismarck at the German headquarters in Versailles about the American proposal. After Bismarck had consulted King William I, who verbally agreed to the idea to convert the factual Franco-German agreement "into a formally concluded suspension of hostilities and continued collaboration of the fleets to protect European interests", War and Navy Minister von Roon also consented to the plan. This gave Bismarck a free hand to have the North German foreign ministry positively reply to Bancroft's enquiry and to consequently enable the Americans to approach the French government on the issue.[117]

On 24 November 1870, Minister Washburne submitted his request to Navy Minister Fourichon and, on 2 December 1870, sent a letter of enquiry to Foreign Minister Favre. In his reply, Favre based his decision on the judgement of the French naval ministry. Hinting at the current circumstances "when Prussia uses with such extreme harshness all the advantages which in the present war the fortune of arms has until now given her upon the land, that we can give up those which our superiority upon the sea assures to us". He even predicted negative counter-effects should France agree to the suspension of hostilities in China and Cochinchina: "All concession on our part would be looked

[117] BAB, R 901-86576: Secretary of State Fish (Washington, DC) to Minister Bancroft (Berlin), 1 November 1870; Minister Bancroft (Berlin) to State Secretary von Thile (Berlin); State Secretary von Thile (Berlin) to Minister Bancroft (Berlin), 2 November 1870; State Secretary von Thile (Berlin) to Chancellor von Bismarck (Versailles), 4 November 1870; Chancellor von Bismarck (Versailles) to War and Navy Minister von Roon (Versailles); War and Navy Minister von Roon (Versailles) to Chancellor von Bismarck (Versailles), 13 November 1870; Chancellor von Bismarck (Versailles) to Foreign Ministry (Berlin), 14 November 1870.

upon as a mark of inferiority and would not fail to be represented as such by the Germans themselves". With this verdict, the case was definitely settled. Before receiving this final message from Berlin, Minister von Brandt was already convinced that the American approach would fail. Pointing to earlier decisions of Fourichon and Admiral Dupré and also "to the entire attitude of the French government and its administrations, even in East Asia", he was absolutely certain that Paris would reject the proposal: "I only need to allude to the expulsion of Germans from Saigon".[118]

All in all, the Franco-German agreement on the temporary suspension of hostilities in Chinese and Japanese waters resulted in most German merchant vessels operating in this region being able to escape into neutral ports. According to information of Rehfues, there was no case of privation which also seemed improbable to him "as long as the shipmasters would remain faithful to the principle not to leave port which was observed since the beginning of the war". However, with altogether 133 vessels, of which 57 alone were lying idle in Hong Kong for almost one year, the Franco-German War caused severe financial losses for German shipmasters and shipping companies. Therefore, for Consul Walter Annecke in Shanghai, the consequences were obvious, as he wrote to Bismarck: "This number should give a picture of the importance of German shipping interests in East Asia and of the need to reinforce the local naval station as soon as possible so that in times of war the presence of a small number of enemy warships is able to entirely terminate merchant shipping".[119]

Such fears proved to be unfounded in the years to come. German steam coasters, probably chartered by the French firm A. R. Marty in Hong Kong, even assisted operations of the French navy during the Sino-French War (1884–1885). On the other hand, the French embargo on rice shipments from Southeast Asia to China (except from French Indochina) during this conflict caused severe financial losses to German merchant vessels. Yet, concerned German shipowners found little support

[118] PAAA, Peking II-261: Foreign Minister Favre (Paris) to Minister Washburne (Paris), 5 December 1870. BAB, R 901-86576: Minister von Brandt (Yokohama) to Chancellor von Bismarck (Berlin), 7 January 1871.

[119] PAAA, Peking II-261: Minister von Rehfues (Beijing) to Chancellor von Bismarck (Berlin), 27 December 1870, Consul Annecke (Shanghai) to Minister von Rehfues (Beijing), 24 November 1870, Consul Annecke (Beijing) to Chancellor von Bismarck (Berlin), 6 October 1871.

in Berlin for their compensation claims at a time when Bismarck was eager to back France's war in Tonkin and China in the interest of improved Franco-German relations. It was only in the autumn of 1914, with the outbreak of the First World War, that German merchant vessels encountered widespread confiscation and destruction on all seas, including East Asian waters.

High Politics and German Merchants (1875–1920s)

The Frankfurt Treaty and Its Repercussions

On 10 May 1871, Foreign Minister Jules Favre and Chancellor Otto von Bismarck signed the Franco-German peace treaty in Frankfurt am Main. Based on the peace preliminaries of Versailles of 26 February, the Frankfurt Treaty confirmed, specified and tightened questions such as the French indemnity of five billion gold francs, the evacuation of the occupied territory in France, the status of the inhabitants of the ceased territory and future trade relations. With the cession of Alsace and the northern part of Lorraine, France lost 14,870 square kilometres of land and 1,628 million people. The French national assembly ratified the Frankfurt Treaty on 18 May 1871 with a majority of 433 votes against 98 dissenting votes and 64 abstentions.[120] Historians have provided differing assessments of the treaty. French historian Raymond Poidevin wrote: "Thus, Bismarck's peace terms were very harsh; the Chancellor secured guarantees for Germany which would prevent France rising in anger at her defeat". German historian Klaus Hildebrand stated: "In her revanchist hostility, France refused to accept realities as definitive, as they were fixed in the Treaty of Frankfurt of 10 May 1871". Another German historian, Volker Ullrich, called France's military defeat "bitter" and even "unbearable due to the annexation of Alsace-Lorraine: this remained a thorn wounding French national pride and provoking the need for revenge". For British historian Christopher Clark, demanding Alsace-Lorraine was probably the "worst mistake" of Bismarck's political career since this annexation "traumatised the French political elite and imposed a lasting burden on Franco-German relations". Looking back to Franco-German ties in 1923, another British historian, George Peabody Gooch, noted the following: "Each of the protagonists sought and found

[120] Digeon (1959, 535–542).

allies, until almost the whole of Europe was involved in their implacable vendetta." French historian Pierre Guillen wrote that "anti-French sentiments and anti-German sentiments, mutual suspicion and hostility" were "a fundamental element, solidly rooted in public opinion". Wolfgang Schivelbusch, a German scholar of cultural studies and a historian, assessed the French rallying cry *La Revanche* as "a political religion, foundational myth and integrating force" which was both an "integrating force and mass delusion" of the Third Republic. All historians agreed that the insoluble question of Alsace-Lorraine remained the major stumbling block in Franco-German political relations between 1871 and 1914.[121]

The Frankfurt Treaty constituted the basis for relations up to 1914, which were dominated by France's efforts to regain her lost territories and Germany's attempt to retain them. According to Pierre Guillen, French foreign policy after 1871 encountered several problems: "Strategically, a border which had become vulnerable; economically, the loss of the resources and wealth of Alsace-Lorraine; psychologically, the morale of the people affected by a crisis of confidence, a reassessment of the superiority of the French cultural model and by an inferiority complex vis-à-vis Germany, more powerful demographically, economically, and militarily, whose model tended to replace the French one in the eyes of a large number of European elites". On the other hand, Imperial Germany also carried heavy burdens or "basic dilemmas" (Hildebrand) after its foundation on 18 January 1871 in the Hall of Mirrors the at Palace of Versailles. Faced with rapid international and societal changes, Bismarck was forced to conduct a policy of "self-imposed modesty" to avoid suspicions among European neighbours. This established Bismarck's foreign policy principle that Germany was territorially "saturated" and did not seek new acquisitions either in Europe or overseas. Political tensions with other powers were to be diverted to the peripheries of Europe. The main obstacle was Alsace-Lorraine, the acquisition of which Bismarck regarded already in August 1871 as a mistake; it made German foreign policy to some extent "immobile" when excluding France as a partner.[122]

From 1871, Bismarck's policy towards Paris was basically aimed at politically isolating Republican France as much as possible. This was the result of the insoluble dispute over Alsace-Lorraine. To achieve his

[121] Poidevin and Bariéty (1982, 124), Roth (1990, 607–638), Hildebrand (1995, 18), Ullrich (1999, 75), Clark (2007, 553), Gooch (1923, 5), Guillen and Allain (2007, 146) and Schivelbusch (2004, 128–135, the quotes: 128).

[122] Hildebrand (1995, 21–24) and Mommsen (1993, 18, 30, 56).

goal, Bismarck strived for closer co-operation, and even an alliance with Austria-Hungary and Russia, the two major conservative monarchies in Europe. The Chancellor hoped that the harsh peace terms of 1871 would prevent France from recovering quickly from her defeat. Therefore, France's rapid political and economic consolidation came as a surprise to Bismarck who regarded this development as a threat to German interests, prompting him to take anti-German propaganda in France very seriously.[123] In January 1873, when Elie de Gontaut-Biron became the first ambassador of the French Republic in Berlin, Franco-German diplomatic relations in Europe reached an all-time low. His despatches from Berlin illustrated Franco-German relations as being full of tension and protests, explanations and threats where each party suspected or pretended to distrust the other about having designs to renew the fight. His German counterpart in Paris, Harry Count von Arnim, was even more pessimistic, leading Bismarck, in February 1873, to state the following: "The frankness with which hatred of Germany is proclaimed and encouraged by all parties leaves us in no doubt that any government will regard the *Revanche* [revenge] as its principal task".[124]

Such fears increased after the election as French president of Marshal Patrice de MacMahon, legitimist (or royalist) and devout conservative Catholic, previously commander of France's main army, who had been trapped and wounded during the decisive Battle of Sedan on 1–2 September 1870. However, tensions decreased in November 1873 when Duke Louis Decazes became the new French foreign minister. In March 1874, the Chancellor recalled Ambassador von Arnim for encouraging the French royalists and instead sent Chlodwig Prince von Hohenlohe-Schillingsfürst to Paris. This development ushered in a period of friendlier relations between the two governments which was to some extent reflected in the microcosm of Saigon.[125]

German Consuls in Saigon

News of the signing of peace preliminaries at Versailles on 26 February 1871 soon became known through telegrams received in Hong Kong and other ports of the South China Sea. Already, around mid-March

[123] Mommsen (1993, 18–21).

[124] Gooch (1923, the quote: 9–10) and Kott (2006, 147).

[125] Wienefeld (1929, 19–23), Roth (1990, 627–633) and Guillen and Allain (2007, 146–152).

1871, some of the expelled Germans boarded the steamer *Suwonada* bound for Saigon, hoping that the French port would be reopened to them. However, on their arrival at the mouth of the Saigon River, the colonial government denied them entry to the French colony, forcing them to sail to Singapore. The same fate was encountered by seventeen German merchant vessels, mostly in ballast but with two or three carrying the cargoes of Chinese traders, which had sailed in March 1871 from Hong Kong and Xiamen (Amoy), expecting that the Franco-German peace agreement would be definite by their arrival. Yet, with official news still pending, they were ordered to leave the waters of French Cochinchina, assembling near Cape St. Jacques at the mouth of the Saigon River to await further news. Meanwhile, on 1 March 1871, the French National Assembly had voted in favour of accepting the peace terms, after which Germans troops began leaving France. When in mid-April 1871 this information became known among the waiting Germans shipmasters, they again hoped to be permitted to enter the river, but in vain. Therefore, on 26 April 1871, they signed a joint petition in French to Governor Dupré, pointing to the fact that Chinese firms in Saigon had chartered their vessels to ship cargoes to Hong Kong, Amoy and France, and also warning of considerable financial losses for both ships and charterers should no permission be granted. They explicitly promised the "peacefulness and orderliness of their crews" on their arrival at Saigon. The shipmasters' action proved successful when on 28 April the governor telegraphically confirmed that from that day "German citizens can come back to Cochinchina, and from 6 May also German vessels".[126] On 15 May 1871, Niederberger, who had returned to Saigon from his exile in Singapore, was informed by the head of the governor's cabinet that Dupré was prepared to issue a temporary exequatur to him which would be valid until the French foreign ministry sent the final one. The governor felt pressured by the return of the Germans and found it "indispensable that one of them holds consular functions". Niederberger did not hesitate to accept the offer, pointing to the various German interests in Cochinchina, among them the important shipping in those waters, and

[126] PAAA, Peking II-261: Consul Eimbcke (Hong Kong) to Minister von Rehfues (Beijing), 31 March 1871. ANOM, INDO-GGI-11647: 17 German shipmasters and ships (Cape St. Jacques) to Governor Dupré (Saigon), 26 April 1871, Government telegram of 28 April 1871 (Saigon). *The North-China Herald and Supreme Court & Consular Gazette*, 19 May 1871.

also to the fact that the colony's administration was "extremely accommodating on this occasion". He reopened the German consulate on 19 May 1871, two days before news arrived in Saigon that the Frankfurt Treaty had been signed.[127] On 25 November 1871, Georg Niederberger was formally appointed honorary consul of Imperial Germany in Saigon. He had found strong backing in Hamburg where the various businessmen consulted regarded Niederberger as the only suitable person to be made consul and saw it a matter of honour that he should return to his post after "suffering so much because of his position as representative of the Confederation".[128]

In his first post-war report, on 1870–1871, Niederberger remained highly objective, sticking to the facts without expressing anti-French sentiments, even when elaborating on the situation facing German merchants in Saigon after the outbreak of the war. The Germans had to suffer from "unpopularity and much hostility", which had increased after the proclamation of the French Republic, the consul explained, resulting in the French citizens of Saigon, "partly for other reasons than patriotism", demanding the expulsion of the Germans. Referring to German trading after the war, he described it "as flourishing as before" and hinted especially at the increase in shipping under the German flag. Despite the fact that only a few German companies operated in Saigon, Niederberger said that they "represented first-rank trading firms, closely followed by the English, and with the French ranked in last place". In general, the German consul was optimistic about the situation in Cochinchina. He regarded the colony's trading position as little affected by the war, pointing to newly opened steamship lines, banks and insurance companies, and especially to the new telegraph line to Singapore and Hong Kong inaugurated on 29 July 1871 which he assessed as "outstanding" for Saigon's development.[129] Concerning the Asian residents of the port city, Niederberger was, on the one hand, rather critical of the Vietnamese,

[127] PAAA, R 251848: A. de Montjon, Cabinet of the Governor (Saigon) to Consul Niederberger (Saigon), 15 May 1871, Exequatur of Admiral Dupré (Saigon) for Georg Niederberger (Saigon), 17 May 1871, Consul Niederberger (Saigon) to Bismarck (Berlin), 23 May 1871. In his letter to Bismarck, the consul admitted to having acted without confirmation when reopening the German consulate in Saigon.

[128] PAAA, R 251848: Mayor Kirchenpauer (Hamburg) to Foreign Ministry (Berlin), 8 November 1871, Appointment of Georg Niederberger (Berlin), 25 November 1871.

[129] Baudrit (1936, vol. 1, 60: Session of 2 February 1870: Telegraph station to be established at Cape St. Jacques to link Saigon with Singapore and Hong Kong).

describing them as "lax, sluggish and apathetic" and wondering why, after ten years of contact with Europeans and financial prosperity, "the people still looked so miserably clothed and apparently as poor as before". On the other hand, he thought highly of the Chinese, characterising them as "intelligent and diligent on average".[130]

In 1872, Niederberger went on extended leave to Germany, leaving consular matters to his associate, Emil Saltzkorn. This caused dissatisfaction in the small German community in Saigon who allegedly wished to have "stronger, more intelligent and independent representation of their interests", as A. Dietelbach, clerk of Speidel & Co. in Phnom Penh, explained to Bismarck in May 1873. The trader also disclosed that anti-German sentiments were prevalent in the country: Germans were frequently confronted with French endeavours to create all kinds of difficulties for them, especially over legal issues, warning Vietnamese about dealing with Germans, and spoiling their stay in the colony through continuous spitefulness. Even in Cambodia and Annam the French were making problems, fearful over the settling of German traders in these countries should they entirely be brought under French control. This remark was a reference to the exploratory missions by French merchant Jean Dupuis on the Red River into China and his detention by Vietnamese mandarins in May 1873.[131]

At the end of 1873, Georg Niederberger resigned from his office as consul. Citing "circumstances which arose since my departure from Saigon, but especially the unfavourable climate conditions of Cochinchina", he announced he was taking up residence in Stuttgart, proposing to appoint his partner, Emil Saltzkorn, as consul. This prompted interested business circles in Hamburg to push the Hamburg city state government to appoint a professional German consul in Saigon. Their initiative reflected the great hopes German traders had for the economic development of Cochinchina. In early 1874, the Hamburg senate informed the German government that from the commercial point of view it supported the proposal "in the liveliest manner". This opened the way for bringing the issue before the Committee for Trade and Traffic of the Bundesrat (Federal Council), composed of delegates from

[130] *Preußisches Handels-Archiv* (January 1873, 2, 34–41).

[131] PAAA, R 251848: Ambassador Harry Baron von Arnim (Paris) to Foreign Ministry (Berlin), 2 October 1872; A. Dietelbach (Phnom Penh) to Chancellor von Bismarck (Berlin), [no day] May 1873.

the twenty-five German federal states, which gave the green light in its session of 13 January 1874. In his memorandum to Bismarck, Bernhard Ernst von Bülow, secretary of state for foreign affairs (the Chancellor's most faithful follower), pointed to the fact that besides trading and shipping, Cochinchina was also of interest because of its relations to Siam and Vietnam. "What deserves attention is particularly the French colonial government' s intention, which seems to be already realised, to take possession of the Annamite [Vietnamese] province of Tonkin that opens access to Chinese Yunnan".[132]

On 15 March 1874, the French representative to Hanoi, Lieutenant Paul Philastre, signed a treaty with the Vietnamese government under which France was granted considerable concessions in Tonkin. The "Philastre Treaty" opened up Vietnam to French influence, or so-called protection, with free trade granted on and around the Red River. This event, which had certainly been already anticipated in Berlin at an earlier stage, was reflected in the wording of Bülow's memorandum. He made it clear that the future German representative in Saigon had a political task as well, namely closely observing and reporting on French activities in Vietnam. Therefore, the post needed to be filled by an experienced Foreign Service official acquainted with East Asia, and especially with Vietnam and French Cochinchina. The best candidate for the post was Werner von Bergen (a Prussian by birth), previously consulate secretary in Caracas, Venezuela, and since December 1871 German consul in Bangkok. In his post in the capital of Siam, Bergen had proven to be an attentive observer of the country's domestic and foreign affairs under the control of King Chulalongkorn (Rama V), witnessing expansion by both France and Britain as they increased their colonial territories and encircled Siam. To signal the political importance of the new post and give its occupant a higher status in the eyes of the French authorities in Cochinchina, Bergen was elevated to consul-general, thus securing diplomatic rank. To prevent any possible concerns on the French side, German Ambassador Prince von Hohenlohe-Schillingsfürst was instructed to personally approach Foreign Minister Duke Louis Decazes on the

[132] Brocheux and Hèmery (2009, 28–29). PAAA, R 251848: Georg Niederberger (Stuttgart) to Foreign Ministry (Berlin), 22 December 1873; Gustav Heinrich Kirchenpauer, Second Mayor and Representative of Hamburg at the Federal Council (Hamburg) to Foreign Ministry (Berlin), 26 February 1874; State Secretary von Bülow (Berlin) to Chancellor von Bismarck (Berlin), 4 March 1874.

matter and to inform Berlin by telegram of his reply. Bülow made it clear to Hohenlohe-Schillingsfürst that "the speedy filling of the vacant consulate in Saigon is in official interest". Less than four weeks later, the ambassador reported from Paris on the positive response of the French foreign minister.[133]

On 29 August 1874, Werner von Bergen was appointed consul-general of Imperial Germany in Cochinchina. The new post was vested with the considerable sum of 25,000 marks (for the year 1874), taken from the foreign ministry's disposition fund for newly established professional German consulates.[134] Just three months later, Bergen and his family were travelling to Saigon on board the Messageries Maritimes liner *Sindh* where the consul-general accidentally ran into Admiral Baron Victor Auguste Duperré, the new governor of Cochinchina. The naval officer, "a Bonapartist by inclination",[135] had served in the French navy during the Napoleonic wars, acquiring administrative experience as governor of the French colony of Gorée and Dependencies (now Gabon) and political knowledge as principal private secretary to Navy Minister Chasseloup-Laubat. He made the best possible impression on Bergen who praised him as possessing "the best intentions to raise up this colony, and especially its commerce". The German official went even further, stating that "Cochinchina should congratulate itself for having obtained such an incredibly intelligent, efficient and energetical head, considerably deviating from the usual French routine". After Bergen formally assumed office on 3 December 1874, he was glad to note that the governor had received the owners of three major German companies in Saigon "in the kindest way", assuring them, and also the consul-general, by word of mouth and in writing of his intention to promote their interests "as far as possible".[136]

[133] PAAA, R 251848: State Secretary von Bülow (Berlin) to Ambassador von Hohenlohe-Schillingsfürst (Paris), 23 July 1874; telegram of Hohenlohe-Schillingsfürst (Paris) to the Foreign Ministry (Berlin), 20 August 1874.

[134] PAAA, R 251848: State Secretary von Bülow (Berlin) to Emperor William I (Berlin), 26 August 1874; Appointment of Werner von Bergen (Babelsberg), 29 August 1874.

[135] Corfield (2013, 90).

[136] PAAA, R 251848: Note of German Consulate (Singapore), 25 November 1874. PAAA, R 251849: Consul-General von Bergen (Saigon) to Foreign Ministry, 2 January 1875.

On 1 January 1875, at the New Year reception of the governor, Bergen and Duperré gave speeches they had agreed on earlier. Since the German consul-general had the highest rank among the foreign representatives, he addressed the governor directly, expressing his strong hopes for the future progress of Cochinchina "thanks to an accurate and intelligent administration". Duperré responded by promising his "constant solicitude for the interests of your nationals which I do not separate from those of the colony". Furthermore, he said: "I will expect with confidence the co-operation of all in order to increase the commercial prosperity of this country, the major goal of my efforts". In his concluding remarks, the governor expressively mentioned "the dignified representatives of friendly powers of France" which he addressed that day. This included the German consul-general who, in his report to Berlin, considered the speeches "a picture of the present friendly relations which procuring I regard as my next task".[137]

The strong interest Governor Duperré took in economically developing Cochinchina prompted him to seek close co-operation with German companies, and with the consul-general. On 20 April 1875, at the official dinner in the governor's palace, the seats of honours were reserved for the Germans, with the manager of Behre & Co. being placed in front of high-ranking French military officials. In his reports to the foreign ministry, Bergen was full of praise about the governor's friendly and supportive attitude, which even went beyond commercial matters. In early 1875, when the Hamburg merchant Karl T. Kufahl, clerk in Wm. G. Hale & Company, was arrested for repeated embezzlement and fraud and for bribing a French official, Bergen approached the governor who quickly succeeded in speeding up judicial procedures in Saigon. After Kufahl was sentenced to three years in prison, Bergen asked the governor to endorse the petition for pardon addressed to the French president. He found Duperré not only supportive of his request but also prepared to personally take up the matter with President MacMahon during his planned visit to Paris, promising "to secure" the pardon.[138] This amicable attitude prompted even Bismarck, who had followed Bergen's reports from Saigon, to take up the matter. Bülow wrote to tell the German

[137] PAAA, R 251849: Consul-General von Bergen (Saigon) to Foreign Ministry, 2 January 1875 (with copies of speech texts of 1 January 1875).

[138] PAAA, R 251849: Consul-General von Bergen (Saigon) to Foreign Ministry, 24 April 1875 and 29 January 1876.

ambassador in Paris the Chancellor was satisfied to see that relations had improved "thanks to incentives given by the governor himself". Prince von Hohenlohe-Schillingsfürst was charged with letting Decazes know "how positive the obliging behaviour of the senior French official towards our representative was considered for promoting mutual interests". According to the ambassador, the foreign minister had noticed that "with great pleasure", replying to him that Duperré was full of praise for the good relations between him and Bergen and honouring "the tactful behaviour" of the consul-general. This was "even more pleasing", Decazes stated (as Hohenlohe-Schillingsfürst revealed in his letter), "because Saigon's commerce was largely managed by German companies and its prosperity was highly relevant for the French colony".[139]

At this time, when Berlin and Paris were exchanging such friendly diplomatic gestures, the German government had already recalled Bergen from Saigon. On 12 November 1875, the consul-general, having been informed about the decision, handed over consular matters to Saltzkorn. On 28 February 1876, Bergen and his family left Cochinchina on the Messageries Maritimes liner *Djemnah* bound for Marseille; Bergen (who was married with a Venezuelan) was later made minister-resident for Central America in Guatemala City (in 1895, he was promoted to chargé d'affaires).[140] The concrete reason for recalling Bergen from his post in Saigon after about one year is not apparent from the sources consulted, or any other sources, but certainly relate to severe criticisms directed by State Secretary von Bülow (and thereby by Bismarck) directed against Bergen for seemingly attempting to establish some kind of formal relations with King Norodom of Cambodia (in 1863, the king had placed his country under French protection). When Bergen reported that he had declined Norodom's invitation to come to Phnom Penh, but expressed hopes of getting permission from the German government "sooner or later", alarm bells rang in Berlin. On 9 April 1875, Bülow made it clear that the consul-general, "without a definite directive from here", was not authorised to indicate such a possibility and gave Bergen advice to keep

[139] PAAA, R 251849: State Secretary von Bülow (Berlin) to Ambassador von Hohenlohe-Schillingsfürst (Paris), 10 March 1876; Ambassador von Hohenlohe-Schillingsfürst (Paris) to State Secretary von Bülow (Berlin), 20 March 1876.

[140] PAAA, R 251849: Memorandum concerning the forthcoming abolition of the Imperial Consulate in Saigon as professional consulate, 25 February 1876; Consul-General von Bergen (Saigon) to Foreign Ministry (Berlin), 28 February 1876.

to "the limitations of your tasks attributed to you". The state secretary pointed to the fact that "we do not pursue political goals there, and also not in Annam or Siam, as I seriously need to remind you". Bergen was requested in future not to submit reports containing political recommendations and to strictly keep to his role of "an objective observer".[141] The note from Berlin made it clear that Bismarck wished to pursue a strictly non-interventionist policy towards the French colonial empire in Asia. The Chancellor wanted to be regularly informed about French activities in Indochina, but was careful enough to avoid any sign that Germany was meddling with France's affairs in her empire.

Meanwhile, relations between France and Germany had entered a severely strained phase after rumours became public that senior German officials and parliamentarians were thinking in terms of a preventive war against France. The so-called War in Sight crisis of April–May 1875, the "most dangerous crisis since 1871" (Gooch), remained an episode that raised suspicions over Bismarck's true intentions, even prompting Britain and Russia temporarily into a joint defensive posture against Germany. Wrongly assessing the reactions of European powers, the crisis was a severe blow to Bismarck's diplomacy. The Chancellor obviously tried to put both direct and indirect pressure on France to abolish her rearmament programme, which Paris regarded as intervention into the country's internal affairs. According to Raymond Poidevin, the result was the "first diplomatic victory by France over Bismarck's policy of violence", and also a sign that opinion in leading circles in Germany was divided, with only a minority considering a preventive war. The strategy of isolating France had "completely failed", concluded Wolfgang J. Mommsen, and the coalition of European powers against Imperial Germany, so much feared by Bismarck, had become "a real possibility, even if it was provoked by his own thoughtless politics". Certainly, Bismarck learned from the crisis that only a defensive strategy would preserve peace in Europe and safeguard Germany's geopolitical position in the long term.[142]

[141] PAAA, R 251849: State Secretary von Bülow (Berlin) to Consul-General von Bergen (Saigon), 9 April 1875.

[142] Gooch (1923, 11–15, the quote: 12), Wienefeld (1929, 25–39), Craig (1978, 107–110), Poidevin and Bariéty (1982, 157), Ullrich (1999, 79–83) and Mommsen (1993, 24–25, the quote: 25).

Against this background, any attempt by the German consul-general in Saigon to establish some form of contact with Cambodia, Vietnam or Siam could easily be regarded by France as German intervention in her colonial affairs. This had obviously triggered Bülow's reaction. However, in the long term, a more important reason to recall Bergen, and to return the Saigon post to the hands of German merchants, was the rather negative assessment by the consul-general of the economic importance of Cochinchina for German commercial interests. In his lengthy report of October 1875, Bergen provided exact facts and figures about the situation in German companies, which were "partly concealed as much as possible", as he revealed. Because the wholesale trade was "almost exclusively in Chinese hands", they commissioned German firms for their exports; the Germans also handled insurance and banking transactions for them. Since hardly any industrial goods from Germany, "with the exception of beer and lamps", were imported to Cochinchina, German firms instead traded French, British, Dutch and Belgian products. Their net profits in 1874 were almost nil due to strong competition from Chinese importers. Bergen assessed the entire capital of the three German companies as not being higher than 400,000 dollars. As he noted, they employed fourteen German staff, and there was also a business associate and a clerk [Karl T. Kufahl] with Wm. G. Hale & Co., thus making a total of sixteen German nationals. He concluded as follows: "The relevancy of the German element for this colony, and especially for trading, was well overestimated by interested business circles at a time when this pertinence was at its climax; however, nowadays no one with only fair knowledge of the situation here will have illusions on this point". After the departure of Werner von Bergen in February 1876, the post of German consul was taken over by Emil Saltzkorn, partner in Behre & Company; during his absence, the acting consul was Gustav Nissle, the company's managing clerk. [143]

Increasing Tensions (1875–1914)

The outcome of the so-called War in Sight crisis (1875) resulted in Bismarck's increased efforts to encourage other European powers to

[143] PAAA, R 251849: Report of Consul-General von Bergen (Saigon), 1 October 1875; Consul-General von Bergen (Saigon) to Foreign Ministry (Berlin), 28 February 1876; Consul Satzkorn (Saigon) to Foreign Ministry (Berlin), 16 May 1876.

settle their disputes at the peripheries of Europe and in the colonies. It even led him to encourage France to pursue her imperialist goals in Tunisia, northern Africa. When Paris declared the country a French protectorate in May 1883, Italian stakeholders in Tunisia felt severely hampered, prompting Rome to seek closer attachment to Germany and Austria-Hungary. On 20 May 1882, with the Italian government joining the Dual Alliance (the combination of Germany and Austria-Hungary established in October 1879), the Triple Alliance between Berlin, Vienna, and Rome was created. This did not prevent Bismarck actively searching for a "rapprochement" to overcome the "congenital defect" of estrangement with France (Hildebrand) which had obstructed Imperial Germany since its foundation. The result was Bismarck's support of French Prime Minister Jules Ferry's East Asian policies during the Sino-French War (1884–1885) although Berlin formally remained strictly neutral in the conflict. With Ferry's resignation in March 1885, this brief period of considerably improved Franco-German relations abruptly ended.[144]

With respect to France's colonial empire, Bismarck kept strictly to his non-interventionist policies. In 1887, when the French general tariff was applied to Indochina, placing heavy customs fees on most non-French products, the foreign ministry prepared a memorandum for Bismarck based on information from Consul Karl Theodor Speidel. The foreign ministry official pointed to "the repeated perception" that "France's colonial expansion is synonymous with the elimination of existing foreign interests". However, this notion was not shared by Bismarck who pencilled next to it the following remark: " Of it there is no doubt, even without those facts: East India [Southeast Asia] costs the French a lot of money and people, they do not want to expend that *pour le roi de Prusse* [for the King of Prussia]". With this humorous French expression, the Chancellor expressed his sympathy for France's colonial engagement in Indochina (from which German firms such as Speidel & Co. profited to a large extent), and even for the introduction of the French general tariff in the colony which disadvantaged non-French businesses and imported products.[145]

[144] Poidevin and Bariéty (1982, 181–189), Mommsen (1993, 25–26, 43–51) and Guillen and Allain (2007, 156–159).

[145] BAB, R 901-9501: Memorandum of Legation Councillor Ludwig Raschdau (Berlin) for Chancellor von Bismarck, 29 September 1887, with marginal notes of Bismarck (written in pencil) (Friedrichsruh), 1 October 1887. The German version of Bismarck's

In March 1890, Bismarck's dismissal as German imperial chancellor was received with pleasure in France. This mood was enhanced when Emperor William II declared his passionate wish to enter into cordial relations with France. Yet, French public opinion was not prepared for such move, as fresh anti-German rhetoric and interpellations in the French parliament made obvious. This was greeted with anti-French press articles in Germany. Less than a year after Bismarck had left office, a French naval squadron visited the Russian port of Kronstadt and received a euphoric reception. This was the beginning of the Franco-Russian rapprochement which reached its peak with the conclusion of the Franco-Russian military-political alliance (1893). The alliance opened a new chapter in the history of the Third French Republic, symbolising "complete recovery from the disasters of 1870 and a guarantee against menaces, humiliations and aggression", George Peabody Gooch explained. French politicians loudly celebrated the pact by underlining its significance: security against Germany, and increased influence in global politics. However, as Pierre Guillen and Jean-Claude Allain pointed out, with differing political positions quickly appearing between Paris and St. Petersburg, the practical effect of the alliance was weakened.[146] Considering their eastern border with Germany secured by the alliance with Russia (while Germany faced the dangerous prospect of a two-front war),[147] after almost a decade French policymakers resumed their colonial ambitions. In 1894, Gabriel Hanotaux, an admirer of Jules Ferry, became French foreign minister, launching an expansionist colonial policy in Africa and Asia. For this strategy, Hanotaux hoped to achieve Germany's support and to include her into a European system of equality and

note reads as follows: "Darin ist auch ohne diese Tatsachen kein Zweifel. Hinterindien kostet den Franzosen viel Geld und Menschen, die wollen das nicht *pour le roi de Prusse* aufgewendet haben". The historical expression "travailler pour le roi de Prusse" [working for the King of Prussia] means working for nothing or without being paid for one's efforts or active participation. This humouristic French proverb derives either from alleged practices of King Frederick II (the Great) of Prussia who broke off his alliances with France in 1742 and 1756 or from common practices (as observed by the French) of granting Prussian soldiers only small amounts of pay which were never paid exactly on the last day of the month.

[146] Gooch (1923, 32–35, the quote: 35) and Guillen and Allain (2007, 188–189, 191–192).

[147] Mommsen (1993, 110–111), Hildebrand (1995, 157–161), Kott (2006, 159) and Stovall (2015, 253).

balance. His pragmatic approach involved a truce in the Franco-German conflict, as became evident when France and Germany amicably arranged their frontiers in West Africa in 1894 and both co-operated with Russia in 1895, forcing Japan to abandon her claim on Port Arthur after the Sino-Japanese War. This kind of co-operation was also visible in the tacit concession by Paris of Germany's 1897 seizure of Jiaozhou (Kiaochow) Bay, located in China's Shandong Province, and in the equally tacit acceptance by Berlin of France's 1898–1899 occupation of Guangzhou Bay (Guangzhouwan), situated in China's Guangdong Province.[148]

In the early years of the twentieth century, the break between Paris and Berlin came with French policy in Morocco and German reaction to it. It began with the Anglo-French Entente Cordiale signed on 8 April 1904 by Hanotaux's successor, Théophile Delcassé (French foreign minister from 1898 to 1905), who became best known for his hatred of Germany. Delcassé, a protégé of Leon Gambetta and member of France's Radical Party, strived to provide the country with more security against the Triple Alliance of Germany, Austria and Italy and continue French expansionist policy, especially in northern Africa, with Morocco as the main stake.[149] After Delcassé declared that he and his British counterpart, Lord Lansdowne, had been concerned exclusively with the interests of their own countries, without detriment to those of any other power, German official reaction was at first favourable to the treaty. However, Emperor William II became increasingly concerned about its possible aggressive implications, and among German government officials, the pact was more and more regarded as a severe blow for Germany's foreign policy and as another decisive step by France in leaving behind her international isolation which Bismarck's diplomacy had created since 1870. Friedrich von Holstein, an influential official of the German foreign ministry, found "Germany's prestige diminished in previous years, while our opponents and rivals are about to encircle us".[150] This was probably a misinterpretation, but demonstrated the decisive impact of the Entente Cordiale on Franco-German relations and international politics.[151]

[148] Gooch (1923, 35–38), Poidevin and Bariéty (1982, 217–221), Nipperdey (1998, 654–656) and Guillen and Allain (2007, 193–196, 207–213).

[149] Guillen and Allain (2007, 233–234, 236–239).

[150] Gooch (1923, 41), Hildebrand (1995, 225–226) and Ullrich (1999, 204–206, the quotes: 205).

[151] Mommsen (1993, 167) and Guillen and Allain (2007, 229–231).

What concretely aroused German worries was France's growing control over Morocco, which was in full accordance with the terms of the Anglo-French treaty, but which triggered a German response. The German government's motives for intervening in Morocco in 1905 remain somewhat obscure. As Gordon A. Graig explains: Chancellor Bernhard von Bülow seemed "to have regarded the operation as one in which bluff would carry the day". What seems certain is that Holstein wanted to teach France a lesson.[152] The crisis began with Emperor William II landing at Tangier in March 1904. Addressing the German business community and the representative of the Sultan, the German ruler insisted on a free Morocco open to peaceful competition among all nations, without monopoly or annexation. This certainly challenged French influence in the North African country. The rather dramatic provocation aroused French and German national feeling and caused diplomatic quarrels across Europe, with London closely siding Paris. According to Gooch, it was Delcassé's "fundamental error (...) in not purchasing in advance Germany's assent to French policy in Morocco". Germany had no political interests and aspirations in Morocco, but her trade was rapidly increasing. She possessed treaty rights and preventing them "being disposed of without her consent was a question of prestige". Consequently, mounting pressure in France forced Delcassé to step down from his office, and the French government was required to submit its Morocco politics to an international conference — "a severe humiliation of France", as Wolfgang J. Mommsen put it.[153]

In January 1906, the Algeciras Conference (with Morocco and twelve European countries, including Russia and the Ottoman Empire, and the United States taking part in it) was opened turning into a prolonged struggle between France and Germany, with Britain openly supporting the French side, before the dispute was settled. In the Algeciras Treaty, France was granted the exclusive right to develop Morocco according to

[152] Graig (1978, the quote: 318). This possible motivation of Holstein is confirmed by Mommsen (1993, 168), Hildebrand (1995, 233) and Ullrich (1999, 206).

[153] Graig (1978, 318–3210), Gooch (1923, 42–43, the quote: 47) and Mommsen (1993, 169–170, the quote: 170).

her plans.[154] The most important result of the Moroccan crisis was the opening of the path to the creation of the Triple Entente (the informal understanding between France, Russia, and Britain) in 1907.

Another result of the Moroccan crisis was France's heightened self-confidence. It became common to speak of "la nouvelle France" (the New France) after this turning point. Britain's moral support throughout the crisis helped to strengthen the position of France as a great power. This became obvious from the start of the second Moroccan crisis when France dispatched troops to the North African country (which was a violation of the terms of the Algeciras Treaty) and Germany reacted by dispatching the gunboat *Panther* to the Moroccan port of Agadir in July 1911. According to Wolfgang J. Mommsen, this "spectacular act of imperialist gunboat diplomacy intended to force France to the negotiating table and to convince her of Germany's seriousness to demand compensations elsewhere". The French government, not being impressed by the open threat, found full support in Britain, while the German foreign minister, Alfred von Kiderlen-Wächter, remained isolated in Europe and even inside his own country; neither the Emperor nor Chancellor Theobald von Bethmann Hollweg (in office since 1909) or the navy high command were prepared to back his aggressive course. In the end, both countries agreed on a compromise, with Germany refraining from any political influence on Morocco, and receiving some territory in French Congo. Gooch wrote that both France and Germany "repeated the mistake of 1905", and encountered the same result: "Once again Germany alienated the sympathies of the world, and once again France found comfort and support in her English friends." Germany's high-risk policy, which led to grave embarrassment for her international prestige, was a triumph for France, strengthening her determination not to submit to any more humiliations and not to enter into an entente with Imperial Germany, as long as the question over Alsace-Lorraine remained unsolved.[155] This attitude was

[154] According to Klaus Hildebrand (1995, 234), the conference was "a clear defeat of the Germans". As Guillen and Allain (2007, 241) explain, Germany stopped French expansion, "at least in the form she had followed, but this success was limited because the privileged position of France was formalised" in certain important sectors of Morocco's political system and economy.

[155] Mommsen (1993, 219–227, the quote: 220), Gooch (1923, 55–58, the quote: 56) and Guillen and Allain (2007, 264–267).

embodied by Raymond Poincaré, the French prime minister and right-winger (whose family had fled Lorraine after its annexation by Germany). Single-handedly controlling French foreign policy since January 1912, Poincaré emphasised a new policy of toughness vis à vis Berlin. Towards the French ambassador in Berlin, Jules Cambon (who was supportive of a détente with Germany), he made it clear that the consequences would be dire: "We would fall out with England, and with Russia, we would lose all the benefits of a policy that France has been following for many years, we would obtain for Alsace only illusory satisfactions and we would find ourselves the following day isolated, diminished and disqualified." In January 1913, Poincaré was elected president of the French Republic.[156]

In 1913–1914, strained Franco-German relations and the tense political atmosphere in Europe were to a certain extent reflected in Saigon. It became public when local celebrations by both the French and German communities accidentally took place on the same day, 27 January 1913. This coincidence caused the local French press to regard the matter as highly symbolic for Franco-German relations. The background was that since November 1912, French authorities in Cochinchina had been preparing for the official visit of Admiral Alfred Winsloe, commander-in-chief of Britain's China Station in Hong Kong. On 22 January 1913, the Admiral landed on board his flagship *Minotaur* in Saigon accompanied by the *Kent*, another armoured cruiser. In the port of Saigon, the French navy had assembled an impressive number of men-of-war of the Naval Squadron of the Far East and the Pacific. To specially honour the British officer during the grand festivities lasting days, Governor-General Sarraut travelled from Hanoi to Saigon and, as German consul Felix Reinsdorf reported, "Saigon and the newspapers got into the usual frenzy". This event coincided with the annual reception of the German consulate celebrating the 54th birthday of Emperor William II on 27 January 1913. In the eyes of the consul (who did not send out special invitations to the reception), the French authorities had harmed "international decency" by completely ignoring this event when not dispatching any representative. To make things even worse, on the same day the Saigon newspaper *L'Opinion* took up this "curious coincidence" by launching an attack on the Emperor and on Germany: "In

[156] Keiger (1997, 137–138; the quote: 137) and Stovall (2015, 254).

our distant Far Eastern colony, while French and English joyfully celebrate the benefits of their close union, some subjects of the Emperor Wilhelm, probably grouped in the salons of their consulate, far from the distant sounds of the jubilant masses, will raise their glasses, in which will perhaps bubble French champagne, to the health of their sovereign". The journal highlighted France's new international position being "strongly supported by her two great and powerful allies", while Germany was "currently finding herself isolated in the middle of the concert of powers". It concluded that "we are far away from the time when Bismarck and Moltke [the former German Chief of the Great General Staff] spoke as masters to the universe!" In August 1914, Consul Reinsdorf retrospectively noted that "*L'Opinion* has long sworn at everything which is German" and the mood in Saigon was "decisively hostile towards Germany, partly because of professional envy".[157]

The First World War and Its Aftermath

The election of Raymond Poincaré as president of the French Republic enhanced the new spirit of confidence. This was noted by Wilhelm von Schoen, German ambassador in Paris (1910–1914) in his memoirs, stating that "France's general policy was unmistakably dominated by hostility to Germany, with the exception of occasional agreement in individual questions which were totally independent of the great point of disagreement". It was "the great question of Alsace-Lorraine, (…) the wound of 1871 would not heal, the French still demanded satisfaction for the injury to their national pride". As Schoen observed, patriotic excitement had eased over time "but an active minority, with effective means at its disposal, was unremitting in its efforts to keep up the smouldering fire, with a view to its bursting into flames at the given moment".[158] The ambassador's own observations should be supplemented by the assessment of French historian Georges-Henri Soutou explaining that, in 1914, "the memory of the 1870 defeat remained perennial, even if *La Revanche* [the Revenge] did not represent a goal for most of them. We were increasingly worried by the demographic superiority as the economic and

[157] *L'Opinion*, 27 January 1913. PAAA, R 19426: Consul Felix Reinsdorf (Saigon) to Chancellor von Bethmann Hollweg (Berlin), 31 January 1913 and 7 August 1914.

[158] Schoen (1922, 140–142).

military power of Germany, which certain circles suspected to wanting to establish her hegemony on the continent".[159] This mood came to a climax with increasing tensions in Europe after the assassination of Archduke Franz Ferdinand of Austria on 28 June 1914. With Germany declaring war on Russia, and France mobilising on 30 July, public sentiment turned worse in France and her colonies. In Saigon, Consul Felix Reinsdorf noted that on 1 August 1914 the call "à Berlin" (the call to march French troops to Berlin) was already being shouted on Saigon's main street, patriotic French marches were frequently played in local market halls and satirical verses were put up in the main post office.[160]

Since mid-July 1914, the French telegraphic office in Saigon had only released very short and vague messages about the coming European conflict while more concrete news was transmitted by German and British news agencies in Hong Kong and Singapore. This gave German businessmen in the British colonial ports sufficient time to make last-minute personal arrangements and financial transactions before prices fell sharply and banks closed down. "Lacking news prevented the [German] business community of Saigon from seizing such advantages", wrote the consul. When Germany's declaration of war on France (3 August 1914) became known in Saigon the next day, public sentiment of the French community increasingly turned against the German residents. Demonstrations were staged in front of the German consulate when Governor Jules Maurice Gourbeil instructed Reinsdorf to take down the consulate's flag and plate and charged the United States deputy consul, William D. Kraft, local manager of the Standard Oil Company, with looking after German interests. On 6 August, Kraft received the expulsion decree issued by the governor ordering that all Germans had to leave Cochinchina within twenty-four hours. This affected twenty-two persons residing in Saigon and Cholon and eleven crew members of the *Argenfels*, the steamer of the major Bremen shipping company DDG Hansa, which was docking in the naval port of Saigon. According to Reinsdorf, twenty-three residents and eleven sailors liable for German military service had already departed the colony for Manila, Philippines, on board German liners to go on to

[159] Soutou (2007, 287) and Poidevin and Bariéty (1982, 285).

[160] Gooch (1923, 62–63). PAAA, R 19426: Consul Reinsdorf (Saigon) to Chancellor von Bethmann Hollweg (Berlin), 7 August 1914.

Jiaozhou (Kiaochow) to join the struggle against approaching Japanese forces.[161]

Violent riots by French residents against German properties occurred in Saigon on the evening of 6 August 1914. As *L'Opinion* commented the next day, this was "the spontaneous expression of anger felt by all the people of Saigon, which is unfortunately only too understandable". The outrage was sparked by telegraphic news of two Frenchmen being killed during the German advance into Belgium. When protesters found the German consulate vacated, around five hundred of them moved to the premises of the Kegel Club (Bowling Club).[162] With bamboo rods taken from the awnings of the nearby warehouse of Speidel & Co., the crowd moved into the club's building "smashing furniture, the library comes down with an astounding crash, the billiards are knocked over while on the first floor a real bombardment of flower pots breaks the window panes of the verandas". The newspaper found the club "to be ravaged as if by a cyclone", actions which were "probably very violently but perfectly reasoned" and "the expression of strong anger". The next target of the rioters was the seat of Speidel & Co., located in a small street leading to the quay of the Chinese arroyo. "It was the repetition of the looting of the club", remarked *L'Opinion*, adding that only the furniture containing the company registers was spared from destruction. The French flag was hoisted at the corner window and greeted with applause. The other German company, F. Engler & Co., escaped looting because it shared its premises with a British firm and the French shipping company Chargeurs Réunis. One French resident was killed during the riots. "One finds the uproar regrettable which capitalised on the demonstrations, and the other, quite the opposite, maintains that the actions of an enemy attacking us and behaving so cravenly justify all retaliation", concluded *L'Opinion*. "The authorities seem powerless in the face of the mob", reported the *Hong Kong Daily Press* on 17 August, adding some days later that the Germans were rescued by the French military and put

[161] PAAA, R 19426: Consul Felix Reinsdorf (Saigon) to Chancellor von Bethmann Hollweg (Berlin), 7 August 1914.

[162] The "Kegel Club" (Bowling Club) in Saigon was established in the 1890s on the initiative of Friedrich Wilhelm Speidel [Junior], which despite its name was an international association, with German, Swiss, British, American and French members. PAAA, R 19418: Commander Gildemeister (SMS *Irene*, Street of Malacca) to Naval Squadron Command, 13 July 1901.

in prison for safekeeping. According to the police director of Saigon, the material damage to the premises of the club and of Speidel & Co. was estimated at 100,000 piastres.[163]

On 7 August, thirty-three Germans left Saigon for Java on board the Norwegian steamer *Solveig*. The manager of Speidel & Co. in Phnom Penh was permitted by the French authorities to stay in Cambodia because the situation was regarded as safe. Consul Reinsdorf, trying in vain to contact the Germans in Tonkin, learned from the colonial government that they had left for Hong Kong. The next day, Reinsdorf, with the remaining nine Germans (some of whom resided in the interior of Cochinchina and had arrived late in Saigon) was ordered to board the coastal steamer *Donai*, of the River Shipping Company of Cochinchina, anchored outside Saigon. This was a precautionary measure to avoid possible fresh riots at the downtown landing stage. When the consul agreed, three cars drove the expellees, accompanied by the police director and the private secretary of Governor Gourbeil, in a long detour around Saigon to a site of the Public Works department. The group boarded the governor's steam launch bound for Nha Bhe (today a suburban district of Ho Chi Minh City) where the French coaster took on the passengers and shipped them to Bangkok. According to the *Hong Kong Daily Press*, referring to information from Shanghai on 11 August 1914, all Germans were expelled from French Indochina.[164] In his seminal work on the Bordeaux network in Cochinchina, Étienne Denis, the head of Denis Frères (Denis Brothers), the French major trading firm in Cochinchina, quoted the exclamation of "the son of the Speidel of 1873" [Adolf Ulrich Speidel, the son of Karl Theodor Speidel], at the moment of his expulsion in 1914. According to this eyewitness, Speidel was "not afraid of publicly putting forward this boast: after the war, I will be back here as governor-general". Denis concluded his account with the remark that after 1918 the Germans were not able to recapture the considerable position they had in Cochinchina before the First World War "thanks to the vigilance of French merchants". This was indeed the case. In the 1920s, the business sector of the colony was dominated by French

[163] *L'Opinion*, 7 August 1914. PAAA, R 19426: Consul Reinsdorf (Saigon) to Chancellor von Bethmann Hollweg (Berlin), 7 August 1914. *Hong Kong Daily Press*, 17 and 22 August 1914.

[164] PAAA, R 19426: Consul Felix Reinsdorf (on board the *Donai*) to Chancellor von Bethmann Hollweg (Berlin), 8 August 1914. *Hong Kong Daily Press*, 17 August 1914.

firms, with a few exceptions such as Wm. [William] G. Hale & Company (the pioneering British firm established in Saigon in 1858) and Diethelm & Company (which had Swiss owners from Zurich).[165]

The Rice Industry of Cochinchina

Rice had been cultivated since ancient times in tropical and subtropical countries, with South Asia and Southeast Asia as major production centres. The Mekong Delta produced rice for internal consumption as well as for export to southern China. While rice was grown by mainly Vietnamese farmers, Chinese intermediaries collected, milled and exported rice. Until the eighteenth century, Chinese merchants were mainly concerned with long-distance trading of luxury goods between China, Japan and Southeast Asia, something which remained the concern of small businesses and resulted in somewhat scattered commercial relations. This changed with the Chinese switching to local trades in bulk goods such as rice, sugar and salt. The rise of Saigon as a major rice exporting centre was undoubtedly related to this new trend, caused by China's need of surplus rice from Southeast Asia during the eighteenth and early nineteenth centuries. This regional trade in the South China Sea was carried out by localised Chinese merchants in Saigon (founded as a town in 1772) or in Bangkok (founded in 1782), two new commercial centres in close proximity to each other and linked by bustling local shipping and trading activities. This was enhanced with the founding of Singapore (opened as a British free port in 1819), with its large and growing immigrant population stimulating high demand for rice, sugar and salt. By the early 1800s, three hundred junks visited Saigon every year, most of which traded with other ports in Southeast Asia. In the first half of the nineteenth century, Singaporean Chinese merchants exported British manufactures (especially grey shirting) to Saigon which were often bartered at a loss for rice; the trip was made profitable by further exporting most of the rice to China and Southeast Asian ports. This resulted in merchants from Singapore closely co-operating with local Chinese rice traders and largely financing the rice trade of Saigon. Only the most prominent Chinese merchants were engaged in this trade due to the requirement for large capital outlays and storage facilities, as well

[165] Denis (1965, 344) and Morlat (2016, 412–413).

as the risks involved in shipping. Therefore, the process of capital concentration accelerated in the hands of important Chinese rice trading firms based in Saigon, Singapore, Bangkok, Canton and later Hong Kong.[166]

Chinese people have migrated to the Indochinese Peninsula since the earliest times, often as a result of population pressure and political upheavals in China. Most of them came from southern China, predominantly from Xiamen (Amoy), Shantou (Swatow) and Guangzhou (Canton), establishing Chinese family firms that were closely connected through personal relationships. The frequent waves of immigration resulted in the creation of a new Sino-Vietnamese ruling class and strong influence of Chinese culture and thinking on Vietnam. This migration pattern did not change during the French colonial period. As Alain G. Marsot explains, the Chinese were active in both Vietnam's agriculture and trade "from the greater cultural and commercial sophistication of their mother country, in terms of its very size and greater economic development, compared to the small and scattered societies of Southeast Asia. Furthermore, those Chinese merchants continued to maintain close ties with their families and kinship organisations in China, and in general with the trading communities there, thereby occupying a naturally privileged position as intermediaries between the South China markets and those of Southeast Asia. They were to maintain that position throughout the European period".[167]

In the nineteenth century, British rule in India, Singapore and Hong Kong established a large free-trade area in Asia that provided the market base for the considerable expansion of the rice trade, with Singapore and Hong Kong developing into key redistribution centres. Rice from Saigon was almost exclusively exported to southern China, resulting in a considerable volume of shipping and commerce between Vietnam and China in the nineteenth and early twentieth centuries. In port cities around the South China Sea, Chinese merchants could be found at all levels of the highly competitive rice export trade, acting as buying agents, millers and shippers. Being well acquainted with different varieties of rice and their

[166] Wong (1960, 158), Li (2004, 265–269) and Lee (2015, 110–112).

[167] Marsot (1993, 22–34, the quote: 32). On Vietnam's rice industry and rice exports to South China and Hong Kong, see Coquerel (1911, 131–168), Schumacher (1917, 35–50), Caron (1925, 40–41), Tsao (1932), Wong (1960), Owen (1971), Latham (1983), Latham (1988), Nørlund (1986), Faure (1990), Li (2004), Lee (2015) and Durand (2016, 227–229).

various market values, Cantonese rice merchants dominated the South China Sea rice trade. The important role of the Chinese as intermediaries between the Europeans and the indigenous peoples of Southeast Asian countries and regions was made possible by their high degree of adaptation to different geographical and social circumstances. The social structure and commercial organisation of overseas Chinese and the long history of Chinese trade with Southeast Asia are the most important explanatory factors for the economic predominance of the Chinese and the patronage they enjoyed from Western elites.[168]

"Mise en valeur" (development or exploitation) was the basic principle at the founding of the French empire in Asia, remaining valid throughout the entire existence of French Indochina. This included the forceful intrusion of foreign capitalism into Vietnam, an agrarian country little integrated into other Asian markets. Private company owners of various nationalities, often actively supported by French colonial governors, focused on developing economic sectors which produced goods for foreign markets. In the first phase of the economic development of French Indochina (1860s to the early 1900s), the production, processing and exporting of rice from Cochinchina was the most important industry.[169] However, after the French conquest of Cochinchina (1858–1859) rice production and trade sharply decreased in southern Vietnam, causing widespread famine among local populations. This forced French officers (among them Francis Garnier, an officer of the staff of Admiral Léonard Charner) to recruit Chinese merchants in Cholon to supply the Vietnamese with imported rice from the Mekong delta. In 1862, Garnier was appointed administrator of Cholon and developed close relations with the Chinese trading community based in this neighbouring town to Saigon; in 1872, Cholon had c.80,000 inhabitants and was after Saigon the second-largest urban agglomeration of French Indochina. In Saigon's municipal council session of 19 November 1867, Major Bouvet called Cholon "this suburb of Saigon, located at the Chinese arroyo of which the commercial importance surpasses Saigon, at least at this moment".[170] Cholon

[168] On the economic roles of Chinese in French Indochina, see Dubreuil (1910), Nguyen (1941), Purcell (1980, 167–207), Tran (1993, 13–38), Li (2004, 268–269) and Amer (2010, 57–80).

[169] Brocheux and Hèmery (2009, 116–120) and Murray (1980, 100–102).

[170] Baudrit (1936, vol. 2, 78: Session of 19 November 1867) and Goscha (2017, 74, 77, 162).

became the undisputed major rice processing centre of Cochinchina, with its husking mills owned and operated by Chinese and Europeans. This made Saigon one of the major rice exporting hubs of Southeast Asia, surpassed only by Rangoon (Burma) and Bangkok (Siam/Thailand).

The French steadfastly realigned rice production towards the export market. After an all-time low in 1863, when annual rice exports amounted to only 10,897 tonnes, the first peak was reached in 1867, with 197, 589 tonnes being exported. In the early 1870s, when more than eight per cent of the total cultivable land area in Cochinchina was used for rice production, the second peak in annual exports (1871) amounted to 299,422 tonnes.[171] In 1875, Governor Duperré, with his strong focus on economically developing Cochinchina, fostered the establishment of the Banque de l'Indochine (Bank of Indochina) in Saigon, succeeding the Comptoir d'escompte de Paris as the major French credit bank in East Asia. At the time, "France came to assume the position of a world creditor and external supplier of money", explained Guy P. Palmade. The new bank became, on the basis of short-term loans guaranteed by secured commodities stocks and the traders' reputation, "an efficient tool" in financing international commercial exchanges, as Hubert Bonin put it. With Cochinchina's rice exports generally increasing since the 1870s, the bank provided important financial means to mostly Chinese, and also some German and French rice exporters, controlling the commerce of the most important produce of Cochinchina.[172]

Until 1878, Cochinchina only exported ordinary, shelled brown rice (in French: riz cargo qualité ordinaire) consisting of a mixture of different sorts, namely oval, long, round, big and small, hard and crumbly grains. This was the result of a process in which the rice plant was milled only one time to remove the outer husks of the grain. Its low quality was a major problem in competition with rice from other parts of East Asia; therefore, there were widespread complaints about its bad taste, mediocre preservation, lack of whiteness and transparency, and particularly the too many

[171] Coquerel (1911, 131–133, 204: Table of Annual Exports 1860–1910).

[172] The Saigon branch of the Banque de l'Indochine was established in April 1875, four months after the founding of the bank in Paris. Consequently, the Comptoir de l'escompte de Paris ceased operation in Saigon transferring its assets, premises, and staff to the new bank. Palmade (1972, 174), Meuleau (1990, 65), Corfield (2013, 14, 90) and Bonin (2020, 54–56).

broken grains resulting from faulty hulling. To improve the effectiveness and quality of rice production, in 1869 the first steam-operated rice mill was established at Khanh Hoi, a village in the Mekong Delta, by the company Alphonse Cahuzac from Bordeaux; some months later, Édouard Renard & Company, another Bordeaux-based firm, associated with Andrew Spooner, opened the Rizeries de Cholon (Cholon Rice Factories). However, the appearance of the rice compared to competitors' remained a major obstacle to rice exports, especially after the opening of the Suez Canal (1869) facilitated transports to Europe and also brought an increasing number of steam tramps to the Far East. European and East Asian rice traders frequently refrained from purchasing Saigon rice, pointing specially to broken, dirty and badly cleaned grains, and turning instead to dry, steamed and properly hulled rice as offered in Calcutta, India and other places in the region. Annual rice exports from Saigon decreased by almost 33 per cent, falling from 279,775 tonnes (1873) to 187,734 tonnes (1874), signalling a severe crisis of the most important export article of Cochinchina.[173]

On 12 September 1874, twenty-four merchants of Cholon and Saigon met in the premises of the major French trade firm, Denis Frères (Denis Brothers), located at Rue Catinat, to find a way out of the crisis. Present were fourteen Chinese and ten European merchants including the most important ones, namely Kaltenbach, Engler & Co., Behre & Co., Speidel & Co., and Wm. G. Hale & Co. Minutes were taken reflecting the tense mood in which the assembly took place. Participants felt "rightly alarmed by the depreciation of our rice on all consumer markets as a result of its low quality, which should be attributed to bad cleaning and to mixing done by the indigenous [Vietnamese] and also small Chinese merchants of Cholon". Pointing to the fact that Saigon's entire commerce depended on rice production, the traders unanimously voiced their strong interest in finding ways to improve the quality of the rice. The Chinese merchants promised to seriously monitor the quality of rice coming to the markets of Cholon from the start of the new season, in December 1874. They further announced they would only provide two qualities of rice as samples to European merchants in Saigon: round rice (Go Cong) and long rice (Vinh Long); this should not contain any mixing and not more than three to five per cent of paddy. The European merchants agreed to accept ten per cent

[173] Denis (1965, 230–231, 237), Vorapheth (2004, 383), Morlat (2016, 304) and Coquerel (1911, 204: Table of Annual Exports 1860–1910).

of broken grains for the round rice and fifteen per cent for the long rice. Samples of the two rice qualities would be placed in the Saigon Chamber of Commerce to make comparisons in case of disputes. All deliveries not conforming to signed contracts would result in indemnities.[174]

Five days later, Piquet, Director of the Interior of Cochinchina, issued a note to all provincial heads, the Inspectors of Indigenous Affairs, charging them with informing Vietnamese rice farmers and sellers about the meeting's decisions. To establish tight controls of rice qualities delivered from the interior, Chinese and some French merchants set up a permanent commission in Cholon. However, with the colonial government refraining from authorising the commission to impose fines, any efficient means to prevent the sale of mixed rice was made impossible. Therefore, on 7 June 1875, the Saigon Chamber of Commerce established its own rice commission, which included a government representative, to study all practical means to convince Vietnamese producers and local Chinese traders of their individual best interests in the matter. However, in December 1875, Piquet admitted in a note that the combined efforts of both Saigon and Cholon merchants to improve the situation had been unsuccessful. Instead, he proposed token control, farming committees, persuasion, distribution of grains and model rice fields as remedies to satisfy both the Chinese and European merchants and the Vietnamese farmers, and to maintain rice production as one of the most important sources of income for the colonial government.[175] To further increase revenues from Cochinchina's rice production, the government, on 1 January 1879, introduced an export duty of 10 cents per picul on milled rice and of 7.5 cents per picul on paddy. According to Consul Emil Saltzkorn, the new duty was not at all obstructive to exports, with the extra cost being entirely covered by Vietnamese producers forced to lower the prices of their rice when selling it to Cholon and Saigon merchants. Thus, those labouring in the rice fields were the ones paying the new duty, but not consumers of export markets in East Asia and Europe. As Christopher Goscha clarifies, the increase in exports "could only have come from lowering the supply available for internal consumption or from halting the

[174] Denis (1965, 232–233: Minutes of 12 September 1874).

[175] Denis (1965, 233–237).

pre-existing black market in rice". In this sense, it was obviously the Vietnamese peasant population paying "the highest price for financing French Cochinchina's development in terms of taxes and rice production".[176]

With the Chinese operating the prosperous rice trade in Cochinchina, the French taxed it, providing from the revenues financial and technological support to Chinese and Vietnamese merchants and growers. Steam-operated rice mills were swiftly replacing traditional methods of rice production in Vietnam. In 1876, Chinese merchants established in Cholon the third rice mill of Cochinchina, called Rizerie chinoise (Chinese Rice Factory), and from the start employed much more effective means for collecting rice than their French competitors. As a result, the rice factory of Alphonse Cahuzac, which was facing financial difficulties, transformed itself some months later into the Société française de Saigon pour le décorticage et le blanchissage du Riz (French Company for Rice Hulling and Laundering in Saigon). Capital was provided from financiers in Paris, and also Behre & Co. in Saigon in which Niederberger and Saltzkorn were partners.[177]

When submitting the 1879 annual report to the foreign ministry in Berlin, Consul Emil Saltzkorn, in February 1880, proudly stated that "rice trading done by Europeans was as ever almost entirely in the hands of German companies of which only one (my one) exported last year more than 900,000 picul, thus almost one sixth of total exports". He added that the number of German ships (91, of 58,642 GRT, including 31 steamers) had significantly increased in Saigon compared to 1878 (73 ships, of 56,505 GRT, including 53 steamers). According to the consul, the lesser number of steamers was due to the fact that rice exports to other destinations than Hong Kong, "remarkably enough to Europe", had since increased some years, "with Hamburg and Flensburg vessels again ranking excellently" in Saigon's shipping statistics.[178] However, the next crisis struck very soon after when a major rice disease broke out in Vietnam, resulting in coloured grains. On 21 October 1880, Niederberger (who resided in Hamburg at the time) strongly warned the Saigon Chamber of Commerce of the fact that this would be "a

[176] PAAA, R 251849: Consul Saltzkorn (Saigon) to Foreign Ministry (Berlin), 20 March 1879. Goscha (2017, 77).

[177] Goscha (2017, 162–163) and Denis (1965, 231, 237–238).

[178] PAAA, R 251850: Consul Saltzkorn (Saigon) to Foreign Ministry, 20 February 1880.

defect much graver than the mixing or the too large proportion of broken grains". In that year, annual rice exports from Saigon fell to a mere 287,312 tonnes, thus more than twenty-one per cent compared to 1879 when 364,823 tonnes were shipped.[179] When Saigon's rice exports increased to 368,801 tonnes in 1882, the modest growth was probably due to the fact that Denis Frères had established Cochinchina's most important rice plant this year. The Rizerie Saigonnaise (Saigon Rice Factory) introduced new methods of rice production, such as heating paddy before milling, significantly improving the appearance and quality of Vietnamese rice. Consequently, rice shipped from Saigon reached hitherto unknown heights: annual exports, in 1883, compared to the previous year, rose by almost thirty per cent to 524,948 tonnes; in the following year, the results were almost equal (520,814 tonnes).[180] As the Prussian envoy in Hamburg, in early 1885, learned from Hamburg importers, the appearance of Saigon rice had generally become better through employing modern huller huskers and was expected to improve further; therefore, in 1884, a number of German steamers, among them ships serving the Australian line of Sloman, had called at Saigon to load rice for Hamburg. However, most rice from Cochinchina was shipped to China, with Singapore and the Philippines following as other major purchasers.[181]

In 1887, with the creation of the Indochinese Union, the French general tariff was first applied in French Indochina, providing that French products could enter the colony duty-free while those of other countries were subject to the same tariffs as in France. In return, produce from Indochina could be imported duty-free into France. Since the port of Saigon lost its status as a free port (as established in 1860), with negative repercussions for its shipping and trading, French historian Charles Fourniau called 1887 "a black year" for the local population, causing a considerable increase of prices.[182] For Speidel & Co. and other foreign firms, the general tariff was a hard blow, considerably impacting

[179] Coquerel (1911, 204: Table of Annual Exports 1860–1910) and Denis (1965, 239).

[180] Brocheux and Hèmery (2009, 116–117), Denis (1965, 231, 237–238) and Coquerel (1911, 204: Table of Annual Exports 1860–1910).

[181] PAAA, R 251851: Prussian Envoy von Wentzel (Hamburg) to Chancellor von Bismarck (Berlin), 14 February 1885.

[182] Girault (1916, 201–216), Robequain (1944, 128–136) and Fourniau (2002, 426–427, the quote: 426).

trading and requiring traders to look for other business opportunities. Consequently, in 1887, Karl Theodor Speidel established in Cholon his company's own mechanical rice mill, the Rizerie de l'Union (Union Rice Factory), which seemed to have regularly distributed considerable dividends. At the end of 1895, Speidel & Co. investing capital of 585,000 dollars, set up another and much larger mill in Cholon, the Rizerie de l'Orient (Orient Rice Factory), which was destroyed by fire on the first day of operation but restarted working at the end of 1897. With their rice mills, Speidel & Co. gained a considerable share among Cholon's rice producers when competing against five Chinese mills and an older French mill. The German traveller Moritz Schanz, visiting Saigon in 1898, went to see the Orient mill where he incidentally watched the visit of Édouard Picanon, the new governor-lieutenant of Cochinchina, accompanied by numerous staff. The travel writer observed that the French were "pulling a long face" when observing "German successes in an industry in which their countrymen entirely failed".[183] In 1911, the Bank of Indochina in Saigon noted, there were ten rice factories of which eight were in Chinese hands.[184] Another French account pointed to the fact that Speidel & Co. held the controlling interest in two of them: the Union Rice Factory produced 300 tonnes of white rice per day and the other, and the Orient Rice Factory, 400 tonnes. The reports suggested that before the First World War rice production in Cochinchina was shared between Chinese and German investors, with the French obviously out of this business. After the war, the two rice mills of Speidel & Co. were confiscated by the colonial government and sold to local Chinese merchants "for very high prices"[185] (Fig. 4.3a and b).

Rice exports from Cochinchina to China were almost exclusively handled by Chinese companies based in Saigon, financed by influential Singapore merchants, with sister companies or branches often located in

[183] Devraigne (1920, 42). Schanz (1900/01, 296) said that the Union Rice Factory distributed dividends of 34 per cent in 1897.

[184] Morlat (2016, 306).

[185] According to Vorapheth (2004, 461), the two rice factories of Speidel & Co. produced and exported c. 60,000 tons of shelled rice annually, of an estimated value of nine million francs. Devraigne (1920, 42) informed that, after the First World War, the Union Rice Factory was sold for 570,000 piastres and the Orient Rice Factory for 785,000 piastres.

a

b

Fig. 4.3 The Union Rice Mill of Speidel & Company in Cholon (front and back views), c. 1890 (Courtesy of Eduard Leopold, Coburg)

Hong Kong.[186] The Saigon rice trade considerably contributed to the major capital accumulation in Chinese hands, making the rice industry one of the most important investment sectors for the rich Chinese located in ports of the South China Sea. Based on capital acquired by rice trading, steam shipping companies (such as for river shipping transportation in the Mekong Delta), insurance firms and warehouses were established in Singapore, Bangkok and Cholon. Information networks around Southeast Asia were important preconditions for the rapid development of the rice trading industry which was almost exclusively held in Chinese hands throughout the period of high colonialism in Southeast Asia (1870–1940).[187] This left Europeans little space for profitable business except the shipping of rice on board modern steam tramps.

Speidel & Company in Saigon

Karl (or Carl) Theodor Speidel (1841–1909) was the founder and most important managing partner of the German trade firm Speidel & Company based in French Indochina.[188] In April 1864, Speidel came to Cochinchina and was employed by Kaltenbach, Engler & Co. in Saigon. At the beginning of 1869, he was made partner and managing clerk in this company, which consequently switched its name to Kaltenbach, Engler & Speidel. In association with his brother Friedrich Wilhelm [Senior], he established Speidel & Co. in Saigon in March 1873. He was appointed consul of the Netherlands in Saigon in June 1872 and held this honorary post until February 1894. Additionally, he was honorary German consul in Saigon from July 1885 to June 1894. As Consul Wilhelm Crull later said, Karl Theodor Speidel was reputed for his "very strict point of views". The obituary published by the *Hong Kong Daily Press* (23 March 1909) said that he was "well known in China and the news of his death

[186] Coquerel (1911, 151).

[187] Wong (1960, 154–158) and Li (2004, 265–269).

[188] Karl (Carl) *Theodor* Speidel was born on 11 December 1841 in Langenbeutlingen, District of Heilbronn, Kingdom of Württemberg, as the fourth child of Pastor Jacob Speidel (1802–1871) and Sophie Christine Wilhelmine Winzenburger (1806–?), who was from Stuttgart. He was married to Johanna Ernestine Emma Haid (1844–1920) and had two sons, Alfred Speidel (1872–1901) and Adolf Ulrich Speidel (1886–?). Lutz (2018: Data Index for Karl Theodor Speidel (1841–1909). On 7 March 1909, he passed away in Paris, Rue Desbordes-Valmore 44. AP, Actes d'état civil, 16e Arrondissement de Paris, Décès 1909, no. 474: Speidel, Charles Théodore.

will be received by all who knew him with very great regret".[189] His older brother, Friedrich Wilhelm Speidel [Senior] (1840–1893) arrived in Cochinchina sometime later and also started trading. In June 1870, he was made United States consular agent in Saigon and, in September 1870 was charged by Governor de Cornulier-Lucinière to represent Prussian interests in Cochinchina during the Franco-German War. When he became partner in Speidel & Co., he was appointed consul for Belgium and Denmark. In 1883, he left for Hamburg to establish new business contacts for Speidel & Co. and seemed to have made a good impression on local business circles.[190] According to the obituary in the *Hong Kong Daily Press*, Friedrich Wilhelm Speidel was a well-known Saigon merchant, "highly respected by the whole community, both European and Asiatic, and by the Chinese in particular, he was esteemed on account of the straightforwardness and honesty which characterised all his transactions".[191]

In 1874, Speidel & Co. liquidated the Saigon property of Paul de Faucheur, agent of Denis Frères in Cambodia and also private advisor of King Norodom. Additionally, the firm took over the Saigon premises of A. Eymond & Delphin Henry, the major shipping and wholesale business from Bordeaux and one of the oldest French firms in Cochinchina. According to the information of the Prussian envoy in Hamburg who, in early 1882, had made enquiries in business circles of the port city, due to various lawsuits, Speidel & Co. had lost much money in the first three years. These financial losses seemed to limit the firm's transactions to

[189] PAAA, R 251851: Karl Theodor Speidel (Saigon) to Foreign Ministry (Berlin), September 1884. PAAA, Peking II-976: Karl Theodor Speidel (Saigon) to Minister Schenck zu Schweinsberg (Beijing), 16 June 1894. Denis (1965, 342). PAAA, Saigon 3-B 8: Consul Crull (Saigon) to Chancellor von Bethmann Hollweg (Berlin), 10 January 1912. *Hong Kong Daily Press*, 23 March 1909.

[190] PAAA, R 251851: Prussian Envoy von Wentzel (Hamburg) to Chancellor von Bismarck (Berlin), 14 February 1885.

[191] Friedrich Wilhelm Speidel [Senior] was born on 12 January 1840 in Langenbeutlingen and remained unmarried and seemingly without children. On 1 October 1893, he died in Saigon and was buried in the European cemetery. His gravestone was removed in the 1970s when the cemetery was turned into a public park. Lutz (2018: Data Index for Friedrich Wilhelm Speidel [1840–1893]). PAAA, R 251851: Consul Bauermeister (Saigon) to Foreign Ministry (Berlin), 6 December 1884. *Hong Kong Daily Press*, 17 October 1893.

mainly buying and selling of goods on consignments. However, the Prussian envoy pointed to the fact that the company had a good reputation, and that one of his managers was considered "especially intelligent", an indication of Karl Theodor Speidel's skilful business practices.[192] Speidel & Co. did a lot of profitable rice trading to China, much business with Cambodia and was also supplying the Phnom Penh government. Since 1875, the firm had a branch in the Cambodian capital managed first by the German A. Dietelbach. There is little information on this branch for the time after, and in 1912 Consul Crull noted that Speidel & Co. had two German clerks in Phnom Penh. Since the beginning of 1911, the firm was also established in the port city Da Nang (Tourane) in central Vietnam employing both a German and French clerk. Shipping services were mostly provided by the M. Jebsen Shipping Company operating a line from Hong Kong and Shantou to Da Nang, and further south to Qui Nhon for which the steamer *Helene*, of 1237 tonnes, was employed.[193]

In December 1881, Emil Saltzkorn, partner of Behre & Co., informed Berlin that he wished to resign as honorary consul in Saigon and recommended August Bauermeister, his partner in the firm, as successor and Bruno Röver, manager of the Cholon branch, as deputy consul. This brought up two new candidates for the post. In February 1882, Hermann von Mittnacht, the Prime Minister of Württemberg, spoke up for the Speidel brothers, pointing to the fact that from various sides they — "born Württembergers" — had been called "definitely qualified and very trustworthy figures". With Hamburg business circles strongly advocating Bauermeister and Röver, the foreign ministry finally decided in their favour. However, things changed quickly when Röver suddenly passed away in May 1882 and Karl Theodor Speidel was made deputy of Bauermeister in January 1883. During the time when Bauermeister stayed in Cambodia for businesses, Speidel was acting German consul, from 6 April to 22 October 1883. After his return, Bauermeister praised Speidel as "having looked after the consulate with greatest care and laudable

[192] PAAA, R 251850: Prussian Envoy von Wentzel (Hamburg) to Foreign Ministry (Berlin), 9 March 1882. Denis (1965, 343) and Vorapheth (2004, 28, 66 and 461, with sales figures of the branches of Speidel & Co. for 1913).

[193] BAB, R 901-12813: Consul von Bergen (Saigon) to Foreign Ministry, 10 February 1875 (on the Phnom Penh branch of Speidel & Co.). PAAA, Saigon 3-B 8: Consul Crull (Saigon) to Chancellor von Bethmann Hollweg (Berlin), 10 January 1912. Hieke (1953, 240).

passion". Less than a year later, Bauermeister was forced to liquidate Behre & Co. and to seek partnership with Speidel & Co. In December 1884, he established the Haiphong branch of the firm and become its first manager. When notifying the foreign ministry of his intention to permanently leave Saigon, Bauermeister suggested appointing Karl Theodor Speidel as the new German consul, emphasising the fact that Speidel "enjoyed widespread respect" and, due to his long-term residency, was "very experienced in all matters here".[194] In the autumn of 1884, the liquidation of Behre & Co. not only resulted in Bauermeister switching to his former main competitor but also gave Speidel & Co. the chance to take over the agencies of major Hamburg shipping companies: Robert M. Sloman, the Deutsche Dampfschiffahrts-Gesellschaft Hansa (or DDG Hansa), and A. J. Hertz & Söhne (A. J. Hertz and Sons). All firms had very positive opinions of Speidel & Co., as the Prussian envoy reported from Hamburg. The company "had considerably grown and won trust in recent years". In September 1884, Speidel submitted his application for German consul to Berlin, pointing to the fact that he had also been Dutch consul since 1872 and had temporarily been acting consul of other countries including Germany. After receiving positive news from the Prussian envoy in Hamburg, the foreign ministry supported the application, and, on 9 July 1885, Karl Theodor Speidel was appointed honorary consul for Cochinchina.[195]

The appointment of Karl Theodor Speidel brought about an illuminating correspondence with Berlin and the sending of regular bulletins by Speidel & Co. on the economic conditions of Cochinchina, which are mostly preserved in the German archives. The *Annual Report* of Speidel & Co. published in English for the year 1884, that Karl Theodor Speidel submitted to the foreign ministry, is the firm's earliest preserved economic bulletins. The practice of frequently sending the firm's *Annual Report*

[194] PAAA, R 251850: Prime Minister von Mittnacht (Stuttgart) to Prussian Envoy von Baur-Breitenfeld (Berlin), 9 February 1882, Prussian Envoy von Wentzel (Hamburg) to Foreign Ministry (Berlin), 22 March 1882, Consul Bauermeister (Saigon) to Foreign Ministry (Berlin), 15 May 1882 and 5 April 1883, Ambassador von Hohenlohe-Schillingsfürst (Paris) to Chancellor von Bismarck (Berlin), 10 January 1883, Consul Speidel (Saigon) to Foreign Ministry (Berlin), 11 April 1883. PAAA, R 251851: Consul Bauermeister (Saigon) to Foreign Ministry (Berlin), 22 October 1883 and 6 September 1884.

[195] PAAA, R 251851: Prussian Envoy von Wentzel (Hamburg) to Chancellor von Bismarck (Berlin), 14 February 1885; Emperor William I (Bad Ems): Appointment of Karl Theodor Speidel, 9 July 1885.

to Berlin (which went along with dispatching the annual trading and shipping reports issued on behalf of the German consulate in Saigon) regularly continued until 1911 (with some reports missing from the foreign ministry's records). For the years 1911, 1912 and 1913, special *Yearly Statistics* were issued by the company. In 1912 and 1913, Speidel & Co. published a *Monthly Report* for every single month which reflected the increase in their business operations in French Indochina.

The 1884 report of Speidel & Co. initially dealt with the most important export product — rice — shipped to various destinations, with a table presenting export numbers between 1876 (341.607 tonnes) and 1884 (520.518 tonnes). This made evident the company's engagement in the strongly export-oriented economy of Cochinchina. More information on the rice business was provided when comparing current and past prices of different sorts of rice, for the same period as before, and informing about duties on exporting rice and presenting further outlooks for the new harvest. This was followed by brief production numbers and prices for other exports such as cotton, fish, hides, horns, pepper and salt. The second part of the report provided in a table listed freight rates of both steamers and sailing vessels to Saigon's main export markets, Hong Kong and retour, Singapore, Java and the Philippines between 1876 and 1884. Another table showed the different national flags, distinguishing between steamers and sailing ships calling at Saigon since 1876. The final part of the report presented a table giving average exchange rates for Paris, London, Singapore, Hong Kong and Batavia during the past nine years.[196]

This kind of publication, a common practice for nineteenth-century export markets, increased the flow of information by providing exact data about rice and other exports contributing to promoting international exchanges. Sending out annual, monthly or weekly circulars listing details of markets kept clients informed and stimulated fresh business deals.[197] In 1906, Rudolf Kallen (the professional German consul in Saigon from 1903–1909) pointed to the fact that Speidel & Co. submitted highly reliable information in its regular circulars. He added that "the German firm Speidel & Company here, in their (English) annual reports destined mainly for their circle of business partners, usually also deals thoroughly

[196] PAAA, R 251851: *Speidel & Co.'s Annual Report* (Saigon), 31 December 1884.
[197] Magee and Thompson (2010, 100).

with local shipping. In their circulars, the firm strives for the most meticulous accuracy; and considering the close contact it has with port, customs and daily business matters through its extensive scope of business transactions, especially also in shipping trades, I judge the firm's reports as definitely reliable. Regarding German shipping, the lists set up at the consulate do afford a respective control to me".[198]

In June 1894, when Karl Theodor Speidel permanently left Cochinchina, his nephew, Friedrich Wilhelm Speidel [Junior] (1869–1948), took over his position in Saigon.[199] He was seconded by Hermann Kurz[200] and Max Leopold,[201] both partners in the firm (Fig. 4.4). Speidel & Co. continued to be mainly concerned with operating their rice mills and shipping large quantities of rice on steam coasters to Hong Kong and other destinations. Additionally, as consequence of the application of the French general tariff in Indochina, which since 1887 had placed heavy customs fees on most non-French products, Speidel & Co. diversified their businesses and began to operate as importer of French high-quality beverages, which were mainly consumed by the non-Asian population

[198] BAB, R 901-53283: Consul Kallen (Saigon) to Chancellor von Bülow (Berlin), 12 February 1905.

[199] Friedrich Wilhelm Speidel [Junior] was born on 7 January 1869 in Neuenstadt, District of Heilbronn, Kingdom of Württemberg, as third child of Karl Theodor's eldest brother, Gustav Adolf Speidel (1835–1881), and Julie Vogel (1845–1864). He was married to Elisabeth Stumpf (1873–1916) from Stuttgart. Their son, Franz Willy Speidel (1904–1969), was born in Saigon and later became managing director of river shipping companies operating tug services on the Neckar River. On 13 March 1948, Friedrich Wilhelm Speidel [Junior] passed away in Stuttgart. Lutz (2018–2019: Data Index for Friedrich Wilhelm Speidel [1869–1948]).

[200] Hermann Kurz was managing partner of Speidel & Co. in Saigon and acting German honorary consul when Karl Theodor Speidel was absent. In October 1894, he was appointed German honorary consul in Saigon. In the 1890s, he was charged with supervising the firm's branches in Phnom Penh and Haiphong. On 24 February 1900, Kurz passed away in Nürtingen, Württemberg. ANOM, INDO-GGI-21893: Karl Theodor Speidel (Saigon) to Governor-General Constans (Hanoi), 20 March 1888. *Haiphong illustré* (1895, 20). PAAA, Peking II-976: Otto Kurz (Saigon) to German Legation (Beijing), 4.3.1900.

[201] Max Leopold was born on 4 February 1858 in Stuttgart and married to Anna Charlotte (born Luidenmeyer, 1869–1895); their son, Eduard Leopold [Senior] (1895–1965) was born in Saigon. After his wife's death, Max and his son moved to Haiphong and returned to Germany sometime before the First World War. He died on 16 April 1930 in Stuttgart. Email of Christiane Millenet (the great-granddaughter of Max Leopold and daughter of Eduard Leopold [Junior]), Nuremberg, 19 June 2020.

Fig. 4.4 Staff of Speidel & Company in Saigon, c. 1894. Second row sitting on the bench from the left: Max Leopold; presumably Friedrich Wilhelm Speidel (Junior); presumably Hermann Kurz (Courtesy of Eduard Leopold, Coburg)

of Cochinchina. Newspaper advertisements show that Speidel & Co. was also sole agent in Indochina and importer of French beers from La Brasserie et Malterie, Le "Phenix" (The Brewery and Malt House, the "Phoenix"), of French mineral water from the company La Boucharade located in the Vivarais region of southeast France), of absinthe, the distilled, highly alcoholic beverage and other alcoholic beverages such as cognacs, liqueurs and rums (from the company Cusenier which, before the First World War, produced the highest-priced absinthe).[202] Another imported item was mineral oil from the Dutch East Indies for which the firm built a storehouse in Nha Be near Saigon to properly deposit oil vats[203] (Fig. 4.5).

In 1902, twenty-eight Germans resided in Saigon: twenty-two were staff of Speidel & Co., four of F. Engler & Co., and one of Kloss & Co. For the first time since 1876, when Werner von Bergen had left office, a professional German consul, Dr. Emil Heintges, was posted in Saigon. Despite the fact that the owners of Speidel & Co. were no

[202] *Le Courrier de Saigon*, 27 August 1898.

[203] Chambre de Commerce de Haiphong, *Minutes of the Session of 7 November 1900.*

Fig. 4.5 The private residence of Max Leopold and his family in Saigon, c. 1895 (Courtesy of Eduard Leopold, Coburg)

longer formally charged with consular duties, they still acted as his agents in case of absence. In July 1902, Kloss & Co. approached the consul complaining that in such case, masters of merchant vessels, with cargoes addressed for Kloss & Co., were required to report to Speidel & Co., thus to their main competitors, resulting in the fact that trade secrets would be revealed to their damage.[204] Professional envy and the precarious situation of merchants being charged with duties of consuls were revealed with this issue. However, the dominant role of Speidel & Co. in the German community of Saigon was obvious. According to Captain Kraft, commander of the German East Asia Cruiser Squadron, French residents in Saigon treated Speidel & Co. as more or less synonymous

[204] PAAA, R 140952: Foreign Ministry (Berlin) to Consul Heintges (Saigon), 12 November 1902. The written complaint of Kloss & Co., dated 6 July 1902, is quoted in this letter. According to Consul Heintges, Kloss & Co. established in 1888 and owned by a German and a Chinese, was "not important". PAAA, R 140952: Consul Emil Heintges (Saigon) to Foreign Ministry (Berlin), 16 December 1902.

with the German consulate. Despite the fact that Heintges was the professional German consul, the French Saigon newspapers, in December 1902, labelled the dinner and garden party which Friedrich Wilhelm Speidel organised on behalf of his company, for officers of a German men-of-war, as events arranged by the "German consul".[205]

In his report of 1911, Captain Kraft, the commander of the East Asia Squadron, pointed to the fact that Speidel seemingly enjoyed a good reputation with the French authorities and "obviously had a positive influence on the numerous staff of his company, keeping alive their patriotic spirit by setting an example to them". At the time, Friedrich Wilhelm Speidel was joined by his cousin and partner, Walter Speidel, the head of the Paris office of Speidel & Co.[206] When Friedrich Wilhelm Speidel permanently left Saigon in the summer of 1910 to retire in Germany, he had passed the management of the firm to Walter Speidel. Before departing, Speidel received a letter of thanks from the German foreign ministry praising "the willingness with which you and your company serve the foreign representation of the Empire" and also "the care and labour" devoted to this task. On 12 December 1910, Friedrich Wilhelm Speidel was awarded the Fourth-Class Red Eagle Order, a rather common award in Imperial Germany, which was received with pleasure by Speidel when he paid a personal visit to the German embassy in Paris.[207]

Walter Speidel (1871–1930) became naturalised in France in 1910 and was probably the first manager of the Paris office located in the 9th district, Rue Taitbout.[208] According to Captain Kraft, who met

[205] PAAA, R 140952: Captain Berger (Surabaya) to the Cruiser Squadron Command, 5 January 1903.

[206] PAAA, R 140953: Captain Kraft, Commander of Cruiser Squadron (at sea), to Emperor William II (Berlin), 2 February 1911. Devraigne (1920, 49).

[207] PAAA, R 140953: Foreign Ministry (Berlin) to Friedrich Wilhelm Speidel (Saigon), 17 April 1910. Award of Fourth-Class Red Eagle Order (Berlin), 12 December 1910. Ambassador von Schoen (Paris) to Chancellor von Bethmann Hollweg (Berlin), 21 December 1910. Lutz (2018–2019: Data Index for Jacob Speidel [1802–1871]).

[208] Walter Speidel was born on 26 December 1871 in Hohengehren, in the district of Esslingen, Württemberg. He was the son of Hugo von Speidel (1843–1901), the youngest son of Jacob Speidel (1802–1871), and of Luise Rosalie Christiane Fromann (1846–1920), a native from Rottweil, Württemberg. He was married to Elise Gesine Sofie Fröhlke (1882–1961) from Brake, Grand Duchy of Oldenburg. Walter Speidel died in Stuttgart on 25 March 1930. Lutz (2018–2019: Data Index for Jacob Speidel [1802–1871]).

him in Saigon, Speidel acquired French citizenship "only for business reasons so that his upright German way of thinking should not be called into doubt".[209] In early 1911, Walter Speidel succeeded his elder cousin, Friedrich Wilhelm Speidel [Junior], as head of Speidel & Co. in Saigon and temporarily as German honorary consul after Emil Heintges's successor, Consul Rudolf Kallen suddenly passed away in 1909. When the East Asia Squadron paid another courtesy visit to Saigon in January 1911, Speidel, being in charge of the programme provided several cars for the naval officers, invited them to the club offering a shooting competition and organised a large hotel dinner together with German merchants. The burdens of performing both as merchant and consul, as well as the difficult climate of Cochinchina, made Speidel extremely irritable, which finally had its price: in the summer of 1911, he fell seriously ill with dysen tery and a life-threatening mental crisis. Therefore, he left Saigon for a rehabilitation cure in Europe.[210] After his departure the company was managed by his partners, H. Prescher, a 48-year-old merchant from Württemberg, and Adolf Ulrich Speidel (1886–?), the youngest son of Karl Theodor Speidel. In November 1912, Walter Speidel returned to Saigon and seemed to have stayed until August 1914, together with Adolf Ulrich Speidel, before all German residents were expelled from Cochinchina[211] (Fig. 4.6).

German visitors to Saigon were always full of praise for Speidel & Co. displaying patriotic feelings and national pride which was common at the time. According to Commander Gildemeister, of the German cruiser *Irene*, paying a five-day courtesy visit to Saigon in July 1901, Speidel & Co. was "the most important company in Saigon enjoying widespread respect and considerable reputation, also from the French".[212] Ten years later, this fact seemed not to have changed: Consul Reinsdorf in Saigon

[209] PAAA, R 140953: Captain Kraft, Commander of Cruiser Squadron (at sea), to Emperor William II (Berlin), 2 February 1911.

[210] PAAA, R 140953: Consul Crull (Saigon), 13 October 1911: Report on 1909/10; Consul Crull (Saigon) to Chancellor von Bethmann Hollweg (Berlin), 29 November 1911.

[211] PAAA, R 140953: Consul Reinsdorf (Saigon) to Chancellor von Bethmann Hollweg (Berlin), 25 July 1911. PAAA, Konsulat Saigon 3: Consul Reinsdorf (Saigon) to Chancellor von Bethmann Hollweg (Berlin), 8 November 1912. Lutz (2018–2019: Data Index for Jacob Speidel [1802–1871]).

[212] PAAA, R 19418: Commander Gildemeister (SMS *Irene*, Street of Malacca) to Naval Squadron Command, 13 July 1901. *L'Opinion*, 7 August 1914.

Fig. 4.6 A street scene in Saigon, with Café "La Civette" and Hotel Laval situated close to the office of Denis Frères, the major French trading firm in Indochina, c. 1895 (Courtesy of Eduard Leopold, Coburg)

labelled Speidel & Co. as "the largest and most reputable company of the whole of Indochina". In November 1911, his successor Crull stated that around nine-tenth of all Germans residing in Saigon were employed by Speidel & Co. and that the firm occupied "an outstanding position" in the business sector of the entire colony.[213] This remark related not only to Speidel's branch at Saigon (which served as headquarters of the firm mainly engaged in the rice industry and in rice exports) but also to the firm's branches in Paris, Phnom Penh, Da Nang, Haiphong, Hanoi and two agencies in China's Yunnan Province, namely in Mengzi

[213] PAAA, R 140953: Consul Reinsdorf (Saigon) to Chancellor von Bethmann-Hollweg (Berlin), 25 July 1911, Consul Crull (Saigon) to Chancellor von Bethmann Hollweg (Berlin), 29 November 1911.

and Kunming (Yunnan-Fu).[214] However, despite its importance for the economic development of French Indochina before 1914, there was naturally little interest on the French side after the First World War about preserving any traces of this German company. Therefore, documentation about the firm's long history in French Indochina and China is only available in fragments, with the exception here in this study oft-quoted German consular correspondence with the Saigon and Haiphong branches of Speidel & Co. A few remarks in articles of the contemporary French colonial press (with some noteworthy exceptions) or a number of advertisements in French journals published in Saigon, Hanoi and Haiphong reveal only little about the firm's actual business strategies or concrete operations. In the early 1920s, when the properties of the company were entirely wound up, Speidel & Co., one of the most important European businesses in French Indochina before the First World War, largely vanished from the collective memory.

The Dutch Consulate

In the aftermath of French Emperor Napoleon Bonaparte's defeat in 1815, the Kingdom of the Netherlands was created as an independent European country. After Belgium seceded from the Kingdom in 1830, the Netherlands became a small nation state which continued to govern a very large Asian colony, the Dutch East Indies (now Indonesia), one of the most valuable colonies under European rule. Since 1850, the Dutch government in Den Haag had appointed consular representatives in China, Japan and Siam, and in European colonies in Asia, who were placed under the authority of the governor-general of the Dutch East Indies in Batavia (now Jakarta). The main purpose was to reap more profit for the Netherlands from expanding global trade. Between 1856 and 1867, the Dutch foreign ministry established seven consulates in Southeast Asia, the last one in Saigon after French Cochinchina had been

[214] Devraigne (1920, 49). Vorapheth (2004, 459–461), who offers the most comprehensive overview of Speidel & Co.'s businesses, concluded that the German firm was until 1914 the "most powerful European company" in French Indochina and considered as responsible for the misfortune and financial ruin of numerous French trading companies. In 1913, the Saigon branch imported and sold goods to the value of ten million francs. On the Haiphong branch of Speidel & Co., see the chapter on Haiphong-"Le Grand Port du Tonkin"-Speidel and Company in Haiphong in this book.

forcefully extended in 1866 with the annexation of three southern Vietnamese provinces and France's naval imperialism came to a halt.[215] In 1867, after several applications from Dutch traders in Saigon, the colonial government authorised the appointment of Robert Aemilius Stadnitski, a Dutch-born man, clerk of the Saigon branch of Édouard Renard & Co. in Bordeaux. However, in the following year, Stadnitski fell ill and returned to Europe where he passed away. His successor, the medical doctor and merchant Jan Nicolaas Servaas also fell sick after a short time and, in March 1870, transferred the Dutch consulate to Karl Theodor Speidel before leaving Saigon. With his physical condition not improving, Servaas, in May 1872, tendered his resignation at the Dutch foreign ministry recommending Speidel — "known as solid man there" — as his successor in the Saigon post. On 25 June 1872, Karl Theodor Speidel, at the time a partner of Kaltenbach, Engler & Speidel, was appointed consul of the Netherlands in Cochinchina, an important honorary post he held for twenty-four years, a "period of stability" (Leewes) for Dutch consular affairs in Saigon.[216]

The typical characteristics of Dutch consuls in the first half of the nineteenth century, as described by Albert Kersten and Bert van der Zwan, applied well to Karl Theodor Speidel who held this office in Saigon from 1872 to 1894. "None of them had taken a vocational course for the office of consul, and consular work was rarely their main activity. Most earned a living in the field of commerce. Their appointment was usually related to their wealth and the prominent position they consequently enjoyed in the local community. (...) These consuls considered their office as their personal property and something that enhanced their status (...)".[217] There was no doubt that the honorary office of Dutch consul in Saigon gave Speidel opportunities to enhance the business of his company, namely to establish official links with the colonial government in Batavia and to promote business connections of Chinese firms in Cochinchina doing trade with the Dutch colony. At the time, the

[215] Leewes (2008, 106–108) and Kersten and van der Zwan (2010, 414–417).

[216] NAN, MBZ-3031: Jan Nicolaas Servaas (Marseille) to Foreign Minister van Limburg (Den Haag), 3 May 1870. NAN, MBZ-1359: Jan Nicolaas Servaas (Deurne) to Foreign Minister van Herwijnen (Den Haag), 25 May 1872, Appointment of Karl Theodor Speidel to Consul in Saigon (Den Haag), 25 June 1872. Leewes (2008, 108–109, 238, the quote: 108).

[217] Kersten and van der Zwan (2010, 415).

number of Dutch ships calling at Saigon had considerably increased from ten (1870) to sixteen vessels (1871), making the flag of the Netherlands the fifth most important one in the port. However, in his letter accompanying the first annual report submitted to Den Haag, Speidel admitted that, in 1872, the Dutch flag had more or less kept its position in Saigon, and although considerable rice exports "to certain ports of Java should have brought a certain busy period for Dutch ships, it did so far not work in this way, the required tonnage being provided more promptly on site or from Hong Kong". In the following years, Speidel repeatedly pointed to the fact that shipping was a key factor in enhancing the competitiveness of Dutch commerce in French Indochina; export articles from the Netherlands were almost absent from Saigon and, if they made their way into the colony, they were transported on board foreign vessels.[218]

In March 1875, Jacob Adolf Bruno Wiselius, controller with the colonial administration on the island of Java in the Dutch East Indies, visited Saigon. Shortly later, when back in Holland, he published a book on his travel experiences. The travel account deals with his impressions of Cochinchina and his visit to the German merchant Speidel charged with the consulate of the Netherlands for almost three years. Wiselius wrote about his visit as follows:

> (...) along the quays you find the trading firms. The large ones are in English and German hands, while retail trade, shops and industrial enterprises are run by Frenchmen. The shopping streets *Rue National* [National Street] and *Rue Catinat* [Catinat Street] pass through the entire town, and into these streets lead the most prominent boulevards and avenues. Already on the day of my arrival, and when the rush for the mail was a bit over – the French mail-steamer always remains 24 hours at Saigon – I visited the Dutch consul, Mr [Karl Theodor] Speidel, a Württemberger, at whose house I always enjoyed the friendliest reception. A recommendation letter to the Director of the Interior was not alone the reason that I experienced much courtesy on his side and received information around my planned journey, but also that by his intervention I was granted access to the governor, Rear Admiral Duperré.[219]

[218] Report of the German Consulate in Saigon for 1870–1871. In *Preußisches Handels-Archiv* (2, January 1873, 34–41). NAN, MBZ-1359: Consul Karl Theodor Speidel (Saigon) to Foreign Minister van Herwijnen (Den Haag), 16 February 1873. Leewes (2008, 108–109, 112).

[219] Wiselius (1878, 28).

During his term in office, Speidel frequently submitted reports on rice and other harvests in Cochinchina, shipping movements, port charges, currency exchange rates and other issues to the Dutch foreign ministry. He also provided legal aid to Dutch sailors from ships calling at Saigon and assisted Dutch officials from Batavia when visiting the French colony. Such case occurred in March 1890 when a small delegation from the Dutch East Indies arrived in Saigon. The event was noted down in the travel account of an anonymous Chinese merchant accompanying the Dutch official who was probably charged with negotiating rice purchases for the Dutch colony. Changing vessels in Singapore, the delegation continued their journey to Cochinchina on board a Messageries Maritimes liner. In his travel account, the Chinese trader noted that after that two days, the ship arrived on the Vietnamese coast, with Karl Theodor Speidel being the first person to meet: "The Dutch consul came on board welcoming the envoy". On the third day of the voyage, the French vessel called at Saigon where Speidel invited his Chinese visitor to accommodate himself in the shop of Chan Eng Bok (Zeng Yingmu), clerk of Speidel & Co. In his travel account, the Chinese merchant praised the hospitality he encountered in Chan's house: "They prepared a banquet and arranged a bed, and I was treated generously".[220]

On 24 February 1894, Karl Theodor Speidel tendered his resignation as Dutch consul, announcing he would "leave Cochinchina in around two months, without having an immediate return in mind". As his successor, he recommended Jacob Friedrich (or Fréderic) Daumiller who, as he wrote, "after a long commercial career in Batavia being not only entirely proficient in writing and speaking Dutch but also acquainted with consular affairs". Daumiller, born in 1842 in Wildbad, Kingdom of Württemberg, was a compatriot of Speidel, and, after an apprenticeship in an Amsterdam business firm, in 1865 he moved to Batavia to be employed as clerk by the German trading company C. Bahre & G. Kinder; he was later appointed merchant-consul of Oldenburg, Saxony and Bremen, and later of the North German Confederation, the German Empire and Denmark. In 1875, Daumiller was made managing clerk of C. Bahre & G. Kinder in which his brother was partner; after the bankruptcy of the company, he, in 1882, established the company Fr. Daumiller in Batavia which made business on the coffee market. When risky financial transactions resulted in huge financial losses, he was forced to liquidate his

[220] Lombard-Salmon and Ta (1994, 169).

company and to take up a bank loan. Through the help of a friend of his youth, Daumiller, in 1893, became managing clerk of Speidel & Co. in Saigon. However, the Dutch Resident of Batavia raised objections against him being made consul, pointing to his German nationality and his background and experience in Batavia. With the foreign ministry deciding to take a wait-and-see position, it took almost two years until on 24 March 1896, Daumiller was finally appointed consul of the Netherlands in Saigon.[221]

Only fifteen months later, on 24 June 1897, Consul Daumiller tendered his resignation, justifying the decision to leave Saigon with personal family matters and announcing to later return to the Dutch East Indies. As his successor, he proposed his countryman Friedrich Woelz, partner and managing clerk in Speidel & Co., doing business in Cochinchina and Tonkin. Woelz, born in 1853 in Stuttgart, capital of Württemberg, had joined Speidel & Co. in 1877, and as present head of the firm, was "generally respected", as the Amsterdam Chamber of Commerce and Industry pointed out. After being appointed, Woelz remained in office for less than a year and, on 14 March 1899, tendered his resignation due to his serious state of health. Although he recommended as successor his friend Eugene Meyer, partner in Speidel & Co., the foreign ministry decided to appoint the Dutchman Nicolaas Luykx, managing clerk of the German firm F. Engler & Company in Saigon. The Amsterdam Chamber of Commerce and Industry had warned about taking away the consulate from Speidel & Co., hinting at possible disadvantages for Dutch interests should another Dutch national not be available later for the post of consul; on the other hand, the Chamber was confident that a Dutchman would more actively promote the interests of the Netherlands in Saigon. When, on 22 September 1899, Luykx was appointed Dutch consul in Saigon, Speidel & Co. had lost an honorary post after more than a quarter of a century. However, initial expectations in the Netherlands that the Saigon consulate would contribute to increase direct Dutch exports to French Indochina never materialised.

[221] NAN, MBZ-1359: Consul Karl Theodor Speidel (Saigon) to Foreign Minister van Tienhoven (Den Haag), 24 February 1894, The Resident of Batavia to Governor-General van der Wijck (Batavia), 4 June 1894, Résumé of Friedrich Daumiller (Saigon), 28 July 1894, Appointment of Friedrich Daumiller to Consul in Saigon (Den Haag), 24 March 1896. Leewes (2008, 111–112).

Exports from the Dutch East Indies such as paraffin generally proved to be too costly for the Vietnamese. In the other direction, rice from Cochinchina was the only export article of some importance. In 1880, 85,002 tonnes was exported to the Dutch East Indies, in 1899, rice exports had almost halved to merely 46,174 tonnes.[222] Therefore, the Dutch consulate never ranked high for the business interests of Speidel & Co. but seemed to have enhanced the firm's overall good reputation in French Indochina.[223] According to information acquired by the Amsterdam Chamber of Commerce and Industry, Speidel & Co., in 1898, was regarded "the chief trading firm in Cochinchina and Tonkin". The year after, the Chamber's chairman reconfirmed the high reputation of Speidel & Co. calling it "doubtless the chief trading firm in Saigon, as well as in Haiphong and Phnom Penh".[224]

References

Archival Sources

Archives de Paris (AP)

Actes d'état civil.

Archives nationales d'outre-mer, Aix-en-Provence (ANOM)

Gouvernement-Général de l'Indochine (INDO-GGI).

Bundesarchiv, Berlin (BAB)

Deutsches Reich, Auswärtiges Amt: R 901.

[222] Coquerel (1911, 211).

[223] NAN, MBZ-1359: Consul Daumiller (Saigon) to Foreign Minister Röell (Den Haag), 24 June 1897, Résumé of Friedrich Woelz (Saigon), 15 September 1897, Chamber of Commerce and Industry (Amsterdam) to Foreign Minister de Beaufort (Den Haag), 14 March 1898 and 1 September 1899, Consul Woelz (Saigon) to Foreign Minister de Beaufort (Den Haag), 14 and 25 March 1899, Appointment of Nicolaas G. M. Luykx to Consul of the Netherlands (Den Haag), 22 September 1899. Leewes (2008, 112–113, 124).

[224] NAN, MBZ-1359: Chamber of Commerce and Industry (Amsterdam) to Foreign Minister de Beaufort (Den Haag), 14 March 1898 and 1 September 1899.

Deutsches Reich, Reichskolonialamt: R 1001.

Geheimes Staatsarchiv Preuischer Kulturbesitz, Berlin (GSTA)

Ministerium der Auswärtigen Angelegenheiten: III. HA.

Nationaal Archief, Den Haag (NAN)

Ministerie van Buitenlandse Zaken: MBZ.

Politisches Archiv des Auswärtigen Amts, Berlin (PAAA)

Altes Amt 117: Konsulat Saigon.
Deutsche Botschaft in China: Peking II.
Deutsches Reich: R.

Secondary Sources

Amer, Ramses. 2010. French Policies Towards the Chinese in Vietnam: A Study of Migration and Colonial Responses. *Moussons: Social Science Research on Southeast Asia* 16 (2): 57–80.

Baasch, Ernst. 1915. *Die Handelskammer zu Hamburg 1665–1915*, vol. 2. Hamburg: Lucas Gräfe & Sillem.

Baasch, Ernst. 1925. *Geschichte Hamburgs 1814–1918*, vol. 2. Gotha: Perthes.

Barrelon, Pierre. 1999. Cochinchina in 1859. In *Cities of Nineteenth Century Colonial Vietnam: Hanoi, Saigon, Hue and the Champa Ruins*, ed. Walter E. J. Tips, 1–29. Bangkok: White Lotus Press (First published in French: Barrelon, Pierre. 1860. *Le Tour du Monde*, vol. 1, 49–62).

Bastian, Adolf. 1868. *Die Völker des östlichen Asien: Studien und Reisen, vol. 4: Reise durch Kambodja nach Cochinchina*. Jena: Costenoble.

Bastian, Adolf. 1870. *Deutschlands Interessen in Ostasien*. Berlin: Koebke.

Batsch, Karl Ferdinand. 1890. *Admiral Prinz Adalbert von Preußen: ein Lebensbild mit besonderer Berücksichtigung auf seine Jugendzeit und den Anfang der Flotte*. Berlin: Brachvogel.

Baudrit, Andrè. 1936. *Contribution à l'histoire de Saigon: extraits des registres de délibérations de la ville de Saigon: Indochine française, 1867–1916*, 2 vols. Saigon: J. Testelin.

Baumgart, Winfried. 1982. *Imperialism: The Idea and Reality of British and French Colonial Expansion, 1880–1914*. Oxford: Oxford University Press.

Becker, Bert. 2004. German Business in Hong Kong Before 1914. *Journal of the Royal Asiatic Society Hong Kong Branch* 44: 91–113.

Berneron-Couvenhes, Marie-Françoise. 2000. The Internationalisation of Messageries Maritimes Steamship Company from 1851 to 1914: The Defense of the French Flag Overseas. In *Transnational Companies (19th–20th Centuries)*, ed. Hubert Bonin, et al., 289–300. Paris: Plage.

Bismarck: Die gesammelten Werke, vol. 6b: Politische Schriften. 1931. Ed. Friedrich Thimme. Berlin: Deutsche Verlags-Gesellschaft.

Bismarck: Die gesammelten Werke, vol. 7, 1: Gespräche. 1924. Ed. Willy Andreas. Berlin: Verlag für Politik und Wirtschaft.

Boissarie, Delphine. 2010–2011. Les stratégies de la Maison *Denis Frères* au Cambodge (1863–1962): Perception et structuration du marché khmer par une maison de commerce européenne, *Siksācakr* 12–13: 116–126.

Bonin, Hubert. 1999. *Les Patrons du Second Empire: Bordeaux et la Gironde*. Paris: Éditions A. et J. Picard.

Bonin, Hubert, and Bruno Marnot. 2007. The International Scope of Bordeaux Port: Logistics Economic Effects and Business Cycles in the Nineteenth and Twentieth Centuries. In *Making Global and Local Connections: Historical Perspectives on Ports*, ed. Tapio Bergholm, Lewis R. Fischer, and M. Elisabetta Tonizzi, 1–22. St. John's, Newfoundland: International Maritime Economic History Association.

Bonin, Hubert. 2008. La construction d'un système socio-mental impérial par le monde des affaires ultramarin girondin (des années 1890 aux années 1950). In *L'esprit économique impérial (1830–1970): Groupes de pression et réseaux du patronat colonial en France et dans l'empire*, ed. Hubert Bonin, et al., 243–273. Paris: SFHOM.

Bonin, Hubert. 2020. *French Banking and Entrepreneurialism in China and Hong Kong: From the 1850s to 1980s*. London and New York: Routledge.

Bouault, Jean. 1929. La Cochinchine et la guerre de 1870–71. *Revue d'histoire des colonies* 72 (November): 599–610.

Brandt, Max von. 1901. *Dreiunddreissig Jahre in Ost-Asien: Erinnerungen eines deutschen Diplomaten*, 3 vols. Leipzig: Georg Wigand.

Brocheux, Pierre, and Daniel Hèmery. 2009. *Indochina: An Ambiguous Colonization, 1858–1954*. Berkeley: University of California Press.

Brötel, Dieter. 1996. *Frankreich im Fernen Osten: Imperialistische Expansion und Aspiration in Siam und Malaya, Laos und China, 1880–1904*. Stuttgart: Franz Steiner.

Busch, Moritz. 1899. *Tagebuchblätter*, vol. 1. Leipzig: Grunow.

Cady, John Frank. 1954. *The Roots of French Imperialism in Eastern Asia*. Ithaca, NY: Cornell University Press.

Caron, Paul. 1925. Le Riz. *L'Illustration Économique et Financière* 15: 40–41.

Chambre de Commerce de Haiphong. 1900. *Procès-verbal de la 192e Séance* (7 November). Haiphong: Gallois.

Chevalier, Edouard. 1873. *La marine française et la marine allemande pendant la guerre de 1870–1871*. Paris: Henri Plon.

Clark, Christopher. 2007. *Iron Kingdom: The Rise and Downfall of Prussia, 1600–1947*. Penguin.

Coquerel, Albert. 1911. *Paddys et Riz de Cochinchine*. Lyon: A. Rey.

Corfield, Justin. 2009. *The History of Vietnam*. Westport, CT and London: Greenwood.

Corfield, Justin. 2013. *Historical Dictionary of Ho Chi Minh City*. London and New York: Anthem Press.

Craig, Gordon A. 1978. *Germany 1866–1945*. New York and Oxford: Oxford University Press.

Denis, Étienne. 1965. *Bordeaux et la Cochinchine sous la restauration et le second empire*. Bordeaux: Delmas.

Devraigne, Georges. 1920. *Le Commerce Austro-Allemand en Indochine et dans les Pays Limitrophes*. Hanoi and Haiphong: Imprimerie d'Extrême-Orient.

Dictionnaire des Ministres de 1789 à 1989. 1990. Ed. Benoît Yver. Paris: Perrin.

Digeon, Claude. 1959. *La Crise allemande de la pensée française, 1870–1914*. Paris: Presses Universitaires de France.

Dubreuil, René. 1910. *De la Condition des Chinois et de leur Rôle économique en Indo-Chine*. Bar-sur-Seine: Saillard.

Durand, Guy. 2016. Le Commerce Extérieur de l'Indochine Française. In *Une Vie Pour le Viêt Nam: Mélanges en l'Honneur de Charles Fourniau*, ed. Alain Ruscio, 223–230. Paris: Les Indes Savantes.

Faure, David. 1990. The Rice Trade in Hong Kong Before the Second World War. In *Between East and West: Aspects of Social and Political Development in Hong Kong*, ed. Elizabeth Sinn, 216–225. Hong Kong: Centre of Asian Studies.

Fecht, Ottmar. 1937. Die Wahrung wirtschaftlicher und politischer Belange in Ostasien durch die Norddeutsche Bundesmarine. *Marine-Rundschau* (August): 347–353.

Fichter, James R. 2012. British Infrastructure and French Empire: Anglo-French Steam Interdependency in Asian Waters, c. 1852–1870. *Britain and the World* 5 (2): 183–203.

Fourniau, Charles. 2002. *Vietnam: Domination coloniale et résistance nationale (1858–1914)*. Paris: Les Indes Savantes.

Friedel, Ernst. 1867. *Die Gründung preußisch-deutscher Colonien im Indischen und Großen Ozean mit besonderer Rücksicht auf das östliche Asien*. Berlin: Eichhoff.

Gautier (Fils), Théophile. 1903. Une Visite au Comte de Bismarck (octobre 1870). *La Revue de Paris* (August): 763–792.

Gautier, Théophile fils. 1912/13. Ein Besuch beim Grafen Bismarck. In *Velhagen und Klasings Monatshefte*, vol. 2, 523–528, vol. 3, 65–70.

Giersch, Alexis L. 2009. Die Marine im Deutsch-Französischen Krieg 1870/71. In *Der Deutsch-Französische Krieg 1870/71: Vorgeschichte, Verlauf, Folgen*, ed. Jan Ganschow, et al., 121–177. Graz: Ares.

Gooch, George Peabody. 1923. *Franco-German Relations 1871–1914*. London: Longman, Green.

Girault, Arthur. 1916. *The Colonial Tariff Policy of France*. Oxford: Clarendon.

Goscha, Christopher. 2017. *The Penguin History of Modern Vietnam*. Milton Keynes: Penguin.

Guillaume, X. 1985. Saigon, or the Failure of an Ambition (1858–1945). In *Colonial Cities*, ed. Robert J. Ross and Gerard J. Telkamp, 181–192. Dordrecht: Martinus Nijhoff.

Guillen, Pierre, and Jean-Claude Allain. 2007. La Puissance Recouvrée (1870–1914). In *Histoire de la Diplomatie Française, vol. 2: De 1815 à Nos Jours*, ed. Jean-Claude Allain, et al., 141–283. Paris: Perrin.

Halpern, Paul. 2001. The French Navy, 1880–1914. In *Technology and Naval Combat in the Twentieth Century and Beyond*, ed. Philipps Payson O'Brien, 36–52. Abington and New York: Routledge.

Hansa: Zeitschrift für Seewesen: Organ des "Deutschen Nautischen Vereins" und der "Deutschen Gesellschaft zur Rettung Schiffbrüchiger". 1870.

Hieke, Ernst. 1953. *Die Reederei M. Jebsen A. G. Apenrade*. Hamburg: Hamburgische Bücherei.

Hildebrand, Klaus. 1995. *Das vergangene Reich: Deutsche Außenpolitik von Bismarck bis Hitler 1871–1945*. Darmstadt: Wissenschaftliche Buchgesellschaft.

Howard, Michael. 1967. *The Franco-Prussian War: The German Invasion of France*. London: Collins.

Hsü, Immanuel C. Y. 2000. *The Rise of Modern China*, 6th ed. New York and Oxford: Oxford University Press.

Jenkins, Ernest H. 1973. *A History of the French Navy: From Its Beginnings to the Present Day*. London: Macdonald and Jane's.

Keiger, J.F.V. 1997. *Raymond Poincaré*. Cambridge: Cambridge University Press.

Kelly, Patrick J. 2011. *Tirpitz and the Imperial German Navy*. Bloomington: Indiana University Press.

Kersten, Albert E., and Bert van der Zwan. 2010. The Dutch Consular Service in the 19th Century. In *Consuls et services consulaires aux XIXe siècle/Consulship in the 19th Century/Die Welt der Konsulate im 19. Jahrhundert*, ed. Jörg Ulbert and Lukian Prijac, 413–421. Hamburg: DOBU.

Körner, Gustav. 1908. *Die norddeutsche Publizistik und die Reichsgründung im Jahre 1870*. Hannover: Fr. Diers.

Kolb, Eberhard. 1990. *Der Weg aus dem Krieg: Bismarcks Politik im Krieg und die Friedensanbahnung 1870/71*. Munich: R. Oldenbourg.

Kott, Sandrine. 2006. Bismarckbilder und Frankreichs innere Spaltungen in der zweiten Hälfte des 19. Jahrhunderts. In *Otto von Bismarck im Spiegel Europas*, ed. Klaus Hildebrand und Eberhard Kolb, 141–165. Paderborn: Schöningh.

Kriegsgeschichtliche Abteilung des Großen Generalstabes. 1874. *Der deutsch-französische Krieg 1870–71*, vol. 1, 1. Berlin: Mittler und Sohn.

Latham, A.J.H., and Larry Neal. 1983. The International Market in Rice and Wheat, 1868–1914. *The Economic History Review*, 2nd Series 36 (2, May): 260–280.

Latham, A.J.H. 1988. From Competition to Constraint: The International Rice Trade in the Nineteenth and Twentieth Centuries. *Business and Economic History*, 2nd Series 17: 91–102.

Lee, Seung-Joon. 2015. Rice and Maritime Modernity: The Modern Chinese State and the South China Sea Rice Trade. In *Rice: Global Networks and New Histories*, ed. Francesca Bray, et al., 99–117. Cambridge: Cambridge University Press.

Leewes, Jody. 2008. The Dutch Consuls in Saigon (1867–1946). In *Lion and Dragon: Four Centuries of Dutch-Vietnamese relations*, ed. John Kleinen, et al., 105–126. Amsterdam: Boom.

Li, Tana. 1998. *Nguyễn Cochinchina: Southern Vietnam in the Seventeenth and Eighteenth Centuries*. Ithaca, NY: SEAP.

Li, Tana. 2004. Rice from Saigon: The Singapore Chinese and the Saigon Trade of the Nineteenth Century. In *Maritime China in Transition 1750–1850*, ed. Wang Gungwu and Ng Chin-keong, 261–270. Wiesbaden: Harrassowitz.

Lombard-Salmon, Claudine, and Ta Trong Hiệp. 1994. De Batavia à Saigon: Notes de voyage d'un marchand chinois (1890). *Archipel* 47: 155–191.

Lorenz, Ottokar. 1902. *Kaiser Wilhelm und die Begründung des Reichs 1866-1871 nach Schriften und Mitteilungen beteiligter Fürsten und Staatsmänner*. Jena: Gustav Fischer.

Lutz, Manfred. 2018 (2018–2019). *Data Indexes of the Speidel Family*. Zimmern ob Rottweil (Baden-Württemberg).

Magee, Gary B., and Andrew S. Thompson. 2010. *Empire and Globalisation: Networks of People, Goods and Capital in the British World, c. 1850–1914*. Cambridge: Cambridge University Press.

Marsot, Alain G. 1993. *The Chinese Community in Vietnam under the French*. San Francisco: EM.

Meisner, Heinrich Otto, ed. 1926. *Kaiser Friedrich III.: Das Kriegstagebuch von 1870/71*. Berlin: Koehler.

Meuleau, Marc. 1990. *Des Pionniers en Extrême-Orient: Histoire de la Banque de l'Indochine (1875–1975)*. Paris: Fayard.

Meyer, Charles. 1996. *Les Français en Indochine 1860–1910*. Paris: Hachette.

Meyer, Charles. 1999. La drôle de guerre de 1870 en Cochinchine. *Historia. Revue Mensuelle* 634 (October): 78–83.

Mitchell, Pearl Boring. 1935. *The Bismarckian Policy of Conciliation with France, 1875–1885*. Philadelphia: University of Pennsylvania Press.

Mommsen, Wolfgang J. 1993. *Großmachtstellung und Weltpolitik: Die Außenpolitik des Deutschen Reiches 1870 bis 1914*. Frankfurt am Main and Berlin: Ullstein.

Morlat, Patrice. 2016. *Indochine années vingt: L'âge d'or de l'affairisme colonial (1918–1928): Banquiers, hommes d'affaires et patrons en réseaux*. Paris: Les Indes Savantes.

Murray, Martin J. 1980. *The Development of Capitalism in Colonial Indochina (1870–1940)*. Berkeley: University of California Press.

Nguyen, Quoc Dinh. 1941. *Les Congrégations Chinoises en Indochine Française*. Paris: Recueil Sirey.

Nipperdey, Thomas. 1998. *Deutsche Geschichte 1866–1918, vol. 2: Machtstaat vor der Demokratie*. Munich: Beck.

Nørlund, Irene. 1986. Rice Production in Colonial Vietnam, 1900–1930: Production, Consumption, Market Relations and Social Differentiation. In *Rice Societies: Asian Problems and Prospects*, ed. Irene Nørlund, et al., 203–229. London: Curzon.

Oncken, Hermann, ed. 1927. *Großherzog Friedrich I. von Baden und die deutsche Politik von 1854–1871*, vol. 2. Stuttgart: Deutsche Verlagsanstalt.

Owen, Norman G. 1971. The Rice Industry of Mainland Southeast Asia 1850–1914. *The Journal of the Siam Society* 59 (2): 75–143.

Palmade, Guy P. 1972. *French Capitalism in the Nineteenth Century*. Newton Abbot: David & Charles.

Paz, Maurice. 1965. Regnier, le mystérieux négociateur de 1870. *Revue des travaux de l'Academie des sciences morales et politiques et comptes rendus de ses séances* 118 (1): 227–240.

Pflanze, Otto. 2014. *Bismarck and the Development of Germany*, vol. 3. Princeton, NJ: Princeton University Press.

Pohl, Heinrich. 1918. Die Neutralisation der ostasiatischen Gewässer im deutsch-französischen Kriege 1870–71. *Archiv des öffentlichen Rechts* 38 (2, 4): 390–395.

Poidevin, Raymond, and Jacques Bariéty. 1982. *Frankreich und Deutschland: Die Geschichte ihrer Beziehungen 1815–1975*. Munich: Beck.

Preußisches Handels-Archiv. Wochenschrift für Handel, Gewerbe und Verkehrsanstalten. 1868, 1869 and 1873. Berlin: R. v. Decker.

Purcell, Victor. 1980. *The Chinese in Southeast Asia*, 2nd ed. Kuala Lumpur: Oxford University Press.

Rickmers, Willi Rickmer. 1934. *Rickmers A Century, 1834–1934*. Hamburg: Broschek.

Robequain, Charles. 1944. *The Economic Development of French Indo-China*. London: Oxford University Press.

Roth, François. 1990. *La Guerre de 1870*. Paris: Pluriel.

Schäfer, Erwin. 1901. *Geschichte der Deutschen Kriegsmarine im neunzehnten Jahrhundert*. Berlin: Schneider.

Schanz, Moritz. 1900/01. Handel, Kulturen und Industrien Indochinas. *Beiträge zur Kolonialpolitik und Kolonialwirtschaft* 10: 294–300.

Schivelbusch, Wolfgang. 2004. *The Culture of Defeat: On National Trauma, Mourning, and Recovery*. New York: Picador.

Schoen, [Wilhelm Eduard] Freiherr von. 1922. *The Memoirs of an Ambassador: A Contribution to the Political History of Modern Times*. London: Allen & Unwin.

Schrecker, John E. 1971. *Imperialism and Chinese Nationalism: Germany in Shantung*. Cambridge, MA: Harvard University Press.

Schumacher, Hermann. 1917. *Der Reis in der Weltwirtschaft*. Munich and Leipzig: Duncker & Humblot.

Soutou, Georges-Henri. 2007. Le Deuil de Puissance (1914–1958). In *Histoire de la Diplomatie Française, vol. 2: De 1815 à Nos Jours*, ed. Jean-Claude Allain, et al., 287–409. Paris: Perrin.

Stenographische Berichte über die Verhandlungen des Reichstages des Norddeutschen Bundes. 1870. I. Legislaturperiode (II. Außerordentliche Session 1870). Berlin: Norddeutsche Allgemeine Zeitung.

Stoecker, Helmuth. 1958. *Deutschland und China im 19. Jahrhundert: Das Eindringen des deutschen Kapitalismus*. Berlin: Rütten & Loening.

Stoecker, Helmuth. 1977. Germany and China, 1861–94. In *Germany in the Pacific and Far East, 1870–1914*, ed. John A. Moses and Paul M. Kennedy, 26–39. St. Lucia, QLD: University of Queensland Press.

Stovall, Tyler. 2015. *Transnational France: The Modern History of a Universal Nation*. Boulder, CO: Westview.

Taylor, K.W. 2013. *A History of the Vietnamese*. Cambridge: Cambridge University Press.

Tran, Khanh. 1993. *The Ethnic Chinese and Economic Development in Vietnam*. Singapore: Institute of Southeast Asian Studies.

Tsao, Ellen. 1932. Chinese Rice Merchants and Millers in French Indo-China. *Chinese Economic Journal* 11 (6, December): 450–463.

Ullrich, Volker. 1999. *Die nervöse Großmacht: Aufstieg und Untergang des deutschen Kaiserreichs 1871–1918*. Frankfurt am Main: Fischer.

Vo, Nghia M. 2011. *Saigon: A History*. Jefferson, NC and London: McFarland.

Vorapheth, Kham. 2004. *Commerce et colonisation en Indochine 1860–1945: Les maisons de commerce françaises: Un siècle d'aventure humaine*. Paris: Les Indes Savantes.

Walser, Ray. 1992. *France's Search for a Battle Fleet: Naval Policy and Naval Power, 1898–1914*. New York: Garland.

Wehler, Hans-Ulrich. 1976. *Bismarck und der Imperialismus*. Cologne: DTV.

Wienefeld, Robert H. 1929. *Franco-German Relations 1878–1885*. Baltimore: John Hopkins Press.

Wiselius, Jakob Adolf Bruno. 1878. *De Franschen in Indo-China: Geografisch, Administratief en Economisch Overzicht van Franch Cochin China, Annam en Kambodja*. Zalt-Bommel: Noman.

Wong, Lin Ken. 1960. The Trade of Singapore, 1819–69. *Journal of the Malayan Branch of the Royal Asiatic Society* 33 (4): 11–315.

Zeitschrift der Gesellschaft für Erdkunde zu Berlin. 1871 (6), 91–96. Berlin: Reimer.

CHAPTER 5

Haiphong

Tonkin and the South China Sea (1600s–1885)

The Red River Delta

The Red River (also known as the Hong River, the Hồng Hà and Sông Cái) flows from Yunnan in southwest China through northern Vietnam to the Gulf of Tonkin. In 111 BCE, the Red River region (which was called "Southern Viet" at the time, and later Tonkin) and the area east of it (today Guangxi and Guangdong in south China) came under the control of the expanding Han Empire which laid the basis of Chinese power. In the following one thousand years, China's frontier province of Jiaozhi (Giao chi in Vietnamese) was deeply impacted by Chinese material culture and became integrated into flows of international commerce coming from the South China Sea (or Nanhai), the Indian Ocean, the Middle East and the Mediterranean. The Gulf of Tonkin developed into a major trading zone, and the Red River was one of the commercial arteries into Yunnan and Guangxi. In the tenth century, Jiaozhi ultimately left the Chinese empire to become an independent state. However, in 1406, during the rule of the Ming Dynasty (1368–1644), "Greater Viet" (or Dai Viet) was occupied by China for two decades and essentially furthered Chinese expansion southwards by land and sea. Chinese techniques of dyke-building aided Tonkin in becoming the rice bowl, and during the century the population more than doubled. Finally, the demographic pressures of the Red River Delta pulled the developing Vietnamese state

B. Becker, *France and Germany in the South China Sea, c. 1840–1930*, Cambridge Imperial and Post-Colonial Studies,
https://doi.org/10.1007/978-3-030-52604-7_5

southwards, to ports such as Qui Nhon and Hoi An, the main hubs of Vietnam's trade with the Indian Ocean.[1]

From the fifteenth century, the Red River Delta (or Tonkin Delta) was homogeneously settled by Vietnamese people, of which a large part had earlier emigrated from southern China. In the Age of Commerce of Southeast Asia (1450–1680), Tonkin seemed to have functioned as a major source of primary products for Chinese markets and was probably more developed in economic and cultural terms than Guangdong, Guangxi, Yunnan and Hainan Island.[2] Population growth, interrupted by bad rice harvests and frequent famines, remained typical characteristics of Tonkin's economy and society in the following centuries.[3] Rice was the most abundant good produced in the Red River Delta and a very restricted export. According to a French geographical study (1936), the peasants of the Delta gave the greatest part of their care to rice, with other crops occupying "only the lands and the months in which it is impossible to devote oneself to rice". Rice was not only the basic food of every meal but was also used for the composition of pastries and cakes, for making alcohol and as straw provided roofs for houses, fed oxen and buffalos and provided them with skimpy bedding and was the principal fuel for the household and the essential material to make warm mattresses. Finally, the sale of rice paddies gave the peasants of the Tonkin Delta their principal cash revenue. The population of the Delta (in 1911 around 6.1 million people) lived in a closed-up economy, with families subsisting mainly by consuming their own products. This resulted in the Delta having very paltry exchanges with surrounding regions,[4] but that never terminated the widespread trade in rice which was mainly in the hands of large and small Chinese companies based in Vietnamese ports which shipped rice to southern China. In the eighteenth century, thousands of southern Chinese were dependent, directly or indirectly, on waterborne activities and trading relations with northern Vietnam.[5]

[1] Li (2006, 83–86), Wheeler (2006, 125, 134–137), Reid (2015, 28) and Goscha (2017, 5–24).

[2] Li (2006, 95, 100) and Reid (1988, 7–8).

[3] Sakurai (1997, 150–151).

[4] Sakurai (1997, 133) and Gourou (1955, 420–421, 639).

[5] Luan and Cooke (2011, 147–154).

The Gulf of Tonkin, located between the coast of northern Vietnam, the Guangxi seaboard, the west side of the Leizhou (Luichow) Peninsula in the southernmost part of Guangdong, and the coast of Hainan more or less from the western exit of the Hainan Strait down to the area around the Yinggehai-Song Hong basin was closely interconnected by vibrant junk traffic. This junk trade between China, Vietnam and other parts of Southeast Asia continued to flourish in the first decades of the nineteenth century. The close economic links began to decrease after the British colony of Singapore (founded in 1819) succeeded Bangkok as Guangzhou's major trading partner and modern steamships began to replace junks as major means of transport. Chinese merchants increasingly chartered Western coastal steamers, often in Hong Kong, for faster and more reliable voyages to Singapore, Saigon and other ports in the South China Sea. This growing trend saw the Gulf of Tonkin become something of a backwater in international and interregional shipping. However, small regional junk traders, smugglers and other seafarers continued to operate in the Gulf and were often illegally shipping rice from the Red River Delta to southern China. Aided, in many cases, by the collusion of corrupt local Vietnamese authorities, rice smuggling was flourishing, making it the most important illegal trade in the Gulf of Tonkin. According to reports, over three hundred small Chinese junks, of an estimated capacity of c. twenty-five tonnes each, loaded rice at Ninh Hai (Ninh Hải, near later Haiphong) from 1844 to 1846. Since this occurred during periods when the Vietnamese government had issued a strict export ban, rice smuggling took probably place with the tacit agreement of Vietnamese mandarins who received considerable bribes. Another illicit activity by small junk traders was the smuggling of kidnapped Vietnamese women and children to brothels and households in Guangzhou (Canton) and Hong Kong. Furthermore, piracy by both Vietnamese and Chinese seafarers was rampant, severely threatening shipping in the Gulf after the 1820s. Often caused by political turmoil in both China and Vietnam in the mid-nineteenth century, which had worsened economic and social conditions in the Gulf region by the 1850s and 1860s, smuggling and piracy belonged to the everyday life of tens of thousands of people, with negative effects on the economy of northern Vietnam.[6]

[6] Ptak (2008, 59), Murray (2004, 43–44), Tagliacozzo (2005, 230–243, 318–338) and Luan and Cooke (2011, 147–154).

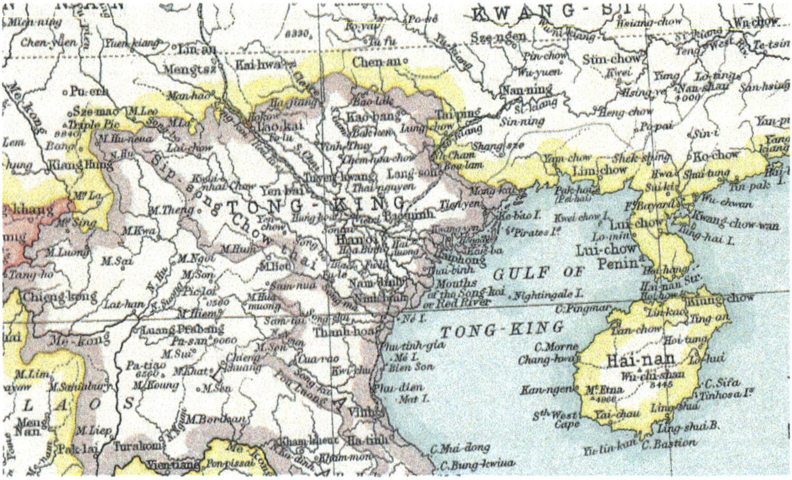

Fig. 5.1 Detail of a map of northern French Indochina and Gulf of Tonkin, 1920s (*Newnes' Citizen's Atlas of the World*, ed. by John Bartholomew, London: The Home Library Book Co., c. 1923/1924)

Hesitant steps by the Vietnamese government to legalise rice exports in the 1860s in order to increase tax revenues proved to be of little success against the flood of smuggling. Another attempt by Hanoi to prevent smuggling involved draining the transit trade from Yunnan by allowing a controlled trade in previously prohibited goods like rice and precious metals. On the other hand, the main concern of Chinese seafarers and merchants trading and living in Tonkin was legal trading. Hanoi reportedly had one thousand Chinese citizens in the 1820s, with the capital's commercial streets full of Chinese selling imported items like silk, herbal medicines, sugar, ceramics, porcelain and so forth. In the mid-nineteenth century, Tonkin was a closely-knit economic zone in which Vietnamese peasants and Chinese traders were the main pillars of the traditionally agricultural economy (Fig. 5.1).[7]

[7] Robequain (1944, 50–51) and Luan and Cooke (2011, 148–151, 155–158).

The Tonkin Crisis of 1873

From the late 1850s, the Red River attracted French attention as a possible gateway into Yunnan which was known for its rich agricultural and mineral produce. The myth of Yunnan remained powerful for the French until the end of the nineteenth century, strongly impacting French imperialist designs on Tonkin and its main waterway. At the time, Britain began exploring land routes between Burma and Yunnan, making it obligatory for the French to explore the Red River as a possible access to Yunnan. A pioneer was the French merchant Jean Dupuis, established in China since the Second Opium War (1858–1860), who was providing arms to Chinese imperial troops fighting the Muslim uprising in Yunnan (1855–1873). Exploiting this opportunity, Dupuis advanced from the Red River into China's south-western region, something that was generally regarded as an impossible mission. In 1867, the German firm Telge, Nölting & Company in Shanghai, of which the Hamburg merchant B. Telge was partner, provided financial support for the expedition. Before departing from Hong Kong, Dupuis secured formal permission from both Vietnamese and Chinese authorities for a commercial expedition to Yunnan which was to begin in October 1872. Admiral Marie-Jules Dupré, Governor of Cochinchina, seemed to have tacitly promoted the plan. When Dupuis sailed up the Red River on board two steamboats loaded with goods from Hong Kong, he was warmly received in China and was able to sell his entire cargo. In March 1873, Dupuis even sent arms to Kunming, the capital of Yunnan. On his retour voyage, he carried samples from Yunnan's rich mineral stocks, planning to sell them in Hong Kong. As Telge related, Dupuis tried to open the region to French trading and sell the minerals from Yunnan to global markets.[8]

However, Vietnamese authorities intervened in this unauthorised transit on the Red River and arrested Dupuis when he passed Hanoi in May 1873, holding him for six months. This gave Governor Dupré the pretext to dispatch the naval officer Francis Garnier and more than two hundred troops to Hanoi on 11 October, charged with enforcing the release of Dupuis. Facing this aggressive action, the Vietnamese court in Hue sent a diplomatic delegation to Saigon with the goal of

[8] Fourniau (2002, 237–246), Brocheux and Hémery (2009, 28) and Goscha (2017, 60). BAB, R 901-12813: Memorandum of B. Telge (Hamburg), 8 January 1874. For more details, see Dupuis (1879).

achieving the restitution of three southern Vietnamese provinces occupied by France in 1866 in return for freeing the French merchant. However, the governor's grand plan of attaining the opening of the Red River to French trade and establishing a French protectorate over Tonkin ended in complete failure when the Vietnamese refused to negotiate anything other than the release of Dupuis. This disappointing result led to Garnier intervening militarily in Tonkin. On 17 November 1873, he declared freedom of navigation on the Red River under French protection, and, three days later, occupied the citadel of Hanoi and other strategically important points in the delta. Installing pro-French authorities in four north-eastern Vietnamese provinces, Garnier aimed to unilaterally impose a French protectorate over Tonkin. But his attempt to permanently establish French control over northern Vietnam failed when his small force was overwhelmed by local Vietnamese commanders and supporting Chinese irregular troops, the so-called Black Flags. Although Emperor Tu Duc had not authorised the hostilities, Garnier was killed in Hanoi on 21 December 1873. However, the French government refrained from retaliation against Vietnam, fearing the possible intervention of China, and ordered Governor Dupré to abstain from any further military action. On 15 March 1874, in Saigon, Vietnamese officials and Lieutenant Paul Philastre signed an agreement (which the French called the "Philastre Treaty") under which the French promised to vacate Tonkin and provide military aid to Vietnam. In return, the Vietnamese court formally abandoned the entire area of Cochinchina, promised to establish jointly administered Vietnamese and French customs houses and concessions in Tonkin and agreed to the posting of a French resident in the capital Hue. Furthermore, Vietnam accepted the establishment of French consulates protected by French garrisons of one hundred men each in Hanoi, Ninh Hai (near the future French colonial port city Haiphong) and Thi Nai (in Binh Dinh Province at the central coast).[9]

The treaty of 15 March 1874 caught the attention of Theodor von Holleben, German Minister in Beijing. "The rather flexible clauses would suffice to make France really master of the country," he wrote to Bismarck in April 1874, adding that his French counterpart kept "unswerving silence on all these questions". When the subsequent commercial treaty of 31 August 1874 between France and Vietnam was published, proclaiming

[9] Fourniau (2002, 246–276), Brocheux and Hémery (2009, 28–29) and Goscha (2017, 61–62).

free trade on and around the Red River, the German government took a positive stance. Rudolf von Delbrück, president of the Reich chancellery, was of the opinion that "it was not yet the time" for separate German-Vietnamese trade negotiations, pointing to the fact that "rights attained by France for all foreigners" would allow German companies "to gain a foothold and to establish contacts" in Vietnam. This development should be awaited "before the question of a particular national protection of such" needed to be considered. Some months later, in January 1875, the State Secretary of Foreign Affairs, Bernhard Ernst von Bülow (known as Bismarck's "right hand"), stressed in his instructions to the newly appointed German ambassador to France, Prince von Hohenlohe-Schillingsfürst, that Berlin "wished to even avoid the impression of pursuing any purpose of thwarting France's political sphere of influence in this country". In order to erase any doubt about the position of the German government, Hohenlohe-Schillingsfürst was instructed to firmly inform French officials "that we do regard the said treaty as progress of civilisation, and also as benefit for the development of German trade in East Asia". In May 1875, Bülow reiterated this position to the ambassador in London: "We have, in short, no interests there and do therefore not intend to oppose France in these far-away regions. On the contrary, it is very desirable when the French, with enthusiasm, bring into action there their funds and powers".[10] Bülow's remark should be seen in the context of the then so-called War in Sight crisis of April–May 1875. At the time, Bismarck had returned to a defensive strategy to avoid conflict and preserve peace with France. It also signalled the Chancellor's intention to encourage other European powers to settle their disputes at the peripheries of Europe and to engage in their colonies. Furthermore, such imperialist commitments, especially in economic fields, promised to provide German private traders with considerable profits. German business in East Asia would be one of the winners in France's naval imperialism and colonial expansion in northern Vietnam.

[10]BAB, R 901-12813: Minister von Holleben (Beijing) to Chancellor von Bismarck (Berlin), 24 April 1874, State Secretary von Bülow (Berlin) to President von Delbrück (Berlin), 6 May 1874, President von Delbrück (Berlin) to Foreign Ministry (Berlin), 21 September 1874, State Secretary von Bülow (Berlin) to Ambassador von Hohenlohe (Paris), 26 January 1875, State Secretary von Bülow (Berlin) to Ambassador von Hohenlohe (Paris) and Ambassador von Münster (London), 5 May 1875.

The Tonkin Campaign 1882/83

For the next eight years, the French held back on expansion on the Indochinese peninsula. This changed when in 1881 French merchants and missionaries in Tonkin demanded military action to free traders held by the Vietnamese authorities. The government of Léon Gambetta, aiming at completely seizing Tonkin, gave the green light to the colonial authorities in Saigon dispatching another naval officer, Captain Henri Rivière, to northern Vietnam with 250 men with the goal of occupying part of the Red River Delta. On 26 March 1882, two French gunboats, with Rivière and three companies of troops, cleared the port of Saigon for Haiphong.[11] The escalating tensions were observed by Consul Gustav Travers in Guangzhou, who had charged the German merchant J. F. Schriever in Haiphong (who was the Haiphong special correspondent of *The Hongkong Daily Press*) to frequently report about the escalating situation. On the night of 31 March to 1 April 1882, three hundred French troops and eight cannons were landed in Haiphong on board the first gunboat to be transhipped to river steamers. Their mission "to temporarily capture the citadel of Hanoi, as well as some other more northern places", as Schriever wrote, seemed well-known in Haiphong at the time; he added that "here [is], of course, bedlam". Around two weeks later, Schriever sent more details about the ongoing preparations for further dispatching troops to Hanoi where the citadel was reinforced by the Vietnamese with extra cannons. On 25 April 1882, Rivière attacked the citadel, only handing back a part of the captured installations five days later. Learning of the successful operation, in his report to Bismarck, Consul Travers showed strong sympathy for the military action when stating that the French government "not only had the right but also the duty to push the Vietnamese government to fulfil its obligations regarding trading, as stipulated in the Franco-Vietnamese treaty of 1874, and, if necessary, to enforce them". He regarded "a more energetic and more resolute appearance" as "the only way to bring about well-ordered circumstances in Tonkin for developing trade and to terminate the maladministration of the [Vietnamese] mandarins".[12]

[11] Brocheux and Hémery (2009, 42), Corfield (2009, 21) and Goscha (2017, 64).

[12] Eastman (1967, 49–51) and Brocheux and Hémery (2009, 42). PAAA, Peking II-53: Consul Röver (Saigon) to German Legation (Beijing), 1 April 1882, J. F. Schriever

The events of spring 1882 in Hanoi marked a decisive turning point when Vietnam's dwindling military power became obvious. In May 1882, Travers reported that among the Chinese in Hanoi a "real panic" had broken out, causing most of them to flee to Haiphong. Obviously basing his account on information received from Schriever, the consul pointed to "efforts of the French authorities to secure as far as possible a favourable opinion among Germans residing in Tonkin, efforts manifesting themselves by a strikingly accommodating disposition of the [French] consul and the Commandant [Rivière], as well as the open and frank way in which they discuss current affairs with Germans". Adding that non-military French circles in Hanoi and Haiphong had sharply condemned such behaviour, Travers attributed verbal criticism and attacks on Germans to "professional envy" and concluded as follows: "They cannot forgive German merchants that they are outdoing other merchants, thanks to their higher routine, fairness, and passion, and now accuse French authorities of favouring the Germans to the detriment of their French countrymen".[13]

France's growing interest in Indochina during the 1870s had not escaped China's attention. Beijing repeatedly stressed Vietnam's tributary relationship to China and, in late December 1880, sent a strong warning to Paris that occupation of Tonkin would cause war; eight months later, the Chinese sent thirty thousand troops to Tonkin. However, France's sudden military seizure of Hanoi came as a complete surprise to the Qing government that on 9 May 1882 questioned the French Minister about the matter. However, Albert Bourée also seemed surprised and lacking in any information from Paris about further plans, his German counterpart in Beijing reported to Bismarck.[14] In mid-1882, the Qing sent troops to their southern border, where they seized major Vietnamese frontier towns such as Lang Son and Son Tay. After negotiations between Li Hongzhang and Bourée, an agreement was made in December 1882 based on a compromise that intended to divide Tonkin into two zones of influence,

(Haiphong) to Consul Travers (Guangzhou), 2 April and 17 April 1882, Consul Travers (Guangzhou) to Chancellor von Bismarck (Berlin), 27 April 1882.

[13] PAAA, Peking II-53: Consul Travers (Guangzhou) to Chancellor von Bismarck (Berlin), 10 May 1882.

[14] Eastman (1967, 57–58) and Brocheux and Hémery (2009, 42–43). PAAA, Peking II-53: Minister von Brandt (Beijing) to Chancellor von Bismarck (Berlin), 13 May 1882.

Chinese to the north, French to the south. The Vietnamese government was not consulted on the Sino-French compromise over Tonkin.[15]

A few weeks later, on 21 February 1883, the second government of Jules Ferry took office, committing France to colonial expansion. Led by the lobby of banking, financial, and insurance interests (among them the Banque de l'Indochine or Bank of Indochina, established in 1875), public agitation for renewed colonial expansion was triggered by economic stagnation in France, with the French economy experiencing a long period of recession which reached a low point in the mid-1880s. Hopes were high that colonial expansion could provide export markets and stimulate economic growth. This notion was combined with justifications such as enhancing France's geopolitical position, promoting her national prestige and fostering a special republican "mission civilisatrice" (France's civilising mission).[16] This encouraged Prime Minister Ferry and Foreign Minister Paul-Armand Challemel-Lacour to take a tough line towards China when sharply criticising Bourée for his deal with the Qing and recalling him from his post in Beijing. To the Chinese government, Paris made it clear that the entire territory of Tonkin should be placed under French control, something which was in accordance with Henri Rivière who had been strictly opposed to the Sino-French compromise over Tonkin. It provided sufficient reason for the naval officer to start a new military campaign, seizing major towns in the Red River Delta including Hon Gay located at Ha Long Bay where coal mines had previously been detected by French engineers. In May 1883, challenged by Black Flag contingents, Rivière's small force of less than five hundred men marched out of Hanoi and were ambushed at Paper Bridge (Pont de Papier) where the commander fell on 19 May. This defeat gave Ferry the opportunity to declare France's commitment to finally achieving victory and to erecting an East Asian empire. With the French parliament immediately voting to provide a huge credit to finance the dispatch of a strong expeditionary force to Tonkin, Admiral Amédée Courbet was sent to Haiphong at the head of naval forces. After the troops of the Far East Squadron had landed and

[15] Eastman (1967, 58–61), Fourniau (2002, 314–317), Brocheux and Hémery (2009, 43–44) and Goscha (2017, 64).

[16] Goscha (2017, 62–63).

been housed in barracks at the port city or transhipped to reinforce the garrisons at Hanoi and Nam Dinh, war resumed in July–August 1883.[17]

In August 1883, Schriever continued his reporting to the German consul about past events. Referring to the death of Rivière, the merchant called the French commander "our best friend in Tonkin" who was "entirely impartial and well-disposed towards Germans". In the aftermath of the French defeat, Hanoi had been fortified against possible attack, with a defence line around the town, the construction of which had involved burning or blowing up surrounding buildings. According to Schriever, the premises of his own company, including all interiors and furniture, were also destroyed. He called the French troops' discipline "miserable" and also criticised French administrators "working against each other". Referring to the surprise attack on Haiphong of 4 July 1883, when Black Flag troops set fire to the blockhouse, forcing the French soldiers to retire, he reported that his own house had also been seriously attacked and almost burnt down. However, the Vietnamese were beaten off, with the loss of two or three men on their side. As the merchant related, the French had accused the local Germans of having provided weapons to the Black Flags and openly displayed "hatred of the Germans". He noted the following: "The French, with a few exceptions, consider us to be enemies".[18]

In the coming months, the French expeditionary forces commanded by General Bouët and Admiral Courbet led the campaign against Vietnamese and Chinese troops. While Bouët overran the Red River Delta, Courbet's naval forces occupied the forts of Thuan An, outside Hue, enabling French gunboats to sail up to Hue. On board was Jules Harmand (the former companion of Francis Garnier in Tonkin), with the rank of general civil commissioner, who delivered a harsh ultimatum to the Vietnamese government. On 25 August 1883, the court gave in and signed a drastic protectorate treaty. The Harmand convention of 25 August 1883 was a prelude to the pure and simple annexation of Vietnam, with a French resident to be installed in Hue. However, the war was not over, with the Chinese holding major positions at Bac Ninh, northeast of Hanoi, and at Son Tay, west of the Tonkin capital. Schriever reported that the

[17] Eastman (1967, 66–73), Bensacq-Tixier (2003, 83–84), Brocheux and Hémery (2009, 44) and Goscha (2017, 64). *The Hong Kong Daily Press*, 19 July 1883.

[18] PAAA, Peking II-54: Schriever (Haiphong) to Legation Secretary von Tattenbach (Beijing), 7 August 1883. *The Hong Kong Daily Press*, 13 July 1883.

15,000 Chinese troops in Son Tay, "allegedly receiving reinforcements from China almost daily", would give the French "a hard nut to crack". The situation in Haiphong was also bad, as the merchant wrote on 10 September 1883: "No one here believes any longer in reinforcements from home, confidence is lost. The Chinese merchants wanting to save their skin are returning in masses to Hong Kong and Guangzhou. (…) The trade is completely ruined. The French are unable to inspire confidence in the people and are feared and hated, even worse than the pirates".[19]

The military situation of the French expeditionary troops worsened in September 1883 after unsuccessful attacks against Black Flag troops in Son Tay. After further reinforcements had been dispatched, Ferry, on 31 October 1883, declared that France intended to seize several new positions on the Red River Delta. Less than two weeks later, the French legation in Beijing informed Christian Count von Tattenbach, Legation Secretary and Acting German Minister, that in the case of war with China, French naval forces were prepared to burn down all ports on the Chinese coast, adding that "single vessels had already been designated and everything could only be a work of 24 hours". Tattenbach immediately contacting his British counterpart, agreeing with him that all foreigners in Chinese ports should be warned by the British and German squadron commanders to save their lives and valuables. On 11 November 1883, he suggested to Bismarck the reinforcing of the German East Asia Squadron, and some days later repeated this request in a second letter to the Chancellor. Tattenbach pointed to the fact that the French fleet in Chinese waters consisted of more than forty men-of-war, while Germany had only four warships, of which three were not operational for various reasons. The only remaining vessel, the steam corvette *Leipzig*, had been charged by Minister Max von Brandt for a voyage to Korea to negotiate a trade and amicability treaty with the Korean government. However, the proposal to considerably boost Germany's naval presence was strongly rejected in Berlin. Rear Admiral Max von der Goltz, the commander of the German Squadron, was only instructed to reach an agreement with the British, American and other naval commanders about measures to

[19] Eastman (1967, 85–89) and Brocheux and Hémery (2009, 44). PAAA, Peking II-54: Consul Speidel (Saigon) to German Legation (Beijing), 30 August 1883, and J. F. Schriever (Haiphong) to Legation Secretary Tattenbach (Beijing), 3 and 10 September 1883. *North China Daily Herald*, 1 September 1883.

be taken to protect foreigners in Chinese ports. Clemens August Busch, undersecretary of state of the foreign ministry, in his telegram to Tattenbach, ordered him to wait until the *Leipzig* had completed the diplomatic mission in Korea before transferring the vessel to the Squadron.[20] It was obvious that Berlin wished to avoid any impression that Germany had tried to interfere in France's war in Tonkin. On 16 December 1883, Son Tay fell after heavy French bombardment. "French and Chinese soldiers committed a lot of cruelties", Schriever told Tattenbach adding that it was "a war to the finish".[21]

When consulting the voluminous records of the former Imperial German legation in Beijing, which contain frequent exchanges of correspondence between German consulates in southern China and Saigon, the legation and the foreign ministry in Berlin, it is obvious that Bismarck was well informed about the Tonkin Campaign of 1882–1883. Consequently, France's colonial expansion in Vietnam was exploited by the Chancellor to achieve a rapprochement with Paris with the goal to establish a kind of colonial Franco-German alliance directed against Britain. His dual strategy aimed at diverting France away from her prime goal of winning back Alsace-Lorraine and towards colonial expansion, and at the same time driving a wedge between Britain and France to hamper any closer Anglo-French cooperation directed against Germany.[22] Already in 1880, Bismarck had instructed the German ambassador in Paris, Prince von Hohenlohe-Schillingsfürst, that "our area of agreement with France spans from Guinea [West Africa] to Belgium". Colonial policies should become the lever to achieve this vision, which meant confrontation with Britain. The first opportunity came when French claims in Madagascar conflicted with the rights the British considered to have established in the island. On 9 December 1882, Bismarck informed Prime Minister Charles Duclerc that Germany would not intervene in Madagascar, and that in case disorder developed on the island, the protection of German

[20] PAAA, Peking II-55: Legation Secretary von Tattenbach (Beijing) to Chancellor von Bismarck, 1 and 11 October 1883, 20 and 26 November 1883, Telegram of Undersecretary of State Busch (Berlin) to German Legation (Beijing), 25 November 1883. Wienefeld (1929, 158) and Brocheux and Hémery (2009, 44).

[21] Eastman (1967, 96–100). PAAA, Peking II-56: J. F. Schriever (Haiphong) to Legation Secretary von Tattenbach (Beijing), 25 December 1883.

[22] Poidevin and Bariéty (1982, 181–189), Mommsen (1993, 67–68) and Guillen and Allain (2007, 156–159).

nationals would be entrusted to the French. After Jules Ferry became prime minister in February 1883, he acknowledged the German position as evidence of the friendly feeling of Germany. Because Ferry pursued the idea of acquiring a great colonial empire instead of regaining Alsace-Lorraine, Bismarck seized the opportunity. The Chancellor was obviously hinting at the fall of Son Tay on 16 December 1883 when making a passing remark to his personal physician, Dr. Eduard Cohen, that "in France, the mood is now improving". As the latter one noted in his journal under the date of 8 January 1884, Bismarck wished the French to gain victories in Tonkin and Madagascar because it would "satisfy their vanity and keep them off from revanche [revenge]". Soon, after discussing the Tonkin affair with Hohenlohe-Schillingsfürst, he instructed the ambassador "to openly declare in Paris that we will be loyal to France and that we will not allow ourselves to relinquish our neutrality: France should wage war on land or at sea (...) and should energetically proceed to occupying some islands". He also announced Tattenbach's recall from his post in Beijing. At the end of March 1884, the diplomat was transferred to a subordinate post in the foreign ministry's division for commercial policy and legation. These actions made it clear the Chancellor was not prepared to allow any interference with his goal of achieving a rapprochement with France.[23]

A strong signal Bismarck sent to France was the refusal to permit the delivery of two ironclad cruisers built for the Chinese government in German yards. In May 1884, when one ship was ready, the Chancellor informed the French ambassador in Berlin, Alphonse Chodron de Courcel, accordingly, giving proof of his benevolent neutrality. Some months later, he laid out to Courcel the reorientation of these foreign policies which had an anti-British alignment and signalled a strong interest in collaborating with France. "I wish to establish a sort of equilibrium on the seas", Bismarck declared to Courcel on 23 September 1884, "and France has a leading role to play in this connection, if she will agree with our views". He wished no war with England but wanted her to accustom herself to the idea "that a German-French alliance is not an

[23] Lepsius (1922, 395): Bismarck (Berlin) to Ambassador von Hohenlohe (Paris), 8 April 1880. Mitchell (1935, 130–132) and Bismarck (1926, 499): Conversation with Dr. Eduard Cohen, 8 January 1884. Curtius (1907, 348): Conversation with Bismarck, 24 January 1884.

impossibility".[24] At the same time, the Chinese minister in Berlin solicited German intervention in Tonkin after Ferry had announced the occupation of Formosa (Taiwan) which resulted in the Battle of Fuzhou (Foochow), with the bombardment of the major Chinese navy yard by Courbet's fleet on 23–24 August 1884. However, Xu Jingcheng was advised by Foreign Minister Paul von Hatzfeldt that China should settle her differences with France. To a similar request for support, Bismarck is said to have remarked: "We stand in too difficult relations with France to do that".[25]

In October 1884, the Chinese minister tried to enlist forty to fifty German officers, especially former artillery and general staff officers, offering them a considerable sum of money for joining the Chinese army. Bismarck promised to prevent the enlistment of men actually in service by refusing to accept their resignations. Yet, he could not stop those not in the reserve. Diplomatic records of the German foreign ministry from 1883 to 1885 related to the background and events of the Sino-French War over Tonkin contain much correspondence on the recruitment of Germans and other foreigners for Chinese military service during that period. When French newspapers published the news that 160 German army officers had enlisted in Chinese service, Ferry asked the Chancellor to have the *Norddeutsche Allgemeine Zeitung*, the semi-official journal and mouthpiece for Bismarck, print the government explanation so that French public opinion would not believe the enlistment to have been authorised. On 4 January 1885, such an article appeared in the journal, stressing that Germany was neutral in the Franco-Chinese conflict and would not allow soldiers in active service or in reserve to take part in it but was unable to forbade ex-service men to enlist.[26]

[24] Wienefeld (1929, 159), Mitchell (1935, 137) and Power (1977, 177–178). The quote in: Gooch (1923, 21) and Hildebrand (1995, 92).

[25] Brocheux and Hémery (2009, 45–46), Mitchell (1935, 137) and Wienefeld (1929, the quote: 160).

[26] BAB, R 901-33637, R 901-33638, R 901-33639. *Norddeutsche Allgemeine Zeitung*, 4 January 1885, *Berliner Tageblatt*, 17 January 1885. Mitchell (1935, 145) and Poidevin and Bariéty (1982, 185).

French Embargoes on Shipments

Although the German government remained strictly neutral during the undeclared Sino-French War (1884–1885), actual events on the spot brought about the real danger of involving German business interests in China in conflict with French military actions. The German firm Blackhead & Company in Hong Kong, which had chartered out its steamer *China* to the Chinese government for many years, was suddenly the focus of German attention after the vessel, in May 1884, had transported Chinese troops and military equipment from Hong Kong to Fuzhou in preparation of a possible French attack. A similar case occurred on 21 August 1884 when *China* shipped seven hundred Chinese officers and soldiers, ammunition and dynamite, and also food supplies including one thousand bags of rice, from Swatow to Fuzhou. According to the memoirs of Max von Brandt, German Minister in Beijing, the Chinese seemed to preferably employ German vessels "thinking that the German flag would provide extra security against their enemies". Captain Adolf Mensing, commander of the cruiser *Prinz Adalbert,* charged by the German admiralty to observe the military events in Fuzhou, reported that on 25 August 1884, the French cruiser *Châteaurenault* and the troopship *Saône* "paid no attention to the *China* landing thereupon in view of the French vessels". On that day, Courbet had received the congratulations of captains of neutral warships on the professionalism displayed by the French squadron during the bombardment of the Chinese naval yard at Fuzhou and the subsequent fighting with Chinese men-of-war. Soon after, the American steamer *Mary Austin*, chartered by the Chinese government, called at Fuzhou with a cargo of dynamite shipped from Hong Kong. Max von Brandt seemed very concerned about the possible threat from such contraband war shipments should France and China officially declare war. He gave strict orders to German consuls in China that in such cases shipowners, shipmasters and merchants should be warned "of violating generally acknowledged principles of international law".[27]

A strong warning signal to merchant vessels under neutral flags was sent out by the commander of the French cruiser *Villars* in August

[27] Brandt (1901, 194) and Power (1977, 179–180). PAAA, Peking II-58: Captain Mensing (Fuzhou) to German Consulate (Hong Kong), 30 August 1884, Consul Travers (Hong Kong) to Captain Mensing (Fuzhou), 6 September 1884, Minister von Brandt (Beijing) to Bismarck (Berlin), 29 September 1884.

1884 when seizing the German steamer *Welle* which had been shipping Chinese troops and supplies to Keelung, the major coal-mining port on the northern coast of Formosa. On 5 August 1884, Admiral Sébastian Lespès had bombarded Keelung, destroying the port's gun emplacements. Although the French tried to occupy the city and the nearby coal mines, they found themselves outnumbered by Chinese troops, which forced Lespès to abandon the undertaking. The ruined attack probably explains the harsh French treatment of the German vessel which was regarded by Consul Travers in Hong Kong as "legally not justified".[28] However, it was only the start of a larger debate on legal issues concerning neutral powers such as Germany during the undeclared Sino-French War. For France, a compelling reason for not declaring war was the problem of logistics for her navy should British colonial ports such as Ceylon, Singapore or Hong Kong be closed to the refuelling and victualling of French warships. Another factor preventing Paris from declaring war was strong criticism from opposition parties of Ferry's government and its East Asian policies. However, the government's official assertion that its military actions against China did not create a state of war with Beijing was unconvincing to foreign opinion.[29]

The Keelung campaign intensified on 1 October 1884 when a small French expeditionary corps drawn from the garrisons in Tonkin and Cochinchina landed at Keelung and occupied the town. However, the important Pei Tao coal mines remained in Chinese hands. Meanwhile, French landing companies under the command of Admiral Lespès attacked the Chinese defences at Tamsui, the other major coal-mining port of Formosa. With the unexpected Chinese victory, the French suffered one of their rare defeats in the war and their control of the island was restricted to Keelung. In the following weeks, disease broke out, causing heavy losses among the French troops, while both soldiers and the small foreign community suffered from the shortfall in outside supplies. The most important lifeline was the shipping connection with Hong Kong which was kept open by two German steamers chartered by a French company that frequently transported provisions, coal and other equipment to Keelung. It is very likely that the unnamed French charterer

[28] PAAA, Peking II-58: Consul Travers (Hong Kong) to Captain Mensing (Fuzhou), 6 September 1884. Eastman (1967, 144–145).

[29] Eastman (1967, 163–164).

in the British colony was the company A. R. Marty because this trading firm was the main supplier to France's forces during the Sino-French War. In January 1885, Consul Travers in Hong Kong, seeking instructions from the German legation in Beijing concerning these shipments was telegraphically instructed by Minister von Brandt "not to interfere". Soon after, Consul-General Johannes Lührsen in Shanghai revealed that the involvement of German merchant vessels in supplying the French forces during the Keelung campaign was publicly well known, even in northern China.[30]

At the end of 1884, the French enforced a limited blockade of Formosa which was nevertheless unable to prevent the Chinese from using the Pescadores Islands as a staging post for landing large numbers of troops in southern Formosa. France's reaction was to substantially reinforce her expeditionary corps, bringing its strength to around 4,000 men in January 1885. In the light of the fact that France used Hong Kong as a major supply base for coal and other provisions, the British colonial government, on 23 January 1885, issued a proclamation that "public ships of the belligerent (French and Chinese) Governments should not be allowed to take on board at Hong Kong supplies, such as would assist naval operations". Coal was banished, and the repairing of French and Chinese warships in the colony prohibited. With the announcement, London made it clear that it would remain strictly neutral in the conflict. Although the British declaration did not explicitly declare coal as contraband of war and limited its possible countermeasures to Hong Kong, the French government was well aware of the consequences. However, both Prime Minister Ferry and Albert Billot, the senior official in charge of political issues in the French foreign ministry, told Ambassador Prince von Hohenlohe-Schillingsfürst that coal supplies in Hong Kong were "without any significance" for the French fleet "possessing coaling stations elsewhere". Such optimism was not shared by Consul Travers who, to the contrary, forecast that the British decision would have a major impact on the French fleet, which "would soon be forced to make Saigon the base of its operations".[31]

[30] Davidson (1903, 221–223) and Eastman (1967, 165–166). BAB, R 901-33639: Minister von Brandt (Beijing) to Bismarck (Berlin), 25 February 1885, Consul-General Lührsen (Shanghai) to Bismarck (Berlin), 24 March 1885.

[31] *The Hongkong Government Gazette Extraordinary*, 23 January 1885. Davidson (1903, 231–232) and Eastman (1967, 166). BAB, R 901-33637: Ambassador von Hohenlohe

France's counter-reaction was swift. In early February 1885, the French government announced that it had instructed its naval officers "to enforce belligerent rights including right of search of neutral ships at sea for contraband of war". On 6 February, Ambassador de Courcel explained to Busch that the British step had forced his government "to exercise such rights which are recognised by the law of nations". When Brandt enquired from Beijing whether German merchant vessels would also be affected by the French measure, the foreign ministry instructed him that the French right to search neutral vessels on the high seas was to be recognised. The German government freely submitted to search and also instructed the East Asia Squadron not to appear at places in Chinese waters where the French squadron was operating. Even Brandt's suggestion of dispatching a larger German warship to Shanghai met with a cautious reception in Berlin. The foreign ministry explained to Leo von Caprivi, chief of the Imperial Navy (the later imperial chancellor), that it did not wish "to provide reasons for misinterpretations about our attitude" at the moment when the French squadron was in Shanghai.[32]

On 20 February 1885, Paris made a further step declaring rice contraband of war during the hostilities with China and specifying two days later that the embargo would be applied only to rice shipments when bound to Chinese ports north of Guangzhou carried out after 26 February 1885. Since rice supplies to Guangzhou itself, and also to Chinese ports south of Guangzhou, were not affected, France obviously wished to avoid any interference with the important rice shipping trade from Indochina to Hong Kong. The same day, Courcel made a gesture of kindness to Berlin when submitting a second letter to Busch providing detailed background information on France's considerations in the conflict with China and specifying that the embargo would only concern rice supplies destined for Chinese troops. Courcel made it clear that his government wanted to take measures which it regarded "the least harmful for third parties when limiting itself to prohibiting rice shipments destined to

(Paris) to Bismarck (Berlin), 24 January 1885, Consul Travers (Hong Kong) to Bismarck (Berlin), 25 January 1885.

[32] *The Hongkong Government Gazette Extraordinary*, 4 February 1885. BAB, R 901-33637: Ambassador de Courcel (Berlin) to Undersecretary of State Busch (Berlin), 6 February 1885, telegram from Minister von Brandt (Beijing), 14 February 1885, telegram from Foreign Ministry (Berlin) to Minister von Brandt (Beijing), 14 February 1885. BAB, R 901-33638: Foreign Ministry (Berlin) to Admiral von Caprivi (Berlin), 2 April 1885.

supplying the enemy" (*la moins dommageable pour les tiers, en se bornant à interdire les expeditions de riz destinées à ravitailler l'ennemi*). With the promise that France would let "freely continue all operations of neutral commerce", the ambassador expressed confidence that the powers interested in trading with China would appreciate France's reasons "dictating her behaviour".[33] On 23 and 28 February 1885, the French official announcements in Courcel's first two letters were successively published by the German government gazette, with an implicit warning to German shipowners and shipmasters. However, the foreign office did not reveal to the public any contents of Courcel's second letter of 22 February which remained confidential.[34]

On 1 March 1885, the Kiel Chamber of Commerce, representing the interests of several major shipping companies based in Schleswig-Holstein, was the first to launch a strong protest against the French embargo on rice shipments. Alluding to the fact that rice was "the staple food of the Chinese people and the main shipping good on the China coast", the chamber's president, August Sartori, said that a number of ships from Apenrade, Sonderburg, Kiel, Heiligenhafen and other port cities had operated in China for many years, and that it would mean "an extremely severe strike" when excluding them from the rice shipping business.[35] After newspaper articles with a similar critical position were published in the German press, Busch, on 4 March 1885, let Prince von Hohenlohe-Schillingsfürst in Paris know Bismarck's attitude towards the French embargo on rice. Explicitly referring to Courcel's second letter of 22 February, the undersecretary of state instructed the ambassador to make at a suitable occasion a statement to the French government with the following in mind:

> The reasons which the French government puts forward for its order appear convincing to the Imperial Chancellor, and he does not find it unjustified if rice shipments destined for supplying the enemy ("destinées à ravitailler l'ennemi", as it is said in the letter of 22 of the month) are cut

[33] BAB, R 901-33637: Ambassador de Courcel (Berlin) to Undersecretary of State Busch (Berlin), 20 and 22 February 1885.

[34] *Deutscher Reichs-Anzeiger*, 23 and 28 February 1885. Eastman (1967, 169).

[35] BAB, R 901-33638: August Sartori (Kiel) to Prussian Ministry of Trade and Industry (Berlin), 1 March 1885.

off by the French. On that score, it is similar to food supplies which one would try to bring to a beleaguered fortress.[36]

On 7 March 1885, the German foreign ministry learned of the British cabinet's refusal to recognise rice as contraband of war. Ambassador Prince von Hohenlohe-Schillingsfürst was immediately instructed to enquire about Ferry's position to this denial and to make it clear that Germany was prepared to recognise rice as contraband "under special circumstances" but wished to have German ships treated as equal to others. In the meeting, Ferry declared that he would continue treating rice as contraband towards Britain and inform London accordingly. He also asked for a copy of Busch's letter of 4 March 1885, in which the attitude of the Chancellor was laid out, to have it published in the *Livre Jaune* (Yellow Book), a collection of diplomatic documents related to the Tonkin affair. Hohenlohe-Schillingsfürst, who had earlier informed Billot about the letter, found himself in a difficult position, answering evasively that Bismarck's statement "contained only a few words for occasional notification". His faux pas of mentioning the said letter to Billot found little understanding in Berlin. Foreign Minister von Hatzfeldt admitted frankly that Ferry's wish "could not be fulfilled". On 17 March 1885, the ambassador informed Bismarck that both Ferry and Billot had not come back to the matter, adding that it was very difficult for him to discuss with the French a pending question and thereby creating the impression that he would only express his personal opinion. Hohenlohe-Schillingsfürst pointed to the fact that "the respect which the French ministers have for you is so great that they consider it impossible that an ambassador could bring out an opinion which was not stipulated to him by an ad hoc decree".[37]

Meanwhile, North German shipowners went on to protest against the French embargo on rice shipments in China and were supported by newspapers critical to the government. The Flensburg Shipowners' Association

[36] BAB, R 901-33637: Foreign Ministry (Berlin) to Ambassador von Hohenlohe (Paris), 4 March 1885.

[37] BAB, R 901-33637: Wolffs Telegraph Bureau (Berlin), 7 March 1885, Telegram from Foreign Ministry (Berlin) to Ambassador von Hohenlohe (Paris), 8 March 1885. BAB, R 901-33638: Telegram from Ambassador von Hohenlohe (Paris) to Foreign Ministry (Berlin), 9 March 1885. Telegram from Foreign Minister von Hatzfeldt (Berlin) to Ambassador von Hohenlohe (Paris), 10 March 1885, Ambassador von Hohenlohe (Paris) to Bismarck (Berlin), 17 March 1885.

and the Flensburg Chamber of Commerce warned of severe damage for the industry should a large numbers of ships be forced to terminate operation. On 10 March 1885, the Munich *Allgemeine Zeitung* published an article by Ludwig Gessner, a retired legal advisor to the foreign ministry, who provided a detailed analysis of the issue, concluding that "according to European international law, food and also rice are on no condition contraband of war". Gessner even approached Herbert von Bismarck (the eldest son of the Chancellor, who had returned to the foreign ministry after his term as ambassador in the Netherlands). Referring to his newspaper publication, which he added to the letter, Gessner reiterated his opinion that the French measure was violating international law. However, on 17 March 1885, Hatzfeldt submitted to the Chancellor the draft of a newspaper article "set up according to your regulation" in which the matter was laid out.[38]

On 18 March 1885, this article was published in the semi-official *Norddeutsche Allgemeine Zeitung*, arguing that there was war between China and France and that therefore "the French regulation was an act of warfare". Firmly rejecting claims that treating rice as contraband of war was illicit according to international law, the anonymous article writer called the measure "justified" when destined to shorten the war by hampering food supplies to the enemy which could contribute to a peaceful solution of the conflict. However, "such means were only justified when executed equally to all nations", the article stated. The appeal was a strong warning to not exclude British vessels from the French embargo which would result in unfair and ruinous competition for German shipowners. This signalled support for the concerned industry which was confirmed with a personal letter from Bismarck addressed to the Kiel and Flensburg chambers of commerce. On 30 March 1885, the Chancellor warned of meddling in a war which could result in more severe damage for German trade than the temporary obstruction of rice trading in Chinese waters. He reiterated the view voiced in the newspaper article

[38] BAB, R 901-33638: Chairman Hansen, Shipowners' Association (Flensburg) to Bismarck (Berlin), 8 March 1885, Chairman Dethleffsen, Chamber of Commerce (Flensburg) to Bismarck (Berlin), 9 March 1885, Ludwig Gessner (Berlin) to Herbert von Bismarck (Berlin), 12 March 1885, Foreign Minister von Hatzfeldt (Berlin) to Bismarck (Berlin), 17 March 1885. *Allgemeine Zeitung* (Munich), 10 March 1885.

that the French measure was "a justified means, as long as it is equally applied to all neutral vessels".[39]

Establishing French Rule Over Tonkin

On 30 March 1885, panic spread in Paris after an anguished telegram from Tonkin was made public by the press. In his message, General Louis Brière de l'Isle, the new French commander-in-chief in Tonkin, announced the withdrawal of his troops before the Chinese forces in Lang Son and asked for fresh reinforcements to repel a feared Vietnamese and Chinese attack in the Red River Delta. Although it was militarily a minor incident, the news sparked deep-seated anger and fear about Ferry's maximalist strategy and the possible danger of a long war with China and of what *Le Temps* called "a colonial Sedan" (a reference to the Battle of Sedan from 1 to 2 September 1870 which effectively decided the Franco-German War in favour of Prussia and its German allies). Equating 1885 with 1870 also hinted at the growing mistrust among the political opposition about Ferry's attitude to Bismarck and his colonial policy, regarded by some as incompatible with the claim to the ultimate recovery of Alsace-Lorraine. Since the autumn of 1884, rumours had spread that France and Germany had some sort of agreement concerning Chinese affairs, and that the Chancellor had agreed to allow the French government *carte blanche* in East Asia. The impression grew that Bismarck was supporting Ferry in Tonkin in order to draw him closer to Germany and bolster his own hegemony in Europe. Among the main opponents of the expansionist policy was Georges Clemenceau, the leader of the far left in the French Chamber of Deputies. On 25 November 1884, during the course of the debate, he again warned colleagues about Bismarck's friendship, and recommended a return to the policy of peaceful seclusion. Both the socialist and monarchist press continued to decry Ferry's colonial policy, which they believed was favoured by the Chancellor. When the telegram from Tonkin was made known, Clemenceau accused the prime minister of high treason,

[39] *Norddeutsche Allgemeine Zeitung (evening edition)*, 18 March 1885. BAB, R 901-33638: Bismarck (Berlin) to the Kiel Chamber of Commerce, 30 March 1885 (identical text with the same date to the Flensburg Chamber of Commerce). According to Guillen and Allain (2007, 164), Bismarck initially had demonstrated his goodwill to France, but invoked Germany's economic interests in the region to protest against the French naval operations in the China Seas and the blockade of Formosa. This statement contradicts actual events.

asking for his indictment before the High Court. Ferry was overthrown the same day. It was "the hour of Clemenceau", declared George Peabody Gooch. According to Klaus Hildebrand, Ferry's affinity for collaborating with Germany contributed "in no small measure to the fact that he fell under humiliating circumstances".[40]

Ironically, at the very moment of his fall, Ferry had almost completed negotiations for a peace treaty with China. In August 1884, Xu Jingcheng, the Chinese minister in Berlin, had sought German mediation, only to be bluntly told by Bismarck that any action on his part would only raise opposition, and that he should discuss his propositions with the French ambassador in Berlin. The meeting with Courcel took place in the home of Foreign Minister von Hatzfeldt, but ended without a result. To come to a kind of compromise, Ferry accepted unofficial British mediation and a plan for a peace agreement, secretly finalised on 15 March 1885. When the telegraphic despatch about the French reverse at Long Son arrived in Paris on the evening of 28 March, Ferry, fearing that China might withdraw from the preliminary engagement urged Courcel, in strict confidence, to seek the mediation of Germany. He was obviously trying to put pressure on China from another angle so that she would not refuse to sign since she had gained a military victory. After Ferry's resignation, Minister Xu approached Hatzfeldt to advise peace, but was told that German relations with France would not let the government intervene. However, on 3 April, when the Chinese minister announced that he was waiting for definite instructions concerning the peace talks, Hatzfeldt agreed with Courcel that he would act as mediator and arrange, if necessary, another meeting between the two diplomats in Berlin. Although this did not occur, it revealed a very surprising association between the French and German officials in view of the many years of hostility and distrust between the two countries.[41]

The compromise between France and China on Indochina was sealed in two separate treaties: first, the Treaty of Hue (or Patenôtre Treaty, named after France's minister to China, Jules Patenôtre) of 6 June 1884 (ratified by France on 9 June 1885) with the Vietnamese government at Hue permitting the French to occupy the whole of Vietnam. It ended the

[40] Wienefeld (1929, 161–162), Mitchell (1935, 138–141), Eastman (1967, 171–172), Power (1977, 180–182), Gooch (1923, 23), Hildebrand (1993, 93), Guillen and Allain (2007, 156–159) and Brocheux and Hémery (2009, 46).

[41] Wienefeld (1929, 163–164) and Mitchell (1935, 145–147).

Hue court's tributary relationship with the Chinese emperor in favour of establishing a French protectorate over Annam and Tonkin. Second, the formal Franco-Chinese peace treaty (or Treaty of Tianjin) of 9 June 1885 acknowledged this French protectorate, ended Vietnam's tributary position in the East Asian order and agreed to the opening of Yunnan, Guangxi and western Guangdong to commerce and railroad construction. In charge were the new French government headed by Prime Minister Henri Brisson and Foreign Minister Charles de Freycinet, with the latter determined to carry on the colonial policy of his predecessors. Yet, the anxiety caused by the events in Tonkin did not diminish before the French national elections in October 1885, which were a defeat for the "Tonkinois" (Tonkinese), the supporters of Ferry's maximalist policy in Indochina. The tensions with the anti-colonialist opposition reached a new climax in the parliamentary debate of 21–24 December 1885, when the government sought approval for a new credit for Tonkin. Camille Pelletan, a Radical leftist, had drafted a report on the matter strongly pleading for evacuating Tonkin. On the last day of the debate, Clemenceau came to his support after Brisson had declared that it would be "impossible to evacuate Tonkin without dishonour". Following a provocative comment from another deputy, Clemenceau replied that it was humiliating to read in the *Livres Jaunes* a despatch in which, after the Lang Son affair, Ferry had invoked the help of Bismarck. Clemenceau, without knowing details of the confidential negotiations of late March 1885, read out telegrams exchanged between Ambassador de Courcel and Prime Minister Ferry. The deputies were scandalised to learn that Ferry had obviously proposed German mediation in the preparation of the treaty with China, while, as Stephen Pichon, an associate of Clemenceau, told parliament, rejecting three times the good offices of the United States. The uproar was so huge that Ferry could hardly defend himself. At the end of the heated debate, the government's request for fresh credits for operations in Tonkin was approved by a majority of only four votes. The hostile attitude of the French Chamber of Deputies caused Brisson to resign on 30 December 1885, with Freycinet taking over as head of government some days later.[42]

The question as to whether Bismarck was seeking a Franco-German alliance has been answered in the negative. French historian Raymond

[42] *Journal Officiel de la République française: Débats parlementaires: Chambre de Députés* (24 December 1885, 379). *The Times*, 25 December 1885, *The Hong Kong Daily Press*,

Poidevin conceded that Bismarck had been aiming for "a real rapprochement" with France since 1878 when, at the Congress of Berlin, the Chancellor had strongly signalled his encouragement of France's colonial policies in Tunisia. The return of Ferry as prime minister gave Bismarck the chance to pursue this line. However, Ferry and Courcel became involved in this "seductive policy" only "with much reservation", Poidevin said, because it was clear from the beginning that they did not wish to discuss Alsace-Lorraine, an alliance or too strong a rapprochement with Germany. The French public were not prepared for such an eventuality, the historian added, and French diplomats feared "being outmanoeuvred by Bismarck" whom they suspected of exploiting improved French-German relations in order to put pressure on London. German historian Klaus Hildebrand pointed to Bismarck's own advice, of October 1884, to Emperor William I to remain far distant from the idea of a Franco-German alliance and to abstain from the notion of putting "our future policy on such insecure foundations". In May 1885, the Chancellor explained to Ambassador Prince von Hohenlohe-Schillingsfürst that the French government could never agree to "a firm dependence" on Germany and that therefore "a temporary one" should not be scorned: "However, we cannot build houses on that; the [French] mistrust towards us will always be stronger than their annoyance with England." Therefore, as Hildebrand concluded, the Chancellor decided to return to his former strategy of isolating France, a move which seemed justified by the new surge in "hatred of Germans" and "revanchism" after Ferry's fall. According to Wolfgang J. Mommsen, with the rise of Georges Clemenceau "a new thrust in nationalist thinking" emerged, resulting in the reorientation of French policy towards Germany.[43]

28 December 1885, 1 and 6 January 1886. Mitchell (1935, 146), Eastman (1967, 200–202), Fourniau (2002, 349–350), Brocheux and Hémery (2009, 47) and Goscha (2017, 66–67).

[43] Poidevin and Bariéty (1982, 181–189, the quotes: 181 and 186–187). Hildebrand (1995, 93–94) refers to Bismarck's letter to Emperor William I, dated 9 October 1884, and to Bismarck's letter to Ambassador Prince von Hohenlohe-Schillingsfürst (Paris), dated 25 May 1885. Mommsen (1993, 78).

"Le Grand Port du Tonkin"

The Unimposing Settlement

Up to the early 1870s, Haiphong was merely a native village with a market located at the confluence of the Song Cua Cam (Sống Cửa Cấm, Forbidden River) and the Song Tam Bac (Sống Tâm Bắc). Situated twenty-five kilometres from the sea, and well connected by river traffic with its hinterland over a considerable distance — the Song Cua Cam is interlinked with the Red River, the main waterway of Tonkin — Chinese and Vietnamese junk traders had frequently visited Haiphong since the 1850s, primarily to purchase rice. The rivers provided access to the French military forces led by Francis Garnier which in 1873 entered northern Vietnam and occupied Hanoi (Hà Nội) and other strategic sites on the Red River Delta. On 15 September 1875, the Franco-Vietnamese treaties of March/August 1874 formally opened Haiphong to foreign commerce. Louis Turc, a navy physician and experienced administrator from Saigon, was appointed the first French consul in Ninh Hai and a mixed French-Vietnamese customs office was set up to impose a 5 per cent duty by value on imports and exports, plus 10 per cent for salt. Opium imports were strictly controlled by the Vietnamese government, while rice exports needed a special temporary official licence and attracted a 10 per cent duty. The small French concession of Haiphong, comprising of an area of 0.15 square kilometre, entered a kind of transitional or proto-colonial phase which would last for about ten years.[44]

The first European vessel on the run between Hong Kong and Haiphong was the steamer *Pernambuco*, chartered by Chinese merchants, which left the British colony on 16 September 1875. The small ship was owned by Mr. Landstein, a Russian merchant (probably from the Baltic region of the Russian Empire, with a considerable German population) who had offered to make a trial voyage, according to Joseph Plichon, the French consul in Hong Kong. Landstein seemed rather surprised when his vessel left the colony almost fully loaded with goods such as cotton fabric and Chinese pharmaceutical products. The Russian merchant intended to operate with his small steam coasters a monthly shipping service between

[44] *Les Ports Autonomes de l'Indochine* (1931, 30), Maybon (1931, 77), Raffi (1994, 71–77), Brocheux and Hémery (2009, 29), Ptak (2008, 62), Luan and Cooke (2011, 157) and Tran (2017, 17–18).

the British colony and Haiphong. On 20 September, he established an agency of his company in the port city and made the French trader Georges Constantin his agent. His vessels, *Washi* and *City of Whampoa*, commanded by European masters, were frequently chartered by Chinese merchants. Constantin's negotiations with Consul Turc about setting up a subsidised mail service between Haiphong and Saigon resulted, in March 1876, in the steamer *Washi*, of c. 300 tons, obtaining a monthly subsidy of 3,000 dollars. For shipping French troops and provisions, the firm received extra payments. The company's unrivalled position ended when, in August 1877, the British firm Herton, Ebell & Company expediting two steamers from Hong Kong, opened a warehouse in Haiphong; its local agent's names and whereabouts remain unknown. After 1877, Landstein's shipping service faced even more competition when a small number of British, German and French firms based in Hong Kong established branches in the French concession, shipping all kinds of products to Haiphong and in return transporting bulk goods such as rice and other agricultural produce from northern Vietnam to the British colony.[45]

The first French firm established in Haiphong was Roque Frères (Roque Brothers, founded in 1862 in Saigon), which, in September 1879, was made an agent of Denis Frères (Denis Brothers), the other pioneering French trading firm in Cochinchina. In 1884, Denis Frères set up their own agency in Haiphong. The French and other foreign firms combined shipping and trading: in 1880, exports were mainly rice (39 per cent), raw silk and silk fabrics (21 per cent), tin (16 per cent) and lacquering oils (6 per cent); imports were mostly English cotton and cotton fabrics (34 per cent), opium (21 per cent), Chinese medicines and drugs (11 per cent), prepared Chinese tobacco (9 per cent) and tea (5 per cent).[46] The first German company established in Haiphong, at an unknown date, was Schriever & Company, the German owner of which, J. F. Schriever from Bremen, was a trader in Hong Kong. His firm in the British colony, which had branch offices in Hanoi and Haiphong, became an industrial pioneer in northern Vietnam, being the first company to begin exporting raw silks from Tonkin to China and Europe. In the late 1870s, to further improve

[45] Raffi (1994, 106) and Brocheux and Hémery (2009, 29). MAE, CCC-137-2: Consul Plichon (Hong Kong) to Foreign Minister Duc Decazes (Paris), 17 September 1875. BAB, R 901-12807: Consul Travers (Guangzhou) to Chancellor von Bismarck (Berlin), 6 May 1882.

[46] Kergaradec (1881, 265–269).

the quality of exported silks, Schriever purchased modern reeling machine winders and hired experienced workers in Hanoi and Guangzhou for its new production sites. Consequently, by producing more uniform silk threads, the company was able to further increase exports of silk fabrics, prices for which could be increased by 15 per cent, and promote the development of silk manufacturing in Vietnam. According to information received from Schriever & Co., Consul Travers in Guangzhou, in May 1882, pointed to the fact that the firm's role model had inspired local Vietnamese silk producers "to pay much more attention to spinning yarns, with the result that nowadays, almost exclusively only unreeled silk for obviously much lower prices can be exported". In early 1878, Schriever & Co. was made the local agent of Bosman & Company, the marine insurance firm in Hong Kong owned by Dutch businessman Charles Henry Maurice Bosman. In the years up until 1885, Wilhelm Schriever, a relative of J. F. Schriever, joined the firm, with Oscar von der Heyde from Bremen as partner.[47]

In 1880, the French shipping company Messageries Maritimes established a bimonthly feeder line between Saigon and Haiphong serviced by steamships. Its first local agent was Georges Constantin who had set up his own firm after separating from Landstein and purchasing the steamer *Washi*.[48] In the same year, rice shipping from Haiphong reached a climax with 25,630 tonnes exported after the Vietnamese government had lifted the export ban. Since 1876, Hue had issued a series of bans on the export of rice from Haiphong to obviously disadvantage the French concession and to favour exports from neighbouring Nam Dinh (Nam Định) which was under its full control. In 1880, 128 vessels called at Haiphong, most of which sailed under the flags of China (38, including junks) and Britain (34) followed by the United States (22), Germany (17) and France (6).[49] As C. de Kergaradec, the French consul in Hanoi, noted in his Haiphong report for the year 1880, the number of Chinese steamers had considerably increased in the past, which he attributed to the stronger presence of the China Merchants Steam Navigation Company operating modern

[47] Raffi (1994, 106, 112, 183). BAB, R 901-12807: Consul Travers (Guangzhou) to Chancellor von Bismarck (Berlin), 6 May 1882. GSTA, I. HA, Rep. 81 Bremen, Nr. 81: Prussian Minister von Kusserow (Hamburg) to Prussian Consulate-General (Bremen), 3 September 1885.

[48] Raffi (1994, 106, 112–113, 117–118, 130).

[49] Raffi (1994, 602: table B-1).

vessels commanded by mostly British captains. The Chinese shipping firm operated an agency in Haiphong which was, however, closed in April 1883 after severe tensions broke out between France and China during the Tonkin campaign. According to Consul Gustav Travers in Guangzhou, about five British, American and Chinese ships frequently serviced the route between Haiphong and Hong Kong in 1881, with frequent calls at the ports of Beihai (Pakhoi) and Haikou (Hoihow) to take extra cargoes or board Chinese passengers. He added that the British steamers were almost exclusively chartered by Chinese merchants in Hong Kong, sailing with Chinese crews and European masters.[50]

Haiphong's early development was frequently documented by German consuls in Saigon and Guangzhou who were charged with observing French activities in northern Vietnam. When Kergaradec's 1881 Haiphong report was published in March 1882, Consul Bruno Röver in Saigon immediately sent copies to Berlin and to the German embassy in Paris.[51] The most important contact to obtain information on the city was the German merchant J. F. Schriever who submitted "very commendable corrections and additions" to the report of Kergaradec, as Consul Travers in Guangzhou put it, praising the trader as "very helpful". Furthermore, Schriever had hinted at several obstacles to entering the port of Haiphong such as the too weak beacon at the entrance, but especially excessive port fees that resulted in "a crippling impact on the advantageous development of shipping and trading". However, collectively submitting complaints from merchants and shipmasters to the French consul had remained unsuccessful, as Travers noted. Summing up his information, the consul concluded that Haiphong was merely a place of transshipment where goods arriving on ocean-going vessels were transferred to river ships, while cargoes sent on river ships were loaded onto seagoing steamers. Compared to Haiphong, the real trading hubs of northern Vietnam were Hanoi and Nam Dinh, "the great entrepôts for distributing goods to various parts of the interior; there, trading firms have their places of business, whereas in Haiphong, only branches or agents are established". The remark throws light on the modest development of proto-colonial Haiphong, which had around five thousand citizens in

[50] Kergaradec (1881, 270) and Raffi (1994, 129–130, 158). BAB, R 901-12807: Consul Travers (Guangzhou) to Chancellor von Bismarck (Berlin), 6 May 1882.

[51] PAAA, R 251850: Consul Röver (Saigon) to Foreign Ministry (Berlin), 15 July 1881.

1883, of which about 850 were Chinese. The main reason for the weak presence of Chinese merchants — the traditional controllers of Indochina's rice trading industry — was the commercial policy of the Vietnamese government, keeping rice export figures from Haiphong to a minimum to the disadvantage of the French concession. At the time, Haiphong was also a dangerous place to reside, a fact which was clearly demonstrated when the town was attacked by large gang of pirates on 5 July 1883. Its inhabitants were only saved because of the stockade surrounding the settlement (except on the river and canal sides) which kept the attackers away while the French opened fire from their men-of-war anchored in the river.[52]

In 1884, the British travel writer James George Scott, paying a visit to Haiphong, summed up his impressions as follows:

> The trim, white houses of the French Concession give Haiphong quite a pretty appearance as one steams up the fourteen miles or so of river which separates it from the sea; but when one passes the mouth of the Song Tam Bac Canal, and still more when one lands, there is a revulsion. From opposite the store-sheds, which used to be the China Merchants [Steam Navigation] Company's godowns, the place looks very desolate, and gives the newly arrived stranger the impression of a two-or-three-month-old settlement in a newly discovered country. (...) The town perhaps grows, though even this is open to dispute; but under no circumstances can it grow fast, for building sites are only to be obtained by laboriously collecting mud and clay from the surrounding fields, and piling it up to form a foundation on which a house may stand a foot or two above the swamps into which the greater part of the town is converted by a high tide. (...) It seems to be only the brackish water which saves Haiphong from being a regular grave to the Frenchmen. (...) As it is, every house is practically the centre of a cesspool, and if there is not sooner or later some serious epidemic it will be a matter for wonder.[53]

The Port as Problem

As Scott's description makes evident, Haiphong, after almost ten years of French settlement, still looked unimpressive and even neglected.

[52] BAB, R 901-12807: Consul Travers (Guangzhou) to Chancellor von Bismarck (Berlin), 6 May 1882. Scott (1885, 213) and Raffi (1994, 158).

[53] Scott (1885, 212–213).

However, with major political changes on their way in Vietnam, the city and its surrounding region underwent a rapid transformation. With the establishment of the protectorates of Annam and Tonkin (1884), new administrative structures and commercial organisations were established at both provincial and local level in northern Vietnam. To promote the economic development of the port of Haiphong, General Ernest Millot, commander-in-chief of France's expeditionary corps, advised the French Resident (or mayor) of Haiphong, Raoul Bonnal, to assemble the local merchants. On 19 August 1884, fourteen traders came together and founded the Consultative Chamber of Commerce of Haiphong, with Edmond Constantin (the agent of Messageries Maritimes who had succeeded his relative Georges Constantin in this function) made president. After Paris had agreed, the Resident-General in Annam and Tonkin, Victor Lemaire, decreed the establishment of the Haiphong Chamber of Commerce on 23 November 1884. It was a purely consultative body with limited powers but soon developed into an important voice in local politics and the most ardent mouthpiece of the French local business community.[54] The Haiphong Chamber's first major struggle concerned the future of the port city as a maritime hub of Tonkin. On 14 November 1885, the Hanoi newspaper *L'Avenir du Tonkin*[55] published an article announcing the intended abandonment of Haiphong for a future port in the Ha Long Bay. The editor was supposed to have been inspired by Pierre Silvestre, the influential director of Affaires civiles et politiques (the department of Civil Affairs and Politics in the colonial government) in Hanoi whose mouthpiece was said to have been the said journal. For some unknown reason, Silvestre had a strong dislike of Haiphong and used all means to discredit the city as the future naval and commercial port of Tonkin. The article was probably another attempt to make the French commander-in-chief aware of the disadvantages of Haiphong and to take up the cudgels for Hon Gay or Quang Yen in Ha Long Bay. "There is no longer any question of Haiphong", the newspaper

[54] Villemagne (2008, 697–704), Brocheux and Hémery (2009, 45), Goscha (2017, 66–67) and Raffi (1994, 173, 179–180).

[55] This newspaper, sold in Hanoi and in Haiphong, was the mouthpiece of the French rural settlers (in French: colons) in Indochina, printed "racist aspersions on the indigenous peoples, impractical suggestions designed to forward the interests of their readers and castigations, justified or not, of metropolitan and colonial policies and personalities". Laffey (1977, 93).

Fig. 5.2 The premises of the Haiphong Chamber of Commerce, with its clock, c. 1900 (Private collection Bert Becker)

editor stated, hinting about the report of the hydrographic commission of Tonkin which had chosen a point in the bay as the site of a naval arsenal and harbour of refuge. The account went on to describe the present status of Haiphong as miserable, with "no wharves" and "with the rough roads which pass between the houses" and "the lane pompously called the Marty Boulevard". Creating the Haiphong Chamber of Commerce was branded as "premature" due to the fact that a few days later, the Consultative Chamber of Commerce for Tonkin was founded by the protectorate's administration which, in the eyes of the editor, was representing "the whole of the merchants of the country". Lashing out in all directions, the article denied Haiphong any commercial future calling the town "unhealthy, where the mortality is enormous, and where enormous sums of money would have to be spent to arrive at a result which after all would only be mediocre" (Fig. 5.2).[56]

[56] *L'Avenir du Tonkin*, 14 November 1885 and *The Hong Kong Daily Press*, 16 January 1886.

The open attack on Haiphong's commerce and industry caused a strong backlash from local business. On 1 December 1885, major French and German companies issued a protest letter. At the head of the list was Camille Gauthier, owner of La Compagnie Française du Tonkin et de l'Indochine (French Company of Tonkin and Indochina); Ernest Bancal, agent of the Lyon-based firm Ulysse Pila et Cie; Oscar von der Heyde, the representative of Schriever & Co.; August Bauermeister, the manager of Speidel & Co.; Mr Vincent, agent of Denis Frères; and Loricourt Dierx, director of the Banque de l'Indochine in Haiphong. Furthermore, there were fourteen other French traders (including Constantin, Roque and Marty), two Chinese and one British merchants, and a shipmaster called Georges. The protest note pointed to the fact that the Chinese had been the first to establish themselves at Haiphong, long before the arrival of European merchants. The reason for them to choose Haiphong was explained as follows: "It is because Haiphong is plainly indicated by its geographical situation; it is the entrance to the delta, it is there that all the principal rivers unite, which serve for transportation of the products of the country (...). Haiphong is on one side the terminus for small boats and on the other side is a port in which seagoing vessels drawing 20 feet can enter". With respect to the difficult entrance and anchorage of the port, the writers alluded to the fact that at present Haiphong was accessible to the largest ships of the Messageries Maritimes and could be further improved by digging a channel through the mud bar. The letter rejected claims about the city's lack of boulevards, stating that "absolutely nothing has been done at Haiphong" by the civil or military administration: "No attempt is made to sanitate the town (...). With some filling in and drainage works our town might be made the healthiest in Tonkin, and for this not much money is required". Financial considerations were also employed when declaring that Hon Gay or Quang Yen would need enormous investment to set up suitable establishments which would need time to be developed. Finally, the Haiphong traders called for conducting most urgent works at this "suitable season of the year", warning of the outbreak of an epidemic with the return of the hot weather.[57]

Soon after, Silvestre was recalled from his post in Hanoi and returned to France. However, with attacks on Haiphong continuing and the danger threatening its very existence, French merchants including

[57] The letter dated Haiphong, 1 December 1885, was translated and published in *The Hong Kong Daily Press*, 16 January 1886.

Auguste Raphael Marty, decided to found a daily newspaper in the port city which they called *Le Courrier d'Haiphong*. The capital subscribed by shares was quickly oversubscribed, and a committee was appointed to obtain the necessary printing press from France and make all other arrangements. The newspaper had its first office and printing machine in the "Cité Marty" (Marty Town). The first issue of the paper appeared in April 1886 and proclaimed an outspoken policy of supporting the interests of the town and port of Haiphong. *Le Courrier d'Haiphong* became the mouthpiece of the French community, representing its members' specific views and opinions, with an emphasis on promoting local business interests. One of its frequently discussed issues was the fight against the project to replace Haiphong as the main port hub of Tonkin with another nearby location.[58]

The French traveller Pierre Sauvaire, Marquis de Barthélemy visiting the port in 1901, noted with evident sarcasm that Haiphong was being developed like other French colonial towns "without bothering about the commercial future which it could take".[59] His comment referred to the difficult entry to the port. From the beginning, its inconvenient location as a riverine port with its approaches from the sea blocked by two bars (the outer one sand, the inner one mud) at the mouth of the Cua Cam caused great concern about its future. Visitors arriving on larger ships at the Tonkin Delta had to change onto smaller vessels to go up to Haiphong. Officially, the French announced that Haiphong would rival Shanghai as a port of commerce by becoming "Le Grand Port du Tonkin" (The Great Port of Tonkin), the principal port of commerce of northern Indochina. This notion was enthusiastically backed by the Haiphong Chamber of Commerce which demanded considerable investment by the colonial government in making the port easier to access, to enable ships drawing 18 to 20 feet (5.5–6.1 metres) of water to come up to the city and to improve the ports' facilities. In 1885, the first port improvement works started, and in the following year several landing places were constructed along the banks of the Cua Cam to enable the

[58] *The Hong Kong Daily Press*, 16 January 1886. *Bulletin Trimestriel de la Société Amicale des Anciens Tonkinois* (1940, 11) and Gantès (1994, vol. 2, 271–273).

[59] Barthélemy (1901, 7).

disembarkation of troops and goods.[60] In 1892, the landing places were enlarged and a small port was created, with a short quayside reserved for ships of the French major lines Messageries Maritimes and Chargeurs Réunis. The latter company, which had ferried French troops to Tonkin in 1884 and to China in 1899–1900 when France took part in the suppression of the Boxer Rebellion, initiated a monthly regular service to Saigon, Tourane (Da Nang) and Haiphong in 1901.[61] However, full port installations did not exist even in 1906, as a visitor to Haiphong noted. This situation required other vessels to moor at buoys in the middle of the river when discharging and loading cargoes. Considerable improvements were achieved after the Haiphong Chamber of Commerce, in late 1911, subscribed to a loan of 1.5 million francs to modernise port facilities.[62]

In 1896, the city faced a serious crisis when the increasing silting of the Cua Cam threatened to cut off Haiphong from the sea. When the French administration planned to transfer Tonkin's principal port to another location, local merchants launched angry protests to avert such harm to the city. This led to another solution, the cutting of a canal between the Cua Cam and the Cua Nam Trieu, another river leading to the Tonkin Delta, finalised in 1901. Due to financial constraints, deepening the Cua Nam Trieu and removing its sand bar could not be carried out, allowing only vessels of a maximum six metres draught to pass the bar at low tide; ships with deeper draughts had to await high tide to go up to Haiphong.[63] Of the several projects being developed to ease access to the port, the most ambitious was unveiled during the term (1897–1902) of Governor-General Paul Doumer. The plan comprised a gigantic canal to connect Haiphong to Ha Long Bay with its deep-water inlet. However, due to

[60] *The Directory & Chronicle* (1910, 1214), *Les Ports Autonomes de l'Indochine* (1931, 31) and Tran (2017, 126–127). PAAA, Peking II-72: Report of Captain Müller (Tsingtao), 2 April 1906.

[61] The Chargeurs Réunis' large steamer *Amiral Duperré*, of 6.500 tons, employed for the initial voyage and carrying only goods from France, left Marseille on 12 October 1901 and called Haiphong on 18 November 1901. Agents in Haiphong was Denis Frères. *Le Courrier d'Haiphong*, 5 November 1901 and Michael S. Smith (1994, 20).

[62] Cunningham (1902, 43–44), *Les Ports Autonomes de l'Indochine* (1931, 32–33) and Michael S. Smith (1994, 20). PAAA, Peking II-72: Report of Captain Müller (Tsingtao), 2 April 1906. PAAA, Konsulat Saigon 3-B 8: Consul Crull (Saigon) to Chancellor von Bethmann Hollweg (Berlin), 10 January 1912.

[63] Cunningham (1902, 43–44).

the enormous building costs, estimated at 21 million francs, the project never materialised.[64]

The 1890 review of the port's shipping published by *Le Courrier d'Haiphong* provides a spotlight glimpse of shipping companies and their vessels calling at Haiphong. First of all, the report mentions the liners of Messageries Maritimes servicing the subsidised feeder line between Haiphong and Saigon, with stopovers at smaller Vietnamese coastal ports. On the run between Haiphong and Hong Kong, the major French shipping company operated a non-subsidised service regularly bringing from the British colony the English mail from Europe and northern China. In 1890, the five steamers employed on the service, *Haiphong*, *Aréthuse*, *Saigon*, *Volga* and *Tibre* made forty-eight voyages, thus four return trips per month, shipping 1,502 French conscripts, most of them placed on deck, and 20,146 tonnes of cargoes, almost half of which originated from Europe. The route was also serviced by the company A. R. Marty in Hong Kong, employing three chartered Jebsen steamers: *Marie*, *Clara* and *Else*. According to *Le Courrier d'Haiphong*, the German ships transported to-and-from Haiphong 1,881 passengers, including eighty-seven Europeans, which meant that almost all voyagers were Asians, probably mostly Chinese merchants. The vessels shipped 27,840 tonnes of goods on fifty-five voyages, thus making almost five return trips per month. This was a somewhat higher frequency than the one offered by the steamers of Messageries Maritimes on the same route. Furthermore, Wang-Tai Frères (Wang-Tai Brothers), a Haiphong firm trading in ships' equipment, coal and Japanese porcelain, the Chinese owner of which was a naturalised Frenchman, had chartered *Triumph*, a Jebsen steamer, and two more ships under the German flag, *Cosmopolit* and *Presto*. With these vessels, the firm made eight annual return voyages in 1890, shipping 172 passengers and 3,766 tonnes of freight. All in all, six German and five French steamers regularly serviced the main run between Hong Kong and Haiphong, occasionally joined by single British, Japanese and French ocean-going vessels arriving from different directions at the French colonial port. Four government-owned vessels, with unknown cargoes, made nine voyages. Regular coastal shipping services were provided by the Service Subventionné des Correspondances Fluviales du Tonkin (Subsidised River Shipping Service of Tonkin), the

[64] PAAA, Konsulat Saigon 3-B 8: Consul Crull (Saigon) to Chancellor von Bethmann Hollweg (Berlin), 10 January 1912.

Fig. 5.3 The commercial port of Haiphong, with parts of the head office and the landing stage of the Subsidised River Shipping Service of Tonkin (Marty et d'Abbadie), c. 1900 (Private collection Bert Becker)

major affiliate of Marty et d'Abbadie, operating steam coasters between the Vietnamese coastal ports of Mon Cay and Vinh. Finally, 645 Chinese junks, of totally 22,541 tons, with all kinds of goods, were plying between Haiphong and Beihai (Pakhoi), the major Chinese port at the northern shore of the Gulf of Tonkin. Numerous junks moved around the archipelago of the Ha Long Bay, the Red River Delta and the rivers of Tonkin (Fig. 5.3).[65]

By the early twentieth century, the riverine port had undisputedly become Tonkin's most important commercial outlet, being well connected to its hinterland by river shipping services and railway lines, and overseas via coastal and ocean-going shipping links. The port's prosperity was increased by the frequent water regulation and improvements works undertaken in the Red River Delta, the construction of modern and steam-driven rice mills, the availability of enough efficient steam shipping tonnage for the bulk transportation of rice and last but not least,

[65] *Le Courrier d'Haiphong*, 30 April 1891.

the installation of telegraphs for the rapid ordering of rice shipments. However, despite its economic development, Haiphong's shipping did not reach the levels of Saigon and Hong Kong, its neighbouring port cities in the South China Sea. In 1913, the total number of ocean-going ships entering the port of Tonkin was 377, at 487,139 net register tons; in the same year, Saigon counted 583 vessels, at almost 1.7 million tons, and Hong Kong 21,867 vessels, at almost 23 million tons. Haiphong was certainly "The Great Port of Tonkin", and even the second-largest port in French Indochina, but at the same time it was considerably dwarfed by the striking preponderance of Hong Kong. This position did not alter after the First World War. In 1931, an official French publication called the port of Haiphong "the start of all domestic routes" in Tonkin, handling all external commerce and the largest part of domestic trade.[66]

French Colonial Port City

In 1885 and 1886, Raoul Bonnal, Haiphong's first Resident (or mayor), gave the urban development of Haiphong major impetus by focusing on having filled in unhealthy swamps penetrating every part of the town and on constructing a large number of buildings on the reclaimed land. In 1886, construction began of the Canal de Ceinture (Ring Canal, sometimes called Canal Bonnal) separating the old Vietnamese settlement of Haiphong from the new French colonial city. This permitted the establishment of a riverine port for junks and barks at the Song Tam Bac which came to be regarded as the Chinese port. Since this smaller river served as a waterway to Hanoi and Nam Dinh, the new port facilitated inland river shipping in the region. Furthermore, dredging the canal provided sediment which was used to fill in swamps and reclaim new land for developing Haiphong's urban infrastructure (Fig. 5.4).[67]

In the same year, 1886, the French contractor Ch. Vézin erected the first military buildings, and Auguste Raphael Marty developed the "Cité Marty" (Marty Town), an array of office blocks in traditional French style, accommodating European trading companies, at the end of Rue du Commerce. On 1 April 1886, the Banque de l'Indochine opened its

[66] Raffi (1994, 494–496), Brocheux and Hèmery (2009, 130) and *Les Ports Autonomes de l'Indochine* (1931, 47).

[67] Cunningham (1902, 49), Martínez (2007a, 87), Raffi (1994, 206–208) and Tran (2017, 126–127).

Fig. 5.4 Map of Haiphong, c. 1915 (*An Official Guide to Eastern Asia*, *vol. 5*, ed. by The Imperial Government Railways of Japan, Tokyo, 1917)

Haiphong agency in one of these buildings, expecting the port to become the major business hub for Tonkin's export and import trades.[68] On 9 July 1888, Haiphong became administratively a French colonial city when the consultative commission (established on 22 June 1886) was transformed into the municipal commission, with all the features of a French town.[69] In the following years, Haiphong turned into a French-style colonial city similar to the administrative capital of Indochina, Hanoi, but to a more limited extent. As Hanoi developed into "a grand city attesting to France's superiority and successful colonial enterprise in Asia" (Drummond), the port city was intended to become "Le Grand Port du Tonkin" (The Great Port of Tonkin), France's answer to British Hong Kong, although on a smaller scale.[70] The new town was built from scratch next

[68] *Haiphong illustré* (1895, 2, 7), *Bulletin Trimestriel de la Société Amicale des Anciens Tonkinois* (1940, 9–10), Meuleau (1990, 123) and Raffi (1994, 182).

[69] *Haiphong illustré* (1895, 2).

[70] Drummond (2013, 207–208, the quote: 225) and Osterhammel (2014, 284–286).

to the old Vietnamese Haiphong and placed in the midst of an extensive rice swamp, with low lying swampy land all around it for kilometres. New streets and boulevards were laid in a grid pattern and provided with a paved surface. Government premises, numerous office buildings, Parisian-style department stores, villas for top bureaucrats and merchants, a cathedral, an opera house, schools and other French-type buildings were constructed. Street and squares were named after "heroes" of the French conquest or great historical or contemporary Frenchmen. The British journalist Alfred Cunningham, after paying a visit to Haiphong in spring 1902, praised the city as "a monument to French labour and enterprise" which was not "as fine a city as Hanoi yet, considering the initial difficulties under which it was built, it may be regarded as a greater triumph of French colonisation".[71]

The most spectacular residential building of the riverine port city was probably the private villa of Auguste Raphael Marty. Although named "Villa Marguerite" (seemingly after Marguerite Garréta, Marty's mother), the popular nickname "La Folie Marty" (Marty's Folly) was common among French residents. According to the anonymous author of Marty's obituary, "it seemed strange at this time that one did more than the strictly necessary" when constructing one of the first summer residences of Haiphong.[72] The house, built in 1889, with ten rooms on the ground floor and three upper floors, was surrounded by a beautiful garden; the total area on which the house and garden stood was 67,340 square metres. It had an office and from 1893 was connected to the headquarters of Marty et d'Abbadie by a direct telephone line of 1.8 km length.[73] Strangely, it was situated close to Haiphong's slaughterhouse at Rue de l'Abbatoir (Slaughterhouse Street). The slaughterhouse had been built by the city of Haiphong three years earlier and was leased for ten years to the French firm Crétin et Leroy et Cie. After the railway line between

[71] Cunningham (1902, 47–48). The best overview of Haiphong's urban development up until 1921 provides Raffi (1994, 190–237 and 336–358); for a comprehensive survey of the city's industrialisation from the late nineteenth century to 1929, see Tran (2017).

[72] On French contemporary postcards, Marty's villa is also labelled as "Chalet Marty" or "Pagode Marty". Raffi (1994, 182 and 219) erroneously states that "La Folie Marty" was the nickname of "Cité Marty" (Marty Town). *Bulletin Trimestriel de la Société Amicale des Anciens Tonkinois* (1940, 10).

[73] VNA1, RST-74: Auguste Raphael Marty (Haiphong) to Chef of Post and Telegraph Service of Annam and Tonkin (Hanoi), 1 April 1893.

Haiphong and Hanoi was opened on 25 June 1902, the tracks formed a kind of dividing line between these very different sites. The house, which became a favourite postcard theme, was described by Cunningham in 1902 as follows (Fig. 5.5):

> It is very elaborately constructed, most of the materials being brought specially from Guangzhou, with the workmen who built it. It is a house that its equal it would be difficult to find in South China and must have cost an enormous sum. It is naturally the delight of every Chinaman who sees it, and it is furnished throughout in the Chinese fashion, being full of curious and expensive articles which Mr Marty has collected during his long residence in China. He is immensely proud of it, and with good reason (...).[74]

The Chinese articles which Cunningham mentions probably came from the shops of A. R. Marty in Hong Kong operated by the brothers Marty. After the owner's death in 1914, an obituary in the Hong Kong press highlighted Marty's "beautiful villa, with its splendid collection of Chinese porcelain and curios" as "one of the sights" of Haiphong.[75]

Haiphong's main characteristics were briefly summarised in the 1910 edition of the *Directory & Chronicle* (the most comprehensive overview of cities and businesses in East Asia) which was published by *The Hong Kong Daily Press*. It reads as follows:

> Most of the native buildings are wretchedly constructed of mud, bamboo, and matting, but a well-built European town with broad boulevards, lighted by electricity, has sprung up and is fast assuming the aspect of a prosperous city. Industries are developing, a cotton mill has produced yarn since 1900 and a cement factory has delivered cement and hydraulic lime since the end of 1901. There is a very pretty theatre, built in 1900 by the Municipality. The Hotel du Commerce is a large and handsome structure, its lofty mansard roof dominating every building in the town. There is a church attached to the Roman Catholic Mission. A small dock and some fine wharves and godowns have been made. A Public Garden of rather limited area with a bandstand in the centre has been neatly laid out at the end of the Boulevard Paul Bert. The Cercle du Commerce, which is a well-managed Club, has its domicile in the Boulevard Paul Bert,

[74] Cunningham (1902, 53–54).

[75] *South China Morning Post*, 17 December 1914.

a

b

Fig. 5.5 The private residence Villa Marguerite of Auguste Raphael Marty in Haiphong, c. 1900. On the back of the image, the sender, in 1909, observed the following: "Cette carte représente un chalet, ou plutôt une forteresse. Très curieuse parait-il, le propriétaire est [à] moitié fou" [This card shows a chalet or rather a fortress. It appears very curious, the owner is a bit fanciful] (Private collection Bert Becker)

> the Cercle Banian, another prosperous Club, has its house in Boulevard Sontay. The Race Course is about a mile from the town on the Do Son road.[76]

Others were less impressed by the port city. In January 1906, Jacob Jebsen, co-owner of Jebsen & Company, arrived in Haiphong on board his steamer *Amigo*, of 1186 tons, which was sufficiently light to overcome the bars at the entrance of the Song Cua Cam. Jebsen was welcomed by his business partner, C. Galland, the local manager of Speidel & Co., and accommodated in his private house. One evening, Jebsen visited the municipal theatre to watch a French comic opera which he found "mediocrely played", as he noted in his travel diary. After a dinner with German friends in the Hotel du Commerce, he assessed the food as "very bad". However, in Hanoi and especially at his journey in Ha Long Bay, Jebsen had better impressions.[77] Other visitors were much more positive about Haiphong. Captain Müller, a German naval officer stationed at Jiaozhou (Kiaochow, the German leased territory in China's Shandong Province), arriving on an official mission in Haiphong in February 1906, called the city "a small-scale Hanoi, noticeable as the latter one for elegant European buildings and cleanliness of the indigenous quarters".[78] In January 1907, Vice Admiral Alfred Breusing, commander of the German East Asia Squadron, had to switch from the cruiser *Fürst Bismarck*, with a draught of c. 25 feet (7.80 metres), to the gunboat *Tiger*, with a draught of 11.7 feet (3.56 metres), to steam upriver for an official visit to Haiphong. According to *Le Courrier d'Haiphong*, Breusing, speaking French "just enough to make himself understood", declared himself excited about what he had observed during his short visit to Tonkin: "Particularly, our town Haiphong charmed the admiral who expressed his thanks to the mayor for the friendly way his men were received here". Breusing felt "especially kindly" treated by Mayor Pierre Tournois, who drove his guest in his own car around the town and its surroundings for some hours. He had the impression that Tonkin was a "well-administered and productive colony". The German naval officer found paths, roads and public buildings "in good condition", observed

[76] *The Directory & Chronicle* (1910, 1214–1215).

[77] JJHA, B10-02-0041: Travel report of Jacob Jebsen (Hoihow and Haiphong), January 1906.

[78] PAAA, Peking II-72: Report of Captain Müller (Tsingtao), 2 April 1906.

Fig. 5.6 The Grand Hotel du Commerce in Haiphong, c. 1900 (Private collection Bert Becker)

towns "with busy life everywhere, while immeasurable rice fields were diligently cultivated by hard-working Vietnamese".[79] When Mayor Tournois made a return visit on board the *Tiger*, the French newspaper praised both receptions as "quotations of the greatest courtesy and the liveliest cordiality" (Fig. 5.6).[80]

Chinese Merchants in Haiphong

After the French conquest of northern Vietnam in 1884, Haiphong saw a steady rise in population, mainly of Vietnamese people. The town's total population was 15,100 in 1890, 18,325 in 1902, 55,811 in 1913, 79,090 in 1923 and 97,620 in 1929. While between 1890 and 1902 the

[79] PAAA, R 19425: Report of Vice Admiral Breusing (Banjoewangi), 13 February 1907.

[80] *Le Courrier d'Haiphong*, 17 and 18 January 1907.

percentage of Vietnamese inhabitants rose from 58 to 65 per cent, the percentage of Chinese fell from 37 to 29 per cent and the percentage of Europeans rose slightly from 4 to 5 per cent. In 1913, the Vietnamese constituted 81 per cent of the local population, the Chinese 15 per cent and the Europeans 3 per cent; in 1929, the Vietnamese had a 76 per cent share of Haiphong's population, the Chinese 21 per cent and the Europeans 2 per cent. There was also a very marginal group, consisting of just 72 people, in 1913 (which, however, rose to 705, until 1929), who may have been people of mixed Chinese-Vietnamese origin known as Minh-Huong (French: métis) who were not born in Haiphong, Hanoi or Tourane. Relations between the Vietnamese and the Chinese were generally friendly, symbolised by the Vietnamese term "khach chu" (guest uncle) to designate the Chinese, while in earlier periods the term "khach tru" (immigrant guest) was more common.[81]

With the Sino-French treaty of 9 June 1885, Chinese settlers were granted the right of free entry and were allowed to run commercial operations in Indochina. In the same year, an immigration office and information bureau were set up in Haiphong to tackle the influx of foreigners. With this step, the French continued the practice of the Vietnamese emperors, who had given a privileged status to Chinese residents. Following the French occupation of Indochina, which established order and security and stimulated economic activity, Chinese immigration was further encouraged, especially from the southern Chinese provinces of Guangdong, Fukien and the island of Hainan to promote commercial relations between Tonkin and southern China. On their arrival, Chinese immigrants were admitted into a congregation (in Vietnamese: bang truong, in French: congrégation), a self-administered Chinese community based on their dialect and/or province of origin in China. Initially, there was merely one congregation for all Chinese in Tonkin, but in 1899, the Hokkien were permitted to establish their own organisation. In 1894, the Guangzhouese Kah On Club of Haiphong, with forty merchants and their staff, was launched, followed in 1896 by the Phoc On Club, with eighteen Hokkien merchants as members. Congregations were not permitted to engage in commercial activities and played a central role in the fields of public order and taxation, and in social and cultural activities. They

[81] Minh-Huong born in these cities had their fathers' nationality, according to the decree of 1888 issued by the governor-general of Indochina. Amer (2010, 64–65) and Brocheux and Hèmery (2009, 199).

also allowed the French to more effectively control and tax the Chinese in Indochina.[82]

In the economic sector, the Chinese were active in agriculture and trade, benefiting, as Alain G. Marsot said, "from the greater cultural and commercial sophistication of their mother country, in terms of its very size and greater economic development, compared to the small and scattered societies of Southeast Asia. Furthermore, those Chinese merchants continued to maintain close ties with their families and kinship organisations in China, and in general with the trading communities there, thereby occupying a naturally privileged position as intermediaries between the South China markets and those of Southeast Asia". What seems to have further contributed to the strong position of the Chinese in Vietnam were certain human capacities, most importantly flexibility and great adaptability. Compared to the Vietnamese, as Marsot states, "they often shared the qualities of the local people, though to a higher degree perhaps, combining them with greater astuteness, obstinacy and method". In his doctoral thesis of 1910, René Dubreuil explained that "the Chinese indeed behave in Indochina as a kind of germ stimulating production and, through that, creating wealth", whereas the Vietnamese "do neither possess the initiative nor the mental curiosity honed by the lure of profit, something that drives the Chinese to search for new products which are likely to provide them with a profit" (Fig. 5.7).[83]

Rice was the Indochina's most important export product, and its production was divided between very large numbers of Vietnamese peasants. Because the Chinese were prohibited from engaging in any industry that directly competed with French investments, they mainly engaged in the fishing sector, in trade and in industries related to rice. In 1905 in Haiphong, 270 Chinese and 147 Europeans held "patents" (trading licences); of the 1,657 licences issued to Vietnamese, most were in retail trades. Rice exports from Haiphong were dominated by local Chinese merchants, most of them Guangzhouese, essentially assuring the commercial success of the port. In 1901, 23 Chinese rice merchants were listed in the official records of Haiphong, all but one of whom were located in the Rue Chinoise (Chinese Street), in close proximity to the Chinese port

[82] Dubreuil (1910, 27–30, 33–40), Nguyen (1941), Marsot (1993, 104–111, 114), Amer (2010, 57–62, 68–73) and Martínez (2007a, 88).

[83] Marsot (1993, 22–34, the quote: 32, and 136–137, the quote: 137) and Dubreuil (1910, 1–20, 111–112, the quote: 111).

Fig. 5.7 French postcard showing Chinese women and merchants in Haiphong, c. 1900 (Private collection Bert Becker)

at Song Tam Bac.[84] Their dominant position in the local rice trading industry was highlighted in early 1903 in an article in *The Hong Telegraph*, which was critical of the French colonial government's position towards the Chinese in Tonkin. The article assessed the organisation of Chinese rice buyers and shippers in Tonkin as "one of the best in the East, and the real commerce of that place, both import and export, depends mainly on the enterprise and industry of the Celestial [Chinese]". The writer was critical of the French authorities, accusing them of frequently raising duties on Chinese rice exporters with flimsy excuses, the "squeezing" of fees from smaller Chinese shopkeepers by the police and charging poorly paid Chinese coolies exaggerated licence fees and taxes. It also pointed to campaigns in the local press against the entire Chinese community, accusing them of being liars and swindlers in their commerce, of being allied with Vietnamese rebels and Black Flags (irregular Chinese troops operating in Tonkin), selling arms and ammunition and inciting

[84] Raffi (1994, 337), Martínez (2007a, 89) and Amer (2010, 72).

and supporting insurrections in Indochina. To contradict such allegations, the article praised the "proverbial integrity of the Chinese merchant" in Tonkin, concluding with the statement that "for truly they are the strength of the land, this hard-working uncomplaining race".[85] Less than three weeks later, a French translation of the article was reprinted by *La Revue Indochinoise*, the monthly journal published in Hanoi and edited by Alfred Raquez, which mainly focused on cultural issues, but sometimes presented political topics concerning French Indochina and neighbouring countries. Since articles written by Raquez displayed a clear pro-colonial attitude in favour of French interests, the reprinting of the English article in the French journal, without any accompanying comment by the editor, shows that the critical position was regarded as somewhat justified.[86]

The dominant position of Chinese merchants in the Haiphong rice trade included control of the bulk of rice shipments, which were conducted by shipping hongs, with trading and shipping typically carried out by the same firm. These Chinese shipping hongs arranged transport, which made them comparable to freight forwarders in other parts of the world. As Michael M. Miller established when evaluating the business operations of Butterfield & Swire in Asia: "The range of services" of Chinese hongs, "from banking to documentation, was so comprehensive that few shippers were prepared to save on commissions and negotiate directly with foreign shipping companies".[87] In this way, hongs located in Haiphong and Hong Kong provided business services and connections when managing shipments. These services enhanced their already powerful economic position within the local Chinese community of Haiphong and among other rice traders.

Speidel and Company in Haiphong

In December 1884, August Bauermeister, an associate of Speidel & Co. in Saigon, established the Haiphong branch and became its first managing partner. Some time earlier, on 7 November 1884, the firm had told the M. Jebsen Shipping Company that they "would be glad to often see your steamers [in Haiphong], which are indeed very well

[85] *The Hong Kong Telegraph*, 3 January 1903: The Chinese in Tongking.

[86] La *Revue Indochinoise*, 16 February 1903, 143–144: Les Chinois au Tonkin.

[87] Miller (2012, 90).

suited for this trade at our place". This was a clear hint that the low draught of the Jebsen vessels permitted them to sail up to the port of Haiphong without difficulties. The shipowner replied on 18 December 1884, expressing the hope that "you will often find opportunities to profitably employ my steamers, all the more since you installed the branch in Haiphong".[88] The correspondence indicated that Speidel & Co. had been made an agent of the M. Jebsen Shipping Company, providing the firm with an important tool to manage their imports and exports. On the other hand, the "Haiphong-Linie" (Haiphong Line), the oft-used label for the run between Hong Kong and Haiphong in Jebsen's business correspondence, developed up to the First World War into one of the main pillars of the intra-Asian coastal shipping network of the M. Jebsen Shipping Company. However, Speidel & Co. did not rely on Jebsen alone, but kept a free hand, frequently chartering steam coasters of other shipping companies. In 1891, the annual Haiphong shipping report (published by *Le Courrier d'Haiphong*) listed Speidel & Co. as a charterer of steam coasters. According to these accounts, the firm had chartered six different steamers, four German vessels (but none from Jebsen) and two British ones, with most of them shipping Tonkin rice to Manila, Singapore and Phan Rang in southern Vietnam. Some of the chartered steam tramps transported petroleum, showing that the Haiphong branch of Speidel & Co. was importing this fuel to Tonkin.[89] The Haiphong port statistics reveal that, from 1886 to 1914, the German flag, with very few exceptions, frequently ranked second after the French flag, followed by the British one. After a personal visit to the port, Consul Walther Rößler (Guangzhou) noted that, in 1910, the German steamers calling at Haiphong were "without exception" owned by the M. Jebsen Shipping Company (Fig. 5.8).[90]

Speidel & Co. in Haiphong and elsewhere in French Indochina actively participated in the basic principle of the founding of the French empire in Asia: "mise en valeur" (development or exploitation).[91] In Haiphong,

[88] Becker (2012, 330: Speidel & Co. (Saigon) to M. Jebsen Shipping Company (Apenrade), 7 November 1884). JJHA, A01-01-215: Michael Jebsen (Apenrade) to Speidel & Co. (Saigon), 18 December 1884.

[89] *Le Courrier d'Haiphong*, 1 May 1892.

[90] Raffi (1994, 602). PAAA, Konsulat Saigon 3-B 8: Consul Rößler (Guangzhou) to Chancellor von Bethmann Hollweg (Berlin), 30 March 1911.

[91] Brocheux and Hèmery (2009, 116–120) and Murray (1980, 100–102).

Fig. 5.8 The Haiphong office of Speidel & Company, located at the corner of Boulevard Paul Bert and Boulevard Amiral Courbet, c. 1900 (Private collection Bert Becker)

the firm quickly gained a strong position, developing into one of the port city's largest trading firms although no concrete numbers about the real volume of business are available due to the entire loss of company archives. Occasional remarks in the protocols of the Haiphong Chamber of Commerce, or advertisements in the local French press, indicate the scope of the firm's businesses. In October 1901, Speidel & Co. was an agent in Haiphong of several shipping companies and of the Chartered Bank of India, Australia and China, handling imports and exports, banking commissions, consignations and insurance. Imports included various products such as fabrics, flour, canned foodstuffs, fluids, wines in bulk, beer, milk powder, pianos, furniture, scrap metal, ironworks, iron and steel of all kinds, corrugated sheet metals, oil, paint, cordage, sail canvas, cement, American pine wood, teak and lime wood and petroleum from Russia and Borneo.[92]

In the 1890s, Speidel & Co. in Haiphong was managed by Hermann Kurz and Max Leopold who had earlier worked in the firm's headquarters in Saigon. In 1896, Franz Dobrowohl (who was from Silesia, Prussia) joined the Haiphong branch as assistant.[93] In 1897, Leopold was co-operating with the British shipping company Gellatly, Hankey, Sewell and Company (established in London in 1862) which had addressed a cargo to Haiphong and enquired about the possibility of discharging heavy goods in the port. However, the only available crane was the one operated by Marty et d'Abbadie, firmly installed in their workshops on the banks of the Song Cua Cam, and therefore on a spot inaccessible for large vessels. In previous years, the Haiphong Chamber of Commerce had several times discussed the acquisition of a floating steam crane, of 25 tons, but its requests to the protectorate remained unanswered. Following Leopold's initiative, the chamber took up the matter again and in its session on 23 November 1897 unanimously voted to urgently submit the case directly to the governor-general of Indochina. The case demonstrated the important position Speidel & Co. had in Haiphong and the interests of the chamber as the representative of local businesses in promoting the port's development.[94] On 1 July 1904, Speidel & Co. established a branch in Hanoi. Dobrowohl was made authorised signatory and took over management of this office which was mainly charged with imports for the administrative capital of French Indochina.[95] From 1911 to the outbreak of the First World War, the firm's sole German competitor in Hanoi and Haiphong was F. Engler & Company (headquartered in Frankfurt am Main, with the main office in Saigon). This trading firm

[92] Chambre de Commerce d'Haiphong, Minutes of Session of 14 February 1898. *Le Courrier d'Haiphong*, 8 October 1901. According to Vorapheth (2004, 461), the Haiphong branch of Speidel & Co. sold goods to the value of eight million francs in 1913 which came closest to the sales figures of the firm's Saigon branch (ten million francs).

[93] PAAA, R 140964: Dobrowohl (Haiphong) to Foreign Office (Berlin), 25 December 1907. PAAA, Konsulat Saigon 3-B 8: Consul Crull (Saigon) to Chancellor von Bethmann Hollweg (Berlin), 10 January 1912.

[94] Chambre de Commerce d'Haiphong: Minutes of Session of 23 November 1897.

[95] Devraigne (1920, 50–54). In 1913, the Hanoi branch of Speidel & Co. imported and sold goods to the value of 3.3 million. Vorapheth (2004, 461).

Fig. 5.9 Max Leopold (1858–1930), partner of Speidel & Company, in Haiphong, c. 1910 (Courtesy of Eduard Leopold, Coburg)

imported fabrics in bulk and anilines, and manufactured rubber on a rather modest scale (Fig. 5.9).[96]

In the early twentieth century, Speidel & Co. employed ten clerks in Haiphong and five in Hanoi, which clearly reflected the port city's more important position in trading, shipping and mining. Haiphong remained the major location for Speidel & Co. in the Tonkin region, selling mainly bulk goods and assuring their transit to their Chinese agencies in Mongze and Kunming (Yunnan-Fu). When the German officer Captain Müller, charged by the Jiaozhou (Kiaochow) colonial government with paying a visit to Indochina, came to Haiphong in February 1906, he labelled Speidel & Co. "the only German business firm here and, at the same time, the largest one".[97] On 1 July 1907, Dobrowohl became managing partner of the Haiphong branch; the other managing partners in Haiphong before him were H. Prescher and later C. Galland. In

[96] Devraigne (1920, 49–50).

[97] PAAA, Peking II-72: Report of Captain Müller (Tsingtao), 2 April 1906.

1911, Consul Walther Rößler in Guangzhou called Dobrowohl "director of the largest local trading firm", who had "good relations to French authorities" and was "very well-acquainted with the entire economic situation".[98] In May 1912, Consul Crull in Saigon reported that Speidel & Co. in Haiphong was the local agent of the Hamburg-Amerika Linie, Germany's major shipping company, and tried to convince the firm's headquarters in Hamburg to establish a regular inter-continental shipping service between Europe, Saigon and Haiphong. This would give "German shipping in Indochina, and especially in Haiphong, a new and welcome upturn", Crull pointed out. He further praised Speidel & Co. as "one of the biggest and richest trading firms in the entire East, with its business contacts spreading around the whole globe; there is no other company in Indochina comparable to it". However, he found that Denis Frères (Denis Brothers), the important French trading house in Indochina, came closest to the German firm. At the time, Speidel & Co.'s overall exports from Tonkin had a value of around 2.5 million francs annually; in its Haiphong and Hanoi warehouses, the firm kept stocks of goods each worth about 1.5 million francs.[99]

In December 1907, Franz Dobrowohl, the new manager of Speidel & Co. in Haiphong, applied to the foreign ministry in Berlin to be appointed consul of Imperial Germany in the port city. He justified his plea by highlighting the strongly increasing German shipping and trading interests in the entire region. Pointing to the upcoming opening of the Yunnan Railway, which promised to considerably open up south-western China to trading, he also drew attention to the fact that families of Germans or former German nationals serving in considerable numbers in the Foreign Legion had often made enquiries about them at Speidel & Co. However, due to the lack of contacts between the private firm and French military authorities, such investigations had remained fruitless. Dobrowohl was convinced that a German consul "well-acquainted with local conditions" would be able to find proper means "for that delicate matter", and to put some of those German legionnaires "back on the

[98] PAAA, Konsulat Saigon 3-B 8: Consul Rößler (Guangzhou) to Chancellor von Bethmann Hollweg (Berlin), 30 March 1911.

[99] PAAA, Konsulat Saigon 3-B 8: Consul Crull (Shanghai) to Chancellor von Bethmann Hollweg (Berlin), 21 May 1912.

straight and narrow", thereby retaining them for the German nation.[100] However, the most powerful factor in establishing a German consulate in Haiphong was the increasing economic importance of Tonkin and Yunnan for European business interests. In the spring of 1904, the British government had appointed Tom Ffennell Carlisle, first assistant of the Bangkok legation, to be Britain's first professional consul in Hanoi. London justified the decision with the ongoing construction of the Yunnan Railway, which was expected to boost the commercial position of Tonkin's major city, regarded as important for British trading interests.[101] Belgium and Norway were due to follow the British example, something finally realised in 1908 when the two countries appointed consuls in Haiphong. However, when he did not receive a reply from Berlin, Dobrowohl instead looked for outside support and found it among German shipmasters, mostly officers of Jebsen steamers who frequently visited the port city or even permanently resided in Haiphong with their families due to the lower costs of living compared to Hong Kong. In February 1909, the masters and several other Germans, or German-speaking Swiss nationals, filed a petition to the German government demanding the setting up of a consulate in Haiphong. This plan was supported by Michael (Magge) Jebsen who regarded the idea as being "in the interest of the [M. Jebsen] Shipping Company".[102]

The joint action finally attracted the attention of the German foreign ministry which instructed their consuls in neighbouring ports to collect information on the matter. According to Consul Rößler in Guangzhou who had visited Haiphong ten years ago, the position of the French port city had considerably increased: "Its location in the delta of the

[100] PAAA, R 140964: Franz Dobrowohl (Haiphong) to Foreign Office (Berlin), 25 December 1907. The ranks of the French Foreign Legion included a number of German nationals, mostly from Alsace-Loraine, to whom Dobrowohl was referring. After the Franco-German War (1870–1871), pro-French volunteers from Alsace-Lorraine had joined the Legion's ranks and taken part in the seizure and so-called pacification of Tonkin from 1883 to 1897. In 1913, Germans made up 17.6 per cent of the Foreign Legion (Michels 2006, 37–46).

[101] *Hong Kong Daily Press*, 12 May 1904 and Corfield (2013, 44).

[102] PAAA, Peking II-976: Foreign Ministry (Berlin) to German Minister von Rex (Beijing), 31 March 1908. PAAA, R 140964: Franz Dobrowohl (Haiphong) to Foreign Ministry (Berlin), 22 September 1908 and 6 September 1909 (with the petition of 1 February 1909). JJHA, PS-6343: Michael (Magge) Jebsen (Hong Kong) to Jacob Jebsen (Apenrade), 1 June 1911.

Red River branching out in watercourses makes it the natural distribution centre of Tonkin". He also pointed to the construction of numerous new traffic routes, voluminous new irrigation and drainage systems in Tonkin and increasing transit trade with Yunnan, resulting in rising exports and imports at Haiphong. Due to the greater importance of the port for Tonkin and the neighbouring Chinese provinces, Rößler pleaded strongly for Dobrowohl to appoint edbe German consul in Haiphong. His call was fully supported by his colleague Consul Crull in Saigon, who concluded that "Germany is the only power which has larger interests in Tonkin, but without a consulate there".[103] In spring 1913, Franz Dobrowohl was commissioned with the consulate. In this function, he was subordinated to the German consul in Saigon who remained charged with general matters concerning the whole of French Indochina.

Before taking home leave in September 1913, Dobrowohl temporarily commissioned Oskar Bezold, his partner in Speidel & Co., with the consulate. Shortly after, an incident happened which shed some light on the relations between French and German residents in Haiphong. On 1 November 1913, *Le Courrier d'Haiphong* published an article titled "Ces bon Célestes!" ("Those Good Celestials!"), in which the journal accused some Chinese of having committed a fraudulent operation, with the help of "nos amis d'outre-Rhin" ("our friends across the River Rhine"). The brief account did not provide any concrete facts or figures and was clearly aimed at the Chinese of Haiphong, labelled as "si bons enfants" ("so good children") who supposedly had frequently defrauded the Haiphong Customs administration of revenues when providing falsified customs declarations. However, alluding to unnamed Germans collaborating with Chinese smugglers was sufficient reason for Acting Consul Bezold to submit a complaint to Henri Tirard, the newspaper's director and editor-in-chief. In his letter, he strongly protested against "lumping together the Germans and the Chinese as smugglers". Pointing to his official function and titling himself "the representative of shipowners targeted by this article", Bezold requested specification of the facts "which inspired the insinuations of your editor". In his report to Consul Reinsdorf in Saigon, he labelled the article "another impertinent piece of French journalism

[103] PAAA, Konsulat Saigon 3-B 8: Consul Rößler (Guangzhou) to Chancellor von Bethmann Hollweg (Berlin), 30 March 1911, Consul Crull (Saigon) to Chancellor von Bethmann Hollweg (Berlin), 10 January 1912.

towards Germany", explaining that "Haiphong was much more chauvinistic than Saigon". Tirard seemed not to have replied to the complaint because the foreign office records do not contain any such answer.[104]

In 1910–1911, to further diversify their business, Speidel & Co. established several metal mining companies in Tonkin.[105] Most of the metal deposits had been worked by Chinese miners before the French occupation and were taken over by French and other firms after the late 1890s for systematic working and outfitting. Zinc and tin were far ahead of all the other metals, both in value and in continuity of extraction. Between 1905 and 1910, the principal zinc deposits were found and exploitation started. In 1912, Speidel & Co. together with other German firms in East Asia, formed a study group headed by the Frankfurt banking house Beer, Sontheimer & Company to explore the productivity of tin, copper and coal mines for future exploitation or for joining foreign mining companies. At Speidel & Co.'s invitation, the Frankfurt bank and the Belgian Compagnie Générale des Minerais de Liège (General Company for Ore of Liège) dispatched special engineers equipped with complete laboratories to Indochina. This initiative was taken shortly after the mining law of Indochina was established on 26 January 1912, stipulating that foreigners could neither own nor manage mines, but the nationality of the capital was not subject to regulation. This gave German investors the chance to become purchasers of the output of the most important mines in Indochina, providing considerable capital for securing sales agreements with durations of about ten years beginning in 1913. In almost all tin and tungsten mines, Speidel & Co. bought the mineral production or served as forwarding agent arranging sales of the minerals at the embarkation at Haiphong, with advantageous freight rates. After the first deposits of calamine (a combination of zinc and ferric oxides) were discovered, the

[104] PAAA, Konsulat Saigon 3-B 8: Consul Dobrowohl (Haiphong) to Consul Reinsdorf (Saigon), 19 August 1913 and 12 September 1913. *Le Courrier d'Haiphong*, 1 November 1913. PAAA, Konsulat Saigon 4-C 5: Acting Consul Bezold (Haiphong) to Henri Tirard (Haiphong) and to Consul Reinsdorf (Saigon), 4 November 1913. In the final correspondence of the short-lived Haiphong consulate before the outbreak of the First World War, Bezold confirmed reception of the consulate shield which was fixed at the entrance of the office building of Speidel & Co. in Haiphong. PAAA, Konsulat Saigon 3-B 8: Acting Consul Bezold (Haiphong) to Consul Reinsdorf (Saigon), 12 January 1914.

[105] PAAA, Konsulat Saigon 3-B 8: Consul Rößler (Guangzhou) to Chancellor von Bethmann Hollweg (Berlin), 30 March 1911.

company took a close interest in the exploitation of this mineral before the First World War brought an end to such diversified business activities.[106]

After the war, the French understandably had little enthusiasm about Speidel when critically re-evaluating their Austrian and German competitors in Indochina and the neighbouring region. However, Georges Devraigne, head of the Economic Department of Cochinchina, admitted that Speidel & Co. was "solidly capitalised and laid out, representing in Indochina an indisputable commercial power". French historian Raymond Poidevin pointed to the fact that German commercial methods which proved to be successful, "were known but found no school in France: French trade, being tied to its habits, did not yet comprehend the need to turn its methods upside down to face the increasingly strong German commercial competition".[107]

Marty et d'Abbadie

The Subsidised River Shipping Service of Tonkin

On 15 June 1886, Resident-General Paul Bert, the most senior French official in the Protectorate of Annam-Tonkin, formally issued the requirements for the projected River Shipping Service of Tonkin. The subsidised service should establish six regular lines in the waterways networks of the Red River and in the more eastward located Song Thai Binh (Thai Binh River). The main run between Haiphong and Hanoi, covering 120 sea miles, was also the longest and had to be serviced three times weekly. Vessels operating the service were prescribed to have a length of 35–40 metres, a maximum draught of 1.60 metres and to run at 9.5 knots when tested but on average not slower than 6 knots. All river boats had to fly the French flag and to sail with French or Asian crews; in the latter case at least, the master had to be French. For the comfort of at least twelve first-class passengers, a restaurant with prices fixed by the protectorate was to be operated on all ships, and a roof installed on the bridge of each vessel covering sofa beds for sleeping. To protect these and other passengers against sunshine and rainfall, the installation of roofs and curtains was stipulated for all vessels. Concerning cargoes, first-class passengers had a baggage allowance of 100 kilograms,

[106] Devraigne (1920, 42–43) and Robequain (1944, 249–250).

[107] Devraigne (1920, 55) and Poidevin (1998, 168–174, the quote: 174).

the others only 30 kilograms. The concessionaries were obliged to transport protectorate and Indochina mail and gold and silver cash, without charging fees. The vessels should also allow the convenient transporting of troops and horses. There were several detailed stipulations on transporting mail, passengers and freight, penalties for contract violations and on other legal issues including the payment of the subsidy. The concessionaries were offered a contract terminating on 1 January 1897, hence for a period of ten years.[108]

However, the detailed stipulations about the size of the vessels for the River Shipping Service soon aroused concerns about the prompt availability of such specific ships. On 29 July 1886, in a letter to the Resident of Haiphong, Bert limited the requirement on sizes to the most important two shipping lines and made it clear that on the other lines, smaller and slower vessels with lesser comfort could be employed. Since political and economic pressures to open up the service as soon as possible were obviously growing, Bert made it clear that the concessionary who won the contract was obliged "to immediately organise a provisional service under conditions to be discussed by mutual agreement with the administration".[109] When the government commission of four met on 17 August 1886 to formally review the submissions and take a decision, it emerged that just three firms had submitted offers, of which the one by the local French merchant, Édouard Jules d'Abbadie, was "the most advantageous one for the administration". His request for 349,000 francs of subsidy (4,648 francs per sea mile), put Abbadie far below the claims of his competitors, and even below the rate fixed by the resident-general. As a result, he won this important contract.[110] Yet, it was obvious that a single French merchant, who did not possess proper financial means, would hardly be able to launch the construction and maintenance of a whole fleet of river ships and operate them on a large scale. Such concerns were certainly prevalent when Auguste Raphael Marty and Édouard Jules d'Abbadie, both experienced in shipping logistics and acquainted with the Tonkin river systems, agreed to join forces and found a partnership

[108] *Annuaire de l'Indo-Chine* (1890, 1195–1201): Cahier des charges pour un service de correspondances fluviales sur les rivières du Tonkin, 15 June 1886.

[109] ANOM, INDO-GGI-6274: Telegram of Resident General (Hanoi) to Resident of Haiphong, 29 July 1886.

[110] *Annuaire de l'Indo-Chine* (1890, 1202–1203): Procès-verbal d'adjudication, 17 August 1886.

company under the name of Marty et d'Abbadie. Not only from the order of names but also from the different energies and mindsets of the two men, it seems that Marty, with his company A. R. Marty in Hong Kong, which had made considerable profits during the Sino-French War (1884–1885), was the driving force behind the idea. The partnership was entered into in pursuance of an instrument under private seal with the joint company's name "Marty et d'Abbadie" on 11 September 1886. The firm (initially located in Haiphong, Rue de la Marine) served as head office (siège social) of the Service Subventionné des Correspondances Fluviales du Tonkin (Subsidised River Shipping Service of Tonkin) and was set to last for the term of the subsidy contract issued by the administration of the Protectorate of Annam-Tonkin, namely from 15 October 1886 to 1 January 1897. The partnership was extended, again under private seal with the name of Marty et d'Abbadie from 1 January 1897 to 31 December 1906, which exactly matched with the duration of the new subsidy contract. After the death of Abbadie, the company name was, in August 1907, formally deleted from the registers, with Marty operating the businesses as "A. R. Marty", the name of his trading firm based in Hong Kong and Haiphong (Fig. 5.10).[111]

On 15 September 1886, the protectorate entered into an agreement with Marty et d'Abbadie on immediately starting operating provisional river shipping services. The company promised to launch six shipping lines within a month and was in return permitted to operate different types of vessels than stipulated in the requirements. Even the obligatory inspection of the boats by a special commission named by the resident-general was dropped to speed up the opening of the service. Newly built vessels were to be put into operation on the two main lines by 20 July 1887 at the latest; for the other lines, the date was fixed as 20 September 1887. It was obvious that Bert was pushing hard to get the service started quickly and to have a fleet of new steamers built in a short time. Since Édouard Jules d'Abbadie was the winner of the contract, he was made director of the River Shipping Service of Tonkin.[112] On 16 October 1886, the state monopolist was officially inaugurated in Hanoi at the banquet of the

[111] *L'Avenir du Tonkin*, 18 September 1886. United States State Department (1901, 147–150). VNA1, SEDT-10534: Auguste Raphel Marty (Haiphong) to Director-General of Finances and Accounts of Indochina (Hanoi), 7 August 1907.

[112] *Annuaire de l'Indo-Chine* (1890, 1203–1204): Convention entre le Protectorat et les messageries fluviales, 15 September 1886.

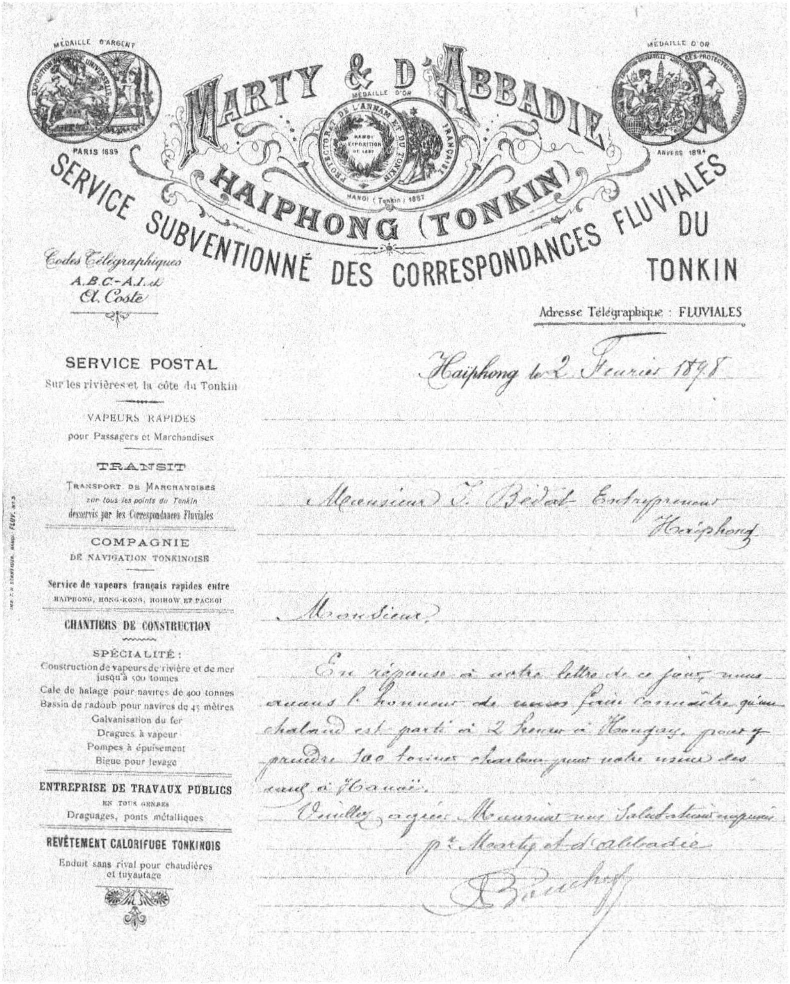

MÉDAILLE D'ARGENT PARIS 1889 — MÉDAILLE D'OR ANVERS 1894

MARTY & D'ABBADIE

MÉDAILLE D'OR — HANOI (Tonkin) 1887

HAIPHONG (TONKIN)

SERVICE SUBVENTIONNÉ DES CORRESPONDANCES FLUVIALES DU TONKIN

Codes Télégraphiques
A.B.C.–A.I. et
A. Coste

Adresse Télégraphique : FLUVIALES

SERVICE POSTAL
Sur les rivières et la côte du Tonkin

VAPEURS RAPIDES
pour Passagers et Marchandises

TRANSIT
Transport de Marchandises
sur tous les points du Tonkin
desservis par les Correspondances Fluviales

COMPAGNIE
DE NAVIGATION TONKINOISE

Service de vapeurs français rapides entre
HAIPHONG, HONG-KONG, HOIHOW ET PACKOI

CHANTIERS DE CONSTRUCTION

SPÉCIALITÉ :
Construction de vapeurs de rivière et de mer jusqu'à 500 tonnes
Cale de halage pour navires de 400 tonnes
Bassin de radoub pour navires de 45 mètres
Galvanisation du fer
Dragues à vapeur
Pompes à épuisement
Bigue pour levage

ENTREPRISE DE TRAVAUX PUBLICS
EN TOUS GENRES
Dragages, ponts métalliques

REVÊTEMENT CALORIFUGE TONKINOIS
Enduit sans rival pour chaudières et tuyautage

Haïphong le 2 Février 1898

Monsieur J. Bédat Entrepreneur
Haïphong

Monsieur,

En réponse à votre lettre de ce jour, nous avons l'honneur de vous faire connaître qu'un chaland est parti à 2 heures à Hongay, pour y prendre 100 tonnes charbon pour votre usine des eaux à Hanoï.

Veuillez agréer Monsieur nos salutations empressées
p. Marty et d'Abbadie

Fig. 5.10 Letter of Marty et d'Abbadie, Haiphong, dated 2 February 1898 (Private collection Bert Becker)

Chamber of Commerce in the presence of Resident-General Bert. As *L'Avenir du Tonkin* reported, chamber members, merchants, manufacturers and settlers wanted to show Bert their gratitude for his consistent efforts to develop Tonkin's commerce and industry. For setting up a preliminary landing stage, a former Norwegian three-mast bark had been stripped out in Haiphong and towed to Hanoi to serve as a pontoon in the Red River.[113] For the downstream route from Hanoi to Haiphong, fourteen hours had been estimated, and in the opposite direction it was eighteen hours upstream. When, for the first time, the itinerary of the service was published in Hanoi's local newspaper on 23 October 1886, the six lines of the new network were seemingly fully operational.[114]

Around five years earlier, the direct counterpart of this new shipping service, the Messageries fluviales de Cochinchine (River Shipping Company of Cochinchina), had been created as public limited company in Paris on 1 June 1881. Initiated by Jules Rueff, a French shipowner in Saigon, the firm had a proper capital of 1.5 million francs divided into 3,000 shares. According to Gilles de Gantès, the River Shipping Company of Cochinchina developed into "the most powerful enterprise in Indochina of the time". Having been granted a considerable subsidy from the colonial government in Saigon to ship mail and French troops, the firm operated a fleet of river ships and coastal steamers in the Mekong Delta and on the Mekong up to Laos and its estuaries as far as Cambodia and Siam. With its quasi-monopoly (which it exploited to frequently raise transport fees), the River Shipping Company of Cochinchina played an important political role in France's naval imperialism and colonial expansion in southern Vietnam, and in her foreign policy towards Siam.[115] In northern Vietnam, the Subsidised River Shipping Service of Tonkin was to play an even more extended role, focusing on developing basic transport infrastructures and turning the Red River into an important transit route to the south-western provinces of China.

[113] *L'Avenir du Tonkin*, 16 October 1886.

[114] *L'Avenir du Tonkin*, 23 October 1886.

[115] Gantès (2008, 744) and Brocheux and Hèmery (2009, 128, 157). For more details, see: www.entreprises-coloniales.fr.

Paddle Steamers

For centuries, Southeast Asia had a river-based shipping tradition using a variety of ships, probably even more diverse than those in the Mediterranean or Atlantic. Between 1290 and 1500, a hybrid Sino-Southeast Asian shipbuilding style was developing after thousands of Chinese sailors, soldiers and traders emigrated to the region due to political turmoil in China. The large junks, which were known to Western explorers when they first arrived in the region, were the Southeast Asian variant of these Chinese ships, dominating the seas and rivers.[116] European traders based in Macao, Manila and other parts of East Asia probably transferred some of their shipbuilding technology to Chinese and Vietnamese craftsmen when ordering new vessels at Dong Nai (the area near modern Bien Hoa) where the Vietnamese shipbuilding industry had been centred since the eighteenth century. Other dockyards operated by the state were located northeast of Saigon, along the riverbank. Under Emperor Gia Long (1762–1820), almost 1,500 ships of different types (including war junks, bigger galleys and Western-style vessels or schooners) were constructed between 1778 and 1819. In 1838, his successor, Tu Duc, acquired a Western steamship and instructed his engineers to study how to build one to prepare the Vietnamese fleet for modern naval warfare. However, with the arrival of the French the shipbuilding industry in Vietnam became almost entirely a colonial matter.[117]

At first, the River Shipping Service relied on a wide variety of small and simple steamboats. In the light of the need to have constructed special vessels of very low draughts able to navigate the shallow rivers of Tonkin, the company founders turned to Hong Kong. The construction plans for new ships were drawn up by the British engineer William Charles Jack, since 1887 superintendent engineer (or chief engineer) of the workshops of Marty et d'Abbadie. The British, who were generally the undisputed leaders in shipbuilding, had little experience of constructing river vessels and found workable types only in the United States. The big paddle steamers operating on American rivers and lakes were unique in their appearance and construction and were a source of amazement to the marine engineers of other nations. Between 1820 and 1880, more than 6,000 paddle wheelers totalling over a million tonnes had been built for

[116] Reid (2015, 80–81).

[117] Li (2004, 120–125) and Goscha (2017, 54–55).

Western rivers in dockyards located on the upper Ohio River between Pittsburgh, Pennsylvania and Louisville. Almost all of the Western river steamboats were constructed there to ply the Mississippi-Ohio River and its tributaries. Because of the shallowness of these streams, they were smaller and usually considerably lighter than other steam-driven vessels, with as little draught as possible. Referred to as the "spoonbill mountain boats", owing to their extremely light draught and the shape of their bow, single-deck steamboats were built in the 1870s to navigate the upper reaches of the trans-Mississippi tributaries. The American writer Mark Twain, who served as a pilot on a Western river boat, allegedly said that a good Missouri riverboat could sail on a heavy dew. Most of the Ohio-built vessels were stern-wheelers although they were initially considered inferior to side-wheelers for technological reasons. However, the utilisation of much larger wheels, and of twin wheels, became possible after builders began to place the wheels beyond the stern. Stern-wheelers had certain advantages over side-wheelers such as substantial protection from driftwood, logs and rocks, and the ability to "grass-hopper" over shallows bars because the rear-mounted paddles would raise the level of water under the hull when operated in reverse. They were generally faster and beamier, which reduced their draught and allowed the vessels to carry more cargo.[118]

In 1887, three stern-wheelers named *Dragon*, *Phénix* and *Tigre* were constructed by the Hong Kong & Whampoa Dock Company, the major dockyard of the British colony, on behalf of Marty et d'Abbadie. The new paddle steamers were immediately assigned to the river lines between Haiphong and Hanoi, and between Haiphong and Phu-lang Thuong. Each of the vessels, equipped with cabins, bathrooms and a luxurious salon, all lit by electricity, could take on board forty first-and second-class passengers, three hundred deck passengers and three hundred tonnes of goods. The largest, the *Dragon*, was 43 metres long and 7.30 metres wide, having a draught of only 1.50 metres; it achieved with its two-screw propeller a maximum speed of 10.5 knots. According to an English newspaper report, the vessels gave "every satisfaction" to Marty et d'Abbadie, which sent a letter of thanks and praise to the Dock Company. The new light-draught steamers, which were put into operation in the summer of 1887, were soon followed by two smaller ones constructed by Fenwick &

[118] Still et al. (2000, 63–67).

Fig. 5.11 River Paddle Steamers of Marty et d'Abbadie, Haiphong, c. 1910 (Private collection Bert Becker)

Company in Hong Kong. They started operating in the autumn of 1887, serving the other four less frequented lines (Fig. 5.11).[119]

The new vessels soon proved so efficient and convenient that demand grew for increased frequency. In February 1888, an additional act to the 1886 convention was signed by the protectorate and Marty et d'Abbadie. On the line between Haiphong and Hanoi, the company promised to raise the number of weekly voyages from three to six, which meant that this route was served almost daily. On the other lines, the number was increased slightly from two to three weekly voyages, while two additional lines were created on a weekly basis. The longest route, covering a distance of 168 miles from Nam Dinh on the lower Red River down to Vinh, the northern seaport of Annam, was both a river and a coastal line. The seagoing vessel of 250 tons, named *Annam*, was assigned to the coastal service and could carry twelve first-class passengers; with its

[119] *The London and China Telegraph*, 31 October 1887, *South China Morning Post*, 25 July 1906, and *Haiphong illustré* (1895, 8). For a comprehensive overview of Marty et d'Abbadie, with details on the fleet of the Subsidised River Shipping Service of Tonkin, see Dubois (1900, 288–294, 295–301).

low draught, it could also pass bars in rivers. The new scheme almost doubled the overall distance to be covered to 210.392 miles (108.264 miles in 1886) for which the firm was granted an extra annual subsidy of 250.000 francs (3.26 francs per mile), providing Marty et d'Abbadie with the impressive sum of 599.000 francs of subsidy. Furthermore, the ships of the service were to be exempt from all light tower and anchorage fees, as well as from all other navigation fees set up since the opening of the service, and even from new ones established in the future. The company received an exclusive right to ship all transports of the protectorate, including troops, passengers, cargoes and ammunition on the routes covered by the service. Additionally, Marty et d'Abbadie was assured that until 1 January 1897, when the additional act expired, no other shipping company would be subsidised on the lines serviced by its vessels.[120] However, such precautions seemed unnecessary. Because the difficult natural conditions of the waterways of Tonkin required specially fitted vessels to navigate them, no serious competitor emerged in the period up to the end of 1906 when the firm operated on the Tonkin waterways.

With its position as a state monopolist confirmed by the new subsidy treaty, Marty et d'Abbadie developed into Tonkin's largest pioneering enterprise. On the banks of the Cua Cam, at Haiphong's almost exclusively European port (called Port de Commerce), and next to the headquarters of the French navy in the Protectorate of Annam-Tonkin (Station locale de l'Annam et du Tonkin), the joint company established its own shipyard for building different kinds of vessels for its fleet of river ships, and for the French administration and naval units stationed in Indochina.[121] The shipyard also built dredgers employed in the rivers of Tonkin, and offered repair services for all sorts of vessels. The workshops were fully equipped with machines and tools for working on metals and woods needed for constructing ship hulls, engines and boilers, plus a 130-metre steam slipway on which two ships of three hundred tonnes each

[120] *Annuaire de l'Indo-Chine* (1890, 1204–1210): Acte Additionnel au contrat en date du 15 septembre 1886, passé avec M.M. Marty et d'Abbadie pour l'exploitation du service des Messageries fluviales, 18 February1888. *Haiphong illustré* (1895, 8).

[121] PAAA, Peking II-72: Report of Captain Müller (Tsingtao), 2 April 1906, PAAA, R 19425: Report of Vice Admiral Breusing (Banjoewangi), 13 February 1907.

could be towed at the same time; a hold with railing for ships of forty-five metres of length; and a wharf with a crane able to lift 30,000 kilograms. The workshops were under the management of chief engineer Jack who supervised European sub-engineers, petty officers and on average 400–500 Chinese and Vietnamese workers.[122]

The following example demonstrates the usual procedure for constructing and delivering a paddle steamer destined for the upper Mekong River, which was contracted by Governor-General de Lanessan on behalf of the Protectorate of Annam-Tonkin. According to the contract signed on 19 February 1894, the single-wheel paddle steamer was pre-fabricated in single pieces, the sheets of metal screwed in place and labelled according to their respective positions. The sides and other parts of the bridge were built to enable them be taken apart and packaged for transport. The fixed price for the ship pre-assembled in the workshops in Haiphong ready for delivery was 60,000 francs. Marty et d'Abbadie received an additional 15,000 francs after promising to get the ship onto the Mekong or the most suitable arroyo leading to it.[123]

Marquis de Barthélemy, a French traveller passing through Haiphong in January 1896, praised Marty et d'Abbadie for its "real efforts to assure river services", pointing to the fact that shipping on the Red River increased every day "thanks to new vessels leaving the shipyard each year". When British journalist Alfred Cunningham visited Haiphong in 1901, he called the shipyard of Marty et d'Abbadie the "chief industry" of the port, "well-appointed and prosperous, and turns out vessels up to 500 tons". As Cunningham noted, "undoubtedly Haiphong owes not a little of its prosperity to the extensive and convenient service of river steamers of this company, which connect it with all the important places in the interior". In the 1890s, Marty et d'Abbadie built its impressive new headquarters at the junction of the rivers Song Tam Bac and Cua Cam. The favourably located buildings accommodating offices, shops, flats and other facilities were placed at the dockings for the paddle steamers. It became a popular postcard theme and, in a certain way, the symbol of French efforts to rapidly introduce modern means of transport to Indochina. In the eyes of

[122] *Haiphong illustré* (1895, 9).

[123] VNA1, RST-6603: Contract with Marty et d'Abbadie for supplying a paddle steamer (chaloupe monoroue) for the Upper Mekong River. Issued in Haiphong, 19 February 1894.

Fig. 5.12 The Haiphong head office of the Subsidised River Shipping Service of Tonkin (Marty et d'Abbadie), c. 1900 (Private collection Bert Becker)

Cunningham, the company headquarters "constitute the most imposing block of business buildings in the port" (Fig. 5.12).[124]

In the illustrated brochure *Haiphong Illustrè* issued as supplement to the thousandth number of the local newspaper *Le Courrier d'Haiphong*, Marty et d'Abbadie was the first private company to be presented, on 24 December 1895. The publication highlighted France's colonial endeavours and successes in the port city and was therefore a public relations issue. On the first pages, the richly illustrated text provided a detailed description of Haiphong's development since 1886, followed by information on local military installations and the Customs and Administration offices of Annam and Tonkin. This was followed by the chapter on Marty et d'Abbadie, with its history and current situation laid out over more than two pages, including images of the owners, key staff members and of vessels of its fleet. The prominent position was justified by the fact that in 1895 the impressive fleet of the River Shipping Service consisted of twenty steamers, various small launches for exploration tasks and several

[124] Cunningham (1902, 58–59, 160–161).

barges. Its vessels were operating twelve different lines, frequently shipping 300 first-class passengers, 200 second-class, 4,500 deck passengers and 3,500 tonnes of goods. Detailed information was also provided on the affiliates of Marty et d'Abbadie, the Compagnie de Navigation Tonkinoise (Tonkin Shipping Company) which since 1893 had operated two self-owned steamers in the South China Sea; the shipyard, with its Ateliers de constructions navales (Shipbuilding Workshops), and the Service des Travaux publics (Public Works Service).[125]

Explorations

The low-draught stern-wheelers constructed by Fenwick and Co. were specially assigned to shipping on the upper Red River requiring extremely low draughts. These paddle steamers served as a model for an entire series of vessels of the same type which since 1888 had been built in the workshops of Marty et d'Abbadie after the designs of chief engineer Jack. In August 1888, the keel of the first stern-wheeler built by private industry in Tonkin was laid. With a hull made of wood with a copper layer, the ship was equipped with many comforts and conveniences for passengers, as well as certain safety installations such as specially fitted bullet shields on the sides as a protection against pirate attacks; in the same manner, steel plates protected the stoke-hold and the engine room. To adjust to the requirements of transport for the government, there was ample space amidships for horses and troops which made the cargo space very large for a boat of its size. The object of the constructors, as an English newspaper explained, was "if possible, open up the Red River as a waterway as far as Yunnan, the chief obstacle to the accomplishment of which is the shallowness of the water".[126] The ship was appropriately named *Lao-kay*, signalling the wish of its owners to ascend the upper Red River as far as Lao Kay, the border town to China's Yunnan Province.

When the *Lao-kay* was launched in December 1888, its trial run fully justified expectations. The vessel, 33 metres long, 6.4 metres wide and with only 0.90 metres draught when loaded, passed the Song Tam Bac in Haiphong at low tide, "the depth of water being so little that at times

[125] *Haiphong illustré* (1895, 7–10) and Gantès (2008, 744).

[126] *The London and China Telegraph*, 29 June 1887, *South China Morning Post*, 25 July 1906. Tran (2017, 127).

the vessel was actually working her wheel over several inches of mud, leaving traces on either side like a steam digger, the engineers having great difficulty in keeping water in the boiler, as the cocks and roses on the ship's bilge were immersed in liquid mud".[127] When it entered the Cua Cam, the ship sailed with a speed of 9.5 knots, displaying excellent steering qualities. From April 1889, it was stationed in Viet Tri to serve lines on the Red River upstream to Yen Bay, on the Clear River to Tuyen Quang and on the Black River to Cho Bo. With the beginning of the heavy summer rains and the increasing water volume in the Red River, Abbadie decided to make the attempt to reach Lao Kay on the border with China. On 7 July 1889, the shipowner, accompanied by Mr Aka, the Vietnamese shipmaster, and an army and a naval officer, left Hanoi on board the *Lao-kay*. On 10 July, the day after departing from Yen Bay, the steamer reached the most dangerous rapid, known as Tac Cai (or Tac Van Cai), when the water was falling. It grounded a little above the rapid and was unable to move for nine days. Yet the most difficult part of the voyage was accomplished, and after another grounding lasting about three hours, the vessel reached Lao Kay on 24 July, anchoring at 8.30 a.m. in front of the citadel. As for the local reactions, *The China Mail* reported soon later: "Being the first steamer that has penetrated so far, the vessel was an object of great curiosity to the natives."[128]

The same day, Abbadie sent a telegram from Lao Kay to Marty who was at the time staying in Paris, immediately informing Eugène Étienne, sub-secretary of state for trade, industry and colonies about the success of his mission. Marty emphasised the lucky and important achievement of the ship "that we had specially built in our workshops of Haiphong, with the goal of overcoming the up to now insurmountable difficulties which the navigation of the upper Red River presented". Governor-General Jules Georges Piquet, in his letter to Étienne, pointed to the mission's wider implications when stating that the success of Abbadie "assures us soon the long-awaited opening of the trade route between Tonkin and Yunnan". In Hong Kong, the press was less enthusiastic, concluding that Abbadie had demonstrated the navigability of the Red River as far as Lao Kay, "at any rate, in certain seasons of the year". This statement echoed

[127] *The London and China Telegraph*, 29 June 1887.

[128] *The China Mail*, 16 July 1889 and *The Hong Kong Daily Press*, 16 and 27 July 1889. ANOM, SG-AF-V-84 (2): Marty et d'Abbadie, *Rapport sur le voyage du vapeur "Lao-Kay" à Lao-Kay* (Haiphong), August 1889.

the observations later made in the report from Abbadie, in which he made it clear that urgent works had to be carried out to specially clear the worst rocks in the river. He hinted at the fact that such improvements, which would not take too much time, should be made when the river's water volume was low. In the meantime, additional steamers of this special type should be constructed by Marty et d'Abbadie.[129]

The next vessel of the same type was named *Yunnan*, signalling the wider political-commercial goals in which the River Shipping Service was involved. After this stern-wheeler proved very effective, its successor was directly modelled after it. Named *Cho-bo*, the composite stern-wheeler was 40 metres long, 6.70 metres wide and had an average maximum draught of only 0.61 metres when unloaded. At its launch from the dockyard of Marty et d'Abbadie, on 15 September 1891, the honours were performed by the most senior French naval officer in the region, Rear Admiral François Ernest Fournier, the commander of the Far East Naval Squadron, and Marty's daughter, Clotilde Emmanuelle, the wife of the Haiphong manager of A. R. Marty, Etienne Rousé.[130] Another vessel of the same type was the *Pho-lu*, 35 metres long and 6.50 metres wide, having when empty a draught of only 0.60 metres and when loaded of 0.95 metres. With its condenser compound engine and single propeller, it reached a speed of 9.5 knots. To protect the ship against impact from rocks with which the rapids of the upper Red River were scattered, the hull, made of soft steel, was divided into watertight compartments which were regarded as an indispensable precaution for shipping on these parts of the river.[131]

There is very little documentation on the crews of the paddle steamers, mostly occasional remarks in correspondence, travel reports and newspaper articles. Since shipmasters had to be French nationals (according to the stipulations of the subsidy contract), the Service employed naturalised Vietnamese and Chinese captains. British journalist Alfred Cunningham, when travelling on board a paddle steamer of the Service,

[129] ANOM, SG-AF-V-84 (2): Marty (Paris) to Sub-Secretary of State Étienne (Paris), 25 July 1889; Governor-General Piquet (Saigon) to Sub-Secretary of State Etienne (Paris), 1 September 1889; Marty et d'Abbadie, *Rapport sur le voyage du vapeur "Lao-Kay" à Lao-Kay* (Haiphong), August 1889. *The China Mail*, 31 July 1889.

[130] *The London and China Telegraph*, 3 November 1891.

[131] *Haiphong illustré* (1895, 8).

obviously encountered saving measures concerning crews when referring to "the commissaire, the official in charge who is captain and purser combined".[132] In the travel report by Marquis de Barthélemy, after his journey through northern Indochina in 1896–1897, the following information was provided about crews and routine procedures on board a paddle steamer:

> The vessels of the River Shipping Service operate in a real special and rather economic way. No French captain is on board but a purser (commissaire) charged with collecting the price of the passage, the food supplies, in one word everything administrative. Furthermore, the purser arranges departure times and stopovers. The Chinese captain is charged with the management of the ship and commands everything concerning shipping. The crews are entirely Chinese; from time to time, Annamites [Vietnamese] are employed.[133]

Experiences

At the time of the French conquest in 1884, northern Vietnam was an area almost lacking any roads at all and in which the numerous marshes and rice fields constituted a perpetual obstacle to fast communication between different places. Waterways were the main transport routes, but their natural conditions hardly made them suitable for navigation by steamships. The volume of the Red River, the main waterway of Tonkin, was frequently increased by heavy summer rains, which usually reached their climax in August. Furthermore, the river carried a great deal of sediment because of the large proportion of friable soils in the river basin. One cubic meter of river water had five hundred grams of silt during the dry season and three and a half kilograms during the floods. This led to changes in the river bed which was obstructed by shoals, which greatly hampered shipping.[134] Therefore, it seemed indispensable to the French colonial administration to improve shipping conditions on the Red River, its estuaries and other Tonkin watercourses and to establish a modern transport infrastructure. In the first phase of "mise en valeur" (1860s to the early 1900s), basic transport infrastructures were

[132] Cunningham (1902, 162).
[133] Barthélemy (1901, 10).
[134] Robequain (1944, 106–107).

needed to boost the economic development of the French colony, especially the trading sector. This project included an extended network of river shipping services, providing fast and reliable communication in order to economically develop the country and to further penetrate beyond its borders into the neighbouring Chinese provinces of Yunnan, Guangxi and Guangdong. The exploitation of northern Vietnam and penetration into south-western China went hand in hand when initiating an effective riverine network in Tonkin.

In the late nineteenth century, France could boast long experience in improving her waterways. In the pre-industrial economies of Europe, inland waterways had formed the backbone of the transport system. In the absence of useable roads, long haul of passengers and goods via rivers, lakes and canals was the preferred, and often, the only mode of transport available. In the eighteenth century, the improvement of these lines became the basic concerns of mercantile policies, especially in France and Prussia. Throughout most of Europe, the importance of river and canal transport increased in the early nineteenth century with the beginning of industrialisation. In France, shipping on rivers and canals was until the mid-nineteenth century almost exclusively carried out by boats hauled by horses. Therefore, a voyage from Rouen, the port city on the River Seine in Normandy, to Paris, of around 150 kilometres, usually took fifteen to eighteen days. During the Second Empire of Napoleon III (1852–1870), considerable government loans were granted to carry out improvements works on the Seine which helped to speed up river transport. To make shipping more reliable, the first haulage companies (still employing horses) and steam traction systems were operated on French rivers and canals from the 1850s to the early 1870s. After the French government had agreed to the so-called Freycinet Plan (named after Charles de Freycinet, Minister of Public Works), France's large network of waterways was considerably developed and extended from 1879, including the construction of canals and locks. The most important works were undertaken on the Lower Seine to facilitate communications with the capital Paris.[135]

Tonkin river improvement schemes were carried out by the Public Works Service of Marty et d'Abbadie (headed in 1895 by the French engineer Brossard), charged with canalisation, dredging and other general

[135] Merger (1995, 182–196).

amelioration projects, particularly on the Canal des Bambous (Bamboo Canal) connecting Haiphong with Nam Dinh. At the Red River, banks were frequently strengthened to limit changes in the river's course.[136] With large improvement works continuing on the upper Red River, the River Shipping Service was able to considerably expand its operations.[137] Therefore, in 1893, Governor-General de Lanessan, on behalf of the Protectorate of Annam-Tonkin, began new negotiations with Marty et d'Abbadie. The contractual requirements of 1886 and 1888 had to be adjusted to the changing conditions of the Service's river network. The number of voyages on the main route between Haiphong and Hanoi was reduced by half (from six to three weekly departures), and six new lines serving the upper Red River, the Clear River and the Black River were introduced. The longest route remained the river and coastal line from Nam Dinh to Vinh, covering a distance of 202 miles. The total distance to be covered was slightly increased to 212.368 miles (210.392 miles in 1888) and the overall subsidy was fixed at an annual 690,196 francs (599,000 francs in 1888), with 3.25 francs paid per travelled mile, which implied a slight decrease. The main conditions were almost equal to those of 1886 and 1888, but the protectorate reserved the right to reduce certain voyages or to completely remove one or several lines, without the number of anticipated miles being reduced by more than a sixth. Furthermore, the protectorate had the right to demand the creation of supplementary lines or an increase in the number of anticipated voyages. In return, Marty et d'Abbadie retained their exclusive rights and monopoly on river shipping in Tonkin, while the protectorate promised not to subsidise any other river shipping company. Marty et d'Abbadie announced they would continue improvement and maintenance work on the rivers of Tonkin and Annam. For this, the protectorate granted them the impressive sum of more than three million francs,

[136] *Haiphong illustré* (1895, 9–10), Robequain (1944, 106) and Tran (2017, 136–137).

[137] The 1891 edition of the *Guide des Voyageurs* (Travellers' Guide) published by Marty et d'Abbadie contained a comprehensive overview of the fleet of 21 river ships, with detailed information on ticket prices for passengers and cargoes, times of departures, customs regulations of Haiphong and fees for mail and telegrams. A few advertisements for private businesses in Haiphong, Hanoi, Hong Kong and Macao obviously contributed to the printing costs of the booklet, totally comprising 66 pages and an additional hand-drawn map at the end showing the main destinations of the River Service.—Marty et d'Abbadie (1891).

paid annually and including materials.[138] When the subsidy contract expired on 31 December 1896, it was extended for another ten years, from 1 January 1897 to 31 December 1906.[139]

In 1902, Alfred Cunningham was full of praise about the River Shipping Service, referring especially to the owners of Marty et d'Abbadie "to whose energy and commercial acumen its success is due". He summed up his impressions of the river ships as follows:

> The steamers of this company provide the means of personal communication with the interior; they transport the troops and carry the traveller; they convey the mails and cargo to the inner-most of the colony, and where at last the rivers are too shallow to admit of stern-wheel steamers drawing two feet of water, the service is resumed by native boats of this Company and others working with it. The fleet is subsidised by the Government; the vessels are well equipped and provide an amount of comfort that is surprising considering the size of some of them.[140]

According to Vietnamese historian Van Kien Tran, the improvement of the waterways was a more economical investment compared to railways and fixed roads because the merchants knew very well how to make the most of the steamers. Before the construction of the railway from Haiphong via Hanoi to Yunnan, the paddle steamers connecting Haiphong and the Red River Delta with other parts of the country were not only useful and less costly than other means of transport, but above all they took up less time than the rudimentary means of the Vietnamese such as dump trucks, ox or buffalo carts and wheelbarrows. Even in the 1920s, when the railway network had been considerably extended, many agricultural centres in northern Vietnam depended on steamships

[138] ANOM, INDO-GGI-7526: *Contrat pour le Service des Correspondances Fluviales du Tonkin, Marty et d'Abbadie, Haiphong – Service Postal Fluvial et Côtier*, F.-H. Schneider, Haiphong, 1893.

[139] ANOM, SG-AF-V-84 (2): *Contrat passe avec M. M. Marty et d'Abbadie le 16 septembre 1893. Acte additionnel au dit contrat, en date du 2 novembre 1893.* ANOM, INDO-GGI-6275: Marty et d'Abbadie (Haiphong) to Resident Superior Rodier (Hanoi), 23 September 1893, Resident Superior Rodier (Hanoi) to Governor-General de Lanessan (Hanoi), 28 September 1893.

[140] Cunningham (1902, 160–161).

to transport their products to market towns, which made it necessary to constantly improve and secure the waterways.[141]

The character of Marty et d'Abbadie as a state monopolist involved close government supervision over its operations, which becomes obvious in the following example. When the Bamboo Canal waters were low, making it necessary in early March 1893 to quickly amend the operation times of the line from Haiphong to Nam Dinh and Vinh, the Service was obliged to formally request authorisation from the Resident Superior, François Pierre Rodier, which was granted after ten days.[142] The company's privileged character did not spare it from friction with Vietnamese people, as the following case demonstrates. According to Marty et d'Abbadie, the River Shipping Service repeatedly met with "the worst passion" of Vietnamese local authorities and residents. This wording was used in a letter from Marty et d'Abbadie in September 1892, in which the firm complained that in almost all cases when one of their vessels ran aground and junks and "coolies" were needed to refloat it (for which they were largely remunerated by the company), the village authorities were absent and the inhabitants either fled or withdrew into their houses. "In short, we cannot get anything, and we are limited to write to the [French] Resident of the province and wait sometimes for a long time before getting the necessary help", the letter explained. Therefore, Marty et d'Abbadie requested that the viceroy of Tonkin [the Vietnamese Imperial Commissioner of Tonkin, *kinh luoc*] should issue a requisition with his seal for each ship which the company's representatives, in case of need, could present to the villages closest to the stranding to obtain help and assistance of junks, coolies and other things. On 10 October 1892, the imperial commissioner did, as requested, provide a letter which instructed all responsible Vietnamese authorities of villages located on rivers used by vessels of the River Shipping Service to provide active support in cases of stranding. Consequently, the Resident Superior recommended to Marty

[141] Tran (2017, 139) and Maybon (1931, 82).

[142] VNA1, RST-63: Subsidised River Service of Tonkin, Marty et d'Abbadie (Haiphong), to Resident Superior (Hanoi), 8 March 1893 (the reply dated 18 March 1893).

et d'Abbadie that they should provide this document to their representatives posted in the provinces of the Red River Delta so that they could make use of it should the need arise.[143]

The concrete reasons for the negative attitude of the Vietnamese towards the River Shipping Service are not evident from the file. Another case made it obvious that the alleged poor service and exaggerated fees were responsible for a complaint by a French resident. While Marty et d'Abbadie encountered almost no competition on rivers due to the difficult conditions on these waterways that required specially fitted vessels, the situation was different on the coastal route to Vinh on which, in 1892, the French firm Roque Frères turned up as a rival, with the merchant steamer *Agnès* transporting all kinds of cargoes for lower fees than the *Annam* and the other Marty et d'Abbadie vessels charged. One of the clients of the *Agnès* was the wood trader Frédéric Mange, based in Ben Thuy, a small port in the mouth of the Ca River near Vinh. In October 1895, he was confronted with a situation where the vessel was not available due to repair works in Hong Kong. When approaching the agency of the River Shipping Service in Vinh to enquire about fees for shipping certain kinds of heavy woods, he was informed that the transport fees were twice as high as before and that his cargo was not suitable to be shipped. The merchant used the opportunity to launch a major complaint against Marty et d'Abbadie, criticising the overall technical condition of the *Annam*, inefficient insurances for cargoes and the bad handling of shipped goods by negligent staff. The case was followed up by the deputy mayor of Vinh who, in his letter to Ernest Albert Brière, Resident Superior of Annam, confirmed the validity of the complaints, suggesting the imposition of stricter obligations on the River Shipping Service to remedy the deficiencies of its ships and services. In January 1896, the company defended itself, rejecting the complaints as groundless and saying that Mange had been compensated for his losses. The reply did not comment on the complaints in detail but praised the vessels of the Service, pointing

[143]VNA1, RST-2420: Marty et d'Abbadie (Haiphong) to the Resident Superior of Tonkin (Hanoi), 22 September 1892; Order of Kinh Luoc of Tonkin (Hanoi), 10 October 1892; Resident Superior of Tonkin (Hanoi) to Marty et d'Abbadie (Haiphong), 19 October 1892. The Kinh Luoc [imperial commissioner] was invested with a delegation of Vietnamese imperial power, imposed by the French on the court of Hue on 27 July 1886. This act separated Tonkin from the direct control of Annam and established a kind of opposition between the Vietnamese in Tonkin and in Annam, which considerably contributed to France's full control over Indochina. Brocheux and Hèmery (2009, 61).

to the fact that they were preferred by Chinese and Vietnamese who were guaranteed fast and secure voyages.[144]

During the Sino-Japanese War (1894–1895), when a large number of merchant steamships commonly available in the South China Sea were hired for transports by the belligerent powers, Marty tried to make the most gain from the temporary monopoly of the Compagnie de Navigation Tonkinoise (Tonkin Shipping Company) on the run between Haiphong and Hong Kong to drastically increase freight rates of shipments on his vessels. This prompted Chinese loaders in Beihai (Pakhoi) and Haikou (Hoihow) to establish a boycott syndicate which chartered German steamers. A similar action by the Chinese targeted the River Shipping Service which was confronted with an extended boycott directed against its fleet. The Chinese company Kouoang-Yun-Pang, based in Mengzi, Yunnan Province, required its members in China and in Tonkin by statute and under penalty of punishment not to load any cargoes onto Marty's river ships making transit voyages on the Red River across the Chinese province of Yunnan. The action seemed well-co-ordinated on the Chinese side, increasing the effectiveness of the shipping boycott in the South China Sea.[145]

Railways as Competitors

In June 1897, after the Lyon trading mission (which explored opportunities to promote French trade with China) had returned to France, the Lyon Chamber of Commerce published a preliminary report about its findings which was sent to various French banks and industries. One of the most important results was the finding that the Red River was regarded as the most suitable way to penetrate China from Tonkin. This notion was consequently supported by the French minister in Beijing, Auguste Gérard, and Foreign Minister Gabriel Hanotaux who gave the

[144] ANOM, INDO-GGI-3336: Frédéric Mange (Ben Thuy) to Resident of France (Vinh), 23 October 1895; Vice Resident of France (Vinh) to Resident Superior Brière (Hue), 25 October 1895; Resident Superior Brière (Hue) to Governor-General Fourès (Hanoi), 5 November 1895; Governor-General Fourès (Hanoi) to Marty et d'Abbadie (Haiphong), 24 December 1895; Marty et d'Abbadie (Haiphong) to Governor-General Fourès (Hanoi), 15 January 1896.

[145] ANOM, INDO-GGI-19925: Minister Gérard (Beijing) to Governor-General Fourès (Hanoi), 27 November 1895. *L'Extrême-Orient*, 21 November 1895: Le Chinois au Tonkin.

green light to begin negotiations with the Chinese government for the concession of building a railway into Yunnan.[146] In December 1897, Governor-General Paul Doumer presented his visionary and ambitious programme of a large Indochinese railway system in the session of the Superior Council of Indochina. However, his plan, comprising a network of 3,200 kilometres to be built for the estimated sum of 400 million francs, was drastically reduced and then adopted by the Superior Council in September 1898. The project comprised four lines covering 1,700 kilometres: the first one, in north-westerly direction, from Haiphong via Hanoi to Lao Cai; the second one, as an extension of the first one, on Chinese territory, from Lao Cai to Kunming (Yunnan-Fu); the third one, in a southerly direction, from Hanoi to Vinh via Nam Dinh, and the fourth in the south from Saigon to Lang Bian via Khan Hoa. After Doumer had successfully promoted the plan before the French Chamber of Deputies in December 1898, with an impressive speech which won the small majority of 298 votes against 243 votes, his reduced railway building project was principally agreed by parliament. On Christmas Day 1898, French President Felix Faure signed the respective law legally formalising the launch of the Indochinese railway building programme.[147]

In early 1899, the railway project started with the construction of 104 kilometres of line between Hanoi and Haiphong, through the densely populated Tonkin Delta with its numerous rice fields and irrigation trenches. The tracks had to be put down on embankments to safeguard the line from flooding by the Red River, as well as on several iron bridges. After the official opening on 25 June 1902, the line was initially served by two trains in each direction making the voyage in five hours; a few months later, due to the high demand, the frequency was increased to three trains per direction. The loss of business to the new railway line was soon felt by Marty et d'Abbadie and its Subsidised River Shipping Service, which in the early fall of 1902 were forced to increase their ticket fees for passengers and goods.[148]

[146] ANOM, SG-AF-V-84 (4): Colonial Ministry (Paris) to Governor-General Doumer (Hanoi), 27 February 1897; Governor-General Doumer (Hanoi) to Foreign Minister Lebon (Paris), 29 January 1898. Martonne (1897, 275) and Eli (1967, 118–119). For the Lyon trading mission, see Chapter 6 of this book.

[147] Eli (1967, 122–132), Rousseau (2014, 3–5) and Tran (2017, 140–142).

[148] *Bulletin du Comité de l'Asie française* (1902, August, 373), (1902, October, 453), (1902, December, 535–536: Beau's speech on 18 October 1902), Kolbe (1911, 203)

The next line to open was the 113-kilometre stretch from Hanoi to Nin Binh, which took place on 8 January 1903 in presence of the governor-general. It formed the first part of the longer line in a southern direction which was to connect Tonkin with Annam. The overall railway network, comprising at the time 385 kilometres, was increased to 450 kilometres with the opening, on 9 March 1903, of the line in a north-western direction from Hanoi to Vietri along the Red River. In his speech on the railway building project given at Hanoi on 20 March 1903, Robert de Caix, editor-in-chief of the *Bulletin du Comité de L'Asie Française*, France's major lobbyist organ for Indochina, called the lines of the Red River Delta a true success after personally gaining an excellent impression of its operation: the three trains on the line between Hanoi and Haiphong, and also the ones on the line from Hanoi to Nam Dinh, were nearly always full, especially the long wagons of the fourth class with Vietnamese and Chinese passengers and their belongings. The high demand meant that the Hanoi-Haiphong line, in both directions, was on the path to become profitable and was expected to almost remunerate its capital. On the other hand, as Caix admitted, the success of the railways had forced several vessels of the Subsidised River Shipping Service to cease operations on the route between Hanoi and Nam Dinh.[149]

In these circumstances, the governor-general was quick to make use of certain clauses of the subsidy contract with Marty et d'Abbadie permitting a reduction in the number of travelled miles of lines which had experienced decreasing demand from passengers and cargoes. The frequency of the River Shipping Service from Haiphong to Hanoi was cut from six to only two weekly voyages, other lines on which railways competed were also reduced, bringing down the overall number of 212.004 miles to 178.776 miles and resulting in considerable savings for the administration. These modifications decreed and signed by Governor-General Beau on 14 April 1903 were put into effect on 1 May 1903. Because of the building of the Tonkin railways parallel to the river way, as Marty later complained, the colonial administration had cancelled passenger and cargo transports on his ships three years before the 1897 contract

and Tran (2017, 142–143). ANOM, INDO-GGI-3342: Marty et d'Abbadie (Haiphong) to Governor-General Beau (Hanoi), 15 October 1902.

[149] *Bulletin du Comité de l'Asie française* (1903, February, 77) and (1903, April, 135–139). Rousseau (2014, 13, table 2).

terminated. This remark reflected the deep impact the railway building programme had on the operation of the paddle steamers' network.[150]

On 1 November 1903, the line from Hanoi to Vietri, the first part of the Yunnan Railway along the upper Red River, was inaugurated. Its extension up to Yen Bay, opened on 1 May 1904, had been impatiently awaited, as stated in the June 1904 edition of the *Bulletin du Comité de l'Asie française*, because it took steam launches three to four days to make the voyage from Hanoi to Yen Bay, with frequent groundings to be expected. Some months earlier, on 28 December 1903, the 54-kilometres extension line from Ninh Binh to Than Hoa was opened, connecting Hanoi with northern Annam. At the time, the growing Tonkin railway network, with Hanoi at the centre, comprised a total of 620 kilometres, with around fifty trains daily frequenting the central station of the capital city. The further extension from Than Hoa to Vinh, the major commercial centre and port of northern Annam, began in early 1904 and was completed on 17 March 1905, allowing travellers to go there directly from Hanoi without making any transfer; the overall length of the line was 326.7 kilometres. It also rendered almost superfluous the coastal line of the River Shipping Service operating once a week on the 202-miles route between Haiphong and Vinh.[151]

Facing the rapid development of the railway network, and the subsequent decrease in profits of the River Shipping Service resulting in financial losses of the entire river shipping network, it seemed sheer desperation when in early 1904, Marty et d'Abbadie offered to sell the government-general their entire fleet, workshops and real estate. The offer was combined with the proposal that the administration should operate such services on its own. The eight-page table the company submitted contained a detailed catalogue of its possessions, with facts and figures including concrete proposals for distributing them among different administrative units such as civil services, customs, public works and military services. At the end, in the section titled memorandum, the subsidy of 1.45 million francs, to be paid from 1 July 1904 to 31

[150] ANOM, INDO-GGI-3342: Decree of Governor-General Beau (Hanoi), 14 April 1903, with respect to the Subsidised River Shipping Service of Tonkin. ANOM, INDO-GGI-3402: August Raphael Marty (Haiphong) to Governor-General Beau (Hanoi), 8 December 1907.

[151] *Bulletin du Comité de l'Asie française* (1903, February, 77), (1904, February, 101), (1904, June, 301) and (1905, May, 195). Kolbe (1911, 264–265) and Tran (2017, 143).

December 1906, when the current contract expired, was specified. It concluded with the summary of overheads of the River Shipping Service for 1902 and 1903, combined with the indication that overall expenditure would be much lower should the administration no longer be contractually obliged to pay the subsidy, but would instead operate such services on its own behalf.[152]

It was obvious that the proposal had fallen on stony ground when in spring 1904 both the colonial government's Financial Control Section and Secretary-General Stanislas Broni strongly rejected the proposed comprehensive and immediate acquisition of the Service. The administration did not see any real advantage in such a deal, in light of the decreasing importance of transport on river ships competing with railways operating on the continuously increasing network. To invest capital in river shipping was regarded as rather useless, even though regions where railway lines were not at the planning stage would also in future depend on water transport. To satisfy such needs, it was argued, other private companies could later offer such services, but the administration should not charge itself with water transports, which were not lucrative and which tended to diminish the income of railways.[153]

After another round of consultations with different administrative services, Broni, in October 1904, submitted his final verdict to the governor-general, suggesting an immediate start to negotiations with Marty et d'Abbadie about cancelling or at least radically modifying the current contract. His prime goal was to achieve considerable cuts in subsidy payments, but also to keep up certain regular river shipping lines which were not competing with railways. Therefore, his proposal hinted that a number of lines should be abolished and others should be extended for a certain period of time; he further recommended purchasing some of the real estate of Marty et d'Abbadie which some administrative units had requested, but at more favourable prices than originally demanded by the company. Finally, he suggested rejecting the sales offer by Marty et d'Abbadie and waiting until the current contract expired. At that time, he hoped, the company would be less demanding when being

[152] ANOM, INDO-GGI-3340: Table *Distribution and Usage of Material of the River Shipping Service by the Administration*, not dated.

[153] ANOM, INDO-GGI-3340: Director of Financial Control (Hanoi) to Governor-General Beau (Hanoi), 30 April 1904; Secretary-General Broni (Hanoi) to Governor-General Beau (Hanoi), 8 May 1904.

urgently forced to sell its belongings on conditions more advantageous for the administration. With that letter, any correspondence about the issue ends, which suggests that negotiations were not entered into, obviously after Marty et d'Abbadie had rejected accepting any modifications to the current subsidy contract.[154] Some weeks later, in December 1904, Édouard Jules d'Abbadie passed away in Haiphong, leaving it to his partner to continue negotiations with the government about the final end of the River Shipping Service.

In July 1906, with the looming termination of the current subsidy contract, the government-general launched the invitation to tender for the next contract of river shipping services in Tonkin. The tender put in by the French firm Roque Frères was finally accepted. While the stipulations of the subsidy contract required Roque Frères to operate ships on the Red River and its estuaries below Hanoi, the subsidiary lines on the higher reaches of the rivers above Hanoi were contracted with another French firm, L'Union commercial indochinoise (The Indochinese Commercial Union), headquartered in Hanoi, which already possessed two newer paddle steamers and was able to start operating the lines quickly. Since the Roque Frères contract required the firm to employ an entirely new fleet of paddle steamers, it decided to contract four light-draught steel stern-wheel vessels in Hong Kong.[155]

In view of the fact that the entire river shipping service of Tonkin would in future be operated by a fleet of new paddle steamers, it was obvious that the river and costal steamers of Marty et d'Abbadie would become superfluous and needed to put on sale as soon as possible. Sales negotiations started in autumn 1906 when Jules Morel, managing director of Customs and Monopolies of Indochina, informally agreed with Marty on the purchase of the seagoing steamers *Vinh* and *Licorne* which were to be used for surveillance services on the coasts of Indochina, and of the river boats *Dragon*, *Cerf* and *Phénix* which were to be assigned to the administration's salt and alcohol transports in Cochin China and Cambodia. Since technical modifications were regarded as indispensable, Marty promised to carry out the requested alterations, refurbishments

[154] ANOM, INDO-GGI-3340: Secretary-General Broni (Hanoi) to Governor-General Beau (Hanoi), 10 October 1904.

[155] The further operation of the river shipping services in Tonkin after 1907 is documented in *Bulletin Économique de l'Indochine* (1914, September) and in *Annuaire Général de l'Indochine* (1915, 80).

and repairs of the vessels in the workshops of Marty et d'Abbadie and to hand over the ships in a perfect state. Yet, the final purchase prices were still to be fixed after a technical commission had carefully examined the modified vessels. With Governor-General Beau principally accepting the deal, Marty announced the delivery of the first finished ships, the *Vinh* and the *Phénix*, as early as 1 January 1907, and of the others during the first quarter of that year.[156]

Such intentions came to nothing when in early 1907 sales negotiations were suddenly terminated, leaving Marty with an investment of around 30,000 dollars for amending his ships. The possible reason for the breakdown of talks was the appearance of a new competitor, the Societé Générale de Remorquage et Transports in Formation in Cochinchina (General Company of Towing and Transports in Formation in Cochin China), with a capital of six million francs which in the autumn of 1906 had offered its services to Saigon. When the firm-to-be was finally charged with shipping salt on behalf of the Customs Administration of Cochinchina, it seemed superfluous to invest large sums in purchasing Marty's ships. After the shipowner was finally able, in October 1907, to sell the *Vinh* to an unknown purchaser, two months later, he made a final attempt at a deal, offering the administration the chance to buy the remaining four vessels. This offer was combined with demands for an extraordinary subsidy for the Guangzhouwan postal steamer service, which was no longer profitable, and for a navigation bonus for his vessels operating on the route between Haiphong and Hong Kong. Of his fleet of river and coastal steamers, he proposed the *Phénix* as a suitable yacht for the king of Cambodia, and the *Licorne*, *Dragon* and *Cerf* as appropriate for the Customs of Indochina. Although the sales offer found some sympathy among administrators, pointing to the need to financially support the French firm in its competition with other flags, Governor-General Beau put an end to such hopes in early 1908 when pointing to the fact that such "proposals are unrealisable in the current state of the budget of Indochina".[157]

[156] ANOM, INDO-GGI-3340: Jules Morel, Managing Director of Customs and Monopolies (Hanoi), to Governor-General Beau (Hanoi), 17 November 1906 and 6 December 1906.

[157] ANOM, INDO-GGI-3402: Auguste Raphael Marty (Haiphong) to Governor-General Beau (Hanoi), 8 December 1907; Director of Commercial and Industrial Services

Édouard Jules d'Abbadie (1853–1904)

On 18 June 1853, Édouard Jules d'Abbadie was born in Tonnay-Charente, a river port commune in Charente-Inférieure (Lower Charente), a maritime department of south-western France on the Atlantic Ocean coast. His father Antoine Édouard d'Abbadie, born 19 February 1820, the son of a local merchant, was a shop assistant (commis négociant), and his mother was the 24-year-old Johanne Juliane Böhlke (probably a German). The witnesses present at the official birth registration act were the 62-year-old broker (courtier) Arnaud Auguste Constantin and the 22-year-old assistant broker Antoine Ernest Constantin.[158]

At the time, around 3,500 people lived in the small town located on the right bank of the Charente River. Ever since the seventeenth century, Tonnay-Charente had stood economically in the shadow of Rochefort, the renowned site of a major navy and military arsenal and a "new town" created by the French kings. As Rochefort's small neighbour, by the mid-nineteenth century Tonnay-Charente had developed into a kind of warehouse for "eaux de vie" (brandies and cognacs), exported primarily to London and Liverpool. From 1840, the port operated a fleet of coastal ships which specialised in shipping English coal, wood (firewood, pedicle, planks and rings) and iron bars to the cognac distilleries at Rochefort and La Rochelle. This important trade grew steadily during the Second Empire of Napoleon III, especially after 1867, when Tonnay-Charente was connected to France's railway system and developed industries closely linked to trading and shipping (shipbuilding, brandy-distilling, iron founding and machine construction) as well as producing chemicals and coke. From 1880, cognac distilleries were established in Tonnay-Charente, exporting most of their products to Britain. An important feature of the department's internal communications was, and still is, the large number of navigable streams which water it. In the early twentieth century, five rivers furnished 143 miles of navigable waterways, with an additional 56 miles of coastal canals. The

(Hanoi) to Governor-General Beau (Saigon), 20 December 1907; Governor-General Beau (Saigon) to Director of Agriculture, Forests, and Trade (Hanoi), 17 January 1908.

[158] ACM, 2 E 472/24 – Tonnay-Charente, Collection du greffe, État civil, Naissances 1853–1862, no. 39: Édouard Jules d'Abbadie.

specific geographical and economic features of his home region certainly left a deep impression on the young Édouard Jules d'Abbadie.[159]

On 6 June 1865, his father Antoine Édouard passed away in Tonnay-Charente; at the time, his mother Johanne Juliane resided in Angoulême, capital of the Charente department. She later moved to Hamburg, and eventually lived in Stuttgart, Germany, where she passed away on 6 January 1882.[160] Therefore, Édouard Jules was listed in the registers of the Lower Charente department as a resident of Stuttgart when in 1873 he was called up to serve in the French military. Because he was residing abroad at the time, he was temporarily exempted from military duty in France. At an unknown date, he went to France to serve in the Infantry Regiment No. 693 stationed at La Rochelle, and on 1 July 1879 was transferred to the regular army's reserve. On 1 July 1883, he was reactivated for a time before leaving for Indochina. At the time, his official place of residence was in Rue de Berlin 4 in Paris. On 3 May 1884, Abbadie arrived in Haiphong. He became an interested employee in the trading firm operated by his uncle, Edmond Constantin, established in 1881 and agent of the major French shipping company Messageries Maritimes which operated the line from Saigon to Hong Kong via Haiphong. On 19 August 1884, Constantin was made president of the Consultative Chamber of Commerce of Haiphong at its creation by the Resident. However, for unknown reasons, he was not a member of the Chamber after its official establishment in November 1884. When in 1886 Messageries Maritimes opened its own office in Haiphong, Constantin lost the important agency. In February 1886, Abbadie became owner of his uncle's company. After winning the subsidy contract of the Protectorate of Annam-Tonkin, in September 1886, he became partner of Auguste Raphael Marty, in the joint company Marty et d'Abbadie, and director of the Subsidised River Shipping Service of Tonkin.[161]

159 https://fr.wikipedia.org/wiki/Tonnay-Charente (visited on 1 May 2020). Hercule (1985, 587). *The Encyclopaedia Britannica* (1910, V, 858).

160 ACM, 2 E 472–22: Tonnay-Charente, État civil – Mariages (1843–1852); ACM, Tonnay-Charente, Collection communale, État civil, Naissances Mariages Décès, 1864–1866: Antoine Édouard d'Abbadie.

161 *Haiphong Illustré* (1895, 7, 10), Imbert (1885, 157–158) and Raffi (1994, 130, 179–182).

Édouard Jules d'Abbadie had three sisters, the youngest of whom was Elisabeth (1863–1935), born in Angoulême on 9 December 1863. From around 1884/1885 to 1887, she stayed with her bachelor brother in Haiphong and acted as his hostess when he entertained guests at his home. In 1887, she came to know her later husband, the English engineer James Knight Rebbeck who was based at the Victoria Foundry in Hong Kong and designed and installed the braking system on the Peak Tram, the first cable car in Asia, built to link the commercial centre of Hong Kong with the summit of Victoria Peak. After Marty et d'Abbadie's first river ships had been built at the Hong Kong & Whampoa Dock Company, Rebbeck supervised the delivery of one of the paddle steamers to Haiphong where his first meeting with Elisabeth apparently took place.[162]

On 21 April 1892, Édouard Jules d'Abbadie married Clémentine Marie Guerrier in Tonnay-Charente.[163] The couple took up residence in Haiphong and had four children. In the years 1893 and 1897, Abbadie returned to France to take part in military exercises by an infantry unit in La Rochelle. In 1899, he formally switched his place of residence from France to French Indochina and enrolled into the Hanoi military list.[164] In the colony, Abbadie served in several honorary positions. For a long period, he was a member of the Conseil Supérieur (Upper Council) of Tonkin, the most important decision-making body in the Protectorate

[162] After the couple fell in love, Rebbeck returned to Hong Kong and sent a series of letter to his fiancée. Elisabeth d'Abbadie laid down her impressions of this time, mostly about land and people in Tonkin, in a book in English titled *The Home of the Dragon: A Tonquinese Idyll,* published in 1893 under the pseudonym Anna Catharina and dedicated to her husband, James Knight Rebbeck. The book's seven chapters contain some anecdotes from her stays in Haiphong and Hanoi, but are entirely silent about her brother, his partner Marty and their business activities in Tonkin. For detailed information, see: https://www.st-antonin.fr/document1/index.html (visited on 8 May 2020).

[163] ACM, Base État civil, Laval – 4 E 159/306 – (1892): Édouard Jules d'Abbadie - Clémentine Marie Guerrier. His wife was the 21-year old daughter of academic inspector Henri Simon Guerrier and Clémentine Josephine Bonaventur from Montluçon, an industrial town in the Allier Department of central France.

[164] ACM, 1 R 38, Classe 1873, Contingent départemental, matricules 1-1671, table alphabétique – La Rochelle: Édouard Jules d'Abbadie; ACM, Base État civil, Laval – 4 E 159/306 (1892): Édouard Jules d'Abbadie and Clémentine Marie Guerrier, 21 April 1892.

of Annam-Tonkin, the de facto government cabinet headed by the Resident Superior.[165] Additionally, he was an ordinary member, vice-president and finally president of the Haiphong Chamber of Commerce.[166] In the latter position, as *L'Avenir du Tonkin* wrote, he "gave this assembly a very active direction, solicitous about the important interests of the great port of Tonkin".[167] Additionally, he was tasked by the government-general in November 1902 with heading the state commission examining the situation in the French merchant navy in Indochina.[168] Abbadie achieved a senior position in local politics when, on 22 July 1902, with six out of seven votes, he was elected vice-president of Haiphong's municipal commission (Fig. 5.13).[169]

According to Marty, by 1903–1904 his partner Abbadie was clearly aware of the hopeless situation the River Shipping Service was in, facing increasing competition from the railways. Seeing his life's work coming to an end, Abbadie decided to take his wife and children back to France where the family took up residence in Rue Marbeuf 5 in Paris. Soon after, Abbadie returned to Haiphong.[170] It remains unclear when or where he became infected with hepatitis, an inflammation of the liver tissue resulting in persistent dysentery, which seems to have proved fatal. At 11.50 a.m. on 26 December 1904, at the age of fifty-one, Abbadie passed away in his house in Rue Jules Ferry in Haiphong.[171]

[165] *L'Avenir du Tonkin*, 29 December 1904. Brocheux and Hémery (2009, 81).

[166] *Haiphong Illustré* (1895, 7), *L'Avenir du Tonkin*, 29 December 1904. Raffi (1994, 304) and Villemagne (2008, 699–701).

[167] *L'Avenir du Tonkin*, 29 December 1904.

[168] *Le Courrier d'Haiphong*, 11 November 1902.

[169] VNA1, RST-3562: Extract of minutes of the extraordinary session of the municipal commission of the town of Haiphong, 22 July 1902; telegram of Resident Mayor (Haiphong) to Resident Superior (Hanoi), 23 July 1902. From 1898 to 1908, Haiphong had eleven town councils and three municipal commissions, demonstrating that municipal management was "chaotic and interrupted by a number of dissolutions". Brocheux and Hèmery (2009, 112).

[170] ANOM, INDO-GGI-3402: Auguste Raphael Marty (Haiphong) to Governor-General Beau (Hanoi), 8 December 1907.

[171] ANOM, Actes de l'État Civil: Tonkin, Haiphong, 1904–1905, Décès 1904: Édouard Jules d'Abbadie. The following day, the municipal officer, Alfred Logerat, prior to issuing the death certificate, consulted Auguste Raphael Marty and Lucien Marie Guerrier (the 36-year old brother-in-law of Abbadie and a state instruction officer at Quang Yen).

Fig. 5.13 Édouard Jules d'Abbadie, c. 1895 (ANOM, Aix-en-Provence: *Haiphong illustré: Supplément au Millième Numéro du Journal: Le Courrier d'Haiphong*, 24 December 1895—all rights reserved)

Abbadie's funeral took place in Haiphong two days later. High-ranking administrators from the port city and Hanoi joined members of the municipal council, the Haiphong Chamber of Commerce, army and navy officers and almost the entire European population in attending the ceremony. Julien Fourès, Resident Superior of Tonkin, gave the first oration, reminding his audience that Abbadie had been a member of the superior council of the protectorate for many years and had taken a keen interest in developing Tonkin's trade and industry. Furthermore, he described him as "an energetic and eloquent defender of Haiphong's commercial and maritime interests". Fourès also characterised Abbadie as "one of these robust pioneers", hailing him as "a bold and courageous initiator in commercial and industrial matters" who "organised this network of river shipping which, during almost twenty years, was one of the most important systems of economic and administrative life".[172] In contrast, Marty later wrote in a letter that his partner was "without fortune, but with some debts" which obliged him to care for Abbadie's four children who were left without sufficient financial means. After Marty had sold the entire fleet of river ships of Marty et d'Abbadie in 1906–1907, he gave the earnings to his late partner's widow, Clémentine, 125,000 dollars paid in three equal instalments by the end of 1908.[173]

The Tonkin Shipping Company

French Coastal Steamers in the South China Sea

In 1884, the trading firm A. R. Marty in Hong Kong began chartering tramp steamers of the M. Jebsen Shipping Company. At the time, the French merchant Auguste Raphael Marty was the agent of Roque Frères (Roque Brothers), the main supplier of France's naval squadron operating at different locations on the Vietnamese and Chinese coasts. The Jebsen vessels were obviously employed to transport provisions to French naval forces engaged in the South China Sea during the Sino-French War (1884–1885). According to the records of the M. Jebsen Shipping Company, the first vessel hired under time charter contract by Marty was the big steamer *Amigo*, of 821 tons. The rather short duration of this charter, which was noted but not further specified in the letter, and the chartering of a very small steamer, *Alwine*, of 400 tons, the following year, indicated that Marty needed to flexibly adjust to limited transport needs in order to operate the vessels profitably. When the war ended, the French merchant in early 1886 re-chartered *Alwine*, clear evidence to Jebsen that Marty was satisfied with the ship and its master.[174]

[172] *Le Courrier d'Haiphong*, 29 December 1904.

[173] ANOM, INDO-GGI-3402: Auguste Raphael Marty (Haiphong) to Governor-General Beau (Hanoi), 8 December 1907.

[174] JJHA, A01-01-215: Michael Jebsen (Apenrade) to Wieler & Co. (Hong Kong), 7 January 1885. JJHA, A01-01-217: Michael Jebsen (Apenrade) to Captain Peter Moos (Hong Kong), 14 April 1886 and 9 August 1886.

Haiphong's rapid development as a French colonial port city triggered increasing shipping traffic with Hong Kong. Using the German shipbroker Siemssen & Company in Hong Kong as middleman, in 1887 Marty hired the medium-sized Jebsen steamers *Marie*, of 704 tons, for the agreed monthly rate of 2,800 dollars, and *Clara*, of 675 tons, at an even lower rate, which Jebsen found too little. "The gentleman usually gets his steamers for cheaper rates than the Chinese, partly because he is financially more secure", Jebsen remarked of Marty's solidity in business. *Clara* was again chartered by Marty the following year under a twelve-month time charter contract, at the much higher monthly rate of 3,200 dollars, and operated by Roque Frères in Haiphong. After paying a visit to Haiphong in June 1888, Captain Jacob Hohlmann, master of *Marie*, was confident that his ship would be offered 3,400 dollars monthly by Marty because "our type of ship is in short supply here at the coast". Smaller steamers were in high demand, as Hohlmann commented one month later, but hardly available. This situation obliged the French merchant to finally agree to a monthly charter rate of 3,600 dollars over a period of twelve months. In early 1889, Marty, who was operating both *Marie* and *Clara* on time charter contracts, asked to hire the steamer *Else*, of 747 tons, for which Wieler & Co. demanded 4,200 dollars monthly for a period of twelve months. When the French merchant finally agreed to the request in March 1889, Michael Jebsen was convinced that this charter rate paid by a "financially solid" Marty would result in a considerable dividend for his shipping company. When the charter contract period for the Jebsen steamers expired in the early summer of 1890, Marty re-chartered the vessels for almost the same rates.[175]

According to *Le Courrier d'Haiphong*, the Jebsen steamers *Marie*, *Clara* and *Else*, chartered by the company A. R. Marty, were frequently plying between Hong Kong and Haiphong in 1890, transporting different kinds of goods and passengers, as well as the mail. In some editions, the French newspaper published detailed lists of cargoes, obviously to demonstrate Marty's efforts to promote Tonkin's trading and

[175] JJHA, A01-01-219: Michael Jebsen (Apenrade) to Siemssen & Co. (Hong Kong), 1 December 1887 (here the quote). LAA-SG090-2235-3-1: Captain Jacob Hohlmann (Hong Kong) to Michael Jebsen (Apenrade), 20 June 1888 and 27 July 1888. JJHA, A01-01-221: Michael Jebsen (Apenrade) to Jacob Diederichsen (Hamburg), 19 March 1889. JJHA, A01-01-222: Michael Jebsen (Apenrade) to Wieler & Co. (Hong Kong) and to Siemssen & Co. (Hong Kong), 8 July 1890.

improve the economic situation and living conditions of Haiphong residents. On 23 June 1890, *Else* carried from Haiphong to Hong Kong 18,454 bags of rice, 2,387 boxes of tin, 652 of guano (bird droppings), 226 of rattan, 69 of dried vegetables, 59 of oil, 41 of silk, and several other agricultural products. Three days later, *Marie* brought from the British colony 465 bags of coal, 400 boxes of petroleum, 306 bags of flour, 223 boxes of potatoes, 188 of medicine, 162 of tea, 118 bales of spun cotton, 82 boxes of furniture, 61 of vegetables, 50 bags of scrap iron, 48 boxes of milk, 29 of alum, 24 of tobacco and of vermicelli, and several other industrial products and foodstuffs.[176] Some details on passengers were provided when the newspaper reported the voyage of *Clara* which departed from Haiphong for Hong Kong on 28 September 1890 with ten Chinese males, one woman and six children, an Indian and six sailors from the British vessel *Kitty*. On her next voyage the steamer encountered minor engine trouble on the route, forcing Captain C. H. Christensen to return to Haiphong, where the steamer arrived on 24 October to be repaired at the wharf of Marty et d'Abbadie.[177]

In January 1891, the company A. R. Marty in Hong Kong chartered the Danish steamer *Activ*, of 355 tons, employing the vessel on the route between Hong Kong and Haiphong for transporting cargoes and mail. The small ship was owned by the Dampskibsselskabet Activ (Activ Steamship Company), established in Randers, the Danish port city on the northern Jutland peninsula, in 1872. Another vessel plying the China Seas was the steamer *Frejr* of the Randers Dampskibsselskab af 1866 (Randers Steamship Company of 1866). The two ships represented 87 per cent of Denmark's share of Hong Kong shipping in 1887; the remainder was divided between the single steamer of the Store Nordiske Telegrafselskabs (Danish Telegraph Company) and the Copenhagen steamer *Norden*. In 1889, the Danish consul in Hong Kong told the foreign ministry in Copenhagen that the Randers vessels' earnings were "particularly good". The success of its vessel encouraged the Activ Steamship Company to order another steamer fitted specially for coastal shipping in East Asia. The steamer named *Ask*, of 670 tons, built on the B & W Shipyard in Copenhagen in 1891, made its maiden voyage to Saigon, where it was chartered by Denis Frères and sent with cargoes to Hong Kong,

[176] *Le Courrier d'Haiphong*, 3 July 1890.

[177] *Le Courrier d'Haiphong*, 2 and 26 October 1890.

arriving on 28 January 1892. Marty was next to hire the brand-new ship instead of re-chartering Jebsen's *Clara,* operating the Danish vessel on the route between Hong Kong and Haiphong.[178]

On 1 May 1892, *Le Courrier d'Haiphong,* publishing the annual shipping overview, stated that Haiphong's entire coastal trade with China was operated by foreign vessels in 1891. The newspaper went on as follows: "We saw very often, with a feeling a sadness, that of eight to ten ships anchoring in Haiphong's harbour, not a single one was flying the French flag. This situation is not specific in Tonkin because it recurs in even sharper form in the way of abstention in all Far Eastern ports".[179] The weak presence of the French flag in East Asia was a sore point in the eyes of the Tonkin press and appealed to the national pride of French communities around the South China Sea. Such public backing provided sufficient motivation for Marty to acquire his own vessels, which would fly the French Tricolour flag. His order of two new steamers was placed at the Sunderland Shipbuilding Company. Sunderland, a north-eastern English port city, had an important shipbuilding industry in the nineteenth century, with several wharfs producing a large number of wooden, and later, steel ships. Yet, the main reason for Marty to order vessels in Britain and not in France certainly had to do with the fact that British shipyards offered more competitive prices than their French counterparts. In spite of generous shipbuilding bounties granted in France's subsidy law of 29 January 1881, higher costs made French yards unable to compete with British shipbuilders. Therefore, it was more advantageous for French shipowners to have their vessels built on British stocks and to receive half the navigation bounty for long sea voyages (navigation au long cours), as fixed in the law of 1881, than to pay the prices demanded in France. The two vessels built to the Marty order were specially constructed for the difficult shipping conditions in Tonkin, with a draught of water of only 13 feet 6 inches, to enable them to pass the bar at Haiphong on any tide with a full cargo. The first vessel, named *Hanoi*, of 658 tons, arrived in Hong Kong on 16 June 1893 and was immediately put into service. Her slightly larger, but otherwise identical, sister ship named *Hongkong*, of 738 tons, followed soon after. Both vessels were fully equipped with electric light,

[178] *Le Courrier d'Haiphong*, 5 and 15 February 1891, 12 March 1891, 4 February 1892 and 28 April 1892. Bach (2014, 54–55).

[179] *Le Courrier d'Haiphong*, 1 May 1892.

cabins and a salon for twenty-four first class passengers and special deck arrangements for other passengers. With modern triple-expansion engines of 1,050 horse power, the steamers reached a maximum speed of 12.5 knots. After the acquisition of the two vessels, Marty established the Compagnie de Navigation Tonkinoise (Tonkin Shipping Company), an affiliate of Marty et d'Abbadie. The company A. R. Marty in Hong Kong and Haiphong was made main agent of the Tonkin Shipping Company.[180]

The presence of Marty's new vessels under the French flag was reflected in Haiphong's shipping statistics. In 1894, the port authority registered 115 entries of ships flying the French flag, the highest ever number, while the German flag considerably decreased to a mere twenty ships, and thus to third-ranked place after the British flag, which had twenty-six vessels in the harbour. On 29 December 1894, to further boost the development of French shipping in Indochina and China, the colonial ministry instructed the governor-general of Indochina to grant navigation bounties to French vessels operating in those waters. With the decree of 15 March 1895, Acting Governor-General François Pierre Rodier granted a bounty of 60 cents per ton of freight exported by French vessels from any port of the Protectorate of Annam-Tonkin. This was direct monetary support for the Tonkin Shipping Company, which shared traffic under the French flag only with the mail liners of Messageries Maritimes calling frequently at Saigon, Haiphong and smaller ports on the coast of Indochina. A French steamer of 600 tons, receiving 360 dollars for the two day voyage from Haiphong to Hong Kong, would cover most of its expenses, Peter Kempermann, German consul-general in Bangkok, told the foreign ministry in Berlin. He expected that "French shipping on this route will again take up the struggle with German and British vessels". However, the diplomat pointed to the fact that Chinese merchants, who dominated traffic in the region, usually preferred German and British vessels when chartering foreign ships to transport cargoes and passengers, including "coolies". Kempermann noted that French masters had the reputation of being pernickety and rarely accommodating, probably due to stricter regulations concerning the usage of holds, cabins and decks for storing cargoes. Furthermore, Chinese merchants had "no confidence in the ability of French masters as seamen". Therefore, the consul-general did not expect any long-lasting impact of the new bounty on shipping

[180] *The London and China Telegraph*, 8 August 1893. Raffalovich (1888, 154) and Dubois (1900, 294–295).

markets in Indochina.[181] However, the M. Jebsen Shipping Company did not accept the situation so easily. In January 1895, Michael Jebsen asked his son Jacob to pay a personal visit to Marty in Hong Kong to reach an agreement, adding that the French shipowner "should be pleased if you would talk French with him, of which Wielers [the German shipping agent Wieler & Company based in Hong Kong] have no clue". This remark pointed to Jacob Jebsen's French language skills which he had acquired at school. Yet, there is no further correspondence on the matter.[182]

Marty's fleet was soon growing further. On 7 April 1896, the Danish steamer *Activ*, hired by A. R. Marty under a time charter contract, was stranded some ten sea miles from Hainan Island, while on the voyage from Beihai to Haikou. The cargo and passengers were shipped on junks to Haikou and transferred to Marty's vessel *Hongkong* which brought them to the British colony. After Hong Kong dock officials had examined the ship, the Danish owners decided to abandon it as being in too bad a condition to be saved. The wreck was put up for auction in Hong Kong on 6 May 1896 and sold to Marty for only 1,500 dollars, "so the purchaser is to be congratulated upon his successful speculation", wrote *The London and China Telegraph*. Subsequently, the French shipowner entrusted chief engineer Jack with saving and repairing the ship. After the wreck had been beached and examined on Hainan Island, it was towed to the British colony by the *Hongkong* on 16 June 1896 and transferred to the Hong Kong & Whampoa Dock Company for further repairs. Michael Jebsen was rather unhappy about Marty purchasing the ship, predicting increased competition in the shipping market of the South China Sea. The *Activ* "is very well-known and also very popular on the route, and I am wondering why you did not have your eye on it", he blamed his son Jacob. After the repairs were finished, the ship was renamed *Hailan* and

[181] Raffi (1994, 602: Table 1). *Journal Officiel de l'Indochine Française: Deuxième partie* (1895, 18 March). BAB, R 901-12956: Consul-General Peter Kempermann (Bangkok) to Chancellor von Hohenlohe-Schillingsfürst (Berlin), 16 April 1895.

[182] JJHA, A01-01-318: Michael Jebsen (Apenrade) to Jacob Jebsen (Hong Kong), 3 January 1895.

put under the French flag, with a Danish master and two Danish officers and mechanics each.[183]

The huge compensation paid by the Chinese government for the losses the Tonkin Shipping Company encountered during the Chinese boycott of 1895–1896 provided sufficient funds for Marty to purchase three older medium-sized tramp steamers, namely the *Hoihow* (formerly *Fokien*), of 508 tons, a British vessel bought from the Douglas Steamship Company in Hong Kong, the *Haeting* (formerly *Smith*), of 705 tons, and the *Hue* (formerly *Cass*), of 703 tons, launched in June 1888 by the British shipyard Hawthorn, Leslie & Company in Newcastle-on-Tyne, which had serviced a Chinese trading house. According to Jacob Jebsen's information, Marty paid between four thousand and five thousand British pounds for each of the used vessels, prices the German shipowner was not willing to pay for them. He told his father: "One of them is always in the dock for repair". Comparing Marty's new vessels, which he knew in some detail, Jebsen was not very impressed, declaring that the *Else* [747 net and 974 gross tonnes] had more loading capacity than the *Hue*, the *Haeting* and the *Hailan* in total and was consuming less than half the coal; however, the *Hue* and the *Haeting* were four miles faster than the *Else* (Fig. 5.14).[184]

With these acquisitions, the Tonkin Shipping Company fleet reached its peak in 1898, comprising six steam coasters, the highest number in its more than twenty-year existence.[185] However, without sufficient capital in hand to acquire newer ships, Marty refrained from regularly modernising his fleet by replacing older vessels with newer ones. This practice resulted in costly repairs and extra costs for chartering other ships

[183] *The Singapore Free Press and Mercantile Advertiser*, 21 April 1896, *The Hong Kong Telegraph*, 30 May 1896 and *The London and China Telegraph*, 7 July 1896. JJHA, A01-01-314: Michael Jebsen (Apenrade) to Jacob Jebsen (Hong Kong), 23 July 1896. *The Chronicle & Directory* (1899, 589).

[184] *The Chronicle & Directory* (1894, 458), (1899, 589). JJHA, A01-01-294: Jacob Jebsen (Hong Kong) to Michael Jebsen (Apenrade), 25 November 1898. Hieke (1953, 226).

[185] In the obituary for Marty (published in 1940), the anonymous author mentioned that the Tonkin Shipping Company was operating "the first liners of the China seas carrying the French flag and greatly facilitating our relations with Hong Kong. To there, they transported tens of thousands of tons of rice because at that time a lot of rice left Tonkin for China. The 'Marty ships' were universally known and appreciated." *Bulletin Trimestriel de la Société Amicale des Anciens Tonkinois* (1940, 12).

Fig. 5.14 Steamship *Hue* of the Tonkin Shipping Company, c. 1910 (ANOM, Aix-en-Provence, INDO-GGI-1868—all rights reserved)

serving as temporary replacements. In July 1900, at the end of the rice exporting season, when rice prices decreased in Hong Kong due to oversupply from Tonkin, the *Hanoi* had to undergo major repairs, prompting Marty to charter a steamer of the China Merchants Steam Navigation Company (the major Chinese shipping company) for the high freight rate of monthly 7,500 dollars. Johann Heinrich Jessen believed that "in the current situation of the Hong Kong rice market, with supplies from Haiphong going to be diminished", this charter would mean losses for Marty.[186]

In early 1900, the Tonkin Shipping Company was granted a ten-year postal subsidy contract to operate a postal steamer service between Haiphong and Guangzhouwan, France's leased territory intended to serve as a military outpost in southern China. Under the stipulations of the contract, the company was obliged to frequently conduct shipments of mail, troops and cargoes to and from Guangzhouwan. As became evident, these transports were the only profitable element of the service operating in the highly competitive shipping market of the South China

[186] LAA, SG090-2252-4: Johann Heinrich Jessen (Hong Kong) to Jacob Jebsen (Apenrade), 29 July 1900.

Sea. The unexpected decision to abandon plans for the territory significantly impacted the Guangzhouwan postal steamer service, making the line no longer profitable for the Tonkin Shipping Company. With the line deprived of its main source of income, the service became a financial burden to Marty who was unable to amend or terminate the subsidy contract, which finally passed into the hands of the Compagnie de l'Est Asiatique française (French East Asiatic Company) in 1910. However, the subsidised Guangzhouwan postal steamer service proved economically unattractive to travellers and cargoes, apparently serving only to bolster feelings of prestige and honour among French politicians, administrators and shipowners alike. Yet, with the stipulations of the new subsidy contract amended, the service offered stable income, encouraging Marty to again secure the service for his firm. The Guangzhouwan postal steamer service operated by the Tonkin Shipping Company from 1913 to 1918, and finally relinquished for financial reasons, was the last visible activity of Marty's small fleet of steam coasters.[187]

The Tonkin Shipping Company was also affected by severe losses. In July 1904, the *Hoihow* ran aground in the Hainan Strait. After discharging her cargo, the ship later sank in deepwater and attempts to salvage the wrecked vessel were unsuccessful.[188] The loss of the *Hoihow* meant that the strength of Marty's ocean-going fleet was decreased to five steamships, while its main competitor, Jebsen & Co., had seventeen. With the Guangzhouwan postal steamer service generating huge losses after the withdrawal of most of the territory's troops, and with the unexpected death of Édouard Jules d'Abbadie, the company was reeling from three fateful setbacks in 1904. Furthermore, the global oversupply of shipping tonnage in the first decade of the twentieth century obliged an increasing number of shipping companies to send their steamers to East Asia, resulting in fiercer competition in Chinese shipping markets. Consequently, freight rates decreased and steamship companies saw very low earnings between 1904 and 1911.[189] For Marty, the situation in his Tonkin Shipping Company, operating exclusively between Haiphong and Hong Kong, was even further heavily impacted by the M. Jebsen

[187] For details of the Guangzhouwan postal steamer service, see Chapter 6 of this book.

[188] *The Hong Kong Telegraph*, *South China Morning Post*, *The China Mail*, all dated 25 May 1904.

[189] Gregg (1921, 613–614).

Shipping Company's strong performance. In February 1907, the French shipowner suffered a fresh disaster when the *Haeting* went ashore on Hainan Island and was lost.[190]

While the M. Jebsen Shipping Company had only two vessels on this run in 1896, it operated a regular line between Hong Kong and ports in the Protectorate of Annam-Tonkin (Haiphong, Tourane and Quin Hon) with seven vessels in 1907, frequently shipping rice and other agricultural produce to the British colony. According to Johann Heinrich Jessen, co-owner of Jebsen & Co., his firm succeeded in "significantly increasing this initially not very important trade" providing "regular and profitable employment" for its steamers.[191] An agreement between Jebsen and Marty on keeping freight rates at a certain level (20 cents per rice bag) on the route from Haiphong to Hong Kong avoided a ruinous price war and secured profitable business for both sides. The unexpected appearance of the China Navigation Company, the shipping arm of the British firm Butterfield & Swire, in the rather closed shipping market between Hong Kong and French Indochina in April 1907 caused considerable concern, prompting Jebsen and Marty to reach an agreement with Butterfield on a 20 per cent decrease in rice shipment freight rates. While Jebsen & Co. was able to compensate for lower profits on this route with higher earnings on other routes in East Asia, the French shipowner was left with few other options. According to Jacob Jebsen, Marty's company operated "less economically than ours and the one of Butterfield".[192]

As a result, Marty tried to sell his ships, but as the British consul Savage in Qiongzhou reported, they were "more or less worn out", making it difficult to find buyers.[193] Dr. Rudolf Walter, the German consul in Beihai, wrote that the Tonkin Shipping Company was "only barely keeping above water" in 1907, having repeatedly offered its vessels to other shipping companies. "Because of the excessive coal consumption, and consequently the costly maintenance of the ships, the offers

[190] *The Straits Times*, 4 March 1907.

[191] BAB, R 901-17972: Johann Heinrich Jessen: Report on the situation of coastal shipping in South China, 3 October 1907.

[192] PAAA, Peking II-1174: Jacob Jebsen (Hong Kong) to Consul von Varchmin (Beihai), 13 February 1908. Becker (2020, 948–949).

[193] TNA, FO 228-1661: Consul V. L. Savage (Qiongzhou, Hainan) to Minister Sir John Jordan (Beijing), 26 April 1907.

were always turned down", the consul explained.[194] The Tonkin Shipping Company fleet's technical lag becomes even more glaring when considering that the M. Jebsen Shipping Company operated thirteen steamers in 1907. Seven of them, built between 1901 and 1904, boasted considerably larger tonnages than earlier vessels and were equipped with the latest ship technology.[195]

From 1891 to 1904, coal supplies for both river and ocean-going vessels of the Tonkin Shipping Company came from the Édouard Mine located in Hai Duong Province, north-west of Haiphong, owned by Marty et d'Abbadie. In 1901, Auguste Raphael Marty became sole proprietor of the Mao Khe coal mine located in Quang Ninh Province, north of Haiphong, and close to the rich coal fields of Hon Gay. The mine was managed by the engineer Duclos, assisted by a mining master and an accountant. It had a monthly output of 2,000 to 2,500 tonnes of riddled coal in tiny pieces which, in 1909, was almost exclusively used for fuelling Marty's steam tramps. The coal extracted from the mine's galleries was transported on a shunter way of sixty cubic metres up to the river where it was put into junks and shipped to Haiphong. When in July 1909 Marty sold the mine to a large syndicate in Paris, he was guaranteed the annual delivery of 10,000 tonnes of coal to his coal depot in Haiphong.[196]

On 23 August 1907, the first rumours about Marty contemplating retiring and seeking to sell his remaining four steam coasters, the *Hongkong*, *Hue*, *Hailan* and *Hanoi* appeared in *The China Mail* in Hong Kong. Three days later, this was denied in the same newspaper which instead reported that the French firm intended "to engage vessels more suitable to this trade and other lines". The matter was taken up by *L'Avenir du Tonkin* on 8 September, informing readers that the announcement by "one of our fellows (French: confrères) in Haiphong" concerning the sale of the Tonkin Shipping Company to a Japanese shipping line was untrue. According to the newspaper, Marty had tried in vain to find a purchaser for both the ocean-going steamers and the river

[194] BAB, R 901-17971: Consul Dr. Walter (Beihai) to Chancellor von Bülow (Berlin), 25 August 1907.

[195] Hieke (1953, 219–243).

[196] ANOM, INDO-GGI-2813: Note of Acting Governor-General Broni (Hanoi) for the Director-General of Public Works (Hanoi), 26 August 1905; Acting Resident Superior of Tonkin (Hanoi) to Governor-General Klobukowski (Hanoi), 6 July 1909; Moulié, Resident of France (Hai Duong), to Resident Superior of Tonkin (Hanoi), 13 July 1909.

ships of Marty et d'Abbadie, with the intention of retaining in Haiphong only the trading firm A. R. Marty. This news alarmed French Consul Joseph Beauvais in Haikou who, in his report to Paris expressed the hope that Marty would use the proceeds of the sale to build up a fleet "with steamers of much larger tonnage than the previous ones, 1,800 to 2,000 tons". The consul was confident that the shipowner, with "an experience of a quarter century at least", would not sell his fleet at a loss and would not let his flag disappear from the China seas.[197]

By 1910, the Tonkin Shipping Company operated four older vessels, the *Hailan*, the *Hanoi*, the *Hongkong* and the *Hue*.[198] Since the vessels were flying the French Tricolour flag, their frequent operations on the route from Hong Kong to Haiphong, often with stopovers at Haikou, Guangzhouwan and Beihai, contributed to enhancing France's maritime presence in the South China Sea. However, this result was achieved with a small fleet of rather outdated steamships, reflecting the general decline of France's mercantile marine in the early twentieth century. After winning the new subsidy contract for the Guangzhouwan postal steamer service in 1912, Marty was obliged to build two large steamers for the line. His search for a shipyard in France which was prepared to construct his vessels proved difficult at a time when, after the end of the economic depression, shipbuilding reached new heights and dockyards had full order books. Rumours about a possible military conflict or war in Europe further quickened the shipbuilding programmes of European navies. After contacting shipbuilders in Britain and Germany, Marty eventually received an offer from an unknown French shipyard with which he concluded the deal.[199] Yet, these vessels were not completed before the outbreak of the First World War. With the uncertainties of the autumn of 1914, when France's northern regions were attacked and occupied by German troops, and the economies of the belligerent countries were adapted to the needs of the war, any prospect of Marty's ships being finished became unrealistic. In November 1914, the Indochinese Postmaster laid down in an internal note that Marty had been informed that, within a period of six months after the end of the war, he was obliged to put into operation two

[197] *The China Mail*, 23 and 26 August 1907. *L'Avenir du Tonkin*, 8 September 1907. MAE, CPC-219: Consul Beauvais (Haikou) to French Minister (Beijing), 6 October 1907.

[198] *The Chronicle & Directory* (1910, 1524).

[199] PAAA, Peking II-1176: Consul Metzelthin (Haikou) to Chancellor von Bethmann Hollweg (Berlin), 25 November 1912. *L'Éveil de l'Indochine*, 30 March 1930.

new ships for the postal steamer service between Haiphong and Hong Kong. Until then, the shipowner was permitted to continue the line with his two older vessels.[200]

On 15 December 1914, Auguste Raphael Marty passed away in Haiphong. His son-in-law, Raymond René Sallé (the second husband of Marty's only daughter Clotilde Emmanuelle), prosecutor-general of Saigon, quit the judicial service of French Indochina to take over the management of the Tonkin Shipping Company and the commercial operations of his late father-in-law's firm, A. R. Marty.[201] As the First World War had severely reduced shipping operations in the South China Sea, the firm was no longer profitable and depended entirely on subsidies provided by the government-general for operating the Guangzhouwan postal steamer service.[202] When the company's liquidation was finalised in 1922, Sallé and his family left Indochina. Subsequently, any clues to the existence of Marty et d'Abbadie and its affiliates in the Tonkin press and other publications vanished completely. The last traces of the firm disappear from the files of the government-general of Indochina in the mid-1920s when long-term judicial issues over compensation payments were finally resolved.[203]

Asian and European Crews

The coastal steamers of the Tonkin Shipping Company had Asian crews on board. This was common practice in Western shipping companies operating in East Asian waters. Since the extremely low salaries paid to Asians allowed European tramp steamers to enjoy profitable voyages, the French tried to employ Vietnamese sailors for their merchant ships, but with little success. According to the French legal scholar Ambroise

[200] ANOM, INDO-GGI-17022: Director of Posts and Telegraphs, Government-General of Indochina (Hanoi), to the Governor-General (Hanoi), 2 November 1914.

[201] MAE, CPC-552: Vice Consul Hauchecorne (Haikou) to Foreign Minister Delcassé (Paris), 31 December 1914 and 27 July 1915.

[202] *L'Éveil économique de l'Indochine*, 30 March 1930.

[203] ANOM, INDO-GGI-17022: Note of Van Vollenhoven, Posts and Telegraphs Administration, Government-General of Indochina (Hanoi), 2 November 1914; Governor-General Maurice Long (Saigon) to Lapicque & Cie. (Haiphong), 28 August 1920; Lapicque & Cie. (Ben Thuy) to Governor-General (Hanoi), 25 September 1920. *L'Éveil économique de l'Indochine*, 8 October 1922. The voluminous file ANOM, INDO-GGI-38190 contains final judicial issues of Marty et d'Abbadie.

Colin, they were "lacking indispensable nautical qualities" and proved capable only for coastal shipping within sight of land, but were "absolutely unsuitable" for long voyages. Therefore, "Messageries Maritimes could only recruit two Vietnamese for their crews on board vessels operating coastal services in East Asia". When these men were discharged after several voyages, the major French shipping company concentrated on employing Chinese, Japanese and Malayans for their ships because they were known for their "endurance and intelligence".[204]

According to the French law for the merchant navy of 21 September 1793, captains and all the officers were to be citizens of the French Republic, and also three-fourths of the crew on vessels under the French flag. This latter requirement was found to be specifically difficult to French vessels operating in the Far East, particularly in the Indian Ocean and the China Seas. In these waters, British and German sailing ships employed African and Asian crews, who not only endured the climate much better than Europeans but were paid wages very much below those demanded by Europeans. Following the acquisition of Cochinchina and increasing French merchant shipping in the South China Sea, repeated complaints from French shipowners on this point led to an agreement between the ministries of the navy, foreign affairs and finance in 1865. The arrangement stipulated that French ships operating in distant waters, and never returning to France, were permitted to fly the French flag without having to comply with the usual requirements as to the personnel of the crew. The only condition required was that these vessels be furnished with annual navigation permits granted by the colonial authorities or by the French consul at their home port. This led to very liberal regulations regarding Asian crews decreed by the governor of Cochinchina in 1865 which were later applied to the whole of French Indochina. Concerning the nationality of the crews, the law of 1793 was further modified by the law of 7 April 1902, providing that the crews of vessels operating in the international coasting trade with any of the French colonies, and never returning to continental France, might be made up of foreign seamen of any proportion desired. Since French laws generally did

[204] Colin (1901, 405–406).

not require any test of efficiency or qualification for merchant seamen, the hiring of Asian crews proved even more advantageous for shipowners.[205]

Concerning the stipulation of the law of 1793 that the shipmaster and all the officers of French vessels should be citizens of France, subsequent modifications did not change this basic precondition. The French law of 26 February 1862 concerning qualifications of shipmasters on coasters in French colonies was applied to French Indochina by decree of the governor-general on 22 November 1895. With respect to the supervision of steam engines on board seagoing vessels by steamship mechanics, the French law of 2 February 1893 went into effect for Indochina by a decree of 29 December 1893. These two laws were the ones relevant for French shipowners in Indochina being generally exempted from regulations for the French merchant navy as applied in France. This principle, applying to all French vessels operating in "distant seas" (mers lontaines), was announced in the navy ministry's circular of 25 November 1885. In the South China Sea, the basic requirement to fly the French flag was the renewal of the annual permit issued by French consulates or the Maritime Inscription offices at Saigon and Haiphong.[206]

France's policy of flexibly applying her maritime laws to overseas shipping markets did not solve the basic problem of French shipping companies exclusively operating in East Asia, namely the grave deficiency of qualified maritime personnel eligible for the posts of shipmaster, officer or mechanic. Suitable Frenchmen were hardly available in Indochina or neighbouring ports. This forced French shipowners in East Asia to hire officers through the help of agents in French ports, without learning much about their personal background, character or physical condition. According to a survey by the French consulate in Hong Kong in 1897, there were sufficient ship officers in French ports seeking employment, but most disliked committing themselves to long-term contracts requiring them to remain for three to five years in distant regions such as East Asia. Those with good qualifications and references who were willing to serve in such faraway locations usually demanded higher salaries. In this case, the shipowner was inclined to replace the officers after

[205] *Hansa. Deutsche Nautische Zeitschrift* (10 July 1897, 334–335), Colin (1901, 405–406) and Jones (1916, 77–79, 82, 96–100, 109).

[206] ANOM, INDO-GGI-3388: Commissioner of the Colonies (Saigon) to Director of Civil Affairs of Indochina (Saigon), 28 July 1899. VNA1, RST-8624: Consul Liébert (Hong Kong) to Governor-General of Indochina (Hanoi), 12 March 1908.

several months, which involved indemnity payments, return travel costs and management fees. To avoid such extra expense, French shipowners were disposed to hire less qualified officers for marginally increased salaries. This often caused problems in ships' daily operation and seriously disadvantaged French shipping companies vis-a-vis foreign competitors. Consulate Chancellor A. Giraud summed it up as follows: "Abundance of officers in France, anaemia in our colonies, permanent worries for shipowners established in our overseas possessions".[207]

After the establishment of an official examination site based in Saigon in 1895, it became possible for Frenchmen in Indochina to obtain the French shipmasters' diploma for short and long coastal shipping (cabotage). Small cabotage concerned river shipping and short distances along the coast of French Indochina, while long cabotage comprised shipping in the maritime region between Saigon, Batavia, Singapore, Hong Kong and Siam. Since other neighbouring destinations in East Asia such as northern China or Japan were not covered by the said certificates, French shipping companies employing masters possessing such diplomas found themselves in the awkward position of not being able to accept charter contracts covering ports in these regions. This was a serious disadvantage in the very competitive shipping markets of East Asia.[208]

Under these conditions, French shipowners in the Far East probably had no other choice than to circumvent or ignore regulations concerning the qualifications of shipmasters and officers. This was not even punished by the higher authorities. In July 1899, the French administration of Cochinchina, in an internal correspondence, admitted that the colonial ministry frequently gave instructions "to observe the greatest tolerance with respect to shipowners and shipping companies" but that "these liberal arrangements" were "very often used and misused in Indochina".[209] In April 1903, Governor-General Paul Beau told

[207] MAE, CCC, 137-6 Hong Kong 1897–1901: Consulate Chancellor A. Giraud (Hong Kong): Report on creating examinations for obtaining diplomas for captains and mechanics on long-distance voyages, 15 July 1897.

[208] MAE, CCC, 137-6 Hong Kong 1897–1901: Consulate Chancellor Giraud (Hong Kong): Report on creating examinations for obtaining diplomas for captains and mechanics on long-distance voyages, 15 July 1897. ANOM, INDO-GGI-3388: Commissioner of the Colonies (Saigon) to Director of Civil Affairs of Indochina (Saigon), 28 July 1899.

[209] ANOM, INDO-GGI-3388: Commissioner of the Colonies (Saigon) to Director of Civil Affairs of Indochina (Saigon), 28 July 1899.

the Federal Association for Shipmasters and Officers of the Mercantile Marine, the responsible body, that he had given orders not to apply in Indochina any longer the regulations about hiring captains in the Far East "should it be impossible to appoint French masters". He informed the naval ministry that the association had complained about "certain shipowners in Indochina, particularly the company Marty et d'Abbadie in Tonkin, taking foreigners as captains and officers on their vessels".[210]

The French law of 17 April 1907 stipulated that French ships making voyages "au long cours" and of more than 700 gross tonnes register were required to have, in addition to the captain, at least one second officer and a lieutenant, both duly certificated.[211] More detailed regulations regarding security of shipping and health and safety on board French merchant vessels were decreed on 20/21 September 1908. However, since the practicability of such rules in French colonies was doubtful, the colonial minister asked the governor-general in Hanoi about the practicability of introducing them for French shipping in Indochina. In earlier public discussions in France, the naval minister had made it clear that the interests of both crews and passengers and of shipping companies needed to be considered, pointing to the inferiority of the French mercantile marine vis-à-vis foreign competition. Consequently, the Haiphong Chamber of Commerce was charged with the enquiry, appointing one of its members, the merchant Paul Roque of Roque Frères, to prepare a report on the situation in Indochina.[212]

The account published in the newspaper *L'Avenir du Tonkin* on 27 May 1909 concluded that the proposed regulations were not applicable in the Far East. Pointing to very different climate conditions and the fact that only small freights were transported on ships under the French flag, the report frankly admitted that only two, three or four officers in all, mostly foreigners, were available per ship and that engines on French ships were supervised by Chinese mechanics working under special conditions. Shipping companies operating in the Far East had

[210] VNA1, RST-9177: Governor-General Beau (Hanoi) to Président de l'Association fédérative des Capitaines au long cours et Officiers de la Marine marchande (Marseille), 30 April 1903, and to Naval Ministry (Paris), 23 June 1903. There is the note by the Resident Superior of Hanoi, of 7 October 1903, that further information on the issue will be collected, but subsequent correspondence is not contained in the file.

[211] Jones (1916, 82).

[212] *L'Avenir du Tonkin*, 8 May 1909.

crews consisting entirely of Asians and followed established customs on board ships. Changing such habits would "unfailingly" result in crews leaving the few French ships and either finding easily work elsewhere or increasing the labour force of Indochina. Concerning food, the report made it clear that Asian crews nourished themselves in their own way, and with respect to hygiene and healthiness, it pointed to local customs and requirements in different climates. Regarding security on board ships, the account made it clear that there were control commissions supervising steam machines, shipping equipment, rescue engines, medical material, draughts and passenger numbers. Local conditions could not be adapted to regulations drafted for France. Furthermore, the account alluded to the fact that the governor-general was able to decree local rules based on administrative and commercial expertise (especially of the chambers of commerce), something that would better fulfil the goals of the proposed regulations. Finally, the report warned of possible negative ramifications for French shipping in Indochina:

> We cannot too much pay particular attention to the consequences of competition given the tiny number of French ships in the Far East. Shipmasters and shipowners all have interests in treating their crews well, since otherwise they would leave at the next port of call. It would be very dangerous to seek to amend general rules which result from experience in these regions and will always be law whatever France can decree. To sum up, if we do not want to definitely hamper French merchant shipping, which is already so limited, it seems vital to us to respect established practices, and to allow the governor-general the necessary freedom to decree measures deemed indispensable by taking his inspiration from proposals of the chambers of commerce.[213]

The report was adopted by the Haiphong Chamber of Commerce and sent to the Resident Superior in Hanoi. Taking the close business relationship of the company A. R. Marty with Roque Frères into account, it seems very likely that the French shipowner had largely inspired the wording of the account. The detailed information on conditions in French shipping in the South China Sea was based on expertise which was hard to find among Haiphong's trading firms but was certainly at the Tonkin Shipping Company. "It is in particular important to imbibe the little

[213] *L'Avenir du Tonkin*, 27 May 1909.

importance of the French element in Far Eastern waters", the report claimed, pointing to the fact that Tonkin currently possessed only four small merchant ships. This number exactly matched the current size of the Tonkin Shipping Company's fleet, consisting of four vessels. Although the account hinted at the fact that another four French steamers from Saigon frequently called at the port of Haiphong, the overall result was still modest, especially with respect to foreign competition. "What can they do in the presence of about two hundred big steamers of English, American, German, Japanese, Norwegian, Danish shipping companies operating in the China seas only? And in this number are included neither units of the lines from India to Japan, and from America to China, nor the mail liners from Europe".[214]

When looking at the list of officers of the Tonkin Shipping Company, as published annually by *The Directory and Chronicle*, it seems obvious from the surnames that most of them were not Frenchmen but Scandinavians, Germans, Iberians or Italians. The only positions on his vessels which Marty was required to fill with Frenchmen, as stipulated in the contract with the government-general issued on 1 June 1900, were "at least" the ones of captain and First Mechanic of the *Hue* servicing the subsidised postal steamer line between Haiphong and Guangzhouwan from 1900 to 1910 and from 1913 to 1918. According to the list of 1906, J. Godineau was captain and Mr Azema was First Mechanic on the *Hue*. After the contract expired in 1910, the captain was Mr Foyn (possibly a naturalised Norwegian) and the First Mechanic was J. MacDonald (possibly a Scotsman). When Marty won back the subsidy contract in 1912, the decree of 21 December 1911 was in force stipulating that shipmasters, officers being second in command and mechanics of French vessels should be French citizens or "protégés". This regulation, included in the new subsidy agreement beginning on 1 March 1913, made it necessary to replace MacDonald and to have a Frenchman as First Mechanic of the *Hue*.[215]

[214] *L'Avenir du Tonkin*, 27 May 1909.

[215] *The Directory and Chronicle for China* (1906, 1320) and (1910, 1524). ANOM, INDO-GGI-3388: Agreement on executing a maritime postal service between Haiphong and Guangzhouwan, issued at Hanoi, 1 June 1900, chapter 3, article 11. ANOM, INDO-GGI-17022: Contract of Mutual Agreement for the operation of a maritime postal steamer service from Haiphong to Hong Kong via Haikou and Guangzhouwan from 1 March 1913 to 28 February 1923, issued at Saigon, 4 October 1912, chapter 9, article 50.

The best alternative for MacDonald seemed to be the Norwegian Lorentz Olaf Reitan, who was well-acquainted with Marty's vessels, being the First Mechanic of the *Hanoi* in 1908, and of the *Hongkong* in 1910. After agreeing to the French shipowner's idea of becoming naturalised, Reitan was transferred to the *Hue*.[216] On 16 November 1912, the Haiphong police station issued the certificate of good conduct for the 36-year-old Reitan after Mayor Pierre Tournois had fully backed his application. Reitan originated from the Haugesund-Stavanger region in south-western Norway and had resided in Hong Kong before arriving in Tonkin in August 1907 and taking up the post in the Tonkin Shipping Company. Governor-General Sarraut, having enquired "about the morality and background of the petitioner", was very supportive of the application, as he told the colonial ministry. On 15 February 1913, Reitan became naturalised, making him eligible to serve on Marty's subsidised postal steamer *Hue*.[217]

When the vessel started operating the Guangzhouwan postal steamer service (1 March 1913), the shipmaster, Captain Abraham Corneliussen, the Third Officer, Lieutenant Amable Balisoni, and the Third Mechanic, Marcel Masse, were French citizens; Reitan was naturalised, the Second Officer, A. Nielsen, was a Dane and the Second Mechanic, Thomas Dobbie, was a Scot. This composition, even when conforming to the stipulations of the subsidy contract, still reflected the highly multinational character of French merchant vessels operating in East Asia, which was compounded by the fact that the remaining crew of the *Hue* consisted entirely of Vietnamese and Chinese sailors.[218]

[216] VNA1, RST-9036: Auguste Raphael Marty (Haiphong) to Head of Maritime Inscription Office (Haiphong), 13 March 1913.

[217] *The Directory and Chronicle for China* (1908, 1423) and (1910, 1524). VNA1, RST-1836: Mayor Tournois (Haiphong) to Resident Superior (Hanoi), 6 November 1912; Haiphong Police Station: Personal Bulletin of Reitan, Lorentz Olaf (born on 22 April 1876), 16 November 1912; Governor-General Sarraut (Hanoi) to Colonial Ministry (Paris), 11 December 1912; Telegram from Colonial Ministry (Paris) to Governor-General (Hanoi), 2 April 1913.

[218] VNA1, RST-9169: Principal Foreman Simonin, Public Works Office (Fort Bayard), to Chief Engineer Giltay, Maritime Services of Tonkin (Haiphong), 21 April 1913, Head of Maritime Inscription Service (Haiphong): Composition of Management and Crews of the Ships of A. R. Marty, 22 July 1913.

On 19 April 1913, the *Hue* became stranded off Guangzhouwan and was towed to Haiphong to be repaired in Marty's workshops. This accident provided sufficient reason for the Maritime Inspection Office at Haiphong to make a thorough investigation into the personnel of the Tonkin Shipping Company's fleet, consisting at the time of the steamers *Hongkong*, *Hanoi* and *Hue*. The result was rather frustrating: besides the fact that not all officers were French citizens or "protégés", none of the diplomas of the foreigners had been acquired in France. This concerned Nielsen, Dobbie, Reitan and even Masse on board the *Hue*. Furthermore, "for good reason, paradoxical" seemed the fact that the Third Officer of the *Hongkong*, Adolph Golde, was a German. Admitting that it was difficult, if not impossible to hire French officers in Indochina, the report nonetheless pointed to the fact that employing foreigners should only be an exceptional case, "whereas at Haiphong the provisional arrangement became the rule and is always permanent". Therefore, the report addressed to the Resident Superior of Tonkin and judging the ships' composition as "heterogeneous" suggested improvements to the situation such as granting shipowners a fixed period of six to twelve months to find personnel in France or to establish regular rotations among ships' officers and mechanics to avoid a shortage of staff. Whether these ideas were regarded as practicable remains an open question since the records consulted do not contain any reply to the report.[219]

Shipping Boycotts in the South China Sea

The Boycott of 1895 and Sino-French Diplomacy

The French consulate in Hong Kong, in its internal shipping report issued in December 1895, noted that thanks to the liners of Messageries Maritimes and vessels of A. R. Marty, the French share of shipping in the British colony was around 4 per cent, while the number of German tonnages was four-and-a-half times higher, a sign of "the minor importance of our flag vis-à-vis those of other nations" and "of our marked inferiority as transporters". The report also explicitly dealt with the situation in French shipping in the South China Sea between Hong Kong

[219] *Weekly Sun*, 3 May 1913. VNA1, RST-9169: Head of Maritime Inscription Service (Haiphong) to Resident Superior (Hanoi), 23 July 1913.

and the Chinese ports of Haikou and Beihai. On this route, Marty operated his own two ships under the French flag and two chartered Danish vessels, *Ask* and *Active,* which had encountered competition from Chinese merchants chartering two German steamers in the second semester of 1895. In that year, as the port statistics of Beihai reveal, French and Danish flags had a share of 3 and of 56 per cent respectively, thus almost 60 per cent combined, while the German flag had 38 per cent. Compared to 1893, when the German flag had a share of 49 per cent, the proportion had changed considerably in favour of Marty. This was the direct result of the Sino-Japanese War (1894–1895), with the high demand for coasters to provide transport and supply provisions for Chinese troops in northern China. In the spring and summer of 1895, Marty's shipping line between Haiphong and Hong Kong faced almost no competition. Consequently, the French shipowner used the favourable situation to gain extra profits for the Tonkin Shipping Company.[220]

Marty's direct competitor on the line was the Chinese merchant Chau Kwang Cheong (hereafter K. C. Chau). In Hong Kong, Chau owned the shipping company Yuen Cheong Lee & Company and in Haikou its branch house Yuen Fat Lee & Company. Beginning in 1885, Chau frequently employed coasters of the M. Jebsen Shipping Company on time charter, conveying passengers and cargo to Hong Kong, Haikou and Beihai. However, in the final phase of the Sino-Japanese War (1894–1895), Chau moved his time-chartered vessels to other, more profitable routes in East Asia — especially on the route to and from Singapore — where steam tonnage could yield considerable gains. Facing such favourable conditions, Marty drastically raised the freight rates for all shipments of passengers and cargo. The sudden increase in transport costs caused heavy losses for Chinese shippers in the port of call who had no alternative but to ship their merchandise on coasters of the Tonkin Shipping Company.[221] The situation caused by the French shipowner's profit-driven business attitude provoked a strong reaction from the major

[220] MAE, CCC-137-5 Hong Kong: Consulate Chancellor A. Giraud (Hong Kong): Commercial Situation of Hong Kong, 31 December 1895. Becker (2015, 573: Table 1). PAAA, Peking II-1169: E. L. B. Allen (Beihai) to Consul Knappe (Guangzhou), 24 January 1896.

[221] PAAA, Peking II-1169: Consul Knappe (Guangzhou) to Minister Schenck zu Schweinsberg (Beijing), 3 January 1896. PAAA, Peking II-1170: Memorandum of Wilhelm Knappe, *Die französische Konkurrenz in Hoihow und Pakhoi* , December 1896.

Chinese commercial guilds at Haikou and Beihai, whose principal goal was to watch over the commercial interests of its members; the reaction was a locally initiated boycott.

In consular files, business correspondence and contemporary newspapers, the events of 1895–1896 and the subsequent ones in 1907 and 1909–1910 are exclusively referred to as "shipping boycotts" or just "boycotts", terms that are also used in this book to characterise these conflict-laden business interactions. Early local boycotts in China — often called "taboos" in English-language sources — were not directed against the ships of a particular nation but against those of a particular company. In this respect, such boycotts were different from the well-known greater boycotts used by the Chinese to target Japan, the United States and Britain in particular from the 1840s to the 1930s. The early boycotts can be regarded as the weaponry of one of the most powerful and organised social groups in late Qing China, namely, the Chinese merchant guilds. Guild members made agreements that involved ceasing to purchase or deal in goods, or abstaining from using ships of the boycotted country.[222] A similar practice, but with the aim of targeting a specific shipping company, can be observed when looking at the boycott of 1895–1896. Confronted with an exceptionally unfavourable situation, the worst-hit Chinese guilds in Haikou and Beihai established the syndicate Tsap Yet Company [also known as Chi I Company or Chak Yik], with the sole purpose of breaking the monopoly of the Tonkin Shipping Company. After statutes had been set up, the syndicate commenced its operations in Beihai in October 1895, chartering two steamers under the German flag, the *Triumph* of the M. Jebsen Shipping Company, of which Jebsen & Co. in Hong Kong were agents, and the *Cosmopolit* of the Reederei Wahl (Wahl Shipping Company), of which Wieler & Company were agents. All partners of Tsap Yet were obliged to ship their cargo exclusively on the two coasters, according to the statutes, while the freight rates of the two syndicate vessels were set lower than Marty's.[223]

On 15 October 1895, Marty experienced the effects of the boycott when one of the Danish steamers called twice at Haikou and Beihai, but

[222] On boycotts in China, see Morse (1909, 55–56), Liu (1956, 147–148), Remer (1966, 1–20), Tsai (1993, 182–237) and Wong (2002).

[223] PAAA, Peking II-1169: Consul Knappe (Guangzhou) to Minister Schenck zu Schweinsberg (Beijing), 3 January 1896, including *Articles of the Chak Yik Steamship Company* (in English).

received absolutely no cargo. Although the French shipowner immediately reacted by considerably lowering his freight rates, his ships were boycotted by Chinese shippers in the ports of Hong Kong, Haikou and Beihai, causing huge financial losses for the Tonkin Shipping Company.[224] The case was taken up by Minister Auguste Gérard in Beijing, an ardent supporter of France's interests in China. The diplomat launched an official protest at the Chinese foreign ministry (Tsungli Yamen), pointing to the alleged violation of the liberty of commerce, as granted by the Sino-French Treaty of 1858 (notably Article 14). The Chinese government, acknowledging the French position in principle, instructed the highest official in the southern coastal provinces, Viceroy Tan Chung-Lin, to ban the syndicate. Under this immense pressure, Tsap Yet was immediately dissolved. In early November 1895, the syndicate's statutes were scrapped, and new regulations were drafted by legal experts in Hong Kong. In the newly established Chinese company in Hong Kong that operated under the same name, the German-owned trading firm Schomburg & Company, based in Beihai, became a shareholder as well as the formal shipping agent of *Triumph* and *Cosmopolit*.[225]

Such steps by the Chinese had little impact on the conviction of French consul Camille Gauthier in Guangzhou and Marty that Tsap Yet was still in operation and that its association with the German firm was only a new complot directed against the Tonkin Shipping Company. After the first meeting with local Chinese merchants at Beihai on 4 December 1895 had ended without any results, the second gathering on 15 January 1896 was accompanied by the presence of the French gunboat *Alouette*, which had been deliberately dispatched to intimidate the Chinese negotiators. This worked better than the French had hoped. Local Chinese officials forced Chinese merchants to exclusively ship their cargo on the vessel of the Tonkin Shipping Company anchored in the harbour which cleared fully loaded. Consul Gauthier even went further, demanding a complete ban of any future shipping on the two chartered German steamers and massive

[224] ANOM, INDO-GGI-6153: Auguste Raphael Marty (Haiphong) to Governor-General Beau (Hanoi), 2 June 1903.

[225] MAE, CCC, 235-1 Pakhoi 1888–1895: Report of Consul Gauthier (Beihai) to Foreign Minister Berthelot (Paris), 20 November 1895. The new rules of Tsap Yet's head firm in Hong Kong, *The Rules of the Chak Yik Steam-Ship Company*, were printed, with one copy enclosed in Gauthier's report.

compensation for Marty for losses caused by Tsap Yet. The Chinese officials quickly gave in, requiring the destruction of the Tsap Yet statutes and promising to severely punish merchants should similar boycott actions reoccur. On 22 January 1896, Tsap Yet formally ceased to exist. This was indeed a remarkable French diplomatic success in advancing their position vis-à-vis the Chinese. To safeguard the fulfilment of their demands, the French again dispatched *Alouette* to Beihai in early February 1896. Facing the combined political and military pressures, the merchants surrendered: the time charters of *Triumph* and *Cosmopolit* were cancelled, resulting in huge contractual penalties for Chinese shippers.[226]

France's intervention in the liberty of shipping and commerce in the South China Sea caught the attention of German shipowners and consuls. After being approached by Jacob Jebsen, Consul Dr. Wilhelm Knappe in Guangzhou solicited support from Viceroy Tan. Although the Chinese official was in favour of the German demands, his actions failed to achieve results. Therefore, Jebsen paid a personal visit to Beihai in early 1896, confidentially announcing to E. L. B. Allen, the British consul in charge of German interests, his intention of establishing a shipping line between Hong Kong, Haikou and Beihai with the steamers *Doris*, *Triumph* and *Michael Jebsen*. He made it clear that he would operate them solely under the name of his company, Jebsen & Co. in Hong Kong, to avoid giving the French the impression that he intended to employ tactics similar to those that Schomburg & Co. had used as agents of Tsap Yet. His initiative brought the hoped-for success: after local Chinese authorities in Beihai had issued a public announcement which made it clear that shippers could ship goods on any vessels of their choice, *Doris* and *Triumph* were charged with shipments of goods from Beihai shippers. The Chinese merchants were well aware that Marty's attempt to exploit his temporary monopoly in the regional shipping market to their economic disadvantage had caused the crisis. It was also plain that the crisis had been exacerbated by the intervention of French officials, who plainly had their own political intentions in mind in supporting the interests of the Tonkin Shipping Company. The best solution to prevent a similar crisis recurring in future seemed to depend on a foreign shipping company which was free of any pressure from the French and Chinese authorities and

[226] PAAA, Peking II-1170: Memorandum of Wilhelm Knappe, *Die französische Konkurrenz in Hoihow und Pakhoi*, December 1896. *Le Courrier d'Haiphong*, 25 January 1896. *The Hong Kong Daily Press*, 1 February 1896. Becker (2015, 576–580).

was firmly backed by German consular staff in China in securing reliable shipments. The only precondition the Chinese made was that the arrangement should be in the form of a partnership between Jebsen and K. C. Chau, the former operator of the line. The plan, which was kept strictly confidential, resulted in an agreement between the two companies signed on 3 February 1896. Jebsen & Co. promised to "undertake the line of steamers running between Haikou, Hong Kong and Beihai (…) on their own account" and appoint Chau's firm in Hong Kong and its branch house in Haikou as "their agents for securing cargo and doing the other ship's business". To prevent any mutual competition in the line, Yuen Cheong Lee & Co. agreed "not to charter any steamers or accept the agency or to be otherwise interested in any steamers trading to Haikou and Beihai without the express consent" of Jebsen & Co.[227]

K. C. Chau's partnership with Jebsen & Co. resulted in the fact that Chinese merchants gave the maximum of cargoes to Jebsen's vessels and the minimum to Marty's, fearing fresh French intervention. However, with such small profits the French shipowner saw no solution to the crisis and decided to see Gérard in Beijing. He was received coldly, with the minister suggesting an understanding between the concerned parties, which Marty furiously refused. His insistence led to a fresh French diplomatic initiative: on 17 June 1896, Gérard approached the Tsungli Yamen, stating that Tsap Yet was still in operation and requesting compensation of 100,000 taels (approximately 153,000 Mexican dollars) for Marty. When Michael Jebsen, at the time a member of the German National Parliament, learned about the French demand, he pleaded with the foreign ministry to prompt Viceroy Tan "not to favour or to harm any line in any way, but to let competition take its course".[228] Consequently, Foreign Minister Adolf Baron Marschall von Bieberstein, who was friendly with Jebsen, instructed the German minister in Beijing to communicate the German position to the Tsungli Yamen accordingly. In Hong Kong, Jebsen & Co. increased competition against Marty to force him to come to a joint solution to the ongoing crisis. However, facing huge losses, Marty again put pressure on French officials, even claiming much higher

[227] PAAA, Peking II-1170: Memorandum of Wilhelm Knappe, *Die französische Konkurrenz in Hoihow und Pakhoi*, December 1896. Becker (2015, 580–582). The agreement (in English) is reprinted in Hänisch (1970, 46–47).

[228] BAB, R 901-12956: Michael Jebsen (Berlin) to Undersecretary of State von Rotenhan (Berlin), 25 June 1896.

compensation, and finally achieved an agreement signed on 4 June 1897 which was a brilliant diplomatic victory. The huge sum of 200,000 taels granted by the Chinese government provided sufficient funds for Marty to purchase three used steam coasters in October 1898 and to considerably enlarge the fleet of the Tonkin Shipping Company.[229]

Even so, Marty had only won the battle and not the war, damaging in the long term his relations with Chinese business circles. His reputation as a businessman was severely harmed in the eyes of the Chinese, who regarded him as greedy, unreliable and untrustworthy. This had become evident in petitions from the Haikou and Beihai merchants of October 1896 to the governor-general of Guangdong Province. The French shipowner was accused of having strived for a monopoly in the shipping market, with the intention of harming Chinese merchants by increasing freight rates. His subsequent attempt to get monetary compensation was regarded as "entirely unfounded". Therefore, the Beihai traders warned that "if Marty should treat us again so badly, then we merchants will rather give up our businesses than to accept his digs in the ribs". Consequently, French officials in China strongly recommended that Marty should restore trust as soon as possible and avoid any future confrontation and animosity.[230]

When Chinese officials began to recover a part of Marty's compensation from shippers in Beihai, Prefect Liu instructed Chinese merchants on pain of punishment not to give the larger part of their cargoes to Jebsen's ships. Under these threats, Chinese firms in Beihai instructed their branches in Hong Kong not to give German vessels more cargo than French ones. Therefore, the Jebsen coasters serving the line received less than half, or no cargo at all, from mid-August to early November 1897. The subsequent French intervention in the freedom of shipping and commerce in the South China Sea prompted Jebsen & Co. to submit in October 1897 its first claim for damages to Consul Ludwig von Loeper in Hong Kong, justifying this demand by declaring the actions

[229] ANOM, INDO-GGI-6153: Auguste Raphael Marty (Haiphong) to Governor-General Beau (Hanoi), 2 June 1903.

[230] PAAA, Peking II-1169: Petition of Haikou merchants, including the reply to calumnious accusations against them, undated [October 1896], petition of Beihai merchants, undated [October 1896]. ANOM, INDO-GGI-56222: Colonial Minister Lebon (Paris) to Governor-General Doumer (Hanoi), 11 September 1897, Governor-General Doumer (Hanoi) to Colonial Minister Lebon (Paris), 2 November 1897.

of Chinese officials to be contrary to commercial freedom. Although Chinese authorities acted quickly, proclaiming that shippers were free to use any ship for transporting cargo, the merchants, obviously afraid of any retaliatory action from the French, continued to give most of their cargo to the vessels of the Tonkin Shipping Company. Consequently, Jebsen & Co. submitted another claim for damages to Consul von Loeper who supported the case before Minister Edmund Baron von Heyking in Beijing. The consul even suggested dispatching a ship of the German East Asia Squadron from Jiaozhou to Haikou and Beihai to increase pressure on the Chinese.[231]

However, such a forceful demonstration of military power in the South China Sea was out of the question due to the recent seizure of Jiaozhou (Kiaochow) Bay by German naval troops. Therefore, Heyking's reaction was terse and frank. In his telegram of 26 December 1897, he advised the foreign ministry "not to comply" with the consul's plea, "because it would now unnecessarily annoy the French against us". Soon later, the minister, who was involved in intensive negotiations with the Chinese government about leasing Jiaozhou, admitted that, "despite my fervent wish to be helpful to German interests and especially to the shipping company which was particularly commended to me, I may not disregard that in order to avoid as much as possible a clash with French political claims in those ports, thus special caution is imperative in this matter". Therefore, a show of might over a rather irrelevant issue such a compensation payment for a private shipping company was out of the question in the interests of higher political goals. In the end, Jebsen & Co. received no monetary compensation from the Chinese government for its losses in the South China Sea. However, the German company was in some way compensated when, in 1898, it won the subsidy contract for operating a shipping line between Shanghai and Jiaozhou which provided the German leased territory in Shandong Province with its major maritime connection.[232]

[231] PAAA, Peking II-1170: Jebsen & Co. (Hong Kong) to Consul von Loeper (Hong Kong), 25 November 1897; Consul von Loeper (Hong Kong) to Minister von Heyking (Beijing), 4, 17, and 29 November 1897. Becker (2015, 587–588).

[232] PAAA, Peking II-1170: Draft telegram of Minister von Heyking (Beijing) to the Foreign Ministry (Berlin), 26 December 1897. PAAA, Peking II-1171: Minister von Heyking (Beijing) to Consul Knappe (Guangzhou), 11 February 1898. On the subsidised Jiaozhou (Kiaochow) postal steamer service operated by the M. Jebsen Shipping Company from 1898 to 1901, see Becker (2009, 205–229).

Marty and the "Chinese League of Tonkin Merchants"

In June 1900, the Tonkin Shipping Company began operating the Guangzhouwan postal steamer service after winning the ten-year subsidy contract initiated by Governor-General Doumer. Despite the considerable financial support from Indochina, the increasing competition from other vessels on the lucrative run between Haiphong and Hong Kong resulted in lower profits for the Tonkin Shipping Company. According to Marty, freight rates for rice shipments in 1901 had decreased from the usual 20 cents per rice bag (equivalent to one Chinese picul or 82 kilograms) to 10 cents, and finally to 6,5 cents which resulted in the total loss of 3,000–4,000 dollars per month for his steamer fleet. In November 1900, at the start of the rice exporting season, Marty approached Doumer warning of "a situation threatening the existence of our Tonkin Shipping Company comprising six steamers flying the French flag [Marty's five vessels and one chartered steamer, the *Taishun*] and operating exclusively on the route from Haiphong to Hong Kong and the intermediate ports of Beihai, Haikou and Guangzhouwan". As Marty explained, this situation was created by several rice merchants based in Tonkin chartering Jebsen's vessel *Clara* (of which Speidel & Co. was the agent) for the run between Hong Kong and Haiphong. Reminding the governor-general of the boycott of 1895–1896, the French shipowner expressly accused the Haiphong rice merchant Kwong Sang Yuen of being "the real agent instead of Speidel & Company". He even presumed that the Chinese trader was behind the French firm Denis Frères in Haiphong which had chartered two steamers of the Douglas Steamship Company in Hong Kong. Marty believed that Kwong was putting the British ships on the run to increase competition against the Tonkin Shipping Company, presuming that "the Chinese league of Tonkin merchants" had promoted "the implantation of the English flag". To members of this association, Marty counted the Chinese comprador of Douglas in Hong Kong who was allegedly supported by some Guangzhou "capitalists" and seven Haiphong rice merchants, including Kwong.[233]

Facing such powerful Chinese combinations seemingly waging unfair competition on him when chartering German and British vessels, Marty was very pessimistic when evaluating the present condition of his shipping

[233] VNA1, GGI-3158: Auguste Raphael Marty (Hong Kong) to Governor-General Doumer (Saigon), 20 November 1900.

company. As he explained to Doumer, the future was "little reassuring and if the current ruinous situation will persist and last beyond the new Chinese year, 19 February 1901, we are forced to withdraw from the Tonkin line after having been there, not without hard work, for more than twenty years". In his letter, the shipowner expressed the common concerns of French businessman in Indochina facing strong commercial rivalry from Chinese traders, saying: "I do not have the ambition to prevent free and loyal competition against which it would be inappropriate to protest. However, it is not the same with secret coalitions and societies, to which the Chinese are accustomed". Warning of a Chinese corporation "causing Chinese exporters in Tonkin to follow sooner or later the way recommended by the current leaders, their compatriots and their colleagues", the shipowner accused the Chinese of "aiming to ruin French enterprises". To avoid this happening, Marty asked Doumer "to take necessary measures to block their attempts".[234]

The expert report on the matter was issued by M. A. Frézoule, the Customs director in Haiphong. The French official concluded that there was indeed a Chinese coalition intending "to exploit an entire trading sector to the exclusive profit of their congregation". Pointing to the fact that the Customs administration had for four years fought against the Chinese to stop them monopolising the trade in salt, indigenous alcohol, opium and tobacco in Indochina, Frézoule called it "even more formidable should they [the Chinese] succeed in chasing away the French flag from the ports of Tonkin solely represented by Marty's vessels; apart from major shipping companies such as Messageries Maritimes and Compagnie nationale [de navigation; Compagnie Fraissinet])". However, he regarded this combination as "a purely commercial operation", explaining that "we must well admit that each merchant has the right to choose his transporters and to charter the vessel that he likes for the price suited to him". Therefore, Frézoule was against restrictive measures, calling them "a constraint to the development of trade which would provoke complaints from shipowners and shipping agents of whom some, like the company Denis Frères, are Frenchmen going along, a bit naïve perhaps, with the manoeuvres of the Chinese". He recommended only that Marty be assisted by granting to his vessels "all favours compatible

[234]VNA1, GGI-3158: Auguste Raphael Marty (Hong Kong) to Governor-General Doumer (Saigon), 20 November 1900.

with the regulations".[235] Since the file does not contain a reply from Doumer, this verdict certainly settled the case.

In 1900, the French reaction to Marty's complaint reflected a considerable deviation from France's high-handed political approach, as it was expressed in the diplomatic negotiations with Beijing over financial compensations for Marty after the boycott of 1895–1896. The French authorities in Indochina regarded the matter as a purely commercial one, refraining from any political intervention. In the same year, the Boxer Rebellion in northern China (1899–1901) sent a strong warning call to imperial powers that anti-imperialism and nationalism in China were on the rise. In the years to come, the unequal imperial power relations of the West with China increasingly underwent changes. A token of the awakening of national sentiments was a public discourse started by Chinese nationalist activists on the recovery of shipping rights, focusing on eradicating foreign shipping power in Chinese waters and replacing it with self-sufficient Chinese shipping companies. In 1908, a new generation of small private Chinese shipping companies strongly committed to shipping nationalism emerged, mostly operating on small inland rivers. Financed by Chinese capital and flying the Chinese flag, the operations of these firms provided arguments for shipping autonomy when demonstrating that China could fulfil its own shipping needs without foreign involvement. The discourse on shipping rights recovery went hand in hand with similar efforts in other arenas such as railways or mining, signalling the beginning of a new anti-imperialist era in China in which the old intellectual, social and economic order increasingly altered while a new one became more and more visible.[236]

The Haiphong Shipping Boycotts of 1907 and 1909–1910

In the early twentieth century, the firms of Jebsen and Marty shared almost all traffic on the run between Haiphong and Hong Kong, with their steam tramps predominantly chartered by Chinese merchants based in the two port cities. In 1905, a total of 248 ships called at the port of Haiphong, of which 92 flew the German flag; 86, the French flag;

[235] VNA1, GGI-3158: M. A. Frézoule (Hanoi) to Governor-General Doumer (Hanoi), 10 December 1900.

[236] Reinhardt (2018, 16–19, 183–187).

29, the British flag; and two, the American flag; the remaining ones were unidentified and probably consisted of local junks and other small carriers.[237] Through a kind of informal agreement between Jebsen and Marty, the freight and passage prices of their steam tramps were more or less equal, fixed at 25 cents per rice bag, and they also granted shippers the return commission of 10 per cent on the amount of freight, to be paid at the end of every year. This practice prevented ruinous competition against each other, which was the case in other shipping markets in East Asia, with often relentless rivalries. In this light, the agreement between Jebsen and Marty was a special case, but it certainly prevented a price war, as the following events clearly made obvious.[238] The expectation that serious competitors would not emerge in this rather closed shipping market was violated with the sudden appearance of the China Navigation Company, the shipping arm of Butterfield & Swire, at the time generally regarded as the most powerful shipping company in East Asia. Until then, the firm had mainly been active in northern China, where it competed with Japanese shipping companies for lucrative freight. However, with the worst recession in decades hitting the world's shipping industry at the time, and fresh Japanese competition in the form of a new rival, the Nisshin Kisen Kaisha (Japan-China Steamship Company), soon dominating the Yangzi River (Yangtze) business, the China Navigation Company seemed to have hoped to obtain higher profits in southern China. This finally triggered the decision to launch a new shipping service between Hong Kong, Haikou and Haiphong.[239]

The British firm officially informed Jebsen & Co. about the planned step beforehand in April 1907, and received information about the German firm's freight tariffs. By agreeing with Jebsen on a reduction from 25 to 20 cents per bag, thus on a decrease of 20 per cent, Butterfield obviously expected to quickly find sufficient transports to position itself firmly

[237] Raffi (1994, 602).

[238] MAE, CPC-548: Consul Teissier-Soulange (Hong Kong) to Foreign Minister Pichon (Paris), 24 April 1907. *The Hong Kong Telegraph*, 17 April 1909.

[239] In French, German and British consular files the China Navigation Company is exclusively referred to as Butterfield & Swire or only as Butterfield, a modus operandi that is also used in this book. Since the company papers of Butterfield & Swire for that specific business during this period are not available, the concrete reasons for the firm's decision to send its ships to southern China remain unclear. The Swire Archives, kept by the School of Oriental and African Studies (SOAS), University of London, do not contain any relevant papers on such aspects.

in the rice shipment market and to stave off the much-feared competition from Japanese shipping companies. Jebsen agreed to the deal, fearing a ruinous price war with Butterfield should he, with his smaller firm, not agree. Marty consented as well, having little flexibility due to his rather small fleet, consisting of four older steamers of which one, the *Hue,* operated the Guangzhouwan postal steamer service on a fixed timetable. However, the low freight rate agreed upon by the three companies resulted in continuously low profits which most severely affected Marty, who announced that he would ask the government-general for a subsidy should the situation not improve. Jacob Jebsen, fearing that such support would give his rival unfair advantages, was even more concerned about Marty being forced to withdraw from the line "and that another, perhaps more energetic French company would enter his inheritance". In his letter to Consul Hans von Varchmin in Beihai, the German shipowner made it clear that "the necessary consideration for Marty complicates our position towards the English competition: A price war would cause the said complications with the French firm, a rise in freight would provide good profits but have the danger that Butterfield would flood us with tonnage. Therefore, for the time being we are endeavouring to keep a middle line".[240]

On 10 November 1907, obviously on Marty's initiative, the three companies came to a new joint agreement on a revised uniform freight rate of 25 cents per bag. This actually restored the rate to the same level before Butterfield entered the market some months earlier. However, Chinese rice shippers in Haiphong regarded this decision as unacceptable and immediately decided to boycott the ships of the three firms. The prominent Shun-Tai rice company at Haiphong, through its Hong Kong agent Po Hing Tai, chartered two Norwegian steamers — the *Fritjof* and the *Dagny,* offering rice shippers the cut-rate price of 19 cents per rice bag. According to Haiphong's mayor, Pierre Tournois, in his later report on the case, the major Japanese shipping company Nippon Yusen Kaisha (N.Y.K.) which frequently chartered Norwegian ships, was behind the matter, offering Chinese shippers all the tonnage they needed for their exports to Hong Kong and imports to Tonkin; in such a case, the Japanese company may have been induced to establish itself in Tonkin. However, with such expansionist plans of the N.Y.K. being abolished

[240] PAAA, Peking II-1174: Jacob Jebsen (Hong Kong) to Consul von Varchmin (Beihai), 13 February 1908.

at the end of 1907, the outcome of the boycott was also affected. In December 1907, a joint conference of concerned shipowners and principal rice merchants was held in Hong Kong, during which both sides tried to find an amicable solution to the crisis. Finally, the three shipping companies agreed to reverse the price increase and to again fix the freight rate at 20 cents per bag, which ended the Chinese boycott of their ships.[241]

As a result of the agreement, Butterfield & Swire, facing low profits on the run, withdrew one of their three steamers from the route between Hong Kong, Haikou and Haiphong. Jacob Jebsen was convinced that the British firm was unhappy with the results so far, but would not entirely give up the trade.[242] This prediction came true when Butterfield initiated a conference in Hong Kong on 23 March 1909 with its two rivals, in which it was agreed that the freight rate on rice should be increased to 26 cents per bag, thus being raised by more than 23 per cent. Additionally, it was agreed that each of the three firms should put only a certain number of ships on the line to avoid an oversupply of tonnage. The companies were confident that the Chinese rice shippers, whether they liked it or not, would accept the increased freight rate when faced with both the coming rich rice harvest of spring 1909 and the difficulty in employing alternative steamers for their rice shipments.[243]

However, such hopes were promptly frustrated. For the new boycott, six large rice trading firms in Haiphong formed a syndicate or charter combine and subsequently established the Lien Yi Chinese Steamship Company in April 1909. The initiator was the major rice merchant Tam Sec Sam, the founder and owner of the rice company Shun-Tai, headquartered in Hong Kong with a branch in Haiphong, as well as sister companies in Hong Kong, Tonkin and Yunnan. Tam, who also served as president of the Chinese Chamber of Commerce in Haiphong, frequently called meetings with other major local Chinese rice merchants to discuss boycott measures. The Chinese combine collected a huge sum from its member firms, which allowed it to offer a cut-rate price of ten cents per

[241] *The Hong Kong Telegraph*, 28 November 1907 and 9 December 1907. On Norwegian merchant steamers operating in East Asia, see Brautaset and Tenold (2010, 207, 217–222) and Becker (2020, 952–953). For the N.Y.K., see Wray (1984, 379–380).

[242] JJHA, B10-01-017: Jacob Jebsen (Hong Kong) to Johann Heinrich Jessen (Apenrade), 29 April 1908.

[243] *The Hong Kong Telegraph*, 17 April 1909. Becker (2020, 954–955).

bag, a considerable decrease (over 61 per cent) of the price fixed by the three European firms. Consequently, the firm chartered three Norwegian steamers on trip charters and the *Victoria* under the Swedish flag on time charter; in July 1909, when these charters expired, it again time-chartered the *Victoria* and also the *Fri* under the Norwegian flag, along with (on trip charter) the *Landrat Scheiff* of the German trading firm Siemssen & Co. in Hong Kong. The Chinese position was complicated by several factors, of which the lack of return cargoes was the most immediate one. *The Hong Kong Telegraph* hinted at this problem: "There is the question of return cargoes to be weighted, for if the entrants in the trade have to bring their vessels back to Haiphong in ballast the venture may prove to be an exceedingly costly one for them. Therein lies the power of the three shipping firms against whose interest the boycott has been instituted". Consequently, the actual freight rate of the Lien Yi Chinese Steamship Company for the round trip increased to around 15 cents per bag.[244]

Faced with the ongoing boycott, Jebsen and Butterfield decided to lower their freight rate to ten cents per rice bag, and even granted a return commission of 10 per cent on the amount of freight at the end of every year. Their hope of undercutting prices and ultimately defeating the rival ships of the Chinese charter combine seemed to pay off when Shun-Tai and two other rice trading firms decided to leave the charter combine and to again provide cargoes to vessels of the three shipping companies. This decision resulted in an angry reaction: in August 1909, Shun-Tai received an anonymous threatening letter accusing the firm of destroying the boycotting union and being a traitor. The letter was channelled to Marty, who took the opportunity to directly approach Governor-General Antony W. Klobukowski about the matter. Hinting that the note was the work of the Chinese in the boycott society (called in Marty's letter "la societé de boycottage"), the shipowner regarded the document as clear proof that the Chinese boycotting combine intended to severely harm the three shipping companies. He also sent another copy of the letter to the prosecutor of the French Republic in Haiphong hoping, as he said in his accompanying letter, that the French authorities would launch a serious investigation into the incident and consequently end the boycott. Marty's action prompted Haiphong's mayor, Pierre Tournois, to collect

[244] Becker (2020, 955–958). *The Hong Kong Telegraph*, 23 April 1909.

information from different sources and produce a lengthy report in which he concluded that this particular case did not constitute a boycott in the true meaning of the term and consequently could not constitute an offence according to the penal code. He advised the shipping companies to take suitable measures to combat their opponents in the field of free competition. With this verdict, the case was settled for the French authorities.[245]

In October 1909, Michael (Magge) Jebsen, head of the shipping department of Jebsen & Co., reported that the Chinese themselves admitted to having lost 10,000 dollars for their chartering during the last months. Therefore, he recommended "to wait until the people get worn out, which will not take too long, if we continue the struggle in the previous form".[246] Yet, it took seven more months before the Chinese merchants finally gave in. The boycott ended after Johann Heinrich Jessen, the co-owner of Jebsen & Co., paid a visit to Haiphong to meet the rice shippers. On 10 May 1910, six Haiphong rice shipping company representing another twelve rice exporting firms and the three European shipping companies signed an agreement fixing freight rates on rice at 22 cents per bag. The three firms also granted the shippers a return commission of 10 per cent on the amount of the freight, to be paid at the end of every year. Compared to the price fixed in March 1909, which had ignited the boycott, this resulted in a more than 15 per cent decrease in the freight rate on rice, which was obviously sufficient for the Chinese shippers. The most important clause was that the rice shippers promised not to charter any other steamer or steamers for the Haiphong-Hong Kong run while the agreement was in force. They also agreed that a restricted number of steamers belonging to the three firms should operate on the run so that competition would be reduced and freight rates could be maintained at the same level. The agreement was put in force on 23 May 1910 for a period of three years and was to automatically continue for another year, if any party did not give notice to each other two months before its expiration.[247]

[245] Becker (2020, 958–960).

[246] JJHA, PS-1502: Michael (Magge) Jebsen (Hong Kong) to Jacob Jebsen (Apenrade), 9 October 1909.

[247] Becker (2020, 963–965). The only remaining evidence of the agreement is a document in typewritten form, titled "Copy of Translation" and called "Memorandum of

The Chinese shipping boycotts of 1907 and 1909–1910 prompted a very different reaction from Western powers than the boycott of 1895–1896. While in the latter case, the French imperial power intervened with the Chinese government on behalf of a French shipping company, the later boycotts did not provoke the intervention of Western powers. Already in 1900, when Marty was very confident of being in a strong position after winning the ten-year subsidy contract of the government-general for operating the Guangzhouwan postal steamer service, his attempt to get support from Doumer against the alleged return of the boycott society of Chinese shippers in Haiphong remained unsuccessful. French authorities regarded boycotts as purely economic struggles in which they saw no reason to intervene. This changed attitude was again obvious during the boycotts of 1907 and 1909–1910, clearly reflecting profound changes in the dynamics of imperial power and Chinese reactions. In the latter case, although the Europeans prevailed in the final struggle, the Chinese shippers won concessions from them. This was a clear evidence of a new Chinese nationalism as it became obvious in the Boxer Rebellion (1899–1901) and growing nationalism in China, expressed in public discourse on the recovery of shipping rights, with economic instead of political means being employed by the Chinese in their struggle against foreign domination. French and German shipping companies learned that economic, not imperial force majeure, determined the outcome of the struggles.

With the Tonkin Shipping Company winning the new subsidy contract of the government-general for operating the Guangzhouwan postal steamer service (which was due to start in March 1913), Jacob Jebsen was very concerned that this would make it more difficult "to push through the urgently needed increase of freight rates" when the agreement of 23 May 1910 expired. He predicted that Marty was less interested in increasing freight rates because he had the financial support of Indochina and would probably receive less cargo from Chinese traders due to the fact that the postal steamers were bound to fixed timetables, and had therefore frequent and rather long stays in the ports of call.[248] However,

Agreement", at the beginning of the text. It was issued in Haiphong, 10 May 1910, and is in English. JJHA, B10-02-0086.

[248] JJHA, A01-01-301: Jacob Jebsen (Apenrade) to Gustav Diederichsen (Hamburg), 20 November 1912.

after lengthy talks with the Haiphong rice shippers, Jebsen and Butterfield, in June 1913, achieved a new agreement on freight rates on rice fixed at 25 cents per bag, thus the same rate on which Jebsen and Marty had informally agreed before Butterfield entered the market in 1907. The shipowners again granted a return commission of 10 per cent on the amount of freight should the shippers refrain from chartering other steamers "outside Tourane" [south of Da Nang in central Vietnam]. This had obviously been practiced by Chinese merchants to circumvent the term of the agreement of 1910, in which they promised to exclusively give their cargoes to vessels of the three companies. Since the Chinese shippers were not prepared to sign a contract for the duration of several years, Jebsen and Butterfield insisted on the stipulation that they were bound to the current rate "only until further notice". This finally settled the new agreement to which Marty transmitted his consent by telegraph. According to Johann Heinrich Jessen, any further increase of freight rates was unrealistic for the time being.[249] With that, any correspondence from Jebsen & Co. on the issue ended. In the following year, with the outbreak of the First World War, shipping under the German flag entirely ceased operating in East Asia.

Steamships and Illicit Trades

Illicit trades such as selling of women and children was prevalent in the South China Sea long before France established her rule in Indochina. This trade in slaves had been pursued for centuries, but with France's presence it became more widely known. As early as 1873, French Catholic missionaries in Tonkin had reported that Vietnamese women and children were frequently being kidnapped. At the time, marketplaces already existed where such illegal transactions took place. In January 1887, the French government-general in Hanoi learned of the massive extent of women trafficking (in French: traite des femmes) in Tonkin. The newspaper *L'Avenir du Tonkin* reported that French and indigenous forces had liberated more than two hundred women and children held captive by Chinese armed bands. According to Eric Tagliacozzo, human trafficking was linked to smuggling, especially of opium, with women being "one of

[249] JJHA, PS-8418: Johann Heinrich Jessen (Hong Kong) to Jacob Jebsen (Apenrade), 14 June 1913.

the most important subsets of people smuggled into and around South-east Asia at the turn of the century (…) to be used for sexual purposes". Vietnamese women especially seem to have developed a reputation among purchasers, mainly Chinese, for being hardworking, quiet and docile, making them attractive as potential concubines. Furthermore, women and older girls were doomed for prostitution in brothels or as "singing girls" working in restaurants and clubs, while older boys were prepared for different criminal jobs, such as thief or brothel pimp. Younger girls transferred to port cities such as Guangzhou or Hong Kong were sold at a considerable profit, often becoming *mui tsai* (little younger sisters), young female domestic bondservants or "slave girls", while young boys and babies were often taken into Chinese families under the guise of adoption. In the late 1870s, the Hong Kong government itself was aware of this practice and the first prosecutions for the kidnapping and detention of children with the intent to sell them into bond service were going ahead in the British colony. In January 1880, the Po Keung Kuk, the Society for the Protection of Women and Children, was established with the goal of helping the victims of slavery.[250]

The poverty of peasant societies in Indochina was the root cause of this phenomenon which was exploited by Chinese and Vietnamese players involved in trafficking of poor, uneducated and often illiterate Vietnamese women and of children of almost all ages. A complex network of countless armed bands travelling in junks or sampans along the coastal and river regions of Indochina and China transported the victims to urban centres in the South China Sea region. Others were clandestinely boarded in Haiphong on vessels heading to Hainan Island or Hong Kong, concealed in the holds of junks or other ocean-going vessels. In April 1880, eighteen Vietnamese children aged five to thirteen, all except one of them girls, were discovered hidden on board the British steamer *Conquest* anchored in the port of Haiphong. Some were rolled in blankets, while others were in closed baskets covered in clothes. According to the harbourmaster's investigation, the children had been transported on riverboats and taken from several places along the Red River to be transhipped on the vessel bound to Hong Kong. The *Conquest,* flying the British flag, was owned by Kwong Li Yuen, obviously a Chinese residing in the

[250] *L'Avenir du Tonkin*, 15 January 1887. Lessard (2009, 4, 9–10), Tagliacozzo (2005, 231–232), Martínez (2007b, 205), Pomfret (2008, 181) and Sinn (1994, 147–148; 2013, 229–240).

British colony. In his report to Cochinchina's Governor, Charles Le Myre de Vilers, French consul Louis Palasme de Champeaux admitted that it was impossible to track the influential people behind the traffic, both in Haiphong and Hong Kong.[251] This added fuel to ongoing investigations in Saigon prompted by the governor after severe criticisms of the pace of anti-slavery reform in Cochinchina had been made public in France by a former magistrate of Saigon. The administrator charged with the inquiry recorded a "veritable trade in children" into situations that equated to "nothing less than slavery".[252]

In the 1880s, the existence of human trafficking was reported by several French missionaries in Tonkin and travellers to the areas bordering China. This practice became even better known after the Sino-French War (1884–1885) and the establishment of the Protectorate of Annam-Tonkin, when French newspapers in Hanoi and Haiphong published numerous reports about literally hundreds of cases of such kidnappings. During the so-called "pacification" campaigns in the early 1890s, the journals frequently reviewed French military and police operations in northern Vietnam and often mentioned the freeing of women and children from Chinese and Vietnamese bandits. In May 1891, the Resident Superior of Tonkin, Ernest Albert Brière, required that all local French residents and vice-residents of the protectorate be highly vigilant when issuing travel papers to Chinese in Tonkin, especially to those travelling with children. He declared that "all our efforts must be directed at trying to stop this ignoble trafficking (trafic infâme)" and that French authorities needed to be vigilant, not careless and to avoid becoming the unwitting accomplices of this trade.[253] His call did not go unheeded. In the following years, there were serious attempts on the part of the French administration, the military and French consuls in ports of the South China Sea to hamper and stop this illicit trade. Such efforts were recorded in files of the Resident Superior, one of which contains telegrams dispatched between 1889 and 1899 concerning the repatriation

[251] Martínez (2007b, 204, 206–207) and Luan and Cooke (2011, 148).

[252] The article titled "Une Colonie esclavagiste" (A Slave Colony) was published anonymously (though known to be by Raoul Postel) in *La Lanterne* on 14 January 1880. The inquiry of Jules Silvestre titled "Rapport sur l'esclavage" (Report on Slavery) in *Excursions et rennaissances*, ii, 3 (1880; repr. 1894), 50–51. Pomfret (2008, 175–176, 181–182, the quote: 181).

[253] Lessard (2009, 11–15, the quote: 13).

of Vietnamese women abducted by Chinese pirates. In April 1889, two women who had been kidnapped three and sixteen years before were discovered by the French consul in Beihai and shipped back to their home towns of Ninh Binh and Thanh Hoa, located south of Haiphong. Thirteen Vietnamese women found on board Chinese junks arriving in Beihai from Haiphong in August 1892 were immediately sent to Haikou on the Jebsen steamer *Triumph* at the expense of the Resident Superior. From there, they were transported back to Tonkin on the first steamer from Haiphong. In April 1899, Marty's steamer *Hue* was recorded as being charged in Beihai with a similar repatriation of Vietnamese women.[254] In November 1901, several Chinese traffickers were arrested in the port of Haiphong when boarding the *Danube* (probably a British steamer), accompanied by Vietnamese women and children disguised as Chinese and holding falsified passports.[255]

In 1904, the French government signed an international agreement in Paris for the suppression of the "White Slave Traffic" which made reference to suppressing "the procuring of women and girls for immoral purposes abroad" and referred broadly to women "of foreign nationality". France promised that it would apply the terms of the agreement to its colonies as well.[256] At the time, it had become obvious in Indochina that human trafficking was prevalent in Haiphong and other ports in northern Vietnam, with many of the captured women and children covered in the holds of junks or steamers which shipped them to Beihai, Haikou or Hong Kong. After such cases occurred more frequently, the Resident Superior of Tonkin, Elie Jean Henri Groleau, announced in 1906 that he was ordering the surveillance of all ports of Tonkin and the searching of every single steamer and junk. This did not prevent the hiding of twenty-seven children of both sexes on French and German steamers. When Marty's vessel *Hanoi* called at Haikou in early September 1906, French consul Joseph Beauvais embarked and discovered eighteen Vietnamese children accompanied by Chinese "robbers" (voleurs) intent on bringing them to Haikou, Hong Kong and Guangzhou. When the

[254]VNA1, RST-2417: Telegram of Resident Superior (Hanoi) to Resident (Ninh Binh), 23 April 1889; telegram of Mayor Baille (Haiphong) to Resident Superior (Hanoi), 22 August 1892; Telegram of Consul Liébert (Beihai) to Resident Superior (Hanoi), 18 April 1899.

[255]*Le Courrier d'Haiphong*, 14 November 1901.

[256]Martínez (2007b, 205) and Lessard (2009, 18).

Carl Diederichsen of the M. Jebsen Shipping Company, chartered by Speidel & Co. in Haiphong, arrived soon afterwards, Beauvais found nine children in the hold. In his report to the governor-general, the consul suspected that the boarding was done "with the complicity of crew members, and perhaps also of the Chinese shipping comprador" (the shipping comprador was usually in charge of all transactions concerning Chinese passengers such as sales of tickets and reservations of cabins). Nevertheless, he judged the fact that such a large number of children could be secretly embarked in Haiphong "a deplorable negligence and so extraordinary a lack of care by our police and Customs personnel" and even cast suspicion on the Vietnamese staff of these administrations as being involved as accomplices. The consul was convinced "that every German or French steamer leaving Indochina bound for Hong Kong carries on board a cargo of this nature".[257]

As an immediate result of this report, Acting Governor-General Stanislas Broni established a special police force to monitor activities in the port of Haiphong. However, on 12 December 1906, Consul Beauvais learned that the Jebsen steamer *Mathilde,* arriving from Haiphong, had ten Vietnamese children on board. This time, he immediately contacted the German consulate and secured the support of the secretary who instructed the shipmaster to allow staff of the Imperial Maritime Customs Service (the Chinese governmental tax collection agency and information service) to inspect the vessel. They discovered ten children dressed in Chinese clothes and accompanied by three Chinese women who were well-known in Haikou for being engaged in this trade. According to Beauvais' information of 17 December 1906, he had been able to rescue thirty-six children of both sexes during the previous ten days. Three days later, in his letter to France's Minister Edmond Bapst in Beijing, the consul enclosed copies of correspondence with the governor-general and summed up his tireless efforts over weeks to free trafficked Vietnamese women and children. Praising the goodwill of local Chinese authorities in bringing the perpetrators of such crimes to justice, he was nevertheless realistic enough to admit that this was "a horrible but very lucrative trade".[258]

[257] MAE, CPC-218 Hainan 1899–1906: Consul Beauvais (Haikou) to Acting Governor-General Broni (Hanoi), 13 September 1906. Lessard (2009, 23–24).

[258] MAE, CPC-218 Hainan 1899–1906: Acting Governor-General Broni (Hanoi) to Consul Beauvais (Haikou), 22 October 1906; Consul Beauvais (Haikou) to Acting

Soon later, Consul Beauvais secured the support of Chas. Kliene, who, according to the staff list of *The Directory and Chronicle* for 1906, ranked first in the list of assistant commissioners of the Imperial Maritime Customs Service at Haikou. The two officials agreed to take certain measures to end the trafficking of Vietnamese children, regarding it as "absolutely necessary" to achieve an agreement between the different foreign consuls in Haikou to ensure that not just French ships were surveyed when calling at the port. With respect to the considerable share of the German flag calling at Haikou, it was obvious to Beauvais and Kliene that "our efforts" would be "absolutely illusionary" without the co-operation of the German consulate. Since Consul Hans von Varchmin, with whom Beauvais had "the most cordial relations", had left for Beihai, Dr. Rudolf Walter was acting head of the consulate in Haikou. According to Beauvais's report, at the meeting on 14 January 1907 Walter insisted that the case concerned only French and Chinese but not German interests and so he regarded any agreement as useless. However, when British Vice-Consul Victor Laurent Savage signalled his support for a joint declaration by the three consuls, Walter gave in, demanding that the drafted regulations should later be submitted for formal approval by the respective legations at Beijing. Therefore, at the meeting on 21 January, the three consuls agreed on the regulations being a "working basis" that was to be submitted to the three ministers "for consideration and approval". The convention's stipulations required masters of British, French and German ships to ensure that Chinese and Vietnamese women of any age, and boys up to the age of fifteen, calling Haikou had valid travel documents or were at least able to provide "a satisfactory account of themselves and their business". After the agreement was signed by the three consuls, it was dispatched to Beijing where it met with strong reservations, even at the French legation. On 26 February 1907, Bapst told Beauvais that any official accord would give "this entirely local question an exaggerated importance" and that it seemed preferable to use, without ostentation, an ordinary agreement without an official protocol. As this position was shared by the British and German ministers, none of the three ministers approved the Haikou regulations. However, Beauvais did not inform

Governor-General Broni (Hanoi), 17 December 1906; Consul Beauvais (Haikou) to Minister Bapst (Beijing), 20 December 1906.

Kliene of that fact, believing that the "tacit" agreement between the three consuls would work without any problems.[259]

On 24 January 1908, staff of the Chinese Maritime Customs in Haikou discovered four young Vietnamese women aged between fifteen and eighteen years hidden in the front holds of the *Carl Diederichsen* Jebsen steamer arriving from Haiphong. Accompanied by a Chinese couple from Beihai, the females were destined to be transported to Hong Kong. Since no regular passports could be provided for the Vietnamese passengers, the shipmaster was required to release them to Customs Commissioner Kliene who brought them to Beauvais. When Theodor Metzelthin, interpreter and acting consul, learned about the events, he strongly protested against Kliene's "irregular" action, especially the detention of a Chinese couple and the Chinese ship's cook who was their accomplice. According to Beauvais, the German consul's complaint basically derived from an earlier personal conflict between his wife and the mother of Kliene. When Consul von Varchmin arrived from Beihai (at the time, the German consulates at Haikou and Beihai were jointly managed by the consul, who usually resided in Beihai, and an acting consul in Haikou), he immediately came down on Metzelthin's side. The underlying personal conflict seemed to be the motivating factor for the hardened positions on both sides, resulting in voluminous correspondence between the customs commissioner and the two German officials — Klienes's letter to Varchmin dated 12 February 1908 consisted of eighteen typewritten pages, while one of 7 March had thirteen typed pages. The correspondence was written in a somewhat cordial, very polite and entirely factual tone, without any political connotations or nationalist terminology, predominantly hinting at administrative regulations and responsibilities, juridical concerns and, to a limited extent, to the business interests of private shipowners. Indeed, both sides insisted they were right, but they did not care about the fate of the trafficked Vietnamese females. On 24 March, in very friendly tones, a full consensus was reached about future formal proceedings. In his letter to Paris, dated 20 June 1908, French Minister Bapst admitted that the Germans had acted properly when protesting against the way the customs commissioner had arrested the Chinese ship's cook. However, "this real error would not have been

[259] *The Directory and Chronicle of China* (1906, 848). MAE, CPC-219 Hainan 1907–1912: Consul Beauvais (Haikou) to Minister Bapst (Beijing), 27 January 1907; Consul Beauvais (Haikou) to Foreign Minister Pichon (Paris), 17 February 1908 (the letter, of 26 February 1907, from Minister Bapst was quoted here).

revealed, if there had not been personal barbs between the German administrator [Metzelthin] and the customs commissioner [Kliene]".[260]

Kidnapping cases were frequently reported in French newspapers published in Hanoi and Haiphong. The sheer volume of shipping and trade in the South China Sea made it impossible to stop this illicit trade. Whether the Chinese traffickers in Haiphong had "business connections with British and German steamer companies", as suggested by Julia Martínez, remains an open question because concrete evidence of such practices rarely found its way into government files or newspaper articles.[261] However, when two new trafficking cases came to light in January 1912, and were extensively documented and commented on by the Tonkin press, the German consulate in Saigon launched a thorough inquiry, contributing detailed insights into this specific issue. The vessel twice involved was the Jebsen steamer *Carl Diederichsen*, which frequently shipped rice from Haiphong to Hong Kong. This was the same vessel affected by trafficking cases four years earlier, but it is possible that more cases went undiscovered. The ship, built at the Howaldt Dockyard in Kiel in 1901, of 774 net and 1243 gross tonnes, had large holds able to take voluminous bulk cargoes. The shipmaster, Christian Jürgensen, thirty-nine years old, from Apenrade, was a very experienced officer who had served as master of four other steamers in the M. Jebsen Shipping Company.[262] On 3 January 1912, a Vietnamese

[260] MAE, CPC-219 Hainan 1907–1912: Consul von Varchmin (Beihai) to Customs Commissioner Kliene (Haikou), 4 February 1908; Consul von Varchmin (Beihai) to Consul Beauvais (Haikou), 6 February 1908, 1 and 24 March 1908; Customs Commissioner Kliene (Haikou) to Consul Beauvais (Haikou), 10 February 1908; Consul Beauvais (Haikou) to Customs Commissioner Kliene (Haikou), 11 February 1908; Customs Commissioner Kliene (Haikou) to Consul von Varchmin (Beihai), 12 February 1908 and 7 March 1908; Consul Beauvais (Haikou) to Foreign Minister Pichon (Paris), 17 February and 30 March 1908; Consul Beauvais (Haikou) to Consul von Varchmin (Beihai), 19 March 1908; Minister Bapst (Beijing) to Foreign Minister Pichon (Paris), 20 June 1908. — See also Lessard (2009, 20–21) who suggests a different interpretation of the matter, shifting the blame entirely to Varchmin for "placing petty jurisdictional issues above the need for action against the trafficking of women and children".

[261] Martínez (2007b, 209–210).

[262] Captain Jürgensen was master on the *Jacob Diederichsen* (1900–1901), the *Apenrade* (II, 1903–1904), the *Knivsberg* (1906–1907) and the *Germania* (1908–1910) before taking over the command of the *Carl Diederichsen* in June 1910. After the Haiphong trafficking cases were settled, the *Carl Diederichsen* was put under the command of Eduard Pahren (1912–13). Jürgensen was made master of the *Clara Jebsen* and remained in this

staff member of the Haiphong harbour police force was finishing his shift at one o'clock in the morning when he heard Chinese voices talking about the boarding of children. At four o'clock, he watched these people embark on a sampan to go to the *Carl Diederichsen* which was anchored in the port. The staff immediately warned M. Gentil, a French police officer, who went onto the vessel and discovered eight or nine Vietnamese children aged from seven to fourteen years hidden in the holds and boiler rooms. Tragically, one of the Vietnamese girls fell into the water and drowned during the rescue operation. Gentil freed the others and arrested a Chinese woman from Hanoi and her accomplice, a Chinese sailor of the *Carl Diederichsen*; two other sailors fled the scene. The newspaper *L'Opinion*, published in Saigon, in reporting the case, admitted that "this shameful trade" was practiced on a large scale in Saigon, Haiphong and other port cities of Tonkin by "vile traffickers of human flesh", risking only minimal penalties. It called for "energetic measures" such as "a very rigorous surveillance" of ports and strict sentences, even deportation of perpetrators and their accomplices to French Guiana, the penal colony located on the northeast coast of South America where prisoners were sentenced to forced labour. Yet, since other French newspapers did not follow up the matter, the incident soon fell into obscurity.[263]

Less than four weeks later, public excitement in Indochina was stirred up to a crescendo when the same ship was again involved in a trafficking case. This time, the harbour police officer, Gentil, discovered a large number of trafficked Vietnamese women and children on board the *Carl Diederichsen.* On the morning of 29 January 1912, the officer woke up to the sound of sampans moving around the ship and immediately went on board with Vietnamese police staff. Deep in the bottom of the steamer, at the entrance to the chain stopper hold, he found large coal sacks which he and his assistants were clearing away when they heard children crying for help. A Chinese passenger found in the hold was immediately arrested. Also found were two Vietnamese women aged eighteen and twenty, the latter being the mother of one of the eleven Vietnamese girls and boys aged between four and six. Two more Chinese passengers were arrested, but the Chinese boatswain who was suspected

position until the *Clara Jeb*sen was confiscated in 1914 at the beginning of the First World War. — Hieke (1953, 236–237, 249–253).

[263] *L'Opinion*, 11 January 1912.

of being an accomplice, escaped from the ship. This time, the incident caused a storm of indignation in Haiphong which was echoed in the press. According to *Le Courrier d'Haiphong*, the children were bound for Hong Kong and the "bateaux de fleurs" ("flower boats") of Guangzhou. The journal expressed the hope "that the shipowners and consignees will give the most severe orders to their captains so that an end is brought to the trafficking of the Yellows which has been occurring on board German ships for almost twenty-five years".[264]

The next day, Speidel & Co. in Haiphong, the loader of the *Carl Diederichsen*, informed Jebsen & Co. by postal mail that the vessel had been waiting for very profitable freight, especially a deck cargo for Haikou. The firm's manager, Franz Dobrowohl, enclosing a copy of *Le Courrier d'Haiphong*, strongly urged Jebsen, "in the interests of German shipping", to establish "forceful regulations" such as replacing and holding accountable the Chinese ship comprador of the steamer as he was "undoubtedly someone who was in the know". Dobrowohl admitted that "in the light of the actual incidents", he was unable to launch a protest and had invited the shipmaster to discuss the situation with him. The possible involvement of the captain in the new trafficking case was mentioned the following day by *L'Avenir du Tonkin*. The French journalist found it astonishing, and even unjust, that "given the repetition of such an event" neither the ship's sailors nor its officers had been punished under the law. He strongly criticised the deficiencies of the French penal code, especially over the "complicity" of masters of ships on which such trafficking cases had been discovered. In an article published by *L'Opinion* in Saigon on 6 February, the writer went even further, accusing "certain seafarers visiting our ports" of being "slave traders" and demanding a full inquiry into "the two affairs of the *Carl Diederichsen* (…) to end this vile trade of children", with "the culprits, whoever they are, Europeans or natives, having to learn the full severity of our laws".[265]

The detailed reports and comments in the Indochina press concerning this specific incident failed to mention that similar cases had occurred

[264] *Le Courrier d'Haiphong*, 30 January 1912, *L'Avenir du Tonkin*, 31 January 1912 and *L'Opinion*, 6 February 1912. BAB, R 901-17976: Consul Crull (Saigon) to Chancellor von Bethmann-Hollweg (Berlin), 15 February 1912.

[265] PAAA, Konsulat Saigon 5-1: Franz Dobrowohl, Speidel & Co. (Haiphong) to Jebsen & Co. (Hong Kong), 30 January 1912. *L'Avenir du Tonkin*, 31 January 1912 and *L'Opinion*, 6 February 1912.

on board British and French vessels in recent years. The rise in trafficking cases that peaked in the early twentieth century was also due to the perpetrators' improved chances of being able to ship their victims on the increasing number of modern steamships operating on the route from Haiphong to Hong Kong. The sheer presence of numerous vessels under the German flag in the ports of Indochina not only triggered negative feelings among French residents, but also made these ships very vulnerable to illicit trades such as trafficking. Therefore, the German consulate in Saigon decided not to get involved in a press campaign, expecting "the chauvinism of local newspapers", as Consul Felix Reinsdorf called it later. This was probably recommended by Speidel & Co., who were anxious to avoid more calamity for their business in the French colony. Explicitly labelling themselves agents of the Jebsen line, on 2 February 1912 the firm promised Haiphong's mayor, Felix Paul Hauser, "to remind captains and compradors to conduct detailed and rigorous surveillances of ships and the Chinese crews on board" and "to help the police in crushing this criminal traffic". On the other hand, Dobrowohl did not forget to ask the French official for "an efficient surveillance of the harbour" in order "to prevent clandestine boarding". However, the mayor's immediate reply made it clear that the captain could not be easily relieved of his responsibility for thoroughly controlling the ship, especially after the previous incident that had occurred not long ago.[266]

Consul Wilhelm Crull in Saigon was keenly interested in quickly and comprehensively investigating the matter. His first steps were to urge Captain Jürgensen to submit a detailed account of the event and to beg the French prosecutor in Haiphong to release to him the results of the questioning of the arrested Chinese. In his report to Berlin of 15 February 1912, the consul stressed that the incident had "utterly harmed the reputation of the German flag in Haiphong, and generally in Indochina". He asked the German government to "remonstrate in the most serious way about the issue with the M. Jebsen Shipping Company in Apenrade and to explicitly commit them to send strict orders guard the *Carl Diederichsen,*

[266] Martínez (2007b, 205). BAB, R 901-76661: Consul Reinsdorf (Saigon) to Chancellor von Bethmann-Hollweg (Berlin), 6 March 1913. PAAA, Konsulat Saigon 5-1: Speidel & Co. (Haiphong) to Mayor Hauser (Haiphong), 2 February 1912. BAB, R 901-17976: Consul Crull (Saigon) to Chancellor von Bethmann-Hollweg (Berlin), 15 February 1912 (this report quoted the reply by Mayor Hauser to Speidel & Co., which was not included in the files).

so that a repetition of the case would be impossible". In the meantime, the Prosecutor of the French Republic in Haiphong, Daniel Dain, notified Crull that his investigation had not provided any evidence of the involve ment of European staff, adding that, in the first trafficking instance, it was the captain himself who had called the police after the First Officer had detected the children during the regular investigation some hours before the ship was due to leave Haiphong. This fact was confirmed soon after by Captain Jürgensen adding that in the second instance, the police had come on board the day before the departure, at a time when the usual examination by the ship officers had not yet been conducted. "We would have found the children even without the police intervening, because it was still twenty-four hours before departure", he explained.[267]

On 12 March 1912, Captain Jürgensen and the First Officer, August Böhmer (who filled this post since December 1908), were questioned in Hong Kong by Consul Ernst Arthur von Voretzsch. According to Böhmer, special precautions against such incidents had not been taken on board the *Carl Diederichsen*, except for announcements in English and Chinese posted in the crew quarters warning about the smuggling of passengers without passports and threatening to hand over perpetrators to the police. The officer pointed to the fact that Vietnamese children were brought on board "only at night", prompting ship officers and the Haiphong police to examine vessels shortly before their departure. He admitted that Chinese crew members were "very likely" involved in the trade because they needed to feed the children during the voyage of eight to ten days from Haiphong to Hong Kong, with a stopover at Haikou. "It is even possible that the traders leave their hiding place with the children after the departure to buy regular tickets", Böhmer said, adding that it was "common practice with passengers arriving during the last night before departure, without billets". These tickets were sold by the Chinese shipping comprador, "without the captain, the officers or the shipping company having any control over that".[268]

[267] BAB, R 901-17976: Consul Crull (Saigon) to Chancellor von Bethmann-Hollweg (Berlin), 15 February 1912. PAAA, Konsulat Saigon 5-1: Consul Crull (Saigon) to Daniel Dain, Prosecutor of the Republic attached to the Court of First Instance (Haiphong), 6 February 1912; Prosecutor Dain (Haiphong) to Consul Crull (Saigon), 14 February 1912; Captain Jürgensen (Hong Kong) to Consul Crull (Saigon), 11 March 1912.

[268] BAB, R 901-17976: Consul Voretzsch (Hong Kong): Interrogation Protocol, 12 March 1912.

Whether the Chinese shipping comprador or another member of the Chinese crew was involved in these trafficking cases remained an open question during the official enquiry. Captain Jürgensen cast suspicion on the Chinese boatswain, who had disappeared when the police entered the vessel on 29 January. Admitting that special precautions against such incidents had not been taken until then, the shipmaster pointed to the fact that he had in the meantime instructed the First Officer to supervise the upper deck, the First Mechanic to monitor the engine room and the shipping comprador to watch the holds and passenger cabins. This unsatisfactory situation prompted Consul Crull to directly approach Jebsen & Co. in Hong Kong, asking to find out which members of the Chinese crew were involved in trafficking and to remove from the steamer those responsible, or even merely susceptible. As he informed the foreign ministry on 21 March 1912, he deemed the instructions of Captain Jürgensen "to be entirely insufficient to serve their purpose". To demonstrate that he was determined to stamp out such incidents in the future, on the same day the consul issued a formal injunction on all ships of the M. Jebsen Shipping Company sailing between Hong Kong and Haiphong. The directive, which captains were obliged to add to the ship's papers, required masters and officers to carry out regular investigations and compile reports about such matters. Furthermore, the six-point list strictly required captains to post guards on each side of the ship should it be loaded at night. If children were brought on board at night, even with an escort holding valid tickets for them, they had to be put into a separate room where the shipping comprador was obliged to find out whether or not they had been kidnapped. The injunction made it clear that "the officer of the watch (Chinese) and the shipping comprador are to be made responsible for strictly meeting this regulation".[269]

When Jacob Jebsen was informed by the foreign ministry about the trafficking cases, he was considerably annoyed, reproaching Captain Jürgensen for lacking order and control on board the *Carl Diederichsen*. He was dismayed to learn from the Apenrade district administrator about Crull's procedure towards Jebsen vessels on the Haiphong-Hong Kong run. Acknowledging that he was prepared "to support each measure suitable to terminate this atrocious trade", Jebsen still felt angry about the way the consul had acted. Since Crull's directive targeted only his

[269] BAB, R 901-17976: Injunction of Consul Crull (Saigon), dated 21 March 1912.

steamers, the shipowner construed it as "indirectly accusing my shipping company of at least passively supporting the Mädchenhandel [White Slave Trade]". Adding that "for fifteen years, my shipping company had given the German flag an outstanding position in the shipping of Tonkin and Annam, and also prevailed under difficult circumstances", he asked for "some more consideration" of the matter, requesting that the injunction either be restricted to the *Carl Diederichsen* or be extended to every German steamer calling at Haiphong. Regarding his company in Hong Kong, the shipowner admitted that "Captain Jürgensen lacked the necessary caution since otherwise this incident would not have been repeated after a short time". He told his brother, Michael (Magge) Jebsen, that the incidents had caused "much annoyance to me because Berlin seemingly took the case very seriously". Furthermore, he appealed to Magge (who was head of the shipping division of Jebsen & Co.), "to take serious precautions to avoid any reoccurrences".[270]

Jebsen's formal complaint was channelled through the Schleswig-Holstein administrations and finally reached the foreign ministry in Berlin. The head of the trade division, Paul von Koerner, decided to contact Consul Felix Reinsdorf in Saigon (who had replaced Wilhelm Crull in the meantime) asking to learn whether the captains of Jebsen's vessels were complying with the injunction of 21 March, and if so, informing them that the regulation should be repealed. In December 1912, Reinsdorf paid a personal visit to Jebsen & Co. in Hong Kong and was probably received by Michael (Magge) Jebsen who assured him that the captains of steamers serving the Haiphong line were abiding by the directive. This was confirmed by Captain Jürgensen reporting in January 1913 that the *Carl Diederichsen,* while in Haiphong, was guarded day and night by the Chinese helmsman, with one or more ship officers joining him during loading and unloading. He added that the Haiphong police and the ship officers would carry out a thorough inspection before the ship left port. Should trafficked children be found during the voyage, they

[270] JJHA, A01-01-269: Jacob Jebsen (Apenrade) to Captain Jürgensen (Hong Kong), 10 April 1912. BAB, R 901-17976: Jacob Jebsen (Apenrade) to District Administrator von Uslar-Gleichen (Apenrade), 27 June 1912. JJHA, A01-01-320: Jacob Jebsen (Apenrade) to Jebsen & Co. (Hong Kong), 28 June 1912. JJHA, PS-8400: Jacob Jebsen (Apenrade) to Michael (Magge) Jebsen (Hong Kong), 25 June 1912.

would be handed over to the French consulate at the next port of call, the captain concluded.[271]

In his report of 6 March 1913, Consul Reinsdorf directly referred to Jebsen's complaint that his company's steamers had been exclusively targeted by Crull's injunction of 21 March 1912. He pointed to the fact that the Jebsen ships were the only ones flying the German flag frequently shipping passengers from Haiphong to Hong Kong. However, not a single case of children being trafficked on board a Jebsen steamer had been discovered or had become known for more than a year. This was sufficient reason for Foreign Minister Gottlieb von Jagow to instruct the consul in Saigon to repeal the directive. Furthermore, he recommended adequately informing and "calming" the shipowner. Reinsdorf acted quickly, revoking the injunction on 1 July 1913. On behalf of Jebsen & Co., Michael (Magge) Jebsen promised that "everything will, of course, be done to the best of our abilities to take precautions against future repetitions of the *Carl Diederichsen* incident".[272]

Crull's opinion that the French authorities, and especially the Haiphong press, had "exaggerated the incident in an inappropriate way" was certainly justified when considering the harsh public reaction immediately after the second trafficking case in January 1912. The underlying trigger for the press campaign was the fact that German vessels largely dominated Haiphong's shipping and that the French had few options for changing that fact. Professional envy in French business circles, frustration about the inability of the Haiphong authorities to effectively control the port and deep-rooted anti-German sentiment were probably the major reasons for the public outburst by the Tonkin newspapers. All the more, Consul Crull was anxious "to avoid all conflict with the authorities", something Speidel & Co. promised to observe as far as

[271] PAAA, Konsulat Saigon 5-1: Director von Koerner (Berlin) to Consul Reinsdorf (Saigon), 31 October 1912; Captain Jürgensen (Hong Kong) to Consul Reinsdorf (Saigon), 12 January 1913. BAB, R 901-76661: Consul Reinsdorf (Saigon) to Chancellor von Bethmann Hollweg (Berlin), 6 March 1913.

[272] BAB, R 901-76661: Consul Reinsdorf (Saigon) to Chancellor von Bethmann Hollweg (Berlin), 6 March 1913; Note of Foreign Minister von Jagow (Berlin), 31 May 1913; Consul Reinsdorf (Saigon) to Chancellor von Bethmann Hollweg (Berlin), 7 July 1913. PAAA, Konsulat Saigon 5-1: Michael (Magge) Jebsen (Hong Kong) to Consul Reinsdorf (Saigon), 14 July 1913.

possible.[273] The public outcry was actually helpful in prompting a thorough investigation into the affair which established the fact that Chinese crew members were obviously helping traffickers smuggle Vietnamese children on board.

After shipmasters and the Haiphong police had introduced stricter control measures, the situation clearly improved for the M. Jebsen Shipping Company, which was most directly concerned. No further correspondence on such incidents is found in German or French government files or the Jebsen company records. However, as continued newspaper reporting about such cases both before and after the First World War makes apparent, the highly lucrative clandestine trade found other vessels for trafficking Vietnamese women and children to China.[274]

References

Archival Sources

Archives départementales de la Charente-Maritime (ACM)

Base État Civil.

Archives nationales d'outre-mer, Aix-en-Provence (ANOM)

Gouvernement-Général de l'Indochine (INDO-GGI).
Actes de L'État Civil.

British National Archives, Kew/Surrey (TNA)

Foreign Office (FO).

273 BAB, R 901-17976: Consul Crull (Saigon) to Chancellor von Bethmann Hollweg (Berlin), 14 March 1912. PAAA, Konsulat Saigon 5-1: Consul Crull (Saigon) to Speidel & Co. (Haiphong), 15 February 1912; Speidel & Co. (Haiphong) to Consul Crull (Saigon), 6 March 1912.

274 See Martínez (2007b, 208, 211–218), Pomfret (2008, 185–198) and Lessard (2009, 22–28). In Hanoi, the newspaper *L'Avenir du Tonkin* frequently reported on "enfants disparus" (missing children) in the city: in one week in March 1913, five Vietnamese children aged eight to thirteen were reported missing. Drummond (2013, 213).

Bundesarchiv, Berlin (BAB)

Deutsches Reich, Auswärtiges Amt: R 901.

Centre des Archives Diplomatiques du Ministère des Affaires Étrangères, Paris (MAE)

Correspondance consulaire et commerciale, 1793–1901 (CCC).
Correspondance politique et commerciale, 1896–1918. Nouvelle Série: Chine (CPC).

Geheimes Staatsarchiv Preuischer Kulturbesitz, Berlin (GSTA)

Gesandtschaft Bremen: Rep. 81.

Jebsen and Jessen Historical Archives, Aabenraa (JJHA)

Letter Copy Books (A01-01).
Family Archives (B10).
Miscellaneous files (PS).

Landsarkivet for Sønderjylland, Aabenraa (LAA)

SG090 Rederi M. Jebsen.

Politisches Archiv des Auswärtigen Amts, Berlin (PAAA)

Altes Amt 117: Konsulat Saigon.
Deutsche Botschaft in China: Peking II.
Deutsches Reich: R.

Vietnamese National Archives One, Hanoi (VNAi)

Gouvernement-Général de l'Indochine (GGI).
Résidence Supérieur au Tonkin (RST).
Service de l'Enregistrement, des Douanes et du Timbre de l'Indochine (SEDT).

Secondary Sources

Amer, Ramses. 2010. French Policies Towards the Chinese in Vietnam: A Study of Migration and Colonial Responses. *Moussons: Social Science Research on Southeast Asia* 16 (2): 57–80.

Annuaire de l'Indo-Chine, IIe Partie: Annam et Tonkin. 1890. Hanoi: F.-H. Schneider.

Annuaire Général de l'Indochine: Commercial, Industriel, Administratif. 1915. Hanoi and Haiphong: Imprimerie d'Extrême-Orient.

Bach, Mette Haugaard. 2014. Randersskibe på Kinakysten. In *Årbog 2014*, ed. Museum Østjylland, 53–63. Randers: Narayana.

Barthélemy, Marquis de. 1901. *En Indo-Chine 1896–1897: Tonquin, Haut Laos, Annam Septentrional*. Paris: Plon.

Becker, Bert. 2009. The German Colony of Kiaochow and Its Postal Steamer Service, 1898–1914. *International Journal of Maritime History* 21 (1): 201–238.

Becker, Bert. 2012. *Michael Jebsen: Reeder und Politiker 1835–1899: Eine Biographie*. Kiel: Ludwig.

Becker, Bert. 2015. France and the Gulf of Tonkin Region: Shipping Markets and Political Interventions in South China in the 1890s. *Cross-Currents: East Asian History and Culture Review* 4 (2): 560–600.

Becker, Bert. 2020. The Haiphong Shipping Boycotts of 1907 and 1909–10: Business Interactions in the Haiphong-Hong Kong Rice Shipping Trade. *Modern Asian Studies* 54 (3): 930–969.

Bensacq-Tixier, Nicole. 2003. *Dictionnaire du corps diplomatique et consulaire français en Chine (1840–1911)*. Paris: Les Indes Savantes.

Bismarck: *Die gesammelten Werke, vol. 8, 2: Gespräche*. 1926. Ed. Willy Andreas. Berlin: Stollberg.

Brandt, Max von. 1901. *Dreiunddreißig Jahre in Ost-Asien: Erinnerungen eines deutschen Diplomaten*, vol. 3. Leipzig: Georg Wigand.

Brautaset, Camilla and Stig Tenold. 2010. Lost in Calculation? Norwegian Merchant Shipping in Asia, 1870–1914. In *Maritime History as Global History*, ed. Maria Fusaro and Amélia Polónia, 203–221. St. John's, Newfoundland: International Maritime Economic History Association.

Brocheux, Pierre, and Daniel Hèmery. 2009. *Indochina: An Ambiguous Colonization, 1858–1954*. Berkeley: University of California Press.

Bulletin du Comité de l'Asie française. 1902, 1903, 1904 and 1905. Paris: Au Siège du Comité.

Bulletin Économique de l'Indochine. 1914. Hanoi and Haiphong: Imprimerie d'Extrême-Orient.

Bulletin Trimestriel de la Société Amicale des Anciens Tonkinois, vol. 9. 1940. Un des créateurs de Haiphong, 8–12. Hanoi: G. Taupin.

Catharina, Anna. 1893. *The Home of the Dragon: A Tonquinese Idyll. Told in Seven Chapters.* London: Fisher Unwin.

Colin, Ambroise. 1901. *La Navigation Commerciale au XIXe Siècle.* Paris: Rousseau.

Corfield, Justin. 2009. *The History of Vietnam.* Westport, CT and London: Greenwood.

Corfield, Justin. 2013. *Historical Dictionary of Ho Chi Minh City.* London and New York: Anthem Press.

Cunningham, Alfred. 1902. *The French in Tonkin and South China.* Hong Kong: Hongkong Daily Press.

Curtius, Friedrich, ed. 1907. *Denkwürdigkeiten des Fürsten Chlodwig zu Hohenlohe-Schillingsfürst*, vol. 2. Stuttgart und Leipzig: Deutsche Verlags-Anstalt.

Davidson, James W. 1903. *The Island of Formosa Past and Present: History, People, Resources, and Commercial Prospects.* Reprinted 1988. Oxford: Oxford University Press.

Devraigne, Georges. 1920. *Le Commerce Austro-Allemand en Indochine et dans les Pays Limitrophes.* Hanoi and Haiphong: Imprimerie D'Extrême-Orient.

Drummond, Lisa. 2013. Colonial Hanoi: Urban Space in Public Discourse. In *Harbin to Hanoi: The Colonial Built Environment in Asia, 1840 to 1940*, ed. Laura Victoir and Victor Zatsepine, 207–229. Hong Kong: Hong Kong University Press.

Dubois, Robert. 1900. *Le Tonkin en 1900.* Paris: Société française d'éditions d'art.

Dubreuil, René. 1910. *De la Condition des Chinois et de leur Rôle économique en Indo-Chine.* Bar-sur-Seine: Saillard.

Dupuis, Jean. 1879. *L'Ouverture du Fleuve Rouge au Commerce et les Évènements du Tong-king, 1872–1873.* Paris: Challamel.

Eastman, Lloyd E. 1967. *Throne and Mandarins: China's Search for a Policy During the Sino-French Controversy 1880–1885.* Cambridge, MA: Harvard University Press.

Eli, Barbara. 1967. *Paul Doumer in Indochina (1897–1902): Verwaltungsreformen, Eisenbahnen, Chinapolitik.* PhD thesis, University of Heidelberg.

Fourniau, Charles. 2002. *Vietnam: Domination coloniale et résistance nationale (1858–1914).* Paris: Les Indes Savantes.

Gantès, Gilles de. 1994. *Coloniaux, gouverneurs et ministres: L'influence des Français du Viet-Nam sur l'évolution du pays à l'époque coloniale 1902–1914.* PhD thesis, Université de Paris VII Denis Diderot.

Gantès, Gilles de. 2008. Le particularisme des milieux d'affaires cochinchinois (1860–1910): Comment intégrer un comptoir asiatique à un empire colonial protège. In *L'Esprit Économique Impérial (1830–1970): Groupes de pression et réseaux du patronat colonial en France et dans l'empire*, ed. Hubert Bonin, et al., 735–752. Paris: SFHOM.

Gooch, George Peabody. 1923. *Franco-German Relations 1871–1914*. London: Longman, Green.

Goscha, Christopher. 2017. *The Penguin History of Modern Vietnam*. Milton Keynes: Penguin Books.

Gourou, Pierre. 1955. *The Peasants of the Tonkin Delta: A Study of Human Geography*. New Haven: Human Relations Area Files. Originally published as Gourou, Pierre. 1936. *Les Paysans du Delta Tonkinois: Étude de Géographie humaine*. Paris: Les Éditions d'Art et d'Histoire.

Gregg, E.S. 1921. Vicissitudes in the Shipping Trade. *Quarterly Journal of Economics* 35 (4): 603–617.

Guillen, Pierre, and Jean-Claude Allain. 2007. La Puissance Recouvrée (1870–1914). In *Histoire de la Diplomatie Française, vol. 2: De 1815 à Nos Jours*, ed. Jean-Claude Allain, et al., 141–283. Paris: Perrin.

Haiphong illustré: Supplément au Millième Numéro du Journal: Le Courrier d'Haiphong, 24 December 1895.

Hänisch, Adolf von. 1970. *Jebsen and Co. Hongkong: China-Handel im Wechsel der Zeiten 1895–1945*. Apenrade: Self-Published.

Hercule, Philippe. 1985. *Paroisses et Communes de France: Dictionnaire d'histoire administrative et démographique, vol. 17: Charente-Maritime*. Paris: Éditions du Centre National de la Recherche Scientifique.

Hieke, Ernst. 1953. *Die Reederei M. Jebsen A. G. Apenrade*. Hamburg: Hamburgische Bücherei.

Hildebrand, Klaus. 1995. *Das vergangene Reich: Deutsche Außenpolitik von Bismarck bis Hitler 1871–1945*. Darmstadt: Wissenschaftliche Buchgesellschaft.

Imbert, Calixte. 1885. *Le Tonkin industriel et commercial*. Paris: Challamel.

Jones, Grosvenor M. 1916. *Navigation Laws: Comparative Study of Principal Features of the Laws of the United States, Great Britain, Germany, Norway, France, and Japan*. Washington: Government Printing Office.

Journal Officiel de l'Indochine Française: Deuxième partie: Annam et Tonkin. 1895. Hanoi: Gouvernement-Général de l'Indochine.

Kergaradec, C. de. 1881. Rapport sur le commerce du port de Haiphong pendant l'année 1880. *Excursions et Reconnaissances* 8: 261–276.

Kolbe, Franz. 1911. Die französischen Kolonialeisenbahnen in Indochina. *Weltverkehr und Weltwirtschaft* (September): 260–268.

Laffey, John F. 1977. Imperialists Divided: The View of Tonkin's Colons Before 1914. *Histoire Social/Social History* 10 (19): 92–113.

Lepsius, Johannes, et al., eds. 1922. *Die Große Politik der Europäischen Kabinette 1871–1914: Sammlung der Diplomatischen Akten des Auswärtigen Amtes*, vol. 3. Berlin: Deutsche Verlagsgesellschaft für Politik und Geschichte.

Les Ports Autonomes de l'Indochine. 1931. Ed. Indochine Française, Section Économique. Paris: Exposition Coloniale Internationale.

Lessard, Micheline. 2009. "Cet ignoble trafic": The Kidnapping and Sale of Vietnamese Women and Children in French Colonial Indochina, 1873–1935. *French Colonial History* 10: 1–34.

Li, Tana. 2004. Ships and Shipbuilding in the Mekong Delta, c. 1750–1840. In *Water Frontier: Commerce and the Chinese in the Lower Mekong Region, 1750–1880*, ed. Nola Cooke and Li Tana, 119–135. Singapore: Singapore University Press.

Li, Tana. 2006. A View from the Sea: Perspectives on the Northern and Central Vietnamese Coast. *Journal of Southeast Asian Studies* 37 (1): 83–102.

Liu, Kwang Ching. 1956. *Anglo-American Steamship Rivalry in China, 1873–85*. Cambridge, MA: Harvard University Press.

Luan Vu Duong, and Nola Cooke. 2011. Chinese Merchants and Mariners in Nineteenth-Century Tongking. In *The Tongking Gulf Through History*, ed. Nola Cooke, et al., 143–159. Philadelphia: University of Pennsylvania Press.

Marsot, Alain G. 1993. *The Chinese Community in Vietnam Under the French*. San Francisco: Edwin Mellen.

Martínez, Julia T. 2007a. Chinese Rice Trade and Shipping from the North Vietnamese Port of Hai Phong. *Chinese Southern Diaspora Studies* 1: 82–96.

Martínez, Julia T. 2007b. La Traite des Jaunes: Trafficking in Women and Children Across the China Sea. In *Many Middle Passages: Forced Migration and the Making of the Modern World*, ed. Emma Christopher, et al., 204–221. Berkeley: University of California Press.

Martonne, Edouard-Guillaume. 1897. La mission lyonnaise d'exploration en China. *Annales de Géographie* 6 (27): 273–276.

Marty et d'Abbadie. 1891. *Guide des Voyageurs sur les Rivières et la Cote du Tonkin – Service Postal*. Hanoi: L'Avenir du Tonkin.

Maybon, Albert. 1931. *L'Indochine*. Paris: Larose.

Merger, Michèle. 1995. The Economic Performance of Inland Navigation in France: The Lower Seine and the Paris-Lens Route in a Comparative Perspective. In *Inland Navigation and Economic Development in Nineteenth-Century Europe*, ed. Andreas Kunz and John Armstrong, 181–212. Mainz: Philipp von Zabern.

Meuleau, Marc. 1990. *Des pionniers en Extrême-Orient: Histoire de la Banque de l'Indochine (1875–1975)*. Paris: Fayard.

Michels, Eckard. 2006. *Deutsche in der Fremdenlegion 1870–1965: Mythen und Realitäten*, 5th rev. ed. Paderborn and Munich: Schöningh.

Miller, Michael B. 2012. *Europe and the Maritime World: A Twentieth-Century History*. Cambridge: Cambridge University Press.

Mitchell, Pearl Boring. 1935. *The Bismarckian Policy of Conciliation with France, 1875–1885*. Philadelphia: University of Pennsylvania Press.

Mommsen, Wolfgang J. 1993. *Großmachtstellung und Weltpolitik: Die Außenpolitik des Deutschen Reiches 1870 bis 1914*. Frankfurt am Main and Berlin: Ullstein.
Morse, Hosea Ballou. 1909. *The Guilds of China*. London: Longmans, Green.
Murray, Dian. 2004. Piracy and China's Maritime Transition, 1750–1850. In *Maritime China in Transition, 1750–1850*, ed. Wang Gungwu and Ng Chin-keong, 43–60. Wiesbaden: Harrassowitz.
Murray, Martin J. 1980. *The Development of Capitalism in Colonial Indochina (1870–1940)*. Berkeley: University of California Press.
Nguyen, Quoc Dinh. 1941. *Les Congrégations Chinoises en Indochine Française*. Paris: Recueil Sirey.
Osterhammel, Jürgen. 2014. *The Transformation of the World: A Global History of the Nineteenth Century*. Princeton: Princeton University Press.
Poidevin, Raymond, and Jacques Bariéty. 1982. *Frankreich und Deutschland: Die Geschichte ihrer Beziehungen 1815–1975*. Munich: Beck.
Poidevin, Raymond. 1998. *Les relations économiques et financières entre la France et l'Allemagne de 1898 à 1914*. Paris: Comité pour l'histoire économique et financière de la France.
Pomfret, David M. 2008. 'Child Slavery' in British and French Far-Eastern Colonies 1880–1945. *Past and Present* 201: 175–213.
Power, Thomas F., Jr. 1977. *Jules Ferry and the Renaissance of French Imperialism*. New York: Octagon.
Ptak, Roderich. 2008. The Gulf of Tongking: A Mini-Mediterranean? In *The East Asian 'Mediterranean': Maritime Crossroads of Culture, Commerce and Human Migration*, ed. Angela Schottenhammer, 53–72. Wiesbaden: Harrassowitz.
Raffalovich, M. Arthur. 1888. The Effects of Shipping Bounties. *Journal of the Royal Statistical Society* 51 (1): 141–154.
Raffi, Gilles. 1994. *Haiphong: origines, conditions et modalités du développement jusqu'en 1921*. PhD thesis, Université de Provence.
Reid, Anthony. 1988. *Southeast Asia in the Age of Commerce 1450–1680, vol. 1: The Lands Below the Winds*. New Haven and London: Yale University Press.
Reid, Anthony. 2015. *A History of Southeast Asia: Critical Crossroads*. Chichester, West Sussex: Wiley Blackwell.
Reinhardt, Anne. 2018. *Navigating Semi-Colonialism: Shipping, Sovereignty, and Nation-Building in China, 1860–1937*. Cambridge, MA: Harvard University Press.
Remer, C.F. 1966. *A Study of Chinese Boycotts: With Special Reference to Their Economic Effectiveness*. Taipei: Cheng-Wen.
Robequain, Charles. 1944. *The Economic Development of French Indo-China*. London: Oxford University Press.

Rousseau, Jean-François. 2014. An Imperial Railway Failure: The Indochina-Yunnan Railway, 1898–1941. *The Journal of Transport History* 35 (1): 1–17.
Sakurai, Yumio. 1997. Peasant Drain and Abandoned Villages in the Red River Delta Between 1750 and 1850. In *The Last Stand of Asian Autonomies: Responses to Modernity in the Diverse States of Southeast Asia and Korea, 1750–1900*, ed. Anthony Reid, 133–152. Houndsmill and London: Macmillan Press.
Scott, James George. 1885. *France and Tongking: A Narrative of the Campaign of 1884 and the Occupation of Further India*. London: T. Fisher Unwin.
Sinn, Elizabeth. 1994. Chinese Patriarchy and the Protection of Women in Nineteenth-Century Hong Kong. In *Women and Chinese Patriarchy: Submission, Servitude and Escape*, ed. Maria Jaschok and Suzanne Miers, 141–170. Hong Kong: Hong Kong University Press.
Sinn, Elizabeth. 2013. *Pacific Crossing: California Gold, Chinese Migration and the Making of Hong Kong*. Hong Kong: Hong Kong University Press.
Smith, Michael S. 1994. Unlikely Success: Chargeurs Réunis and the Marine Transport Business in France, 1872–1914. *Entreprises et Histoire* 6: 11–27.
Still, William N., Gordon P. Watts, and Bradley Rogers. 2000. Steam Navigation and the United States. In *The Advent of Steam: The Merchant Steamship Before 1900*, ed. Robert Gardiner and Basil Greenhill, 44–82. Edison, NJ: Chartwell.
Tagliacozzo, Eric. 2005. *Secret Trades, Porous Borders: Smuggling and States Along a Southeast Asian Frontier, 1865–1915*. New Haven and London: Yale University Press.
The Chronicle & Directory for China, Corea, Japan, The Philippines, Indo-China, Straits Settlements, Siam, Borneo, Malay States, & c. 1894. Hong Kong: The "Daily Press" Office.
The Directory & Chronicle for China, Japan, Corea, Indo-China, Straits Settlements, Malay States, Siam, Netherlands India, Borneo, The Philippines, & c. 1899, 1906, 1908 and 1910. Hong Kong: The "Daily Press" Office.
The Encyclopaedia Britannica: A Dictionary of Arts, Sciences, Literature and General Information. 1910, 11th ed. Cambridge: Cambridge University Press.
Tran, Van Kien. 2017. *L'Industrialisation de la Ville de Haiphong de la Fin du XIXe siècle jusqu'à l'Année 1929: L'Invention d'une Ville Industrielle en Asie du Sud-Est*. PhD thesis, Université Aix-Marseille.
Tsai, Jung-fang. 1993. *Hong Kong in Chinese History: Community and Social Unrest in the British Colony, 1842–1913*. New York: Columbia University Press.
United States State Department. 1901. *Paper Relating to the Foreign Relations of the United States, with the Annual Message of the President Transmitted to the Congress*, 3 December.
Villemagne, Claire. 2008. Les Chambres de commerce du Tonkin, 1884–1894: Sociabilité culturelle ou mission économique? In *L'Esprit Économique Imperial*

(1830–1970): Groupes de pression et réseaux du patronat colonial en France et dans l'empire, ed. Hubert Bonin, et al., 697–714. Paris: SFHOM.

Vorapheth, Kham. 2004. *Commerce et colonisation en Indochine 1860–1945: Les maisons de commerce françaises: Un siècle d'aventure humaine*. Paris: Les Indes Savantes.

Wheeler, Charles. 2006. Re-thinking the Sea in Vietnamese History: Littoral Society in the Integration of Thuận-Quảng, Seventeenth-Eighteenth Centuries. *Journal of Southeast Asian Studies* 37 (1): 123–153.

Wienefeld, Robert H. 1929. *Franco-German Relations 1878–1885*. Baltimore: John Hopkins Press.

Wong, Sin Kiong. 2002. *China's Anti-American Boycott Movement in 1905: A Study in Urban Protests*. New York: Peter Lang.

Wray, William D. 1984. *Mitsubishi and the N.Y.K., 1870–1914: Business Strategy in the Japanese Shipping Industry*. Cambridge, MA: Harvard University Press.

CHAPTER 6

Guangzhouwan

French Politics in the South China Sea (1898–1904)

France's Sphere of Influence in Southern China

In May 1894, the diplomat Gabriel Hanotaux was appointed French foreign minister. Except for a period of six months, he was France's key figure in foreign politics for the next four years. American historian William L. Langer described Hanotaux and Delcassé (who directed French policy from 1898 to 1905) as the two outstanding statesmen of their time, adding that of the two, "Hanotaux, historian and student of Richelieu, was undoubtedly the more significant". As Langer observed, Hanotaux a "disciple of Jules Ferry" who dominated French policy from 1894 to 1898 was "immensely impressed with the need for empire". Among the foreign ministers of the Third Republic, he was rather exceptional because of his long career in the foreign service but minimal experience in political life. A moderate Republican, politically close to Léon Gambetta and Jules Ferry, he believed that France would increase rather than diffuse her resources by becoming a great imperial and colonial power. Despite the unusual handicap of having little practical political experience (he was member of parliament for the department of Aisne from 1886 to 1889 before losing his seat to a monarchist), he probably had as much autonomy in the conduct of external affairs as any French minister since Talleyrand, Napoleon Bonaparte's chief diplomat. Foreign ministers enjoyed something of a free hand because their colleagues had

B. Becker, *France and Germany in the South China Sea, c. 1840–1930*, Cambridge Imperial and Post-Colonial Studies,
https://doi.org/10.1007/978-3-030-52604-7_6

little time for, interest in or knowledge about international relations. For the forty months Hanotaux was in power France read to the world through him since the foreign minister lacked public speaking skills and instead focused on writing French history (he was a trained archivist and a scholar of Early Modern History, winning in 1896 the highest prize for historical writing of the Académie Française for his biography of Cardinal Richelieu). Usually, he discussed and guided his policies with the help of a small group of high functionaries and ambassadors. As a great admirer of Ferry, he again pursued colonial expansion by designing an empire centred on Africa and the Mediterranean and a wide sphere of influence in East Asia. The "mission civilisatrice", France's civilising mission, was a guiding principle for the foreign minister who was driven in his imperialism less by economic than by political motives. In realising the colonial project, the only real opponent for Hanotaux was Britain, while Germany was regarded in a very pragmatic way even though he had disliked this country since the War of 1870–1871. Therefore, the question of Alsace-Lorraine was less important for the French foreign minister than his overseas ambitions.[1]

When Hanotaux assumed office, the Franco-Russian military–political alliance (1893) had already been formalised as a response to the formation of the Triple Alliance (1882) headed by Germany. In Europe, two opposing imperialist blocs had formed, dominating politics up to the First World War. The alliance between Paris and Saint Petersburg resulted in close collaboration in political, military and economic matters which was helped by the fact that Hanotaux was an intimate friend of Russian foreign minister, Aleksey Lobanov-Rostovsky. With the victory of Japan in the Sino-Japanese War (1894–1895), the two powers offered support to the Chinese government in meeting the enormous indemnity of 200 million taels (ca. 150 million US dollars) which Beijing was compelled to pay following the terms of the peace treaty of Shimonoseki. The result was a loan of 400 million francs provided by a combination of Russian and French banks, formally concluded on 6 July 1895. Hanotaux left no room for doubt that the loan was intended to obtain from Beijing concessions for building railways in southern China and to gain Russia's support for this approach. Seeking privileges in China in exchange for Chinese

[1] Langer (1960, 796), Iiams (1962, 13–27), Grupp (1972, 16–84), Guillen (1984, 339–340) and Guillen and Allain (2007, 193–195).

gratitude was the basic principle of the Russo-French political–financial combination.[2]

Hanotaux's like-minded counterpart was the French Minister in Beijing, Auguste Gérard, an admirer of Jules Ferry, who embodied France's new expansionist policy in China from 1893 to 1897. Before he left Paris to take over the legation in China, Gérard was instructed by Hanotaux to remind Indochina's Governor-General Jean Marie de Lanessan and Auguste Pavie (the commissioner general of the government of the newly formed French colony of Laos) that the Protectorate of Annam-Tonkin was intended as a trade route into the south China market. Gérard passed on his voyage via Haiphong, Hainan Island and Hong Kong, arriving in Beijing in May 1894 to begin a vigorous, sometimes even aggressive, term as French minister. In his memoirs, Gérard wrote that his first obligation was to preserve and maintain all rights, concessions, advantages and privileges France had acquired since her first treaty with China in 1844. "France did not let China forget whose money it was that financed the 1895 indemnity," declared Thomas M. Iiams. The minister's push for a treaty with Beijing containing many major concessions from China in her relationship with Tonkin was finally approved by Emperor Kwang Hsu on 20 June 1895. In the convention, China promised to treat as intra-Chinese trade all goods shipped in and out of China and through the ports of French Indochina, to call on French engineers and industrialists first to carry out any mining operations in the three adjacent provinces Yunnan, Guangxi and Guangdong and to permit a trunk line of the Tonkin railroads to be built in Chinese territory. This convention permitted France to develop economic interests between Tonkin and southern China and to establish her sphere of influence in the region.[3]

In September 1895, Hanotaux charged Gérard to demand from China the concession for the railway from Tonkin to Longzhou (Longchow or Lungchow, the Chinese town in Guangxi Province bordering northern Vietnam), proposing to employ French capital and engineers for the construction (this contract was finally approved by Beijing in March 1896). Furthermore, Gérard was to inform the Chinese government

[2] Langer (1960, 186–189), Iiams (1962, 72–73), Guillen (1984, 370–376) and Hsü (2000, 344–348).

[3] Gérard (1918, vii–xiii), Iiams (1962, the quote: 73) and Guillen (1984, 374–377).

about the Lyon trading mission which planned to explore opportunities to promote French trade with China. The study tour initiated by the Lyon Chamber of Commerce and actively promoted by Governor-General Paul Armand Rousseau consisted of delegates from six major French cities (Bordeaux, Lille, Lyon, Marseille, Roubaix and Roanne). Their goal was to explore and study suitable ways for commercially penetrating China from Tonkin, to determine capacities of production and consumption in the visited Chinese provinces and to endeavour to show ways and means suitable for diverting to Tonkin the traffic of the West River (Xijiang, Sikiang) and Guangzhou. Arriving in Haiphong on 16 October 1895, the mission formed three groups, paying visits to the Chinese provinces of Yunnan, Guizhou (Kweichow) and Szechwan (Sichuan) and to major trading centres in southern China (Hong Kong, Macao, Guangzhou and Beihai) and along the Yangzi River (Shanghai and Hankow), travelling altogether more than 20,000 kilometres. In 1898, the detailed report of the Lyon mission was published. The journalist and economist, Henri Brenier, secretary-general of the Lyon mission, concluded that commercial relations between French Indochina and China were "less bad than we generally imagine", pointing to the colony's second place in China's foreign trade. In spite of that fact, "public opinion and mind in France for external questions is unfortunately almost completely absent", Brenier stated. Continental France imported from China "almost forty times more trading value" than she exported to her, with silk being the absolutely dominant import. In the other direction, there were "unfortunately, insignificant numbers" of French exports to China comprising mainly silk fabrics, trimmings and ribbons and stuffing. According to the French expert, the basic problem seemed to be the lack of available manpower in East Asia: "It is the tiny number of French companies and representatives in the Far East being the major reason, or at least one of the crucial reasons for the inferiority of our role in this field as anywhere else".[4]

This opinion was shared by Minister Gérard, who blamed the "indifference" of French financiers and businessmen who still had to be persuaded to take advantage of the valuable concessions acquired by the minister's diplomacy. In February 1897, an official technical delegation was dispatched from France to visit mines in Yunnan producing copper, tin

[4] Guillen (1984, 376), Martonne (1897, 273–276), Brenier (1898, 443–451, the quotes: 444–445, 448), Murray (1980, 103–105) and Brötel (1996, 441–444).

and silver and to explore options to build a railway linking the Chinese mines with the coal mines of Tonkin. At the time, French industrialists were actively searching for new markets after the large railway construction projects in France had been largely completed. Their intentions were vigorously supported by Paul Doumer, Governor-General of Indochina (in office from 1897 to 1902). For Doumer, one of the major means to enhance Indochina's economic situation was to closely link Tonkin with southern China, and especially with Yunnan by a railroad. This found active support in France's foreign and colonial ministries. Mainly due to the combined efforts of Hanotaux and Gérard, the pressure mounted on Beijing to grant a railway concession and a territorial foothold in southern China, to establish a coaling port for the French Far East Naval Squadron.[5]

Concerning the naval station, the French foreign minister proved the most active supporter of the idea of acquiring Hainan Island for France. This, the second-largest island in China, closed the eastern side of the Gulf of Tonkin, separated by the Qiongzhou (Hainan) Strait from the Leizhou Peninsula of Guangdong Province. With the Strait being the major shipping route between Indochina and Hong Kong (although difficult to navigate), the island was regarded as strategically highly important for fostering France's sphere of influence in southern China. Under the impression that Germany was at the time actively searching for a location to set up a naval station on the China coast, Gérard repeatedly urged the Chinese government not to hand over the island to any other power, as the new German Minister Edmund Baron von Heyking, reported to Berlin in February 1897. In the previous month, Heyking had informed his French and Russian counterparts that Germany was seeking a coaling station along the central Chinese coast, outside both the French and Russian spheres of influence. This prompted another exploratory mission by the French squadron along the Guangdong coast and around Hainan, resulting in a strong recommendation to occupy the island. To prevent suspected German designs on Hainan, Gérard, in his ongoing negotiations to acquire railway and mining concessions in southern China, claimed a formal assurance that the Chinese government "would not alienate to any other Power under any form and in any case the Island of Hainan and the Guangdong coast opposite it". On 15 March 1897,

[5] Iiams (1962, 74–75) and Guillen (1984, 375–378).

the Chinese foreign ministry (Tsungli Yamen) finally signed a declaration with France "concerning Non-Alienation of Island of Hainan". With the French sphere of influence demarcated by that formal assertion, it seemed obvious, as the *Hong Kong Weekly Press* wrote in February 1898, "that the French intend to annex the Island of Hainan sooner or later".[6]

France's possible annexation and permanent control over the island promised to become difficult, with respect to Hainan's large territorial size of 32,900 square kilometres (similar to that of Belgium or slightly smaller than that of Formosa) and considerable German and British commercial interests concentrated in the island's main city, Haikou (Hoihow), and in Qiongzhou (Kiungchow), the centre of Chinese administration and a major port located on the Hainan Strait. This caused the French to examine alternative locations along the China coasts. In 1894, Naval Minister Félix Faure instructed Rear Admiral Jean-Olivier de la Bonninière, Comte de Beaumont, the commander-in-chief of the naval squadron, to support Gérard's initiatives towards the Chinese government by actively searching for a suitable location for the planned French naval station which would provide the chance to extend the range of French warships and to reinforce France's sphere of influence in the region. On 7 February 1895, Beaumont reported about his findings to Paris, proposing Guangzhou Bay (Guangzhouwan) on the coast of Guangdong Province, which had been visited by French warships earlier. He described the bay, located halfway between Tonkin and Hong Kong, as an anchorage of good size, with deep water, "a kind of Asian Bizerte" [a large naval port in French-controlled Tunisia], being little known and not having attracted much attention. If occupied, it should provide the navy "with a superb closed-up port at the China Sea" commanding the entry of the Hainan Strait. His account also pointed to the future option of creating a territorial link between Guangzhouwan, the Leizhou Peninsula and the provinces of Guangxi and Guangdong that "would establish an uninterrupted line of seacoast, turning the Gulf of Tonkin into a French lake".[7]

[6] PAAA, R 19417: Minister von Heyking (Beijing) to Chancellor von Hohenlohe-Schillingsfürst (Berlin), 17 February 1897. MAE, CPC-217: Report of Commodore Gigault de La Bedollière, 18 April 1897. *Hong Kong Weekly Press*, 19 February 1898. MacMurray (1921, 98), Joseph (1928, 185) and Iiams (1962, 76–77).

[7] MAE, CPC-193: Report of Rear Admiral Jean-Olivier de la Bonninière, Comte de Beaumont, 7 February 1895, as quoted in the note of the Foreign Ministry (Paris), 28 March 1898. Herriou (1994, 120) and Vannière (2020, 56–57).

Beaumont's idea was taken up by Hanotaux, classifying his letter to Naval Minister Armand Besnard as very confidential when suggesting that "instead of focusing our view on the central coasts of China (…) it would perhaps be better to concentrate on the southern region, and especially on the bay of Guangzhou which high strategic importance your ministry has several times pointed out".[8] Yet, the foreign minister's idea met with little interest when soon after Captain Hippolyte Boutet, commander of the man-of-war *Alger*, visited Guangzhou Bay and explicitly warned of the sand bar situated at the entrance of the main passage. In his account of 18 December 1896, Boutet stated that a naval port for refuge and supplying could not be created since many men-of-war would have no access to the bay; he also turned down the notion that the bay had any economic value for France.[9]

In November 1897, German naval troops occupied Jiaozhou (Kiaochow) Bay in Shandong (Shantung) Province. In the following weeks, the naval and foreign ministries in Berlin co-operated closely to secure Jiaozhou as a future German naval base, shipping and trading hub and starting-point from which the coal-rich hinterland in Shandong could be exploited. Such hopes were buoyed by the fact that both Naval Minister Alfred Tirpitz and Emperor William II were ardent supporters of such economic goals. Tirpitz wanted to strengthen the navy because he regarded a powerful fleet as the major basis for demonstrating not only Imperial Germany's national strength and global impact but also for fostering its economic power. Jiaozhou was to become a German trading and shipping centre based upon free trade for which British Hong Kong served as a model. Prompted by the German military action, Russian troops, in December 1897, seized Port Arthur and Dairen on Liaodong (Liaotung) Peninsula, under the pretence of protecting China from the Germans. In the following month, Russia claimed the two ports and their adjacent areas for building railways and began negotiations with the Chinese foreign ministry.[10]

[8] Herriou (1994, 120: Foreign Minister Hanotaux [Paris] to Naval Minister Besnard [Paris], 29 May 1896).

[9] MAE, CPC-193: Report of Captain Boudet, 18 December 1896, as quoted in the note of the Foreign Ministry (Paris), 28 March 1898.

[10] Hsü (2000, 348--350), Schrecker (1971, 19–27), Mühlhahn (2000, 65–111) and So (2019, 58–60).

The German and Russian military operations and diplomatic negotiations were carefully watched in Paris. While tacitly backing Russia's actions, Hanotaux made use of the Franco-Russian alliance for his own imperial purposes, prompting him to take part in the so-called "scramble for concessions" of European powers in China. In contrast to Jules Ferry, who was mainly interested in the economic profits of colonialism, Hanotaux regarded imperial expansion as necessary for enhancing French greatness. This prompted the foreign minister to also demand from China various concessions, privileges and preferable treatments in order not to fall behind the other great powers.[11] On 20 January 1898, the foreign ministry finished a memorandum in which the possible annexation of Hainan was evaluated, but finally rejected because of the island's large size and possible problems in permanently controlling it. Instead, Guangzhouwan was recommended as a fine and good defendable harbour that should be made France's centre for expanding into the China Seas and the hinterlands of western China.[12] On 5 February 1898, Hanotaux stated in parliament that France's diplomats in China were on alert with the goal of increasing the nation's influence and defending her rights.[13] Strong support for immediate action came from Doumer who, in his telegram of 17 February 1898 to Colonial Minister André Lebon, offered to send Indochinese troops in the case that the government decided to occupy Hainan, Guangzhouwan and also Beihai (Pakhoi). In the accompanying letter, he explained that taking possession of Guangzhouwan would only be worth doing when also adding "the entire Gulf of Tonkin and at least a part of Guangdong [Province] into France's exclusive sphere-of-interest".[14] However, Doumer's far-reaching plan was openly criticised in the *Hong Kong Weekly Press* on 19 February 1898, reflecting official British opinion on France's ambitions. The newspaper warned that if France annexed Hainan Island Britain would claim the valley of the West River from China. This request, frequently made since 1895, had

[11] Grupp (1972, 39–63), Guillen (1984, 374–383) and Guillen and Allain (2007, 193–195, 199–201).

[12] MAE, CPC-217: Anonymous note "On the subject of Hainan" to Foreign Minister (Paris), 20 January 1898.

[13] Guillen (1984, 382).

[14] MAE, CPD-208: Telegram from Governor-General Doumer (Hanoi) to Colonial Minister Lebon (Paris), 17 February 1898. ANOM, INDO-GGI-21849: Governor-General Doumer (Hanoi) to Colonial Minister Lebon (Paris), 17 February 1898.

been opposed by France which was interested in attracting the trade of southwest China to Tonkin. Controlling the main lines of communications in this region, the West River and its tributaries and also the city of Nanning — the main distribution centre for eastern Yunnan and western Guangxi — had been an objective for both France and Britain.[15]

In the meantime, German and Chinese diplomats hammered out the final details of the lease treaty of Jiaozhou which granted Germany sovereignty over the area for ninety-nine years. Germany's economic privileges involved a concession to build three railway lines and to operate mines within ten miles of the roadbeds on either side. On 6 March 1898, the Sino-German convention on Jiaozhou was signed in Beijing.[16] The following day, Hanotaux instructed Georges Dubail, the new French Minister and Gérard's successor in Beijing, to present France's demands to the Chinese government. Apart from claiming certain concessions and privileges in China, Hanotaux demanded the "freedom of France to install on the southern coast of China a coal depot under the same conditions as a most-favoured nation", arguing that this would not harm the integrity of China and constitute the minimum compensation to France for advantages already granted by China to other countries. When the minister presented the demands on 13 March 1898 in the form of an ultimatum, the Tsungli Yamen reacted indifferently, and even negatively, which prompted Dubail to insist that China handle the issue seriously. The Chinese newspaper *Kuo wen-pao* was outraged, sharply criticising "the joint actions of Russia and France in the North and South", making it impossible for China to defend herself "against plot and scheme" by powers still pretending to protect China. Therefore, the journal asked the following rhetorical question: "How to find words for such a shamelessness"?[17] In this interim, Russia proceeded on her talks with the two Chinese negotiators, Li Hongzhang and Chang Yin-huan, who seem to have been bribed with large sums by Russian Finance Minister Sergei

[15] *Hong Kong Weekly Press*, 19 February 1898. Young (1970, 88–89).

[16] MacMurray (1921, 112–116); Schrecker (1971, 33–42) and Mühlhahn (2000, 107–110).

[17] MAE, CPC-193: French Minister Dubail (Beijing) to Foreign Minister Hanotaux (Paris), 16 March 1898. PAAA, Peking II-13: *Kuo wen-pao*, 23 March 1898 (translated from Chinese into German by Dr. Peter Merklinghaus, interpreter of the German Legation in Beijing).

Witte. On 27 March 1898, Russia was granted the Liaodong Peninsula and concessions to construct railways.[18]

In the meantime, Hanotaux had reached an agreement with Naval Minister Besnard on acquiring Guangzhouwan for France. It was obvious that for Hanotaux political factors such as upholding France's geopolitical status in the "scramble for concessions" mattered more than thoroughly evaluating the economics or geography of the territory. Relying on the optimistic comments in Beaumont's report of 1895, the foreign minister discounted the warnings in Boutet's account of 1896 about the bay's limited accessibility and the low economic value of its hinterland. On 31 March 1898, Dubail was instructed to convey to the Chinese government France's desire to establish herself at Guangzhouwan. After three rounds of negotiations, it was agreed that, as Dubail wrote in his report, "the bay of Guangzhou is ceded to us on bail for ninety-nine years. We have the right to establish there a naval station with a coal depot. (…) It allows to take us the entire bay, what means we establish ourselves on such a point we judge as convenient". On 9 and 10 April 1898, the French minister exchanged diplomatic notes with the Tsungli Yamen concerning the concession for building a railway from Tonkin to Yunnan and the lease of Guangzhouwan. This was joined by the supplementary declaration "concerning Non-Alienation of Chinese territory bordering Tonkin" which was intended to reject possible British claims on the Chinese provinces of Yunnan, Guangxi and Guangdong. The Sino-French convention of 27 May 1898 on the lease of Guangzhouwan to France (signed in Beijing on 29 May 1898) completed the talks, formally opening up to France the path to establishing her sphere of influence in south-western China.[19]

Military Seizure and Chinese Resistance

On 23 March 1898, France's demands on China became publicly known in Hong Kong when the *Hong Kong Daily Press* warned in a leading

[18] MacMurray (1921, 119–121), Hudson (1937, 103) and Hsü (2000, 348–349).

[19] MAE, CPC-193: Telegram from Foreign Minister Hanotaux (Paris) to Minister Dubail (Beijing), 31 March 1898. MAE, CPC-194: Minister Dubail (Beijing) to Foreign Minister Hanotaux (Paris), 11 April 1898. *The London and China Telegraph*, 18 April 1898. MacMurray (1921, 124–125) and Vannière (2020, 68–70).

article that this was "a pretty wide programme" of power and "the preliminary step towards the acquisition of the whole of Leizhou Peninsula, in order to control the trade of the West River". Hanotaux was reproached for entirely divesting himself "of any shred of political modesty or bashfulness that may once have clung on him". The newspaper reflected British official opinion when frankly stating: "We have no objection to fair competition, but we shall certainly oppose the cession of exclusive rights to another Power, especially when that Power adopts the selfish and silly policy of closing every port by means of hostile tariffs." This was an obvious verbal attack on the French customs policy in Indochina which had long been critically commented on in the Hong Kong press. The leader ended by strongly warning that "England may perhaps not be unwilling to assist China to repel aggression".[20] The day before the article was published, the British minister in China, Sir Claude Maxwell MacDonald, was instructed by London to warn the Chinese government that Britain and other powers might make similar demands should China agree to the French claim. With Germany, Russia and France being granted leased territories in China, the British government proceeded to request compensatory concessions. On 2 April 1898, MacDonald demanded an extension of the boundaries of Hong Kong. The readjustment of the Hong Kong frontier for naval and military reasons had been discussed since 1895, but had met with a divided response in British government circles due to fears that any action could provoke France to retaliate. The French lease of Guangzhouwan made it necessary, and also possible, for Britain to launch negotiations with the Chinese government about the lease of additional land to the British colony. In the subsequent Sino-British convention of 9 June 1898, the area that remained known as the New Territories was regarded as "necessary for the proper defence and protection of the Colony" and leased for a period of ninety-nine years. However, for the British minister, the lease of the New Territories presented a permanent cession in disguise. The takings on lease indeed marked a new development in the methods of European imperialism in China.[21]

[20] *Hong Kong Daily Press*, 23 March 1898.

[21] Catalogue of Treaties (1919, 186), Hudson (1937, 103), Wesley-Smith (1980, 30–31), Welsh (1997, 321–326), Tsang (1997, 7–9) and Becker (2019a, 192).

In the interim, French naval forces had set up a flagstaff on the old Chinese fort of Hoitow (Xiying, later the French administrative town Fort Bayard) on the right bank of the Maxie River near the bay. Four men-of-war were anchored in the river's estuary when the French Tricolour was hoisted by Rear Admiral Lucien Pierre Jean-Baptiste Gigault de La Bedolière, commander of a division of the Far East Naval Squadron, to the music of a ship's band and amid hurrahs and cheers from crews. *Le Courrier d'Haiphong* noted the absence of Chinese authorities, "but on the other hand a considerable Chinese crowd witnessed the ceremony, being delighted in advance about the idea of exploiting us and of selling goods as expensive as dubious to our men".[22] On the left bank of the river, in the town of Maxie, French naval officers posted the "very urgent special proclamation" (in Chinese) which, referring to the friendly relationship between France and China, announced the opening of coal mines in the region and promised local residents that "your trade will be more and more prosperous every day". Stating that "everything is done with peace intentions" and calling for all to live "peacefully together as in ordinary times", the declamation warned nevertheless that touching the French flag would be "considered a punishable offence".[23] The Chinese authorities in Guangzhou were not informed of the event, reported German consul Dr. Wilhelm Knappe in Guangzhou, charged with observing France's activities in southern China. Speaking of "a certain secrecy" with which the ceremony was performed, Knappe, in his report to Berlin, considered the proclamation "colourless". Indeed, only four days after the event, on 26 April 1898, two Chinese officials from neighbouring districts arrived in Maxie charged with formally handing over the place to the French naval forces.[24]

[22] *Le Courrier d'Haiphong*, 28 April 1898.

[23] The French proclamation of 22 April 1898, as English translation from Chinese, in TNA, FO 228–1289: Enclosure no. 1 in Acting Consul Pierre Essex O'Brien Butler's dispatch no. 11 (Qiongzhou), 3 May 1898, and as German translation from Chinese, in PAAA, Peking II-13: Consul Knappe (Guangzhou) to Chancellor von Hohenlohe-Schillingsfürst (Berlin), 8 May 1898. For the full text of the proclamation (English translation), see Becker (2019a, 185). The original French or Chinese versions could not be found.

[24] PAAA, Peking II-13: Consul Knappe (Guangzhou) to Chancellor von Hohenlohe-Schillingsfürst (Berlin), 8 May 1898. Herriou (1994, 121–122), Fourniau (2002, 523–533) and Vannière (2020, 75–76).

The armed occupation of the bay met with stiff resistance by local Chinese forces which was much stronger than the French expected. According to French Consul Gaston Kahn, the Chinese population of the territory feared mass expropriations, an exorbitant capitation and seizures of their properties for the sake of Chinese Christians. French historian Antoine Vannière pointed to the fact that existing documentation hardly permits drawing a comprehensive picture of the attitudes of the local Chinese population towards the French occupation of the territory. On 4 October 1898, Governor-General Doumer dispatched colonial troops — two naval infantry companies and a section of mountain artillery — in order to quell intensifying fighting. The number of troops was increased to a four-company battalion of around eight hundred troops in June 1899, repelling additional attacks and seizing other parts of the territory.[25] After negotiations on demarcating the territory resumed in October 1899, local Chinese resistance was still so fierce that further troops were dispatched from Indochina. On 16 November 1899, a sudden, final agreement was reached on the demarcation of Guangzhouwan, with concrete outlines and figures included into the Sino-French convention of 27 May 1898 on the lease of Guangzhouwan to France (which was ratified by China on 5 January 1900). With the final agreement signed on 16 November 1899, France clearly had withdrawn from her key territorial demands: the marked territory was much smaller than planned and difficult to defend. Originally, French planning had envisaged three options, drafted by Beaumont and passed through the French legation in Beijing to the foreign ministry. The first option was the most limited one, encompassing a surface area around Guangzhou Bay of about 1,800 square kilometres, whereas the second possibility covered a large area of around 3,800 square kilometres. This would have extended the French territory in a westerly direction from the bay region across the Leizhou Peninsula up to the eastern shores of the Gulf of Tonkin. It would have permitted ships loaded with coal and other cargoes from Indochina to circumvent the Hainan Strait (which was difficult to navigate) when sailing to the French territory. To connect the two seashores, the plan suggested constructing a steam tram or railway which would have provided Guangzhouwan with a secure and fast way to import coal from Indochina needed for operating a naval base and a coal depot. On

[25] Vannière (2020, 97, Table 1).

the other hand, it would have led to the division of the peninsula into a French part in the north and a Chinese area in the south, with the latter isolated from the Chinese continent. Beaumont was reasonable enough to remark that this option would be hardly acceptable to the Tsungli Yamen. The third possibility was presented as a compromise between the others; however, it was basically the first, very modest option combined with the exclusive right to build a railway from Guangzhouwan to the Gulf of Tonkin where a landing place was in a way reserved for France.[26]

On 16 November 1899, Rear Admiral Courrejolles, commander-in-chief of the Far East Naval Squadron, and General Su Yuan Chun, supreme commander of Chinese troops in the region, signed the agreement on the demarcation of Guangzhouwan. With the last troops dispatched from Haiphong arriving at Fort Bayard on 26 November 1899, the French military presence reached its greatest extent. The troops were needed to safeguard the final demarcation of the territorial borders of Guangzhouwan, which ended on 10 December 1899. This caused alarm at the German legation in Beijing. In January 1900, Minister Clemens Baron von Ketteler approached Li Hongzhang who had been appointed as the viceroy of the two Guang Provinces and was about to leave to Guangzhou. "I very especially recommended to him the protection and promotion of German trading aspirations within his official duties", Ketteler reported to Berlin, adding that Li asked him "to directly get in contact with him in an emergency". On 3 and 4 February 1900, Governor-General Doumer and General Gustavie Borgnis-Desbordes, supreme commander of the troops in Indochina, paid a visit to Guangzhouwan to gather information on the new territory and to inspect troops of the future outpost of the Reserve Brigade of the Occupation Corps of China, headquartered in Haiphong. The leased territory, including the bay, which the French called "Kouang-Tchéou-Wan" (Guangzhouwan or Kwang-chow-wan, present-day Zhanjiang), encompassed an area of 842 square kilometres. This was considerably larger than Jiaozhou (Kiaochow) which had 552 square kilometres, but slightly smaller than the New Territories of Hong Kong, which covered 953 square kilometres. The leasehold provided France with the

[26] MAE, CPC-209: Note of the French Legation (Beijing) for the Political Direction, Foreign Ministry (Paris), undated, attached to the letter of Minister Stephen Pichon (Beijing) to Foreign Minister Delcassé (Paris), 20 November 1899. Bonhoure (1900, 326–330), Pieragastini (2017, 113–114) and Vannière (2020, 88–93).

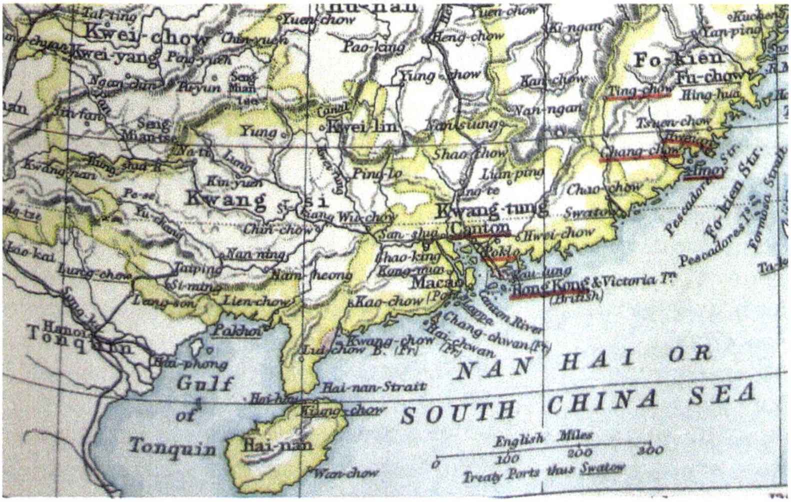

Fig. 6.1 Detail of a map of south China, showing the northern shore of the South China Sea, with Guangzhouwan ["Kwang-chow B. (Fr.)" on the map] situated between Hong Kong and Haiphong, early twentieth century (*The Hundred and Twentieth Report of the London Missionary Society*, 1915.)

chance to establish a naval hub in the South China Sea and to draw the Chinese provinces of Yunnan, Guangxi and Guangdong into her exclusive sphere of influence in southern China. In 1900, Eugène Bonhoure, the former secretary of the French parliament, said of Guangzhouwan that its possession was "a guarantee, almost a mortgage to safeguard our interests in case – quite likely – of serious eventualities. We have now 'taken a good position'. We can wait" (Fig. 6.1).[27]

The Distant Outpost

In June 1899, Jean Marie de Lanessan, former governor-general of Indochina (1891–1894), was made French naval minister. His primary

[27] Herriou (1994, 126–129) and Vannière (2020, 74–102, text of the Convention: 649–651). PAAA, Peking II-70: Minister von Ketteler (Beijing) to Chancellor von Hohenlohe-Schillingsfürst (Berlin), 11 January 1900. Bonningue (1931, 22) and Bonhoure (1900, 330).

goal was to bolster the French navy after the Fashoda Incident in 1898 — the climactic episode in imperial territorial disputes between France and Britain in East Africa — had demonstrated how far France lagged behind Britain in battleship power. Distancing himself from the naval doctrines of the French "Jeune École" ("Young School"), which focused on the construction of small warships and various other types of vessels, the minister set up a comprehensive programme for a new fleet of battleships and numerous other men-of-war. In January 1900, the naval project was approved by the French parliament.[28] As a consequence of the Boxer Rebellion (1899–1901), which had shown the crucial importance of France's naval forces operating in Chinese waters, the minister issued the reorganisation decree of 1 April 1902, with the goal of merging four different naval units into the newly created "Force Navale des Mers d'Orient" (Eastern Seas Naval Force) which was given both defensive and offensive tasks and put under a joint supreme command; the main field of its operation was the China Seas and rivers in China and French Indochina.[29] According to the report by German Consul Dr. Emil Heintges in Saigon, the new French naval force was intended to turn Guangzhouwan into one of the important naval hubs in East Asia.[30] In February 1902, Governor-General Doumer (who had nearly reached the end of his term in Hanoi) submitted a bill on the project to develop Guangzhouwan into a naval port to the Conseil Supérieur (Upper Council) of Indochina. The plan included improved access to the territory's port for large French warships, the construction of a landing stage, a light tower on Naozhou (Nau Chau) Island, barracks for troops and the installation of defensive artillery batteries. The bill was adopted without modifications and submitted to Paris. The Upper Council's position was welcomed in the Tonkin press which expressed hopes that the development of the leased territory would finally secure French influence on the West River, the major access route into southern and central China.[31] The next month saw Doumer's successor, Paul Beau, arrive in Indochina. The new governor-general followed a drastically less-expansionist policy

[28] Taylor (1971, 380), Baumgart (1982, 63–68), Walser (1992, 27–45) and Halpern (2001, 44).

[29] Peyre (1902, 216).

[30] PAAA, R 19420: Consul Heintges (Saigon) to Chancellor von Bülow (Berlin), 15 February 1903.

[31] *Bulletin du Comité de l'Asie française* (1902, September, 407).

regarding French influence in southern China. However, he promised to continue the projects which had been started by his predecessor. The project to develop Guangzhouwan into a naval hub was not abandoned, and was even continued into early 1903. As Consul Heintges reported, the Guangzhouwan garrison, in 1902, consisted of around 1,000 naval and artillery troops, in addition to a French gunboat stationed at the port. In February 1903, the consul was convinced that the works at Guangzhouwan would soon begin after construction plans were fixed, and that, if required, further funding would be unhesitatingly granted by France.[32]

However, France's national elections in the spring of 1902 were to be a political turning point that, in turn, would alter her naval policies. The results were a great victory for the Leftists, and the cabinet Emile Combes formed in June 1902 was the most leftist in the history of the Third Republic. The Combes cabinet was dominated by the so-called Radical Democrats who had only the year before become a national party. Since the 1880s, Radicals had dominated the parliamentary committees in the bicameral legislature of the French Republic, the Chamber of Deputies and the Senate, and by around 1900 they had gained a dominant position in the committees. Prominent Radical politicians included Théophile Delcassé (1898–1905 foreign minister), the naval ministers Édouard Lockroy (1895–1896 and 1898–1899) and Jean Marie de Lanessan (1899–1902) and also Paul Doumer. From their political stance, the Radical Democrats were very much committed to popular sovereignty expressed through universal male suffrage, but less to the legitimacy of parliamentary institutions. The extreme Leftist Radicals included Camille Pelletan who was highly critical of the Chamber of Deputies and the Senate, which he regarded as discredited by corruption and intrigue and unwilling to reform. However, by the late 1880s, Radical leaders such as Pelletan and Georges Clemenceau (later French prime minister), had

[32] *Bulletin du Comité de l'Asie française* (1902, October, 449). According to Heintges' report the following troops were stationed in Guangzhouwan: At Fort Bayard, an artillery direction, the 15th battery of the colonial artillery and the battalion headquarters of the 10th colonial infantry regiment; at Chekam, two companies of the 10th regiment; at Hoitow, two companies of the 10th regiment and a company of the 2nd Tonkinese infantry troops (local Annamite soldiers); and at Pointe Nivet, another company of the 10th regiment. PAAA, R 19420: Consul Heintges (Saigon) to Chancellor von Bülow (Berlin), 15 February 1903.

toned down their opposition to parliament and began to identify themselves with the parliamentary system of the Third Republic. They took aim at the highly centralised administration of the French state, especially in the ministries of the army, navy and foreign affairs where important positions were occupied by men who had little regard for the Republic and its democratic institutions. For Pelletan, a Radical Member of the French parliament since 1881, the organisational reform of the French state, and especially the importance of reducing government administrative costs, remained a chief concern. By the 1890s, he had become a key figure in the struggle between the Chamber and the administration, especially after 1885 when he was a member of the Budget Committee, the most powerful body in the Chamber.[33] Pelletan's main interest during his time on this committee was the navy, the army, public debt, large banks and the railroads; it was over these matters that he demonstrated his great mistrust of state administration and major private companies. In the 1902 national election campaign, the Left associated itself with the defence of the Republic while the Right took a protective stance over the army, and especially the church. Electoral success, with 233 Radicals controlling the 589 seats of the Chamber of Deputies, was seen as a powerful call for the implementation of a radical programme by the government of Emile Combes.[34]

The reorientation of French naval policy in the Far East began after Pelletan assumed office as naval minister in 1902. He quickly overturned Lanessan's naval programme, returning to what many saw as the worst excesses of the Jeune École. This was in sharp contrast to France's neighbour, Germany, whose navy under Admiral Alfred Tirpitz was steadily constructing large battleships. In the autumn of 1902, and in February 1903, Pelletan laid out his programme for the navy which focused on a reduction in expenditure, democratisation and a complete reassessment of France's international naval position. Driven by the ideas of the Jeune École, and his own political beliefs, the minister called for the cancellation of all offensive policies, not only in Europe but also in the French colonies, finding it impossible for France to match the

[33] On Camille Pelletan, see *Dictionnaire de la Politique Française* (1972, 530), *Dictionnaire des Ministres de 1789 à 1989* (1990, 565), Bloch (1972, 123–126) and Stone (1996, 219–227, 230–231, 261). According to the journal *La Dépêche de Toulouse*, organ of the Radicals' leftist wing, Pelletan was the incarnation of the Left. Mayeur (1984, 189).

[34] Rebérioux (1975, 56–63) and Stone (1996, 261–266).

naval expenditure of Britain or Germany. Pelletan's ultimate goal was to convert the French navy into a model cost-effective republican state service, with an emphasis on a defensive strategy.[35] This considerably impacted the great plans for Guangzhouwan and resulted in shifting the focus of France's defence efforts back to Indochina. In January 1903, Governor-General Beau announced the creation of a special committee of the Haiphong Chamber of Commerce charged with promptly submitting detailed proposals for improving access to the port of Haiphong.[36] In the following month, after visiting the leased territory, the supreme commander of Indochina's colonial troops, General Pierre-Guillaume-Paul Coronnat, decided to abandon plans for the further fortification and development of Guangzhouwan. The *Châteaurenault*, a first-class cruiser of France's East Asia Naval Squadron, was ordered to fetch one hundred tonnes of artillery shells and other war materials which had been brought to the territory only a few months earlier. The unexpected move was greatly criticised in the Tonkin press, and in late February 1903 the newspapers accused the naval ministry of playing politics in France, but being unprepared for a possible war. In April 1903, Consul Heintges pointed to exclusively military reasons for France's decision to abandon Guangzhouwan as a military outpost in southern China: the French had recognised that the isolated territory could not be defended without the support of massive naval forces.[37]

Naval Politics and the Defence of Indochina

When Imperial Germany relinquished the political heritage of Chancellor Otto von Bismarck, who had strived to maintain cordial relations with St. Petersburg, France formed her alliance with Russia (1893). In the aftermath of the Sino-Japanese War (1894–1895), the two nations staged

[35] Stone (1996, 261–266, 273–285), Walser (1992, 113–25) and Halpern (2001, 44–46).

[36] *Bulletin du Comité de l'Asie française* (1903, March, 121). Similar efforts were made at the port of Saigon where in September 1903 more than seven hundred workers were employed day and night to facilitate the access to the harbour. *Bulletin du Comité de l'Asie française* (1903, December, 552).

[37] *Le Courrier d'Haiphong*, 27 January 1903, 17 February 1903 and 28 February 1903. PAAA, R 19420: Consul Heintges (Saigon) to Chancellor von Bülow (Berlin), 21 April 1903.

impressive naval demonstrations to temper Japanese ambitions in China. For European geopolitical reasons, but also because of other political and economic motives, France made concern for her alliances her top priority, as Hanotaux explained in a speech in the French parliament on 10 June 1895. His successor, Delcassé, was overheard saying in February 1899 that he would give priority to reinforcing the alliance with Russia which meant, de facto, activating it. "Alliance" soon became the official term for defining France's relationship with Russia. Between 1900 and 1904, the tangible consequence of Franco-Russian co-operation in the Far East was the regular sharing of intelligence on the latest developments in the Japanese navy and army. French diplomats and military attachés stationed in Tokyo provided blueprints of Japanese ships under construction in dockyards and handed over reports about actual conditions in the Japanese navy. Yet with increased Japanese secrecy, estimates of the size of the country's forces varied considerably. While the French warned that Japan possessed reorganised and lavishly equipped troops, the Russian assessment predicted a steady decline in the Japanese military threat which led to a fatal underestimation of Japan's actual military power prior to the outbreak of hostilities in 1904. Despite such differences, French assistance in providing observations and conclusions about the Japanese forces, especially the navy, was very useful to the Russians. In his secret memoirs, the later foreign minister of Japan, Tadasu Hayashi, at the time resident minister to Great Britain, pointed to the close existing relations between France and Russia which had shaped the French attitude towards Japan before and during the Russo-Japanese War.[38]

A few weeks after the outbreak of war between Russia and Japan, France, on 8 April 1904, entered into the Entente Cordiale with Britain. This agreement conclusively settled colonial disputes between them and also ended the intense rivalry over their respective spheres of interest in China. Anglo-French negotiations began in October 1903 and were stepped up after the outbreak of hostilities in East Asia. With the much-improved relationship, it was in both France and Britain's strong interests not to get involved in the war between Russia and Japan, to strictly observe neutrality and provide only minimal support for their respective partners. This attitude considerably impacted the French position in the Russian war effort which remained rather modest.

[38] Pooley (1969, 213), Taylor (1971, 334–345), Guillen and Allain (2007, 218–219) and Menning (2007, 53–60).

However, the naval ministry decided to allow the Russian Baltic fleet into Indochina ports to load coal and other fuels. The deep-water Cam Ranh Bay (about 290 kilometres northeast of Saigon) became the staging area for the forty-strong Russian fleet prior to the crucial Battle of Tsushima (27–28 May 1905). However, as Hayashi wrote in his secret memoirs, this logistical aid was regarded by Japan as flagrant disregard of international law and neutrality. As he observed, most French people feared the Japanese would one day attack Indochina because of this breach of neutrality.[39]

Although France's support for Russia during the war was mostly financial and logistical, French political and military circles became increasingly concerned about the danger of a possible Japanese attack on French Indochina. In February 1904, after Japanese forces had bottled up the Russian fleet at Port Arthur, French public opinion reacted nervously, warning of immediate danger for French Indochina should Japan establish herself as a first-class naval power. Such fears soon manifested themselves as the "yellow danger", the term which appeared in French newspapers. Plans for the defence of Indochina were brought forward by the Comité de l'Asie Française (Committee of French East Asia), the Indochina section of the French colonial lobby, and published in the *Bulletin du Comité de L'Asie Française*. In the leading article of the February 1904 edition, the anonymous writer (who was in fact its editor Robert de Caix) warned Japan was a power which was believed to be capable of fighting the greatest powers. Concerning Indochina, he called for the creation of a military force with sufficient strength to repulse any forces threatening the colony. Returning to the matter sometime later, the Indochina lobby stated that it was impossible to protect everything and requested that only the colony's most important and wealthiest parts (the Red River Delta of Tonkin and the Mekong River Delta of Cochinchina) should be defended at all costs. Earlier projects carried out in Guangzhouwan, in Da Nang (Tourane) or at other locations should be definitely shelved as such scattered ports would not compensate for the numerical inferiority of France's squadrons and could only be defended by a French fleet superior to its opponent.[40] In view of such frank recommendations, it was clear that

[39] Guillen and Allain (2007, 242), Bloch (1972, 149), Goscha (2016, 162) and Pooley (1969, 213–214).

[40] *Bulletin du Comité de l'Asie française* (1904, February, 68–76). Barnère (1904, 142–146).

the French colonial lobby had decided the defence of Indochina's mainland was its top priority. Consequently, Guangzhouwan as a defendable military post had to make way for the protection of Indochina.

In his reports of February and March 1904, Major von Hugo, the German military attaché at Paris, informed his government that four March Battalions of French colonial infantry regiments, of around 600 men each, were ready to be transferred from France to Haiphong together with two batteries of colonial infantry, increasing the total number of troops stationed in Tonkin by 3,300 soldiers. Furthermore, a commission of French engineer-officers had been ordered to construct fortifications in the area between the coastline and Hanoi to serve as troop bases and for the protection of Europeans, which Hugo judged an indication of growing French concerns for Indochina. This was soon confirmed by Lieutenant-Commander Rudolf Siegel, the German naval attaché at Paris, who also reported that a new French transport torpedo boat had been put into service to transport submarines from France to Saigon. In early June 1904, Alfons Mumm von Schwarzenstein, the German minister in Beijing, was informed by the French military attaché that troops, artillery material and two submarines had arrived at Saigon, whereupon the attaché had again voiced his fears about the potential threat to Indochina should Japan win the war against Russia.[41] In the same month, Pelletan's plans for Indochina became obvious in a conversation with German Ambassador Hugo Count von Radolin-Radoliński. Having recently returned from an official visit to Algeria, the naval minister spoke about the North African colony's natural beauty, explaining that it had been a mistake of French colonial policy not to focus on nearby Morocco, but instead on Indochina. He confessed that he had tried his best to work against the Tonkin Campaign (1882–1883) during his time as an opposition member in the French parliament, but in vain. The ambassador noted that Pelletan had exclaimed with a laugh: "Je vous l'aurais cédé volontiers." ("I would have ceded it to you with pleasure."). However, the French naval minister made clear that at that time, and also in future,

[41] PAAA, R 19421: Reports of German Military Attaché, Major von Hugo (Paris), 22 February 1904 and 10 March 1904; reports of German naval attaché, Lieutenant-Commander Siegel (Paris), to Admiral von Tirpitz (Berlin), 4 and 5 March 1904; German Minister Mumm von Schwarzenstein (Beijing) to Chancellor von Bülow (Berlin), 4 June 1904.

there was no other option than to protect France's East Asian possession against Japan.[42]

From February to December 1904, when naval actions between Japanese and Russian forces occurred at Port Arthur, French newspapers continued to express deep concern about the seemingly insufficient military protection of French Indochina. On 25 August 1904, Governor-General Beau explained before the Upper Council in Hanoi that the defence of Indochina was his major concern. Consequently, he revealed information about the ongoing fortification works in Saigon and at the mouth of the Saigon River, the strengthening of coastal and maritime defences and the much improved access to the port of Haiphong. In his view, the political situation in Indochina and in Guangzhouwan was excellent, with none of the reports from different regions showing any disturbance of public order or security. Concerning Guangzhouwan, Beau announced that the demarcation of the bay should be finished promptly and that the building of landing stages would be considered, but he remained completely silent about the future military position of the leased territory. In the following month, André Mévil, the influential French journalist, published an article expressing his firm opinion that after the war with Japan, Russia would not be able to regain her former naval dominance. It was therefore imperative to make France's East Asia Naval Squadron as strong as possible and to create another Port Arthur in Indochina in order to repulse a possible Japanese attack and provide French warships with refuge and repair facilities. Although Mévil did not specify a concrete location, it was evident that such a major naval base should be situated on the coast of Indochina.[43]

Final steps to improve the defence of the Indochinese peninsula were made when almost the entire Reserve Brigade of the Occupation Corps of China was withdrawn from Guangzhouwan, affecting three out of four infantry companies and leaving behind only an artillery section. In October 1904, the number of troops, around 1,000-strong, was drastically reduced to 150, a decrease of eighty-five per cent.[44] In the *Bulletin*'s

[42] PAAA, R 19421: Ambassador von Radolin-Radoliński (Paris) to Chancellor von Bülow (Berlin), 19 June 1904.

[43] *Bulletin du Comité de l'Asie française* (1904, October, 476, 464–481) and *L'Eclaire*, 28 September 1904.

[44] According to *Territoire de Kouang-Tchéou (Chine)* (1906, 51), there were c. 1,000 troops in Guangzhouwan in 1904. In early 1905, German Consul Hans von Varchmin in

November 1905 edition, the editor-in-chief once and for all put an end to plans for Guangzhouwan as a French naval hub in southern China. Reminding readers of the Sino-French lease convention of 1898, and of France's initial plans for her territory in China, Caix wrote the following:

> It does not seem that we have ever understood in France which precise use would be made of the territory thus obtained. We had put ourselves on the same rank as the other powers; in case the system of the "spheres of influence" prevailed, we had reduced the limits of ours to the Leizhou Peninsula. But in regard to the use of Guangzhouwan itself, the greatest uncertainty continued. We did not seem any more disposed to consider this acquisition as having any more value than the British theirs of Weihaiwei. Soon we recognised it would be foolish to want to establish in Guangzhouwan the naval base which we still project to create in the Far East. It would have been there a passing situation. It would be better to use some good Indochinese bay, leaning directly against the mass of our Asian possessions, than to risk a naval base in a small territory without means of defence, without features particular to it. And we decided to administer Guangzhouwan as any colonial dependence, sometimes even quite badly, as the significant incidents of a few months ago have shown. It is clear, today, that Guangzhouwan does not stand out either as a naval base, nor as a cover of a sphere of influence since no one thinks of spheres of influences in China anymore, admitting even that we had never really seriously thought of it. This does not mean that we must abandon this point. One must never abandon anything to one's name, at least without compensations that leave it intact. The British themselves give us its example in Weihaiwei, lost at the end of Shandong [Province], dominated by the German companies, possession we never knew what to do with and that Britain continues to declare itself determined to keep, if only as an undefended stopover port and as a sanatorium for the British squadron of the China seas. But, by keeping Guangzhouwan, we must make of it an enclave as inexpensive as possible for us and also as non-bothersome as possible for China".[45]

Beihai reported that the former number of about 1,000 troops stationed at Fort Bayard had included colonial infantry, Vietnamese infantrymen and some artillery. As he noted, this number was considerably reduced, with barely 200 French and perhaps twice as many or a few more Vietnamese soldiers remaining in Guangzhouwan. PAAA, Peking II-72: Consul von Varchmin (Beihai) to Chancellor von Bülow (Berlin), 18 February 1905. Bonningue (1931, 22) reports that the only artillery section left at Guangzhouwan was transferred back to Tonkin in 1906.

[45] Caix (1905, 425).

Caix's advice hinted to a certain extent at the future of Guangzhouwan, the ambitious plans for which, drawn up by Governor-General Doumer in 1899–1900, were set aside. Doumer had wanted the leased territory to develop into an important trading centre for the neighbouring Chinese provinces of Guangdong and Guangxi, after major commercial flows had been redirected to it. For this purpose, Guangzhouwan was declared a free port in 1900, with the goal of developing into a transit hub from which French-built railways could penetrate into southern China to facilitate the exploitation of coal mines and to exchange all kinds of goods. The status of free port, without any customs regime (which was not even mentioned in the Sino-French convention of 27 May 1898 on the lease of Guangzhouwan to France), allowed all products to enter Guangzhouwan without paying any customs fees and to be stocked and resold later. All imported and exported goods were free of any duties, even the ones crossing the border into China, without undergoing any controls or paying any duties. In January 1900, when Doumer put Guangzhouwan under the complete control of the governor-general of Indochina (with the territory's chief administrator becoming a member of Doumer's cabinet in Hanoi), he announced that he did not intend to impose, "at least at first", any duties or customs regulations on imports and exports. With no customs regime permanently in place, Guangzhouwan remained a blank sheet to the Chinese Imperial Maritime Customs Administration. In July 1901, Guangzhouwan's chief administrator Gustave Alby, made it clear to the Chinese trading company J. Charles et Cie in Haiphong that the port of Guangzhouwan was "open to all ships without distinction of the flag, and that all stopover services which could be established there are assured of receiving the most favourable welcome".[46] With such an announcement, there were high hopes that Guangzhouwan, with its free port, would develop into a trading and shipping centre similar to Hong Kong. However, from the beginning, the territory's free port status provided a stark contrast with the directly neighbouring, and extremely impoverished parts of Guangdong and Guangxi. To develop Guangzhouwan into a flourishing commercial hub of southern China, as Doumer had planned, it required a rich hinterland or important maritime links, as was the case with Saigon or Hong Kong. This meant that Guangzhouwan, with its free port but lack

[46]ANOM, INDO-GGI-23450: Chief Administrator Gustave Alby (Guangzhouwan) to Messrs J. Charles & Cie. (Haiphong), 8 July 1901.

of options for becoming a thriving commercial hub, could only acquire a more important economic role when it became an opium trading hub. This promised to be a very lucrative business for the dozen or so opium producers established in the territory and, through revenues on opium sales, for the French administration as well. Consequently, raw opium from British India was imported duty free from Hong Kong, and some of the raw opium from Yunnan usually traded down the West River was redirected to Guangzhouwan. Since local consumption of the drug was always too limited to provide considerable profits for opium producers in Guangzhouwan, most of the opium produced was to be exported by land or sea to neighbouring Chinese regions, where demand for the drug was frequently high, despite new opium suppression campaigns by the Qing government after 1901. This resulted in around two-thirds of Guangzhouwan's produced and registered opium (with probably a larger proportion of smuggled opium) being shipped to Hong Kong, and from there to Macao, the Chinese mainland and overseas destinations such as the United States. With French authorities turning a blind eye to favour the territory's only profitable commerce, Guangzhouwan developed into a major redistribution centre for opium trading and a hub of opium trafficking (Fig. 6.2).[47]

Despite the fact that Guangzhouwan was administratively made an integral part of French Indochina, commercial links remained extremely limited. Most important was the fact that the entire trading sector was dominated by Chinese merchants acting as agents of Chinese companies based in Hong Kong, Macao or Guangzhou. This resulted in very close economic links to ports in the Pearl River Delta. In terms of trading, Guangzhouwan and Haiphong, the Vietnamese port closest to the territory, generally had very little to exchange due to the almost identical economic structures of their respective hinterlands. A very large amount of exports from Tonkin consisting mainly of rice and other agricultural goods, and shipped from Haiphong, went first to Hong Kong from where it was transported further to China or other East Asian destinations, and even to Guangzhouwan. This made the direct Haiphong-Hong Kong run the more profitable route for shipping companies (such as the Tonkin Shipping Company or the M. Jebsen Shipping Company) operating in this part of the South China Sea. Most exports

[47] Fourniau (2002, 536–538), Pieragastini (2017, 115–116) and Vannière (2020, 129–130, 187–197).

Fig. 6.2 Guangzhouwan [spelt on the postcard as Quang-Tchéou-Wan, one of many variations of the French territory's name in different languages]: Administrative Building in Fort Bayard, the administrative centre of Guangzhouwan, c. 1910 (Private collection Bert Becker.)

from Guangdong and Guangxi, mainly agricultural produce and some processed goods, channelled through Guangzhouwan, were directed to the British colony, with its large free port, or to Singapore and Macao, but not to Haiphong which was heavily burdened by customs fees imposed by French Indochina. In the other direction, Guangzhouwan imported most of its needs from Hong Kong, predominantly opium, cotton yarns, wood, matches and even rice as re-exports from Indochina, as mentioned earlier.[48]

[48] In 1902, total exports of Guangzhouwan had the value of 1,287,370 piasters, and total imports of 4,040,902 piasters. Of the total exports, the share of Hong Kong, Singapore and Macao was 845,137 piasters (65.65 per cent). Of the total imports, the share of Hong Kong was 3,255,526 piasters (80.56 per cent), while the share of Haiphong was merely 208,251 piasters (5.15 per cent). *Bulletin du Comité de l'Asie française* (1903, July, 308) and Vannière (2020, 135–136). In 1914, 99.6 per cent of Guangzhouwan's exports were sent to Hong Kong and Guangzhou, with 96.3 per cent of imports coming from these two ports; merely 0.4 per cent of Guangzhouwan's exports went to Haiphong, with 3.7 per cent (mainly rice) being imported from there. Vannière (2020, 384, Table 11).

Shipping and Politics

Maritime Links

At the time of the French occupation of Guangzhou Bay (1898), shipping was dominated by Chinese junks, some of them of fifty to one hundred tonnes, which frequently called at the harbour. The junks served shipping routes along the southern Chinese coast up to Guangzhou and Hong Kong, in a south-westerly direction along the coast of Leizhou Peninsula up to Qiongzhou (Kiungchow), the main port of Hainan Island, into the Gulf of Tonkin and further south to Saigon, Bangkok and Singapore. Their main destination for exports remained Hong Kong from where they brought back cotton fabrics, petrol, matches, noodles and numerous other industrial goods. Inside the French territory, junks operated on the Maxie River up to Chikan (the major port and commercial centre of Guangzhouwan). However, the large number of trading vessels calling at the harbour made them vulnerable to frequent attacks by pirates. Piracy was a centuries-old phenomenon in the northern South China Sea during periods of dynastic upheaval or decline in China or Vietnam. As Luan and Cooke pointed out, "most local people were involved in piracy or smuggling to some extent". During the reign of the Vietnamese Emperor Tu Duc (1848–1883), Quang Yen Province in north-eastern Vietnam was the main centre for piracy, with more than half of all cases reported in the Gulf of Tonkin, although the number was probably even higher if the attacks of China-based pirates from Guangxi Province were included. For their operations, pirates exploited geographical advantages such as numerous coves along the Guangdong coastline serving as hideouts. In 1877, French authorities in Haiphong initiated an anti-piracy programme and removed the Chinese from Cat Ba Island in northern Vietnam. By the 1890s, many larger pirate bands had been destroyed by French eradication measures, while the increasing employment of steam coasters made it more difficult for smaller pirate communities to successfully attack merchant vessels. In August 1898, when French military operations in Guangzhouwan reached their first climax, French Consul Gaston Kahn in Haikou reported that piracy was "very lucrative in these regions", with the local population colluding with pirates. However, Kahn added that many pirates had recently been driven back to the southern Chinese coasts by the large number of French men-of-war operating off the coast of Hong Kong.[49]

After Guangzhouwan was declared a free port in 1900, the French territory saw a considerable increase in ocean-going shipping and overseas trading. French companies pioneered the introduction of steamships, adding a new component to the territory's maritime connections. The earliest shipping service operating between the British colony and Guangzhouwan was initiated by the French merchant Louis Sculfort, who had taken part in the exploratory mission of the Lyon Chamber of Commerce (1895–1896) and was thereafter the founder of the trading firm L. Sculfort & Company in the British colony. After acquiring a small steamer, of 98 tonnes (built in 1899), to which he gave the name *Nau Chau* (probably after Naozhou Island located inside Guangzhouwan), Sculfort, on 14 February 1900, inaugurated the first shipping service from Hong Kong to Macao and Guangzhouwan, departing immediately after the arrival of the French mail liner of Messageries Maritimes. The small ship, which required twenty-six hours for the voyage, carried thirteen passengers and nine hundred boxes of goods, and on the return voyage eleven passengers and eight hundred boxes of Chinese products such as oil, sugar, pork and mats. The *Nau Chau* made four return voyages per month, leaving Hong Kong shortly after the French mail liner had called at this port, so that letters sent from Marseille arrived at Guangzhouwan after twenty-nine days. The ship had stopovers at Macao and smaller Chinese ports of call along the Guangdong coastline. When the Boxer Rebellion in northern China caused a strong demand for vessels shipping European troops, this led to an extraordinary shortage of available vessels in the South China Sea. As a result, Sculfort was unable to find a vessel of more than five hundred tonnes. Although the *Nau Chau* proved inadequate from the start, the ship provided good profits for its owner, as French Consul Charles-Edmond Hardouin in Guangzhou reported. However, the vessel frequently fell victim to Chinese pirate attacks, as on 12 October 1900. The newspaper *La Chine Nouvelle: Revue Illustrée d'Extrême Orient*, published by Sculfort in Hong Kong, reported that the *Nau Chau*, with a crew of eighteen Chinese sailors and several passengers on board, among them six pirates, had departed Guangzhouwan carrying a cargo of cotton yarn and 32,000 dollars in

[49] Luan and Cooke (2011, 152–154), Pieragastini (2017, 110–111) and Vannière (2020, 48–49, the quote: 49).

cash. When the pirates on board started attacking the crew and passengers, they were joined by an armed junk, with thirty more pirates, robbing the ship of its entire cargo.[50]

Around 1899, Sculfort established the French-Chinese Syndicate, a joint-stock company registered in Hong Kong, associated with the French trading firm Racine, Ackermann & Cie, in which Chinese merchants from Guangzhouwan and Guangdong held one-quarter of the shares. The first visible presence of the Syndicate in Guangzhouwan was the construction of a warehouse on Naozhou Island serving as storage for French and other foreign goods imported from Hong Kong and Macao.[51] According to an overview published in July 1900, the Syndicate imported cotton fabric from Britain, window glass and iron from Belgium, cotton yarn and opium from British India, aniline, woolen fabric, drawstrings and toys from Germany, matches and cotton yarn from Japan, cement from Macao and petrol from the United States. In the following month, the French-Chinese Syndicate was taken over by P. Lemaire & Company headquartered in Paris, with branches in Hong Kong and Guangzhouwan.[52] Additionally, the French merchant became the owner of the *Nau Chau*, operating the small vessel for some time before selling it to the Customs Administration of French Indochina. In June 1901, he purchased the steamer *Paul Doumer*, which carried three hundred tonnes of goods and three hundred to four hundred passengers. To operate the large ship on the route between Guangzhou and Guangzhouwan, Lemaire was granted from the government-general shipping subsidies of 2,000 piasters per month (10,800 francs per month) or 24,000 piasters (129,000 francs) annually.[53] The *Paul Doumer* made three voyages per month between

[50] ANOM, INDO-GGI-5087: Note of Louis Sculfort (Naozhou, Guangzhouwan), 19 February 1900; note of Louis Sculfort (Hong Kong), 25 February 1900. ANOM, INDO-GGI-19563: Consul Hardouin (Guangzhou) to Governor-General Doumer (Paris), 14 April 1901. *La Chine Nouvelle* (1900, August–September, no. 9).

[51] ANOM, INDO-GGI-5087: Note of Louis Sculfort (Naozhou, Guangzhouwan), 19 February 1900; Louis Sculfort (Hong Kong) to Governor-General Doumer, 25 February 1900. Vannière (2020, 131).

[52] *La Chine Nouvelle: Revue Illustrée d'Extrême Orient* (1900, July, no. 8, Special Issue) and (1900, August–September, no. 9).

[53] ANOM, INDO-GGI-55365: Governor-General Doumer (Hanoi) to Consul Leroux (Hong Kong), 9 November 1900; Consul Leroux (Hong Kong), to Acting Governor-General Broni (Saigon), 3 July 1901. ANOM, INDO-GGI-19563: Consul Hardouin (Guangzhou) to Governor-General Doumer (Paris), 14 April 1901.

Guangzhou and Guangzhouwan, calling at Hong Kong, Macao and small ports of the Leizhou Peninsula which were known as hotbeds of piracy. According to German consul Hans von Varchmin in Beihai, Lemaire's line's operations were interrupted in 1904 for unknown reasons and resumed only in the following year.[54]

The break was probably due to the fact that, during the Russo-Japanese War, Guangzhouwan had been abandoned as a French military outpost, which considerably impacted the territory's trade and shipping. Chinese junks and other vessels, most of them owned by three Chinese shipping companies, filled the gap, fiercely competing against each other on the thriving run between the ports of the Pearl River Delta and Guangzhouwan, the maritime lifeline of the French territory. Since August 1900, one of their vessels, the steamer *La Seine*, of 250 tonnes, had obtained the French flag at Guangzhouwan and was under the management of a Chinese firm based in Guangzhou. According to *Le Courrier d'Haiphong*, in 1906, sixty-five Portuguese, fifty-seven French and twenty-five German vessels called at the French territory doing mostly transit trade between Guangzhouwan and Macao.[55] Facing strong competition, the shipping service to the French territory provided by the *Paul Doumer* seemed to have little profitability for Lemaire, even with the Indochina subsidy. When the *Paul Doumer* was shipwrecked, and the insurance had provided full compensation, Lemaire relinquished the entire shipping business in 1907. From then on, Chinese junks and steam coasters, Portuguese steam tramps from Macao and German vessels serviced the route to Guangzhouwan. There were, in addition, a small number of vessels owned by the Tonkin Shipping Company of Marty and the Compagnie de l'Est Asiatique française (French East Asiatic Company), both flying the French flag in the South China Sea.[56]

[54] PAAA, Peking II-72: Consul von Varchmin (Beihai) to Chancellor von Bülow (Berlin), 18 February 1905.

[55] ANOM, INDO-GGI-5087: Note of Chief Administrator Alby (Fort Bayard), 8 August 1900. PAAA, R 19420: Consul Heintges (Saigon) to Chancellor von Bülow (Berlin), 15 January 1903. *Le Courrier d'Haiphong*, 20 February 1907.

[56] ANOM, INDO-GGI-3403: Chief Administrator Fernand Gautret (Fort Bayard) to Acting Governor-General Bonhoure (Hanoi), 5 June 1908; Lucien Fontaine (Saigon) to Acting Governor-General Bonhoure (Hanoi), 14 May 1908.

The Guangzhouwan Postal Steamer Service

On 27 January 1900, Governor-General Doumer issued a decree on the call for tenders for the operation of a subsidised postal steamer service between Haiphong and Guangzhouwan. The service was planned to closely tie Guangzhouwan to Tonkin by safeguarding swift and reliable shipping connections. The route, with stopovers at Beihai and Haikou, was to cover a distance of 138.66 sea miles (or 210.76 kms).[57] This attracted considerable attention among French and even German firms involved in shipping in the South China Sea. Although Jacob Jebsen was realistic enough to recognise that "because of our flag", the M. Jebsen Shipping Company had "very little chance to win the contract", he announced the offer of a steamer for the monthly charter rate of 5,000 dollars, and was even prepared to put the ship under the Belgian flag. Jebsen seemed to have high hopes for the fast development of Guangzhouwan, as his following remark makes evident: "Calling at the new French place would very well fit into our [Haiphong] line and I believe we must go there sooner or later, even without a subsidy". The German shipowner was concerned that "our competitor Marty, the only possible French shipowner", would find "new support against us with the subsidy".[58]

On 21 March 1900, a seven-member commission reconvened in Haiphong's city hall to examine the eight offers which had been received from French firms for the Guangzhouwan postal steamer service (Jebsen was not among the bidders). With the others regarded as risky, two companies, Marty et d'Abbadie and Roque Frères, emerged as fron-trunners but the former's security and service regularity was viewed as advantageous.[59] With this clear vote for Marty et d'Abbadie, the path was open to further discussions during which the company not only agreed to the proposed price reduction (finally fixed at 22 francs per actual trav-elled sea mile) but also the French navy's right to transport personnel and

[57] ANOM, INDO-GGI-3388: Governor-General Doumer (Hanoi), 27 January 1900: Decree for the call for tenders for the operation of a maritime postal service from Haiphong to Guangzhouwan.

[58] JJHA, A01-01-294: Jacob Jebsen (Hong Kong) to Gustav Diederichsen (Hamburg), 5 February 1900.

[59] ANOM, INDO-GGI 3388: Protocol of commission session of 21 March 1900.

cargoes on the route on vessels of its own choice.[60] Apart from this exception, Marty et d'Abbadie, with the government-general of Indochina agreeing to reserve all its transports to the company's subsidised steamer, had the monopoly on the route between Haiphong and Guangzhouwan for which the subsidy was paid; the government promised not to subsidise any competitor on the route. The contract stipulated return voyages once every fortnight, with the option of extending the route to Hong Kong and back as long as the regular service between Haiphong and Guangzhouwan would not suffer from the detour.[61] The annual subsidy finally paid by the Indochinese government to the firm was 77,379.04 piasters (158,627.04 francs) for which 52 voyages were to be made by the postal steamer.[62]

The Guangzhouwan postal steamer service was inaugurated on 16 June 1900, with the first departure of the *Hue* from Haiphong.[63] The steamer, which came from the Tonkin Shipping Company's fleet, had been carefully chosen by the government-general because it had special installations which offered a far higher standard of comfort for passengers and the transporting of troops, compared to other merchant vessels. The *Hue* shipped mainly military personnel and supplies, in addition to a variety of goods, and was the most important traffic link to the new French territory, where the outpost of the Reserve Brigade of the Occupation Corps of China, headquartered in Haiphong, was based. This function, according to Marty et d'Abbadie, generated serious traffic for the transporting of military staff as well as military supplies and other materials destined for Guangzhouwan.[64] The opening of the Guangzhouwan postal steamer service, equipped with a ten-year subsidy contract, was a

[60] Such a clause for military transports, in which the navy reserved this option, was common and also applied in the case of the German postal steamer line in northern China which had been launched two years earlier to connect Germany's leasehold Jiaozhou (Kiaochow) with Shanghai and northern Chinese ports. Becker (2009, 205–208).

[61] ANOM, INDO-GGI-3388: Mr Brou, Director of Post and Telegraphy (Hanoi), to Marty et d'Abbadie (Haiphong), 30 April 1900; Agreement on executing a maritime postal service between Haiphong and Guangzhouwan. Issued in Hanoi, dated 1 June 1900.

[62] ANOM, INDO-GGI-3396: Auguste Raphael Marty (Haiphong) to Mr Lourme, Director-General of Post and Telegraphy (Hanoi), 15 April 1903.

[63] ANOM, INDO-GGI-3390: Announcement by A. R. Marty (Haiphong), undated.

[64] ANOM, INDO-GGI-3400: Marty et d'Abbadie (Haiphong) to the Governor-General of Indochina (Hanoi), 18 April 1906.

clear reflection of Doumer's keen interest in developing the territory into a military and economic outpost of Indochina. After Guangzhouwan was declared a free port in 1900, it was obvious that a commercial profile equal to Hong Kong was also projected for the territory. In this respect, the postal steamer service clearly served to boost not only France's imperialist political and economic goals but also the country's prestige in China. Marty was more pragmatic, reminding Governor-General Beau in June 1903 of the fact that "the line was established to comply with the political goals in south China of the French colonial government of Indochina and to make profits for his company".[65] This argument helped Marty play the national card when referring to his interests as a private French shipowner.

The main competitor of the subsidised postal steamer service was the M. Jebsen Shipping Company of which Jebsen & Co. in Hong Kong was the sole agent. In mid-1899, Jebsen & Co. admitted that due to the numerical superiority of his fleet in the Gulf of Tonkin region, Marty was able to frequently match their own ships with one of his vessels. With Marty dominating the route in the number of ships, Jebsen & Co. reported in July 1899 that the French shipowner was always able to make arrangements to ensure that one of his vessels was docking at Haiphong when a Jebsen steamer was arriving in the port.[66] However, by putting more ships on the line, Jebsen was able to match Marty's subsidised steamer. In 1902, the M. Jebsen Shipping Company had a fleet of fourteen medium-sized and large steam coasters in China while Marty's fleet only comprised six mainly smaller vessels. At the time, Consul Karl Lang in Guangzhou pointed to the fact that a large part of the shipping route between Hong Kong, Haikou, Beihai and Haiphong had come into the hands of Jebsen & Co. On the other hand, as Lang noted, Marty, in spite of receiving a huge government subsidy and therefore being in a more financially comfortable position than his competitors, had not been able

[65] ANOM, INDO-GGI-6154: Auguste Raphael Marty (Haiphong) to Governor-General Paul Beau (Hanoi), 2 June 1903.

[66] JJHA, A01-01-294: Jacob Jebsen (Hong Kong) to Michael Jebsen (Apenrade), 13 May 1898; JJHA, A01-02-0047: Jebsen & Co. (Hong Kong) to M. Jebsen Shipping Company (Apenrade), 7 July 1899.

to chase away Jebsen's vessels from the route, or even stop them from expanding their transport services.[67]

The competitive situation for the postal steamer service was even more intense on the extension route from Guangzhouwan to Hong Kong and back, for which the Tonkin Shipping Company did not receive any subsidy. However, this run was more profitable because of the strong commercial flows between the British colony and the French territory. Apart from competition from vessels flying the German, British, Chinese and other flags, of which most were Chinese junks, the French flag was also present on that route, with the French traders Sculfort and Lemaire operating a steamer service between the Pearl River Delta and the French territory. With Lemaire's and Marty's steamers frequently calling at the British port, the number of vessels flying the French flag increased slightly to five ships, totalling 10,000 tonnes, in 1902. According to information from the French consulate in Hong Kong, this positive development was particularly due to Marty and his postal steamer service.[68]

In 1904, France's unexpected abandonment of Guangzhouwan as a military outpost of Indochina severely impacted the Tonkin Shipping Company and the subsidised postal steamer service. The withdrawal of troops had a grave impact on Marty's firm, which faced a huge loss in profits, after passengers and cargoes destined to and from Guangzhouwan were significantly reduced. According to Marty et d'Abbadie, the transporting of troops and their equipment to and from the French territory had constituted the only profitable element of the postal steamer service.[69] The fall in shipping directly impacted the overall value of imports and exports of Guangzhouwan in 1904 which decreased by almost 23 per cent compared to the previous year; the downward trend accelerated in the following year with a decrease of almost 27 per cent compared to the year before.[70] The numbers make it clear that Guangzhouwan's shipping and trading was considerably impacted by the withdrawal of the major part of its troops. In the official 1906 report on Guangzhouwan, the government-general

[67] BAB, R 901-16758, Consul Lang (Guangzhou) to German Legation (Beijing), 24 March 1902.

[68] Réau (1903, 452).

[69] ANOM, INDO-GGI-3400: Marty et d'Abbadie (Haiphong) to the Governor-General of Indochina (Hanoi), 24 August 1906.

[70] *Territoire de Kouang-Tchéou (Chine)* (1906, 49, 51) and Becker (2019b, 420–421).

of Indochina observed that the territory's commercial transactions had progressed consistently until 1904, when they had been disrupted by the Russo-Japanese War. Although initially accounting for the decline in Guangzhouwan's trade on the measures taken by Chinese authorities in neighbouring ports, the report admits, in a footnote, that the reduction in troops was responsible for such an outcome.[71]

The new situation made the Guangzhouwan postal steamer service a heavy financial burden for the Tonkin Shipping Company. According to Marty, in 1904, the overall profits of the *Hue* fell by 45,000 dollars. When losses extended into the following year, the company asked Governor-General Beau to provide financial compensation. The request was deemed valid, but Beau was unable to grant it as the 1906 budget for Indochina had already been drawn up, recommending instead that the company submit a fresh application which would be approved in 1907. The annual profits of the *Hue* were reduced by 60,000 dollars in 1905, and also in 1906. In April 1906, the company wrote to Beau, suggesting the extension, with immediate effect, of the subsidised service up to Hong Kong, and also to add two years to the current subsidy contract. Receiving no reply, they sent a reminder in August 1906, writing of "the precarious circumstances done to our steamer *Hue*". This time, in October 1906, the government-general looked into the matter, considering that "there is an unquestionable political interest in favouring the shipping company which carries most honourably the French flag in this part of the China Seas". In spite of this, the administration finally decided the reduced transporting of troops did not give the company a right to any compensation. Additionally, with Guangzhouwan regularly served every week by two or three steamers which had their port-of-call in Hong Kong, the requested subsidy to extend the postal steamer service to the British colony was seen as groundless. The government-general concluded that an additional subsidy would only be of benefit to the company.[72] This made it obvious that pragmatism, and especially financial considerations, dominated the attitude of French authorities, with France's ambitious imperial projects

[71] *Territoire de Kouang-Tchéou (Chine)* (1906, 51).

[72] ANOM, INDO-GGI-3400: The Inspector-General, Director-General of Post and Telegraphs of Indochina (Hanoi), to the Secretary-General of Indochina (Hanoi), 13 June 1906; Administrative Service of the Government-General of Indochina (Hanoi) to the Governor-General of Indochina (Hanoi), 5 October 1906; Governor-General of Indochina p. i. (Hanoi) to Marty et d'Abbadie (Haiphong), 8 October 1906.

being largely abandoned in the aftermath of the Russo-Japanese War. It was clear that not even political prestige could woo the financially strained government-general after France had retreated from its former economic and political goals in southern China and relinquished the defence of Guangzhouwan for that of Indochina. To make matters even worse, at the beginning of that year, Marty had lost the contract of the Subsidised River Shipping Service of Tonkin. In early 1908, the government-general decided that a further subsidy for Marty was "unrealisable in the current state of the budget of Indochina".[73] This resulted in Hanoi declining to pay any compensation for the financial losses suffered by the Tonkin Shipping Company (the government-general was not legally required to do so). Furthermore, it was not prepared to subsidise the shipping route between Guangzhouwan and Hong Kong. Internal deficiencies of the Tonkin Shipping Company added to its decreasing competitiveness, as Jacob Jebsen pointed out in 1908 when he remarked that Marty's firm would work less economically than Jebsen & Co. or Butterfield & Swire.[74]

The Guangzhouwan postal steamer service's continuing financial losses also demonstrate the more general problem of transport services which are contractually required to operate on fixed schedules. Even with little or no cargoes and passengers available at ports, the postal steamer is forced to adhere to its timetable to safeguard the regular and punctual transporting of mail. This restricts the shipping company's ability to take advantage of market opportunities or strike up profitable business deals whenever they turn up and, in turn, forces it to reduce the running costs of the postal steamer as much as possible. It often results in saving expenditures for the ship itself, for its crew or for passenger services on board.[75] Writing from Beihai in early 1910, French Vice-Consul Amédée Guibert, observing Marty's postal steamer *Hanoi* calling at the port, reported that "by the nature itself of its service, the postal ship is compelled to a regularity which is a hindrance to the good commercial operation of the line". Without mentioning Jebsen by name, he further

[73] ANOM, INDO-GGI-3402: Administrative Service of the Government-General of Indochina (Saigon) to the Director of Agriculture, Forests and Trade (Hanoi), 17 January 1908.

[74] JJHA, B10-01-017: Jacob Jebsen (Hong Kong) to Consul von Varchmin (Beihai), 13 February 1908.

[75] Sturmey (2010, 25–26) and Thieß (1907, 103).

remarked that foreign shipping companies, especially German ones, being acquainted with the *Hanoi*'s schedule, would often send their vessels to the port one or two days in advance of the steamer's arrival to take away lucrative freights.[76] In view of his company's worsening financial situation, Marty reduced services for passengers on board the vessels to save costs. This had immediately negative consequences. On 17 February 1910, several passengers who had recently sailed from Haiphong to Hong Kong on the *Hanoi*, penned a joint complaint to the governor-general of Indochina. In the letter, they criticised the poor accommodation, bathroom facilities, meals and even the presence of rats. Hinting that conditions had been even worse on the *Hue*, the complainants asked the governor-general for appropriate measures "to put an end to the shameful procedures of the French flag". When French Consul Gaston-Ernest Liébert in Hong Kong authenticated the complaints, an enquiry was launched by the government-general of Indochina which resulted, in April 1910, in a strong warning to Marty to carefully observe the terms of the 1900 contract.[77] At the time it was already widely known that another company than Marty's had won the new postal steamer contract. Whether the complaint had contributed to this result remains uncertain since there were already various rumours circulating in Tonkin about the poor services on vessels operating the Guangzhouwan postal steamer service. This certainly harmed Marty's reputation as a shipowner.[78]

With Marty's contract for operating the postal steamer service approaching its termination in 1910, the Tonkin press launched a public discussion about the future of French shipping services in the China Seas. In May 1909, the Hanoi Chamber of Commerce led the public discussion and proposed the establishment of a regular line from Haiphong to Shanghai. It would be served by fast steamers, quickly transporting the mail bound for Paris on the Siberian Railway and increasing the exports of Indochina's products to the Shanghai market. In addition to the Messageries Maritimes mail liners already plying between Hong

[76] MAE, CPC-551, Vice-Consul Guibert (Beihai) to Governor-General Klobukowski (Hanoi), 6 January 1910.

[77] ANOM, INDO-GGI-19311: Passengers on board of the *Hanoi* (Hainan Strait) to the Governor-General (Hanoi), 19 February 1910; Consul Liébert (Hong Kong) to the Governor-General (Hanoi), 25 February 1910; Acting Governor-General Picquié (Hanoi) to Consul Liébert (Hong Kong), 11 April 1910.

[78] *Bulletin du Comité de l'Asie française* (1910, April, 198).

Kong and Shanghai, the new line would increase shipping services under the French flag on this route. While Tonkin business circles welcomed the idea of improved transport services, the local press criticised the estimated subsidy amount of around 1.2 million francs and pointed out that due to time constraints in Hong Kong, cargoes from Indochina could not be charged or discharged during stopovers at this important port. To speed up the line, the press suggested permitting the Tonkin Shipping Company to establish a direct link between Haiphong and Hong Kong in weekly or biweekly intervals, without making any stopovers on the route. This would allow passengers and mail to catch the Messageries Maritimes mail liners leaving Hong Kong for Shanghai.[79] The views of the press were supported by the new governor-general Antony Klobukowski, with the important exception that the postal steamers should also call Guangzhouwan on a biweekly basis. Having learned that the subsidy contract of Messageries Maritimes for the Hong Kong-Shanghai service was due to expire in 1912, and that the large French shipping company was interested in possibly launching an extended line in the Gulf of Tonkin, the government-general was only prepared to grant a new contract for a period of two years for the service between Haiphong and Hong Kong.[80] Klobukowski's arrival in October 1908 had almost coincided with that of Paul-Edgard Dufrenil, the new chief administrator of Guangzhouwan. Detailing Dufrenil's future tasks in the territory, Klobukowski emphasised that Guangzhouwan had to be kept going "under honourable conditions" and that it was necessary to give the impression to the local Chinese and to the Chinese authorities in the vicinity that the territory had "a very great value" for France. The colonial ministry went even further, asking the governor-general not to demolish the vacated military buildings in Guangzhouwan as it was feared that it would upset the Chinese and possibly weaken French influence in the region.[81] In view of these political considerations, along

[79] *L'Avenir du Tonkin*, 9 and 14 May, 7/8 June and 28 October 1909.

[80] ANOM, INDO-GGI-3403: The Chief Director of the Post and Telegraphs Service of Tonkin charged with the expedition of matters of the Direction-General (Hanoi) to the Governor-General (Saigon), 2 December 1909.

[81] ANOM, INDO-GGI-2376-2: Governor-General Klobukowski (Hanoi) to Chief Administrator of Guangzhouwan (Fort Bayard), 11 December 1908; General Lasserre, Director of Military Services, on behalf of the Colonial Minister and by order (Paris) to the Governor-General (Hanoi), 6 May 1909.

with the restricted budget of Indochina, Klobukowski finally approved the biweekly stopover at Guangzhouwan for the new Haiphong–Hong Kong line in the autumn of 1909. Although it meant better connections for mail, passengers and cargo bound to and from Hong Kong, it also brought an end to any stopovers in Beihai and Haikou. The cuts in funding for various projects after the abolishment of France's imperialist designs was finally felt among the small local French communities in the region.[82]

Although Marty had the support of the Tonkin press, which praised his efforts in representing the French flag in the Gulf of Tonkin,[83] it was the Compagnie de l'Est Asiatique française (French East Asiatic Company) which won the new subsidy contract in March 1910. The French East Asiatic Company was a subsidiary of the Danish-owned Det Østasiatiske Kompagni or Ø.K. (East Asiatic Company, EAC) founded in Copenhagen in 1897 by Hans Niels Andersen and Isak Glückstadt. In 1902, the French East Asiatic Company was established in Paris by a group of French and Danish businessmen with the active support of Princess Marie of Denmark (the wife of Prince Valdemar, a younger brother of King Frederick VIII of Denmark). As France already possessed a major shipping company, specifically the Messageries Maritimes which had a network of shipping lines to and from the Far East, the founding of the French East Asiatic Company was executed in close collaboration with Messageries Maritimes. The latter company even provided office space and two managers to the new firm in Paris. Its capital was derived from Danish and French investors, the latter predominantly based in Marseille where the company headquarters was situated.[84] In French Indochina, the French East Asiatic Company had the Messageries Maritimes' agency whose subsidy contract for the lines to the Far East was due to expire in 1912. To give its principals a better position in future negotiations regarding subsidised services in East Asia, the French East Asiatic Company wanted to bring the line between Haiphong and Hong Kong under its own management. Although Marty purportedly had been promised by the government-general of Indochina that his contract would be extended, he

[82] *Bulletin du Comité de l'Asie française* (1909, October, 452).

[83] *L'Avenir du Tonkin*, 9 May 1909.

[84] Hansen (1970, 46) and Andersen (1914, 54–56). *Paris-Capital*, 9 July 1902 and 18 March 1903 and *Le Figaro*, 22 September 1903. For more details, see Becker (2019b, 430–433).

received a rude shock when competitors appeared and demanded that the service be put to auction. When the government-general finally conceded to these requests, three firms submitted offers. Marty demanded a subsidy of 9,520 francs for each return trip from Haiphong to Hong Kong, while the French East Asiatic Company requested 8,874 francs, which proved to be the most economical one. Marty, as he later stated, had to accept defeat.[85]

The new subsidy contract of the French East Asiatic Company stipulated a biweekly service between Haiphong and Hong Kong, with a stopover at Guangzhouwan, to be made in 53 hours in order to provide the immediate connection with Messageries Maritimes liners bound for Shanghai. For its service, the French East Asiatic Company was granted a yearly subsidy of about 230,000 francs in view of the longer distances, in comparison to the route which had been formerly served by Marty et d'Abbadie (160,000 francs annually). The new subsidy covered the entire route to Hong Kong via Guangzhouwan, thus combining the former independent lines of Marty et d'Abbadie and Paul Lemaire. However, Beihai and Haikou were no longer ports of call, a factor which was criticised in the Tonkin press and seen as neglecting French interests in the region when local French expatriate communities were no longer connected with each other and Indochina by a regular shipping service under the French flag. Therefore, most criticism in the Tonkin press about the new arrangements came from French residents in Haikou and Beihai who were forced to board steamers under the German flag when travelling to Indochina, Guangzhouwan or Hong Kong, which was regarded as a severe blow to France's national prestige and influence in the region.[86]

The French East Asiatic Company launched its new service on 29 May 1910 with the steamer *Hai Mun* purchased in Hong Kong. After the steamer was declared technically unfit for service, the company put the larger Messageries Maritimes steamer *Manche* on the line. It then purchased the used steamer *Touareg*, of 1,274 gross register tonnes, with a speed of 11 knots. It was renamed the *Sikiang* and in September 1910 put on the line. Built in around 1889, the vessel with its tonnage

[85] PAAA, Peking II-1176: Consul Dr. Merklinghaus (Beihai) to Chancellor von Bethmann Hollweg (Berlin), 26 March 1910. ANOM, INDO-GGI-17022: Auguste Raphael Marty (Haiphong) to the Governor-General (Saigon), 26 October 1911.

[86] *L'Avenir du Tonkin*, 29 June 1910 and 25 August 1910 and *Le Courrier d'Haiphong*, 1 July 1910.

equalled other merchant steamers of its age, but was inferior to modern steamers operating in East Asia, which on average were more than 2,500 gross registered tonnes. Its relatively small size (in Hong Kong, it was known as the "Baby") meant it was unable to handle sufficient and profitable cargoes, even during the rice harvest seasons when demand for merchant vessels was highest.[87] Furthermore, the *Sikiang* was relatively slow and uncomfortable for passengers, resulting in travellers in Hong Kong opting for the vessels of its British (Butterfield & Swire) and German (Jebsen & Co., the sole agent of the M. Jebsen Shipping Company) competitors for trips to Indochina or Guangzhouwan. Writing to Colonial Minister Albert Lebrun in October 1912, Governor-General Albert Sarraut stated that the *Sikiang*'s inadequacy was well known and that its bad reputation constituted an absolute obstacle to the development of relations between Tonkin and south China.[88] This remark hinted at Sarraut's "policy of progress and development" which he regarded as important in making French interests in the region yield a profit by assuring with increasingly stronger means France's colonial rule over Indochina and expanding French influence in East Asia.[89]

At the beginning of 1912, it was certain that the company Messageries Maritimes would launch a new and direct shipping line between Marseille and Haiphong, but without extending its service up to Hong Kong so that the feeder in the Gulf of Tonkin needed to be operated by another French shipping company.[90] German Consul Dr. Peter Merklinghaus in Beihai later said that Marty had never given up on recovering the subsidy contract and had pulled strings to get the Tonkin press on his side. As the consul observed, the shipowner seemed to be more interested in regaining it all and less interested in the amount of the subsidy. In preparation, Marty had already approached Chinese rice merchants in Haiphong and

[87] PAAA, Peking II-1175: Johann Heinrich Jessen (Hong Kong) to German Minister von Rex (Beijing), 30 May 1910 (on the *Hai Mun*). PAAA, Peking II-1176: Consul Dr Merklinghaus (Beihai) to Chancellor von Bethmann Hollweg (Berlin), 29 June 1910 and 5 September 1910; Consul Dr Merklinghaus (Beihai) to Chancellor von Bethmann Hollweg (Berlin), 12 October 1912.

[88] ANOM, INDO-GGI-17022: Governor-General Sarraut (Saigon) to Colonial Minister Lebrun (Paris), 30 October 1912.

[89] On 19 November 1913, Governor-General Sarraut outlined his policy before the Government-Council of French Indochina. Fourniau (2002, 750) and Vannière (2020, 304–317).

[90] *Bulletin du Comité de l'Asie française* (1912, February, 198).

in other ports of Tonkin to exclusively provide him with their cargoes, declaring he would transport them on two new high-speed steamers, and also on his three older vessels.[91] Apart from economic factors, Marty's intense efforts to regain the subsidised line was also personally motivated by hopes of restoring his pride and reputation as the most prominent French shipowner in the region. Therefore, his approach to the Chinese merchants in Tonkin was directed against his main competitor, Jebsen & Co., which at the time operated twelve modern steam coasters in East Asia, while three ships in Marty's fleet had been sold or wrecked, with only the *Hanoi*, *Hongkong* and *Hue* remaining. After the Haiphong Chamber of Commerce had voiced strong opposition to certain details of the planned contract, the formal call for tenders for the new service was postponed to 2 September 1912 when four firms submitted their offers, of which only two were accepted for further consideration: those of the Tonkin Shipping Company and the Compagnie Maritime Indochinoise (Indochinese Shipping Company, the subsidiary of the French East Asiatic Company,[92] which seemed only to have been established for legally acquiring the subsidy contract). However, both firms demanded a subsidy which was higher than the maximum amount fixed by the government-general. Fearing a halt in the negotiations, Marty asked to immediately begin talks with the administration, emphasising that his firm had been the originators of the service and had defended the interests of the French flag in the Gulf of Tonkin for more than twenty years. After this appeal, he promised to have within two years two new large steamers built for the service, and, in addition, was prepared to accept a reduced subsidy. With the administration and Marty finally agreeing on a subsidy of 22.50 francs per sea mile between the administration and Marty, Governor-General Sarraut was convinced that better financial conditions could not have been achieved in the interests of Indochina.[93]

On 4 October 1912, the ten-year contract for the Guangzhouwan postal steamer service beginning on 1 March 1913 was signed, with specifications stipulating a weekly service of two postal steamers of which one

[91] PAAA, Peking II-1176: Consul Dr Merklinghaus (Beihai) to Chancellor von Bethmann Hollweg (Berlin), 12 October 1912.

[92] Morlat (2016, 448).

[93] ANOM, INDO-GGI-17022: Governor-General Sarraut (Saigon) to Colonial Minister Lebrun (Paris), 30 October 1912. *Bulletin du Comité de l'Asie française* (1912, October, 438–439).

should serve the route from Haiphong to Hong Kong, with a stopover at Guangzhouwan, and on its return trip, call at Haikou; the following steamer should sail to Hong Kong via Haikou, and on the way back call at Guangzhouwan. At least two steamers, each of around 2,500 gross register tonnes, with a speed of 12 knots, were to operate on the line. The large vessels which had to be relatively new, also had to have a standard comparable to modern French liners, with full comfort for passengers.[94] For the time being, Marty continued to use the *Hue* which was completely overhauled, and the *Hanoi*. To Jacob Jebsen, it was clear that Marty's new contract with a substantial subsidy of around 9,000 dollars per voyage would give the French shipowner "certainly very considerable moral support". The German shipowner predicted that Marty would be able to make a surplus "at all events", although his new steamers were "more expensive than ours in building costs and operation".[95]

In February 1914, the French lawyer Henri Cucherousset, the later founder of the journal *L'Éveil Economique du Tonkin* (1917), wrote an article on Guangzhouwan detailing his observations during a visit. The territory's port was not lively, with the *Hue* calling Guangzhouwan every second Saturday on her way to Hong Kong, and every second Friday on her way back to Haiphong.[96] Despite this, the postal steamer line continued to operate as scheduled in the contract. While the *Hue* serviced the line to Guangzhouwan, the larger steamer *Hongkong,* and occasionally also the *Hanoi,* operated on the direct line between Haiphong and the British colony.[97] After Marty died in Haiphong on 15 December 1914, his son-in-law, Raymond René Sallé, continued the Guangzhouwan postal steamer service during the First World War, but gave it up in 1918 when his request for an increased subsidy to cover his operational expenses was

[94] ANOM, INDO-GGI-17022: Contract of Mutual Agreement for the operation of a maritime postal service from Haiphong to Hong Kong via Haikou and Guangzhouwan, issued at Saigon, 4 October 1912.

[95] JJHA, A01-01-301: Jacob Jebsen (Apenrade) to Gustav Diederichsen (Hamburg), 20 November 1912.

[96] *L'Avenir du Tonkin*, 19 February 1914.

[97] ANOM, INDO-GGI-17022: Government-General of Indochina, Director of Posts and Telegraphs (Hanoi), to the Governor-General of Indochina (Hanoi), 17 May 1913.

rejected by the government-general.[98] The service passed into the hands of the Haiphong-based shipping company, P. A. Lapicque & Company (owned by Paul Augustin Lapicque, a French officer, then captain and then shipowner, who had come to East Asia in 1904 as representative of a major French trading firm). After conducting several geographical expeditions in China and Indochina, with an emphasis on studying major rivers, Lapicque founded his own shipping and trading firm in Hong Kong in 1910. In partnership with the French engineer F. Walthert he established the firm P. A. Lapicque & Co. in Haiphong in September 1918, operating Marty's former vessel *Hanoi* and also the steamer *Song-Ma* on the line.[99] However, in the autumn of 1923, Lapicque went bankrupt after the global economic crisis of the early 1920s put an end to the post-war shipping and trade boom.[100] In order to temporarily safeguard the operation of the service, a syndicate of major French colonial firms of Indochina was formed which, in November 1923, founded La Compagnie indochinoise de navigation (The Indochinese Shipping Company). After taking over the subsidised weekly service between Haiphong and Hong Kong, and also the biweekly service between Haiphong and Guangzhou via Guangzhouwan, the Indochinese Shipping Company operated three steamers, the *Hanoi* (Marty's former vessel), the *Tonkin* and the *Song Bo*.[101] Although the territory had almost completely lost its economic and political importance for France, remaining primarily a prestigious symbol for the country's position in China, the government-general of Indochina, with the considerable subsidy for the postal steamer service, retained the most important lifeline of Guangzhouwan during the 1920s and 1930s.

[98] VNA1, RH-4725: Company A. R. Marty, R. Sallé (Successor), Timetable of 1916 for the Subsidised Service Haiphong-Hong Kong via Guangzhouwan or Haikou corresponding with the Trans-Siberian. *L'Éveil économique de l'Indochine*, 30 March 1930.

[99] *L'Éveil économique de l'Indochine*, 22 September 1918 and 5 February 1922 and *Annuaire général de l'Indochine française* (1920, 87).

[100] *L'Éveil économique de l'Indochine*, 5 August 1923 and 19 August 1923, *Les Annales coloniales*, 5 October 1923 and 12 October 1923 and Morlat (2016, 448).

[101] The Indochinese Shipping Company was headed by Maxime Getten, engineer and vice-president of La Compagnie française des chemins de fer de l'Indochine et du Yunnan (The French Railway Company of Indochina and of Yunnan), and by managers from leading companies of Indochina and France, among them French banks based in Paris. It derived its capital from Indochinese and French firms in the shipbuilding and banking sectors. Morlat (2016, 448–449).

Guangzhouwan in German Government Records (1898–1914)

For many years, Guangzhouwan (1898–1946) remained barely researched. Important fresh initiatives were provided by the seminal academic study of French historian Antoine Vannière and a large number of conference papers given by historians at international conferences on the history and culture of Guangzhouwan organised in 2016 and 2019 by Wang Qin Feng, professor at Lingnan Normal University in Zhanjiang, in the People's Republic of China.[102] With respect to primary sources related to the history of the French territory, the unsorted collection of documents preserved in German government archives is a useful addition to the well-known records kept in French, Vietnamese and Chinese archives. Such documents were authored by German diplomatic and consular staff posted in Beijing and in port cities of the South China Sea, namely Hong Kong, Guangzhou, Beihai, Haikou and Saigon. German consuls in these port cities were charged to frequently observe French activities in southern China and to consequently submit their accounts to the legation in Beijing and neighbouring German consulates, or directly to the foreign ministry in Berlin. It should be noted that collecting information on political, economic and all kinds of activities of other states is part of the normal and routine-like work of foreign ministries and of embassies, legations and consulates worldwide. Therefore, documentation on Guangzhouwan was primarily intended to provide the government in Berlin, the German legation in Beijing and German consulates in the region around Guangzhouwan with accurate and reliable information on all sorts of internal and external factors impacting the French territory. However, the reports were also politically motivated. Although Imperial Germany's political, economic and cultural interests focused on northern China and striving to develop Jiaozhou (Kiaochow) into a "model colony" or a "German Hong Kong",

[102] The eminent study of Vannière on Guangzhouwan (2020) (founded on the author's PhD thesis of 2004) provides the most comprehensive and detailed historical account of the French leased territory based on extensive and meticulous research in French and Vietnamese archives. The papers presented at the First International Academic Conference on Guangzhouwan's History and Culture (Zhanjiang, 2016) were published by Wang Qin Feng (2019); the papers of the follow-up conference are in the unpublished *Conference Proceedings* of the Second International Academic Conference on Guangzhouwan's History and Culture (Zhanjiang, 2019).

German steam shipping and trading companies continued to thrive in the South China Sea, in the entire Gulf of Tonkin region and in the ports of French Indochina. This fact made it obligatory for German diplomats and consuls to promote and even defend the shipping and trading interests of German companies seemingly challenged by France's claim of her sphere of interest in southern China. Such conflicting Franco-German interests had a twofold impact: On the one hand, due to Germany's more extended shipping and trading interests in the northern South China Sea, there was a much keener desire for the Germans, than for example for the British, to remain well informed about the French territory in China; on the other hand, the Germans always maintained a very critical stance towards the French territory when providing facts and figures and expressing their own opinions about its fate. Some correspondence and reports were even coloured by suspicion, mistrust, condescension and disdain, especially after Guangzhouwan seemed not to develop into a "French Hong Kong", as some contemporaries had hoped. However, despite some highly critical comments, occasionally tainted by traditional anti-French prejudices, German reporting on Guangzhouwan principally gave accurate and reliable information to the foreign ministry in Berlin. Except for providing useful facts and figures (which are sometimes difficult to find elsewhere), the documents offer unique analyses from contemporary observers, and even visitors to the territory, about Guangzhouwan's retarded development from 1898 to 1914.

In November 1902, the German foreign ministry appointed Arthur Mudra as professional consul in Beihai and Haikou. He was told that "your main task is to observe the doings of the French in southern China in connection with their colony of Indochina and their leased territory of Guangzhouwan". His first task was to travel from Beihai to the leased territory in order to monitor its development and to set up a report about the future naval port. For unknown reasons, this document is not to be found in the records of the foreign ministry.[103] In December 1902, in a kind of parallel action, Consul Heintges in Saigon was assigned by Berlin to pay close attention to any future plans for Guangzhouwan by Doumer's successor, Governor-General Beau.

[103] PAAA, R 141855: Consul Dr. Knappe (Guangzhou) to Consul Mudra (Shanghai), 9 November 1902.

However, the consul's subsequent reports were entirely based on information collected in Cochinchina and not on personal observations of Guangzhouwan. In January 1903, the first account was completed, with a second one following in the next month in which Heintges pointed to the fact that "Guangzhouwan and the creation of a first-class naval hub there is valued very much here [in Saigon] and in Paris because the maritime defence of Indochina is based upon that". In April 1903, Heintges reported that, as result of General Coronnat's inspection tour to Guangzhouwan, "further fortification and enforcements will be abandoned". This decision was the consequence of France's revised naval policy under Naval Minister Pelletan. The consul made it clear that French authorities and residents in Indochina had their specific interests in the matter and were of the opinion that "in case of war between France and another power the colony [French Indochina] would be the prime objective target. Therefore, the question of defending the coasts and some ports occupies a large part of public discussions in the newspapers and elsewhere", Heintges concluded.[104]

The German East Asia Naval Squadron also took an interest in Guangzhouwan. When the gunboat *Tiger* paid a courtesy visit to Haiphong in early 1903, Captain Schrader asked Captain de la Ruelle, commander of the French naval station (Station locale de l'Annam et du Tonkin) whether a trip to Guangzhouwan would be permitted. The French officer told him that "he would be happy about a German ship calling at this port: surveying is ended and maps should be issued soon". He also offered to provide a pilot should the arrival be announced in advance. From the office of Speidel & Co. in Haiphong, Schrader finally obtained "privately" a copy of the map of the harbour of Guangzhouwan. Whether the visit took place was not recorded in the files of the foreign ministry.[105]

[104] PAAA, 117, Konsulat Saigon, 5–1: Otto Mühlberg, Undersecretary of State of the Foreign Ministry (Berlin), to Consul Heintges (Saigon), 17 December 1902. PAAA, Peking II-72: Consul Heintges (Saigon) to Chancellor von Bülow (Berlin), 15 January 1903. PAAA, R 19420: Consul Heintges (Saigon) to Chancellor von Bülow (Berlin), 15 February 1903; Consul Heintges (Saigon) to Chancellor von Bülow (Berlin), 21 April 1903.

[105] PAAA, R 19420: Captain Schrader (Hanoi) to Headquarters of German East Asia Naval Squadron, 19 January 1903; Commander Geissler (Hong Kong) to Chief of Naval Staff (Berlin), 20 January 1903.

The first and very detailed German eyewitness account of Guangzhouwan was created by the military attaché of the German embassy in Tokyo, Baron von Ritter zu Grünsteyn (or Grünstein). In December 1902 and January 1903, the army officer took part in the Congress of Orientalists in Hanoi, and later made a round tour through Indochina which included Guangzhouwan. His observations focusing on military matters also encompassed monitoring the territory's geographical and infrastructural features. Grünsteyn concluded his findings as follows: "From all that I have seen in Guangzhouwan, I gained the impression that the government of Indochina had been very generous with funds to promote the development of this new French leased territory in order to attract the French merchant as well as the Chinese. This place will only gain a higher strategic value when linked by train with Haiphong, a line, however, which would run through unsafe Chinese territory".[106]

Another German official paying a personal visit to Guangzhouwan was Consul Hans von Varchmin of Beihai. His rather lengthy account dated 18 February 1905 was based on his personal observations during two separate stays in the territory in 1904. Furthermore, Varchmin added some information taken from official French publications and from unnamed sources, probably from talks with French residents in Guangzhou. His report mainly dealt with Guangzhouwan's topographical features, agricultural produce, imports and exports (including opium) and shipping conditions, and also described and evaluated the installations of the indigenous guard, the various construction works carried out in Fort Bayard and Maxie (including the ones for developing Guangzhouwan into a French naval hub) and railway building projects. The consul did not forget to point to the fact that violent attacks by gangs of robbers frequently occurred in the territory. Furthermore, he sharply criticised large-scale opium smuggling activities in Guangzhouwan, which, in his view, were harming intermediate trading in neighbouring port cities such as Beihai and Haikou (where considerable German trading interests were concerned). Blaming French authorities for not taking effective measures against smuggling, Varchmin concluded his findings as follows:

[106] PAAA, R 19420: Report of Baron von Ritter zu Grünsteyn (Tokyo), 30 March 1903.

> Furthermore, it can be assumed that the [French] leading circles are uncertain about Guangzhouwan's future and tend to make experiments. Should the [French] government seriously intend to develop Guangzhouwan into a trading hub in the extreme south [of China], even into a second- or third-class Hong Kong only, then the current indifference towards its eventual military importance will pass – or there is another factor behind it because no government is capable of developing a flourishing colony in order to throw it into the lap of the enemy at the earliest opportunity. We must now keep to the present state of affairs and - to repeat it - the demand seems justified that French [commercial] competition in Guangzhouwan is conducted in decent ways and not shying away from daylight. Each success in this direction is not imaginary or merely morally but is immediately and directly of benefit for the respective treaty ports and our [German] interests there.[107]

On 15 August 1905, Consul von Varchmin submitted another account of Guangzhouwan based on second-hand information, presumably from newspapers published in Indochina and from French residents in Guangzhou. Referring to his earlier report of February 1905, he stated that it followed that "previous achievements of the French in their leased territory are minor, but not as insignificant as often portrayed from the French side". However, in the focus of his new coverage was a political scandal concerning Guangzhouwan's chief administrator Gustave Alby and one of his most senior officers, adjunct administrator Henry Liégeot who was supposed to have committed crimes against humanity when dealing with Chinese prisoners and witnesses during court trials. The "rather dirty affair", as Varchmin called it, had resulted in the death of Liégeot and consequently in Alby's dismissal from his post. Alby had been accused of "incapability, inactivity and gruffness in dealing with his charges [the Chinese]" but also of "secretly collaborating with the Chinese and taking bribes from them to foster their projects and enterprises to the disadvantage of his own fellow citizens [the French]", the consul said. He was convinced that Alby was incapable of doing his duties and had been treated as a "scapegoat" for certain deficiencies of Guangzhouwan for some time. Therefore, Varchmin doubted whether Alby's successor, Fernand Gautret, would be able to begin "a new era of the flourishing of the colony on all fields". His reporting on the political

[107] PAAA, Peking II-72: Consul von Varchmin (Beihai) to Chancellor von Bülow (Berlin), 18 February 1905.

scandal continued in March 1906 when he evaluated the Hanoi court trial involving two French-Chinese non-commissioned officers stationed in Guangzhouwan and several Chinese citizens from the French territory. In the end, the defendants confessed to all accusations (aiding in a murder case and assaulting with fatal results) and, after declaring that they had acted in direct command of their superior, Liégeot, were acquitted. The consul concluded his account as follows: "The Alby case is certainly an instructive piece of history of administering colonies with a half-civilised population".[108]

In April 1907, Varchmin's successor in Beihai and Haikou, Dr. Rudolf Walter, referred to the Alby case when reporting on "another colonial drama from the time of the Alby regiment in Guangzhouwan". This time the former chief justice of Guangzhouwan's second district, Louis Tiersonnier, and the previous police officer attached to the district court, Gilles, were involved in the scandal. Based on information published in *Le Courrier d'Haiphong*, Walter reported in detail about the Hanoi court trial, summing up his impressions as follows: "The picture that unfolded during the trial can only provoke general indignation. Only the worst colonial scandals show similar cruelties as the ones of Tiersonnier and Gilles". However, in the end, the consul noted that "in contrast to public opinion and each sense of justice, Tiersonnier and Gilles were acquitted. All journals were furious". For this reason, as he recorded, voices again became louder "calling the acquisition of Guangzhouwan an evil mistake and urgently recommending relinquishing the "naval station" or, if possible, exchanging it for another territory – perhaps Hainan [Island]?"[109]

In January 1906, the German legation in Beijing informed the foreign ministry in Berlin that in exchange for certain commercial and industrial concessions from China, France was allegedly prepared to abandon Guangzhouwan. This news soon proved to be purely speculative but prompted more detailed reports from Consul von Varchmin on the current situation of Guangzhouwan. Based on second-hand information

[108] PAAA, Peking II-72: Consul von Varchmin (Beihai) to Minister Mumm von Schwarzenstein (Beijing), 15 August 1905. On this affair, see Vannière (2020, 241–242).

[109] *L'Avenir du Tonkin*, 17 March 1907. BAB, R 901-1088: Consul Dr. Walter (Beihai/Haikou) to Chancellor von Bülow (Berlin), 20 April 1907. For details of the affair and French reform efforts in Guangzhouwan, see Vannière (2020, 248–258).

derived from acquaintances who had recently passed through the territory, the consul, in February 1906, reported that Fort Bayard seemed to have been almost abandoned after the French military had withdrawn from Guangzhouwan, with barracks standing empty. "The Chinese started to remove roofs from the few houses in Fort Bayard which they themselves had built", Varchmin said. This seemed to indicate to him "that it is slowly coming to an end with Guangzhouwan", and that "many persons are already firmly convinced of that, which I however regard as premature". The consul pointed to the fact that after Gautret took office as chief administrator, it became "peculiarly silent in Guangzhouwan" and there was "nothing disclosed on any remarkable progress on whatever field". Furthermore, he said that there were fresh rumours in the French Indochinese and Hong Kong press that France intended to exchange Guangzhouwan for another place — allegedly Hainan Island. In the following month, Varchmin added to this report that, despite rumours concerning Hainan, Guangzhouwan seemed to be in a safe position: "As we all know, France jealously guards this advanced post of her alleged sphere of interest".[110]

From May 1909 to November 1912, Consul Dr. Peter Merklinghaus in Beihai and Haikou turned his attention to the reorganisation of French steamship services in the South China Sea. According to his initial letter of 27 May 1909, he regarded French action in this respect as an attempt "to better position the sparsely represented French flag in East Asian waters and make it independent, to a certain extent, from foreign shipping and competition".[111] Another topic was ongoing changes in Guangzhouwan's administration. In July 1912, Acting Consul Theodor Metzelthin in Haikou observing the reorganisation of Guangzhouwan's financial administration pointed to the fact that "in addition to exploiting new sources of revenue, it was also tried to make former ones more

[110] BAB, R 901-1087: Telegram from Minister Mumm von Schwarzenstein (Beijing) to Foreign Ministry (Berlin), c. 17 January 1906. PAAA, Peking II-72: Consul von Varchmin (Beihai) to Chancellor von Bülow (Berlin), 12 February 1906; Consul von Varchmin (Beihai) to Minister Mumm von Schwarzenstein (Beijing), 5 March 1906.

[111] PAAA, Peking II-1176: Consul Dr. Merklinghaus (Beihai) to Chancellor von Bülow (Berlin), 27 May 1909, 10 July 1909 and 11 September 1909, and to Chancellor von Bethmann Hollweg (Berlin), 9 December 1909, 26 March 1910, 29 June 1910, 5 September 1910, 16 February 1911, 29 May 1911 and 25 November 1912; Acting Consul Metzelthin (Haikou) to Chancellor von Bethmann Hollweg (Berlin), 12 October 1910.

productive". In May 1914, Metzelthin alluded to another, far-reaching modification of Guangzhouwan's financial policy: the opium and salt monopolies formerly leased to Chinese private entrepreneurs had been placed under the Customs and *Régie* Administration of Indochina; this public company was also empowered to import and to sell Chinese rice liquors, perfumed liquors and wines. According to his account, the abundant income from the opium monopoly for Chinese leaseholders provided enough reason for the administration to introduce these amendments. Concerning the salt monopoly, the consul reported that the concerned Chinese leaseholder, who had provided salt to buyers in Hong Kong and Singapore, had lost profits due to the extensive smuggling activities of salt works owners. Therefore, Metzelthin was convinced that the reason for the new regulations was as follows: "By suppressing smuggling and improving production methods and organisation, the Administration hopes to substantially increase the salt works' profits".[112]

In May 1914, the final German reports were issued based on a series of articles titled "Notes on Guangzhouwan" written by the French lawyer Henri Cucherousset. After visiting the territory, in February 1914, he began publishing his personal impressions in the Hanoi newspaper *L'Avenir du Tonkin*. At the time, Guangzhouwan was a very closed place which becomes evident in the following comment by Acting Consul Metzelthin in Haikou: "Even, if it would not be extremely difficult at present, if not almost impossible, to get hold of reliable news on the development of Guangzhouwan, the observations and judgments of this French traveller should be of general interest because they bring forth an in-depth reflection and seem to describe conditions in an unbiased way". Metzelthin's account, predominantly based on Cucherousset's observations and on other, unnamed sources, concluded as follows:

> After describing all that, it cannot be disputed that some progress becomes apparent in the development of the leased territory; however, the French should not be particularly proud when considering the meagre overall result of their sixteen years of administration. Most of the now projected numerous improvements and new installations were already on the work programme ten years ago, with even some more far-reaching plans of which

[112] BAB, R 901-1090: Acting Consul Metzelthin (Haikou) to Chancellor von Bethmann Hollweg (Berlin), 11 July 1912 and 6 May 1914. See Vannière (2020, 310–317).

> nowadays nothing can be heard of, for example, the construction of railways (…). According to earlier French plans, Guangzhouwan was expected to become a trading emporium of southwest China and to enter into competition with Hong Kong. Remembering that and comparing it with today's Guangzhouwan, then the territory's development must be labelled as rather miserable.[113]

The Almost Forgotten French Territory

With the abandonment of France's larger imperialist projects in the aftermath of the Russo-Japanese War (1904–1905), various projects to create a French sphere of influence in southern China were abolished. The funding of schools, hospitals or post offices designed to promote France's influence in southern China were successively cut back in 1907–1908. When looking at the goals French officials had in mind with Guangzhouwan, it can be concluded that only modest achievements were made in the almost fifty-year long history of the territory. Several factors impacted the development of France's only colony in China. The most important one, or the core problem of Guangzhouwan, was its administrative attachment to the government-general of Indochina. After Governor-General Doumer, who was mainly responsible for realising this linkage, had left office in 1902, the territory lacked any political vision and was administered by Hanoi in order to derive the maximum profits from its opium trade. Guangzhouwan was reduced to a financial source for Indochina's general budget. The territory's own budget was extremely simple and did not include any expenses for economic and social matters. This made it impossible for any chief administrator of Guangzhouwan, if he had wished so, to set up an independent policy of economic promotion or social development. Therefore, Guangzhouwan remained an outside post of Indochina, dependent on it but not fully integrated into it.[114]

Furthermore, a naval station or a coal depot was not established. France had a first-class port in Saigon and a second-class port in Haiphong. From a military-strategic point of view, Guangzhouwan actually did not enhance Indochina's defence potential. This became obvious

[113] PAAA, R 19426: Consul Metzelthin (Beihai) to Chancellor von Bethmann Hollweg (Berlin), 17 May 1914.

[114] Pieragastini (2017, 114–125), Vannière (2020, 557–561) and Qu (2019, 57).

when the territory was abandoned as military outpost during the Russo-Japanese War. Governor-General Doumer's plan to make the territory a starting-point or centre of a French sphere of influence in southern China was not realised. Guangzhouwan was hindered by the government-general of Indochina in developing into such an important economic and cultural base because it would have meant opening the territory to French, Chinese and other investors, something that could have disrupted the strict government control over the highly profitable opium trade. Therefore, the notion of connecting Guangzhouwan with its hinterland by railways was never realised. French capital was not encouraged by the government-general of Indochina to invest into such projects, and the Chinese were not prepared to co-operate with the French, fearing that this would be the first step in France's colonial acquisition of the entire coastline of southern China between the Tonkin border and Hong Kong. In the South China Sea, the territory remained an economic satellite of British Hong Kong throughout its existence, being much closer connected to the Pearl River Delta than to the Red River Delta. For the maritime route from Fort Bayard to Hong Kong, a passage of 233 sea miles, a steamer needed around twenty-two hours, whereas the route from Fort Bayard to Haiphong, 320 sea miles, was serviced in about forty-eight hours. For this and various other reasons, Guangzhouwan continued to be economically dependent on Hong Kong. Concerning the territory's domestic economy, the French invested in urban projects and created modern facilities which were unknown in this part of China. Nevertheless, the local economy continued without much interference by the colonial power. In political terms, the French permitted local self-government to a certain extent. All in all, the economic and social development of Guangzhouwan was appreciable, but remained rather modest in comparison to German Jiaozhou (Kiaochow) or Hong Kong's New Territories. During the Second World War in Asia, the French territory was for a short period the safe haven for refugees from China and Hong Kong fleeing Japanese forces. In 1942, a large number of Chinese teachers from the University of Hong Kong, with a considerable number of their family members and students, escaped from the British colony (which was occupied by Japan in December 1941) via Macao to Guangzhouwan.

After its occupation by Japanese forces in 1943, Guangzhouwan was returned to China in 1945 and renamed Zhanjiang.[115]

Looking back at its nearly fifty-year existence, this leasehold colony, acquired in 1898 from the legal point of view in the same way as its British, German and Russian counterparts, developed in a very different manner. Its history certainly demonstrates certain characteristics of French colonial–imperial and geopolitical politics in East Asia at the time, which should be equally taken into consideration when evaluating the territory's history. In the eyes of most French of today, this territory is regarded as a deadlock of their colonisation, as a "clandestine colony" (the subtitle of Antoine Vannière's seminal study of Guangzhouwan) or even a failed state. However, in the eyes of many Chinese, the history of Guangzhouwan often looks much more positive, especially when contrasted with the turbulent events in mainland China during the same period. During turmoil in China, Guangzhouwan offered a safe haven for refugees and immigrants, something that was appreciated by Chinese residents and newcomers. Such differing but not antagonistic views do offer space for the re-evaluation of the history of Guangzhouwan.

References

Archival Sources

Archives nationales d'outre-mer, Aix-en-Provence (ANOM)

Gouvernement-Général de l'Indochine (INDO-GGI)

British National Archives, Kew/Surrey (TNA)

Foreign Office (FO)

Bundesarchiv, Berlin (BAB)

Deutsches Reich, Auswärtiges Amt: R 901

115 Cunich (2012, 405) and Vannière (2019, 202–232).

Centre des Archives Diplomatiques du Ministère des Affaires Étrangères, Paris (MAE)

Correspondance politique et commerciale, 1896–1918. Nouvelle Série: Chine (CPC)

Politisches Archiv des Auswärtigen Amts, Berlin (PAAA)

Altes Amt 117: Konsulat Saigon
Deutsche Botschaft in China: Peking II
Deutsches Reich: R.

Vietnamese National Archives One, Hanoi (VNA1)

Résidence Supérieur au Tonkin (RST)
Résidence de Hadong (RH)

Secondary Sources

Andersen, H.N. 1914. *Tilbageblik*. Copenhagen: Hertz.

Barnère, Jean. 1904. La défense de l'Indochine. *Bulletin du Comité de L'Asie Française* 36: 141–146.

Baumgart, Winfried. 1982. *Imperialism: The Idea and Reality of British and French Colonial Expansion, 1880–1914*. Oxford: Oxford University Press.

Beasley, W.G. 1991. *Japanese Imperialism 1894–1945*. Oxford: Clarendon Press.

Becker, Bert. 2009. The German Colony of Kiaochow and Its Postal Steamer Service, 1898–1914. *International Journal of Maritime History* 21 (1): 201–238.

Becker, Bert. 2019a. French Guangzhouwan and British Hong Kong: Politics and Shipping, 1890s–1920s. In *British and French Colonialism in Africa, Asia and the Middle East: Connected Empires Across the Eighteenth to the Twentieth Centuries*, ed. James R. Fichter, 181–221. Cham: Palgrave Macmillan.

Becker, Bert. 2019b. French Indochina and the Guangzhouwan Postal Steamer Service, 1900–1918. In *Études Historiques et Culturelles de Kouang-Tchéou-Wan: Actes de la Première Conférence Académique Internationale sur l'Histoire et la Culture de Kouang-Tchéou-Wan*, vol. 1, ed. Wang Qin Feng, 390–456. Zhanjiang: Lingnan Normal University.

Bloch, Charles. 1972. *Die Dritte Französische Republik: Entwicklung und Kampf einer parlamentarischen Demokratie (1870–1940)*. Stuttgart: Köhler.

Bonhoure, Eugène. 1900. *L'Indo-Chine*. Paris: Challamel.

Bonningue, Alfred. 1931. *La France à Kouang-Tchéou-Wan*. Paris: Berger-Levrault.

Brenier, Henri. 1898. Rôle actuel et possible de la France. In *La Mission Lyonnaise d'Exploration Commerciale en Chine 1895–1897*, ed. Chambre de Commerce de Lyon, 431–451. Lyon: A. Rey.

Brötel, Dieter. 1996. *Frankreich im Fernen Osten: Imperialistische Expansion und Aspiration in Siam und Malaya, Laos und China 1880–1904*. Stuttgart: Franz Steiner.

Bulletin du Comité de l'Asie française. 1902, 1903, 1904, 1909, 1910 and 1912. Paris: Au Siège du Comité.

Catalogue of Treaties 1814–1918. 1919. Ed. Department of State, United States of America. Washington: Government Printing Office.

Caix, Robert de. 1905. La Politique Française à Kouang-Tchéou-Ouan. *Bulletin du Comité de L'Asie Française* 56: 425–427.

Conference Proceedings: The Second International Academic Conference on Guangzhouwan's History and Culture. 2019. Unpublished manuscript. Zhanjiang: Lingnan Normal University.

Cunich, Peter. 2012. *A History of The University of Hong Kong, vol. 1: 1911–1945*. Hong Kong: Hong Kong University Press.

Dictionnaire de Bio-Bibliographie Générale, Ancienne et Moderne de l'Indochine Française. 1935. ed. Antoine Cabaton. Paris: Société d'Éditions Géographiques, Maritimes, et Coloniales.

Dictionnaire de la Politique Française, vol. 2. 1972. ed. Henry Coston. Paris: Publications Henry Coston.

Dictionnaire des Ministres de 1789 à 1989. 1990. ed. Benoît Yvert. Paris: Perrin.

Eversheim, Franz. 1958. *Effects of Shipping Subsidization*. Bremen: Institut für Schiffahrtsforschung.

Fourniau, Charles. 2002. *Vietnam: Domination coloniale et résistance nationale (1858–1914)*. Paris: Les Indes savantes.

Gérard, Auguste. 1918. *Ma Mission en Chine (1893–1897)*. Paris: Plon.

Goscha, Christopher. 2016. *The Penguin History of Modern Vietnam*. Milton Keynes: Penguin Books.

Grupp, Peter. 1972. *Theorie der Kolonialexpansion und Methoden der imperialistischen Außenpolitik bei Gabriel Hanotaux*. Frankfurt am Main: Peter Lang.

Guillen, Pierre. 1984. *L'Expansion 1881–1898*. Paris: Imprimerie Nationale.

Guillen, Pierre, and Jean-Claude Allain. 2007. La Puissance Recouvrée (1870–1914). In *Histoire de la Diplomatie Française, vol. 2: De 1815 à Nos Jours*, ed. Jean-Claude Allain, et al., 141–283. Paris: Perrin.

Iiams, Thomas M., Jr. 1962. *Dreyfus, Diplomatists and the Dual Alliance: Gabriel Hanotaux at the Quai d'Orsay (1894–1898)*. Geneva: E. Droz.

Halpern, Paul. 2001. The French Navy. In *Technology and Naval Combat in the Twentieth Century and Beyond, 1880–1914*, ed. Philipps Payson O'Brien, 36–52. Abingdon and New York: Routledge.

Hansen, Svend Aage. 1970. *Early Industrialisation in Denmark*. Copenhagen: Gad.

Herriou, Yann-Firmin. 1994. La participation de la Marine à la prise de possession de Kouang-tcheou-wan (avril 1898-janvier 1900). *Revue Historique des Armées* 197: 117–129.

Hishida, Seiji. 1940. *Japan Among the Great Powers: A Survey of Her International Relations*. London and New York and Toronto: Longmans, Green and Co.

Hudson, G.F. 1937. *The Far East in World Politics: A Study in Recent History*. London: Oxford University Press.

Hsü, Immanuel C.Y. 2000. *The Rise of Modern China*, 6th ed. New York and Oxford: Oxford University Press.

Joseph, Philip. 1928. *Foreign Diplomacy in China 1894–1900: A Study in Political and Economic Relations with China*. London: Allen & Unwin.

Langer, William L. 1960. *The Diplomacy of Imperialism 1890–1902*, 2nd ed. New York: Alfred A. Knopf.

Luan, Vu Duong, and Nola Cooke. 2011. Chinese Merchants and Mariners in Nineteenth-Century Tongking. In *The Tongking Gulf Through History*, ed. Nola Cooke, et al., 143–159. Philadelphia: University of Pennsylvania Press.

MacMurray, John V.A. 1921. *Treaties and Agreements with and Concerning China 1894–1919, vol. 1: Manchu Period (1894–1911)*. New York: Oxford University Press.

Martonne, Edouard-Guillaume. 1897. La mission lyonnaise d'exploration en China. *Annales de Géographie* 6 (27): 273–276.

Mayeur, Jean-Marie. 1984. *La vie politique sous la Troisième République 1870–1940*. Paris: Édition du Seuil.

Menning, Bruce W. 2007. Miscalculating one's Enemies: Russian Intelligence Prepares for War. In *The Russo-Japanese War in Global Perspective: World War Zero*, vol. 2, ed. David Wolff, et al., 45–80. Leiden and Boston: Brill.

Morlat, Patrice. 2016. *Indochine années vingt: L'âge d'or de l'affairisme colonial (1918–1928): Banquiers, hommes d'affaires et patrons en réseaux*. Paris: Les Indes Savantes.

Mühlhahn, Klaus. 2000. *Herrschaft und Widerstand in der „Musterkolonie" Kiautschou: Interaktionen zwischen China und Deutschland, 1897–1914*. Munich: R. Oldenbourg.

Murray, Martin J. 1980. *The Development of Capitalism in Colonial Indochina (1870–1940)*. Berkeley: University of California Press.

Petersson, Niels P. 2000. *Imperialismus und Modernisierung: Siam, China und die europäischen Mächte 1895–1914*. Munich: De Gruyter Oldenbourg.

Peyre, Jean de la. 1902. La Force navale des mers d'Orient et son role en Extrême-Orient (à propos d'un récent décret). *Bulletin du Comité de L'Asie Française* 14: 216–220.

Pieragastini, Steven. 2017. State and Smuggling in Modern China: The Case of Guangzhouwan/Zhanjiang. *Cross-Currents: East Asian History and Culture Review* 25 (December): 108–139 (E-Journal).

Pooley, A.M., ed. 1969 (1st edition 1915). *The Secret Memoirs of Count Tadasu Hayashi*. New York: G. P. Putnam's Sons.

Qu, Kanghui. 2019. Le Chikan de Kouang-Tchéou-Wan en période de La Guerre anti-japonaise. In *Études Historiques et Culturelles de Kouang-Tchéou-Wan: Actes de la Première Conférence Académique Internationale sur l'Histoire et la Culture de Kouang-Tchéou-Wan*, vol. 2, ed. Wang Qin Feng, 46–58. Zhanjiang: Lingnan Normal University.

Réau, Raphaël. 1903. Le rôle économique de Hong-kong. *Bulletin du Comité de L'Asie Française* 31: 451–455.

Rebérioux, Madeleine. 1975. *La République radicale? 1898–1914*. Paris: Édition du Seuil.

Schrecker, John E. 1971. *Imperialism and Chinese Nationalism: Germany in Shantung*. Cambridge, MA and London: Harvard University Press.

So, Fion Wai Ling. 2019. *Germany's Colony in China: Colonialism, Protection and Economic Development in Qingdao and Shandong, 1898–1914*. Abingdon and New York: Routledge.

Stone, Judith F. 1996. *Sons of the Revolution: Radical Democrats in France 1862–1914*. Baton Rouge and London: Louisiana State University Press.

Sturmey, S.G. 2010. *British Shipping and World Competition*. St. John's, Newfoundland: International Maritime Economic History Association.

Taylor, A.J.P. 1971. *The Struggle for Mastery in Europe 1848–1918*. Oxford: Oxford University Press.

Territoire de Kouang-Tchéou (Chine): Notice publiée à l'occasion de l'exposition coloniale de Marseille. 1906, ed. Gouvernement Général de l'Indo-Chine. Hanoi and Haiphong: L. Gallois.

Thieß, Karl. 1907. *Deutsche Schiffahrt und Schiffahrtspolitik der Gegenwart*. Leipzig: B. G. Teubner.

Tsang, Steve. 1997. *Hong Kong: Appointment with China*. London: I. B. Tauris.

Vannière, Antoine. 2004. *Le Territoire à Bail de Guangzhouwan: Une Impasse de la Colonisation Française en Asie Orientale, 1898–1946*. PhD thesis, Université Paris 7 Denis Diderot.

Vannière, Antoine. 2019. Urbanisation et transformations socio-économiques à Guangzhouwan sous l'occupation française (1898–1945): Essai sur les voies de la modernisation locale. In *Études Historiques et Culturelles de Kouang-Tchéou-Wan: Actes de la Première Conférence Académique Internationale sur l'Histoire et la Culture de Kouang-Tchéou-Wan*, vol. 1, ed. Wang Qin Feng, 188–232. Zhanjiang: Lingnan Normal University.

Vannière, Antoine. 2020. *Kouang-Tchéou-Wan, colonie clandestine: Un territoire à bail français en Chine du Sud 1898–1946*. Paris: Les Indes Savantes.

Walser, Ray. 1992. *France's Search for a Battle Fleet: Naval Policy and Naval Power, 1898–1914*. New York: Garland.
Wang, Qin Feng, ed. 2019. *Études Historiques et Culturelles de Kouang-Tchéou-Wan: Actes de la Première Conférence Académique Internationale sur l'Histoire et la Culture de Kouang-Tchéou-Wan*, 2 vols. Zhanjiang: Lingnan Normal University.
Welsh, Frank. 1997. *A History of Hong Kong*. London: HarperCollins.
Wesley-Smith, Peter. 1980. *Unequal Treaty 1898–1997: China, Great Britain and Hong Kong's New Territories*. Hong Kong: Oxford University Press.
Young, L.K. 1970. *British Policy in China 1895–1902*. Oxford: Oxford University Press.

CHAPTER 7

Conclusion

The South China Sea was a closely interconnected maritime region of vibrant commercial exchange for centuries. Economic rivalry between the ports of southern China, Vietnam and other regions was driven by seafarers and merchants, making the South China Sea a kind of Asian Mediterranean. This process was given further impetus in the Age of Commerce of Southeast Asia (1450–1680) in which the major trade boom provided wealth to port cities in the South China Sea and neighbouring urban centres. In this period, Chinese and Vietnamese shipowners and traders were joined by Portuguese merchants who established Macao as a major entrepôt and early modern cosmopolis. Cantonese and Portuguese seafarers and merchants collaborated on intra-Asian trade. The Dutch United East India Company (VOC), the most powerful trading company of the seventeenth century, established a network stretching from Persia to Japan, with its centre in the Dutch East Indies (now Indonesia) and a strong base in Tonkin, the northern region of Vietnam. After the opening of Guangzhou (Canton) to foreign trading in 1684, the English East India Company emerged as a new economic power in East Asia. In 1698, private French merchants, leasing the trade monopoly of the French East India Company (sponsored by King Louis XIV), opened a warehouse in Guangzhou. The so-called Canton Trade era coincided to a large extent with the Chinese Century of Southeast Asia (1740–1840) in which large numbers of Chinese migrants made

B. Becker, *France and Germany in the South China Sea, c. 1840–1930*, Cambridge Imperial and Post-Colonial Studies,
https://doi.org/10.1007/978-3-030-52604-7_7

their way southward, stimulating economic growth in regions around the South China Sea.

The Kingdom of Prussia sent its first merchant vessel to Guangzhou in 1752, thus opening up German trade with East Asia. The first Prussian consul in the Chinese port city was an English trader, appointed in 1787, who wished to circumvent the monopoly of the English East India Company. At the time the first ship from Hamburg set sail for China in 1797, the South China Sea was experiencing a period of strong and mutually influential economic upturns that led to increasing prosperity in Southeast Asia. In Europe, the Napoleonic era (1799–1815) severely interrupted French and Prussian commercial relations with East Asia. In the First Opium War (1839–1842), Anglo-French imperialism enforced the further opening up of China to foreign commerce. Thanks to her strong naval forces operating in the China seas, France played a pivotal role during the conflict. The French trade mission to China led by the diplomat Lagrené succeeded in signing with China the Treaty of Whampoa (1844), which gave France the same privileges as Britain. However, initial hopes of opening up considerable French commerce with China were soon disappointed. Prussia came to the same conclusion after sending the economic expert Grube to China in 1843, who assessed the trade prospects as very limited.

German merchants, established in Chinese port cities since 1843 and increasingly trading via London, clearly benefited from the unequal treaties Britain and France had signed with China. Sailing ships from Hamburg were transporting British and German goods to East Asia, and after discharging their freights, engaged in intra-Asian trading along Chinese and other Asian coasts. The right of coastal shipping (or cabotage) had been tacitly granted by China to Britain and France in the treaties of 1842/1844 and was explicitly confirmed in the subsequent treaties of 1858. After Prussia had signed a treaty with China in 1861, which included the members of the Customs Union and smaller German states, German flags ranked third in China's shipping market. This stimulated the further establishment of German traders in Guangzhou, Hong Kong and other port cities in the South China Sea. France, which signed another treaty with China in 1858, was able to secure certain rights for her Catholic missionaries, but benefited little from economic concessions, meaning French shipping and trade in China and Southeast Asia were almost non-existent.

The Prussian trading expedition to East Asia (1861–1862) led by Count zu Eulenburg resulted in the signing of treaties with Japan, China and Siam and the establishment of long-lasting shipping and trading relations between Germany and these countries. Another goal of the expedition was to create a Prussian naval station, or even a Prussian settlement colony, for which the island of Formosa (now Taiwan) was initially regarded as the most suitable place. However, the plan by King William I (the later German Emperor), motivated by French naval expansion in the South China Sea and the subsequent seizure of southern Vietnam (Cochinchina) including Saigon in 1859–61, was finally dropped for several reasons. The project of a Prussian naval station materialised soon after when for this purpose a plot of land was leased in Yokohama, Japan, in 1867 and two warships flying the flag of the North German Confederation were permanently stationed in East Asian waters in 1869. After the acquisition of Jiaozhou (Kiaochow) Bay, located in China's Shandong Province, the German East Asia Squadron possessed a proper naval base from 1898 to 1914.

Hong Kong, since 1842 a British crown colony in China, with its free-market economy and social non-interventionism, developed into the first meeting place of foreign and Chinese social networks of capital in Asia. This unique position, backed by the principles of the rule of law and, last but not least, protected by British military power attracted people from around the world. German trading firms initially established in Guangdong gradually opened branches in Hong Kong and began competing against British companies at a time when Germany's global foreign trade quadrupled between 1860 and 1913. On the other hand, German merchants invested capital in British firms or served as board members of major British industries in Hong Kong. This "participatory colonialism" contributed to promoting Britain's imperialist position in East Asia. Like most foreign companies, German firms employed Chinese merchants as compradors (middlemen) who were crucial for import–export transactions in China. One such example of a successful business relationship between a Western company and a Chinese comprador was the co-operation between Jebsen & Company (founded in Hong Kong in 1895 as a shipping agency and trading firm) and the Chau family. Despite their considerable economic potential in the British colony, Germans in Hong Kong remained a very small group of expatriates whose numbers never exceeded 359 (in 1906). Three distinct professional groups — merchants, seafarers and missionaries — can be identified who contributed in different ways to the colony's economic and social life. The most remarkable social institutions were probably the German Club Germania (modelled after British clubs) and the German Church and School Congregation which for some years operated a small school for exclusively European children subsidised by the foreign ministry in Berlin. As a result of the outbreak of the First World War, most German residents were expelled from Hong Kong or interned in prisoner-of-war camps, and their properties were confiscated. After the war, a number of German firms were re-established in Hong Kong and focused on trading and shipping in southern China. However, shipping operations did not fully recover and the number of vessels flying the German flag had declined drastically by 1930 compared to pre-war figures.

Tramp shipping markets in East Asia were dominated by three big British and Chinese shipping companies in the late nineteenth and early twentieth centuries. However, a number of firms from Germany that operated small and medium-sized steam tramps played a considerable role in intra-Asian coastal shipping. After the opening of the Suez Canal (1869), steamers successively replaced sailing ships as the main carriers of bulk goods shipped on behalf of predominantly Chinese merchants based in ports on the South China Sea and beyond its shores. Steam coasters were chartered on trip (or voyage) charter or time charter, with the latter permitting the operation of regular lines in coastal shipping. The M. Jebsen Shipping Company headquartered in Apenrade, Schleswig-Holstein, serves as an example of the operation of a fleet of steam tramps which had Hong Kong as its base. With the shipowner, Michael Jebsen, remaining in Imperial Germany (where he became a shipping lobbyist during his terms as a national liberal parliamentarian in Berlin in the 1890s), his eldest son, Jacob Jebsen, with an associate, founded Jebsen & Company in Hong Kong in 1895, acting as sole agent for the M. Jebsen Shipping Company, and later as a trading firm. For their vessels operating in East Asia, the firm employed European officers and Asian crews, mostly Chinese seafarers hired in Hong Kong, for reasons of costs. Professional relations with the far-away captains remained a constant concern for Michael Jebsen, who was mistrustful of his masters and constantly called for more economy aboard his ships.

The French business community in Hong Kong consisted of three groups, namely Catholic missionaries, representatives of larger French companies and retailers. While the last group focused on imports and sales of French luxury goods or Chinese and Japanese artworks, the weak presence of French industrial products in Asian markets remained the main concern for French consuls posted in Hong Kong. Auguste Raphael Marty and his brother Pierre Augustin Marty, at the time the most important French traders in Hong Kong, profited from France's military campaign in Tonkin and undeclared war with China (1882–1885) as main suppliers of the French troops. Such earnings allowed the trading firm A. R. Marty to open a regular shipping service between Hong Kong and Haiphong, the northern Vietnamese port city. In 1886, Auguste Raphael Marty, together with his partner Édouard Jules d'Abbadie, established the shipping company Marty et d'Abbadie in Haiphong in order to operate river shipping services in Tonkin. In 1893, Marty founded the Tonkin Shipping Company, which competed with the M. Jebsen Shipping Company on ocean-going routes. Another important French businessman in Hong Kong was the Lyon merchant and banker Louis Sculfort, a member of the trading mission of the Lyon Chamber of Commerce which had explored export and import markets for French products in China and French Indochina in 1895–96. Sculfort established a trading firm in Hong Kong and the joint French-Chinese Syndicate, with French and Chinese shareholders, which constructed the first warehouse in Guangzhouwan, the French leased territory in Guangdong Province. Additionally, Sculfort produced a short-lived French newspaper in Hong Kong promoting France's trading with China. However, such initiatives could not significantly increase the weak performance of the French flag in East Asia, which has always been attributed to wrong-headed government policies, especially the system of subsidies to shipbuilders and shipping companies first set up in 1881 and subsequently renewed in 1893, 1902 and 1906. The decline of France as a maritime power in the late nineteenth century, which was due to interrelated geographical, cultural, political and economic factors, was also felt in the South China Sea. Postal subsidies granted by the colonial government of Indochina strongly impacted the business of the French shipping company Marty et d'Abbadie and of its main affiliates operating river shipping and ocean-going shipping services. While such subsidies were crucial to fostering the infrastructural development of northern Vietnam under French rule, they made the firm dependent on fluctuating political programmes and also prevented shipowners from investing in modern technology and successfully competing against their rivals in cut-throat shipping markets.

Saigon, since 1859/1861 capital of the French colony Cochinchina and the centre of rice production in southern Vietnam, saw a rapid influx of foreign traders, mostly French merchants from Bordeaux, British firms from Hong Kong and individual German traders. Among the early German firms, Behre & Company and Kaltenbach, Engler & Company, achieved profitable business by supplying the French colonial government and the navy with basic provisions. Georg Niederberger, partner in Behre & Co., was appointed Prussian honorary consul for Cochinchina in 1865 and served eight years in the post during a most tumultuous time when the Franco-German War (1870–1871) led to the forceful expulsion of German residents from Saigon. Before the war, the consul had provided Berlin with somewhat optimistic reports on the state of the French colony and was even appointed by the governor to serve as member of the municipal commission (later called the municipal council) of Saigon. Combined with the involvement in the local Chamber of Commerce, this political office provided German traders with the chance to actively participate in the economic and urban development of the French riverine port city. This engagement was to a certain extent comparable to the forms of participatory colonialism practised by German merchants in Hong Kong. With the outbreak of war between France and Germany, such active involvement came to an abrupt end and (as a consequence of the Frankfurt Treaty and continuing Franco-German frictions) was not resumed after the return of the Germans to Saigon in 1871.

During the Franco-German War (1870–1871), the public debate in a number of German states about war aims and peace terms had focused on France's cession of Alsace and parts of Lorraine, but there were also voices that discussed the acquisition of French colonies like Cochinchina by a victorious Germany. This idea, which appeared for several months in articles in German newspapers, may have prompted French Empress Eugenie to send a personal messenger, Théophile Gautier, to Otto von Bismarck, Chancellor of the North German Confederation, from her exile in England. However, the offer to cede this French colony in lieu of Alsace-Lorraine was rejected by the Chancellor. Already in the 1860s, Bismarck had shown little interest in acquiring colonies for Prussia and had focused instead on establishing a Prussian naval station in East Asian waters in order to protect German shipping and trading interests in the region. Since Eugenie's initiative remained secret at the time, the public debate in the North German Confederation (which even involved high-ranking aristocrats) about acquiring Cochinchina with its major commercial centre, Saigon, continued for several weeks until Bismarck put an end to such ideas. The Franco-German War and its repercussions directly affected not only the small number of German traders expelled from Saigon, but also the French and North German navies operating in East Asia. Facing the overwhelming dominance of French naval forces and their threat to capture merchant vessels flying the North German flag, the German commander offered to cease hostilities and declare the Chinese and Japanese waters neutral during the war. This idea initially found support from his French counterpart, who was interested in maintaining a free hand vis-à-vis China after the Tianjin Massacre, the deadly attack by Chinese on a large number of French Catholic missionaries in the summer of 1870. Although Britain and the United States supported the idea (which had been embraced by Bismarck), for the sake of demonstrating European and American solidarity vis-à-vis China, the new French government rejected the plan because it feared negative counter-effects for France during the ongoing war. The temporary halting of hostilities in East Asian waters provided North German merchant vessels with the chance to escape confiscation by fleeing to neutral ports, which mainly caused financial damage to the shipowners concerned.

After the return of the German traders to Saigon in the wake of the Franco-German War, relations between local French and German residents were severely impacted by the overall political tensions between the two countries. Bismarck's goal of diplomatically isolating Republican France as much as possible and distract her from taking revenge for the loss of Alsace-Lorraine led him to tacitly and later actively support French naval expansion in China and Indochina. After the first professional German consul-general, Werner von Bergen, was appointed to the post in Saigon in 1874, the Chancellor kept a close eye on restricting him to his duties in Cochinchina, and even recalling him the following year after his apparent attempt to establish some kind of formal relations with King Norodom of Cambodia, who had placed his country under French protection. Seeking a rapprochement with France to overcome the estrangement since 1871, Bismarck followed a strict policy of non-interventionism towards the French colonial empire. This principle led him to actively support Prime Minister Jules Ferry's East Asian policies during the Tonkin campaign (1882–1883) and the subsequent Sino-French War (1884–1885). His rigorous political line even saw the Chancellor express his sympathies for Paris when the French general tariff applied to Indochina in 1887 placed heavy customs fees on most non-French products and severely disadvantaged German trade with Indochina. After Bismarck's dismissal (1890), Franco-German political relations took a turn for the worse as a consequence of the Franco-Russian rapprochement in 1893, but came to a kind of truce during the term of French Foreign Minister Gabriel Hanotaux, who focused on imperialist-expansionist policies in Africa and East Asia instead of European affairs. During this period, Germany, in 1898, leased Jiaozhou (Kiaochow) Bay in China's north-eastern Shandong Province and turned the territory into a kind of model colony for Germany's industrial achievements, while France, in 1898, succeeded in leasing Guangzhou Bay (Guangzhouwan) in Guangdong Province, planned as a naval hub controlling the South China Sea. With increasing tensions between the Triple Alliance of Germany, Austria-Hungary and Italy (established in 1879/1882) and the Entente Cordiale of Britain and France (formed in 1904 and complemented by the Triple Alliance with Russia in 1907), the political confrontations between the governments in Paris and Berlin became more severe, resulting in the two Moroccan crises of 1904 and 1911. France's increasingly stronger international position, and therefore heightened self-confidence, was expressed in Prime Minister, and later, President Raymond Poincaré's domination of French foreign policy from 1912 and his steering of a new policy of toughness vis-à-vis Berlin. The tense political atmosphere between the two countries was reflected in the microcosm of Saigon where anti-German sentiments were openly displayed by the French press and local French citizens. After the outbreak of the First World War (1914), Saigon witnessed violent riots by French residents, the destruction of German-owned properties and the forceful expulsion of German traders from Cochinchina.

In the inter-war period from 1871 to 1914, German merchants gained a small share of the rice industry of Cochinchina dominated by Chinese traders, who acted as the traditional purchasers of raw rice from Vietnamese peasants and oversaw the milling and exporting of the produced rice to destinations in the South China Sea region. These Chinese merchants, whose ancestors had been emigrating to the Indochinese peninsula since ancient times, maintained close ties with their families and kinship organisations in China, thereby creating human networks across the South China Sea. Since the eighteenth century, China's need for surplus rice from Southeast Asia had led to the rise of Saigon (founded as a town in 1772) to a major rice exporting centre in which local Chinese merchants established shipping and trading links to port cities in southern China. With the founding of Singapore as a British colony in 1819, demand for rice further increased, with Singaporean Chinese merchants largely financing the rice trade of Saigon. After British rule in India, Singapore and Hong Kong had established a large free-trade area in Asia, several major Chinese trading firms based in Saigon, Singapore, Bangkok, Guangzhou and Hong Kong dominated the South China Sea rice trade in the nineteenth and early twentieth centuries. The French conquest of Cochinchina caused a sharp decrease in local rice production and trading though it recovered from the mid-1860s, with French governors, banks such as the Banque de l'Indochine (Bank of Indochina) and major trading firms such as Denis Frères (Denis Brothers) strongly promoting the rice industry. To enhance the quality of the rice from Cochinchina and provide the colonial government with extra revenues, steam-operated rice mills were set up by French entrepreneurs and a special rice commission of the Saigon Chamber of Commerce was created. The German firm Speidel & Company (established in Saigon in 1873) succeeded in gaining a small share of the rice industry of Cochinchina dominated by Chinese merchants. Initially focusing on exporting rice to ports in the South China Sea and importing German and other produce into Cochinchina (often with steam tramps of the M. Jebsen Shipping Company), Speidel & Co., in the late 1890s, began operating two rice mills in Cholon and distributing luxury products from France after the French general tariff had been applied to her colonies in 1887, discriminating against foreign imports other than French ones. Until the First World War, the owners of Speidel & Co. (additionally representing over a long period of time both Imperial Germany and the Netherlands in consular matters) kept an important share of the rice producing and trading sectors of Cochinchina.

The Red River (or Tonkin) Delta region of northern Vietnam, settled since the earliest times by Vietnamese people who mainly farmed rice, was closely interconnected by vibrant junk traffic with China. With modern steamships partly replacing junks since the mid-nineteenth century, Chinese merchants established direct links with economic hubs such as Singapore, Bangkok and Saigon, causing the Gulf of Tonkin to become something of a backwater in international shipping. Piracy, rice smuggling and human trafficking were rampant in this part of the South China Sea. In the 1870s and 1880s, French naval expansion on the Indochinese Peninsula focused on the Tonkin Delta, the border region to southern China and a possible gateway to Yunnan, a

Chinese province rich in agricultural produce and minerals. The military intervention by the French naval officer Francis Garnier resulted in the so-called Philastre treaty signed with the Vietnamese government on 15 March 1874. This agreement granted to France three concessions in northern Vietnam, among them at Ninh Hai near Haiphong, which was later to become the most important French colonial port city in Tonkin. The German government took a positive stance towards French imperialist approaches because Bismarck had a strong interest in distracting France from European affairs (especially from striving to win back Alsace-Lorraine) while encouraging and promoting German shipping and trading in the northern South China Sea.

Such an attitude also characterised the Chancellor's foreign policy movements during the Tonkin Campaign (1882–1883) and the subsequent Sino-French War (1884–1885). France's colonial expansion in Vietnam was clearly exploited by Bismarck to achieve a rapprochement with Paris and establish a kind of colonial Franco-German alliance, hampering any closer Anglo-French co-operation directed against Germany. After Jules Ferry became prime minister in 1883, Bismarck sent strong signals to Paris that he supported France's political and military efforts directed against China. Officially, Berlin remained strictly neutral in the undeclared Sino-French War, even when the French government declared rice contraband of war, threatening shipments bound for Chinese ports north of Guangzhou. Strong protests by German shipping companies did not impress the Chancellor, who warned against meddling in a war which could result in more severe damage for German trade than the temporary obstruction of rice trading in Chinese waters. After Ferry's fall, the short phase of improved Franco-German relations came to an abrupt end, with Bismarck returning to his former strategy of isolating France. A new wave of nationalist thinking in France, as enunciated by Georges Clemenceau, further triggered this reorientation.

The treaties of 1884–1885 with Vietnam and China granted France the right to establish a protectorate over Annam and Tonkin and to open up southern China to French trading and railroad construction. This gave Haiphong, which had remained an unimposing settlement since it was opened to foreign commerce in 1874, a new push. French firms based in Saigon and British firms based in Hong Kong, and Chinese and American merchants, were the first to start trading in Tonkin, with J. F.

Schriever from Hong Kong becoming the first German trader and industrial producer based in Haiphong and Hanoi. From the beginning, due to its difficult accessibility from the sea, Haiphong encountered vociferous critics who questioned the future of its port. Despite such odds, with the strong support of the local Chamber of Commerce, Haiphong succeeded in developing into the major port of Tonkin, without ever being able to rival Hong Kong or Saigon in terms of shipping and trading volumes. Built from scratch, with all the features of a French town, Haiphong became a French-style colonial city similar to Hanoi, the administrative capital of French Indochina, but on a smaller scale. One of the most remarkable buildings was the private residence of Auguste Raphael Marty (called Villa Marguerite and nicknamed Marty's Folly), reflecting the important position the company Marty et d'Abbadie had gained in the shipping and transport industries of northern Vietnam.

"Mise en valeur" (development or exploitation), the basic principle of the founding of the French empire in Asia, had in its first phase (1860s to the early 1900s) emphasised the rice industry and the building of basic transport infrastructures. This feature also marked the economic development of Haiphong. Among the local inhabitants, mostly Vietnamese people, Chinese merchants played an important economic role in trading with rice, the major export product of French Indochina. With the French continuing the practice of Vietnamese emperors in granting a privileged status to Chinese residents, Chinese immigration to Tonkin was encouraged, resulting in their merchants becoming controllers of the rice trade. This left non-Chinese merchants such as Speidel & Co. (which established in Haiphong in 1884 a branch of their Saigon firm) relatively little room for the rice business except for shipping large quantities to Hong Kong on board steam tramps. Speidel & Co. in Haiphong was the principal agent of the M. Jebsen Shipping Company in French Indochina, frequently chartering steamers for the highly profitable Hong Kong-Haiphong run. Furthermore, the firm, in conjunction with their Hanoi branch, imported and exported a wide range of products other than rice, and became active in handling banking commissions, consignations and insurance issues related to their own and other companies' commercial transactions. In 1913, Franz Dobrowohl, the local manager of Speidel & Co. in Haiphong, was appointed to honorary consul of Imperial Germany in Tonkin.

In the second phase of "mise en valeur" (from the first years of the twentieth century to the 1930s), other industries added to rice production and trading in French Indochina, such as companies focusing on the mining and exporting of coal and other minerals, processing and manufacturing industries and firms developing modern urban facilities and transport infrastructures. The former focus was clearly embodied by Speidel & Co. further diversifying its business when establishing several metal mining companies in Tonkin. After the outbreak of the First World War, the company was forced to cease operations in Indochina, with its properties being liquidated. The latter focus of "mise en valeur" was undoubtedly represented by Marty et d'Abbadie (established in Haiphong by Auguste Raphael Marty and Édouard Jules d'Abbadie), with its main affiliates, the Subsidised River Shipping Service of Tonkin, the Tonkin Shipping Company and their workshops in Haiphong. Operated by Marty et d'Abbadie from 1886 to 1906, the River Shipping Service subsidised by the Protectorate of Annam-Tonkin initially developed basic water transport infrastructures and opened up the transit route on the Red River to Yunnan. This made the service a political tool of France's development programme for northern Vietnam and its expansionist plans for southern China. For a period of twenty years, the River Shipping Service of Marty et d'Abbadie was a state monopolist, operating an impressively large fleet of paddle steamers and steam coasters on the Tonkin rivers and canals and along the coastline of northern Vietnam. With the start of the railway network construction programme (initiated by Governor-General Paul Doumer), the new railway lines developed into serious competitors of the riverboats, leading to constantly shrinking profits for the subsidised service. When the last subsidy contract expired, Auguste Raphael Marty (Édouard Jules d'Abbadie had died in 1904) dissolved the firm of Marty et d'Abbadie and sold the entire fleet of riverboats in 1907.

The other major affiliate of Marty et d'Abbadie, the Tonkin Shipping Company, was established in 1893 after Marty had purchased two new British-built steam tramps. After several used steamers had been added to the fleet, Marty's shipping company reached its peak, possessing six vessels in 1898. As was common among European tramp shipping companies operating in East Asia, the vessels had Asian crews and European officers on board. Since suitable Frenchmen were rarely available in Indochina or neighbouring ports, most of Marty's officers were from Scandinavia, Germany, the Iberian Peninsula or Italy. His crews consisted of Chinese and Vietnamese seamen, which helped to cut costs. With his rather outdated fleet, the French shipowner faced rising costs for repairs and for chartering other vessels as temporary replacements. Due to these financial burdens, Marty lacked the capital to regularly modernise his fleet. This dire situation temporarily improved in 1900 when the Tonkin Shipping Company was granted a huge subsidy from the government general of Indochina for operating the Guangzhouwan postal steamer service shipping troops and goods between Haiphong and the French territory in China. However, with the sudden withdrawal of most of the troops during the Russo-Japanese War (1904–1905), Marty's vessels operating the service were no longer profitable. Contributing to the further decline of the shipping company was the strong competition from the M. Jebsen Shipping Company and the shipping boycotts by Chinese merchants in Haiphong in 1907 and 1909–1910. After Marty's death (1914), the Tonkin Shipping Company continued to operate the Guangzhouwan postal steamer service (which was temporarily in the hands of the French East Asiatic Company) before it was dissolved shortly after the First World War.

Shipping boycotts by Chinese merchants were directed against foreign shipping companies when Chinese ship charterers felt unfairly treated. The boycott of 1895–1896 was inspired by Marty's profit-driven attempt to drastically raise freight rates when the Sino-Japanese War (1894–1895) caused a temporary shortage of available shipping tonnage in Hong Kong and in Haikou and Beihai, the Chinese treaty ports located in the north-western part of the South China Sea. In retaliation, Chinese merchants set up a syndicate to break the monopoly of the Tonkin Shipping Company by chartering steamers under the German flag including a steam tramp of the M. Jebsen Shipping Company. Although Marty immediately lowered his freight rates, Chinese shippers continued to boycott his ships, causing severe financial losses for his firm. The case was taken up by French Minister Auguste Gérard in Beijing who protested against the alleged violation of the liberty of commerce and requested compensation from the Chinese government. The concerned merchants reacted promptly by promoting the establishment of a partnership between a Chinese shipping company based in Hong Kong and the M. Jebsen Shipping Company, with the intention of operating Jebsen's steam tramps on the run between Hong Kong, Haikou and Beihai to which they gave a maximum of cargoes. This caused a fresh French diplomatic intervention on Marty's behalf, demanding an even higher amount in compensation from Beijing. The French succeeded in redirecting some of the cargoes to Marty's vessels and in getting massive compensation for the shipowner which provided sufficient funding for purchasing three used steam coasters in 1898, considerably enlarging the Tonkin Shipping Company's fleet. However, the French political intervention ruined Marty's business relations with Chinese merchants for many years to come. In stark contrast to Marty, the M. Jebsen Shipping Company had a long-lasting partnership with the Chinese shipping company, from which the first comprador of Jebsen & Company was recruited. When Jebsen & Co. demanded compensation for the damage it had suffered as a result of the French diplomatic actions of 1896–1898, however, the firm found no support from the German minister in Beijing, who was conducting intensive negotiations with the Chinese government on the lease of Jiaozhou (Kiaochow) Bay in Shandong Province. To avoid any interference from France in the Sino-German talks, the minister remained firm and rejected the idea of any visible political support for the German shipping company.

After the boycott of 1895–1896, Marty remained highly suspicious of Chinese merchants who apparently engaged in unfair competition against him when chartering German and British vessels for all kinds of shipments. His attempt in 1900 to enlist the support of French officials against an alleged league of Chinese merchants in Haiphong who wanted to ruin him failed after the Boxer Rebellion in northern China (1900–1901) sent a strong warning signal to the imperialist powers that anti-imperialism and nationalism in China were growing stronger. This probably prompted French authorities in Indochina to regard the matter as a purely commercial one, refraining from any political intervention on behalf of Marty. Among French officials, this attitude prevailed when the Haiphong shipping boycotts of 1907 and 1909–1910 targeted the vessels of the Tonkin Shipping Company, the M. Jebsen Shipping Company and Butterfield & Swire, the major British shipping company in East Asia. In 1907, Chinese shippers protested against the joint increase of freight rates on rice after the rates had been lowered when Butterfield entered the market some months earlier. Regarding the increase as unacceptable, the Chinese immediately boycotted the ships of the three European shipping companies and chartered two vessels under the Norwegian flag. This eventually led to the agreement to withdraw the price increase and end the Chinese boycott. However, when facing low profitability, Butterfield, shortly before the start of the rice exporting season of spring 1909, initiated a new joint increase of freight rates on rice, expecting

Chinese shippers to agree to this unexpected step. This expectation proved wrong when six major Chinese rice trading firms in Haiphong formed a syndicate or charter combination and established their own steamship company chartering Norwegian, Swedish and German steam tramps. From the beginning, the main difficulty the Chinese firm faced was finding return cargoes from Hong Kong, and they often had to sail in ballast which considerably reduced the profitability of the chartered vessels. The ongoing boycott and price war resulted in Marty's vain attempt to win the support of Governor-General Klobukowski for his complaint against the Haiphong merchants. French officials refused to regard the matter as a boycott in the true meaning of the term and therefore rejected the idea of treating it as an offence against the French penal code. After the Chinese shipping company had suffered heavy financial losses during the boycott, which lasted for over a year, the boycott was ended with the agreement of May 1910 stipulating a reduction of more than 15 per cent in the freight rate on rice, which was obviously sufficient for the Chinese shippers to give in. Economic, not political, factors determined the outcome of the struggle and brought an end to the boycott. Another agreement between the three European shipping companies and Chinese rice merchants in Haiphong was signed in June 1913, restoring the freight rates for rice to the level that had applied before Butterfield entered the market in 1907. Any further increase in freight rates was considered unrealistic by the M. Jebsen Shipping Company for the time being.

Illicit trades such as the selling of Vietnamese women and children of almost all ages to Chinese households and brothels in Hong Kong and Guangzhou were prevalent in the South China Sea long before France seized Indochina. Human trafficking conducted by Chinese and Vietnamese players was often carried out on European steam tramps calling at Haiphong, despite frequent controls on the port by the Haiphong police. Such cases involved vessels of the Tonkin Shipping Company and of other shipping companies, but to an even greater extent the steam tramps of the M. Jebsen Shipping Company, which constantly operated on the run between the French colonial port and the British colony. Even after stricter regulations for travellers and tighter controls of shipmasters were introduced by French authorities, the very lucrative trade did not stop. Alleged business connections between Chinese traffickers and British and German shipping companies could not be confirmed due to lack of any concrete evidence. After two new trafficking cases came to light in 1912, involving a Jebsen steamer and causing an outcry in the Tonkin French press (and also revealing deep-seated anti-German sentiments), the *L'Avenir du Tonkin* sharply criticised inadequate control measures by German shipmasters and the legal shortcomings of the French penal code. This prompted the German consul in Saigon to launch a full investigation into the possible involvement of the captain of the *Carl Diederichsen*, a Jebsen steamer which was frequently sailing between Hong Kong and Haiphong. It emerged that Chinese crew members of this ship were apparently helping Chinese traffickers to smuggle Vietnamese women and children on board. The consul's immediate instruction to enforce stricter control measures on board all Jebsen ships before they left the port of Haiphong prompted Jacob Jebsen, the owner of the M. Jebsen Shipping Company, to protest against a measure directed only against his fleet and to promise to take stricter precautions against such cases. The government files and the M. Jebsen Shipping Company records consulted show that this shipping company, whose vessels almost dominated shipping in Haiphong, was more vulnerable to human trafficking because of the large number of its ships calling at the port. Lack of caution and insufficient control measures by shipmasters and the Haiphong port police, not the active involvement of these players, allowed Chinese traffickers to smuggle their human cargos aboard ships.

Guangzhouwan, the French leasehold in China's Guangdong Province (1898–1945), was the result of France's new imperialist policy during the tenure of Foreign Minister Gabriel Hanotaux. During the so-called "scramble for concessions" in China, Hanotaux felt challenged by the German seizure of Jiaozhou (Kiaochow) Bay in Shandong Province and strived not to fall behind other powers. Co-operating closely with the French minister in Beijing, the foreign minister pushed to acquire Guangzhou Bay on the northern shores of the South China Sea primarily for political reasons, pushing aside concerns about the economic value of the site. Under the Sino-French convention of 27 May 1898, France leased the bay from China for ninety-nine years with the right to establish a coal depot for a naval base and to build a railway to the Gulf of Tonkin. Around one thousand troops of the Reserve Brigade of the Occupation Corps of China headquartered in Haiphong were stationed in the territory which was administratively attached to French Indochina. However, Governor-General Paul Doumer's far-reaching plans to make Guangzhouwan a French naval station and the main transit hub for trade with Guangdong and Guangxi proved premature as most of the troops stationed in the territory were redeployed to Haiphong and Saigon during the Russo-Japanese War (1904–1905) to protect Indochina. This decision was the result of the strategically-led reorientation of France's naval policy under Naval Minister Camille Pelletan and the French colonial lobby. It had a major impact on the territory's shipping and trade and forced the economy to rely increasingly on its most profitable commerce, the sale or smuggling of opium produced within Guangzhouwan to consumer markets in China and elsewhere. The small territory with its mainly agricultural base, its economically poor hinterland and its almost non-existent trade with Indochina developed into an economic satellite of Hong Kong, with which it was linked by the junks and steam coasters of various national flags.

In 1900, Governor-General Doumer initiated the Guangzhouwan postal steamer service to closely link Haiphong with Guangzhouwan for the shipment of troops, other passengers and goods. French Indochina granted a considerable subsidy to the Tonkin Shipping Company of Marty et d'Abbadie which operated the service until 1910, and again from 1913 to 1918. However, after the relocation of most troops from Guangzhouwan, the service was no longer profitable for the shipowners and experienced a steady decline due to strong competition on the run from Guangzhouwan to Hong Kong. In 1910, it was taken over by the Compagnie de l'East Asiatique française (French East Asiatic Company), which had been founded jointly by French and Danish entrepreneurs and which co-operated closely with France's largest shipping company, Messageries Maritimes. Unable to provide proper shipping services, the French East Asiatic Company lost the subsidy contract after only two years of operation, and it was returned to Auguste Raphael Marty's hands. After the death of the shipowner, the new owner of the Tonkin Shipping Company operated the Guangzhouwan postal steamer service until 1918 when the subsidy contract expired. Although Guangzhouwan had almost entirely lost its economic and political importance for France, the service, which continued to be operated by other French shipping companies during the 1920s and 1930s, remaining above all a symbol of prestige for the country's position in China.

The development of Guangzhouwan from 1898 to 1914 was closely monitored by German consuls stationed in Guangzhou, Beihai, Haikou, Hong Kong and Saigon, and by German military officers who reported their findings to the German legation in Beijing. Because of the important economic interests of German shipping companies and trading firms operating in southern China and French Indochina, interest in Guangzhouwan was relatively stronger on the German side than on the British. Driven by traditional Franco-German conflict and rivalry, German consuls and military officers were obliged to carefully evaluate the geopolitical and economic position of the French territory and provide reliable facts and figures to the German government. This led to a particularly rich collection of unpublished documents kept in government archives in Berlin. The German accounts, based mainly on personal visits to Guangzhouwan, articles in the Tonkin press and conversations with French residents in Chinese treaty ports, cover various aspects and provide rare outsiders' insights into the political, military and economic-social conditions of the French leasehold territory. To the relief of German observers, the very modest economic development of Guangzhouwan did not allow the small French territory in China to become a kind of "French Hong Kong". However, the history of Guangzhouwan, which was returned to China in 1945 and renamed Zhanjiang, is not just one of failure, but also of urban and economic-social modernisation driven by the French administration and the territory's important role as a safe haven for Chinese refugees during periods of political turmoil in China. In recent years, the re-evaluation of the history of Guangzhouwan has been inspired mainly by two international conferences organised by the Lingnan Normal University in Zhanjiang, which opened up new perspectives on the almost forgotten French territory in China.

Finally, it can be concluded that the maritime region bordering the British and French empires in East Asia was a crucible of imperial power and an axis of economic struggle for shipowners and merchants from various nations. In the European Century of East Asia (c. 1860–1910s), Hong Kong, the global port city, and the colonial ports of Saigon and Haiphong developed into major hubs of the flow of goods and people, while Guangzhouwan remained a rather insignificant outpost of the French empire in Asia and an economic satellite of the British colony. Combining both imperial history and transnational business history allowed us to evaluate the political or economic impact of outside forces on these port cities such as fluctuating government policies, global or regional economic changes and also unforeseen events such as wars. When assessing the role of private businesses in shaping different connections in conjunction with other actors and institutions, it can be concluded that, despite occasionally stoking up Franco-German tensions in Indochina, both sides — the French colonial state and private French and German companies — certainly profited from each other when jointly driving the economic development of the French colony in Asia.

There are two additional aspects that this book tried to highlight: firstly, the interdependent relationship between private business and colonial governments in the geographical context of French Indochina; secondly, the impact of Franco-German political relations on maritime competition in the South China Sea. Concerning the first aspect, it can be concluded that government measures boosting the operation of shipping companies (be it in the form of preferable treatment or direct state subsidies) were ultimately counterproductive for private businesses and their profitability, even when the firms were prudently and skilfully managed and their owners were well connected in society. The history of Marty et d'Abbadie and its affiliates demonstrates governments' influences in an exemplary manner. The French colonial state enabled the creation and fast development of this state monopolist in Tonkin but provided too few incentives and liberties to allow the firm to survive long-term in highly competitive shipping markets. The M. Jebsen Shipping Company, operating in the South China Sea without any subsidies, provided a stark contrast to its French counterpart. These divergent fates bring a somewhat tragic element to the history of the French companies, and also to the individual biographies of Auguste Raphael Marty and Édouard Jules d'Abbadie. German tramp shipping companies in East Asia, unhampered by state intervention and operating from a free-market environment such as Hong Kong, had better chances to earn huge profits and gain an important share of the shipping market of French Indochina. The M. Jebsen Shipping Company serves as an example of this different mode of doing business. Hong Kong provided ample space to Michael Jebsen and his fleet of steam tramps, which were frequently overhauled and equipped with the latest maritime technology produced by the rapidly advancing modern industries of Imperial Germany and financed by powerful European capital networks, to freely operate from the British colony. This was certainly a success story that helped the company survive after the First World War, even though its fleet had been confiscated or destroyed during the conflict.

Compared to the aforementioned French and German shipping companies, the trading firm Speidel & Company in French Indochina resembled a mixture of different business cultures forced to conform to France's customs laws and Indochina's regulations. To drive their business forward under often difficult economic circumstances and political conditions, the owners took French citizenship and established a branch in Paris, probably not only securing their existence in the French colony, but their further business in various sectors of the economy of Indochina, including their role as agents of various German firms and foreign companies. This economic role was combined with the political function as consuls of Imperial Germany and the Netherlands, which seemed to considerably enhance the firm's status in the French colony. The sudden closure of Speidel & Co. at the outbreak of war in 1914 and the subsequent complete disappearance of this major trading firm from Indochina (the exact circumstances of which remain unknown) adds a tragic element to its corporate history.

Concerning the second aspect, it can be concluded that the strained Franco-German relations were hardly felt in Hong Kong where business communities from several different nations lived together under British rule, with daily routine interaction in the economic and other sectors but without much in private spheres. What mattered most for European shipping and trading companies was being on good terms with their main customer base, namely Chinese and other merchants. The case studies of Speidel and Company in Saigon and Haiphong, of A. R. Marty in Hong Kong and Haiphong, of the M. Jebsen Shipping Company in Hong Kong and of Marty et d'Abbadie in Haiphong demonstrated patterns of co-operation and of conflict between various transnational actors in the South China Sea. This was certainly nothing new or unusual, but always worth investigating in order to shed more light on transnational interactions on the ground: Private companies and their individual owners and employees in port cities in this region operated mostly on a routine basis with Chinese traders, loaders and ships charterers, but sometimes they encountered disruption such as price wars or boycotts or even illicit trades such as human trafficking.

In the South China Sea, Franco-German relations have been shaped since the 1840s by French military officers and officials who acquired, secured and developed France's Asian colonial empire, and by German shipowners and merchants who actively participated and considerably profited from France's imperialist endeavours. At the same time, successive German governments were carefully observing this process, but without ever intervening. The strong economic performance of Imperial Germany in world markets and, on the other hand, the relatively less power of the export industries of Republican France certainly enhanced mutual negative perceptions and contributed to poisoning relations on both sides of the River Rhine. On the other hand, the hard economic factors that showed an asymmetrical development of the German and French economies cannot be blamed for the mutual negative perceptions or even the outbreak of the First World War, in which other factors were decisive. The bigger picture was more complex, although it was certainly true (but difficult to evaluate) that the tense political climate in some way affected, and even poisoned, the daily business operations of Germans and French traders in Saigon and Haiphong. The First World War terminated the presence of German firms in Indochina, which, unlike Hong Kong during the 1920s, was not restored. The post-war period and especially the Ruhr Crisis of 1923 (when French and Belgian troops occupied the western German industrial hub) brought Franco-German relations to a new abyss. However, the subsequent relaxation of tensions between Paris and Berlin highlighted by the Locarno Treaties (1925) and the Franco-German trade agreement (1927) ended the long-term economic warfare between the two countries. The Locarno agreements led to the award of the Nobel Peace Prize to both the German Foreign Minister Gustav Stresemann and French Prime Minister Aristide Briand, opening a (short-lived) period of more harmonious relations between France and Germany.

Index

B. Becker, *France and Germany in the South China Sea, c. 1840–1930*, Cambridge Imperial and Post-Colonial Studies,
https://doi.org/10.1007/978-3-030-52604-7

D

E

T

MIX
Papier aus verantwortungsvollen Quellen
Paper from responsible sources
FSC® C105338

Printed by Books on Demand, Germany